COMPUTERS, COMMUNICATIONS, AND INFORMATION

A USER'S INTRODUCTION

COMPREHENSIVE VERSION

REVISED EDITION

Sarah E. Hutchinson

Stacey C. Sawyer

with contributions by
Glen J. Coulthard
Okanagan University College

Boston   Burr Ridge, IL   Dubuque, IA   Madison, WI   New York   San Francisco   St. Louis
Bangkok   Bogotá   Caracas   Lisbon   London   Madrid
Mexico City   Milan   New Delhi   Seoul   Singapore   Sydney   Taipei   Toronto

Irwin/McGraw-Hill

A Division of The McGraw·Hill Companies

This book is printed on acid-free paper.

1 2 3 4 5 6 7 8 9 0 VH/VH 9 0 9 8 7

ISBN 0-07-109327-3 (core version)
ISBN 0-256-25277-7 (comprehensive version)

Vice president and editorial director: *Michael W. Junior*
Senior sponsoring editor: *Garrett Glanz*
Development: *Burrston House*
Marketing manager: *James Rogers*
Senior project manager: *Gladys True*
Production supervisor: *Karen Thigpen*
Production: *Stacey C. Sawyer, Sawyer & Williams*
Designer: *Michael Warrell*
Electronic makeup: *GTS/Stacey C. Sawyer*
Art and composition: *GTS Graphics, Inc.*
Photo research: *Monica Suder/Stacey C. Sawyer*
Typeface: *10/12 Times New Roman*
Printer: *Von Hoffmann Press*

Library of Congress Cataloging-in-Publication Data

Hutchinson, Sarah E.
  Computers, communications, and information : a user's introduction
/ Sarah E. Hutchinson, Stacey C. Sawyer: with contributions by Glen
J. Coulthard. — 2nd ed.
    p.   cm.
  Includes index.
  ISBN 0-07-109327-3 (core version : acid-free paper). — ISBN
0-256-25277-7 (comprehensive version : acid-free paper)
  1. Computers. 2. Information technology. I. Sawyer, Stacey C.
II. Coulthard, Glen J. III. Title.
QA76.5.H867 1998
004—dc21   97-32174

http://www.mhhe.com

BRIEF CONTENTS

1 OVERVIEW: THE FOUNDATION FOR YOUR FUTURE 1.1

EPISODE 1: STARTING A WEB BUSINESS E1.1

2 PROCESSING HARDWARE: TURNING DATA INTO SOMETHING YOU CAN USE 2.1

3 INPUT/OUTPUT HARDWARE: INTERFACES BETWEEN YOU AND THE COMPUTER 3.1

4 STORAGE HARDWARE: PRESERVING DATA AND INFORMATION 4.1

EPISODE 2: DECIDING TO START YOUR WEB BUSINESS E2.1

5 SYSTEM SOFTWARE: THE DIRECTOR 5.1

6 APPLICATIONS SOFTWARE: THE USER'S TOOLS 6.1

EPISODE 3: PLANNING FOR COMMERCE AT YOUR SITE E3.1

7 COMMUNICATIONS TECHNOLOGY: STARTING ALONG THE INFORMATION HIGHWAY 7.1

8 USES OF COMMUNICATIONS TECHNOLOGY: TELECOMMUTING, ONLINE RESOURCES, AND THE INTERNET 8.1

EPISODE 4: PROMOTING TRAFFIC TO YOUR SITE E4.1

9 INFORMATION SYSTEMS ANALYSIS AND DESIGN: THE SYSTEMS DEVELOPMENT LIFE CYCLE 9.1

10 SOFTWARE PROGRAMMING AND LANGUAGES: WHERE YOUR SOFTWARE COMES FROM 10.1

11 INFORMATION MANAGEMENT: WHO NEEDS TO KNOW WHAT, AND WHEN? 11.1

12 FILES AND DATABASES: ORGANIZING AND MAINTAINING DIGITAL DATA 12.1

13 TRENDS IN COMPUTING: MULTIMEDIA AND DEVELOPMENTS IN INFORMATION TECHNOLOGY 13.1

14 ETHICS, PRIVACY, SECURITY, AND SOCIAL QUESTIONS: COMPUTING FOR RIGHT LIVING 14.1

EPISODE 5: THE FUTURE OF YOUR WEB BUSINESS E5.1

PREFACE

Why We Wrote This Book: Meeting the Needs of Users

Computers, Communications, and Information: A User's Introduction, Revised Edition, is written for future computer users—people who will use the computer as an everyday tool for working with reports, spreadsheets, databases, and the like. It is not intended only for students who will eventually write programs or design computer systems.

We wrote this book in order to provide instructors and students with the most useful information possible in an introductory computer course. Specifically, we offer the following five important features:

1. Complete coverage, avoiding unnecessary detail

2. Practical orientation

3. Interesting, readable explication

4. Learning reinforcement

5. Complete course solutions: supplements that work

We elaborate on these features below.

Feature 1: Complete Coverage, Avoiding Unnecessary Detail

This book offers complete coverage of core concepts of computers and information technology. We have tried to be neither too brief nor too encyclopedic, offering users just what they need to know to use a computer competently. Moreover, we have avoided the cluttered, over-illustrated look and style that many instructors tell us they find objectionable in other texts. Thus, you will not find icons, margin notes, cartoons, or similar distractions.

IMPORTANT NOTE—Core and Comprehensive Versions: This book is available in two versions: the Core Version includes Chapters 1–8 and Episodes 1–4; the Comprehensive Version includes all 14 Chapters and Episode 5.

Feature 2: Practical Orientation

The text presents information on capabilities of microcomputers that users can apply at work, home, and school. For example, we provide up-to-date, practical discussion of . . .

■ Use of the Inernet and the World Wide Web

■ PC and Macintosh hardware, addressing upgrading and compatibility issues

■ Buying and maintaining a microcomputer system

■ Computer-related health and safety matters

■ Ethics, privacy, and security

■ Common features of applications software

■ Object-oriented programming, expert systems, virtual reality, and digital convergence

Feature 3: Interesting, Readable, Style

We are gratified that over many editions reviewers, instructors, and students have found our writing style praiseworthy. Our primary goal is to reach students by making our explanations of concepts as clear, relevant, and interesting as possible.

The book has also been completely redesigned, and all the art has been recreated, to provide a modern, accessible look.

Feature 4: Learning Reinforcement

We have developed a variety of learning aids to provide learning reinforcement:

- **Chapter objectives and previews:** Each chapter opens with a list of chapter *learning objectives* and an introductory section entitled *Why Is This Chapter Important?*

- **Section previews:** Each section heading is followed by a short *preview* of the text to come.

- *New Format!* **Chapter summaries:** Each chapter concludes with a *Summary* section to help students review. All the important terms appearing in a chapter—and the page numbers where they appeared—are also included. We also connect each summary item with its related numbered learning objective from the beginning of the chapter.

- **Self-tests, exercises, and critical thinking questions:** End-of-chapter *fill-in-the-blank tests, short-answer exercises,* and *critical thinking questions* enable students to test their comprehension and encourage them to learn more about microcomputers on their own.

- *New Feature!* **Career boxes:** Special boxes show students how computers are used in some common and uncommmon ways in the workplace.

- *New Feature!* **Episodes:** Several *Episodes,* case studies of *Amazon.com,* appear throughout the text to provide students with practical insights into establishing a Web-based business.

Feature 5: Complete Course Solutions— Supplements That Work

Computer concepts are only one part of the course experience. Our instructional package also includes **applications software tutorials, interactive software modules, lecture enhancement software, instructor support materials,** and a **software support program.** We elaborate on these below.

Support for Students

Applications Software Tutorials: Our publisher, Irwin/McGraw-Hill, offers five different series of software applications tutorials, which present five different hands-on approaches to learning software. Check with your local sales representative to learn about the specific software covered in each series.

- The **Advantage Series** *for Computer Education by Sarah Hutchinson and Glen Coulthard:* Averaging 224 pages per manual, the *Advantage Series* provides software tutorials for a large number of popular software packages, including the latest versions of Microsoft Office. Each tutorial leads students through step-by-step instructions not only for the most common methods of executing commands but also for alternative methods.

  Each session within a manual begins with a case example and concludes with case problems showing real-world application of the software. Quick-reference guides appear throughout. Boxes introduce unusual functions that will enhance the user's productivity. The *Advantage Series* will train your students to become proficient users of today's key productivity tools.

■ In partnership with MindQ Publishing, Irwin/McGraw-Hill brings you **Advantage Interactive Software Tutorials:** Based on the printed *Advantage Series* texts described above, these CD-ROMs combine sight, sound, and motion into a truly interactive learning experience. Video clips, simulations, hands-on exercises, and quizzes reinforce every important concept. *Advantage Interactive* CDs are available for Microsoft Office 95 & 97 Professional, and are designed to be used independently or with the corresponding manuals.

■ The **O'Leary Series** *by Linda and Timothy O'Leary:* Designed for application-specific short courses, each manual offers a project-based approach that gives students a sense of the real-world capabilities of software applications. Extensive screen captures provide easy-to-follow visual examples for each major textual step, while visual summaries reinforce the concepts, building on students' knowledge. O'Leary Series manuals are available for a wide variety of software applications, including the latest versions of Microsoft Office.

■ **Interactive Computing Skills** *by Ken Laudon and Azimuth Multimedia:* This series of CD-ROM-based tutorials offer complete introductory coverage of software applications. Each lesson takes 45–60 minutes to complete, and is narrated and highly interactive. With up to 4 lessons per disk, you'll find *Interactive Computing Skills* a valuable addition to your courseware package or an excellent self-study tool. Each CD features a "SmartQuiz"at the end of lessons to actively test software skills within a simulated software environment. Available for Microsoft Office 4.3 and 97.

■ The **Effective Series** *by Fritz J. Erickson and John A. Vonk:* Written specifically for the first-time computer user, the *Effective Series* is based on the premise that success breeds confidence and confident students learn more effectively. Exercises embedded within each lesson allow students to experience success before moving on to a more advanced topic. The "why" as well as the "how" is always carefully explained. Each lesson features several applications projects and a comprehensive problem for student practice.

Interactive Software: *InfoTech Interactive* provides students with an expanding number of self-paced learning modules, on topics from the system unit to multimedia. Combining text, illustrations, animations, and audio narration, this tool runs in a Web browser and is available in both networked and CD-ROM-based versions. It is primarily intended for student lab use, but may also be used by instructors for additional visual explanation in a lecture setting.

InfoTech Interactive will include the following modules:

■ Applications Software—Office Suites   ■ Peripherals
■ Applications Software—Other Apps   ■ Multimedia
■ System Unit   ■ Internet
■ Secondary Storage   ■ Networks

Additional modules will be developed on an ongoing basis. Please consult your Irwin/McGraw-Hill sales representative for details on the latest *InfoTech* offerings.

Each module provides three levels of learning: (1) The *Introduction level* provides text and animated enhancement of computer concepts. (2) The *Explore level* allows the user to experiment with various scenarios and see the immediate results. (3) The *Practice level* poses cases and problems for which the user must provide solutions based on the Intro and Explore sections.

Minimum System requirements: (a) IBM PC or compatible with a Pentium processor, 4X CD-ROM drive and at least 16 MB of RAM, running Windows 3.1 or later, or (b) Power Macintosh with at least 16 MB of RAM and 4X CD-ROM drive, running System 6.01 or later.

Support for Instructors

■ The *CIT Classroom Presentation Tool* is a graphics-intensive set of electronic slides created to enhance any lecture. This CD-ROM-based software helps to clarify topics that may otherwise be difficult to present. *Minimum System requirements:* IBM PC or compatible with a Pentium processor, 4X CD-ROM drive and at least 16 MB of RAM, running Windows 3.1 or later. An LCD panel is needed if the images are to be shown to a large audience.

■ *Instructor's Resource Manual:* This complete guide supports instruction in any course environment. The Instructor's Resource Manual includes: *a student questionnaire, course planning and evaluation grid, suggestions for writing course objectives, suggested pace and coverage for courses of various lengths, suggestions for using the exercises in various class structures,* and *projects for small and large classes.*

   For each chapter, the IRM provides an overview, chapter outline, lecture notes, notes regarding the boxes from the text, solutions, and suggestions and additional information to enhance the project and critical thinking sections.

■ *Test bank:* The test bank contains more than 1500 different questions, all referenced to the text. Specifically, it contains *true/false, multiple-choice,* and *fill-in questions,* categorized by difficulty and by type; *short-essay questions; sample midterm exam; sample final exam;* and *answers to all questions.*

■ *Computerized testing software:* Called *Computest,* this popular computerized testing software is a user-friendly, menu-driven, microcomputer-based test-generating system that is free to qualified adopters. Containing all the questions from the test bank described above, Computest allows instructors to customize tests, entering their own questions and generating review quizzes and answer keys.

   Available for DOS, Windows, and Macintosh formats, Computest has advanced printing features that allow instructors to print all types of graphics; Windows and Macintosh versions use easily remembered icons.

   System requirements: (a) IBM PC or compatible with at least 2 MB of RAM running Windows 3.1, or (b) Macintosh with at least 2 MB of RAM running System 6.01 or later; CD-ROM drive or 3.5-inch floppy-disk drives.

   Instructors interested in administering networked tests should read the following description of the *McGraw-Hill Learning Architecture.*

■ *Videos:* A broad selection of 20 videos segments from the acclaimed PBS television series, *Computer Chronicles,* are available. Each video is 30 minutes long. The videos cover topics ranging from computers and politics, to online financial services, to the latest developments in PC technologies..

■ *Technical support services:* Irwin/McGraw-Hill's Technical Support is available to you on any of our software products, such as InfoTech Interactive or the CIT Classroom Presentation Tool. You can use the Online Helpdesk by linking to *http://www.mhhe.com/helpdesk.* If you can't find your answer there, call us at 800-331-5094.

■ *McGraw-Hill Learning Architecture:* This exciting new Web-based software provides complete course administration. *MHLA* is available to students using a standard Web browser and allows for content customization, authoring, and delivery. Students can take online quizzes and tests. Their scores are automatically graded and recorded. *MHLA* also includes useful features like e-mail, message boards, and chat rooms, and it easily links to other Internet resources. The future of interactive, networked education is here today! Ask your sales representative for more information on the *McGraw-Hill Learning Architecture.*

Acknowledgments

Two names are on the front of the book, but a great many others are powerful contributors to its development.

First, we thank Glen Coulthard for his educational and technical expertise in his role as consulting editor. (Take a break, Glen!) We are also grateful to many people at Irwin/McGraw-Hill: Tom Casson and Garrett Glanz in Editorial, and Gladys True, Karen Thigpen, Michael Warrell, and all others in the Production Department who helped us get this book out on time. Special thanks go to the designer, Ellen Pettengell, for our sharp new text design and to Matt Baldwin for the cover design. Glenn Turner, Meg Turner, Cathy Crowe, and others at Burrston House provided invaluable assistance by analyzing manuscript reviews and establishing revision needs. Our student friend Jonathan Lippe expertly prepared the summaries. Anita Wagner once again did an excellent copyediting job. Monica Suder was our invaluable photo researcher, and David Sweet took professional care of permissions fulfillment. And GTS Graphics in Los Angeles provided the best prepress services in the business (special thanks go to Bob Marinas and Donna Machado).

Finally, we appreciate the helpful comments and suggestions provided by the following reviewers:

Beverly Amer, *Northern Arizona State University*
Hashem Anwari, *Northern Virginia Community College*
Gregg Boalch, *Curtin University* (Australia)
Ruth Bond, *Lake County Community College*
Kris Chandler, *Pikes Peak Community College*
Donald L. Dershem, *Mountain View College*
George Federman, *Santa Barbara City College*
Richard Fox, *University of Texas— Pan American*
A. E. Geldenhuys, *Technikon SA* (South Africa)
Albert G. Haddad, *University of North Texas*
C. Michael Hassett, *Fort Hays State University*

Rose M. Laird, *Northern Virginia Community College*
James F. LaSalle, *University of Arizona*
Paul Lou, *Diablo Valley College*
Sharad K. Maheshwari, *Hampton University*
Mike Michaelson, *Palomar College*
George A. Mundrake, *Ball State University*
Steve Murtha, *Tulsa Community College*
Merrill Parker, *Chattanooga State University*
Roy Martin Richards, Jr., *University of North Texas*
Evelyn Rosengarten, *Burlington County College*
Eddie Sanders, Jr., *Chicago State University*
Shannon Scanlon, *Henry Ford Community College*
Suzanne Shores, *Tulsa Community College*
Meenu Singh, *Kentucky State University*
Don Voils, *Palm Beach Community College*

And the following students:

Mary Bellino, *College of Dupage*
Paul Hieber, *Moraine Valley Community College*
Karen Jones, *College of Lake County*

Ericka Kriese, *Oakton Commmunity College*
Don Martell, *College of Lake County*
Sue Rodriguez, *Triton Community College*
Cynthia Thornton, *Chicago State University*

SEH
SCS

DETAILED CONTENTS

1 Overview: The Foundation for Your Future   1.1

Why Is This Chapter Important?   1.2

Who Is the User? Mostly People Like You   1.2

The Importance of Becoming Computer Literate and Computer Competent   1.3

What Is a Computer-Based Information System?   1.4

The Digital Basis of Computers   1.6

The Analog Basis of Life   1.7

Computer Hardware   1.8

Input Hardware   1.8

Processing and Memory Hardware   1.9

Output Hardware   1.11

Storage Hardware   1.11

Communications Hardware   1.11

Computer Software   1.11

System Software: The Computer's Boss   1.12

Applications Software: Your Servant   1.12

Types of Computer Systems: What's the Difference?   1.13

● *Career Box: Using Computers in . . . Weather Forecasting or Firefighting*   **1.16**

Milestones in Computer Development   17

The Evolution of Computers: March of the Generations   1.18

The Information Explosion: Data Overload or Knowledge   1.20

Computing Trends: Connectivity, Online Access and the Internet, Interactivity, and Digital Convergence   1.21

Connectivity: The Examples of Telecommuting, Teleshopping, and E-mail and Voice Mail   1.21

Online Information Access: The Examples of Databases, Online Services and Networks   1.23

● *Career Box: Using Computers in . . . Web Publishing*   **1.24**

Interactivity: The Examples of Multimedia Computers, TV/PC "Smart Boxes," Network Computers, and Personal Digital Assistants   1.25

Digital Convergence: The Way of the Future   1.28

Summary   1.29

Exercises   1.35

EPISODE 1: Starting a Web Business   E1.1

2 Processing Hardware: Turning Data into Something You Can Use   2.1

Why Is This Chapter Important?   2.2

How Data and Programs Are Represented in the Computer   2.3

Binary Coding Schemes   2.4

The Parity Bit: Checking for Errors   2.5

Machine Language: Your Brand of Computer's Very Own Language   2.5

● *Career Box: Using Computers in . . . Medicine*   **2.6**

How Computer Capacity Is Expressed: Bit by Bit   2.8

The Processor, Main Memory, and Registers   2.9

The Processor: In Charge   2.9

Specialized Processor Chips: Assistants to the CPU   2.12

Main Memory: Working Storage Area for the CPU   2.12

Registers   2.13

The Machine Cycle: How a Single Instruction Is Processed   2.14

Telling Computers Apart: RAM Capacity, Word Size, and Processor Speed   2.15

RAM Capacity   2.15

Word Size   2.15

Processing Speeds   2.16

● *Career Box: Using Computers in . . . Agriculture*   **2.17**

Focus on the Microcomputer: What's Inside?   2.18

The Power Supply   2.20

The Motherboard   2.20

The Microprocessor   2.20

RAM Chips   2.21

ROM Chips   2.22

Other Forms of Memory   2.22

Ports: Connecting Peripherals   2.23

Expansion Slots and Boards   2.25

Buses   2.25

Coming Attractions?   2.27

Summary   2.30

Exercises   2.35

3 Input/Output Hardware: Interfaces Between You and the Computer   3.1

Why Is This Chapter Important?   3.2

I/O, I/O, It's Off to Work We Go   3.2

Input Hardware   3.4

Keyboard Input   3.4

Pointing Devices   3.7

Pen-Based Systems   3.10

Source-Data Entry   3.11

● *Career Box: Using Computers in . . . Photography Careers   3.19*

Multimedia Input Needs   3.20

Input Controls: Preserving Data Integrity   3.21

Output Hardware   3.21

Impact Printers   3.22

Nonimpact Printers   3.22

Plotters   3.25

Installing a Printer or Plotter   3.26

Multifunction Printer Technology: One for All   3.26

Monitors   3.26

Future Display Technology   3.30

Audio Output Hardware   3.30

● *Career Box: Using Computers in . . . Self-Employed, Home-Based Careers   3.31*

Multimedia Output Needs   3.33

In and Out: Devices That Do Both   3.33

Terminals   3.33

Smart Cards and Optical Cards   3.35

Touch Screens   3.36

Now You See It, Now You Don't   3.36

Summary   3.38

Exercises   3.44

4 Storage Hardware: Preserving Data and Information   4.1

Why Is This Chapter Important?   4.2

Storage Fundamentals   4.2

Data Representation and Data Storage Capacity   4.3

Types of Files   4.3

What Can You Do with Files Besides Filing Them?   4.5

Data Access Methods   4.5

Tape Storage   4.8

Diskette Storage   4.9

The Disk Drive   4.10

How a Disk Drive Works   4.10

Characteristics of Diskettes   4.11

Taking Care of Diskettes   4.13

Hard Disks   4.13

Microcomputer Internal Hard Disk Drives   4.14

Microcomputer Hard Disk Variations: Power and Portability   4.17

Virtual Memory: Using Disk Space to Increase RAM   4.18

Hard Disk Technology for Large Computer Systems   4.18

Future Hard Disk Technology: The MR Head   4.19

Optical Disks   4.19

CD-ROM Disks   4.19

CD-R Disks   4.23

Erasable Optical Disks (CDE)   4.25

DVD-ROM: The "Digital Convergence" Disk   4.25

The Importance of Backup   4.27

Other Forms of Secondary Storage   4.28

Flash-Memory Cards   4.28

Advanced Storage Technology   4.29

● *Career Box: Using Computers in . . . Finance and Banking Careers   4.30*

Summary   4.31

Exercises   4.35

EPISODE 2: Deciding to Start Your Web Business   E2.1

5 System Software: The Director   5.1

Why Is This Chapter Important?   5.2

Two Basic Software Types: For the Computer and for the User   5.3

System Software Components   5.4

Operating System: In Control   5.5

Data Management: Tracking Data   5.6

TP Monitor: Input Management   5.6

Network Operating System: Traffic Management   5.6

Communications Protocols: Details for Data Transmission   5.6

Messaging Protocols: Details for E-Mail Transmission   5.6

Drivers: Peripheral Management   5.7

Utility Programs: Helping Hands   5.7

Language Translators   5.11

Other System Software Capabilities   5.11

System Software Interfaces   5.13

Common Operating Systems: Platforms   5.14

DOS   5.15

● *Career Box: Using Computers in . . . Law Enforcement*   **5.16**

Windows 3.x   5.17

Windows 95   5.17

Windows NT   5.19

OS/2   5.20

Unix   5.21

Macintosh Operating System   5.22

NetWare   5.23

Multimedia Support   5.24

The Future: Is the Web Changing Everything?   5.24

Bloatware or the Network Computer?   5.26

The Jolt from Java   5.27

Onward: Toward Compatibility   5.28

Summary   5.29

Exercises   5.33

6 Applications Sofware: The User's Tools   6.1

Why Is This Chapter Important?   6.2

Applications Software Tools   6.2

Common Features of Applications Software   6.4

Compatibility Issues: What Goes with What?   6.6

Productivity Software Tools   6.7

Word Processing Software   6.7

Spreadsheet Software   6.11

Personal Finance Software   6.13

Presentation Graphics   6.15

Database Management System Software   6.15

Communications Software   6.18

Groupware   6.19

Desktop Accessories and PIMs   6.20

Integrated Software and Software Suites   6.21

Web Browsers   6.22

● *Career Box: Using Computers in . . . Transportation*   **6.23**

Specialty Applications Software Tools   6.24

Desktop-Publishing Software   6.25

Project Management Software   6.26

Computer-Aided Design (CAD) and Manufacturing (CAM)   6.27

Drawing and Painting Software   6.29

Hypertext and Web Site Management   6.30

Multimedia Authoring Software   6.30

Installing and Updating Applications Software   6.33

Installing Applications Software   6.33

Applications Software Versions and Releases   6.33

Ethics and Intellectual Property Rights: When Can You Copy?   6.34

What Is a Copyright?   6.34

Piracy, Plagiarism, and Ownership of Images and Sounds   6.35

Public Domain Software, Freeware, and Shareware   6.36

Proprietary Software and Types of Licenses   6.37

The Software Police   6.38

Summary   6.39

Exercises   6.45

EPISODE 3: Planning for Commerce at Your Site   E3.1

7 Communications Technology: Starting Along the Information Superhighway   7.1

Why Is This Chapter Important?   7.2

Using Computers to Communicate Technological Basics   7.2

Analog Signals: Continuous Waves   7.3

Digital Signals: Discrete Bursts   7.3

The Modem: The Great Translator   7.4

Communications Software   7.6

ISDN, Cable Modems, ADSL, and Dishes:
Faster, Faster, Faster!   7.7

Communications Channels: The Conduits of Communications   7.9

The Electromagnetic Spectrum   7.9

● *Career Box: Using Computers in . . .
Education Careers*   7.11

Twisted-Pair Wire   7.12

Coaxial Cable   7.13

Fiber-Optic Cable   7.13

Microwave and Satellite Systems   7.13

Other Wireless Communications   7.14

The Next Generation of Wireless
Communications   7.17

Factors Affecting Communications Among Devices   7.20

Transmission Rate: Higher Frequency, Wider
Bandwidth, More Data   7.20

Line Configurations: Point-to-Point and
Multipoint   7.21

Serial and Parallel Transmission   7.21

Direction of Transmission Flow: Simplex,
Half-Duplex, and Full-Duplex   7.22

Transmission Mode: Asynchronous Versus
Synchronous   7.23

Packet Switching: Getting More Data on a
Network   7.24

Multiplexing: Enhancing Communications
Efficiencies   7.25

Protocols: The Rules of
Data Transmission   7.26

Communications Networks   7.27

Types of Networks: Wide Area, Metropolitan
Area, and Local   7.28

Some Features: Hosts and Nodes, Downloading
and Uploading   7.28

Advantages of Networks   7.29

Local Networks   7.30

Types of Local Networks: PBXs
and LANs   7.30

Types of LANs: Client-Server and
Peer-to-Peer   7.31

Components of a LAN   7.32

Topology of LANs   7.34

The Impact of LANs   7.36

What's Next?   7.36

Summary   7.37

Exercises   7.43

8 Uses of Communications Technology: Telecommuting, Online Resources, and the Internet   8.1

Why Is This Chapter Important?   8.2

The Practical Uses of Communications and Connectivity   8.2

Tools of Communications and Connectivity
8.3

Telephone-Related Communications Services   8.4

Fax Messages   8.4

Voice Mail   8.5

E-Mail   8.6

Video/Voice Communication: Videoconferencing and Picture Phones   8.8

Videoconferencing and V-Mail   8.8

Picture Phones   8.9

Online Information Services   8.9

Getting Access   8.10

Offerings of Online Services   8.11

Will Online Services Survive the Internet?
8.12

The Internet   8.13

Where Did the Internet Come From?   8.13

Connecting to the Internet   8.14

Internet Addresses   8.16

Features of and Tools For Navigating the
Internet   8.19

World Wide Web   8.22

What Can You Find on the Web?   8.25

Speed of Web Data Transfer: How to Get Old
Fast   8.27

Marketing and Business on the Web: If You
Build It, Will They Come?   8.27

Life After Browsers: Push/Pull   8.28

Net Loss?   8.30

Shared Resources: Workgroup Computing, EDI, and Intranets and Extranets   8.31

Workgroup Computing and Groupware   8.32

Electronic Data Interchange 8.32

Intranets and Extranets 8.33

Portable Work: Telecommuting and Virtual Offices 8.33

Telecommuting and Telework Centers 8.34

The Virtual Office 8.34

● *Career Box: Using Computers in . . . Job Searches* **8.36**

Summary 8.37

Exercises 8.41

EPISODE 4: Promoting Traffic to Your Site E4.1

9 Information Systems Analysis and Design: The Systems Development Life Cycle 91

Why Is This Chapter Important? 9.2

User Participation in Systems Development: Helping to Avoid System Failure 9.3

Systems Development Life Cycle (SDLC) 9.7

Are Phases Clearly Distinct from One Another? Not Always 9.8

Who Participates? Basically, Everyone 9.9

The First Phase: Conduct a Preliminary Investigation 9.11

1. Conduct the Preliminary Study 9.11

2. Propose Alternative Solutions 9.12

3. Describe Costs and Benefits 9.13

4. Submit a Preliminary Plan 9.13

The Second Phase: Do a Detailed Analysis of the System 9.13

1. Gather Data 9.14

2. Analyze the Data 9.15

3. Write a Report 9.19

The Third Phase: Design the System 9.20

1. Do a Preliminary Design 9.20

2. Do a Detail Design 9.22

3. Write a Report 9.23

The Fourth Phase: Develop the System 9.23

1. Acquire Software 9.24

2. Acquire Hardware 9.24

3. Test the System 9.24

The Fifth Phase: Implement the System 9.25

1. Convert to the New System 9.26

2. Compile Final Documentation 9.26

3. Train the Users 9.28

The Sixth Phase: Maintain the System 9.28

● *Career Box: Using Computers in . . . Sales and Marketing Careers* **9.29**

Summary 9.30

Exercises 9.33

10 Software Programming and Languages: Where Your Software Comes From 10.1

Why Is This Chapter Important? 10.2

Software Development and Programming Languages 219

Programming: A Five-Step Procedure 10.3

What a Program Is 10.3

The First Step: Clarity the Programming Needs 10.3

The Second Step: Design the Program 10.5

The Third Step: Code the Program 10.10

The Fourth Step: Test the Program 10.11

The Fifth Step: Document and Maintain the Program 10.12

Five Generations of Programming Languages 10.13

First Generation: Machine Language 10.15

Second Generation: Assembly Language 10.15

Third Generation: High-Level Languages 10.16

Fourth Generation: Very-High-Level Languages 10.17

Fifth Generation: Natural Languages 10.17

Traditional Programming Languages 10.18

COBOL: The Language of Business 10.18

C: For Portability and Scientific Use 10.19

BASIC: The Easy Language 10.21

Ada: A Possible New Standard 10.21

Other Programming Languages 10.21

Object-Oriented and Visual Programming 0.22

Object-Oriented Programming: Block by Block 10.23

Visual Programming 10.26

HTML, VRML, and Java   10.26

The Future   10.29

• *Career Box: Using Computers in . . .
Professional Sports Careers*   10.30

Summary   10.31

Exercises   10.35

11 Information Management: Who Needs to Know What, and When?   11.1

Why Is This Chapter Important?   11.2

Trends Forcing Change in the Workplace   11.2

The Virtual Office   11.3

Automation   11.3

Downsizing and Outsourcing   11.3

Total Quality Management   11.3

Employee Empowerment   11.4

Reengineering   11.4

Organizations: Departments, Tasks, Management Levels, and Types of Information   11.5

Departments: R&D, Production, Marketing, Accounting, Human Resources   11.5

Management Tasks: Five Functions   11.7

Management Levels: Three Levels, Three Kinds of Decisions   11.7

Types of Information: Unstructured, Semistructured, and Structured   11.9

Management Information Systems   11.10

Transaction Processing Systems: To Support Operational Decisions   11.12

Management Information Systems: To Support Tactical Decisions   11.12

Decision Support Systems: To Support Strategic Decisions   11.3

Executive Information Systems   11.16

Expert Systems   11.17

Office Automation Systems   11.18

The Future: Going Sideways   11.18

• *Career Box: Using Computers in . . .
Real Estate Careers*   11.21

Summary   11.22

Exercises   11.24

12 Files and Databases: Organizing and Maintaining Digital Data   12.1

Why Is This Chapter Important?   12.2

All Databases Great and Small   12.3

The Database Administrator   12.5

The Data Storage Hierarchy and the Key Field   12.6

The Data Storage Hierarchy   12.6

The Key Field   12.7

File Handling: Basic Concepts   12.8

Two Types of Data Files: Master and Transaction   12.8

Batch Versus Online Processing   12.8

Offline Versus Online Storage   12.9

File Organization: Three Methods   12.9

File Management Systems   12.10

Disadvantages of File Management Systems   12.11

Database Management Systems   12.12

Advantages and Disadvantages of a DBMS   12.12

Types of Database Organization   12.13

Hierarchical Database   12.13

Network Database   12.14

Relational Database   12.14

Object-Oriented Database (OODBMS)   12.16

Features of a DBMS   12.17

Data Dictionary   12.17

Utilities   12.17

Query Language   12.18

Report Generator   12.19

Access Security   12.19

System Recovery   12.19

New Approaches: Mining, Warehouses, and "Siftware"   12.20

Data Mining: What It Is, What It's Used For   12.20

Preparing Data for the Data Warehouse   12.21

"Siftware" for Finding and Analyzing   12.23

The Ethics of Using Databases: Concerns About Accuracy and Privacy   12.23

Matters of Accuracy and Completeness   12.24

Matters of Privacy   12.24

• *Career Box: Using Computers in . . . Information Brokering, Philanthropy, Job Hunting* 12.27

Summary 12.28

Exercises 12.33

13 Trends in Computing: Multimedia and Developments in Information Technology   13.1

Why Is This Chapter Important? 13.2

Multimedia as Part of Your World 13.2

Business and Industry 13.2

Education and Training 13.3

Entertainment and Games 13.3

The Multimedia Computer 13.4

Creating Multimedia 13.4

The Authoring Process 13.8

Multimedia Presentation Software 13.9

Multimedia Authoring Software 13.9

Multimedia CBT Authoring Software 13.11

Career Opportunities in Multimedia 13.12

Artificial Intelligence (AI) 13.14

What Is AI Supposed to Do? 13.14

Robotics 13.14

Perception Systems 13.14

Natural Language Processing 13.16

Fuzzy Logic 13.17

Expert Systems: Human Expertise in a Computer 13.18

Neural Networks 13.21

Genetic Algorithms 13.23

Artificial Life, the Turing Test, and AI Ethics 13.23

Virtual Reality (VR) 13.26

Intelligent Agents, Information Filtering, and Avatars 13.29

Intelligent Agents 13.29

Avatars 13.30

Summary 13.31

Exercises 13.35

14 Ethics, Privacy, Security, and Social Questions: Computing for Right Living   14.1

Why Is This Chapter Important? 14.2

Computer Ethics 14.3

Computers and Privacy 14.3

Databases 14.5

Electronic Networks 14.5

Rules and Laws on Privacy 14.7

The Case for Limiting Privacy: Should We Really Fear "Data Rape"? 14.7

Intellectual Property Rights 14.9

Copyright 14.9

Software and Network Privacy 14.9

Plagiarism 14.10

Ownership of Media 14.11

Truth in Art and Journalism 14.11

Manipulation of Sound 14.11

Manipulation of Photos 14.12

Manipulation of Video 14.12

Manipulation of Facts 14.13

Free Speech, Civility, Pornography, and Censorship 14.14

Civility: Online Behavior and "Netiquette" 14.14

Pornography and Censorship 14.15

Security: Threats to Computer and Communications Systems 14.16

Errors and Accidents 14.17

Natural and Other Hazards 14.19

Crimes and Computers and Communications 14.19

Crimes Using Computers and Communications 14.22

Worms and Viruses 14.23

Computer Criminals 14.25

Security: Safeguarding Computers and Communications 14.28

Identification and Access 14.28

Who You Are—Your Physical Traits 14.30

Encryption 14.30

Protection of Software and Data 14.30

Disaster-Recovery Plans 14.31

Social Questions: Will Information Technology Make Our Lives Better? 14.32

Environmental Problems 14.33

Mental-Health Problems: Isolation, Gambling, Net Addiction, Stresss 4.34

Workplace Problems 14.36

Economic Issues: Employment and the Haves/Have-Nots 14.37

Education and Information 14.39

Health 14.39

Commerce and Electronic Money 14.40

Entertainment 14.40

Government and Electronic Democracy 14.40

Onward: Toward the Future 14.41

Summary 14.42

Exercises 14.47

EPISODE 5: The Future of Your Web Business E5.1

Appendix A: Guide to Purchasing a Microcomputer System A.1

Appendix B: Answers to Selected Exercises A.9

Appendix C: Notes A.11

Appendix D: Credits A.18

Index A.18

CHAPTER 1

OVERVIEW

The Foundation for Your Future

PREVIEW

When you have completed this chapter, you will be able to:

1. Define who the computer user is and what it means to be computer literate and computer competent

2. Explain what the word *digital* means and how it differs from *analog*

3. Explain what a computer-based information system is by focusing on hardware, software, data/information, procedures, people, and communications (connectivity)

4. Describe the five categories of computer hardware: input, processing, storage, output, and communications

5. Describe the main types of computer systems: supercomputers; mainframe, or mid-size, computers; workstations; microcomputers; and microcontrollers

6. Describe some of the major events in the development of computers

7. Describe computing trends: connectivity; on-line access and the Internet; interactivity; and digital convergence

WHY IS THIS CHAPTER IMPORTANT?

This chapter starts you on your way to becoming computer literate and computer competent so that you can find that "lucky job," the one that helps you realize what you want to do. Richard Bolles, author of the perennial best-selling job-hunting book *What Color Is Your Parachute?*, thinks he knows how to find that lucky job. *Luck*, he says, favors people who are going after their dreams—the thing they really want to do most in the world—who work hardest at the job hunt, and who have told the most people what they're looking for. Luck also favors people who are *prepared.*[1]

You can prepare yourself to find your special job by working through this book. Taking this step could make a vast difference in your future. Among workers who were nonusers of computers, according to one survey, 70% reported they were struggling with serious employment problems—layoffs, low pay, dead-end jobs, and the like. By contrast, among those calling themselves "sophisticated" computer users, less than a third reported such problems.[2] Moreover, those who use a computer at work are estimated to make 20% higher wages than those who don't.[3]

This first chapter starts you on your way by presenting a brief overview of computers—hardware, software, and other concepts. Later chapters will cover these topics in detail.

Who Is the User? Mostly People Like You

There is a difference between a "computer professional" and a general computer user.

First things first: Do you really know what a computer user is? Consider the following distinction:

■ A **computer professional** is a person who has a certain amount of experience and/or at least a two-year degree in the technical aspects of using computers. For example, a *computer programmer* designs, writes, tests, and implements the software programs that process the data. A *systems analyst* analyzes, designs,

Students of all ages need to be computer literate and computer competent.

and develops entire information systems for businesses and other organizations. *Computer operators* operate and monitor organizational network and business systems on a 24-hour/7-day basis.

■ The **user** (or *end-user*) is a person perhaps like yourself—someone without much technical knowledge of computers but who uses or wants to use computers to perform work-related or personal tasks, enhance learning and productivity, or have fun. The user is not necessarily a computer expert and may never need to become one. Many companies, for example, prefer to train new employees in the specific computer uses applicable to their job—and these applications may never require the user to have a lot of technical knowledge.

How do you think you will use computers in your career?

Living in what is called the Information Age, you know by now that computers aren't just a passing fad. Many types of organizations depend on them, and you will use them not only in your career but also probably to pursue private interests. To use computers efficiently, however, you must become computer literate and computer competent.

The Importance of Becoming Computer Literate and Computer Competent

By learning certain terminology, concepts, and skills, you can become computer literate and computer competent. These capabilities are now critical to your success in almost any field you choose to work in.

A computer monitors a man being screened for muscle fatigue.

Computer literacy is having an understanding of what a computer is and how it can be used as a resource. Literacy, which refers to having knowledge and understanding, needs to be distinguished from competency, which refers to having a skill. **Computer competency** is applying your skill with computers to meet your information needs and improve your productivity.

It's becoming increasingly difficult to find a professional field or area of work that does not require knowledge of computers. To help you become computer literate and computer competent, in this book and accompanying computer lab tutorials we will help you learn the following:

■ *Terms:* You will master the terminology used to describe computers and their operations.

■ *Functions:* You will learn the functions of the parts of a computer system.

■ *Uses:* You will learn how to use a computer to increase your productivity—to produce the information you need and perform the tasks required—and to meet future job requirements. You will also learn to be flexible—that is, knowledgeable about different kinds of computers and different types of software.

Besides becoming knowledgeable about and skilled in the use of computers, you should also learn to be "information literate"—to be able to find, analyze, and use information in your career.

What Is a Computer-Based Information System?

A computer-based information system is made up of six parts: hardware, software, data/information, procedures, people, and communications (connectivity). Its purpose is to transform raw data to useful information.

Not too long ago, computers were people—"persons who compute"—and machines that computed were "calculators." However, after about 1940, human computers began to be replaced by machines called "electronic computers." Thus the term **computer** now describes a device made up of a combination of electronic and electromechanical (part electronic, part mechanical) components. By itself, a computer has no intelligence and is referred to as **hardware,** which means simply the physical equipment. The hardware can't be used until it is connected to other elements, all of which constitute the six parts of a **computer-based information system** (*see Figure 1.1*):

1. Hardware
2. Software
3. Data/information
4. Procedures
5. People
6. Communications

Software is the term used to describe the instructions that tell the hardware how to perform a task. Without software, the hardware is useless.

The primary purpose of computer systems in most businesses today is to transform data into information that can be used by people to make decisions, sell products, and perform a variety of other activities. Data can be considered the

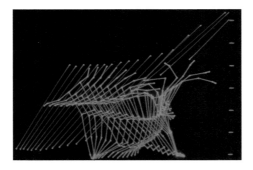

A computer analyzes a javelin thrower's performance.

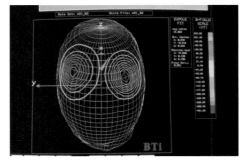

A SQUID (Super Conducting Quantum Interference Device) monitor detects electricity in the brain.

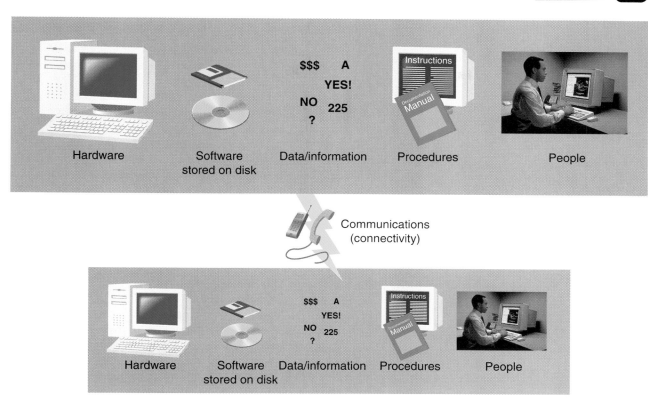

Figure 1.1 A computer-based information system typically combines six elements: hardware, software, data/information, procedures, people, and communications (connectivity).

raw material—whether in paper, electronic, or other form—that is processed by the computer. In other words, **data** consists of the raw facts and figures that are processed into information. **Information** is summarized data or otherwise manipulated (processed) data. For example, the raw data of employees' hours worked and wage rates is processed by a computer into the information of paychecks and payrolls.

Actually, in ordinary usage, the words *data* and *information* are often used synonymously. After all, one person's information may be another person's data. The "information" of paychecks and payrolls may become "data" that goes into someone's yearly financial projections or tax returns.

People, however, constitute the most important component of the computer system. People operate the computer hardware, and they create and use the computer software. They enter the data and use the information the system generates. They also follow certain procedures when using the hardware and software. **Procedures** are descriptions of how things are done, steps for accomplishing a result. Procedures for computer systems appear in *documentation manuals,* also known as *reference manuals* and *user guides,* which contain instructions, rules, and guidelines to follow when using hardware and software. These guides also offer training tutorials and are available in paper-based form and in electronic form (on disk/online). When you buy a microcomputer/software package, it comes with documentation.

What is the purpose of a computer system?

When one computer system is set up to share data and information electronically with another computer system, **communications**—also called *connectivity*—becomes a sixth system element. In other words, the manner in which the various individual systems are connected—for example, by phone lines, microwave transmission, or satellite—is an element of the total computer system.

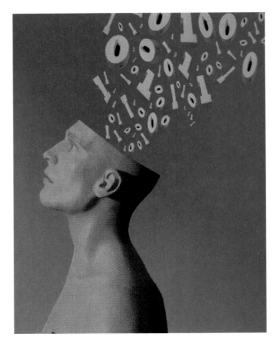

The Digital Basis of Computers

One of the main characteristics of a computer is its digital nature. No doubt you're used to hearing this word often, but what does it really mean?

Computers may seem like incredibly complicated devices, but their underlying principle is simple. When you open up a microcomputer, what you see is mainly electronic circuitry. And what is the most basic statement that can be made about electricity? It is simply this: it can be either *turned on* or *turned off,* or switched between *high voltage* and *low voltage.*

In a two-state on/off, high/low, open/closed, present/absent, positive/negative, yes/no arrangement, one state can represent a 1 digit, the other a 0 digit. People are most comfortable with the decimal number system, which has ten digits (0, 1, 2, 3, 4, 5, 6, 7, 8, 9). Because computers are based on on/off or other two-state conditions, they use the **binary number system,** which consists of only two digits—0 and 1.

The word *digit* simply means "numeral." The word *digital* is derived from "digit," which refers to the fingers people used to count with. Today, however, **digital** is almost synonymous with "computer-based." More specifically, it refers to communications signals or information represented in a discrete (individually distinct) form—usually in a binary or two-state way.

In the binary system, each 0 and 1 is called a **bit**—short for *binary digit.* In turn, bits can be grouped in various combinations to represent characters of data—numbers, letters, punctuation marks, and so on. For example, the letter H could correspond to the electronic signal 01001000 (that is, off-on-off-off-on-off-off-off). In computing, a group of 8 bits is called a **byte,** and each character is represented by 1 byte.

What kind of number system does a computer use? Why is that system also called "digital"?

Digital data, then, consists of data in discrete, discontinuous form—usually 0s and 1s. This is the method of data representation by which computers process and store data and communicate with one another.

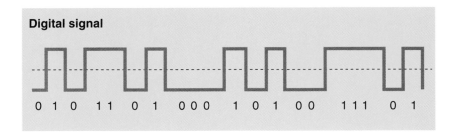

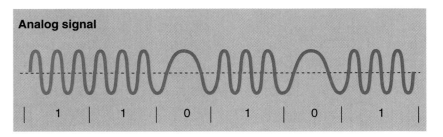

The Analog Basis of Life

Most phenomena of the world are not digital: they are **analog,** having continuously variable values. Sound, light, temperature, and pressure values, for instance, can fall anywhere on a continuum or range. The highs, lows, and in-between states have historically been represented with analog devices rather than in digital form. Examples of analog devices are humidity recorders, thermometers, and pressure sensors, which can measure continuous fluctuations. Thus, analog data is transmitted in a continuous form that closely resembles the information it represents. The electrical signals on a telephone line are analog-data representations of the original voices. Telephone, radio, broadcast television, and cable TV have traditionally transmitted analog data.

The differences between analog and digital data transmission are apparent when you look at a drawing of a wavy analog signal, such as a voice message on a standard telephone line, and an on/off digital signal. (*See opposite page and Figure 1.2.*) To transmit your computer's digital signals over telephone lines, you still need to use a *modem* to translate them into analog signals. The modem provides a means for computers to communicate with one another while the old-fashioned copper-wire telephone network—an analog system built to transmit the human voice—still exists.

Why can't traditional telephone wires directly accept digital signals from a computer?

Modems and communications are covered in detail in Chapter 7. For now, we'll focus on the *basics* of the first part of the typical computer-based information system—the hardware devices. You can use the following discussion to gain an overall perspective, or understanding, of computer hardware. We provide you with more specific hardware discussions in Chapters 2–4 and Chapter 7.

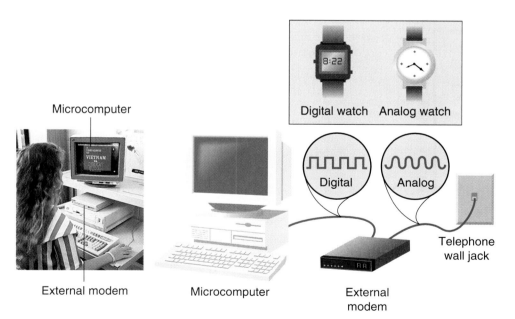

Microcomputer

External modem   Microcomputer

Digital watch   Analog watch

Digital   Analog

Telephone wall jack

External modem

Figure 1.2 Analog versus digital signals, and the modem. (*Top*) On an analog watch, the hands move continuously around the watch face; on a digital watch, the display changes once each minute. (*Bottom*) Note the wavy line for an analog signal and the on/off (or high-voltage/low-voltage) line for a digital signal. The modem shown here is outside the computer. Today many modems are inside the computer and not visible.

Computer Hardware

Computer hardware can be divided into five categories according to the five basic functions of a computer: (1) input, (2) processing, (3) storage, (4) output, and (5) communications.

When Marget Trejo, then 36, was laid off from her job because her boss couldn't make the payroll, she was stunned. "Nothing like that had ever happened to me before," she said later. "But I knew it wasn't a reflection on my work. And I saw it as an opportunity."

Today Trejo Production is a successful desktop-publishing company in Princeton, New Jersey, that uses computers to produce scores of books, brochures, and newsletters. "I'm making twice what I ever made in management positions," says Trejo, "and my business has increased by 25% every year."[4]

To do desktop publishing means first becoming familiar with some fairly sophisticated hardware, the machinery and equipment of a computer system. Hardware—what most people think of when they visualize a computer system—consists of, among other things, the keyboard, screen, printer, and the computer or processing device itself.

In general, computer hardware is categorized according to which of the five computer operations it performs (*see Figure 1.3*):

- Input
- Processing and memory
- Output
- Storage
- Communications

External devices that are connected to the computer cabinet but are not inside the main cabinet are referred to as **peripheral devices.** Thus keyboard, mice, monitors, and printers are all peripheral devices.

Input Hardware

The function of **input hardware** is to accept data and convert it into a form suitable for computer processing. In other words, input hardware allows people to put data into the computer in a form that the computer can use. For example, input may be by means of a keyboard, mouse, or scanner.

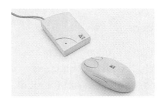

- *Keyboard:* A **keyboard** includes the standard typewriter keys plus a number of specialized keys. The standard keys are used mostly to enter words and numbers. Examples of specialized keys on microcomputers are *function keys,* labeled F1, F2, and so on. These special keys are used to enter software-specific commands. (Some large computers use PF1, PF2, etc. for "programmable function keys.")

- *Mouse:* A **mouse** is a device that is rolled about on a desktop to direct a pointer on the computer's display screen. The pointer is a symbol, usually an arrow, that is used to select items from lists (menus) on the screen or to position the cursor. The **cursor,** also called an *insertion point,* is the symbol on the screen that shows where data may be entered next, such as text in a document.

- *Scanners:* **Scanners**—which are often used in desktop publishing—translate images of text, drawings, and photos into digital form. The images can then

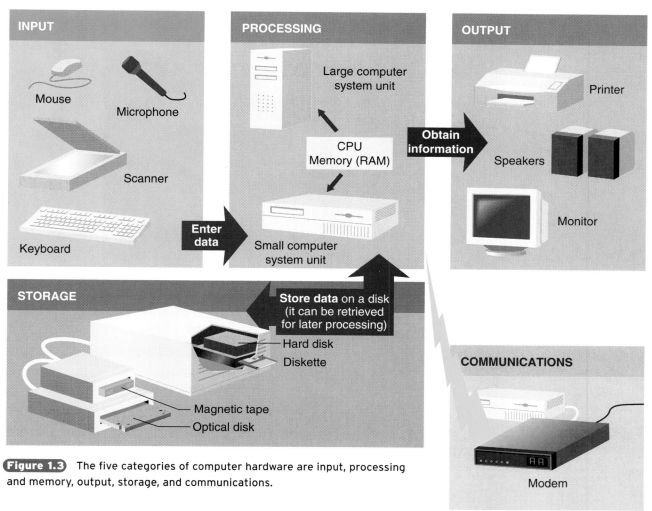

Figure 1.3 The five categories of computer hardware are input, processing and memory, output, storage, and communications.

be processed by a computer, displayed on a monitor, inserted in documents, stored on a storage device, or transmitted to another computer.

Input devices are discussed in detail in the first half of Chapter 3.

Processing and Memory Hardware

The computer's control center is made up of the processing and main memory devices, housed in the computer's system unit. The **system unit,** or *system cabinet,* houses that part of the electronic circuitry that does the actual processing and the memory that supports processing, together called the **processing hardware.** (*See Figure 1.4.*)

■ *CPU—the processor:* The **CPU,** for **central processing unit,** is the processor, or computing part, of the computer. It controls and manipulates data to produce information. In a microcomputer the CPU is a 1.5-inch (3.75-centimeter) or smaller square "chip" called a *microprocessor,* with electrical circuits printed on it. This microprocessor, and other components necessary to make it work, are mounted on a main circuit board called the *motherboard,* or *system board.*

Figure 1.4 The system unit. This cabinet houses the electronic processing circuitry and the memory that supports processing.

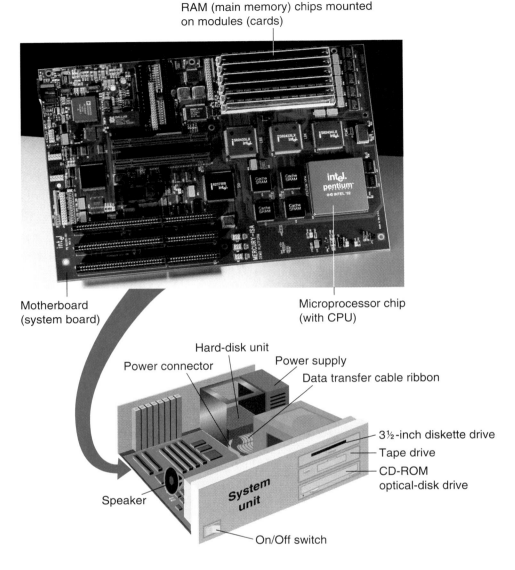

RAM (main memory) chips mounted on modules (cards)

Motherboard (system board)

Microprocessor chip (with CPU)

Hard-disk unit

Power connector

Power supply

Data transfer cable ribbon

3½-inch diskette drive

Tape drive

CD-ROM optical-disk drive

System unit

Speaker

On/Off switch

What is the basis of categorizing hardware devices?

Memory—working storage: **Memory**—also known as *main memory, RAM (random access memory),* or *primary storage*—is temporary working storage. That means memory is the computer's "work space" or "desk area," where data and programs needed for immediate processing are held. Computer memory is contained on memory chips mounted on the motherboard. Memory capacity is important because it determines how much data can be processed at once and how big and complex the program used to process the data can be.

Despite its name, this kind of memory cannot "remember." That is, once the power is turned off, all the data and programs within memory simply vanish—that is, they are *volatile.* This is why data/information must also be stored in relatively permanent form on disks and tapes, which are called *secondary storage* devices to distinguish them from main memory's *primary storage.*

Processing and memory hardware is covered in detail in the next chapter.

Output Hardware

The function of **output hardware** is to provide the user with the means to view and use information produced by the computer system. For example, previously input but unorganized sales figures were processed into meaningful form and now are displayed on a computer screen or printed out on paper.

Information is output in either hardcopy or softcopy form. *Hardcopy output* can be held in your hand—an example is paper with text (words or numbers) or graphics printed on it. *Softcopy output* is typically displayed on a *monitor*, a television-like screen on which you can read text and graphics. Another type of softcopy output is audio output, such as music.

Output hardware is the topic of the second half of Chapter 3.

Storage Hardware

As previously mentioned, the function of secondary **storage hardware** is to provide a means of storing software and data in a form that is relatively permanent, or *nonvolatile*—that is, the data is not lost when the power is turned off—and easy to retrieve when needed for processing. Storage hardware serves the same basic functions as do office filing systems except that it stores data as electromagnetic signals or laser-etched spots, commonly on magnetic disk, optical disk, or tape, rather than on paper.

Secondary storage hardware is discussed in Chapter 4.

Communications Hardware

The function of **communications hardware** is to facilitate the connections between computers and between groups of connected computers called *networks*. Of course, computers can be "stand-alone" machines, meaning that they are not connected to anything else. Indeed many students tote around portable microcomputers that they use for word processing and other programs. However, the communications component of a computer system vastly extends the computer's range and utility.

In general, computer communications is of two types: wired connections, such as telephone wire and cable, and wireless connections, such as microwaves and radio waves. Because the dominant communications media that have been developed during this century use analog transmission, the principal form of direct connection has been via standard copper-wire telephone lines. Hundreds of these copper wires are bundled together in cables strung in telephone poles or buried underground. As we described earlier, a modem is required to translate a computer's digital signals into analog form for transmission over telephone wires. Although copper wiring still exists in most places, it is gradually being supplanted by newer forms of connections that will allow direct transmission of digital signals. We cover these and other aspects of computers and communications in Chapters 7 and 8.

Computer Software

Computer hardware is useless without the electronic instructions—software—that tell it what to do. There are two categories of software: applications software and systems software.

A computer has no intelligence of its own and must be supplied with instructions that tell it what to do and how and when to do it. These instructions are called *software,* because you can't feel it or see it. It flows through the computer's circuits as coded pulses of electricity. The importance of software can't be overestimated. Without software to "breathe life" into the computer, to make it do what you want it to do, the computer will only take up space.

Software is made up of a group of related *programs* written in a specific code called a *programming language* and based on the computer's language of 0s and 1s. In turn, each program is made up of a group of related instructions that perform specific processing tasks. Software acquired to perform a general business function is often referred to as a *software package.* Software is usually created by professional software programmers and comes on disk, CD-ROM, or online, across the Internet.

Software can generally be divided into two categories:

1. System software

2. Applications software

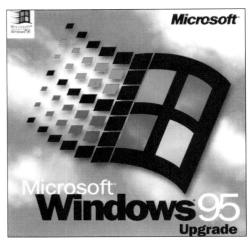

System Software: The Computer's Boss

Software designed to allow the computer to manage its own resources and run basic operations is called **system software.** This software runs the basic operations; it lets the CPU communicate with the keyboard, the screen, the printer, and the disk drive. However, it does not solve specific problems relating to a business or a profession. For example, system software will not help Silicon Valley entrepreneur Jerry Kaplan, self-styled "P.T. Barnum of cyberspace," process data about goods offered by his company ONSALE for online computer auction. It will, however, tell the computer where and how to store and retrieve data used during the processing. System software didn't tell film editor Rob Kobrin how to digitally move mountains in the 1996 family movie *Alaska,* but it helped manage how the special effects were output.

Examples of system software are DOS, Windows, OS/2, Macintosh Operating System, NOS (Novell Operating System), and Unix. (We describe system software in detail in Chapter 5.)

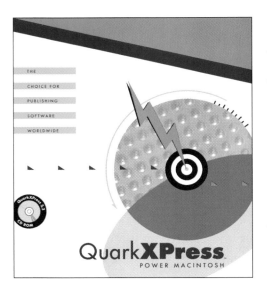

Applications Software: Your Servant

Applications software allows you to increase your productivity and creativity in ways simply not possible without it. **Applications software** is software that performs tasks to directly benefit or assist the user. Examples are programs that do word processing, desktop publishing, payroll processing, or animation. (We cover applications software in Chapter 6.)

Ready-made applications software can be purchased "off the shelf" from a computer store or a mail-order supplier, or it can be created, or customized, to specification by a programmer. If a company has fairly routine payroll processing requirements, it can purchase a payroll software package off the shelf to handle the job. However, if the company has unique payroll requirements, such as a need to handle the records of hourly, salaried, and commissioned employees paid in different countries and in different currencies, then it may need to have its payroll software custom-written by a programmer.

Types of Computer Systems: What's the Difference?

Computers are often classified into general types based mainly on processing speed and storage capacity. Divisions among these types are blurring as technology improves.

Computers have come a long way since the first operational computer in 1940. In 1969 the onboard guidance computer used by the Apollo 11 astronauts, who made the first moon landing, weighed 70 pounds (31 kilograms) and could hold the equivalent of a mere 2000 characters (bytes) of data in its main memory. The Mission Control computer on the ground had only 1 million characters of memory. "It cost $4 million and took up most of a room," says a space physicist who was there.[5]

Fast forward to the present: Today the shrinkage of computer components means that you can easily buy, for a couple thousand dollars, a personal computer that sits on a desktop and has hundreds of times the processing power and about 32 to 64 times the memory of the 1969 Mission Control computer. You have more productivity at your fingertips than the American space program had a generation ago. And computer processing power is doubling every 18 months. In other words, that new computer that you just took out of the box will be only half as powerful as those introduced next year.

Although you may be familiar only with microcomputers, computers still come in a variety of sizes and with a variety of processing capabilities. We may categorize them as:

1. Supercomputers
2. Mainframe computers
3. Workstations
4. Microcomputers
5. Microcontrollers

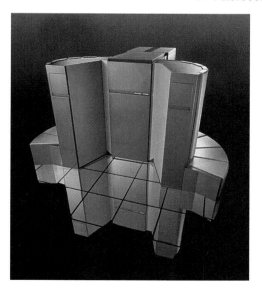

It's hard to give a precise definition to each type because computer speeds and storage capacities change rapidly. Nevertheless, the following definitions will suffice:

■ *Supercomputers:* First developed in the 1970s, **supercomputers** are the fastest and highest-capacity computers. Their cost ranges from several hundreds of thousands to millions of dollars. They may occupy special air-conditioned rooms and are often used for research. Among their uses are worldwide weather forecasting and analysis of weather phenomena, oil exploration, aircraft design, evaluation of aging nuclear weapons systems, and mathematical research. Unlike microcomputers, which generally have only one central processing unit, supercomputers have hundreds to thousands of processors.

One supercomputer named Option red fills 85 locker-size cabinets and 1600 square feet at Sandia National Laboratories in Albuquerque, New Mexico.

- *Mainframe computers:* The only type of computer available until the late 1960s, **mainframe computers** are less powerful than supercomputers, but they are still fast, mid- to large-size, large-capacity machines. Their size varies depending on how many concurrent users they are serving—from a few hundred to thousands of people. Mainframes are used by many banks, airlines, insurance companies, mail-order houses, universities, and the Internal Revenue Service. Mainframes also have many processors.

- *Workstations:* **Workstations,** introduced in the early 1980s, are expensive, powerful desktop computers used mainly by engineers, scientists, and special-effects creators for sophisticated purposes. Providing many capabilities comparable to midsize mainframes, workstations are used for such tasks as designing airplane fuselages, prescription drugs, and movies' special effects. Workstations are often connected to a larger computer system to facilitate the transfer of data and information. The capabilities of low-end workstations overlap those of high-end microcomputers.

- *Microcomputers:* **Microcomputers,** also called *personal computers (PCs),* are small computers that can fit next to a desk, on a desktop, or can be carried around. Some microcomputers, called *tower units,* are higher than they are wide and can be placed on the floor. Whether desktop, tower (floor-standing), notebook, palmtop, electronic organizer, or pen-based, personal computers are now found in most businesses (*see Figure 1.5*). They are used either as stand-alone machines or connected to a network, such as a local area network. A **local area network (LAN)** connects, usually by special cable, a group of desktop PCs and peripheral devices in an office or a building. In most LANs, one PC is assigned the role of **server,** meaning that it stores data and software for use by the other PCs and/or performs services for them, such as printing.

- *Microcontrollers:* Also called *embedded, dedicated,* or *hidden computers,* **microcontrollers** are tiny computers installed in "smart" appliances like microwave ovens and pocket calculators. They are dedicated to performing a restricted number of tasks.

Some companies use a combination of computers, and, indeed, the predominant information system is now a hybrid model, whereby a variety of systems are tied together under a common umbrella. For instance, an insurance company with branch offices around the country might use a mainframe computer to manage companywide customer data. To access information from the mainframe, a local claims

Types of Microcomputers

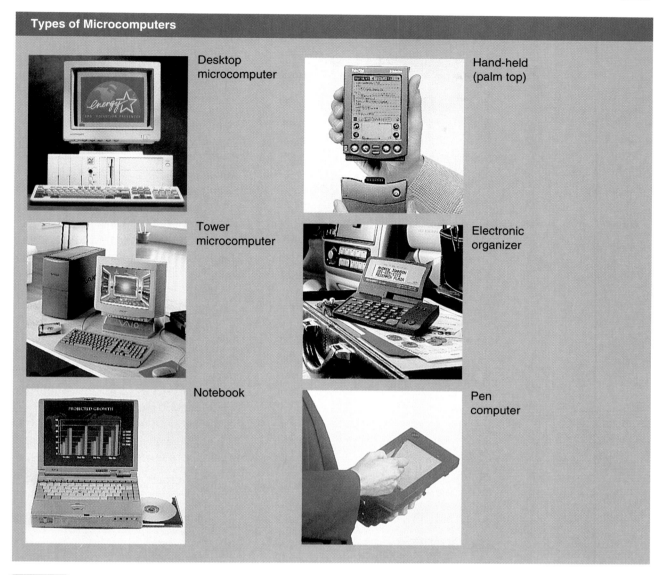

Desktop microcomputer

Hand-held (palm top)

Tower microcomputer

Electronic organizer

Notebook

Pen computer

Figure 1.5 Microcomputers come in different sizes.

adjuster might use a microcomputer on his or her desktop. That same microcomputer can also be used to perform specialized tasks such as generating invoices or drafting letters to customers. Because microcomputers are generally versatile, increasingly powerful, and more affordable than the other types of computers, they are practical tools for organizations wishing to improve their productivity.

Whatever their size, speed, and capacity, all computers operate according to similar principles. In the next section, we present a brief history of computer processing to show why these machines take the form they do today.

What is a server? What is at least one advantage of using a LAN and a server in an office?

Weather Forecasting or Firefighting

"Everyone talks about the weather, but no one does anything about it," quipped Mark Twain.

Now maybe they can—with the help of supercomputers, better weather satellites, and other high-tech tools.

Advance notice of the record-shattering snowstorm that buried the East Coast in 1996 allowed Governor George Allen of Virginia to declare an emergency "before a single snowflake hit his state," according to one account.[6] As a result, for example, airlines were able to divert their planes to safety before the storm, and none were pinned down on the ground by the storm.

"Five years ago, no one would have predicted a record," said the director of the National Weather Service, Elbert Friday. In recent years, however, meteorologists have added a slew of new digital technologies to their arsenal. The result is more accurate forecasts and a public more willing to trust the forecasters' predictions.

Because the data on weather is so complex, supercomputers, the most powerful of the lot, have long been used by the National Weather Service. Now even faster supercomputers are being used to run more sophisticated global-forecast models analyzing more precise kinds of weather data collected from a greater variety of sources.

Wind data has traditionally been collected from balloons released twice daily in different locations. Now additional wind and temperature data are being automatically collected from high-flying jetliners and from new ground-based Doppler weather radar stations. Automated ground sensors are augmented by new high-tech satellites hovering over the equator that measure cloud-top temperatures. The supercomputers plot the data on a grid map and perform recalculations every minute to create predictions. Comparing the forecast of a January 1996 blizzard to that for a similar big storm two years earlier, Friday said, "The difference in response was really spectacular."

Technology is also helping in dry weather by helping change the way wildfires are fought. The California Department of Forestry, for instance, relies on a ring of 24 satellites organized into the country's GPS (global positioning satellite network). The satellites beam down signals that allow people on the ground to immediately plot their positions by activating small handheld units. Using this data, fire crews can produce special data-intensive GIS (Geographic Information System) maps that show spot fires, crew locations, roads, and homes.

Said California firefighter Mark Bisbee, describing the strategy employed in a recent fire in Lake County, "We drove up to each house [in the area] and got a reading from our GPS unit, then used the information to develop accurate GIS maps for our crews. We know where each house is, and that's critical."[7]

Someday, say experts, a lot of this information will not need to be created on the spot. It will be available before the fires start—in the database of a computer.

Milestones in Computer Development

People have been processing data and information in some form since prehistoric times. However, it was the development of the computer that revolutionized information processing. Since the first generation of computers was built, the subsequent three computer generations have produced smaller, more powerful, and less expensive machines—mostly as the result of the development of the integrated circuit.

Over the centuries, people have developed an amazing variety of data processing tools and techniques. Around 3000 B.C., the Sumerians used a box of stones as a device for representing numbers. About 2000 years later, the Chinese took the idea a step farther when they strung stones on threads in a wooden frame, the *abacus*, a device still in wide use in some parts of Asia. Other calculating tools were in use between the mid-1600s and the early 1900s, as described in Figure 1.6. However, the birth of the true electronic computer did not occur until our own century.

Figure 1.6 Which came first—computers or data processing? Many people think that we have been turning data into information only since computers came into use. The truth is that people have been processing data since prehistoric times. This illustration shows a few of the data processing methods used between the mid-1600s and the early 1900s. (a) Pascaline calculator (mid-1600s), the first automatic adding and subtracting machine; (b) Leibniz Wheel (early 1700s), the first general-purpose calculating machine; (c) Jacquard loom (1801), run by punched cards; (d) Thomas's arithnometer (1860), the first commercially successful adding and subtracting machine; (e) Hollerith's tabulating machine, used in the 1890 U.S. census; and (f) early IBM calculating machine (circa 1930).

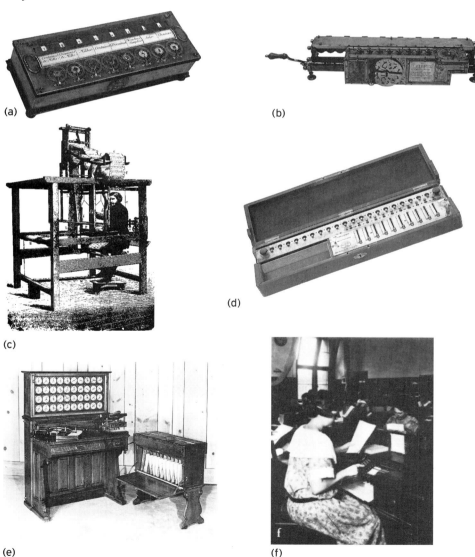

(a)

(b)

(c)

(d)

(e)

(f)

The Evolution of Computers: March of the Generations

The first large-scale electronic computer, the grandparent of today's handheld machines, was the Electronic Numerical Integrator and Computer (ENIAC), which became operational in 1946. (*See Figure 1.7.*) ENIAC contained approximately 18,000 light-bulb-size electronic vacuum tubes that controlled the flow of electric current. It weighed 30 tons (27.2 metric tons) and occupied about 1500 square feet (139 square meters) of floor space—a huge machine by today's standard. It was able to multiply four numbers in the then remarkable time of 9 milliseconds (9/1000 of a second). From that start, computers have developed through four so-called *generations,* or stages, each subsequent one characterized by smaller size, more power, and less expense than its predecessor.

First Generation (1944–1958)

In the earliest general-purpose computers, most input and output media were punched cards and magnetic tape. Main memory was almost exclusively made up

Figure 1.7   ENIAC, the first large-scale electronic computer. ENIAC weighed 30 tons, filled 1500 square feet, included 18,000 vacuum tubes—and it failed about every 7 minutes.

Computer Technology Timeline

1000 BC	200 BC
Abacus used for arithmetic calculations, developed in Orient 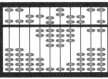	Chinese artisans develop an entire mechanical orchestra

of hundreds of vacuum tubes—although one computer used a magnetic drum for main memory. These computers were somewhat unreliable because the vacuum tubes failed frequently. They were also slower than any microcomputer used today, produced a tremendous amount of heat, and were very large. They could run only one program at a time. ENIAC and UNIVAC I—the UNIVersal Automatic Computer, which was used by the U.S. Bureau of the Census from 1951 to 1963—are examples of first-generation computers. The UNIVAC was priced at $500,000 in 1950; today, you could purchase microcomputer chips with the same processing power for less than $100.

Second Generation (1959–1963)

By the early 1960s, transistors and some other solid-state devices that were much smaller than vacuum tubes were being used for much of the computer circuitry. (A transistor is an electronic switch that alternately allows or does not allow electronic signals to pass.) Magnetic cores, which looked like very small metal washers strung together by wires that carried electricity, became the most widely used type of main memory. Removable magnetic disk packs, stacks of disks connected by a common spindle (like a stack of records), were introduced as storage devices. Second-generation machines tended to be smaller, more reliable, and significantly faster than first-generation computers.

Third Generation (1964–1970)

In the third period, the **integrated circuit**—a complete electronic circuit that packages transistors (signal bridges) and other electronic components on a small silicon chip—replaced traditional transistorized circuitry. Integrated circuits are cost-effective because individual components don't need to be wired directly to the computer's system board.

The use of magnetic disks for secondary data storage became widespread, and computers began to support such capabilities as multiprogramming (processing several programs simultaneously) and timesharing (people using the same computer simultaneously). Minicomputers, priced around $18,000, were being widely used by the early 1970s and were taking some of the business away from the established mainframe market. Processing that formerly required the processing power of a mainframe could now be done on a minicomputer.

Fourth Generation (1971–Now)

Large-scale integrated (LSI) and very-large-scale integrated (VLSI) circuits were developed that contained hundreds to millions of transistors on a tiny chip. In

1642 AD	1832	1843
First automatic adding machine (Blaise Pascal)	Babbage's analytical engine (first "computer")	World's first computer programmer, Ada Lovelace, publishes her notes

1971 Ted Hoff of Intel, developed the microprocessor, which packaged an entire CPU, complete with memory, logic, and control circuits, on a single chip. The microprocessor and VLSI circuit technology caused radical changes in computers—in their size, appearance, cost, availability, and capability—and they started the process of *miniaturization:* the development of smaller and smaller computers.

Also during this time, computers' main memory capacity increased, and its cost decreased, which directly affected the types and usefulness of software that could be used. Software applications like word processing, electronic spreadsheets, database management programs, painting and drawing programs, desktop publishing, and so forth became commercially available, giving more people reasons to use a computer.

The Information Explosion: Data Overload or Knowledge?

What has been the effect of this tremendous increase in processing power? It has made data and information available to us not only more quickly but also in greater quantity.

Before the computer, most business transactions involved the use of paper—creating it, using it, sending it, storing it. One promise of the computer was that it would eliminate paper, but it seems now that there is more than ever. "By 2000," according to a forecast a few years ago, "U.S. businesses will still need a space equivalent to all of the office space in Pittsburgh to file the 120 billion sheets of new paper they will generate every year."[8]

Where do you think you will be able to get help learning how to handle information overload when you have to research term papers?

The catch to information technology is that although it can generate information—mountains of information in both paper and electronic form—it does not always generate knowledge. Thus, we need to learn how to be selective about the information we get—to make sure that, in the classic definition of usefulness, it is *complete, accurate, relevant,* and *timely (CART).* To avoid being buried in an avalanche of unnecessary data, we must be able to distinguish what we *really need* from what we *think* we need.

1890	1900	1930	1946
Electricity used for first time in a data-processing project (punched cards)	Hollerith's automatic census-tabulating machine (used punched card)	General theory of electronic computers	First electronic computer in United States (ENIAC)

Computing Trends: Connectivity, Online Access and the Internet, Interactivity, and Digital Convergence

Connectivity is the ability to connect computers and other information devices to each other by communications lines. It is through connectivity that people have envisioned the "Information Superhighway," whereby everyone on the planet will eventually have the ability to electronically access previously unimagined amounts of information and services.

Lee Taylor is what is known as a "lone eagle." Once he was the manager of several technical writers for a California information services company. Then, taking a one-third pay cut, he moved with his wife to a tiny cabin near the ski-resort town of Telluride, Colorado. There he operates as a freelance consultant for his old company, using phone, computer network, and fax machine to stay in touch.[9]

"Lone eagles" like Taylor constitute a growing number of professionals who, with information technology, can work almost anywhere they want. Many operate out of resort areas and remote towns. Although their income may be less, it is offset by such "quality of life" advantages as weekday skiing or reduced housing costs.

Taylor is one beneficiary of several trends that will probably intensify as information technology continues to proliferate. We examine these trends briefly here.

Connectivity: The Examples of Telecommuting, Teleshopping, and E-Mail and Voice Mail

Just as Telluride's phone system is connected to bigger networks, so can any *telecommunications* network may be connected to larger ones. This is one example of **connectivity,** the ability to connect computers and telephones by telecommunications lines to other devices and sources of information. It is this connectivity that is the foundation of the Information Age.

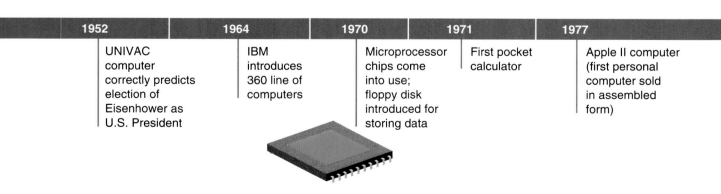

1952	1964	1970	1971	1977
UNIVAC computer correctly predicts election of Eisenhower as U.S. President	IBM introduces 360 line of computers	Microprocessor chips come into use; floppy disk introduced for storing data	First pocket calculator	Apple II computer (first personal computer sold in assembled form)

The connectivity of telecommunications has made possible many kinds of activities, among them telecommuting, teleshopping, and electronic and voice mail. (These topics are covered in detail in Chapter 8.)

■ *Telecommuting:* In standard commuting, one takes transportation (car, bus, train) from home to work and back. In *telecommuting,* one works at home and communicates with ("commutes to") the office by phone, fax, and computer. Already an estimated 9.1 million people telecommute in the United States at least part of the time.[10] Telecommuting is also growing in Europe, Canada, and the Pacific Rim countries.

Telecommuters may be full-time employees—insurance claims processors, typesetters, travel agents—who work at home and seldom go in to the company's main office. Or they may work at home some days and make the trek to the office on others.

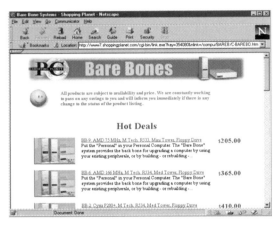

Consultants or freelancers like Lee Taylor resemble these kinds of telecommuters. The difference is that, instead of being tied to headquarters by high technology, they *are* headquarters. That is, they run their own businesses from wherever they want and "telecommute" with clients and suppliers by telephone, fax, and computer.

■ *Teleshopping:* With *teleshopping,* microcomputer users dial into a telephone-linked computer-based shopping service that lists prices and descriptions of products that may be ordered through the computer. Products range from computer hardware and software to flowers, food, and cosmetics. One of the most popular shopping categories is music, with about 10,000 sites around the world; the top five sites sell more than 25,000 CDs each day.[11]

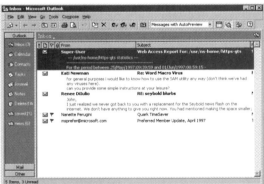

■ *E-mail and voice mail:* E-mail, or *electronic mail,* is a system that links computers by wired or wireless connections. It allows users, through their keyboards, to post messages and to read responses on their computer screens. Whether the network is a company's small local area network or a worldwide network such as the Internet, e-mail allows users to send messages anywhere on the system.

Voice mail acts like a telephone answering machine; incoming voice messages are digitized and stored on your telephone company's server for your retrieval later. Retrieval is accomplished by dialing into

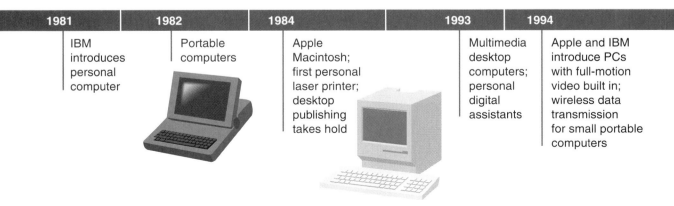

1981	1982	1984	1993	1994
IBM introduces personal computer	Portable computers	Apple Macintosh; first personal laser printer; desktop publishing takes hold	Multimedia desktop computers; personal digital assistants	Apple and IBM introduce PCs with full-motion video built in; wireless data transmission for small portable computers

What might be some of
the limitations of
telecommuting? What do
you think are some of the
disadvantages of using
e-mail and voice mail?

your "mailbox" number from any telephone. One advantage over answering machines is that even while you're on the phone, incoming callers can leave messages in your voice mail box.

Online Information Access: The Examples of Databases, Online Services, and Networks

The term *online,* or *on-line* (with a hyphen), refers to being connected via modem or network to other computers. That is, you are "on the line" with them, taking advantage of your system's connectivity options. Online connections usually are of the wired kind but rapidly are becoming wireless also.

Being online gives you access to resources far beyond those available with a computer sitting by itself unconnected to anything else. The word *access* refers to the ability to connect to a particular database, network, or online service. Being able to access modern information systems can significantly enhance your professional abilities and research capabilities.

■ *Databases:* A **database** is a collection of integrated, or cross-referenced, data. A database may be stored on your own unconnected microcomputer. Here, however, we are concerned with databases located elsewhere, which different people may access to use for different purposes. These are libraries of information at the other end of a wired or wireless connection and available to you through your microcomputer. For example, suppose that a company offered you a job, but you didn't know much about the company. To find out about your prospective employer, you could go online to gain access to some helpful databases. Examples are Business Database Plus, Magazine Database Plus, or TRW Business Profiles. You could then study the company's products, review financial data, identify major competitors, or learn about recent sales increases or layoffs. You might even get an idea of whether or not you would be happy with the "corporate culture."[12]

■ *Computer online services, networks, and the Internet:* Established major commercial online services include America Online, CompuServe, and Microsoft Network. A computer **online service** is a commercial information service that, for a fee, makes available to subscribers various services through their telephone-linked microcomputers.

1998	2000	2009	2012	
Home video computers	Tele-conferencing replaces the majority of business travel	Half of U.S. workers work at home using computer systems	U.S. citizens vote for president at home, online	**The Future**

Web Publishing

Spawned by the punk rock underground of the 1970s, *zines* are printed magazine-like "quirky periodicals that rarely carry ads and usually have only a handful of readers," according to one description. Their main attribute is that they tackle "narrow subjects with unrestrained subjectivity."[13] *Dishwasher,* for instance, is written by someone named "Dishwasher Pete" who chronicles one man's quest to wash dishes in all 50 states.

Opening screen of the E-zine called *Slate*

Now zines have moved to the Internet's World Wide Web, where they are known as *E-zines* or *Webzines.* One of the results of the Web's popularity is that it has enabled almost anyone to become a publisher. Says one writer who goes by the name R. U. Serius, "There are no producers or editors deciding who gets to appear on the Web. . . . You don't need a journalism degree to proffer your version of reality."[14]

What distinguishes a Webzine from a print zine? First, on the Web, articles often include links (underlined words) to other Web resources. That is, using the mouse buttons, you simply "click on" the underlined word to obtain more information. Second, articles feature not only text and graphics but also links to video clips and short bits of sound. Third, you can often type in ("post") questions to the editor and receive feedback via electronic mail. Finally, you can selectively print out on your computer's printer those articles of interest to you.

Many Webzines target specific niches, such as motorcycle, chile-pepper, or Florida lovers. Some—such as *Slate, Salon, HotWired, Word, Feed,* and *Mr. Showbiz*—strive to go beyond simply being idiosyncratic voices and to make money. Many periodicals, including *Time, USA Today,* and *The Wall Street Journal,* have created Web magazines. Many readers have found that scientific journals take too long to report new findings that might affect their health, and scientists are now being urged to post research papers electronically first, and only then to submit them to journals.

Still, Web publishers are still trying to figure out how to attain profitability, since many Internet users are used to paying zero and advertisers are wary of the new medium. *The Web Review,* for instance, had to stop publishing after nine months and appeal to readers to pay for its information. However, a few online publishers are starting to make money, such as the *San Jose Mercury News*'s Mercury Center. Alex Brown Research and the McCann-Erickson Advertising Agency found U.S. advertising revenues on the Net in 1996 to be between $150 million and $200 million. They forecast $2 billion in revenues by 2000.[15] Other estimates run as high as $5 billion by 2000.[16]

Among other things, consumers can research information in databases, participate in subject-specific discussion groups, make airline reservations, shop, and send messages via e-mail.

A computer online service also provides one way of accessing the greatest network of all, the Internet. The **Internet** is an international network of tens of thousands of smaller networks that link computers at academic, industrial, and scientific institutions. An estimated 23.5 to 26.4 million people around the world are currently using the Internet. With the proper software and access, you can do anything on the Net that you can do via an online information service—research, investing, shopping, e-mail, travel reservations, real-time conversation, and so on. The most well-known part of the Internet is the **World Wide Web,** which stores information on the Internet in multimedia form—that is, in sound, photos, and video, as well as text. People and companies who maintain Web locations on the Internet do so in sites called *Web pages* that are stored on servers connected to the Internet. To view Web pages, users need special software called a *Web browser*—such as Netscape Navigator or Communicator, or Microsoft Explorer. (Information Services, the Internet, and the Web are covered in detail in Chapter 8.)

Interactivity: The Examples of Multimedia Computers, TV/PC "Smart Boxes," Network Computers, and Personal Digital Assistants

Developed by ImagiNation Network, CyberPark is an online game service, a virtual (3-D) theme park where members can wander around, chat with other members, and play various games via computer. This is an example of interactivity. **Interactivity** means that the user is able to make an immediate response to what is going on and modify the processes. That is, there is a dialogue between the user and the computer or communications device. Interactivity allows users to be active rather than passive participants in the technological process.

Among the types of interactive devices are multimedia computers, PC/TV "smart boxes" and "Internet appliances," network computers, and personal digital assistants.

- *Multimedia computers:* The word *multimedia,* one of the buzzwords of the '90s, has been variously defined. Essentially, however, **multimedia,** from "multiple media," refers to technology that presents information in more than one medium, including text, graphics, animation, video, music, and voice.

   Multimedia microcomputers (sometimes called *MPCs*) include sound and video capability, run CD-ROM disks, and allow you to play games or perform interactive tasks.

- *Up-and-coming "smart boxes" and "information appliances":* Already envisioning a world of cross-breeding among televisions, telephones, and computers, enterprising manufacturers are experimenting with developing PC/TV set-top control boxes, or *smart boxes,* and *information appliances. (See Figure 1.8.)* With these devices, consumers presumably could listen to music CDs, watch movies, do computing, view multiple cable channels, and go online. Set-top boxes would provide two-way interactivity not only with video games but also with online entertainment, news, and educational programs. Video-game consoles that can double as set-top boxes to access online offerings are being made by various manufacturers, such as Philips, Sega, Sony, and Thomson. WebTV Networks, Inc., sells a box a bit smaller than a VCR that you connect to your TV and a phone line. Once you subscribe to their WebTV service, you can explore the Web, send and receive e-mail, and watch regular TV. These

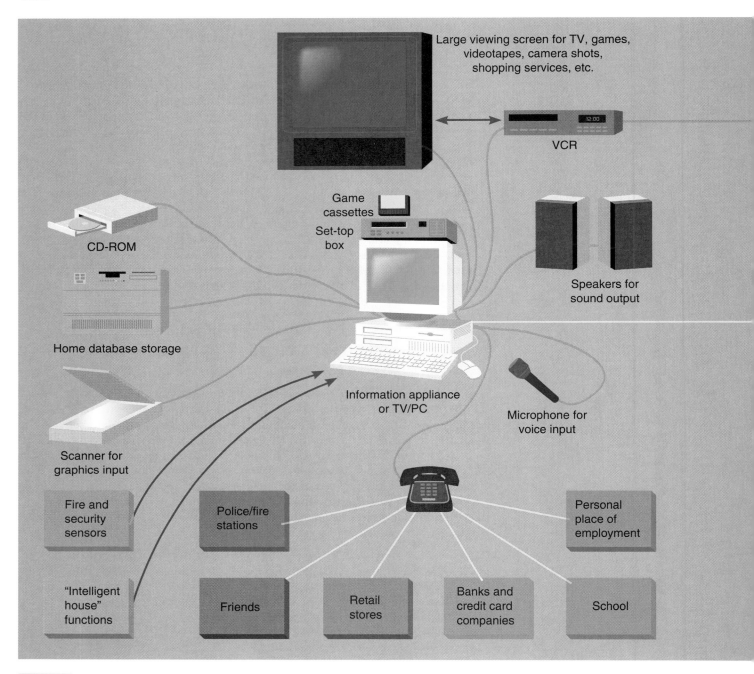

Figure 1.8 Information appliance

types of set-top boxes, however, cannot make your TV set behave like a computer monitor. Because a TV screen has lower resolution than a computer monitor, Web pages can be difficult to read. You also cannot participate directly in the thousands of discussion groups ("chat rooms") on the Internet, and you can't use computer software.

- *Network computers:* The "hollow personal computers," called *network computers* have recently become available. Instead of having complex memory and storage capabilities built in, these inexpensive Net PCs serve as entry points to the online world, supposedly allowing access to all the resources anyone

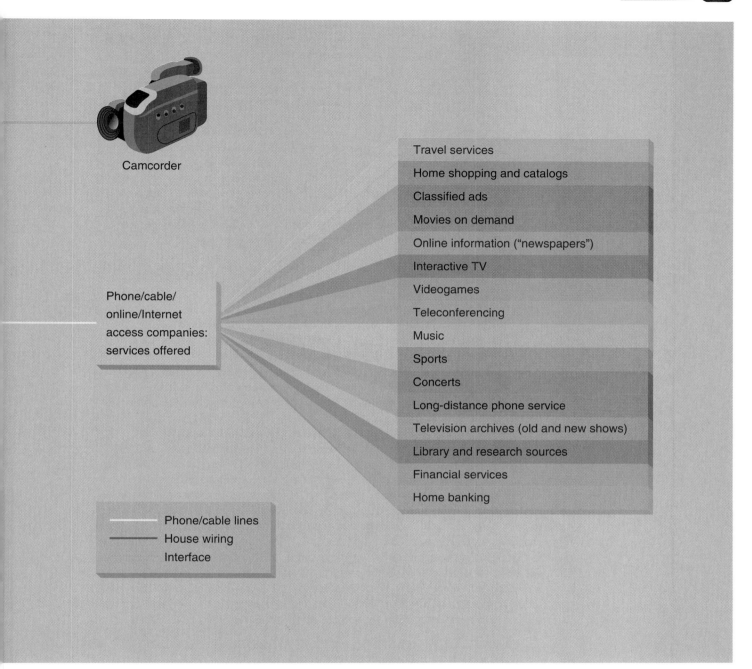

Camcorder

Phone/cable/
online/Internet
access companies:
services offered

Travel services
Home shopping and catalogs
Classified ads
Movies on demand
Online information ("newspapers")
Interactive TV
Videogames
Teleconferencing
Music
Sports
Concerts
Long-distance phone service
Television archives (old and new shows)
Library and research sources
Financial services
Home banking

Phone/cable lines
House wiring
Interface

would need. Says Larry Ellison, chief executive officer (CEO) of Oracle, the world's second largest software company: "We need to make [the gadget] so inexpensive and easy to use that nearly everyone will have a computer, just like they have a TV set or a phone."[17] However, many people point out that until the communications infrastructure becomes more reliable—until most of the old copper-wire telephone lines have been replaced—they do not want to rely on remote locations to supply all their software, processing, and information needs. Net PCs usually come with a monitor, keyboard, mouse, and network connections. To use one, you simply connect it via a phone line to the network you subscribe to (such as an Internet service provider) and turn it on.

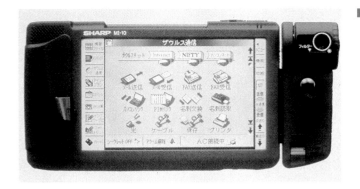

This PDA from Japan includes a digital camera

Personal digital assistants: Since their introduction in 1988, handheld electronic organizers have evolved into *personal digital assistants* (*PDAs*), small pen-controlled, handheld computers that, in their most developed form, can do two-way wireless messaging. Instead of pecking at a tiny keyboard, you can use a special pen to write out commands on the computer screen. The newer generation of PDAs can be used not only to keep an appointment calendar and write memos but also to access the Internet and send and receive faxes and e-mail. With a PDA, then, you can immediately get information from some remote location—such as your microcomputer on your desk at home—and, if necessary, edit it or update it.

What does the term *multimedia* mean? *Interactivity?* What do you think you will use multimedia for?

Digital Convergence: The Way of the Future

"We should all be concerned about the future," said engineer and inventor Charles Kettering, "because we will have to spend the rest of our lives there." *Convergence* is definitely part of our future. Basically, **digital convergence** is the technological merger of several industries through various devices that exchange information in the digital format used by computers. The industries are computers, communications, consumer electronics, entertainment, and mass media.

The direction in which digital convergence is going is illustrated by the PC/TV. In the recent past, it was not possible to use your television set as a computer or to use a personal computer to watch broadcast TV programs. Now, however, the technologies of television and computing are coming together.

Technological convergence has tremendous significance. It means that, from a common electronic base, information can be communicated in all the ways we are accustomed to receiving it. These include the familiar media of newspapers, photographs, films, recordings, radio, and television. However, it can also be communicated through newer technology—satellite, cable, cellular phone, fax machine, or compact disk, for example. More important, as time goes on, *the same information may be exchanged among many kinds of equipment, using the language of computers.* Understanding this shift from single, isolated technologies to a unified digital technology means understanding the effects of this convergence on your life, such as:

- The increased need for continuous learning

- The necessity of adapting to less well defined jobs as "information workers"

- An increased pace of change

- Exposure to relatively unregulated technical and social information from other cultures via global networks

This book will help you get ready.

WHAT IT IS
WHAT IT DOES

WHY IT IS IMPORTANT

analog (LO 2,* p. 1.7)   Refers to nondigital (non-computer-based), continuously variable forms of data transmission, including voice and video. Most current telephone lines and radio, television, and cable-TV hookups are analog transmissions media.

You need to know about analog and digital forms of communication to understand what is required for you to connect your computer to other computer systems and information services. Computers cannot communicate over analog lines. A modem and communications software is usually required to connect a microcomputer user to other computer systems and information services over (via) analog lines.

applications software (LO 3, p. 1.12) Software that you can use to perform useful work on general-purpose tasks; compare with *system software.*

Applications software such as word processing, spreadsheet, database management, graphics, and communications packages are commonly used tools for increasing people's productivity.

binary digit (LO 2, p. 1.6)   1 or 0 in the binary system of data representation in computer systems.

The binary digit is the fundamental element of all data and information stored in a computer system.

binary number system (LO 2, p. 1.6) A two-state system of numbers; contains *binary digits* 0 and 1.

Computer systems use a binary system for data representation; two digits, 0 and 1, refer to the presence or absence of electrical current or pulse of light.

bit (LO 2, p. 1.6)   Short for *binary* dig*it*; a 0 or a 1.

See *binary digit.*

byte (LO 2, p. 1.6)   A group of 8 bits.

A byte holds the equivalent of a character—such as a letter or a number—in computer data-representation coding schemes.

communications (LO 3, p. 1.5)   Also called *connectivity;* becomes an element of the computer-based information system when one computer system is set up to share data and information electronically with another computer system.

Communications technology vastly expands the opportunity for information sharing and increased productivity.

---

*LO refers to the numbered learning objectives on the first page of each chapter.

communications hardware (LO 4, p. 1.11)   Equipment that facilitates connections between computers and computer systems—for example, over phone lines using a modem.

computer (LO 3, p. 1.4)   Programmable, electro-mechanical machine that accepts raw data—facts and figures—and processes (manipulates) it into useful information, such as summaries and reports. The computer and all equipment attached to it are called *hardware;* the encoded instructions that tell the computer what to do are called *software.*

computer competency (LO 1, p. 1.3)   Refers to applying skills in using a computer to meet information needs and improve productivity.

computer literacy (LO 1, p. 1.3)   Refers to having an understanding of what a computer is and how it can be used as a resource. Literacy, which refers to having knowledge and understanding, needs to be distinguished from competency, which refers to having a skill.

computer professional (LO 1, p. 1.2)   Person in a profession involving computers who has had formal education in the technical aspects of using computers; examples are computer programmer, systems analyst, and network administrator.

computer-based information system (LO 3, p. 1.4)   Data processing system with six parts: (1) hardware; (2) software; (3) data/information; (4) procedures; (5) people; (6) communications.

connectivity (LO 3, p. 1.22)   Refers to the act of communicating among computers and information sources via telecommunications devices.

CPU (central processing unit) (LO 4, p. 1.9)   The processor; it controls and manipulates data to produce information. In a microcomputer the CPU is usually contained on a single integrated circuit or chip called a *microprocessor.* This chip and other components that make it work are mounted on a circuit board called a *motherboard* (*system board*). More powerful computers have many processors.

data (LO 3, p. 1.5)   Raw facts and figures that are processed into information; third element in a computer-based information system.

database (LO 7, p. 1.23)   Collection of integrated, or cross-referenced, electronically stored data that different people may access to use for different purposes.

Without communications hardware, users would not be able to transmit/receive data and information to/from other computer systems.

The computer greatly speeds up the process whereby people solve problems and perform repetitive tasks and thus increases their productivity.

It's becoming increasingly difficult to find a professional field or area of work that does not require knowledge of computers.

See *computer competency.*

Computer professionals are to be distinguished from computer *users*—people who use computers to perform professional or personal tasks, enhance learning, or have fun.

The purpose of a computer-based information system is to transform raw data into useful information and quickly transmit it to the people who need it.

Connectivity is the foundation of the latest advances in the Digital Age. It provides online access to countless types of information and services.

The CPU is the "brain" of the computer; without it, there would be no computers.

Users need data to create useful information.

Users with online connections to database services have enormous research resources at their disposal. In addition, businesses and organizations build databases to help them keep track of and manage their activities.

digital (LO 2, p. 1.6) Refers to communications signals or information represented in a binary or two-state way.

With a two-state on/off, open/closed, present/absent, positive/negative, yes/no arrangement, the "on" state can be coded as the digit 1, the "off" state as the digit 0. Computers use digital signals—strings of on and off electrical pulses represented in codes of 1s and 0s—to represent software instructions and data.

digital convergence (LO 7, p. 1.28) Refers to the technological merger of several industries through various devices that exchange information in the electronic, or digital, format used by computers. The industries are computers, communications, consumer electronics, entertainment, and mass media.

From a common electronic base, the same information may be exchanged among many organizations and people.

hardware (LO 3, p. 1.4) The electronic and the electromechanical parts—the first element—of the computer-based information system. Hardware is classified into five categories: input, processing and memory, output, secondary storage, and communications.

Basically, hardware *is* the computer; however, hardware runs under the control of software and is useless without it.

information (LO 3, p. 1.5) Summarized data or otherwise manipulated (processed) data. Technically, data comprises raw facts and figures that are processed into information. However, information can also be raw data for the next person or job. Thus are sometimes the terms used interchangeably. Information/data is the third element in a computer-based information system.

The whole purpose of a computer (and communications) system is to produce (and transmit) useful information.

input hardware (LO 4, p. 1.8) Devices that allow people to put data into the computer in a form that the computer can use; that is, they perform *input operations*. The keyboard, mouse, and scanner are common input devices.

Useful information cannot be produced without input data.

integrated circuit (IC) (LO 6, p. 1.19) Collection of electrical circuits, or pathways, etched on tiny squares, or chips, of silicon about 1½ inches square.

The development of the IC enabled the manufacture of the small, powerful, and relatively inexpensive computers used today.

interactivity (LO 7, p. 1.25) Situation in which the user is able to make an immediate response to what is going on and modify processes; that is, there is a dialogue between the user and the computer or communications device.

Interactive devices allow the user to be an active participant in what is going on instead of just a passive reactor.

Internet (LO 7, p. 1.25) International network connecting approximately tens of thousands of smaller networks that link the computers of millions of users at educational, scientific, military, and commercial institutions and in homes.

The Internet makes possible the sharing of all types of information and services for millions of people all around the world.

keyboard (LO 4, p. 1.8) Input hardware device that uses standard typewriter keys plus a number of specialized keys to input data and issue commands.

Microcomputer users will probably use the keyboard more than any other input device.

local area network (LAN) (LO 5, p. 1.14)   Communications network that connects users located near one another, as in the same building.

LANs have replaced mainframes and other large computers for many functions and are considerably less expensive. Local area networks enable users in the same office, building, or college to share data and information and some peripherals, such as printers.

mainframe computer (LO 5, p. 1.14)   Second most powerful computer, after the supercomputer. There are small, medium, and large-scale mainframes serving from hundreds to several thousands of users.

Mainframes are used by large organizations—such as banks, airlines, insurance companies, and colleges—for processing millions of transactions.

memory (LO 4, p. 1.10)   Also called *main memory, primary storage, RAM* (*random access memory*); the computer's "work space," where data and programs for immediate processing are held. Memory is electronically created by special memory chips mounted on the system board.

Memory size determines how much data can be processed at once and how big and complex a program may be used to process it.

microcomputer (LO 5, p. 1.14)   Also called a *personal computer,* or *PC;* the computer used most by business professionals. Microcomputers range in size from small palmtops, notebooks, and laptops to powerful desktops and floor-standing (tower) models. The microcomputer has a small silicon chip, or microprocessor, as its CPU.

Microcomputers are used in virtually every area of modern life. People going into business or professional life today are often required to have basic knowledge of the microcomputer.

microcontroller (LO 5, p. 1.14)   Also called an *embedded,* or *dedicated, computer;* the smallest category of computer.

Microcontrollers are built into "smart" electronic devices, such as microwave ovens and electronic calculators, as controlling agents.

mouse (LO 4, p. 1.8)   Input hardware device that can be rolled about on a desktop to direct a pointer on the computer's display screen. The pointer is a symbol, usually an arrow, that is used to select items from lists (menus) on the screen or to position the cursor by clicking buttons on the mouse. The cursor is the symbol on the screen that shows where data may be entered next, such as text in a document.

With microcomputers, a mouse is needed to use most graphical user interface programs and to draw illustrations.

multimedia (LO 7, p. 1.25)   Refers to computer technology that presents information in more than one medium, including text, graphics, animation, video, music, and voice.

Use of multimedia is becoming more common in business, the professions, and education as a means of improving the way information is communicated.

online service (LO 7, p. 1.23)   Company that provides access to all kinds of databases and electronic meeting places to subscribers equipped with telephone-linked microcomputers. Popular online services are CompuServe, America Online, and Microsoft Network.

Online information services offer a wealth of services—for example, electronic mail, home shopping, travel reservations, enormous research facilities, discussion groups, and special-interest bulletin boards.

output hardware (LO 4, p. 1.11)   Consists of devices that translate information processed by the computer into a form that humans can understand; that is, they perform *output operations.* Common output devices are monitors (softcopy output) and printers (hardcopy output). Sound is also a form of computer output.

Without output devices, computer users would not be able to view or use their work.

people (LO 3, p. 1.5)   Most important part of the computer-based information system.

People design and develop computer systems, operate the computer hardware, create the software, and establish procedures for carrying out tasks.

peripheral device (LO 3, p. 1.8)   Any hardware device that is connected to a computer. Examples are the keyboard, mouse, monitor, printer, and disk drives.

Most of a computer system's input and output functions are performed by peripheral devices.

procedures (LO 3, p. 1.5)   Descriptions of how things are done, steps for accomplishing a result. Procedures for computer systems appear in *documentation manuals,* which contain the guidelines for using the hardware and software. Procedures for using a particular software package are also often available on disk.

Procedures are the fourth element in a computer-based information system. In the form of documentation, procedures help users learn to use hardware and software.

processing hardware (LO 4, p. 1.8)   Hardware that retrieves and executes (interprets) instructions (software) provided to the computer. The main components of processing hardware are the central processing unit (CPU), which is the brain of the computer, and main memory, where all instructions and/or data ready for processing are held.

Processing hardware forms the essence of the computer; no other hardware would work without it.

scanner (LO 4, p. 1.8)   Input device that translates images of text, drawings, and photos into digital form.

Scanners simplify the input of complex data. The images can be processed by the computer, manipulated, displayed on a monitor, stored on a storage device, and/or communicated to another computer.

server (LO 5, p. 1.14)   Computer shared by several users in a network.

Servers enable users to share data and applications.

software (LO 3, p. 1.4)   Also called *programs;* electronic instructions that tell the hardware how to perform a task. Software represents the second element of a computer-based information system.

Without software, hardware would be useless.

storage hardware (LO 4, p. 1.11)   Hardware that provides a means of storing software and data in a form that is relatively permanent, or *nonvolatile.* This type of storage is referred to as *secondary.* (Data and information in main memory, *primary storage,* is volatile, meaning it is lost when the power is turned off.)

The storage phase enables people to save their work for later retrieval, manipulation, and output.

supercomputer (LO 5, p. 1.13)   Largest, fastest, and most expensive computer available.

Supercomputers are used for research, weather forecasting, oil exploration, airplane building, and complex mathematical operations, for example.

system software (LO 3, p. 1.12)   Software that controls the computer and enables it to run applications software. System software, which includes the operating system, allows the computer to manage its internal resources.

Applications software cannot run without system software.

system unit (LO 4, p. 1.9)   Also called the *system cabinet;* housing that includes the electronic circuitry (processor), which does the processing, and main memory, which supports processing.

The microcomputer was born when processing, memory, and power supply were made small enough to fit into a cabinet that would fit on a desktop.

user (LO 1, p. 1.3)   Someone without much technical knowledge of computers but who uses computers to produce information for professional or personal tasks, enhance learning, or have fun.

See *computer professional.*

workstation (LO 5, p. 1.14)   Expensive, powerful desktop computers used mainly by engineers, scientists, and special-effects creators for sophisticated purposes.

Providing many capabilities comparable to mid-size mainframes, workstations are used for such tasks as designing airplane fuselages, prescription drugs, and movies' special effects. Workstations are often connected to a larger computer system to facilitate the transfer of data and information. The capabilities of low-end workstations overlap those of high-end microcomputers.

World Wide Web (LO 7, p. 1.25)   The most well-known part of the Internet; connected servers store information in multimedia form—that is, in sound, photos, and video, as well as text.

People and companies who maintain Web locations on the Internet do so in sites called *Web pages* that are stored on servers connected to the Internet. To view Web pages, users need special software called a *Web browser*—such as Netscape Navigator or Communicator, or Microsoft Explorer.

SELF-TEST EXERCISES

1. _____ refers to microcomputer users dialing into a telephone-linked computer-based shopping service listing prices and descriptions of products, which may be ordered through the computer.

2. Whereas most of the world is _____, computers deal with data in _____ form.

3. Hardware devices that aren't inside the system unit are referred to as _____ devices.

4. The category of hardware that can be compared to a filing cabinet is _____ hardware.

5. The term _____ is used to describe a device made up of electronic and electromechanical parts.

SHORT-ANSWER QUESTIONS

1. Briefly describe the function of each of the six main components of a computer system.

2. What is the function of the system unit in a computer system?

3. What is the difference between system software and applications software?

4. Why is it important to have a computer with more main memory rather than less?

5. Briefly describe five different types of activities you can perform on the Internet.

MULTIPLE-CHOICE QUESTIONS

1. Which of the following isn't considered a peripheral hardware device?
   a. keyboard
   b. scanner
   c. monitor
   d. printer
   e. memory

2. Which of the following can translate drawings and photos into digital form?
   a. keyboard
   b. mouse
   c. scanner
   d. modem
   e. all the above

3. Which of the following enables digital data to be transmitted over the phone lines?
   a. keyboard
   b. mouse
   c. scanner
   d. modem
   e. all the above

4. Which of the following computer types was available before 1970?
   a. supercomputer
   b. mainframe computer
   c. workstation
   d. microcomputer
   e. microcontroller

5. What hardware category does a scanner fall into?
   a. input
   b. processing and memory
   c. output
   d. storage
   e. communications

TRUE/FALSE QUESTIONS

1. Computers are continually getting larger and more expensive. (true/false)

2. Mainframe computers process faster than microcomputers. (true/false)

3. Main memory is a software component. (true/false)

4. System software tells the computer how to handle the keyboard and other hardware components. (true/false)

5. A local area network connects mainframe computers in an office or a building. (true/false)

KNOWLEDGE IN ACTION

1. Determine what types of computers are being used where you work or go to school. Microcomputers? Workstations? Any mainframe or supercomputers? In which departments are the different types of computers used? What are they being used for? How are they connected to other computers?

2. Identify some of the problems of information overload in one or two departments in your school or place of employment—or in a local business, such as a real estate firm, health clinic, pharmacy, or accounting firm. What types of problems are people having? How are they trying to solve them? Are they rethinking their use of computer-related technologies?

3. Imagine a business you could start or run at home. What type of business is it? What type of computer do you think you'll need? Describe the computer system in as much detail as possible, including hardware components in all five areas we discussed. Keep your notes and then refine your answers after you have completed the course.

4. Can you envision yourself using a supercomputer in your planned profession or job? If yes, how? What other type(s) of computer do you envision yourself using?

5. How would you define *information,* or *knowledge, worker*? What types of skills does an information worker possess? What do you think the future holds for information workers? Do you think you will be an information worker someday? Explain your point of view.

6. How do you think digital convergence will affect you in the next five years? For example, will it affect how you currently perform your job or obtain access to education? Do you think that digital convergence is a good thing? How? How not?

EPISODE 1

Whether you have a business or are planning to start a business, the World Wide Web provides numerous opportunities for reaching customers. It is accessed by millions of people in more than 200 countries and is growing at an astounding rate. International Data Corporation (IDC) estimates that the number of Web users was 35 million at the end of 1996 and will grow to around 163 million by the year 2000. Currently, commercial sites make up the fastest-growing segment of the World Wide Web. One reason is that in return for a minimal investment in creating a Web site, any business—large or small—can reach a worldwide audience. As of December 1996, IDC estimates that the total value of goods and services sold on the Web was $5.4 billion. IDC expects this number to grow to $95 billion by the year 2000.

For most businesses today, including business start-ups, the question isn't *whether* to create a Web site, but *when*. For you, the time is now: in this first of five Episodes, you assume the role of an entrepreneur who has decided to start a Web-based business. For inspiration and guidance as you work through each Episode, we profile the real-life Amazon.com Inc., a Web-based bookstore whose phenomenal success mirrors the expanding popularity of the Web.

Note: The Episodes are not "hands-on" tutorials, although they include some hands-on aspects; instead, they are meant to be thought provoking and to be the basis of discussions. You *can* complete the Episodes without access to the Web. However, you might not be able to answer all the questions at the end of each Episode.

WELCOME TO EARTH'S BIGGEST BOOKSTORE . . . . . .

Amazon.com

In 1994, Jeffrey P. Bezos left a successful career on Wall Street to exploit the potential for electronic retailing on the World Wide Web. Soon thereafter, he founded Amazon.com, Inc. (*www.amazon.com*), an online bookstore that is today one of the leading commerce sites on the Web. For Jeff, success came quickly. Amazon.com sold its first book in July of 1995. By March 1997, Amazon.com had sales of more than $32 million and 350,000 customer accounts in over 100 countries.

THE RATIONALE BEHIND AMAZON.COM

For a number of reasons, Jeff felt that an opportunity existed for online book retailing. First, no traditional bookstore (that is, one confined by four walls) can possibly stock the more than 2.5 million books that are now active and in print. Traditional bookstores must make substantial investments in real estate for retail stores and warehouses, and hire employees for each location. An online bookstore doesn't need retail locations or lots of warehouse space (Amazon.com orders books from the publisher *after* it takes an order), so it can pass savings along to customers in the form of discounts. An online bookstore can obtain demographic information about its customers in order to offer personalized services, a difficult task for traditional bookstores. Amazon.com, for example, alerts customers via electronic mail when books that are of interest to them are published.

Finally, Jeff saw opportunities for customer-customer and customer-author interaction. Today, customers post reviews of the books they read and share ideas with other customers interested in similar books and topics. For those customers interested in finding out more about their favorite authors, Amazon.com facilitates regular interviews with authors. Customers can also easily reach authors by e-mail to provide feedback.

GOING ONLINE WITH AMAZON.COM

Now let's preview some of the functions you as a customer might perform at the Amazon.com site.

Navigate the site. After you enter the store, you click the underlined links in the navigation bar (located on the left side of each page) to move around the site. Links also appear embedded on each page.

Search by Author, Title, and Subject

Performed targeted searches. If you click the Author, Title, Subject link in the navigation bar, the search page above appears.

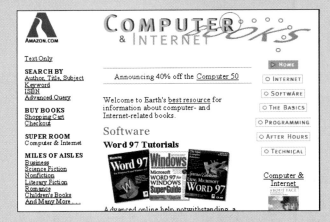

Browse a book category or featured list. For example, if you click the Computer & Internet link, the home page for computer- and Internet-related books appears, as shown above.

Enter an Amazon.com contest. The page above appears after you click the Win Prizes link in the navigation bar. (Note: You must scroll down to see the link.)

Completing Your Order is Easy

We encourage you to enter your credit card number online (why this is safe). However, you also have the option of phoning us with the number after completing the order form. If you have any problems or questions, see the bottom of the page for details on our toll-free (800) customer support number.

1. Welcome.

Please enter your e-mail address:

Please **double check** your e-mail address; one small typo and we won't be able to communicate with you about your order.

○ I am a first-time customer. (You will be asked to create a password later on.)

○ I am a returning customer, and my password is
Have you forgotten your password?

2. Select a payment method.

Make a purchase. At any point while shopping, you simply click a button to proceed to the checkout stand (see above) to provide shipping and credit card details.

THE IMPORTANCE OF CHOOSING A NAME

So how did Jeff Bezos come up with the name *Amazon*? "Earth's biggest river, Earth's biggest bookstore. The Amazon River is ten times as large as the next largest river, which is the Mississippi, in terms of volume of water. Twenty percent of the world's fresh water is in the Amazon River Basin, and we have six times as many titles as the world's largest physical bookstore," explained Amazon.com's founder in a 1996 interview.[1] Since that time, Amazon.com has nearly doubled the number of books it offers.

Just as 1-800-FLOWERS is the world's largest florist because its name is so easy to remember, a memorable domain name (Internet/Web address) such as *amazon.com, ibm.com,* or *television.com* can have a tremendous impact on the success of your Web business. "In 1994, Mike O'Connor registered the Internet domain *television.com* as his own name. Domain names were free back then, and O'Connor had a hunch. He used to work in the radio business, where a station's call letters (like KOOL or WLIV) are one of its most valuable assets. O'Connor figured the same thing would happen to Internet domain names. His foresight paid off in May 1996, when he sold his rights to *television.com* for more than $50,000," says Web author Vince Emery.[2]

For a couple of hundred dollars, your Internet access provider will register your name for you. Your base charge of $100 per name is good for two years, plus a $50 annual fee. Duplicate domain names can't exist on the Web. You can easily check to see if the name you choose already exists using InterNIC's "Whois" search page at *http://rs.internic. net/cgi-bin/whois.*

INTRODUCING YOURNAME.COM

Now it's your turn to come up with an idea for a small business that you would like to start on the Web. We emphasize the word *small* so that you can more easily identify the hardware, software, and communications requirements for the business in later Episodes. For simplicity, assume you will run your business from a single computer and that you will generate revenue from selling a product. It is highly possible that your business idea already exists on the Web. If so, feel free to use the existing business as a source of ideas for your start-up, but

don't forget to come up with a memorable (and unique) name for your business.

Assume you will hire a Web consultant to take care of the technical aspects of designing your Web site and getting it to work online. Your role in these Episodes is to decide *what* you want to do, not *how* you're going to do it. Understanding all the technical details of the Web can be a full-time job in itself, so leave these technical details to your expert assistant.

WHAT DO YOU THINK?

1. Visit the Amazon.com Web site. What are the main features of the site? Is it easy to order a book? How are payment transactions performed? What features of the site do you find especially interesting? Would you consider buying your next book at Amazon.com rather than at your local bookstore? Why? Why not?

2. Visit the Amazon.com Web site and search for a book on a topic you're interested in. In a few paragraphs, describe the process of searching for a book, reading customer reviews, and learning more about the author.

3. Provide a general overview (1–2 paragraphs) of the business you would like to start on the Web. What product are you planning to sell? What advantages will the Web provide you in selling this product? Does a business like yours already exist on the Web? If so, how will your business compare?

4. What kinds of tasks will you need a computer for in your new business? Will you need to keep track of inventory? Payroll? Monthly bills (accounts payable)? Receipts? Will you need a computer to keep tax records? What else?

5. Choose a name for your business. If you have Web access, check to see whether the name already exists by visiting InterNIC's "Whois" search page at *http://rs.internic.net/cgi-bin/whois.* Describe the process of using the site and include a printout of the "Whois Query Results" screen.

6. Some sites are dedicated to providing statistics about the Web. Visit Georgia University's site at *www.cc.gatech.edu/gvu/user_surveys/* to find some interesting statistics.

CHAPTER 2

PROCESSING HARDWARE

Turning Data into Something You Can Use

PREVIEW

When you have completed this chapter, you will be able to:

1. Explain more fully how data is represented in a computer system and explain what machine language is

2. Name the units of measurement used to measure computer capacity

3. Explain the functions of the processor, RAM, and registers

4. Describe processing power in terms of RAM capacity, word size, and speed

5. Describe the components found in a microcomputer's system unit

6. Describe some future processing technologies

Many types of computers are doing their jobs so unobtrusively that we hardly know they're there. "The best computer interface is my car's antilock braking system," says University of Virginia computer science professor Randy Pausch. "I jam on the pedal and a computer makes thousands of complex decisions for me and saves my life."[1]

San Jose Mercury News computing editor Dan Gillmor describes 10 computers he uses on a weekday morning even before he gets to the office. "The alarm clock (1) goes off precisely at 6 A.M. I grumble to myself that I should have gone to sleep earlier, pick up the remote control unit (2) and click on my television (3) to watch a few minutes of morning headlines." He pulls a clean cup from the dishwasher (4), pours coffee from the coffee maker (5), and turns on the microwave (6) for his cereal. After checking his watch (7), he climbs into his car (8) and joins the flow of traffic, stopping at a traffic light (9). As he heads toward work, his cell phone (10) rings.[2]

What all these devices have in common is that they contain microcontrollers (✔ p. 1.14) with *microprocessors,* or processing circuitry on chips. The microprocessor, says Michael Malone, author of *The Microprocessor: A Biography,* "is the most important invention of the 20th century."[3] Quite a bold claim, considering the incredible products that have issued forth during the past nearly 100 years. Part of the reason, Malone argues, is the pervasiveness of the microprocessor in the important machines in our lives, from computers to transportation. However, pervasiveness isn't the whole story. "The microprocessor is, intrinsically, something special," he says. "Just as [the human being] is an animal, yet transcends that state, so too the microprocessor is a silicon chip, but more." Why? The reason is that it can be programmed *to learn and adapt.* Malone writes:

> Implant [a microprocessor] into a traditional machine—say an automobile engine or refrigerator—and suddenly that machine for the first time can learn, it can adapt to its environment, respond to changing conditions, become more efficient, more responsive to the unique needs of its user. That machine now evolves, not from generation to generation but within itself.[4]

This ability to learn and adapt, Malone points out, "is something radically new in human history. The microprocessor constructs its own society; in the emptiness of its millions of transistors awaiting instruction lies a near-infinity of possibilities, from the Space Shuttle orbiting the earth to the toaster on your kitchen counter."

The development of the microprocessor enabled the development of the microcomputer. To understand the tremendous role microcomputers now play in business and life in general, it's helpful to look at how that role has developed. With the introduction of the Apple II and the Radio Shack Model I and II systems in the late 1970s, the business community began to adopt microcomputers. Then a number of additional vendors, including Atari, Commodore, Osborne, and Kaypro, entered the marketplace with computers designed to be used in the office

Computers in medicine.
A hospital technician
monitors cardiac surgery.

or in the home. The interest in microcomputers grew rather slowly at first for several reasons: (1) The starting costs (without peripherals) for some microcomputer systems was quite high, ranging up to $6000; (2) only a limited amount of applications software was commercially available; (3) the average person did not have sufficient background in computer-related subjects to use the computer without difficulty; and (4) there were no industry-wide standards to ensure the common usability of data and software on different brands of microcomputer systems.

However, when IBM introduced the IBM PC in 1981, along with DOS (disk operating system, developed in cooperation with Bill Gates of Microsoft), so many businesses adopted the product that an industry standard was set. Most vendors now design their products to be compatible with this standard; these products are referred to as IBM *clones,* which are based on Intel processor design. The only relatively successful microcomputer product line today that uses a different microprocessor architecture (Motorola) is the Apple Macintosh.

There are now more than 15 billion microprocessors and microcontrollers in use each day on earth. That is more than all the televisions, automobiles, and telephones combined. On those chips are more circuits than raindrops will fall in California this year. And on each of those chips the lines and structures now outnumber the streets and buildings of the largest cities ever built.

Were all these chips to disappear tomorrow, our civilization would be in deep trouble. The lights would go out, the Internet would go silent, TV screens and phone lines would be reduced to snow and static. Emergency rooms would malfunction, as would airplanes, trains, and cars. Commerce would halt.[5]

This chapter covers this amazing device—the processor—and associated processing hardware. But before we examine the topic of processing, we need to discuss the language of computers.

How Data and Programs Are Represented in the Computer

Computers use the two-state, 0/1 binary system to represent data in the form of machine language. Capacity of a computer is expressed in bits, bytes, kilobytes, megabytes, gigabytes, and terabytes. Two

Before we study the inner workings of the processor, we need to expand on Chapter 1's discussion of data representation in the computer—how the processor "understands" data. We started with a simple fact: electricity can be either *on* or *off.*

Other kinds of technology also use this two-state on/off arrangement. An electrical circuit may be open or closed. The magnetic pulses on a disk or tape may be present or absent. Current may be high voltage or low voltage. A punched card or tape may have a hole or not have a hole. This two-state situation allows computers to use the *binary system* to represent data and programs.

The decimal system that we are accustomed to has 10 digits (0, 1, 2, 3, 4, 5, 6, 7, 8, 9). By contrast, the **binary system** has only two digits: 0 and 1. (*Bi-* means "two.") Thus, in the computer the 0 can be represented by the electrical current being off (or at low voltage) and the 1 by the current being on (or at high voltage). All data and programs that go into the computer are represented in terms of these numbers. *(See Figure 2.1.)* For example, the letter H is a translation of the electronic signal 01001000, or off-on-off-off-on-off-off-off. When you press the key for H on the computer keyboard, the character is automatically converted into the series of electronic impulses that the computer recognizes.

What does a bit stand for?

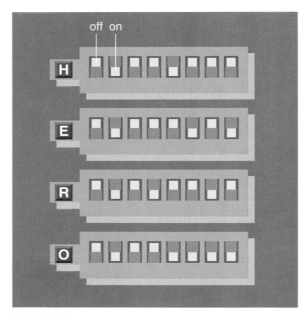

Figure 2.1 Binary representation. How the letters H-E-R-O are represented in one type of off/on, 0/1 binary code.

Binary Coding Schemes

All the amazing things that computers do are based on binary numbers made up of 0s and 1s. The binary digits, bits, are stored as charged and uncharged memory cells in the computer's main memory. On magnetic disk and tape, the bits are stored as positively and negatively charged magentic spots. Display screens and printers convert the binary numbers into visual characters. However, the data that we enter into the computer is not input as random groupings of 0s and 1s; it is encoded, or arranged, by means of *binary,* or *digital, coding schemes* to represent letters, numbers, and special characters.

There are many coding schemes. Two common ones are EBCDIC and ASCII-8. Both use 8 bits to form each byte. *(See Figure 2.2.)* One newer coding scheme uses 16 bits.

■ *EBCDIC:* Pronounced "*eb*-see-dick," **EBCDIC,** which stands for **Extended Binary Coded Decimal Interchange Code,** is commonly used in mainframes.

■ *ASCII-8 or "extended ASCII":* Pronounced "*as*-key," **ASCII,** which stands for **American Standard Code for Information Interchange,** is the most widely used binary code with microcomputers.

ASCII originally used 7 bits, but microcomputers use 8-bit bytes, so a zero was added in the left position to provide an 8-bit code, which provides 256 combinations with which to form letters, numbers, and characters, such as math symbols and Greek letters. Although ASCII can handle the English language well, it cannot handle all the characters of some other languages, such as Chinese and Japanese.

Figure 2.2 Two binary coding schemes: EBCDIC and ASCII. There are many more characters than those shown here. These include punctuation marks, Greek letters, math symbols, and foreign language symbols.

Character	ASCII-8	EBCDIC	Character	ASCII-8	EBCDIC
A	0100 0001	1100 0001	N	0100 1110	1101 0101
B	0100 0010	1100 0010	O	0100 1111	1101 0110
C	0100 0011	1100 0011	P	0101 0000	1101 0111
D	0100 0100	1100 0100	Q	0101 0001	1101 1000
E	0100 0101	1100 0101	R	0101 0010	1101 1001
F	0100 0110	1100 0110	S	0101 0011	1110 0010
G	0100 0111	1100 0111	T	0101 0100	1110 0011
H	0100 1000	1100 1000	U	0101 0101	1110 0100
I	0100 1001	1100 1001	V	0101 0110	1110 0101
J	0100 1010	1101 0001	W	0101 0111	1110 0110
K	0100 1011	1101 0010	X	0101 1000	1110 0111
L	0100 1100	1101 0011	Y	0101 1001	1110 1000
M	0100 1101	1101 0100	Z	0101 1010	1110 1001
0	0011 0000	1111 0000	5	0011 0101	1111 0101
1	0011 0001	1111 0001	6	0011 0110	1111 0110
2	0011 0010	1111 0010	7	0011 0111	1111 0111
3	0011 0011	1111 0011	8	0011 1000	1111 1000
4	0011 0100	1111 0100	9	0011 1001	1111 1001
!	0010 0001	0101 1010	;	0011 1011	0101 1110

■ *Unicode:* **Unicode,** a subset of ASCII developed by several big names in the computer industry, uses 2 bytes (16 bits) for each character, instead of 1 byte (8 bits). Thus Unicode can handle 65,536 character combinations rather than just 256. Although each Unicode character takes up twice as much memory space and disk space as each ASCII character, conversion to the Unicode standard seems likely. However, because most existing software applications and databases use the 8-bit standard, the conversion will take time.

The Parity Bit: Checking for Errors

Dust, electrical disturbance, weather conditions, and other factors can cause interference in a circuit or communications line that is transmitting a byte. How does the computer know if an error has occurred? Detection is accomplished by use of a parity bit. A **parity bit,** also called a *check bit,* is an extra bit attached to the end of a byte for purposes of checking for accuracy.

Parity schemes may be *even parity* or *odd parity.* In an even-parity scheme, for example, the ASCII letter H (01001000) consists of two 1s. Thus, the ninth bit, the parity bit, would be 0 in order to make the byte come out even. With the letter O (01001111), which has five 1s, the ninth bit would be 1 to make the byte come out even. *(See Figure 2.3, page 2.7.)* The system software in the computer automatically and continually checks the parity scheme for accuracy. (If the message "Parity Error" appears on your screen, you need a technician to look at the computer to see what is causing the problem—usually it's bad RAM chips.)

Medicine

"A fundamental change in medicine is coming about right now, " says Army Colonel Rick Satava, who is a laparoscopic surgeon. A laparoscope is essentially a computer-chip camera that can be inserted into the body so that surgeons can watch on a television monitor what they're doing inside a patient.

He continues: "All medical information—X-ray or lab test or blood pressure or pulse monitor—can now be digitized. It can all be brought to the physician or surgeon in digital format. Now we just close the loop and let the surgeon manipulate and act on the patient through the digital world of information."[6]

Digitizing—converting patient data into the 1s and 0s that can be processed by a computer—has long been used on the business side of medicine, as in record keeping. More recently the technology is also being used to help save lives, as well as time and money.

A Palo Alto, California, company named Caliper Technologies has crammed an entire medical laboratory onto a computer chip, designed to run the blood, urine, and other tests that now require expensive machines. At present, routine medical lab work costs $100 or so. Caliper's plan is that a doctor's office would need just a $5000 testing unit and boxes of various test chips for a dollar each. This would significantly lower the cost and increase the reliability. "We want to use new technology to do basic tests already done in hundreds of labs across the world," says the firm's president, Lawrence Block. "Faster. More accurately. Cheaper."[7]

At Duke University, the Medical Center's Databank for Cardiovascular Disease, stored on disks on two ordinary personal computers wired together, contains details of thousands of heart attacks that occurred over 30 years. The data is used by physicians to treat not just heart attacks but other problems as well. "Doctors on five continents dial into the system," says one report, "type in the critical components of their patient's problem, and get a recommendation for treatment based on the thousands of patients who have passed that way before."[8]

"Electronic medicine" is also increasingly being practiced with the help of *expert systems,* which have been in use since 1970. For instance, POEMS (for Post Operative Expert Medical System), in use in England, helps inexperienced medical staff treat patients who have become seriously ill while recovering from surgery. The computer system scans information about a patient and then proposes specific actions.[9] In addition, virtual reality—a kind of computer-generated artificial reality that provides the sensation of three-dimensional space—is now being used to train medical students, as in refining their skills in administering X-rays to cancer patients.

As you might expect, medicine is also going online. Patients, for instance, may draw on over 10,000 health-related Web sites. They may also use electronic mail to join patient forums and exchange views with others with similar conditions. More and more physicians and specialists are volunteering their time online to provide medical advice. University- and government-run Web sites typically provide the most reliable information. (Users should always be careful about information sources on the Web.)

One of the most exciting and far-reaching applications is the collection of long-distance ministrations known as *telemedicine*. Explains systems consultant Dennis Streveler, "Telemedicine is the use of high-speed telecommunications and computers to provide capabilities to extend the reach of the physician."[10] For some time, physicians in rural areas lacking local access to radiologists have used "teleradiology" to exchange digital images such as X-rays via telephone-linked networks with expert physicians in metropolitan areas. Now telemedicine is moving to another level, using digital cameras and sound to, in effect, move patients to doctors rather than the reverse. In the future, says Streveler, "there is the promise of robotic applications and virtual reality applications. For example, robotic control of microsurgical procedures has been attempted. Will there come a time when a surgeon at [a California medical center] performs a surgical procedure on a patient in Sierra Leone [West Africa]? Theoretically this is already possible."

Figure 2.3 Example of a parity bit. This example uses an even-parity scheme.

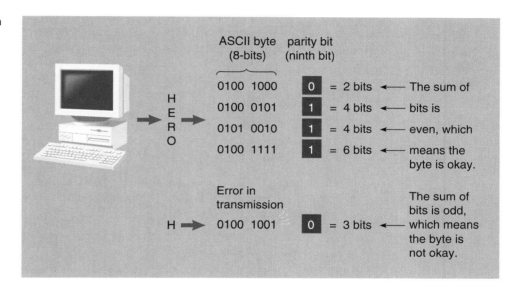

Machine Language: Your Brand of Computer's Very Own Language

So far we have been discussing how data is represented in the computer—for example, via ASCII code in microcomputers. But if data is represented this way in all microcomputers, why won't word processing software that runs on an Apple Macintosh run (without special arrangements) on an IBM PC? In other words, why are these two microcomputer platforms incompatible? It's because each hardware platform, or processor model family, has a unique machine language. **Machine language** is a binary programming language that the computer can run directly. To most people an instruction written in machine language is incomprehensible, consisting only of 0s and 1s. However, it is what the computer itself can understand, and the 0s and 1s represent precise storage locations and operations. Following are only four examples of many different platforms:

- Intel processors, used in most IBM-type PCs

- Motorola processors, used in Macintoshes and other Apple computers

- S/370, used in IBM mainframes

- Unisys, used in Unisys mainframes

Many people are initially confused by the difference between the 0 and 1 ASCII code used for data representation and the 0 and 1 code used in machine language. What's the difference? ASCII is used for *data* files—that is, files containing only data in the form of ASCII code. Data files cannot be opened and worked on without *execution* programs, the software instructions that tell the computer what to do with the data files. These execution programs are run by the computer in the form of machine language. As an analogy, what if all the restaurant menus in the world were written in Esperanto? And what if all the cooks back in the kitchens could read Esperanto but worked only in the native language of their countries—Italian, Chinese, Portuguese, and so on? Although all the restaurant owners could trade menus (the data files) without needing to translate them for themselves, they still would not have any food for their customers; for this, the cooks would have to execute the orders. However, when they execute their orders, they work only in their native language. Thus a cook from a Portuguese kitchen could not work in a Russian kitchen.

Why won't software written for the IBM platform usually run on a Macintosh?

But wouldn't it be horrendously difficult for programmers to write complex applications programs in seemingly endless series of machine-language groups of 0s and 1s? Indeed it would, so they don't. Instead, programmers write in special programming languages that more closely resemble human language. Then, basically, this code is translated by system software programs called *language translators* into the machine language that the computer's particular type of processor can "understand." This translating occurs virtually instantaneously, so that you are not aware of its happening.

How Computer Capacity Is Expressed: Bit by Bit

How many 0s and 1s will a computer's main memory or a storage device such as a hard disk hold? This is a very important matter. The following terms are used to denote capacity:

- *Bit:* In the binary system, the binary digit (bit)—0 or 1—is the smallest unit of measurement.

- *Byte:* To represent letters, numbers, or special characters (such as ! or *), bits are combined into groups. A group of 8 bits is called a **byte,** and a byte represents one character, digit, or other value. (For example, in one scheme, 01001000 represents the letter H.) The capacity of a computer's memory or a diskette is expressed in numbers of bytes or generally in multiples of bytes.

- *Kilobyte:* A **kilobyte (K, KB)** is about 1000 bytes. (Actually, it's precisely 1024 bytes, but the figure is commonly rounded.) The kilobyte was a common unit

Computers in agriculture. An experimental desert farm in Israel uses computers to manage irrigation.

of measure for memory or secondary-storage capacity on older computers. The original IBM PC, for example, had 640 K (about 640,000 characters) of memory. An average printed page of text, such as in this book, would take up about 4100–4200 bytes, or 4.1–4.2 kilobytes of space.

■ *Megabyte:* A **megabyte (M, MB)** is about 1 million bytes (1,048,576 bytes). Many measures of microcomputer capacity—such as for main memory and diskettes—are expressed in megabytes.

■ *Gigabyte:* A **gigabyte (G, GB)** is about 1 billion bytes (1,073,741,824 bytes). This measure is used to measure the capacity of many microcomputer hard disks and the main memory capacity of mainframes and some supercomputers.

Why should units of capacity matter to computer users?

■ *Terabyte:* A **terabyte (T, TB)** represents about 1 trillion bytes (1,009,511,627,776 bytes). This unit of measurement is used for some supercomputers' main memory capacity.

A little later in the chapter we'll go into main memory capacity in more detail.

The Processor, Main Memory, and Registers

The processor, often called the central processing unit (CPU)—the "brain" of the computer—consists of the control unit and the arithmetic/logic unit (ALU). The processor works with main memory (RAM) and registers to turn data into information.

How is the information in "information processing" in fact processed? As we mentioned in Chapter 1, this is the job of the circuitry known as the **processor.** In large computers such as mainframes, this device, along with main memory and some other basic circuitry, is also called the **central processing unit (CPU);** in microcomputers, it is often called the **microprocessor.** The processor works hand in hand with other circuits known as *main memory* and *registers* to carry out processing. Together these circuits form a closed world, which is opened only by connection to input/output devices, covered in Chapter 3.

The Processor: In Charge

The main processor follows the instructions of the software to manipulate data into information. The processor consists of two parts: (1) the control unit and (2) the arithmetic/logic unit. The two components are connected by a kind of electronic roadway called a *bus. (See Figure 2.4.)* (A bus also connects these components with other parts of the microcomputer, as we will discuss.)

■ *Control unit:* The **control unit** tells the rest of the computer system how to carry out a program's instructions. It directs the movement of electronic signals between main memory and the arithmetic/logic unit. It also directs these electronic signals between main memory and the input and output devices.

Figure 2.4 The control
unit and the arithmetic/
logic unit. The two components are connected by a
kind of electronic roadway
called a *bus.* A bus also
connects these compo-
nents to main memory.
Temporary data storage
holding/computation
working areas called
registers are located in the
control unit and the arith-
metic/logic unit.

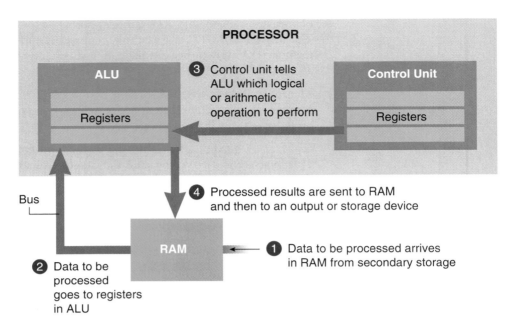

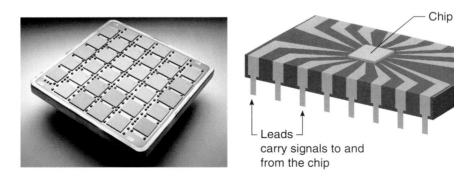

Chips mounted on an IBM
mainframe board

■ *Arithmetic/logic unit:* The **arithmetic/logic unit,** or **ALU,** performs arithmetic
operations and logical operations and controls the speed of those operations.

As you might guess, *arithmetic* operations are the fundamental math operations: addition, subtraction, multiplication, and division.

Logical operations are comparisons. That is, the ALU compares two
pieces of data to see whether one is equal to ($=$), greater than ($>$), or less
than ($<$) the other. The comparisons can also be combined, as in "greater
than or equal to ($\geq$)" and "less than or equal to ($\leq$)."

In the most powerful computers, the CPU is contained on several relatively
large printed circuit boards. In the case of a microcomputer's microprocessor, the
processor circuitry is etched on a thumbnail-size or slightly larger **chip** of silicon.
The chip is mounted on a carrier with metal leads, or pins, on the bottom that
plug into the computer's main circuit board, called the *system board.*

**What are the main
components of the
processor?**

What is silicon, and why use it? *Silicon* is an element that is
widely found in clay and sand. It is used not only because its
abundance makes it cheap but also because it is a *semiconductor.*
A *semiconductor* is material whose electrical properties are intermediate between a good conductor of electricity and a nonconductor of electricity. (An example of a good conductor of electricity is copper in household wiring; an example of a nonconductor

is the plastic sheath around that wiring.) Because it is only a semiconductor, silicon has partial resistance to electricity. As a result, when good-conducting metals are overlaid on the silicon, the electronic circuitry of the integrated circuit can be created. *(See Figure 2.5.)*

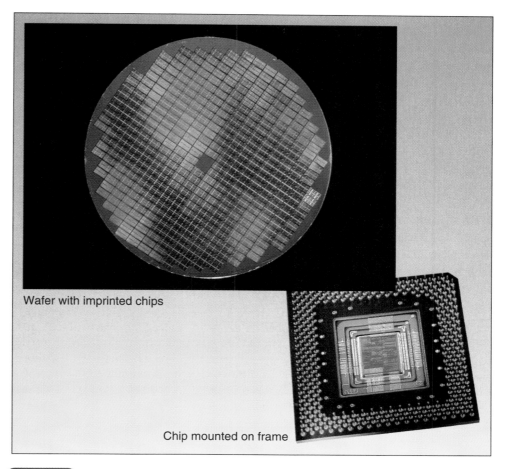

Wafer with imprinted chips

Chip mounted on frame

Figure 2.5 Making of a chip.

In brief, chips are created like this:

1. A large drawing of electrical circuitry is made that looks something like the map of a train yard. The drawing is photographically reduced hundreds of times so that it is of microscopic size.

2. That reduced photograph is then duplicated many times so that, like a sheet of postage stamps, there are multiple copies of the same image or circuit.

3. That sheet of multiple copies of the circuit is then printed (in a printing process called *photolithography*) and etched onto a 3-inch-diameter piece of silicon called a *wafer.*

4. Subsequent printings of layer after layer of additional circuits produce multilayered and interconnected electronic circuitry built above and below the original silicon surface.

5. Later an automated die-cutting machine cuts the wafer into separate *chips,* which can be less than 1 centimeter square and about half a millimeter thick. A *chip,* or *microchip,* is a tiny piece of silicon that contains thousands of microminiature electronic circuit components, mainly transistors. (A transistor is like an electronic "gate," or switch, that opens and closes to transmit or stop electrical current. It can alternate between "on" and "off" millions of times per second.)

6. After being tested, each chip is then mounted in a protective frame with extruding metallic pins that provide electrical connections through wires to a computer or other electronic device.

Specialized Processor Chips: Assistants to the CPU

Actually, modern computers may have a number of processors in addition to the main processor. Each of these **coprocessors** is dedicated to a special job. Two common examples are math and graphics coprocessor chips. A *math coprocessor chip* helps programs using lots of mathematical equations to run faster. A *graphics coprocessor chip* enhances the performance of programs with lots of graphics and helps create complex screen displays. Specialized chips significantly increase the speed of a computer system by offloading work from the main processor. These chips may be plugged directly into the motherboard; however, often they are included on "daughter cards," such as sound cards and graphics cards, used to expand a computer's capabilities.

CISC, RISC, and MPP: Not All Processors Are Created Equal

Not all main processors are constructed exactly the same—a factor that also affects the speed of a computer system.

- *CISC:* CISC (*complex instruction set computer*) processor architecture (design), found in most conventional mainframes and IBM-type microcomputers, offers a machine language that can support a large number of instructions. However, this great number of instructions gets in the way of processing speed.

- *RISC:* In *RISC* (*reduced instruction set computer*) processor architecture, the number of necessary processing instructions is reduced by shifting some of the computational burden from hardware to software. Thus, a RISC computer system operates with fewer instructions than those required in conventional CISC computer systems. Although software for CISC machines must be modified to run on RISC machines, the RISC chip is faster and runs more economically. Macintosh computers and many workstations use RISC technology.

- *MPP:* Computers with a CISC or RISC processor execute instructions one at a time—that is, *serially.* However, a computer with more than one processor can execute more than one instruction at a time, which is called *parallel processing.* Although some powerful microcomputers and workstations are available with more than one main processor, the most powerful computers, such as supercomputers, often use *massively parallel processing* (*MPP*), which spreads calculations over hundreds or even thousands of standard, inexpensive microprocessors of the type used in microcomputers. (Option Red has 9072 processors!) Tasks are parceled out to a great many processors, which work simultaneously.

    A difficulty is that MPP machines are notoriously difficult to program, because each processor has its own memory. Still, with the right software, 100 small processors can often run a large program in far less time than the largest supercomputer running it in serial fashion, one instruction at a time.

Main Memory: Working Storage Area for the CPU

Mentioned briefly in Chapter 1, **main memory**—also known as *memory, primary storage, internal memory,* or *RAM* (*random access memory*)—is working storage. The term *random access* comes from the fact that data can be stored and retrieved at random—from anywhere in the electronic RAM chips—in approximately equal

Memory chip modules
(SIMMs)

amounts of time, no matter what the specific data locations are. This circuitry has three tasks. (1) It holds data for processing. (2) It holds instructions (the programs) for processing the data. (3) It holds data that has been processed (become useful information) and is waiting to be sent to an output, storage, or communications device.

Main memory is in effect the computer's short-term storage capacity. It determines the total size of the programs and data files it can work on at any given moment. There are two important facts to know about main memory:

- *Its contents are temporary:* Once the power to the computer is turned off, all the data and programs within main memory simply vanish. This is why data must also be stored on disks and tapes—called "secondary storage" to distinguish them from main memory's "primary storage."

Thus, main memory is said to be "volatile." As mentioned earlier, *volatile storage* is temporary storage; the contents are lost when the power is turned off. Consequently, if you kick out the connecting power cord to your computer, whatever you are currently working on will immediately disappear. This impermanence is the reason why you should *frequently* save your work in progress to a secondary-storage medium such as a diskette or hard disk. By "frequently," we mean every 3–5 minutes.

- *Its capacity varies in different computers:* The size of main memory is important. It determines how much data can be processed at once and how big and complex a program may be used to process it.

Could a computer work without main memory? Why or why not?

Main memory is contained on chips called *RAM chips* that use CMOS (complementary metal-oxide semiconductor) technology. Memory chips are grouped on *single in-line memory modules,* or *SIMMs*—small circuit boards inserted into slots inside the computer and connected to the processor by a bus.

Common RAM technologies are dynamic RAM (DRAM) and static RAM (SRAM). DRAM chips are used in more computers than are SRAM chips; although they are faster, SRAM chips are more expensive, take up more space, and use more power.

Computers in music. Max Mathews, a computer musician at Stanford University, California, conducts a computer-generated orchestra by waving radio wands.

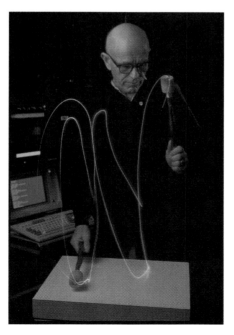

Registers

The control unit and the ALU also contain registers, or special high-speed circuitry areas that temporarily store data during processing and provide working areas for computation. (*Refer back to Figure 2.4.*) It could be said that main memory, which is outside the processor, holds material that will be used "a little bit later." Registers, which are contained in the processor, hold material that is to be processed "immediately." The computer loads the program instructions and data from main memory into the registers just before processing. There are several types of registers, including an instruction register, which holds the instruction being executed; an address register, which holds the addresses (locations) of data to be processed; a program register, which holds status information; and an accumulator, which holds the results of the ALU's logic operations.

The Machine Cycle: How a Single Instruction Is Processed

How does the computer keep track of the characters of data or instructions in main memory? Like a system of post-office mailboxes, it uses addresses. An *address* is the location, designated by a unique number, in main memory in which a character of data or part of an instruction is stored during processing. To process each character, the processor's control unit retrieves that character from its address in main memory and places it into a register. This is the first step in what is called the *machine cycle*.

The **machine cycle** comprises a series of operations performed to execute a single program instruction. It is the shortest interval in which an elementary operation can take place within the processor. The machine cycle consists of two parts: an instruction cycle, which fetches and decodes, and an execution cycle, which executes and stores. *(See Figure 2.6.)*

■ *Instruction cycle:* In the **instruction cycle,** or **I-cycle,** the control unit (1) fetches (gets) an instruction from main memory and (2) decodes that instruction (determines what it means).

■ *Execution cycle:* During the **execution cycle,** or **E-cycle,** the arithmetic/logic unit (3) executes the instruction (performs the operation on the data) and (4) stores the processed results in a register.

The details of the machine cycle are actually a bit more involved than this, but our description shows the general sequence. The machine cycle is important because a processor's speed is often measured by the time it takes to complete one cycle.

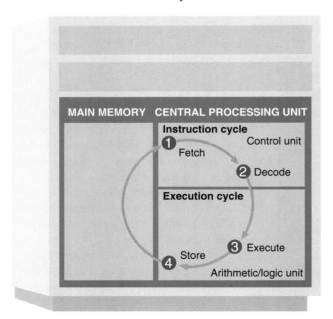 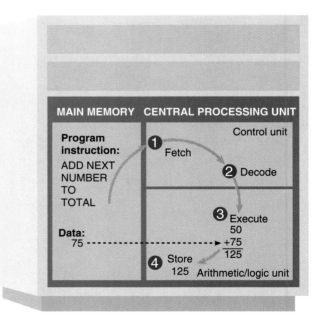

Figure 2.6 The machine cycle. (*Left*) The machine cycle executes instructions one at a time during the instruction cycle and execution cycle, through four steps: fetch, decode, execute, store. (*Right*) Example of how the addition of two numbers, 50 and 75, is processed and stored in a single machine cycle.

Telling Computers Apart: RAM Capacity, Word Size, and Processor Speed

A computer's RAM capacity, the number of bits it can handle at one time, and the speed at which it can execute a machine cycle determine its level of power.

In the 1950s, the head of IBM, Thomas J. Watson, estimated that the demand for computers would never exceed more than five for the entire world.

How far we have come. The world now has millions of computer users. Prices have fallen to the point that not only are computers not considered exotic, they are often considered as indispensable an appliance as a phone or television set. A poll of computer users in southern California asked how much they would miss their machines if they were taken away. About 20% said "some," and nearly two-thirds said "a lot."[11]

"I wouldn't give up my computer for the world," says Kathleen Travers, 39, a computer expert for the Los Angeles Cultural Affairs Department. "I've written a couple of full-length books, and to be able to move a chapter and have it automatically renumber the pages, that is incredibly time-saving. It's a very valuable tool."[12]

Watson's five computers have multiplied into millions. How to distinguish among the various types?

Recall from Chapter 1 that computers are classified according to how powerful they are: supercomputers, mainframes and midsize computers, workstations, microcomputers, and microcontrollers. Their power is measured according to three main units of measurement: RAM capacity, word size capability, and processor speed. Although there are other differentiating factors, these three are the most important.

RAM Capacity

The main memory capacity of most microcomputers is stated in megabytes (MB). If a microcomputer has less than 8 MB RAM, it will not be able to handle some of today's sophisticated software programs. Many software manufacturers recommend 16–32 MB or *more* of RAM for microcomputers. The RAM capacity of many mainframes and some supercomputers is measured in gigabytes (GB). Other supercomputers' RAM capacity is measures in terabytes (TB). (The Option Red supercomputer mentioned earlier has 600 gigabytes of memory.)

Word Size

Processor capacity is expressed in terms of **word size,** which refers to the number of bits it can hold in its registers, process at one time, and send through its internal (local) bus, the electronic pathway between the CPU, memory, and registers. Often the more bits in a word, the faster the computer. An 8-bit processor will work with data and instructions in 8-bit chunks. A 32-bit word processor is faster, working with data and instructions in 32-bit chunks. Other things being equal, a 32-bit computer processes 4 bytes in the same time it takes a 16-bit machine to process 2 bytes.

Note that expansion bus capacity is also measured by word size. Expansion buses connect the processor, RAM, and registers to the computer's peripheral devices. In other words, you can characterize a processor by saying how many bits it can work with at a time *and* how many bits it can send or receive at a time. Thus you can have a microcomputer with a 32-bit local bus but a 16-bit expansion bus. In this case, certain input/output operations would slow down to the speed of 16-bit word size.

Processing Speeds

Computers with a large word size can process more data in each instruction cycle. However, with transistors switching off and on at perhaps millions of times per second, the repetition of the machine cycle occurs at blinding speeds. Just how blinding? There are three main ways in which processing speeds are measured:

■ *For microcomputers:* Every computer contains a system clock—an internal timing device that switches on when the power to the computer is turned on. The **system clock** controls how fast all the operations take place. The system clock uses fixed vibrations from a quartz crystal to deliver a steady stream of digital pulses to pace the processor. The faster the clock, the faster the processing, assuming the computer's internal circuits can handle the increased speed.

   Microcomputer processing speeds are most often expressed in **megahertz (MHz),** with 1 MHz equal to 1 million beats (machine cycles) per second. Microcomputers purchased today commonly run at 133–200 MHz or more. (Note that if two microprocessors have the same MHz rating but different word sizes, the one with the greater word size will process faster.) High-end microprocessor speeds may occasionally be measured in MIPS. *(See next paragraph.)*

■ *Workstations, midsize computers, and mainframes:* Processing speed can also be measured according to the number of instructions processed per second, which today is in the millions. Thus **MIPS (millions of instructions per second)** is a measure of a computer's processing speed. A high-end microcomputer or a workstation might perform at 100 MIPS or higher, a mainframe 200–1200 or more MIPS. (Note that 1200 MIPS is 1.2 BIPS, or billions of instructions per second.) For comparison, a microcontroller, the least powerful type of processor, might perform in the 0.5–1 MIPS range. There is a mathematical relationship between MIPS and MHz. You can derive MIPS from MHz if you know how many machine cycles it takes to execute an instruction in the CPU. For example, a '486 Intel processor takes 1.9 cycles on average. To obtain MIPS for a 66 MHz '486, divide 66 by 1.9, yielding 35 MIPS.[13]

■ *Supercomputers:* Supercomputer processing speed is measured in **flops,** which stands for **floating-point operations per second,** a floating-point operation being a special kind of mathematical calculation. This measure is usually expressed in:
   —*megaflops* (*mflops*), or millions of floating-point operations per second
   —*gigaflops* (*gflops*), or billions of floating-point operations per second (1 billion flops)
   —*teraflops* (*tflops*), or trillions of floating-point operations per second (1 trillion flops)

   The Option Red supercomputer cranks out 1.8 teraflops. In a galaxy of 1000 planets, each planet with as many people as earth, it would take every person in the galaxy, each doing one calculation—at the same time—to equal what that computer can do in 1 second. Or, if you did one arithmetic calculation every second, nonstop, it would take you more than 31,000 years to do what Option Red does in a second.

Agriculture

In 1996, Alan Greenspan, chairman of the Federal Reserve Board, spoke of a historic transition—"one of those rare, perhaps once-in-a-century events"—by which technology was re-ordering the economy. "The advent of the transistor and the integrated circuit," he said, "and, as a consequence, the emergence of modern computer, telecommunication, and satellite technologies have fundamentally changed the structure of the American economy."[14]

Nowhere is the shift more pronounced than in agriculture. A century ago, America changed from an agrarian to an industrial economy. Now it is moving from the Industrial Age to the Information Age—and farmers are decreasing even further, with their numbers expected to drop 273,000 between 1994 and 2005, according to the U.S. Bureau of Labor Statistics.[15] Part of the reason for this decline is computer technology. And for those that remain, agriculture will be high-tech indeed.

Lloyd and Disa McPherson, dairy farmers near Stuarts Draft, a small Virginia town in the Blue Ridge Mountains, own not only milking machines, tractors, and barns. They also have a desktop microcomputer, with which they visit World Wide Web sites to check prices for the grains they feed their Holsteins and Jerseys. "To get this information before," Lloyd says, "we had to make telephone calls—lots of them. On the Internet, it's easy to find and we can check it whenever we want."[16]

Others use Web sites for marketing purposes. Greg Nolan, co-owner of the Bar 5 Simmental Stock Farms cattle ranch in Douglas, Manitoba, Canada, created a series of Web pages to advertise the ranch's breeding stock. On the Net, Nolan figures, he can not only reach potential customers at low cost but also compete better with larger businesses. "On the Internet, it's all the same," he says. "Whether you're IBM or the Bar 5, you're on a level playing field."[17]

Arlen Ruestman's business card lists not only his telephone number but also the exact latitude and longitude of his corn and soybean farm in Toluca, Illinois. It's his way of promoting what is known as *precision farming,* the use of global-positioning-satellite (GPS) technology to control costs and boost crop yields. "With GPS," says one account, "farmers map and analyze their fields for characteristics such as acidity and soil type, feed the data into computers, and pick up signals from space [satellites] that calibrate their actions as they drive over their fields. So instead of covering a large tract with a uniform amount of seeds, fertilizers, or herbicides, for example, they can spread just the right amount needed on each square yard."[18]

Now that we have covered some of the basics relating to computer processing in general, let's focus on the type of computer you will most likely have to work with: the microcomputer.

Focus on the Microcomputer: What's Inside?

The microcomputer system unit, or cabinet, contains the following electrical components: the power supply, the motherboard, the microprocessor, specialized processor chips, RAM chips, ROM chips, other forms of memory (cache, VRAM, flash), expansion slots and boards, ports, bus lines, and PC slots and cards.

As important as the microprocessor is to you, would you recognize it if you saw one? If someone opened up a microcomputer cabinet and let you look inside, could you identify it? And what else is inside the box that we call "the computer"? This section covers these issues.

The box or cabinet that contains the microcomputer's processing hardware and other components is called the **system unit.** *(See Figure 2.7.)* The system unit does not include the keyboard or printer. Usually it also does not include the monitor (display screen). It usually does include a hard disk drive and one or two diskette drives, a CD-ROM drive, and sometimes a tape drive. We describe these secondary storage devices and other peripheral devices in the chapters on input/output devices and storage devices. Here we are concerned with the following parts of the system unit:

- Power supply
- Motherboard

Computers in veterinary medicine. Checking a dog's joint at the Tuskegee University School of Veterinary Medicine.

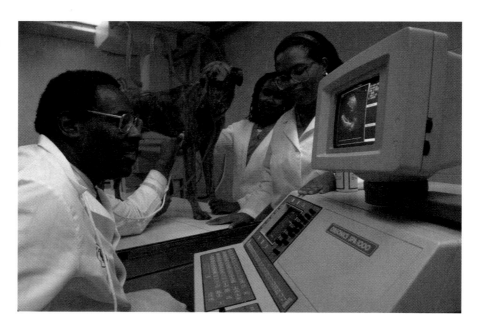

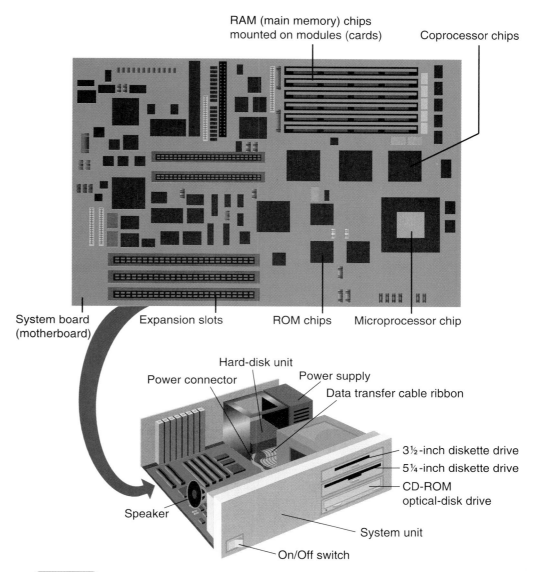

RAM (main memory) chips mounted on modules (cards)

Coprocessor chips

System board (motherboard)
Expansion slots
ROM chips
Microprocessor chip

Hard-disk unit
Power connector
Power supply
Data transfer cable ribbon

3½-inch diskette drive
5¼-inch diskette drive
CD-ROM optical-disk drive

System unit

Speaker

On/Off switch

Figure 2.7 The system unit and its contents

- Microprocessor
- RAM chips
- ROM chips
- Other forms of memory—cache, VRAM, flash
- Ports
- Expansion slots and boards
- Bus lines and PC slots and cards

These are terms that appear frequently in advertisements for microcomputers. After reading this section, you should be able to understand what these ads are talking about.

The Power Supply

The electricity available from a standard wall outlet is AC (alternating current), but a microcomputer runs on DC (direct current). The **power supply** is the device that converts power from AC to DC to run the computer. The on/off switch in your computer turns on or shuts off the electricity to the power supply. Because electricity can generate a lot of heat, a fan inside the computer keeps the power supply and other components from becoming too hot.

Electrical power drawn from a standard AC outlet can be quite uneven. A sudden surge, or "spike," in AC voltage can burn out the low-voltage DC circuitry in your computer ("fry the motherboard"). Instead of plugging your computer directly into the wall electrical outlet, it's a good idea to plug it into a power protection device, which is in turn plugged into the wall outlet. The two principal types are *surge protectors* and *UPS* (*uninterruptible power supply*) units.

The Motherboard

The **motherboard,** also called the *system board,* is the main circuit board in the system unit. *(See Figure 2.7.)*

The motherboard consists of a flat board that fills the bottom of the system unit. This board contains the microprocessor, any coprocessor chips, RAM chips, ROM chips, some other types of memory, and *expansion slots,* where additional circuit boards, called *expansion boards,* may be plugged in.

The Microprocessor

Most microcomputers today use microprocessors of two kinds—those made by Intel and those by Motorola—although that situation may be changing.

■ *Intel chips:* Intel makes chips for IBM and IBM-compatible computers such as Compaq, Dell, Gateway, Tandy, Toshiba, and Zenith. Variations of Intel chips are made by other companies, such as Advanced Micro Devices (AMD), Cyrix Inc., and Chips and Technologies.

Intel used to identify its chips by numbers—8086, 8088, 80286, 80386, 80486: the "x86" series. (SX and DX suffixes attached to these numbers refer to different versions of the same chip. For example, because it lacks a math coprocessor, a '486SX is a slower and cheaper version of the '486DX, which

Computers in space research. Workers at the Mission Control Room at the Johnson Space Flight Center in Houston, Texas, monitor the wavy flight path of a spacecraft.

does have a math coprocessor.) Intel's successor to the x86 chips is the Pentium family of chips—the *Pentium, Pentium Pro,* and *Pentium MMX.* Until recently, microprocessors have tended to double in power and performance every 18 months. (Recent developments by Intel and IBM promise to accelarate this rate.) Whereas microprocessors in the 1970s may have had about 2300 transistors, microprocessors in the late 1990s have more than 5.5 million transistors. In the 1970s a microprocessor may have run at only 1 MHz; now some microprocessors run faster than 200 MHz.

About 90% of microcomputers use Intel-type microprocessors; thus most applications software packages have been written for Intel platforms. New versions of popular applications software and entertainment CD-ROMs have been released to take advantage of the MMX chip, also called the "overdrive chip," which Intel developed with multimedia in mind. This chip runs faster and more smoothly than the Pentium Pro and is expected to play a major role in advancing videoconferencing. Non-MMX chips will be phased out over the next few years.

■ *Motorola chips:* Motorola makes chips for Apple Macintosh computers. These chip numbers include the 68000, 68020, 68030, and 68040. More recently, Motorola joined forces with IBM and Apple and produced the PowerPC family of chips, which uses RISC architecture. With some software and/or hardware add-ons, a PowerPC can run application software whether it's written for the Apple or IBM platform.

For which platform has most microcomputer applications software been written?

Most new chips are "downward compatible" with older chips. *Downward compatible,* or *backward compatible,* means that you can run the software written for computers with older chips on a computer with a newer chip. For example, the word processing program and all the data files that you used for your '486 machine will continue to run if you upgrade to a Pentium machine. Of course, new, sophisticated software programs have minimum processor requirements to run *efficiently.* These requirements are listed on the software box.

RAM Chips

As we described earlier in the chapter, *main memory,* or *RAM* (*random access memory*), is memory that temporarily holds data and instructions that will be needed shortly by the processor. RAM operates like a chalkboard that is constantly being written on, then erased, then written on again.

Like the microprocessor, RAM is made up of circuit-inscribed silicon chips. Microcomputers come with different amounts of RAM. In many cases, additional RAM chips can be added by plugging a memory-expansion card into the system board, as we will explain later. The more RAM you have, the faster the software can operate. If, for instance, you type such a long document in a word processing program that it will not all fit into your computer's RAM, the computer will put part of the document onto your disk (either hard disk or diskette). This means you have to wait while the computer swaps data back and forth between RAM and disk. Microcomputer users need 8–32 MB or more of RAM to run today's software.

Having enough RAM has become a critical matter! Before you buy any software package, look at the outside of the box to see how much RAM is required to run it by itself and to run it at the same time as other programs you commonly use.

ROM Chips

Unlike RAM, which is constantly being written on and erased, **ROM,** which stands for **read-only memory** and is also known as *firmware,* cannot be written on or erased by the computer user. (Firmware is a term used for software permanently stored on a chip.) In other words, RAM chips remember, temporarily, information supplied by you or a software program; ROM chips remember, permanently, information supplied by the manufacturer. One of the ROM chips contains instructions that tell the processor what to do when you first turn on, or "boot," the computer. These instructions are called the *ROM bootstrap,* because they get the computer system going by helping it to "pull itself up by its bootstraps." To get the computer going, ROM performs a "power-on self-test" (POST). Another ROM chip helps the processor transfer information between the keyboard, screen, printer, and other peripheral devices to make sure all units are functioning properly. These instructions are called **ROM BIOS,** or **basic input/ output system.** Fundamentally, ROM BIOS is an interface, a connector, and a translator between the computer hardware and the software programs that you run. (To be a true IBM clone, a computer must have the same ROM BIOS system as an IBM.) Still another ROM chip tells the computer how to construct each character displaying on the screen.

Three variations of ROM chips are used in special situations, *PROM, EPROM,* and *EEPROM:*

■ *PROM: PROM* chips, for *programmable read-only memory,* are blank chips on which the buyer, using special equipment, writes the program. Once the program is written, it cannot be erased. Some microcomputer software packages come on PROM units.

■ *EPROM: EPROM* chips, for *erasable programmable read-only memory,* are like PROM chips except that the contents can be erased, using special equipment, and new material can be written. Erasure is done with a special device that uses ultraviolet light.

What's the difference between RAM and ROM?

■ *EEPROM: EEPROM* chips, for *electronically erasable programmable read-only memory,* can be reprogrammed using special electrical impulses. The advantage of EEPROM chips is that they need not be removed from the computer to be changed.

Other Forms of Memory

In addition to inserting SIMMs in expansion slots, as we mentioned earlier (✔ p. 2.13), a microcomputer's performance can be enhanced by adding other forms of memory, as follows:

Figure 2.8 Diagram of cache memory operation

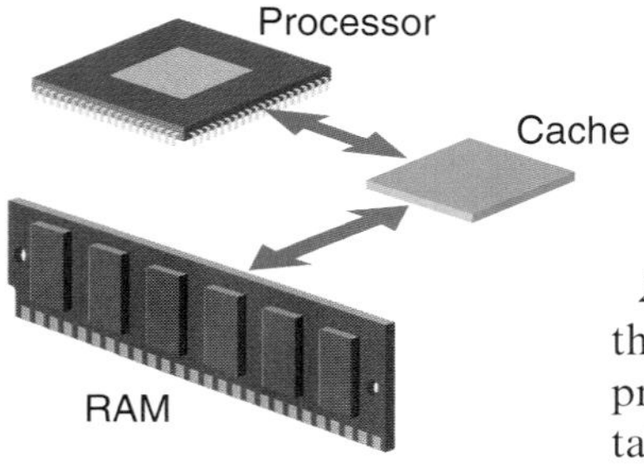

Processor

Cache

RAM

■ *Cache memory:* In the most powerful computers and in high-end microcomputers, RAM is divided into two sections. One section is relatively large (several rows of chips) and is called *main RAM.* The other section is tiny—just a few chips. This is cache memory, which is much faster but also much more expensive than RAM. Pronounced "cash" in the United States and sometimes "caish" in other countries, **cache memory** is a special high-speed memory area that the processor can access quickly. Essentially, cache memory is a bridge between the processor and RAM. *(See Figure 2.8.)* A special "look-ahead program" transfers the data and instructions that were transferred from secondary storage to RAM from RAM to the processor. This allows the processor to run faster because it doesn't have to take time to swap instructions in and out of RAM. Large, complex programs and fast processors benefit the most from having a cache memory available. There are several types of cache memory available. One type you see advertised frequently in computer magazine ads is *pipeline-burst cache,* which allows memory chips to be read from and written to at the same time.

■ *Video memory:* Video memory or **video RAM (VRAM)** chips are used to store display images for the monitor. The amount of video memory determines how fast images appear and how many colors are available. Video memory chips are particularly desirable if you are running programs that display a lot of graphics. VRAM chips are usually located on a special video adapter card inserted in an expansion slot on the system board.

■ *Flash memory:* Derived from EEPROMs and used primarily in portable computers, **flash memory,** or **flash RAM cards,** consist of circuitry on credit-card-size cards that can be inserted into slots connecting to the motherboard. Unlike standard RAM chips, flash memory is *nonvolatile.* That is, it retains data even when the power is turned off. Flash memory can be used not only to simulate main memory but also to supplement or replace hard disk drives for permanent storage. Some experts predict that flash RAM will eventually replace traditional CMOS RAM.

Ports: Connecting Peripherals

Microcomputers have different types of ports, depending on whether they use the PC or the Mac platform and how recent the model is. A **port** is a socket on the outside of the system unit that is connected by a bus to an expansion board on the inside of the system unit or connected directly to integrated circuitry on the motherboard. A port allows you to use a cable to plug in a peripheral device, such as a monitor, printer, or modem, so that it can communicate with the computer system.

Ports are of several types *(see Figure 2.9):*

■ *Parallel ports:* A **parallel port** allows lines to be connected that will enable 8 bits to be transmitted simultaneously, like cars on an eight-lane highway. Parallel lines move information faster than serial lines do, but they can transmit information efficiently only up to 15 feet [5.4 meters]. Thus, parallel ports are used principally for connecting printers.

■ *Serial ports:* A **serial port,** or *RS-232 port,* enables a line to be connected that will send bits one after the other on a single line, like cars on a one-lane highway. Serial lines are used to link equipment that is not close by. Serial ports are used principally for communications lines, modems, scanners, and mice—and, in the case of the Macintosh, the printer. (Serial ports are often called "COM" ports, for communications.) On the back of

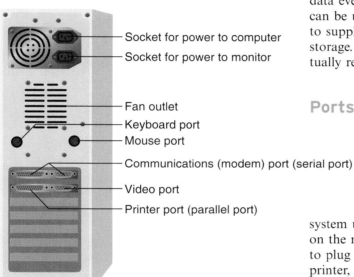

Figure 2.9 Different types of ports. Shown are the backs of an IBM-style computer and an Apple Macintosh.

— Socket for power to computer
— Socket for power to monitor

— Fan outlet
— Keyboard port
— Mouse port

— Communications (modem) port (serial port)

— Video port
— Printer port (parallel port)

IBM-compatible

— SCSI port
— Socket for power to computer
— Socket for power to monitor
— External disk drive port

— Fan outlet

— Video ports

— Adapter card
— Modem port
— Printer port
— Apple desktop bus ports for keyboard or mouse
— Audio jack

Apple Macintosh

Some plugs and sockets

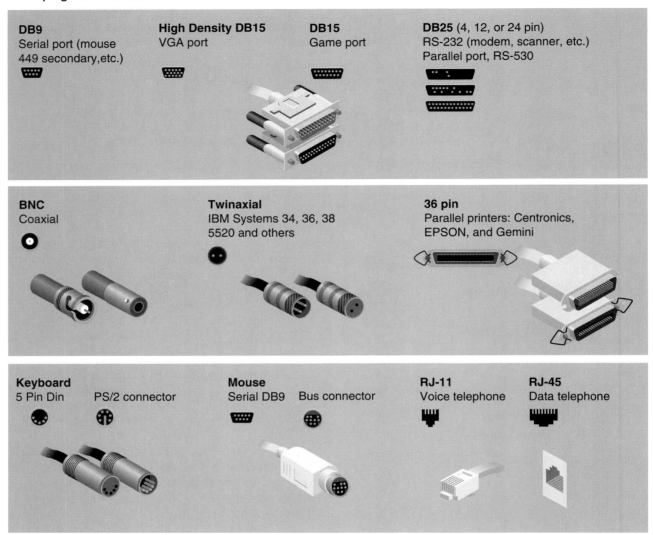

DB9
Serial port (mouse
449 secondary,etc.)

High Density DB15
VGA port

DB15
Game port

DB25 (4, 12, or 24 pin)
RS-232 (modem, scanner, etc.)
Parallel port, RS-530

BNC
Coaxial

Twinaxial
IBM Systems 34, 36, 38
5520 and others

36 pin
Parallel printers: Centronics,
EPSON, and Gemini

Keyboard
5 Pin Din   PS/2 connector

Mouse
Serial DB9   Bus connector

RJ-11
Voice telephone

RJ-45
Data telephone

newer PCs is one 9-pin connector for serial port COM1, typically used for the mouse, and one 25-pin connector for serial port COM2, typically used for the modem.

■ *Video adapter ports:* **Video adapter ports** are used to connect the video display monitor outside the computer to the video adapter card inside the system unit. Monitors may have either a 9-pin plug or a 15-pin plug. The plug must be compatible with the number of holes in the video adapter card.

■ *SCSI ports:* Pronounced "scuzzy" (and short for Small Computer System Interface), a **SCSI port** provides an interface for transferring data at high speeds for up to seven or fifteen SCSI-compatible devices, linked together in what is called a *daisy chain,* along an extended cable. *(See Figure 2.10.)* These devices include external hard disk drives, magnetic-tape backup units, scanners, and CD-ROM drives.

■ *Game ports:* Game ports allow you to attach a joystick or similar game-playing device to the system unit.

Expansion card

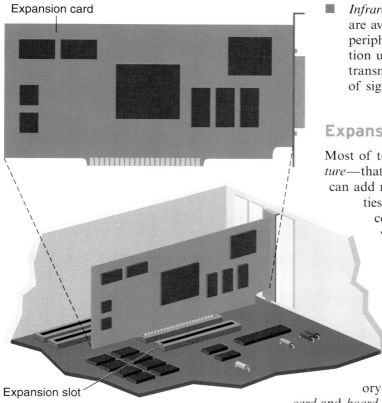

Expansion slot

■ *Infrared ports:* These wireless, data-transfer ports are available on new computers and hardware peripherals such as printers. This type of connection uses a certain frequency of radio waves to transmit data, so it requires an unobstructed line of sight between the transmitter and the receiver.

Expansion Slots and Boards

Most of today's microcomputers have *open architecture*—that is, they can easily be opened, so that users can add new devices and enhance existing capabilities. This spares users from having to buy a completely new computer every time they want to upgrade something. As with ports, microcomputers will have different numbers and kinds of expansion slots, based on the model.

Expansion slots are sockets on the system board into which you can plug expansion cards. (*Refer back to Figure 2.4.*) The sockets connect to buses.

Expansion cards, or *add-on boards,* are circuit boards that provide more memory or control peripheral devices. The words *card* and *board* are used interchangeably. Some slots will be needed right away for ordinary peripherals, but if you have enough free slots open, you can use them for expansion later.

Figure 2.10 Daisy chain illustration

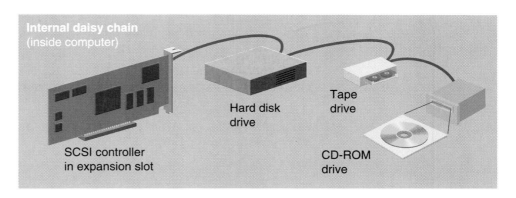

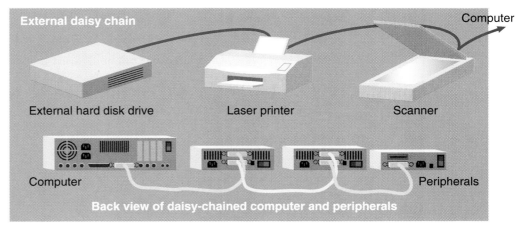

Among the types of expansion cards are the following:

■ *Expanded memory:* As we mentioned in the section on RAM, memory expansion cards (or SIMMs) allow you to add RAM chips, giving you more main memory.

■ *Display adapter or graphics adapter cards:* These cards allow you to adapt different kinds of color video display monitors for your computer.

■ *Controller cards:* Controller cards are circuit boards that allow your microprocessor to work with the computer's various peripheral devices. For example, a disk controller card allows the computer to work with different kinds of hard disk and diskette drives.

■ *Other add-ons:* You can also add special circuit boards for modems, fax, sound, video capture, and networking, as well as coprocessor chips.

Note that each kind of expansion card is designed to work with a particular expansion bus.

Buses

As we mentioned earlier, a **bus line,** or simply **bus,** is a hardware pathway through which bits are transmitted within the processor and between the processor and other devices in the system unit. The computer's internal bus is known as the *local bus,* or *processor bus.* (We discussed this bus in the sections on the processor and on word size.) Other types of buses, called *expansion buses,* connect various types of peripheral devices to the computer via connection to expansion cards inserted in the system board.

A computer bus provides parallel data transfer. For example, a 16-bit bus transfers 2 bytes (16 bits) at a time over 16 wires; a 32-bit bus transmits 4 bytes (32 bits) at a time over 32 wires, and so on. The bus has two parts: the address bus and the data bus.

Today there are several standard bus designs, or architectures:

■ *ISA: Industry Standard Architecture* (*ISA,* pronounced "eye-suh") is a common expansion bus standard used for the plug-in boards that control the video display, disks, and other peripherals in the IBM platform. Unfortunately it is rather slow—a 16-bit bus.

■ *MCA: Micro Channel Architecture* (*MCA*), a more recent expansion bus and an improvement over ISA, is a 32-bit bus.

■ *EISA:* The *Enhanced Industry Standard Architecture* (*EISA,* pronounced "ee-suh") bus is also a 32-bit expansion bus for the IBM platform. MCA and EISA buses are much more expensive than ISA buses, so they are used primarily on high-end microcomputers and network servers.

■ *NuBus:* Apple's *NuBus* is a 32-bit expansion bus used in Apple Macintoshes.

■ *Local buses:* There are two commonly used microcomputer local bus architectures—PCI and VL.

   PCI, for *Peripheral Component Interconnect,* is a local bus using a 64-bit data path. It is used in Pentium-based systems.

   VESA, for *Video Electronics Standard Association,* also called the VL-bus, is a 32-bit bus.

PCI buses are used on high-end microcomputers, and the VL bus is used on more basic models.

■ *SCSI:* Using a SCSI port and a SCSI adapter card inside the computer can provide an alternative to regular expansion buses. Peripheral devices are connected in a daisy chain along an external cable. Devices inside the computer are connected along an internal cable. (SCSI interfaces are used in all sizes of computers.)

■ *Universal Serial Bus:* The previous types of buses do not always allow for easy installation of a peripheral or expansion card, because certain computer settings and software device drivers must be dealt with. (*Drivers* are software programs that let the processor communicate with the peripherals.) The recently developed *Universal Serial Bus,* or *USB,* promises to alleviate this problem by making true "plug and play" a reality. In this case, one simply plugs in the new device, and it is configured automatically—no need to take off the system unit cover, mess with internal settings, or even turn off the computer. And up to 127 USB devices can be daisy chained.

What's the difference between a local bus and an expansion bus?

PC card

■ *PCMCIA:* Short for **Personal Computer Memory Card International Association, PCMCIA** is a bus standard for recent-model microcomputers, notebooks, and palmtops that allows users to insert credit-card-size peripherals (about 2.1 by 3.4 inches), or (5.3 by 8.6 centimeters) called *PC cards*—typically memory cards or modems—into slots in the computer.

Not all slots will take all kinds of peripherals. There are four types of PCMCIA slots, each accepting a different thickness of card. Type I is used primarily for memory cards. Type II is used for fax modems and LAN adapters. Type III is for rotating disk devices, such as hard disk drives. Type IV is for large-capacity hard disk drives.

Coming Attractions?

Future processing technologies may use gallium arsenide, superconductors, optical processing, nanotechnology, and biochips.

The old theological question of how many angels could fit on the head of a pin has become the technological question of how many *circuits* could fit there. Computer developers are obsessed with speed, constantly seeking ways to promote faster processing. Some of the most promising directions, already discussed, are RISC chips and parallel processing. Some other research paths being explored are the following:

■ *Gallium arsenide:* Silicon is the material of choice today for microprocessors, but there are other contenders. One is *gallium arsenide,* which allows electrical impulses to be transmitted several times faster than silicon can. Gallium arsenide also requires less power than silicon chips and thus can operate at higher temperatures. However, chip designers at present are unable to squeeze as many circuits onto a chip as they can with silicon.

■ *Superconductors:* Silicon, we stated, is a semiconductor: Electricity flows through the material with some resistance. This leads to heat buildup and the risk of circuits melting down. A *superconductor,* by contrast, is material that allows electricity to flow through it without resistance. The superconducting materials so far discovered are considered impractical because they are super-conductors only at subzero temperatures. Nevertheless, the search continues for a superconductor at room temperature—which would lead to circuitry 100 times faster than today's silicon chips.

■ *Opto-electronic processing:* Today's computers are electronic, tomorrow's might be *opto-electronic*—using light, not electricity. With optical-electronic technology, a machine using lasers, lenses, and mirrors would represent the on-and-off codes of data with pulses of light.

Light is much faster than electricity. Indeed, fiber-optic networks, which consist of hair-thin glass fibers instead of copper wire, can move information at speeds 3000 times faster than conventional networks. However, the signals get bogged down when they have to be processed by silicon chips. Opto-electronics chips would remove that bottleneck.

■ *Nanotechnology:* Nanotechnology, nanoelectronics, nanostructures, nanofabri-cation—all start with a measurement known as a nanometer. A *nanometer* is a billionth of a meter, which means we are operating at the level of atoms and molecules. A human hair is approximately 100,000 nanometers in diameter.

Nanotechnology is a science based on using molecules to create tiny machines to hold data or perform tasks. Experts attempt to do "nanofab-rication" by building tiny "nanostructures" one atom or molecule at a time. When applied to chips and other electronic devices, the field is called "nanoelectronics."

■ *Biotechnology:* Another possibility is using biotechnology to grow cultures of bacteria, such as one that, when exposed to light, emits a small electrical charge. The properties of this "biochip" could be used to represent the on/off digital signals used in computing.

Imagine millions of nanomachines grown from microorganisms processing information at the speed of light and sending it over far-reaching pathways. What kind of changes could we expect with computers like these?

Common Measurements Used in Computers and Communications

When salespeople or friends rattle on about how fast a computer's "clock speed" is or how many "dpi" the printer uses, how will you know what they're talking about? The following is a quick guide to some common measurement terms.

- **baud and bps** Both terms are used to describe the speed at which a computer can transfer information.

  - *Baud ("bawd"):* A measure of signal changes that take place during 1 second of data transfer.

  - *bps (bits per second):* A measure of the actual number of bits that are transferred during that second. (A bit is a 0 or 1, the smallest unit of information used in computing.)

Baud rates are sometimes erroneously used to specify bits per second for modem speed, but only at low speeds are they the same (for example, 300 baud is equal to 300 bps—only about 6 words per second).

- **capacity—from bits to terabytes** Capacity refers to how much data/information a storage device will hold. Capacity is represented by bits, bytes, kilobytes, megabytes, gigabytes, and terabytes.

  - *Bit:* Short for binary digit; a 0 or 1, which the computer hardware represents as an "on" or "off" (or high-voltage or low-voltage) electrical state.

  - *Byte:* Usually a group of eight bits.

  - *Kilobyte (K or KB):* About 1000 (1024) bytes. Bytes and their multiples are common units of measure for memory or storage capacity of personal computers.

  - *Megabyte (M or MB):* About 1 million (specifically 1,048,576) bytes.

  - *Gigabyte (G or GB):* Pronounced "*gig*-a-bite" (not "*jig*-a-bite"); about 1 billion (1,073,741,824) bytes.

  - *Terabyte (T or TB):* About 1 trillion (specifically 1,009,511,627,776) bytes.

- **clock speed—Hz, KHz, and MHz** *Clock speed* refers to how fast a computer processes. (The CPU, or central processing unit, is circuitry that controls the interpretation and execution of instructions.) The *CPU clock* uses a quartz crystal to generate a steady stream of pulses to the CPU to regulate the system's internal speed. The clock measures speed in hertz, kilohertz, and megahertz as frequency of electrical vibrations (cycles) per second.

  - *Hertz (Hz):* A single clock cycle per second
  - *Kilohertz (KHz):* 1000 cycles per second
  - *Megahertz (MHz):* 1 million cycles per second

The clock speed of a microprocessor (a CPU on a single chip) in a microcomputer is measured in mega-

hertz. For example, for '486 and later microprocessors, speeds range from 25 MHz to 166 MHz or more.

- **dot pitch** Measurement used to describe the clarity of the image on a display screen or of a printer's output.

  - *Pixels:* For display screens, dot pitch is expressed in millimeters as the distance between individual dots, or *pixels (picture elements)*. The smaller the dot pitch, the clearer the image. Typically, display screens vary from .28 to .51 millimeters.

    dpi: For printers, dot pitch is expressed in *dpi*, the number of dots that a printer can print in a linear inch.

- **dpi** *Dots per inch*; dpi is a measurement used to describe the image clarity of printers and scanners. if you look closely, you will see that a printed image is made up of individual dots. The higher the number of dots per linear inch, the clearer the image. A 300 dpi printer prints 300 x 300, or 90,000, dots in 1 square inch. A 400 dpi printer produces 160,00 dots, a 500 dpi printer produces 250,000 dots. Common printer and scanner measurements range from 300 to 600 dpi and up.

- **fractions of a second** In increasing order of rapidity:

  - *Milliseconds (ms):* Thousandths of a second; measures the amount of time the computer takes to access information from a hard disk.

  - *Microseconds (μs):* Millionths of a second; measures instruction execution.

  - *Nanoseconds (ns):* Billionths of a second; measures the speed at which information travels through circuits, as for memory chips (70–60 ns).

  - *Picoseconds (ps):* Trillionths of a second; measures transistor switching.

- **inch** Measurement used to describe size of floppy disks and of monitors.

  - *Diskette sizes:* Diskettes come in two principal sizes: $3^1/_2$ (or 3.5) inches, now the more common standard; and $5^1/_4$ (or 5.25) inches, an older size, now less common.

  - *Monitor sizes:* Like the screens of television sets, computer monitors, or display screens, are measured diagonally from one corner to the other. Common sizes are 14–17 inches or larger.

- **MIPS** *million instructions per second;* MIPS are a measurement of the execution speed of a large computer.

- **word** The standard unit of information natural to a particular system. The unit varies depending on the computer. For a computer with a microprocessor that processes 16 bits at a time, a word would be 16 bits.

WHAT IT IS
WHAT IT DOES

WHY IT IS IMPORTANT

arithmetic/logic unit (ALU) (p. 2.10, LO 3)   The part of the CPU that performs arithmetic operations and logical operations and that controls the speed of those operations.

Arithmetic operations are the fundamental math operations: addition, subtraction, multiplication, and division. Logical operations are comparisons, such as is equal to ($=$), greater than ($>$), or less than ($<$).

ASCII (American Standard Code for Information Interchange) (p. 2.4, LO 1)   Binary code used in microcomputers; ASCII originally used 7 bits to form a character, but a zero was added in the left position to provide an 8-bit code, providing more possible combinations with which to form other characters and symbols (256 possible combinations).

ASCII is the binary code most widely used in microcomputers.

binary system (p. 2.4, LO 1)   A two-state system (*bi-* means "two").

Computer systems use a binary system for data representation; two digits, 0 and 1, refer to the presence and absence of electrical current or a pulse of light. All data and programs that go into the computer are represented in terms of these numbers.

bus (p. 2.26, LO 5)   Electrical pathway through which bits are transmitted within the CPU and between the CPU and other devices in the system unit. There are different types of buses, such as local bus and expansion bus.

The wider a computer's buses, the faster it operates.

byte (p. 2.8, LO 2)   A group of 8 bits.

A byte holds the equivalent of a character—such as a letter or a number—in computer data-representation coding schemes. It is also the basic unit used to measure the storage capacity of main memory and secondary storage devices.

cache memory (p. 2.22, LO 5)   Special high-speed memory area on a chip that the CPU can access quickly. A copy of the most frequently used instructions is kept in the cache memory so the CPU can look there first.

Cache memory, which supplements main memory, allows the CPU to run faster because it doesn't have to take time to swap instructions in and out of main memory. Large, complex programs benefit the most from having a cache memory available.

central processing unit (CPU) (p. 2.9, LO 3) The processor; it controls and manipulates data to produce information. In a microcomputer the CPU is usually contained on a single integrated circuit or chip called a *microprocessor.* This chip and other components that make it work are mounted on a circuit board called a *motherboard* (system board). More powerful computers have many processors.

The CPU is the "brain" of the computer.

chip (microchip) (p. 2.10, LO 3) Small piece of silicon that contains thousands of microminiature electronic circuit components, mainly transistors.

Chips have made possible the development of small computers.

control unit (p. 2.9, LO 3) The part of the CPU that tells the rest of the computer system how to carry out a program's instructions.

The control unit directs the movement of electronic signals between main memory and the arithmetic/logic unit. It also directs these electronic signals between the main memory and input and output devices.

coprocessors (p. 2.12, LO 3) Additional processor chips that extend the capabilities and speed of the microprocessor.

Each coprocessor is dedicated to a special job, such as crunching numbers or handling graphics.

EBCDIC (Extended Binary Coded Decimal Interchange Code) (p. 2.4, LO 1) Coding scheme that uses 8 bits to form each byte.

EBCDIC is commonly used in mainframes.

execution cycle (E-cycle) (p. 2.14, LO 3) Part of the machine cycle during which the ALU executes the instruction and stores the processed results in a register.

The completion time of the execution cycle determines how fast data is processed. The execution cycle is preceded by the instruction cycle.

expansion card (p. 2.25, LO 5) Add-on circuit board that provides more memory or a new peripheral-device capability. (The words *card* and *board* are used interchangeably.) Expansion cards are inserted into expansion slots inside the system unit.

Users can use expansion cards to upgrade their computers instead of having to buy entire new systems.

expansion slots (p. 2.25, LO 5) Socket on the motherboard into which users may plug an expansion card.

See *expansion card.*

flash memory (p. 2.23, LO 5) Used primarily in notebook and subnotebook computers; flash memory, or flash RAM cards, consists of circuitry on credit-card-size cards that can be inserted into slots connecting to the motherboard.

Unlike standard RAM chips, flash memory is nonvolatile—it retains data even when the power is turned off. Flash memory can be used not only to simulate main memory but also to supplement or replace hard disk drives for permanent storage.

floating-point operations per second (flops) (p. 2.16, LO 4) A kind of mathematical calculation usually expressed in megaflops, gigaflops, or teraflops—millions, trillions, and billions of floating-point operations per second.

This measure of computing speed is mainly used with supercomputers.

gigabyte (G, GB) (p. 2.9, LO 2) Approximately 1 billion bytes (1,073,741,824 bytes); a measure of storage capacity.

Gigabytes are used to express the storage capacity of large computers, such as mainframes, although it is also applied to some microcomputer secondary storage devices.

instruction cycle (I-cycle) (p. 2.14, LO 3)   Part of the machine cycle in which a single computer instruction is retrieved from memory and decoded.

"Decoding" means that the control unit alerts the circuits in the microprocessor to perform the specified operation. The instruction cycle is followed by the execution cycle.

kilobyte (K, KB) (p. 2.8, LO 7)   Unit for measuring storage capacity; equals 1024 bytes (usually rounded off to 1000 bytes).

The sizes of stored electronic files are often measured in kilobytes.

machine cycle (p. 2.14, LO 3)   Series of operations performed by the CPU to execute a single program instruction; it consists of two parts: an instruction cycle and an execution cycle.

The machine cycle is the essence of computer-based processing.

machine language (p. 2.7, LO 1)   Binary code (language) that the computer uses directly. The 0s and 1s represent precise storage locations and operations.

For a program to run, it must be in the machine language of the computer that is executing it.

main memory (p. 2.12, LO 3)   Also known as *memory, primary storage, internal memory,* or *RAM* (for *random access memory*); working storage that holds (1) data for processing, (2) the programs for processing the data, and (3) data after it has been processed and is waiting to be sent to an output, secondary-storage, or communications device.

Main memory capacity determines the total size of the programs and data files a computer can work on at any given moment.

megabyte (M, MB) (p. 2.9, LO 2)   About 1 million bytes (1,048,576 bytes).

Microcomputer main memory capacity is usually expressed in megabytes.

megahertz (MHz) (p. 2.16, LO 4)   Measurement of microcomputer processing speed, controlled by the system clock; 1 MHz equals 1 million machine cycles per second.

Generally, the higher the megahertz rate, the faster a computer can process data. Currently microcomputers run at 133–200 MHz or more.

microprocessor (p. 2.9, LO 3)   A CPU (processor) consisting of miniaturized circuitry on a single chip; it controls all the processing in a computer.

Microprocessors enabled the development of microcomputers.

millions of instructions per second (MIPS) (p. 2.16, LO 4)   Another measure of a computer's processing speed.

This measure is often used for large, relatively powerful computers and new sophisticated microcomputers.

motherboard (p. 2.20, LO 5)   Also called *system board;* the main circuit board in the system unit of a microcomputer.

This board contains the interconnecting assembly of important components, including CPU, main memory, other chips, and expansion slots.

parallel port (p. 2.23, LO 5)   Part of the computer through which a parallel device, which transmits 8 bits simultaneously, can be connected.

Enables microcomputer users to connect to a parallel printer.

parity bit (p. 2.5, LO 1)   Also called a *check bit;* an extra bit attached to the end of a byte.

Enables a computer system to check for errors during transmission. (The check bits are organized according to a particular coding scheme designed into the computer.)

PCMCIA (Personal Computer Memory Card International Association) (p. 2.27, LO 5)   Bus standard for portable computers.

This standard enables users of notebooks and subnotebooks to insert credit-card-size peripheral devices called *PC cards,* such as modems and memory cards, into their computers.

port (p. 2.23, LO 5)   Connecting socket on the outside of the computer system unit that is connected to an expansion board on the inside of the system unit. Ports are of five types: parallel, serial, video adapter, SCSI, game ports, and infrared ports.

Ports enable users to connect peripheral devices such as monitor, printer, and modem so that they can communicate with the computer system.

power supply (p. 2.20, LO 5)   Device in the computer that converts AC current from the wall outlet to the DC current the computer uses.

The power supply enables the computer (and peripheral devices) to operate.

processor (p. 2.9, LO 3)   See *central processing unit.*

ROM (read-only memory) (p. 2.22, LO 5)   Also known as *firmware;* a memory chip that permanently stores instructions and data that are programmed during the chip's manufacture and that cannot be changed or erased by the user. Three variations on the ROM chip are PROM, EPROM, and EEPROM. ROM is a nonvolatile form of storage.

ROM chips are used to store special basic instructions for computer operations such as those that start the computer and display characters on the screen.

ROM BIOS (basic input/output system) (p. 2.22, LO 5)   ROM chip that helps the processor transfer information between the keyboard, screen, printer, and other peripheral devices to make sure all units are functioning properly.

ROM BIOS is an interface, a connector, and a translator between the computer hardware and the software programs that you run.

SCSI (Small Computer System Interface) port (p. 2.24, LO 5)   Pronounced "scuzzy"; an interface for transferring data at high speeds for up to seven or fifteen SCSI-compatible devices, connected in a "daisy chain."

SCSI ports are used to connect external hard disk drives, magnetic-tape backup units, and CD-ROM drives to the computer system.

serial port (p. 2.23, LO 5)   Also known as RS-232 port; a port to which a cable is connected that transmits 1 bit at a time, one after the other (instead of in parallel fashion).

Serial ports are used principally for connecting communications lines, modems, and mice to microcomputers.

system clock (p. 2.16, LO 4)   Internal timing device that uses a quartz crystal to generate a uniform electrical frequency from which digital pulses are created.

The system clock controls the speed of all operations within a computer. The faster the clock, the faster the processing.

system unit (p. 2.18, LO 5)   The box or cabinet that contains the electrical components that do the computer's processing; usually includes processing components, RAM chips (main memory), ROM chips (read-only memory), power supply, expansion slots, and disk drives but not keyboard, printer, or often even the display screen.

The system unit integrates and protects many important processing and storage components.

terabyte (T, TB) (p. 2.9, LO 2)   Approximately 1 trillion bytes (1,009,511,627,776 bytes).

The capacities of some forms of mass storage, or secondary storage for mainframes and supercomputers, are expressed in terabytes.

Unicode (p. 2.5, LO 1)   Subset of ASCII developed by several big names in the computer industry. Unicode uses 2 bytes (16 bits) for each character, instead of 1 byte (8 bits). Thus Unicode can handle 65,536 character combinations rather than ASCII's 256.

Although it will take time, conversion to Unicode seems likely because it can handle more character combinations.

video adapter port (p. 2.24, LO 5)   Part of the computer used to connect the video display monitor outside the computer to the video adapter card inside the system unit.

The video adapter port enables users to have different kinds of monitors, some having higher resolution and more colors than others.

video RAM (VRAM) (p. 2.23, LO 5)   Chips that are used to display images for the monitor.

The amount of video memory determines how fast images appear and how many colors are available on the display screen. Video memory chips are useful for programs displaying lots of graphics.

word size (p. 2.15, LO 4)   Number of bits that the processor can store in its registers, process at one time, and send through its internal (local) bus or through expansion buses.

Often the more bits in a word, the faster the computer. An 8-bit-word computer will transfer data within each CPU chip in 8-bit chunks. A 32-bit-word computer is faster, transferring data in 32-bit chunks.

1. A(n) _kilo byte_ is about 1000 bytes (1024) bytes.

   A(n) _mega byte_ is about 1 million bytes (1,048,576 bytes).

   A(n) _giga byte_ is about 1 billion bytes (1,073,741,824 bytes).

2. A(n) _parity_ bit is an extra bit attached to a byte for purposes of checking for accuracy.

3. _Machine language_ is a binary programming language that the computer can run directly.

4. The _ALU_ is the part of the microprocessor that tells the rest of the computer system how to carry out a program's instructions.

5. _Word size_ refers to the number of bits the processor can hold in its registers, process at one time, and send through its local bus.

SHORT-ANSWER QUESTIONS

1. What is the purpose of a parity scheme? How does it work?

2. What is a coprocessor chip? What is the purpose of a graphics coprocessor chip?

3. What is the function of registers in a computer system?

4. What types of chips are typically included on the motherboard of a microcomputer?

5. What is the function of the ALU in a microcomputer system?

MULTIPLE-CHOICE QUESTIONS

1. Which of the following coding schemes is widely used on microcomputers?
   a. EBCDIC
   b. ASCII-8
   c. Unicode
   d. Microcode
   e. all the above

2. What is the main disadvantage of a massively parallel processing (MPP)?
   a. expensive
   b. difficult to program
   c. slow program execution
   d. requires bulky hardware
   e. all the above

3. Which of the following is used to measure a computer's processing power?
   a. RAM capacity
   b. word size capability
   c. processor speed
   d. all the above

4. Which of the following is accessed when you switch on your computer?
   a. RAM chip
   b. ROM chip
   c. coprocessor chip
   d. microprocessor chip
   e. all the above

5. Which of the following can be used in portable computers to replace the hard disk?
   a. cache memory
   b. video RAM
   c. flash memory
   d. ROM
   e. none of the above

TRUE/FALSE QUESTIONS

1. Computer programmers write in programming languages that resemble machine language. (true/false)

2. The bus connects a computer system's control unit and ALU. (true/false)

3. The machine cycle is composed of the instruction cycle and execution cycle. (true/false)

4. Today's microprocessors have more transistors than those in the 1970s. (true/false)

5. Main memory is nonvolatile. (true/false)

KNOWLEDGE IN ACTION

1. Describe the latest microprocessor chip released by Intel. Who are the intended users of this chip? How is this chip better than its predecessor? Perform your research using current computer maga-zines and periodicals and/or the Internet.

2. Develop a binary system of your own (use any two states, objects, or conditions) and encode the following: I am a rocket scientist.

3. Look through some computer magazines and identify advertised microcomputer systems. Decide what microcomputer might be the best one for you to use based on your processing requirements (if necessary, pick a hypothetical job and identify some probable processing requirements). Describe the microcomputer you would choose and why. Compare this microcomputer to others you saw advertised using the following categories: (a) name and brand of computer, (b) microprocessor model, (c) RAM capacity, (d) availability of cache memory, and (e) cost.

4. Look through several computer magazines and list all the coprocessor chips and add-on boards mentioned. Next to each listed item, write down what it does and what type of computer system it's compatible with. Then note an application (task) for which each item could be useful.

5. Using computer magazines and periodicals and/or the Internet, conduct additional research on one of the newer technologies described in the Coming Attractions? section at the end of this chapter. Who will use this technology? For what? When will this technology be available? Who is developing this technology and who is providing the funding?

INPUT/OUTPUT HARDWARE

Interfaces Between You and the Computer

3

WHY IS THIS CHAPTER IMPORTANT?

If, in a sudden fit of anti-technology disillusionment, you decided never to lay hands on a computer for the rest of your life, one system would still be hard to avoid. It's that universal gadget the ATM, the automated teller machine—the "magic money machine," as some people call it, built into the walls of banks, malls, and supermarkets everywhere.

Nearly half of American households already use ATMs at least once a month, and younger consumers use them an average of eight times a month.[1] Now, in a move that will probably affect your future, banks are recognizing that ATMs can be used to deliver all kinds of things besides $20 bills. "Anything that can be printed on paper and can be dispensed is possible," says the marketing vice president of one ATM maker.

ATMs in Las Vegas gambling casinos dispense $100 bills. In the future, look for machines that will cash checks down to the penny. In airports variations on ATMs called *electronic ticketing machines* help travelers avoid lines and airlines save money. Some teller machines act like vending machines, selling plane and theater tickets, traveler's checks, bus passes, postage stamps, phone cards, and other documents. And, in a great leap beyond paper, a device called a Personal-ATM has been unveiled that you can install in your home. With this device, you can use your phone to download funds from your bank account onto a "smart card," a credit-card-like piece of plastic embedded with a computer chip and usable as a cash substitute.[2]

Beyond one important fact—that they deal with money—why are ATMs of interest to us here? The reason is that this device exemplifies the two faces, or interfaces, by which people interact with the computer. These are *input,* as when we deposit a check into the machine, and *output,* as when it dispenses crisp green bills. In this chapter we explore input/output, or I/O, devices.

I/O, I/O, It's Off to Work We Go

Input/output devices are called *I/O devices.* They translate data going into the computer into the Os and 1s of computer language and translate the information coming out of the computer into a form understandable by humans.

Essentially, in a computer every data transfer is an output from one device and an input into another—or vice versa. For example, data stored on a hard disk is output to RAM to be processed in the processor. Data input through the keyboard is processed and output, for example, to disk or printer. In this chapter we focus on the common input/output (I/O) devices that people deal with when they are working with a computer. *(See Figure 3.1.)*

Input hardware consists of devices that translate data into a form the computer can process. The people-readable form may be words like the ones in these sentences, but the computer-readable form consists of 0s and 1s, or off and on signals. **Output devices** consist of hardware that translates information processed by the computer into a form that humans can understand. The computer-processed information consists of 0s and 1s, which need to be translated into words, numbers, sounds, and pictures.

First we'll cover input hardware.

Figure 3.1 Chart of input/output devices

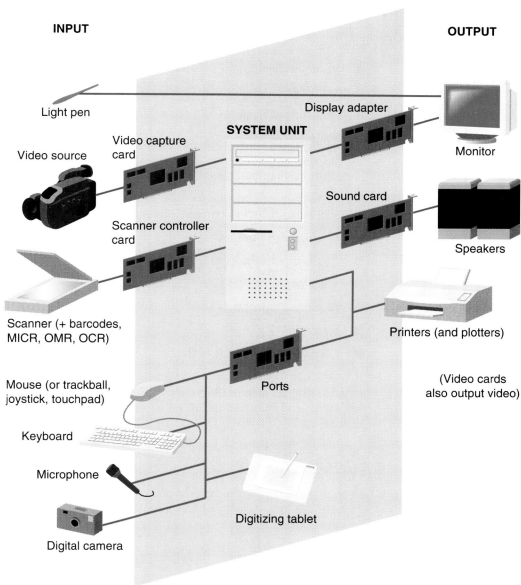

INPUT

OUTPUT

Light pen

Display adapter

Video capture card

SYSTEM UNIT

Monitor

Video source

Sound card

Scanner controller card

Speakers

Scanner (+ barcodes, MICR, OMR, OCR)

Printers (and plotters)

Mouse (or trackball, joystick, touchpad)

Ports

(Video cards also output video)

Keyboard

Microphone

Digitizing tablet

Digital camera

Input Hardware

Input hardware includes keyboards, pointing devices, and source-data entry devices, as well as voice and audio/video input devices.

One input device you will probably have to learn to use is the keyboard. A **keyboard** converts letters, numbers, and other characters into electrical signals that are machine-readable by the computer's processor. The keyboard may look like a typewriter keyboard to which some special keys have been added. Or it may look like the keys on a bank's automatic teller machine or the keypad of a pocket computer used by a bread-truck driver.

You will also probably use some non-keyboard **pointing devices.** These devices control the position of the cursor or pointer on the screen. Pointing devices include:

Cursor   Pointer

■ Mice, trackballs, and joysticks

■ Light pens

■ Digitizing tablets

■ Pen-based systems

Because keyboard entry requires typing by people, the data input this way is less accurate than data input via non-keyboard **source-data entry devices.** These include:

■ Scanners, including bar code scanners, fax machines, and imaging systems

■ Voice-recognition devices

■ Audio input devices

■ Video input devices

■ Electronic cameras

■ Sensors

■ Human-biology input devices

Often keyboard, pointing, and source-data input devices are combined in a single computer system. A basic desktop-publishing system, for example, uses a keyboard, a mouse, and an image scanner. And some microcomputers have built-in scanners.

Keyboard Input

Even if you aren't a ten-finger typist, you can use a computer keyboard. *(See Figure 3.2.)* You should not feel intimidated by the number of keys, because you can easily undo mistakes.

■ *Standard typing keys: Typing keys* are the same familiar QWERTY arrangement of letter, number, and punctuation keys found on any typewriter. QWERTY refers to the alphabet keys in the top left row on a standard typewriter keyboard.

The space bar and Shift, Tab, and Caps Lock keys do the same things on the computer that they do on a typewriter. (When you press the Caps Lock

Only capital letters will be displayed.

Prints what's currently displayed on the screen.

Prevents the screen from scrolling.

The Esc key allows you to exit a command or menu and return to the work screen.

Temporarily suspends the current task.

These status lights indicate when these functions are on or off.

Function keys are used to issue commands specific to the software package being used.

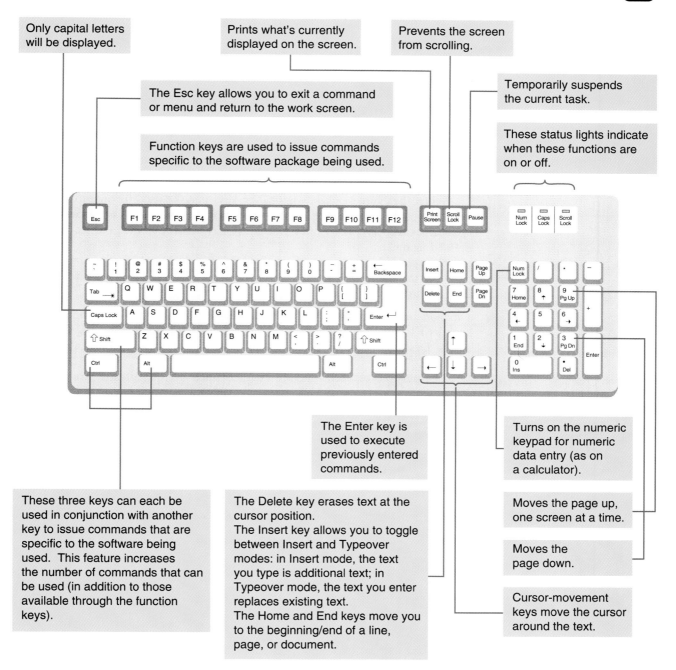

The Enter key is used to execute previously entered commands.

Turns on the numeric keypad for numeric data entry (as on a calculator).

These three keys can each be used in conjunction with another key to issue commands that are specific to the software being used. This feature increases the number of commands that can be used (in addition to those available through the function keys).

The Delete key erases text at the cursor position.
The Insert key allows you to toggle between Insert and Typeover modes: in Insert mode, the text you type is additional text; in Typeover mode, the text you enter replaces existing text.
The Home and End keys move you to the beginning/end of a line, page, or document.

Moves the page up, one screen at a time.

Moves the page down.

Cursor-movement keys move the cursor around the text.

Figure 3.2 Common keyboard layout

key, a light on your keyboard shows you are typing ALL CAPITAL LET-TERS until you press the Caps Lock key again.)

An exception is the Enter (bent left arrow) key. The **Enter key,** sometimes called the Return key, is used to enter commands into the computer, in addition to beginning a new paragraph in a word processing system.

■ *Cursor-movement keys:* The **cursor,** also called the *insertion point,* is the symbol on the display screen that shows where data may be entered next. The

cursor-movement keys, or arrow keys, are used to move the cursor around the text on the screen. These keys move the cursor left, right, up, or down.

The key labeled *PgUp* stands for *Page Up,* and the key labeled *PgDn* stands for *Page Down.* These keys move the cursor the equivalent of one page or one screen at a time up (backward) or down (forward).

■ *Numeric keys:* On a standard 101-key keyboard, previously known as an enhanced AT-style keyboard, a separate set of keys, 0 through 9, known as the **numeric keypad,** is laid out like the keys on a calculator. The numeric keypad has two purposes.

Whenever the Num Lock key is off, the numeric keys may be used as arrow keys for cursor movement and for other purposes such as PgUp, PgDn.

When the Num Lock key is on, the keys may be used for manipulating numbers, as on a calculator. A light is illuminated on the keyboard when the Num Lock key is pressed once and goes off when the Num Lock key is pressed again.

For space reasons, portable computers often lack a separate numeric keypad—or the numeric keys may be superimposed on the typewriter letter keys and activated by the Num Lock key.

■ *Function keys:* **Function keys** are the keys labeled with an F and a number, such as F1 and F2. They are used for issuing commands, not typing in characters. Desktop microcomputers usually have 12 function keys, portables often only 10.

The purpose of each function key is defined by the software you are using. For example, in one program, pressing F2 may print your document; in a different program, pressing F2 may save your work to disk. The documentation manual that comes with the software tells you how to use the function keys. Also, some companies make small templates that fit around or above the function keys and list the commands that the function keys correspond to.

What are function keys used for? How do you know which key does what?

As computers have become more widespread, so has the incidence of various hand and wrist injuries. Accordingly, keyboard manufacturers have been giving a lot of attention to ergonomics. **Ergonomics** is the study of the physical relationships between people and their work environment. Various attempts are being made to make keyboards more ergonomically sound in order to prevent injuries. *(See Figure 3.3.)*

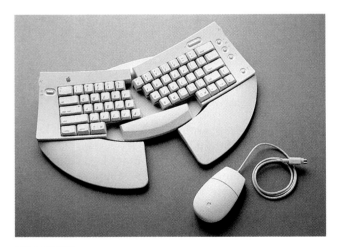 

Figure 3.3 Ergonomic keyboards

Pointing Devices

One of the most natural of all human gestures, the act of pointing, is incorporated in several kinds of input devices.

Mice, Trackballs, Joysticks, and Touchpads

The principal pointing tools used with microcomputers are the mouse, the trackball, the joystick, and the touchpad, all of which have variations. *(See Figure 3.4.)*

■ *Mouse:* A **mouse** is a device that is rolled about on a desktop to direct a pointer on the computer's display screen. The pointer may sometimes be, but is not necessarily the same as, the cursor. The **mouse pointer** is the symbol that indicates the position of the mouse on the display screen. It may be an arrow, a rectangle, or even a representation of a person's pointing finger. The pointer may change to the shape of an I-beam to indicate that it is a cursor identifying the place where text or other data may be entered.

   The mouse usually has a cable that is connected (by being plugged into a special port, or socket) to the microcomputer's system unit. This tail-like cable and the rounded "head" of the instrument are what suggested the name *mouse.* Some newer mouse types are wireless (cordless)—that is, they use battery-powered senders to send infrared signals to a battery-powered receiver hooked up to a serial port on the back of the computer. Some companies make mice in different sizes, to fit hands of different sizes.

   On the bottom side of the mouse is a ball that translates the mouse movement into digital signals. On the top side are one to four buttons. Your

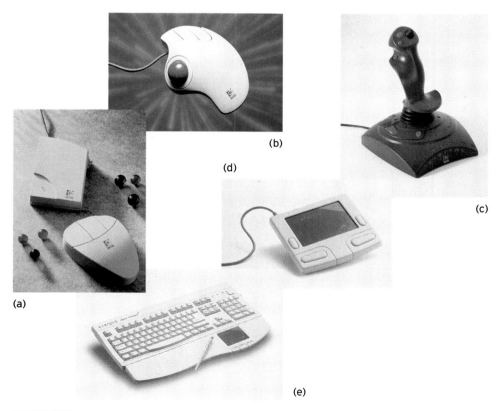

(a)

(b)

(c)

(d)

(e)

Figure 3.4 Giving a few pointers. (*a*) Two types of mouse. (*b*) Trackball. (*c*) Joystick. (*d*) Touchpad. (*e*) Touchpad integrated with a keyboard.

software determines the use of the second, third, and fourth buttons; the first one is used for common functions, such as *clicking* and *dragging*. *(See Table 3.1.)*

Gently holding the mouse with one hand, you can move it in all directions on the desktop (or on a rubber mouse pad, which may provide additional traction). This will produce a corresponding movement of the mouse pointer on the screen.

Depending on the software, many commands that can be done with a mouse can also be performed through the keyboard. The mouse may make it easy to learn the commands for, say, a word processing program. However, you may soon find that you can execute those commands more quickly through a combination of keystrokes on the keyboard.

■ *Trackball:* Another form of pointing device, the trackball, is a variant on the mouse. A **trackball** is a movable ball, on top of a stationary device, that is rotated with the fingers or palm of the hand. In fact, the trackball looks like a mouse turned upside down. Instead of moving the mouse around on the desktop, you move the trackball with the tips of your fingers.

Trackballs are especially suited to portable computers, which are often used in confined places such as on airline tray tables. Trackballs may appear on the keyboard centered below the space bar, as on the Apple PowerBook, or built into the right side of the screen. On some portables the trackball is a separate device that is clipped to the side of the keyboard.

■ *Joystick:* A **joystick** is a pointing device that consists of a vertical handle like a gearshift lever mounted on a base with one or two buttons. Named for the control mechanism that directs an airplane's fore-and-aft and side-to-side movement, joysticks are used principally in video games, in some computer-aided design systems, and in computerized robot systems. Special joysticks, such as SAM-JOYstick from RJ Cooper and Associates, are available for people who have disabilities that don't let them use a mouse or a trackball.

■ *Touchpad:* **Touchpads** let you control the cursor/pointer with your finger. About the same size as a mouse, touchpads are flat, rectangular devices that

Small trackball integrated with a keyboard

Table 3.1

LEARNING MOUSE LANGUAGE	
Term	**Definition**
The directions you are most likely to encounter for using a mouse or a trackball are the following:	
Point	Move the pointer to the desired spot on the screen, such as over a particular word or object.
Click	Tap—that is, press and quickly release—the left mouse button.
Double-click	Tap—press and release—the left mouse button twice, as quickly as possible.
Drag	Press and hold the left mouse button while moving the pointer to another location.
Drop	Release the mouse button after dragging.
Point-and-shoot	Point, then click.

Pros	Cons
• Relatively inexpensive • Very little finger movement needed to reach buttons **Mouse**	• When gripped too tightly can cause muscle strain • Uses more desk space than other pointing devices • Must be cleaned regularly
• Uses less desk space than mouse • Requires less arm and hand movement than mouse **Trackball**	• Wrist is bent during use • More finger movement needed to reach buttons than with other pointing devices
• Small footprint • Least prone to dust **Touchpad**	• Places more stress on index finger than other pointing devices do • Small active area makes precise cursor control difficult

Figure 3.5 Pros and cons re: mouse, trackball, touchpad

What can you do with a mouse? Why would you use a trackball, a joystick, or a touchpad instead?

use a very weak electrical field to sense your touch. As you move your fingertip, the cursor follows the movement. You "click" by tapping your finger on the pad's surface or by pressing buttons on the top, back, or side of the pad. Touchpads are now common on portable computers, built into the keyboard.

Figure 3.5 gives some pros and cons of using mice, trackballs, and touchpads.

Light Pen

The **light pen** is a light-sensitive stylus, or pen-like device, connected by a wire to the computer terminal. The user brings the pen to a desired point on the display screen and presses the pen button, which identifies that screen location to the computer. *(See Figure 3.6.)* Light pens are used by engineers, graphic designers, and illustrators.

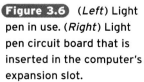

Figure 3.6 (*Left*) Light pen in use. (*Right*) Light pen circuit board that is inserted in the computer's expansion slot.

Digitizing Tablets

A **digitizing tablet** consists of a tablet connected by a wire to a stylus or puck. A stylus is a pen-like device with which the user "sketches" an image. A puck is a copying device with which the user copies, or traces, an image. *(See Figure 3.7.)*

When used with drawing and painting software, a digitizing tablet and stylus allow you to do shading and many other effects similar to those artists achieve

Figure 3.7 Digitizing tablets

with pencil, pen, or charcoal. Alternatively, when you use a puck, you can trace a drawing laid on the tablet, and a digitized copy is stored in the computer.

Digitizing tablets are used primarily in graphic design, computer animation, and engineering.

Pen-Based Systems

Pen-based computer systems use a pen-like stylus to enter handwriting and marks into a computer. *(See Figure 3.8.)* There is a good chance you will use one of these systems if you haven't already.

There are four types of pen-based systems:

■ *Gesture recognition or electronic checklists: Gesture recognition* refers to a computer's ability to recognize various check marks, slashes, or carefully printed block letters and numbers placed in boxes. This type of pen-based system is incorporated in devices that resemble simple forms or checklists on handheld electronic clipboards that have an accompanying electronic pen or stylus. This type of small computer is used by meter readers, package deliverers, and insurance claims representatives.

■ *Handwriting stored as scribbling:* A second type of pen-based system recognizes and stores handwriting. The handwriting is stored as a scribble and is not converted to typed text.

■ *Handwriting converted, with training, to typed text:* Some pen-based devices can recognize your handwriting and transform it into typed text. These systems require that the machine be "trained" to recognize your particular (or even peculiar) handwriting. Moreover, the writing must be neat printing rather than script. The advantage of converting writing to typed text is that after conversion the text can be retrieved and later edited or further manipulated.

■ *Handwriting converted, without training, to typed text:* The most sophisticated—and still mostly elusive—application of pen-based computers converts script handwriting to typed text without training.

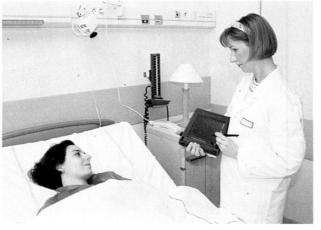

Figure 3.8 Pen-based systems. (*Left*) Stylistic 1000 with a color screen. (*Right*) In some hospitals, pen-based computers are used to enter comments to patients' records.

Source-Data Entry

As we mentioned earlier, source-data input devices do not require keystrokes to input data to the computer. In other words, data is entered from as close to the source as possible; people do not need to act as typing intermediaries. One of the most common source-data entry devices is the scanner.

Scanning Devices

Scanners use laser beams and reflected light to translate hardcopy images of text, drawings, photos, and the like into digital form. The images can then be processed by a computer, displayed on a monitor, stored on a storage device, or communicated to another computer. Scanning devices include:

- Bar-code readers

- Mark- and character-recognition devices

- Fax machines

- Imaging systems

Bar-Code Readers   **Bar codes** are the vertical zebra-striped marks you see on most manufactured retail products—everything from candy to cosmetics to comic books. In North America and some other countries, such as Australia, supermarkets, food manufacturers, and others have agreed to use a bar-code system called the *Universal Product Code.* Other kinds of bar-code systems are used on everything from Federal Express packages to railroad cars.

Bar codes are read by **bar-code readers,** photoelectric scanners that translate the bar code symbols into digital code (ASCII or EBCDIC). *(See Figure 3.9.)* The price of a particular item is set within the store's computer and appears on the salesclerk's point-of-sale terminal and on your receipt. Records of sales are input to the store's computer and used for accounting, restocking store inventory, and weeding out products that don't sell well.

A recent innovation is the self-scanning bar-code reader, which grocers hope will extend the concept of self-service and help them lower costs. Here customers bring their groceries to an automated checkout counter, where they scan them and bag them. They then take the bill to a cashier's station to pay. To guard against theft, the bar-code scanner is able to detect attempts to pass off steak as peas.

Figure 3.9 Bar-code readers in use. (*Left*) A bar-code reader is used to input bar codes to a database. (*Middle*) Bar-code readers are used in clothing stores to read bar-coded data on the back of merchandise. (*Right*) Bar-readers are also used to read clothing tags.

A soldier uses a scanner to check the photo ID of a man after the Gulf War in 1991.

Bar codes are also occasionally used on people. For example, when 1000 runners completed a 1996 relay race from Calistoga to Santa Cruz in northern California, they didn't have to wait four months to find out their times. Instead, they got the information at the finish line. Each runner wore a bar-code T-shirt, and handheld bar-code readers recorded runners' times at each of the race's thirty-six checkpoints.

Mark-Recognition and Character-Recognition Devices There are three types of scanning devices that translate certain types of marks and characters. They are usually referred to by their abbreviations MICR, OMR, and OCR.

■ *Magnetic-ink character recognition:* In **magnetic-ink character recognition (MICR),** a scanner translates the magnetically charged numbers printed at the bottom of bank checks and deposit slips. *(See Figure 3.10.)* MICR characters, which are printed with magnetized ink, are read by MICR equipment, producing a digitized signal. This signal is used by a bank's reader/sorter machine to sort checks.

Figure 3.10 MICR technology

Check reader

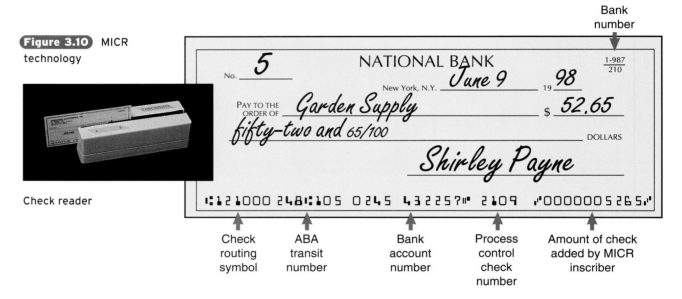

■ *Optical mark recognition:* **Optical mark recognition (OMR)** uses a device that reads pencil marks and converts them into computer-usable form. Well-known examples are the OMR technology used to read the College Board Scholastic Aptitude Test (SAT), the Graduate Record Examination (GRE), and SCANTRON tests.

How do you imagine you might use bar codes and bar-code readers in your profession or career? OCR?

■ *Optical character recognition:* **Optical character recognition (OCR)** uses a device that reads special OCR character sets called OCR *fonts,* as well as typewriter and computer-printed characters, and converts them into machine-readable form. *(See Figure 3.11.)* Examples that use OCR characters are utility bills and price tags on department-store merchandise. The *wand reader* is a common OCR scanning device. Some advanced OCR systems can recognize human handwriting, but generally the letters must be block printed. Because *script* handwriting styles vary so widely, there is no standard to apply to program computers to recognize them.

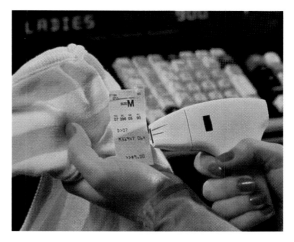

OCR-A
NUMERIC   0123456789
ALPHA   ABCDEFGHIJKLMNOPQRSTUVWXYZ
SYMBOLS   >$/-+-#"

OCR-B
NUMERIC   00123456789
ALPHA   ACENPSTVX
SYMBOLS   <+>-¥

Figure 3.11   Optical character recognition. Sample OCR fonts and price tag with wand reader

Experts say the accuracy rate of OCR programs scanning text pages with different type styles and sizes is about 85%, and they expect it to improve.[3] They also say that using OCR can be five times faster than retyping a document into the computer. The important function of OCR is that, once the text appears on-screen, a user can copy it to a word processing program, make corrections and additions, and save it.

Fax Machines   A **fax machine**—or *facsimile transmission machine*—scans an image on paper and sends it as electronic signals over telephone lines to a receiving fax machine, which re-creates the image on paper. *(See Figure 3.12.)* (*Facsimile* means "an exact copy.") It can also scan and send an image to a fax *modem* (circuit board) inside a remote computer—this fax can be displayed on the screen, stored, or printed out by the computer's printer. In other words, a stand-alone fax machine can scan a paper document but a fax modem cannot. The user of a fax modem must usually create a fax by typing the content into the computer.

Imaging Systems   An **imaging system**—or image scanner or graphics scanner—converts text, drawings, and photographs into digital form that can be stored in a computer system and then manipulated, stored, output, or sent via modem to another computer. *(See Figure 3.13.)* The system scans each image—color or black and white—with light and breaks it into light and dark dots or color dots, which are then converted to digital code. This is called *raster graphics,* which refers to the technique of representing a graphic image as a matrix of dots.

Figure 3.12   Stand-alone fax machine in use and a fax modem board

Imaging systems are used in document management, desktop publishing (DTP), and multimedia development. In DTP, the graphics scanner scans in artwork and photos that can then be positioned on a page of text, using desktop-publishing software. Other

Figure 3.13 Two workers at the U.S. National Research Center for the Identification of Missing Children have just scanned a missing child's photo into a computer.

systems are available for turning paper documents—say, legal transcripts or financial records—into electronic files so that people can reduce their paperwork as well as the space required to store it. Internet and Web users scan photos into their computer systems to send to online friends or to post on Web pages.

Scanners generally are flatbed, sheetfed, or handheld. Flatbed scanners are used for scanning high-quality graphics. Sheetfed scanners are smaller and less expensive and are used by business and home-office users who need a convenient way to convert paperwork to electronic files that can be used with different software applications. Flatbed scanners can scan all sorts of documents, even books.

(*Above*) Portable scanner. (*Above right*) Handheld photo scanner. (*Right*) 3-D scanner.

Most sheetfed scanners can handle only single sheets. Color flatbed scanners scan at higher resolutions—up to 2400 dots per inch (dpi), compared to 400 dpi for sheetfed scanners. (The higher the resolution, the crisper the image but the longer the scanning time and the larger the image file.)

Handheld scanners are rolled by hand over the documents to be scanned. These scanners are generally used to scan in small images or parts of images. Their resolution is not very high.

Some manufacturers are building small scanners into portable computers—one feeds a sheet of paper into a slot in the computer. Also, small scanners used just for snapshots are available. Expensive 3-D scanners are also available that can convert small and medium-size objects into 3-D files.

How do you think you will use an image scanner in your planned career?

Imaging-system technology has led to a whole new art or industry called *electronic imaging.* Electronic imaging is the combining of separate images, using scanners, digital cameras, video capture cards, and advanced graphic computers. This technology has become an important part of multimedia.

Voice-Recognition Systems

A **voice-recognition system,** which typically adds a microphone and audio sound card to a computer system, converts a person's speech into digital code by comparing the electrical patterns produced by the speaker's voice with a set of prerecorded patterns stored in the computer. *(See Figure 3.14.)*

Voice-recognition systems are finding many uses. Warehouse workers are able to speed inventory-taking by recording inventory counts verbally. Blind or paralyzed people can give verbal commands to their PCs rather than use the keyboard. Traders on stock exchanges can communicate their trades verbally. Astronauts who need to use two hands to make repairs in space can activate display screens in their helmet visors with spoken commands. Radiologists spend most of their time interpreting images such as X rays and sending reports of their findings to other doctors. The reports traditionally have been dictated into a recording machine, transcribed by a secretary, and then corrected by the doctor—a process that often took days. Now, however, many radiologists use advanced voice-recognition systems to get their reports out much more rapidly.

Figure 3.14 How a voice-recognition system works. Voice recognition begins with a person speaking into a micro-phone attached to a computer system.

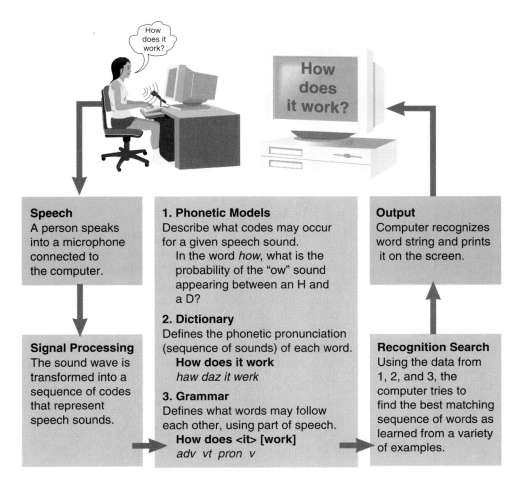

Speech
A person speaks into a microphone connected to the computer.

Signal Processing
The sound wave is transformed into a sequence of codes that represent speech sounds.

1. Phonetic Models
Describe what codes may occur for a given speech sound.
In the word *how*, what is the probability of the "ow" sound appearing between an H and a D?

2. Dictionary
Defines the phonetic pronunciation (sequence of sounds) of each word.
How does it work
haw daz it werk

3. Grammar
Defines what words may follow each other, using part of speech.
How does <it> [work]
adv vt pron v

Output
Computer recognizes word string and prints it on the screen.

Recognition Search
Using the data from 1, 2, and 3, the computer tries to find the best matching sequence of words as learned from a variety of examples.

So far, however, voice-recognition technology has been hindered by three limitations:

■ *Speaker dependence:* Most systems need to be "trained" by the speaker to recognize his or her distinctive speech patterns and even variations in the way a particular word is said. Systems that are "speaker independent" are beginning to appear, but consider the hurdles to be overcome: different voices, pronunciations, accents, slang, and technical vocabulary.

■ *Single words versus continuous speech:* Most systems can handle only single words and have vocabularies of 1000 words or less. However, some newer technologies offer continual-speech recognition so that one need not artificially pause between words when speaking, and they have 30,000-word dictionaries (vocabularies).

■ *Lack of comprehension:* Most systems merely translate sounds into characters. A more useful technology would be one that actually comprehends the *meaning* of spoken words. You could then ask a question, and the system could check a database and formulate a meaningful answer. Some such systems are being developed for the military.

Audio Input Devices

Voice-recognition devices are only one kind of audio input device, which can translate music as well as other sounds. An **audio input device** records or plays analog sound and translates it for digital storage and processing. As we mentioned in Chapter 1, an *analog sound signal* represents a continuously variable wave within a certain frequency range. Such continuous fluctuations are usually represented with an analog device such as a cassette player. For the computer to process them, these variable waves must be converted to digital 0s and 1s, the language of the computer.

There are two ways in which audio is digitized:

■ *Audio board:* Analog sound, say, input through a microphone, goes through a special circuit board called an *audio board,* or a *sound card.* An *audio board* is an add-on (expansion) circuit board in a microcomputer that converts analog sound to digital sound and stores it for further processing and/or plays it back, providing output directly to speakers or an external amplifier. The three major sound standards are SoundBlaster, Ad Lib, and Windows. Some sound cards support all three standards. And some sound cards also have MIDI capability.

■ *MIDI board:* A *MIDI* (pronounced "middie") *board*—MIDI stands for Musical Instrument Digital Interface—provides a standard for the interchange of musical information between musical instruments, synthesizers, and computers. MIDI, which is a set of computer instructions instead of sample sounds, is widely used for multimedia applications. Most high-end sound cards have certain MIDI capability including ports for connecting external MIDI devices. For example, MIDI keyboards, also called *controllers,* and synthesizers can be plugged in to input music, which can then be stored, manipulated, and/or output.

Analog sound is converted to digital data via *sampling,* which refers to the number of times per second analog sound is turned into a binary number by the computer. To digitize voice, the computer samples the sound waves 8000 times per second to attain AM-radio-quality output. Music is sampled 44,000 times per second to attain CD-quality output.

Video and Photographic Input

Video card

As with sound, most film and videotape is in analog form, with the signal a continuously variable wave. Thus, to be used by a computer, the signals that come from a VCR or a camcorder must be converted to digital form through a special video capture, or digitizing, card installed in the computer.

Two types of video cards are the frame-grabber video and the full-motion video:

■ *Frame-grabber video card:* Some video cards, called *frame grabbers,* can capture and digitize only a single frame at a time.

■ *Full-motion video card:* Other video cards, called *full-motion video cards* or *adapters,* can convert analog to digital signals up to 30 frames per second (TV quality), giving the effect of a continuously flowing motion picture. *(See Figure 3.15.)*

Most video cameras are analog, but digital video cameras are also available. Unlike analog video cameras, which convert light intensities into infinitely variable signals, digital video cameras convert light intensities into discrete 0s and 1s. With the appropriate software, digital video can be transmitted (downloaded) directly to the computer. The main limitation in capturing full video is not input but storage. It takes a huge amount of storage space to store just 1 second of video.

Photographs can also be created digitally, avoiding the need for a scanner. The digital camera is a particularly interesting piece of hardware because it foreshadows major change for the entire industry of photography. Instead of using

Figure 3.15 Analog video input is changed to digital form

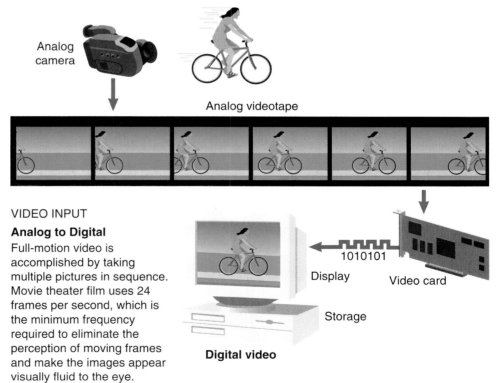

Analog camera

Analog videotape

VIDEO INPUT

Analog to Digital
Full-motion video is accomplished by taking multiple pictures in sequence. Movie theater film uses 24 frames per second, which is the minimum frequency required to eliminate the perception of moving frames and make the images appear visually fluid to the eye.

1010101
Display
Video card
Storage

Digital video

TV video generates 30 interlaced frames per second, which is actually transmitted as 60 half frames ("fields" in TV lingo) per second.

Video that has been digitized and stored in the computer can be displayed at varying frame rates, depending on the speed of the computer. The slower the computer, the jerkier the movement.

Digital camera

Sensor

traditional (chemical) film, a digital camera captures images in electronic form for immediate viewing on a television, computer display screen, or attached LCD screen (such as that used to display charts on a classroom wall).

A **digital camera** uses a light-sensitive processor chip to capture photographic images in digital form on a small disk inserted in the camera. *(See Figure 3.16.)* The bits of digital information can then be copied onto a computer's hard disk for manipulation and printing out. Another type of digital camera stores 16 to 64 to 128 color shots in its flash memory chips, depending on the resolution. This type of camera is connected via a serial port so that (using special software) photos can be downloaded to the computer's hard drive. (Photos can also be input to a computer via a scanner.)

Digital cameras have gone into wide use in journalism and industrial photography because the images are instantly available, can be deleted to make storage available for more photos, and can be transmitted over telephone lines.

Sensors

A **sensor** is a type of input device that collects specific kinds of data directly from the environment and transmits it to a computer. Although you are unlikely to see such input devices connected to a PC in an office, they exist all around us, often in invisible form. Sensors can be used for detecting all kinds of things: speed, movement, weight, pressure, temperature, humidity, wind, current, fog, gas, smoke, light, shapes, images, and so on.

Beneath the pavement, for example, are sensors that detect the speed and volume of traffic. These sensors send data to computers that can adjust traffic lights to keep cars and trucks away from gridlocked areas. In aviation, sensors are used to detect ice buildup on airplane wings or to alert pilots to sudden changes

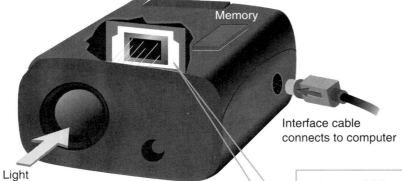

Memory

Light

Interface cable connects to computer

3. The digital information is stored in the camera's electronic memory, either built-in or removable.

4. Using an interface cable, the digital photo can be downloaded onto a computer, where it can be manipulated, printed, placed on a Web page, or e-mailed.

1. Light enters the camera through the lens.

2. The light is focused on the charge-coupled device (CCD), a solid-state chip made up of tiny, light-sensitive photosites. When light hits the CCD, it records the image electronically, just like film records images in a standard camera. The photosites convert light into electrons, which are then converted into digital information.

A look at CCDs
The smallest CCDs are 1/8 the size of a frame of 35mm film. The largest are the same size as a 35mm frame.

Smallest CCD

● Lower-end cameras start with 180,000 photosites.
● Professional cameras can have up to 6 million photosites.

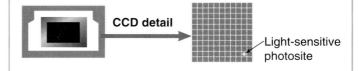

CCD detail

Light-sensitive photosite

Figure 3.16 How a digital camera works

Photography Careers

HOLD IT! *Click!*

Or will the *click* come from a mouse button rather than from a camera shutter? Photography is undergoing radical changes, moving from a film, or chemical-based, medium to a digital one.

Filmless digital cameras, which record images on memory chips, are fast gaining in popularity among news organizations, as by Associated Press photographers covering the Super Bowl. "The cameras really . . . perform quite spectacularly," says the AP's executive photo editor.[4]

The Associated Press, however, can afford top-of-the-line cameras. Many professional photographers have continued to stick with film, since, as one report suggests, "the only digital cameras that come close to film's quality cost as much as a new car."[5] Affordable filmless cameras can sometimes produce somewhat grainy images, and so their initial uses have been for jobs requiring the quick recording or relaying of information. Thus, they have been well received by insurance investigators, real-estate brokers, advertising agencies, aircraft-maintenance shops, and designers of World Wide Web home pages on the Internet. Still, as more and more imaging chips are produced by standard chip-making methods, quality should improve and camera prices fall.

Digital photography has been described by technology writer Stephen Manes as being "like Polaroid photography with a Xerox copier and fax machine attached."[6] With a digital camera, you don't need to visit a photofinisher. Instead, right after you take the picture, as Manes says, "you can transmit your photos of earthquake damage to your insurance agent, incorporate your friends' leering mugs into your home page for all the world to laugh at, or use retouching software and your ink-jet printer to print hundreds of copies of a faked picture proving you are a personal friend of Oprah's."

The ability to use a scanner to input conventional photos into computers has existed for some time. Photo developers can then take the scanned photos and put them on a flexible disk or CD-ROM. With a digital camera, however, photographers can simply transfer the images, via a cable, directly into a Macintosh or Windows-based microcomputer. They can then use imaging software to touch up, stretch, squeeze, distort, or completely alter the pictures. The software also allows photographers to insert photos into greeting cards or into digital "picture postcards" that can be sent to someone via e-mail.[7] In addition, they can plug the digital camera directly into a television set to provide impromptu slide shows.[8] If you have your portrait taken at a professional photographers, with the right digital equipment the proofs can be made available immediately on a computer screen so additional poses can be shot if necessary. Though still in their infancy, desktop photography and digital imaging are clearly giving photographers many new tools.

"Everything—the popularity of digital cameras, cheaper prices for scanners, the popularity of color printers and the Internet, and low-cost photo-editing software—point to a boom in [the photography] market," says the vice president of Life Picture Inc., developer of photo-editing products.[9]

Earthquake sensors being installed in the ground

in wind direction. In California, sensors have been planted along major earthquake fault lines in an experiment to see if scientists can predict major earth movements. Sensors are also used by government regulators to monitor whether companies are complying with air-pollution standards.

Human-Biology Input Devices

Characteristics and movements of the human body, when interpreted by sensors, optical scanners, voice recognition, and other technologies, can become forms of input. Some examples are as follows:

■ *Biometric systems:* *Biometric security devices* identify a person through a fingerprint, voice intonation, or other biological characteristic. For example, retinal-identification devices use a ray of light to identify the distinctive network of blood vessels at the back of one's eyeball. Biometric systems are used in lieu of typed passwords to identify people authorized to use a computer system.

■ *Line-of-sight systems:* Line-of-sight systems enable a person to use his or her eyes to "point" at the screen, a technology that allows physically handicapped users to direct a computer. This is accomplished using a video camera mounted beneath the monitor in front of the viewer. When the user looks at a certain place on the screen, the video camera and computer translate the area being focused on into screen coordinates.

■ *Cyber gloves and body suits:* Special gloves and body suits—often used in conjunction with "virtual reality," or the computer-generated simulation of reality—use sensors to detect body movements. The data for these movements is sent to a computer system. Similar technology is being used for human-controlled robot hands, which are used in nuclear power plants and hazardous-waste sites.

■ *Brain-wave devices:* Perhaps the ultimate input device analyzes the electrical signals of the brain and translates them into computer commands. Experiments have been successful in getting users to move a cursor on the screen through sheer power of thought. Other experiments have shown some users are able to type a letter by slowly spelling out the words in their heads. Although there is a very long way to go before brain-wave input technology becomes practicable, the consequences could be tremendous, not only for handicapped people but for all of us.

Multimedia Input Needs

You'll recall from Chapters 1 and 2 that we stated that multimedia systems have high system requirements. For example, you need a fast, powerful processor and some coprocessors. Throughout the section on input hardware, we mentioned some of the needs of a multimedia system. To recap—in addition to a keyboard and a mouse you need these for multimedia input:

■ *Sound card:* All multimedia presentations now use sound.

■ *Microphone:* The microphone provides sound input to the sound card.

■ *Graphics scanner:* This allows you include photos and art from outside sources.

■ *Video capture card:* This card lets you digitize film and video segments for manipulation.

Input Controls: Preserving Data Integrity

No matter how sophisticated your input hardware is and how well thought out your input methods are, you still run the risk of generating inaccurate or even useless information. The completeness and accuracy of information produced by a computer system depend to a great extent on how much care was taken in capturing the raw data that served as input to the processing procedures. An old computer-related saying summarizes this point: "Garbage In, Garbage Out" (GIGO). If you, the user, input incomplete and inaccurate data (Garbage In), then you can expect the information that is produced to be correspondingly incomplete and inaccurate (Garbage Out). How do you ensure that input data is accurate and complete?

Input controls include a combination of manual and computer-based control procedures designed to ensure that all input data has been accurately put into computer-usable form. A variety of control techniques can be used, depending on the design of the computer system and the nature of the processing activities taking place. System designers study these techniques and build them into systems. For example, computer software (a data entry program) can include instructions to identify incorrect, invalid, or improper input data. Also, the computer can be programmed to run "reasonableness checks" to determine if input data exceeds specified limits or is out of sequence.

Why does source-data entry pose less of a problem for accuracy of input data than does data input via keyboard?

How important are input controls? Consider the modest-living couple who got a phone bill for $450,000 and spent months trying to convince the company it was a mistake. The customer service personnel and the data processing staff were probably trying to identify the glitch in the input control procedures. The computer doesn't make mistakes; the people who input data and monitor input procedures do. Even software writers are not infallible. Without input controls, mistakes might be impossible to detect or correct. Imagine the consequences this could have at the level of international trade, politics, and military activities.

Output Hardware

Output devices translate information processed by the computer into a form that humans can understand. Output devices include printers, plotters, and multifunction devices; display screens; and audio output devices.

One of the most common output devices you will encounter is the monitor; another is the printer. However, there are several types of each of these devices to match the needs of various types of users. First we'll discuss printers.

A **printer** is an output device that prints characters, symbols, and perhaps graphics on paper. (The printed output is generally referred to as *hardcopy.*) Printers are categorized according to whether or not the image produced is formed by physical contact of the print mechanism with the paper. *Impact printers* have contact; *nonimpact printers* do not.

Impact Printers

An impact printer has mechanisms resembling those of a typewriter. That is, an impact printer forms characters or images by striking a mechanism such as a print hammer or wheel against an inked ribbon, leaving an image on paper. Impact

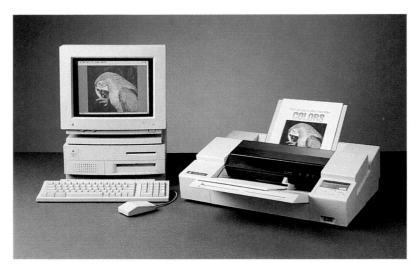

printers are dying out; however, you may still come in contact with a dot-matrix printer. A *dot-matrix printer* contains a print head of small pins that strike an inked ribbon, forming characters or images. Print heads are available with 9, 18, or 24 pins, with the 24-pin head offering the best print quality. Dot-matrix printers can print *draft quality,* a coarser-looking 72 dots per inch vertically, or *near-letter-quality* (*NLQ*), a crisper-looking 144 dots per inch vertically. Students and others find draft quality acceptable for doing drafts of papers and reports. They then usually switch to near-letter-quality when they are preparing a finished product to be shown to other people.

Dot-matrix printers print about 40–300 characters per second (cps) and can print some graphics, although the reproduction quality is poor. Color ribbons are available for limited use of color. Dot-matrix printers are inexpensive and noisy, but they can print through multipart forms, which nonimpact printers cannot do.

Another type of impact printer is not used with microcomputers. Large computer installations use high-speed *line printers,* which print a whole line of characters at once rather than a single character at a time. Some of these can print up to 3000 lines a minute. Two types of line printers are *chain printers,* which contain characters on a rotating chain, and *band printers,* which contain characters on a rotating band.

Nonimpact Printers

Nonimpact printers, used almost everywhere now, are faster and quieter than impact printers because they have fewer moving parts. Nonimpact printers form characters and images without making direct physical contact between the printing mechanism and the paper.

Two types of nonimpact printers often used with microcomputers are *laser printers* and *ink-jet printers.*

■ *Laser printer:* Similar to a photocopying machine, a **laser printer** uses the principle of dot-matrix printers of creating images with dots. However, these images are created on a drum, treated with a magnetically charged ink-like toner (powder), and then transferred from drum to paper. *(See Figure 3.17.)*

There are good reasons why laser printers are the most common type of printer. They produce sharp, crisp images of both text and graphics, providing resolutions from 300 dpi up to 1200 dpi, which is near-typeset-quality (NTQ). They are quiet and fast. They can print 4–32 text-only pages per minute for individual microcomputers, and more than 120 pages per minute for mainframes. (Pages with graphics print more slowly.) They can print in many fonts (type styles and sizes). (We discuss fonts in more detail in Chapter 6.) The more expensive models can print in different colors.

Laser Printer

1 The computer's software sends signals to the laser printer to determine where each dot of printing toner is to be placed on the paper.

2 The instructions from the printer's processor rapidly turn on and off a beam of light from a laser.

3 A spinning mirror deflects the laser beam so that the path of the beam is a horizontal line across the surface of a cylinder called the *drum*. The combination of the laser beam being turned on and off and the movement of the beam's path across the cylinder results in many tiny points of light hitting in a line across the surface of the drum. When the laser has finished flashing points of light across the entire width of the drum, the drum rotates—usually 1/300th of an inch in most laser printers—and the laser beam begins working on the next line of dots.

4 At the same time that the drum begins to rotate, a series of gears and rollers feeds a sheet of paper into the print engine along a path called the *paper train*. The paper train pulls the paper past an electrically charged wire that passes a static electrical charge to the paper. The charge may be either positive or negative, depending upon the design of the printer. For this example, we'll assume the charge is positive.

5 Where each point of light strikes the drum, it causes a negatively charged film—usually made of zinc oxide and other materials—on the surface of the drum to change its charge so that the dots have the same electrical charge as the sheet of paper. In this example, the light would change the charge from negative to positive. Each positive charge marks a dot that eventually will print black on paper. The areas of the drum that remain untouched by the laser beam retain their negative charge and result in white areas on the hard copy.

6 About halfway through the drum's rotation, the drum comes into contact with a bin that contains a black powder called *toner*. The toner in this example has a negative electrical charge—the opposite of the charges created on the drum by the laser beam. Because particles with opposite static charges attract each other, toner sticks to the drum in a pattern of small dots wherever the laser beam created a charge.

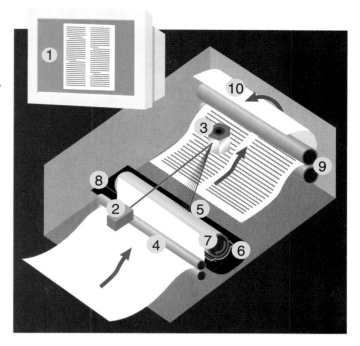

7 As the drum continues to turn, it presses against the sheet of paper being fed along the paper train. Although the electrical charge on the paper is the same as the charge of the drum created by the laser beam, the paper's charge is stronger and pulls the toner off the drum and onto the paper.

8 The rotation of the drum brings its surface next to a thin wire called the *corona wire*. It's called that because electricity passing through the wire creates a ring, or corona, around it that has a positive charge. The corona returns the entire surface of the drum to its original negative charge so that another page can be drawn on the drum's surface by the laser beam.

9 Another set of rollers pulls the paper through a part of the print engine called the *fusing system*. There pressure and heat bind the toner permanently to the paper by melting and pressing a wax that is part of the toner. The heat from the fusing system is what causes paper fresh from a laser printer to be warm.

10 The paper train pushes the paper out of the printer, usually with the printed side down so that pages end up in the output tray in the correct order.

Figure 3.17 Laser printer. A small laser beam is bounced off a mirror millions of times per second onto a positively charged drum. The spots where the laser beam hits become neutralized, enabling a special toner (powder) to stick to them and then print out on paper. The drum is then recharged for the next cycle.

Laser printers have built-in RAM chips to store documents output from the computer. If you are working in desktop publishing and printing complicated documents with color and many graphics, you will need a printer with a lot of RAM (check the printer RAM requirements on your software package). Laser printers also have their own ROM chips to store fonts and their own small dedicated processor. To be able to manage graphics and complex page design, a laser printer works with a page description language, a type of software that has become a standard for printing graphics on laser printers. A *page description language* (*PDL*) is software that describes the shape and position of letters and graphics to the printer. PostScript, from Adobe Systems, Inc., is one common type of page description language; HPGL, Hewlett-Packard Graphic Language, is another.

■ *Ink-jet printer:* Like laser and dot-matrix printers, ink-jet printers also form images with little dots. **Ink-jet printers** spray small, electrically charged droplets of ink from four nozzles through holes in a matrix at high speed onto paper. *(See Figure 3.18.)*

Ink-jet printers can print in color and are quieter and much less expensive than a color laser printer. However, they are slower (about 1–4 text-only pages per minute) and print in a somewhat lower resolution (300–720 dpi) than laser printers. High-resolution output requires the use of special coated paper, which costs more than regular paper. And, if you are printing color graphics at 720 dpi on an ink-jet printer, it may take 10 minutes or more for a single page to finish printing!

A variation on ink-jet technology is the *bubble-jet printer,* which uses miniature heating elements to force specially formulated inks through print heads with 128 tiny nozzles. The multiple nozzles print fine images at high speeds. This technology is commonly used in portable printers.

For people who want the highest-quality color printing available with a desktop printer, thermal printers are the answer. However, they are expensive, and they require expensive paper. Thus, they are not generally used for jobs requiring a high volume of output. *(See Figure 3.19.)*

It's not uncommon these days to receive a crisply printed letter rendered on a word processor—in an envelope with a handwritten address. Why? Because the

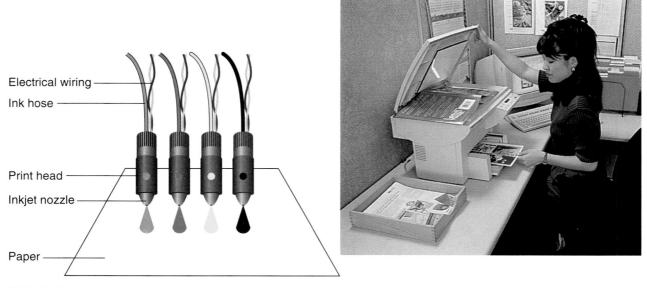

Electrical wiring

Ink hose

Print head

Inkjet nozzle

Paper

Figure 3.18   Ink-jet printer operation

Do I want a desktop or portable printer—or both? You'll probably find a desktop printer satisfactory (and less expensive than a portable). If you're on the road enough to warrant using a portable, see whether a *transportable* or an *ultraportable* would best suit you.

Do I need color, or will black-only do? Are you mainly printing text or will you need to produce color charts and illustrations (and if so, how often)? If you print lots of black text, consider getting a laser printer. If you might occasionally print color, get an inkjet that will accept cartridges for both black and color.

Do I have other special output requirements? Do you need to print envelopes or labels? special fonts (type styles)? multiple copies? transparencies or on heavy stock? Find out if the printer comes with envelope feeders, sheet feeders holding at least 100 sheets, or whatever will meet your requirements.

Is the printer easy to set up? Can you easily put the unit together, plug in the hardware, and adjust the software (the "driver" programs) to make the printer work with your computer?

Is the printer easy to operate? Can you add paper, replace ink/toner cartridges or ribbons, and otherwise operate the printer without much difficulty?

Does the printer provide the speed and quality I want? Will the machine print at least three pages a minute of black text and two pages a minute of color? Is the black dark enough and are the colors vivid enough?

Will I get a reasonable cost per page? Special paper, ink or toner cartridges (especially color), and ribbons are all ongoing costs. Ink-jet color cartridges, for example, may last 100–500 pages and cost $25–$30 new. Laser toner cartridges are cheaper. Ribbons for dot-matrix printers are cheaper still. Ask the seller what the cost per page works out to.

Does the manufacturer offer a good warranty and good telephone technical support? Find out if the warranty lasts at least 2 years. See if the printer's manufacturer offers telephone support in case you have technical problems. The best support systems offer toll-free numbers and operate evenings and weekends as well as weekdays.

Figure 3.19 How to choose a printer

person writing the letter doesn't have, or doesn't know how to use, a printer envelope feeder for printing addresses. Envelope feeders and label printers are only one of several considerations to make when buying a printer. (Specialty printers are also available, useful for businesses that do large mailings, that print nothing but envelopes and labels.)

Plotters

A **plotter** is a specialized output device designed to produce high-quality graphics in a variety of colors. *(See Figure 3.20.)* Plotters are especially useful for creating maps and architectural drawings, although they may also produce less complicated charts and graphs.

The two principal kinds of plotters are *flatbed* and *drum*.

What kinds of printers/plotters do you think you will use in your job or career?

- *Flatbed plotter.* A *flatbed plotter* is designed so that paper lies flat on a table-like surface. The size of the bed determines the maximum size of the sheet of paper. Under computer control, between one and four pens move across the paper, and the paper moves beneath the pens. Plotters can produce color output.

- *Drum plotter.* A *drum plotter* works like a flatbed plotter except that the paper is output over a drum, enabling continuous output, such as that needed to track earthquake activity.

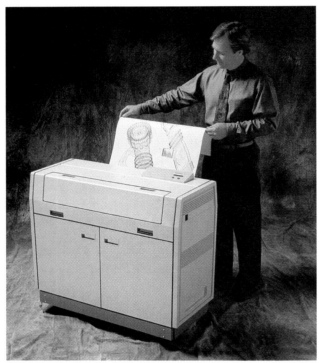

Figure 3.20 Drum plotters

Installing a Printer or Plotter

Printers and plotters, like other peripheral devices such as mice, scanners, sound cards, and the like, must be installed. What does this mean? It means that the device's *driver* must be used to tell the computer what the device is and that it is attached to the system. A **driver** is a software program that links a peripheral device to the computer's operating system. It is written by programmers who understand the device's language and characteristics. The driver contains the machine language necessary to activate the device and perform the necessary operations. Drivers may come on disk with the peripheral device. In the case of fundamental peripherals such as the keyboard, diskette drive, and some hard disks, the drivers are included in the computer's BIOS chip. If you purchase a new peripheral—for example, a scanner—the documentation will tell you what steps to follow to install it. Occasionally a new peripheral's driver will be incompatible with some software already on your computer; in this case, call the company's technical support line for advice.

Multifunction Printer Technology: One for All

Everything is becoming something else, and even printers are becoming devices that do more than print. For instance, fax machines are now available that can also function as an answering machine and a laser or ink-jet printer. Since 1990, Xerox Corp. has sold an expensive printer-copier-scanner that can be hooked into corporate computer networks.

Some recent hardware can do even more. **Multifunction devices,** sometimes called *hydra printers,* combine several capabilities, such as printing, scanning, copying, and faxing, all in one device. *(See Figure 3.21.)* An example is Hewlett-Packard's OfficeJet, which combines four pieces of office equipment—photocopier, fax machine, scanner, and laser printer—in one. By doing the work of four separate office machines at a price below the combined cost of buying these devices separately, the OfficeJet offers budgetary and space advantages. Note, however, that these multifunction devices generally do not perform each of their functions as well as individual hardware devices dedicated to one function.

Monitors

"Softcopy" output generally refers to the display on a monitor, the output device that many people use the most. Monitors run under the control of a graphics display adapter card plugged into an expansion slot on the system board. The adapter allows information to leave the computer and appear on the monitor. (If you are working with graphics and video, such as in multimedia applications, this card will also have a graphics coprocessor, accelerator circuitry, and video sup-

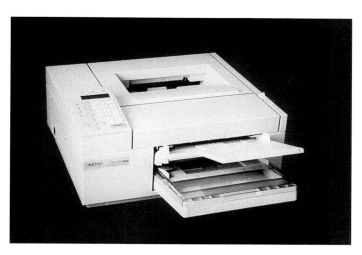

Figure 3.21 The multi-function device combines four machines in one: printer, copier, fax machine, and scanner.

port.) The display adapter comes with its own RAM, called *VRAM,* or *video RAM.* VRAM controls the resolution of images displayed on the monitor, as well as the number of colors and the speed at which the images are displayed. In addition, the more video memory you have, the higher the resolution and the more colors you can display. A video display adapter with 1 megabyte of memory will support 16.7 million colors. Two common types of VRAM are WRAM and EDO RAM.

The size of a screen is measured diagonally from corner to corner in inches, just like television screens. For desktop microcomputers, 12- to 17-inch screens are common sizes. Larger screens are often used by people in desktop publishing and multimedia production in order to view two facing pages of a book or magazine at the same time. Portable computers may have screens ranging from 12.1 inches to 13.3 inches. Pocket-size computers may have even smaller screens. To give themselves a larger screen size, some portable-computer users buy a larger desktop monitor (or a separate "docking station") to which the portable can be connected. Near the display screen are control knobs that, as on a television set, allow you to adjust brightness and contrast.

Cathode-Ray Tubes (CRTs)

The **cathode-ray tube (CRT)** is a vacuum tube used as a display screen in a computer or video display terminal. CRTs are the most common softcopy output devices used with desktop computer systems; this technology is also used in standard TV sets. The CRT's screen display is made up of small picture elements (dots), called *pixels* for short. A **pixel** is the smallest unit on the screen that can be turned on or off or made different shades. A stream of bits defining the image is sent from the computer to the CRT's electron gun, where electrons are activated according to the bit patterns. *(See Figure 3.22.)* The inside of the front of the CRT screen is coated with phosphor. When a beam of electrons from the electron gun (deflected through a yoke) hits the phosphor, it lights up selected pixels to generate an image on the screen.

Flat-Panel Displays

If CRTs were the only existing technology for computer screens, we would still be carrying around 25-pound (12-kilogram) "luggables" instead of lightweight notebooks and pocket PCs. CRTs provide bright, clear images, but they consume power and space and are relatively heavy. The larger the CRT screen, the deeper the unit.

Compared to CRTs, **flat-panel displays** are much thinner, weigh less, and consume less power. Thus, they are used in portable computers, although they are slowly becoming available for desktop computers also. (The current problem is cost: an LCD for a desktop microcomputer costs 4–8 times as much as an equivalent monitor based on CRT technology.[10]) Flat-panel displays are made up of two plates of glass with a substance in between them, which is activated in different ways.

Flat-panel displays are distinguished in two ways: (1) by the substance between the plates of glass and (2) by the arrangement of the transistors in the screens.

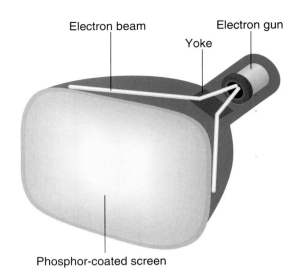

Electron beam

Electron gun

Yoke

Phosphor-coated screen

Pixels

Figure 3.22 How a CRT works. (*Top*) A stream of bits from the computer's CPU is sent to the electron gun, which converts the bits into electrons. The gun then shoots a beam of electrons through the yoke, which deflects the beam in different directions. When the beam hits the phosphor coating on the inside of the CRT screen, a number of pixels light up, making the image on the screen. (*Bottom*) Each character on the screen is made up of small dots called *pixels,* short for *picture elements.*

■ *Substances between plates—LCD or EL:* There are two common types of technology used in flat-panel display screens: *liquid-crystal display* and *electro-luminescent display. (See Figure 3.23.)*

    Liquid-crystal display (LCD) consists of a substance called *liquid crystal,* the molecules of which line up in a way that alters their optical properties. As a result, light—usually backlighting behind the screen—is blocked or allowed through to create an image.

    Electroluminescent (EL) display contains a substance that glows when it is charged by an electric current. A pixel is formed on the screen when current is sent to the intersection of the appropriate row and column. The combined voltages from the row and column cause the screen to glow at that point.

■ *Arrangement of transistors—active-matrix or passive-matrix:* Flat-panel screens are either active-matrix or passive-matrix displays, according to where their transistors are located.

    In an **active-matrix display,** each pixel on the screen in controlled by its own transistor. Active-matrix screens are much brighter and sharper than passive-matrix screens, but they are more complicated and thus more expensive.

    In a *passive-matrix display,* a transistor controls a whole row or column of pixels. Passive matrix provides a sharp image for monochrome (one-color) screens but is more subdued for color. The advantage is that passive-matrix displays are less expensive and use less power than active-matrix displays.

Screen Clarity

Whether for CRT or flat-panel, screen clarity depends on three qualities: *resolution, dot pitch,* and *refresh rate.*

■ *Resolution:* The clarity or sharpness of a display screen is called its **resolution;** the more pixels there are per square inch, the better the resolution. Resolution

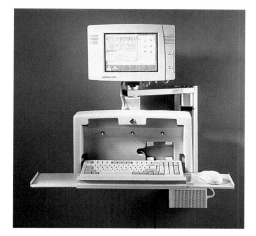 

Figure 3.23 Flat-panel displays. (*Left*) Active matrix LCD, Planar System's CleanScreen compact computer for hospital information systems. (*Right*) Planar EL screen.

is expressed in terms of the formula *columns of pixels × rows of pixels*. Thus a screen with 640 × 480 pixels multiplied together equals 307,200 pixels. This screen will be less clear and sharp than screens with higher resolutions. Standard screen resolutions are 640 × 480, 800 × 600, 1024 × 768, 1280 × 1024, and 1600 × 1200. Some display adapters can handle all these resolutions, while others may go only as high as 1024 × 768.

■ *Dot pitch:* **Dot pitch** is the amount of space between pixels; the closer the dots, the crisper the image. A .28 dot pitch means dots are 28/100ths of a millimeter apart. Generally, a dot pitch of less than .31 will provide clear images. Multimedia and desktop publishing users typically use .25 mm dot pitch monitors.

■ *Refresh rate:* **Refresh rate** is the number of times per second that the pixels are recharged so that their glow remains bright. Refresh is necessary because the phosphors hold their glow for just a fraction of a second. The higher the refresh rate, the more solid the image looks on the screen—that is, it doesn't flicker. The refresh rate should be at least 70 Hz (Hertz).

Color

Display screens can be either *monochrome* or *color.*

■ *Monochrome: Monochrome display screens* display only one color on a background—usually black on white, amber on black, or green on black. The number of shades of the one color that the monitor can display is referred to as *gray-scale.* Monochrome screens are dying out. However, if your principal applications are word processing or number manipulation, a monochrome monitor will probably suit your needs nicely.

■ *Color: Color display screens,* also called *RGB monitors* (for red, green, blue), can display between 16 colors and 16.7 million colors, depending on their type. The number of colors is referred to as the *color depth,* or *bit depth.* Most software today is developed for color, and—except for some pocket PCs—most microcomputers today are sold with color display screens.

There are different standards for monitors, and they support different color depths.

■ *VGA:* **VGA,** for *video graphics array,* will support 16 to 256 colors, depending on resolution. At 320 × 200 pixels it will support 256 colors; at the sharper resolution of 640 × 480 pixels it will support 16 colors, which is called *4-bit color.*

■ *SVGA:* **SVGA,** for *super video graphics array,* will support 256 colors at higher resolution than VGA. SVGA has two graphics modes: 800 × 600 pixels and 1,024 × 768. SVGA is called *8-bit color.*

■ *XGA:* Also referred to as *high-resolution display,* **XGA,** for *extended graphics array,* supports up to 16.7 million colors at a resolution of 1024 × 768 pixels. Depending on the video display adapter memory chip, XGA will support 256, 65,536, or 16,777,216 colors. At its highest quality, XGA is called *24-bit color,* or *true color.*

Note: The more colors and the higher the refresh rate and the resolution, the harder the display adapter has to work, and the more expensive it is. And the higher the settings, the slower the adapter operates. Also, for a display to work, video display adapters and monitors must be compatible. Your computer's software and the video display adapter must also be compatible. Thus, if you are changing your monitor or your video display adapter, be sure the new one will still work with the old. Most monitors today can accommodate resolutions greater than SVGA, depending on the video card connected to them.

> Name at least three factors that determine the quality of a CRT display.

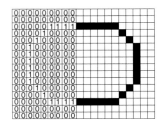

Raster graphics (bitmap)

Bit-Mapped Displays

The computer uses bits (0s and 1s) to describe each pixel's attributes—its color and position. On monochrome screens, one bit represents one pixel on the screen. For color monitors, several bits represent one pixel. Bit-mapped display screens permit the computer to manipulate pixels on the screen individually, enabling the software to create a greater variety of images. Today most screens can display text and graphics—icons, charts, graphs, and drawings.

Future Display Technology

Home TV designs favor image brightness and compact size, whereas computer screens need to be engineered for higher resolution and sharp images.[11] For technical reasons, it's difficult to make the image on a computer screen as bright as one on a TV screen. However, the development of HDTV (high-definition television) may change that and create a convergence between the TV and the computer monitor markets. The reason for this is that HDTV specifications call for resolution of up to 1920 × 1080 pixels, which is more than adequate for desktop computer screen displays.

Another promising new approach for computer screen technology is FED (field emission display). In FED, dozens or hundreds of tiny electron emitters are placed behind each pixel, in a panel in which each pixel is controlled directly—as with an active-matrix LCD—but where the light is emitted by the phosors at that individual pixel, as in a CRT.[12]

Self-Employed, Home-Based Careers

Her job for a software firm—with its long hours and molasses commute—had destroyed her first marriage, and she sometimes wondered if it was destroying her, too. So Jan Jewell, 43, of Hollister, California, quit and started up her own one-woman home-based business—using an electronic knitting machine and software to produce custom-designed baby blankets. She does a half-dozen blankets a day, at $50 to $60 each, selling most of them to customers who come to her through her Web site.[13]

Jewell is one of the 55% of Americans who would prefer to be their own boss, and one of the 19% who actually own their own firms, freelance, or are temporary workers.[14] She is also one of 39 million people—both self-employed and employed by others—in the United States who work out of their homes.[15]

To be sure, there are some drawbacks. An outgoing type, Jewell finds that her work gives her little face-to-face interaction. Her contact with customers is by phone and computer. Her husband works outside the home. Her tasks are always there, all the time. On the other hand, she answers only to her customers. "There are no hidden agendas, no office politics," she says. Her business turned a profit after two and a half years.

Many self-employed people have offices outside the home, especially those whose clients might otherwise view them as amateurish operations. Some take space with other small-business types in an "executive suite," where they can share clerical help and conference rooms. However, technology has made working at home far easier than ever before. "With such advances as voice mail, e-mail, and fax machines," says one freelance business writer, "it's possible to create a much more professional environment at home than was once possible."[16] Add computers, printers, and copiers, and it's clear that these are the glory days for many home workers.

These devices all require power, however, and not all buildings—especially those built prior to World War II, when building codes were different—can satisfy this need. Copiers and computers, for instance, need to be on their own circuit, separate from refrigerators and appliances that can damage equipment by causing power surges. More than two phone lines may also be required to operate fax machine, computer modem, and the dual-line phone that many home office users find essential.

Some operators of work-at-home businesses find they ultimately have to leave home. Michael Prince, an entrepreneur who ran a home-based telephone-selling business specializing in industrial pollution-control materials from his home 85 miles from New York City, became so successful that he had to hire more employees, which forced him to move out to a building in a nearby town.

But he was looking forward to the commute. "Here, I have supper at 6:30, and I can go back to the [home-based] office until 10:30 or 11. Working at home is just too convenient."[17]

Audio Output Hardware

In the following sections we describe the hardware devices that enable voice output and sound output.

Voice Output

Voice output devices convert digital data into speech-like sounds. These devices are no longer very unusual. You hear such forms of voice output on telephones ("Please hang up and dial your call again"), in soft-drink machines, in cars, in toys and games, and recently in vehicle-navigation devices. Two types of voice output technology exist: *speech coding* and *speech synthesis.*

Speech coding uses actual human voices speaking words to provide a digital database of words that can be output as voice sounds. That is, words are codified and stored in digital form. Later they may be retrieved and translated into voices as needed. The drawback of this method is that the output is limited to whatever words were previously entered into the computer system. However, the voice output message does sound more convincingly like real human speech.

Speech synthesis uses a set of 40 basic speech sounds (called *phonemes*) to electronically create any words. No human voices are used to make up a database of words; instead, the computer converts stored text into voices. For example, with one Apple Macintosh program, you can type in *Wiyl biy ray5t bae5k*—the numbers elongate the sounds. The computer will then speak the synthesized words, "We'll be right back." Such voice messages are usually understandable, though they don't sound exactly human.

Some uses of speech output are simply frivolous or amusing. You can replace your computer start-up beep with the sound of James Brown screaming "I feel goooooood!" Or you can attach a voice annotation to a financial analysis document to say "I know this figure looks high, Bob, but trust me."

But some uses are quite serious. For the disabled, for example, computers help to level the playing field. A 39-year-old woman with cerebral palsy had little physical dexterity and was unable to talk. By pressing keys on the laptop computer bolted to her wheelchair, she was able to construct the following voice-synthesized message: "I can do checkbooks first time in my life. I cannot live without my computer."[18]

Sound Output

Sound output devices produce digitized sounds, ranging from beeps and chirps to music. All these sounds are nonverbal. PC owners can customize their machines to greet each new program with the sound of breaking glass or to moo like a cow every hour. Or they can make their computers express the distinctive sounds available (from the book/disk combination *Cool Mac Sounds*) under the titles "Arrgh!!!" or "B-Movie Scream." To exercise these possibilities, you need both the necessary software and the sound card, or digital audio circuit board (such as SoundBlaster). The sound card plugs into an expansion slot in your computer, but it is commonly integrated with the motherboard on newer computers.

A sound card is also required in making computerized music. There are two types of sound output technology for music: *FM synthesis* and *virtual acoustics.*

In *FM synthesis,* a synthesizer mimics different musical instruments by drawing on a library of stored sounds. Sounds are generated by combining wave forms of different shapes and frequencies. This is the kind of music-synthesis technology embodied in the pioneering Moog synthesizer, invented in 1964, and the Yamaha DX-7 synthesizer. It is also used in 95% of the circuit boards that offer advanced sound in IBM-compatible computers. The drawback, however, is that even the best synthesized music doesn't sound truly life-like; electronic instruments can't capture all the nuances of real instruments.

In *virtual acoustics,* instead of storing a library of canned sounds, the device stores a software model of an actual instrument, such as a clarinet. Thus, a set of formulas in the software represent how tightly a musician's lips press against the clarinet's mouthpiece reed (what's called *embouchure*). On a virtual-acoustics synthesizer, the musician can simulate "blowing" on the instrument either by breathing into a sensor or by pushing a pedal. This triggers a special microprocessor that simulates the airflow and resonances of an actual clarinet.

In either case, the digital sound outputs go to a mixer, a device that balances and controls music and sounds. They can then flow through stereo speakers or be recorded. Microcomputers often come with a sound speaker, although these speakers often have a rather tinny quality. For good sound, one needs to connect external speakers.

Multimedia Output Needs

Clearly, the various kinds of audio outputs and their devices are important components of multimedia systems. Some software developers are working on applications not only for entertainment but also for the business world.

The advances and refinements in output devices are producing more and more materials in *polymedia* form. That is, someone's intellectual or creative work, whether words, pictures, sound, or animation, may appear in more than one form or medium. For instance, you could be reading this chapter printed in a traditional bound book. Or you might be reading it in a "course pack," printed on paper through some sort of electronic delivery system. Or it might appear on a computer display screen. Or it could be in multimedia form, adding sounds, animated graphics, and video to the text.

Thus information technology changes the nature of how ideas are communicated.

If you are working in multimedia or want to run multimedia applications on your computer, you will need the following output hardware items:

- ◼ Sound card
- ◼ Headphones

- ◼ External speakers
- ◼ Video output via video capture card

In and Out; Devices That Do Both

Some hardware devices perform both input and output. Three common ones are terminals, smart cards, and touch screens.

Terminals

People working on a large computer system are usually connected to the main, or host, computer via terminals. A **terminal** is an input/output device that uses a keyboard for input and a monitor for output. *(See Figure 3.24.)*

Terminals are either dumb or intelligent.

- ◼ *Dumb:* A *dumb terminal* can be used only to input data to and receive information from a computer system. That is, it cannot do any processing on its own.

Figure 3.24 Terminals in use at a Texas Instruments facility in Bangalore, India

An example of a dumb terminal is that used by airline clerks at airport ticket and check-in counters. Another example is a kind of portable terminal. A *portable terminal* is a mobile terminal that can be connected to a main computer system through wired or wireless communications. A parking control officer might use a handheld wireless dumb terminal to send data about cars to a central computer in order to identify those with unpaid parking tickets.

■ *Intelligent:* An *intelligent terminal* has built-in processing capability and RAM but does not have its own storage capacity. Intelligent terminals are not as powerful as microcomputers and are not designed to operate as stand-alone machines. This type of terminal is often found in local area networks in an office. Users share applications software and data stored on a server. Some companies are marketing a type of intelligent terminal as a "network computer" (✔ p. 1.26). This machine, less expensive than a microcomputer, would be hooked up to the Internet, which would provide necessary software and data via servers also hooked up to the Internet.

Microcomputers are also sometimes used in business as terminals, also called *clients*. This trend is occurring not only because their prices have come down but also because they reduce the processing and storage load on the main computer system.

Some terminals are built specifically to accomplish certain tasks—for example, the point-of-sale terminal and the automated teller machine.

■ A **point-of-sale (POS) terminal** offers the input capabilities of a cash-register-type keypad, an optical scanner for reading price tags, and/or a magnetic stripe reader for reading credit cards and combining them with the output capabilities of a monitor and a receipt printer. Point-of-sale systems may be hooked up to a central computer for credit checking and inventory updating, or they may be stand-alone machines that store daily transactions until they can be downloaded to the main computer for processing. POS terminals are found in most department stores. *(See Figure 3.25.)*

■ The *automated teller machine (ATM)* reads the encoded magnetic stripe on the ATM card and provides output in the form of display on a monitor and printed records of transactions.

Figure 3.25 POS terminal. This point-of-sale terminal is being used at a clothing store. The system not only prints out the customer's receipt but also updates sales records and inventory records.

Smart Cards and Optical Cards

It has already come to this: just as many people collect stamps or baseball cards, there is now a major worldwide collecting mania for used wallet-size telephone debit cards. These are the cards by which telephone time is sold and consumed in many countries. Generally the cards are collected for their designs, which bear likenesses of anything from Elvis Presley to Felix the Cat to Martin Luther King. The cards have been in use in Europe for more than 15 years, and about 500 U.S. phone companies are now selling them.

Most of these telephone cards are examples of "smart cards." An even more sophisticated technology is the optical card.

Telephone smart cards

■ *Smart card:* A **smart card** looks like a credit card but contains a microprocessor and memory chip that are used for identification and financial transactions. When inserted into a reader, it transfers data to and from a central computer, and it can store some basic financial records. It is more secure than a magnetic stripe card and can be programmed to self-destruct if the wrong password is entered too many times.

In France, where the smart card was invented, you can buy telephone debit cards at most cafés and newsstands. You insert the card into a slot in the phone, wait for a tone, and dial the number. The time your call lasts is automatically calculated on the chip inside the card and deducted from the balance of time paid for. The French also use smart cards as bank cards, and some people carry their medical histories on them.

The United States has been slow to embrace smart cards because of the prevalence of the conventional magnetic-stripe credit card. Moreover, the United States has a large installed base of credit-card readers and phone networks with which merchants can check on these cards. However, in some other countries phone lines are scarce, so that merchants cannot easily check over the phone with a centralized credit database. In these places, smart cards make sense because they carry their own spending limits.

Already planners have envisioned a host of future uses for smart cards. For instance, the Department of Defense is looking at replacing traditional

Smart card from Mondex

military dog tags with smart cards that include service and family data. Some observers think that business travelers will soon have a personal smart card that can be used for many purposes. This includes buying airline tickets, reserving rental cars, checking into hotels—even opening the door to their hotel rooms. Once back at the office, they will be able to transfer all their travel expenses electronically onto an expense report. There will be no need to keep paper receipts.

Indeed, smart cards may eventually eliminate the need for cash, as envisioned by many banks, credit card issuers, universities, and the U.S. government. Why? Smart cards can save the cost of collecting, counting, securing, and transferring cash. Some smart "cash cards" come with small handheld readers that tally the card's cash balance.

■ *Optical card:* The conventional magnetic-stripe credit card holds the equivalent of a half page of data. The smart card with a microprocessor and memory chip holds the equivalent of 30 pages. The optical card presently holds about 2000 pages of data. Optical cards use the same type of technology as music compact disks but look like silvery credit cards. Optical cards are plastic, laser-recordable, wallet-type cards used with an optical card reader. Because they can cram so much data (6.6 megabytes) into so little space, they may become popular in the future. With an optical card, for instance, there's enough room for a person's health card to hold not only his or her medical history and health-insurance information but also digital images. Examples are electrocardiograms, low-resolution chest X rays, and ultrasound pictures of a fetus. A book containing 1000 pages of text plus 150 detailed drawings could be mailed on an optical card in a 1-ounce first-class letter. One manufacturer of optical library-card systems suggested that people might wish to store personal information on their cards, such as birth certificates and insurance policies.

> How could using a smart card make your life easier? More complicated?

Figure 3.26 Touch screen being used to enter orders at a restaurant

Touch Screens

A **touch screen** is a video display screen that has been sensitized to receive input from the touch of a finger. *(See Figure 3.26.)* The screen is covered with a plastic layer, behind which are invisible beams of infrared light. The user can, for example, input requests for information by pressing on displayed buttons and then see the requested information displayed as output on the screen.

Because touch screens are easy to use, they can convey information quickly. They are used more often in automatic teller machines, in directories conveying tourist information in airports and hotels, in fast-food restaurants to display menus, and in preschool multimedia education. Some applications are also available for microcomputers, although touch screens are of limited use because they cannot display large amounts of information.

Now You See It, Now You Don't

Of course, as with input technology, improvements are continually being made in output hardware systems. Retinal display systems are one example—images projected pixel by pixel, or point of light by point of light, from an outside source directly onto the retina of a viewer's eye.[19] *(See Figure 3.27.)*

Imagine you are a soldier facing a minefield. You scan the lethal ground in front of you, and suddenly the buried mines appear before your eyes, enabling you to pick a path to safety. Unfortunately, that kind of X-ray road map is not yet available, but within a few years, experts predict, the technology will be ready— not just for the military but also for surgeons, mechanics, and anyone else who needs to visualize complex information on the spot.

Retinal displays allow viewers to see information on what appears to be a translucent computer screen hanging a few feet in front of them. In fact, there is no screen; the image exists only inside the eye. Soldiers will be able to use virtual displays to see mines as they are projected from helmet-mounted, ground-penetrating radar. Surgeons will be able to call up high-resolution X rays of patients as they lie on the operating table. Mechanics will see color-coded diagrams of the miles of wiring under a jet airplane's skin as they work on it.

Figure 3.27 How retinal display works

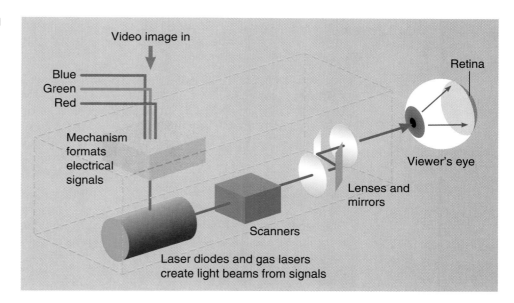

WHAT IT IS
WHAT IT DOES

WHY IT IS IMPORTANT

active-matrix display (p. 3.28, LO 8) Type of flat-panel display in which each pixel on the screen is controlled by its own transistor.

Active-matrix screens are much brighter and sharper than passive-matrix screens, but they are more complicated and thus more expensive.

audio input device (p. 3.16, LO 4) Device that records or plays analog sound and translates it for digital storage and processing.

Audio input devices, such as audio boards and MIDI boards, are important for multimedia computing.

bar codes (p. 3.11, LO 3) Vertical striped marks of varying widths that are imprinted on retail products and other items; when scanned by a barcode reader, the code is converted into computer-usable digital input.

Bar codes may be used to input data about many items, from food products to overnight packages to railroad cars, for tracking and data manipulation.

bar-code reader (p. 3.11, LO 3) Photoelectric scanner, found in many supermarkets, that translates bar code symbols on products into digital code.

With bar-code readers and the appropriate computer system, retail clerks can total purchases and produce invoices with increased speed and accuracy; and stores and other businesses can monitor inventory and services with greater efficiency.

cathode-ray tube (CRT) (p. 3.27, LO 8) Vacuum tube used as a display screen in a computer or video display terminal. Images are represented on the screen by individual dots or "picture elements" called *pixels*.

This technology is found not only in the screens of desktop computers but also in television sets and flight-information monitors in airports.

cursor (p. 3.5, LO 1) The movable symbol on the display screen that shows the user where data may be entered next.

All applications software packages use cursors to show users where their current work location is on the screen.

cursor-movement keys (p. 3.6, LO 1) Also called *arrow keys;* used to move the cursor around the text on the screen.

These keys move the cursor left, right, up, or down.

digital camera (p. 3.18, LO 4) Type of electronic camera that uses a light-sensitive silicon chip to capture photographic images in digital form.

Unlike still-video cameras, digital cameras can produce images in digital form that can be transmitted directly to a computer's hard disk for manipulation, storage, and/or printing out.

digitizing tablet (p. 3.9, LO 2) Tablet connected by a wire to a pen-like stylus, with which the user sketches an image, or to a puck, with which the user copies an image.

A digitizing tablet can be used to achieve shading and other artistic effects or to "trace" a drawing, which can be stored in digitized form.

dot pitch (p. 3.29, LO 8)   Amount of space between pixels (dots); the closer the dots, the crisper the image.

Dot pitch is one of the measures of display-screen crispness.

driver (p. 3.26, LO 7)   Software program that links a peripheral device to the computer's operating system.

The driver contains the machine language necessary to activate the device.

electroluminescent (EL) display (p. 3.28, LO 8) Flat-panel display that uses a substance that glows when it is charged by an electric current. A pixel is formed on the screen when current is sent to the intersection of the appropriate row and column. The combined voltages from the row and column cause the screen to glow at that point.

EL display is used in portable computers.

Enter key (p. 3.5, LO 1)   Also called the *Return key;* used to enter commands into the computer.

Executing commands is a key function of using a computer.

ergonomics (p. 3.6, LO 1)   Study, or science, of the physical and psychological relationships between people and their work environment.

Ergonomic principles are used in designing ways to use computers to further productivity while avoiding stress, illness, and injuries.

fax machine (p. 3.13, LO 3)   Short for *facsimile transmission machine;* input device for scanning an image and sending it as electronic signals over telephone lines to a receiving fax machine, which re-creates the image on paper, or to a fax modem.

Fax machines enable the transmission of text and graphic data over telephone lines quickly and inexpensively.

flat-panel display (p. 3.27, LO 8)   Refers to display screens that are much thinner, weigh less, and consume less power than CRTs. Flat-panel displays are made up of two plates of glass with a substance between them that is activated in different ways. Two common types of technology are used in flat-panel display screens: liquid-crystal display and gas-plasma display. Flat-panel screens are either active-matrix or passive-matrix displays.

Flat-panel displays are used in portable computers, for which CRTs are not practical (because of their large size).

function keys (p. 3.6, LO 1)   Computer keyboard keys that are labeled F1, F2, and so on; usually positioned along the top or left side of the keyboard.

Function keys are used to issue commands. These keys are used differently, depending on the software.

imaging system (p. 3.13, LO 3)   Also known as *image scanner,* or *graphics scanner;* input device that converts text, drawings, and photographs into digital form that can be stored in a computer system.

Image scanners have enabled users with desktop publishing software to readily input images into computer systems for manipulation, storage and output. Imaging systems are also used in document management and multimedia development.

ink-jet printer (p. 3.24, LO 7)   Nonimpact printer that forms images with little dots. Ink-jet printers spray small, electrically charged droplets of ink from four nozzles through holes in a matrix at high speed onto paper.

Because they produce high-quality images on special paper, they are often used by people in graphic design and desktop publishing. However, ink-jet printers are slower than laser printers and print at a lower resolution on regular paper.

input controls (p. 3.21, LO 6)   Combination of manual and computer-based control procedures designed to ensure that all input data has been accurately put into computer-usable form.

Without input controls, mistakes might be impossible to detect or correct.

input hardware (p. 3.3, LO 1)   Devices that take data and programs that people can read or comprehend and convert them to a form the computer can process. Devices are of two types: keyboard entry and source-data entry.

Input hardware enables data to be put into computer-processable form.

joystick (p. 3.8, LO 2)   Pointing device that consists of a vertical handle like a gearshift lever mounted on a base with one or two buttons; it directs a cursor or pointer on the display screen.

Joysticks are used principally in video games, computer-aided design systems, and in computerized robots.

keyboard (p. 3.4, LO 1)   Typewriter-like input device that converts letters, numbers, and other characters into electrical signals that the computer's processor can "read."

Keyboards are the most popular kind of input device.

laser printer (p. 3.22, LO 7)   Nonimpact printer similar to a photocopying machine; images are created on a drum, treated with a magnetically charged ink-like toner (powder), and then transferred from drum to paper.

Laser printers produce much better image quality than dot-matrix printers do and can print in many more colors; they are also quieter. Laser printers, along with page description languages, enabled the development of desktop publishing.

light pen (p. 3.9, LO 2)   Light-sensitive pen-like input device connected by a wire to a computer terminal; the user brings the pen to a desired point on the display screen and presses the pen button, which identifies that screen location to the computer.

Light pens are used by engineers, graphic designers, and illustrators for making drawings.

liquid-crystal display (LCD) (p. 3.28 , LO 8)   Flat-panel display that consists of a substance called *liquid crystal,* the molecules of which line up in a way that alters their optical properties. As a result, light—usually backlighting behind the screen—is blocked or allowed through to create an image.

LCD is useful not only for portable computers but also as a display for various electronic devices, such as watches and radios.

magnetic-ink character recognition (MICR) (p. 3.12, LO 3)   Type of scanning technology that reads magnetized-ink characters printed at the bottom of checks and converts them to computer-acceptable digital form.

MICR technology is used by banks to sort checks.

mouse (p. 3.7, LO 2)   Pointing device that is rolled about on a desktop to position a cursor or pointer on the computer's display screen.

For many purposes, a mouse is easier to use than a keyboard for communicating commands to a computer. With microcomputers, a mouse is needed to use most graphical user interface programs and to draw illustrations.

mouse pointer (p. 3.7, LO 2)   Symbol on the display screen whose position is directed by movement of a mouse.

The position of the mouse pointer indicates where information may be entered or a command (such as clicking, dragging, or dropping) may be executed. The shape of the pointer may change, indicating a particular function that may be performed at that point.

multifunction device (p. 3.26, LO 7)   Single hardware device that combines several capabilities, such as printing, scanning, copying, and faxing.

A multifunction device can do the work of several separate office machines at a price below the combined cost of buying these devices separately.

numeric keypad (p. 3.6, LO 1)   Laid out like the keys on a calculator; used for manipulating numbers and for directional purposes.

The numeric keypad has two purposes: Whenever the Num Lock key is off, the numeric keys may be used as arrow keys for cursor movement. When the Num Lock key is on, the keys may be used for manipulating numbers, as on a calculator.

optical character recognition (OCR) (p. 3.12, LO 3)   Type of scanning technology that reads special preprinted characters and converts them to computer-usable form. A common OCR scanning device is the wand reader.

OCR technology is frequently used with utility bills and price tags on department-store merchandise.

optical mark recognition (OMR) (p. 3.12, LO 3)   Type of scanning technology that reads pencil marks and converts them into computer-usable form.

OMR technology is frequently used for grading multiple-choice and true/false tests, such as parts of the College Board Scholastic Aptitude Test and SCANTRON tests.

output devices (p. 3.3, LO 7)   Hardware that translates information processed by the computer into a form that humans can understand.

Without output devices computer users would not be able to view or use their work.

pen-based computer system (p. 3.10, LO 2)   Input system that uses a pen-like stylus to enter handwriting and marks into a computer. The four types of systems are gesture recognition, handwriting stored as scribbling, personal handwriting stored as typed text, and standard handwriting "typeface" stored as typed text.

Pen-based computer systems benefit people who don't know how to or who don't want to type or need to make routinized kinds of inputs such as check marks.

pixel (p. 3.27, LO 8)   Short for *picture element;* smallest unit on the screen that can be turned on and off or made different shades.

Pixels are the building blocks that allow text and graphical images to be presented on a display screen.

plotter (p. 3.25, LO 7)   Specialized output device designed to produce high-quality graphics in a variety of colors. Two common types of plotters are flatbed and drum.

Plotters are especially useful for creating maps and architectural drawings, although they may also produce less complicated charts and graphs.

pointing devices (p. 3.4, LO 2)   Input devices that control the position of the cursor or pointer on the screen.

Pointing devices include mice, trackballs, joysticks, light pens, digitizing tablets, and pen-based systems.

point-of-sale (POS) terminal (p. 3.34, LO 11)   Terminal that combines the input capabilities of a cash-register-type keypad, optical scanner, and magnetic-stripe reader with the output capabilities of a monitor and a printer.

POS terminals record customer transactions at the point of sale and also store data for billing and inventory purposes.

printer (p. 3.21, LO 7)   Output device that prints characters, symbols and perhaps graphics on paper. Printers are categorized according to whether the image produced is formed by physical contact of the print mechanism with the paper. Impact printers have contact; nonimpact printers do not.

Printers provide one of the principal forms of computer output.

refresh rate (p. 3.29, LO 8)   Number of times per second that screen pixels are recharged so that their glow remains bright.

The higher the refresh rate, the more solid the image looks on the screen.

resolution (p. 3.28, LO 8)   Clarity or sharpness of a display screen; the more pixels there are per square inch, the better the resolution. Resolution is expressed in terms of the formula horizontal pixels × vertical pixels. A screen with 640 × 480 pixels multiplied together equals 307,200 pixels. This screen will be less clear and sharp than a screen with 800 × 600 (equals 480,000) or 1024 × 768 (equals 786,432) pixels.

Users need to know what screen resolution is appropriate for their purposes.

scanner (p. 3.11, LO 3)   Source-data input device that translates hardcopy images of text, drawings, and photos into digital form.

Scanners simplify the input of complex data. The images can be processed by the computer, manipulated, displayed on a monitor, stored on a storage device, and/or communicated to another computer.

sensor (p. 3.18, LO 4)   Type of input device that collects specific kinds of data directly from the environment and transmits it to a computer.

Sensors can be used for detecting speed, movement, weight, pressure, temperature, humidity, wind, current, fog, gas, smoke, light, shapes, images, and so on.

smart card (p. 3.35, LO 11)   Card similar to a credit card but containing a microprocessor and memory chip that can be used to input data.

Telephone users may buy a smart card that lets them make telephone calls until the total cost limit programmed into the card has been reached. Smart cards may eventually take the place of cash.

sound output devices (p. 3.32, LO 9)   Audio output device that produces digitized, nonverbal sounds, ranging from beeps and chirps to music. It includes software and a sound card or digital audio circuit board.

PC owners can customize their machines to announce new programs and certain functions with particular sounds. Sound output is also used in multimedia presentations.

source-data entry device (p. 3.4, LO 3)   Also called *source-data automation;* non-keyboard data-entry device. The categories include scanning devices; magnetic-stripe cards; smart and optical cards; voice-recognition devices; audio input devices; video input devices; electronic cameras; sensors; and human-biology input devices.

Source-data entry devices lessen reliance on keyboards for data entry and can make data entry more accurate.

SVGA (super video graphics array) (p. 3.30, LO 8)   Graphics board standard that supports 256 colors at higher resolution than VGA. SVGA has two graphics modes: 800 × 600 pixels and 1024 × 768. Called *8-bit color.*

Super VGA is a higher-resolution version of video graphics array (VGA).

terminal (p. 3.33, LO 11)   Input/output device that uses a keyboard for input and a monitor for output.

Terminals are generally used to input data to and output data from large computer systems, such as a mainframe.

touchpad (p. 3.8, LO 2)   Flat, rectangular input device that uses a very weak electrical field to sense your touch.

Touchpads let you control the cursor/pointer with your finger.

touch screen (p. 3.36, LO 11)   Video display screen that has been sensitized to receive input from the touch of a finger. It is often used in automatic teller machines and in directories conveying tourist information.

Because touch screens are easy to use, they can convey information quickly and can be used by people with no computer training; however, the amount of information offered is usually limited.

trackball (p. 3.8, LO 2)   Movable ball, on top of a stationary device, that is rotated with the fingers or palm of the hand; it directs a cursor or pointer on the computer's display screen.

Unlike a mouse, a trackball is especially suited to portable computers, which are often used in confined places.

VGA (video graphics array) (p. 3.29, LO 8) Graphics board standard that supports 16 to 256 colors, depending on resolution. At 320 × 200 pixels it will support 256 colors; at sharper resolution of 640 × 480 pixels it will support 16 colors. Called *4-bit color.*

VGA is still a commonly used standard, although SVGA is taking over.

voice output device (p. 3.32, LO 9)   Audio output device that converts digital data into speech-like sound. Two types of voice output technology exist: speech coding and speech synthesis.

Voice output devices are a common technology, found in telephone systems, soft-drink machines, and toys and games.

voice-recognition system (p. 3.15, LO 4)   Input system that converts a person's speech into digital code; the system compares the electrical patterns produced by the speaker's voice with a set of pre-recorded patterns stored in the computer.

Voice-recognition technology is useful for inputting data in situations in which people are unable to use their hands or need their hands free for other purposes.

XGA (extended graphics array) (p. 3.30, LO 8) Graphics board display standard, also referred to as *high resolution;* supports up to 16.7 million colors at a resolution of 1024 × 768 pixels. Depending on the video display adapter memory chip, XGA will support 256, 65,536, or 16,777,216 colors. At its highest quality, XGA is called *24-bit color,* or *true color.*

XGA offers the most sophisticated standard for color and resolution.

1. _input_ _control_ are designed to ensure the accuracy of input data.

2. A(n) _dumb_ terminal is entirely dependent for all of its processing activities on the computer system to which it is hooked up.

3. One of the easiest ways to categorize input hardware is whether or not it uses a(n) _keyboard_.

4. _____ determines what the function keys on a keyboard do.

5. _aragonomics_ is the study of the physical relationships between people and their work environment.

SHORT-ANSWER QUESTIONS

1. What is an imaging system?
2. What does a voice-recognition system do?
3. What three characteristics determine the clarity of a computer screen?
4. What is the main difference between a dedicated fax machine and a fax modem?
5. What is a terminal?

MULTIPLE-CHOICE QUESTIONS

1. Which of the following hardware devices will you need in order to create a multimedia presentation?
   a. sound card
   b. microphone
   c. graphics scanner
   d. fast and powerful processor
   e. all the above

2. A _____ looks like a credit card but contains a microprocessor and memory chip.
   a. sound card
   b. smart card
   c. touch card
   d. point-of-sale card
   e. none of the above

3. Which of the following should you purchase if you have a limited amount of space in your office but need to be able to print, make photocopies, scan images, and fax documents?
   a. printer
   b. fax machine
   c. scanner
   d. multifunction device
   e. all the above

4. Which of the following characteristics affect how brightly images appear on a computer screen?
   a. resolution
   b. dot pitch
   c. refresh rate
   d. screen size
   e. all the above

5. Which of the following should you consider using if you have to work in a confined space?
   a. mouse
   b. digitizing tablet
   c. trackball
   d. keyboard
   e. none of the above

TRUE/FALSE QUESTIONS

1. QWERTY describes a common keyboard layout. (true/false)

2. Scanners use laser beams and reflected light to translate photos into digital form. (true/false)

3. Photos taken with a digital camera can be downloaded to a computer's hard drive. (true/false)

4. On a computer screen, the more pixels that appear per square inch, the higher the resolution. (true/false)

5. Display screens can be either monochrome or color. (true/false)

KNOWLEDGE IN ACTION

1. If you could buy any printer you want, what type (make, model, etc.) would you choose? Does the printer need to fit into a small space? Does it need to print across the width of wide paper (11 × 14 inches)? In color? On multicarbon forms? How much printer RAM would you need? Review some of the current computer publications for articles or advertisements relating to printers. How much does the printer cost? Your needs should be able to justify the cost of the printer (if necessary, make up what your needs might be).

2. Interview someone in your school's or business's computer center and find out what kinds of input controls are used to minimize the amount of errors input to the system. Give a short report.

3. What uses can you imagine for voice output and/or sound output in your planned job or profession?

4. *Paperless office* is a term that has been appearing in computer-related journals and books for over 5 years. However, the paperless office has not yet been achieved. Do you think the paperless office is a good idea? Do you think it's possible? Why do you think it has not yet been achieved?

5. Research the current uses of smart card technology and how companies hope to implement smart card technology in the future. Will smart cards have an effect on shopping over the Internet? The transportation industry? What other industries might be affected? Conduct your research using current periodicals and/or the Internet.

STORAGE HARDWARE

Preserving Data and Information

PREVIEW

When you have completed this chapter, you will be able to:

1. Describe the difference between primary and secondary storage

2. Name the basic types of files and explain what one does with files

3. Explain how data is represented on magnetic tape

4. Describe the characteristics of diskettes and how to take care of them

5. Describe hard disks for microcomputers and large computer systems

6. Describe optical storage technology by focusing on CD-ROM disks, CD-R disks, erasable optical disks, and DVD-ROM

7. Explain how backup is done and why it's so important

8. Describe flash memory

WHY IS THIS CHAPTER IMPORTANT? "Long viewed as mere supporting actors to high-powered computers, storage devices are starting to edge toward center stage," writes a business reporter.[1] Machines for storing programs and data for later retrieval and use, storage hardware—or more formally, secondary storage hardware—has traditionally been used to support a computer's needs. Now, with the explosive growth in World Wide Web sites and business stockpiling of customer and market-research data, the world of computing "is becoming a storage-centric reality," says an analyst at International Data Corp.[2]

L ike scanners and printers, storage devices were once considered "peripheral devices," adjuncts to the computer. Today, states one industry executive, business users "do not think of storage devices as peripherals anymore. They're a fundamental part of business."

As we explain in this chapter, secondary storage devices can range from a personal computer's diskette drive with a diskette holding the text of a letter to a giant video server of the type being developed to store and distribute thousands of first-run movies over cable channels. Before we describe how these and similar devices work, let us cover some storage fundamentals: data representation, capacity, and types of files.

Storage Fundamentals

Data in secondary storage is stored as files. There are many types of files, but sizes are all measured in multiples of bytes.

As you learned in the previous chapter, the data you are working on is stored in RAM (primary storage) in an electrical state during processing. Because RAM is an electrical state, when you turn off the power to your computer, data in RAM disappears. Therefore, before you turn your microcomputer off, you must save your work onto a storage device that stores data permanently (until it is erased)—such as a diskette or a hard disk—rather than electrically. When saved to a **secondary storage** device, your data will remain intact even when the computer is turned off.

In addition to data, computer software programs must be stored in a computer-usable form. A copy of software instructions must be retrieved from a permanent storage device and placed into RAM before processing can begin. The computer's operating system determines where and how data and programs are stored on the secondary storage devices.

In very general terms, a secondary storage device can be thought of as a file cabinet. You store data there until you need it. Then you open the drawer, take out the appropriate folder (file), and place it on the top of your desk (in primary storage, or RAM), where you work on it—perhaps writing a few things in it or throwing away a few pages. Note that in the case of electronic documents on a computer, you are actually taking out a *copy* of the desired file and putting it on the "desktop." An old version of the file remains in the file cabinet (secondary storage) while the copy of the file is being edited/updated on the desktop (in RAM). When you are finished with the file, you take it off the desktop (out of primary storage) and return it to the cabinet (secondary storage). Thus the updated file replaces the old file.

Data Representation and Data Storage Capacity

In Chapter 2, we explained the meanings of kilobytes, megabytes, gigabytes, and terabytes in conjunction with RAM capacity. The same terms are also used to measure the data capacity of secondary storage devices. To repeat:

■ *Kilobyte:* (abbreviated K or KB) is equivalent to 1024 bytes.

■ *Megabyte:* (abbreviated M or MB) is 1 million bytes (rounded off).

■ *Gigabyte:* (G or GB) is 1 billion bytes (rounded off).

■ *Terabyte:* (T or TB) is about 1 trillion bytes.

The amount of data in a file in your personal computer might be expressed in kilobytes or megabytes. The amount of data being stored in a remote database accessible to you over a communications line could well be expressed in gigabytes or terabytes.

Types of Files

A file is a collection of data or information treated as a unit by the computer. However, not all files can be used by all software programs—cross-platform compatibility and applications software compatibility are issues here (✔ p. 2.7). Each file has a unique name, and PC-based (not Macintosh-based) files have "tags," or extension names, added after a period, such as .DOC added onto the name of a word-processed document file (REPORT.DOC). (Typically, the applications software program automatically adds an extension to your file names.)

Some common types of files are these:

■ *Program files:* **Program files** are files containing software instructions. **Source program files** contain high-level computer instructions in their original form, as written by the programmers. These instructions must be translated into machine-language instructions (✔ p. 2.7) in order for the processor to use them. The files that contain the machine-language instructions are called **executable files** (or *binary files*). Source program file names may have the extension .COM; executable files might use .EXE. Certain system support files that also contain machine-language instructions may use .DLL and .DRV.

■ *Data files:* **Data files** contain data, not programs—that is, they contain content that you or someone else has created and stored using applications software programs. Examples are database files. These files often use the extension .DAT, such as TRVLST.DAT for "travel statistics." Other database file

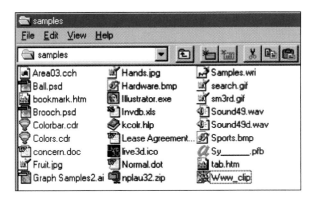

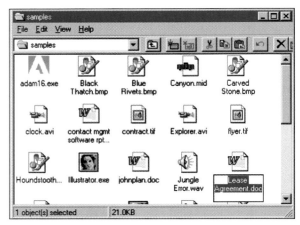

IBM-type PC file extensions and program icons

extensions are .DBF and .MDB. Common spreadsheet extensions are .XLS and .WKS. **Document files** are word-processing or desktop-publishing data files, which may contain some graphics. PC files may use the extension .DOC, such as PSYCRPT.DOC for "psych report."

- *ASCII files:* **ASCII files** are text-only (no formatting, such as boldface or italic, and no graphics). The characters are in ASCII code (✔ p. 2.4). This file format is used to transfer documents between incompatible platforms, such as IBM and Macintosh. Such files may use the .TXT extension.

- *Image files:* **Image files** contain digitized graphics. They may use many different extensions, depending on the software used to create them. Examples are .EPS (encapsulated PostScript), .TIF (tagged image file format), .JPG (still images compressed according to the standards of the Joint Photographic Experts Group), and .GIF (graphics interchange format). .BMP (bitmap) files are standard Windows graphics files.

- *Audio files:* **Audio files** contain digitized sound. Extensions are .WAV and .MID (✔ p. 3.16).

- *Video files:* **Video files** contain digitized video images. One common extension is .MPG (Moving Pictures Expert Groups). .AVI is another common extension.

There are more kinds of files than we list here. For example, some fonts (sets of characters in particular type styles) may be in .FON, .FOT, or .TTF (for "TrueType") files. However, the preceding list describes the most common types of files you will work with. How does the operating system software—called the OS—know where to store and locate all the different types of files on a secondary storage device? Some OSs use **FATs,** or **file allocation tables.** This part of the OS keeps track of where everything is stored on disk by maintaining a sort of indexed table with entries of locations for all file names. Files are not usually stored with all their data intact in one place. Instead, they are stored in *clusters*— that is, in groups of data spread out in different locations on the same disk. The FAT tracks the cluster locations. In Macintosh computers, the tracking of file locations is handled by the part of the OS called the *Finder.* (On the newest disks, each file may indeed be stored in one place.)

Why does it matter what the file extension is? Why do users need to be familiar with file extensions?

How does the user keep track of the files on the computer— that is, how do you find them? The OS uses a filing system that displays the names of the files in each directory (PC) or folder (Mac). Some directories/folders are created by the OS and applications software programs for their own use; others are created by the user as they are needed. For example, you would open the directory or folder called PSYCHOLOGY REPORT (or PSYCRPT) and see the files CHAPT1, CHAPT2, CHAPT3, and so on, listed in order. The type of OS you have determines the filing system (covered in Chapter 6).

What Can You Do with Files Besides Filing Them?

When you work with common applications software packages such as word processing programs, spreadsheets, and graphics programs, you will become familiar with the basic functions of file management. Say you're writing a report. After you key in a bit of text, you'll want to save it (so you don't lose it). Your software program will ask you to name the file. Some programs restrict the number of characters you can use, others don't. You could name your file PEANUT because it contains data on peanuts, then issue the command to save it. Thus you have *created, named,* and *saved* your file—three of the most common file management functions. You continue to work and add a lot of text and make many changes. When it's time to save the report again, you decide you don't want to change the original file (PEANUT), so you use the *Save As* function to save the current updated version in another file under a new name—say, PEANUT-2. Then you continue to update this working file. After you're through for the day, you save the file again under the same name (PEANUT-2) and turn off your computer. The next day, you boot up your computer again and *retrieve* your file so you can *display* it again on your monitor, *update* it, and *print* it. If you're sending your file to someone over the Internet, you can *upload* it to her (send it to her) or you can *download* one of her files via a server and store it on your hard disk.

If you're working with sound, you can also *play* your file. In addition, you can *copy* your files and *delete* (erase) them. If your files are huge, taking up a lot of space on your hard disk, you may also use special software programs to *compress* them (a topic we cover in detail in Chapter 6). If you want to *export* a file to be used by a different application software program or on a different platform (different kind of computer), you need to use a specific software program to convert it to a usable format. The same goes if you want to *import* a file to use on your computer—that means you use a software program to convert it to a format your computer can use.

How would you define "file"? What are five things you can do with a file?

Data Access Methods

Before we move on to discuss individual secondary storage devices, we need to mention one more aspect of storage fundamentals—data access methods. The way that a secondary storage device allows access to the data stored on it affects its speed and its usefulness for certain applications. The two main types of data access are sequential and direct.

Sequential Storage

Sequential storage means that data is stored in sequence, such as alphabetically. *(See Figure 4.1.)* Tape storage falls in the category of sequential storage. Thus, you would have to search a tape past all the information from A to J, say, before you got to K. Or, if you are looking for employee number 8888, the computer will have to start with record 0001, then go past 0002, 0003, and so on, until it finally comes to record 8888. This method is less expensive than other methods because it uses magnetic tape, which is cheaper than disks. The disadvantage of sequential file organization is that searching for data is slow.

Direct Access Storage

Disk storage, by contrast, generally falls into the category of **direct access storage** (although data can be stored sequentially). Direct access storage means that the computer can go directly to the information you want. The data is retrieved

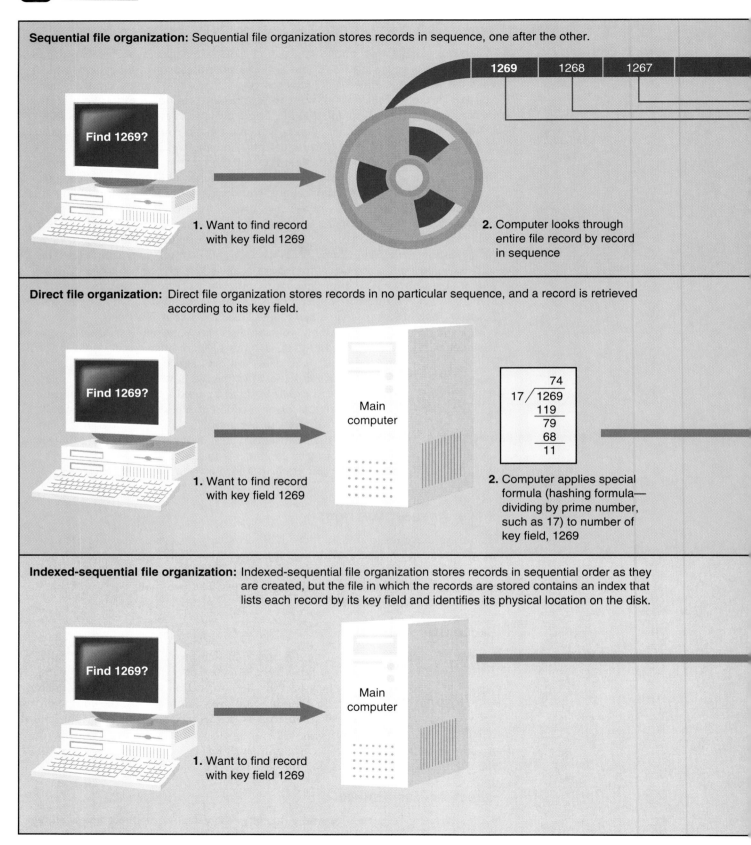

Sequential file organization: Sequential file organization stores records in sequence, one after the other.

| 1269 | 1268 | 1267 |

Find 1269?

1. Want to find record with key field 1269

2. Computer looks through entire file record by record in sequence

Direct file organization: Direct file organization stores records in no particular sequence, and a record is retrieved according to its key field.

Find 1269?

Main computer

$$17 \overline{\smash{\big)}\ 1269} \begin{array}{r} 74 \\ \hline 119 \\ \hline 79 \\ \hline 68 \\ \hline 11 \end{array}$$

1. Want to find record with key field 1269

2. Computer applies special formula (hashing formula— dividing by prime number, such as 17) to number of key field, 1269

Indexed-sequential file organization: Indexed-sequential file organization stores records in sequential order as they are created, but the file in which the records are stored contains an index that lists each record by its key field and identifies its physical location on the disk.

Find 1269?

Main computer

1. Want to find record with key field 1269

Figure 4.1 Three methods of data storage: sequential, direct, and indexed-sequential.

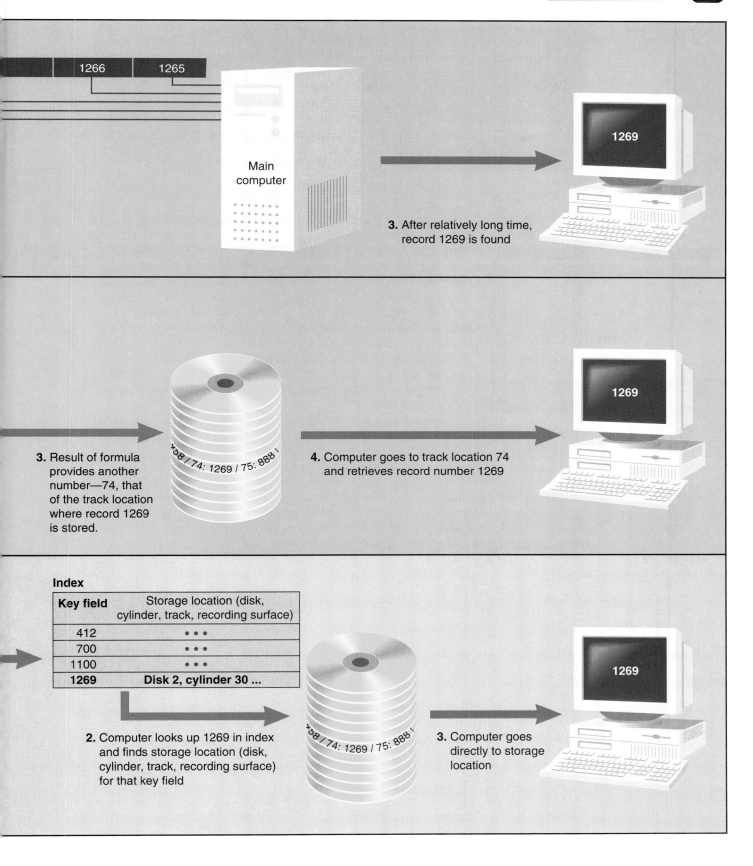

1266   1265

Main computer

3. After relatively long time, record 1269 is found

1269

3. Result of formula provides another number—74, that of the track location where record 1269 is stored.

x58 / 74: 1269 / 75: 888

4. Computer goes to track location 74 and retrieves record number 1269

1269

Index

Key field	Storage location (disk, cylinder, track, recording surface)
412	• • •
700	• • •
1100	• • •
1269	**Disk 2, cylinder 30 ...**

2. Computer looks up 1269 in index and finds storage location (disk, cylinder, track, recording surface) for that key field

x58 / 74: 1269 / 75: 888

3. Computer goes directly to storage location

1269

(accessed) according to a unique identifier called a *key field*. This method of file organization is used with hard disks and other type of disks. It is ideal for applications such as airline reservation systems or computerized directory-assistance operations. In these cases there is no fixed pattern to the requests for data.

Direct file organization is much faster than sequential file organization for finding specific data. However, because the method requires either hard disk or optical disk storage, it is more expensive than magnetic tape. The process resembles what CD players do to play a certain song. Because you can directly access information, retrieving data is much faster with magnetic disk than with magnetic tape.

ISAM

A third, less common type of data storage is the indexed-sequential access method (ISAM), which has some of the advantages of both sequential and direct forms of storage. Indexed-sequential file organization stores data in sorted order. However, the file in which the data is stored contains an index that lists the data by key fields and identifies the physical locations on the disk. This type of file organization requires magnetic or optical disk.

> When you go on the Internet to search for data in a particular database, what kind of storage access do you think the database uses? Why?

For example, a company could index certain ranges of employee identification numbers—0000 to 1000, 1001 to 2000, and so on. For the computer to find the key field 8888, it would go first to the index. The index would give the location of the range in which the key field appears (for example, 8001 to 9000). The computer would then search sequentially (from 8001) to find the key field 8888.

This method is slower than direct file organization because of the need to do an index search. The indexed-sequential method is best when large batches of transactions occasionally must be updated, yet users want frequent, rapid access to records. For example, bank customers and tellers want to have up-to-the-minute information about checking accounts, but every month the bank must update bank statements to send to customers.

Now that we have covered storage and file fundamentals, we turn to the secondary storage devices you are likely to encounter:

- Tape
- Diskette
- Hard disk
- Optical disk

Tape Storage

Magnetic tape is used primarily for backup and archiving.

Magnetic tape used to be a common secondary storage medium for large computer systems. However, these days magnetic tape is used mainly on large systems for backup and archiving (maintaining historical records) and on some microcomputers for backup. Direct access storage devices are used for most other purposes, to provide the necessary quick access to information.

Magnetic tape is thin plastic tape on which data can be represented with magnetized spots. On large computers, tapes are used on magnetic-tape units (reels) and in cartridges. On microcomputers, tapes are used only in cartridges. You may never see the traditional reel-to-reel tape systems used with mainframes (except in 1960s movies), but you may encounter cartridge tape units because they are often used with microcomputers. **Cartridge tape units,** also called *tape streamers,* are used to back up data from a hard disk onto a tape cartridge. *(See Figure 4.2.)*

A cartridge tape unit using ¼-inch cassettes (*QIC,* or *Quarter-Inch Cartridge standard*) fits into a standard slot in the microcomputer system cabinet and uses minicartridges that can store up to 17 GB of data on a single tape. A more advanced form of cassette, adapted from technology used in the music industry, is the digital audio tape (DAT), which uses 2- or 3-inch cassettes and stores 2–4 GB. Redesigned DATs called *Traven* technology are expected to hold as much as 8 gigabytes. Some microcomputer users don't use tape for their backup, which, although relatively inexpensive, is generally a slow process—it takes several hours, for example, to back up a large-capacity hard disk. They prefer instead to make duplicate diskettes of their work and keep them in a separate location. However, it takes many diskettes to back up as much data as can be stored on one tape. That is why other users prefer to use removable hard disk cartridges as backup media, as we will discuss shortly. (Prices of drives and tape/disk cartridges are always factors in deciding on a backup method.)

Diskette Storage

3½-inch diskettes are used to transport data easily.

A **diskette,** or *floppy disk,* is a removable, round, flat piece of mylar plastic that, like tape, stores data and programs as magnetized spots. More specifically, data is stored as electromagnetic charges on a metal oxide film that coats the mylar plastic. Data is represented by the presence or absence of these charges, following standard patterns of data representation (such as ASCII). The diskette is contained in a square plastic case to protect it from being touched. Diskettes are often called "floppy" because the disk within the case is flexible, not rigid.

Figure 4.2 Cartridge tape units. This device is used with microcomputers to back up data from a hard disk.

Internal tape drive with tape cassette

External tape drive

" 'When you lose a disk, you're not only losing the hardware and software,' said John L. Copen, president of Integ, an information protection company in Manhattan. 'The information has to be reproduced, and if you have to reproduce it without a backup...,'

Mr. Copen demonstrates the point by holding up a digital audio-tape (DAT) cassette, . . . used for backing up data on larger hard disk drives, the kind that act as hubs for networks of personal computers in an office.

'I ask people in the audience what it's worth,' he said. 'It's a little cassette about the size of a credit card. The cassette costs about $16. I ask them to guess how much it can store. Forty megs? Eighty megs? It stores four gigabytes.' A gigabyte is roughly a thousand megabytes, or a billion characters of information.

'How much information can you put in four gigs?' Mr. Copen continued. 'About 20,000 big spreadsheets, which translates to about 100,000 days of work, or 800,000 hours. At $20 an hour, that's $16 million. Never before have people been able to reach down, pick up a cassette and walk out the door with $16 million of data in their pocket.' "

— Peter H. Lewis, "Finding an Electronic Safe-Deposit Data Box," *New York Times*

The most common size of diskette is 3½ inches in diameter. *(See Figure 4.3.)* Larger and smaller sizes of diskettes also exist, although they are not standard on most microcomputers.

The Disk Drive

To use a diskette, you need a **disk drive.** A disk drive is a device that holds, spins, and reads data from and writes data to the diskette. In the context of secondary storage, the words *read* and *write* have exact meanings:

- **Read** means that the data represented by the magnetized spots on the disk (or tape) is converted to electronic signals and transmitted to primary storage (RAM) in the computer. That is, *read* means that data is copied *from* the diskette.

- **Write** means that the electronic information processed by the computer is recorded onto disk (or tape). Data—represented as electronic signals within the computer's memory—is transferred *onto* the disk (tape) and is then stored as magnetized spots.

The diskette drive (floppy drive) is usually built into the computer's system cabinet. *(See Figure 4.4.)*

How a Disk Drive Works

A diskette is inserted into a slot, called the *drive gate,* or *drive door,* in the front of the disk drive. *(See Figure 4.5.)* This clamps the diskette in place over the spindle of the drive mechanism so the drive can operate. An access light goes on when the disk is in use. After using the disk, you retrieve it by pressing an eject button beside the drive. (Note: Do not remove the disk when the access light is on!)

Figure 4.3 Diskettes

Figure 4.4 Diskette drive on system unit

Figure 4.5 Cutaway view of a diskette drive

When a diskette is inserted into the drive, it presses against a system of levers. One lever opens the metal plate, or shutter, to expose the data access area.

Other levers and gears move two read/write heads until they almost touch the diskette on both sides.

The drive's circuit board receives signals, including data and instructions for reading/ writing that data from/to disk, from the drive's controller board. The circuit board translates the instructions into signals that control the movement of the disk and the read/write heads.

A motor located beneath the disk spins a shaft that engages a notch on the hub of the disk, causing the disk to spin.

When the heads are in the correct position, electrical impulses create a magnetic field in one of the heads to write data to either the top or bottom surface of the disk. When the heads are reading data, they react to magnetic fields generated by the metallic particles on the disk.

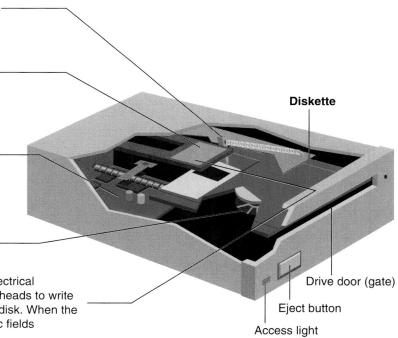

Diskette

Drive door (gate)

Eject button

Access light

Why is a diskette
sometimes called a
"floppy" disk?

What does "read" mean?
"Write"?

The device by which the data on a disk is transferred to the computer, and from the computer to the disk, is the disk drive's read/write head. The diskette spins inside its case, and the read/write head moves back and forth over the data access area, which is under the diskette's metal protective plate. This plate slides aside when you insert the diskette into the drive. (*Refer back to Figure 4.5.*)

Characteristics of Diskettes

Diskettes have the following characteristics:

■ *Tracks and sectors:* On a diskette, data is recorded in rings called **tracks,** which are neither visible grooves nor a single spiral. Rather, they are closed concentric rings. (*See Figure 4.6.*) The number of tracks on a diskette is referred to as *TPI,* or *tracks per inch.* The higher the TPI, the more data the diskette can hold.

Each track is divided into **sectors.** Sectors are invisible wedge-shaped sections used by the computer for storage reference purposes. The number of sectors on the diskette varies according to the recording density—the number

Figure 4.6 Parts of a diskette

Front

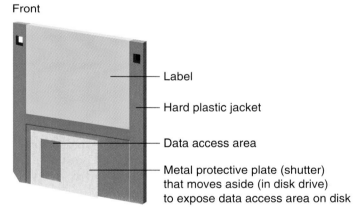

- Label
- Hard plastic jacket
- Data access area
- Metal protective plate (shutter) that moves aside (in disk drive) to expose data access area on disk

Back

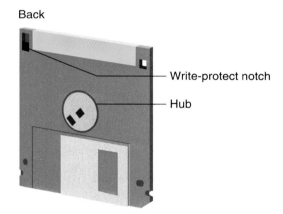

- Write-protect notch
- Hub

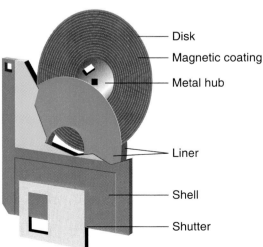

- Disk
- Magnetic coating
- Metal hub
- Liner
- Shell
- Shutter

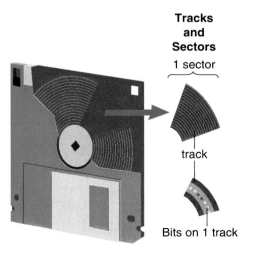

Tracks and Sectors

1 sector

track

Bits on 1 track

of bits per inch (see "Data capacity" in this list). Each sector typically holds 512 bytes of data. When you save data from your computer to a diskette, it is distributed by tracks and sectors on the disk. That is, the system software uses the point at which a sector intersects a track to reference the data location in order to spin the disk and position the read/write head.

■ *Unformatted versus formatted diskettes:* When you buy a new box of diskettes to use for storing data, the box may state that it is "unformatted" (or say nothing at all). This means you have a task to perform before you can use the disks with your computer and disk drive. Unformatted disks are manufactured without tracks and sectors in place. **Formatting**—or **initializing,** as it is called on the Macintosh—means that you must prepare the disk for use so that the computer's operating system software can write information on it. This includes defining the tracks and sectors on it as well as setting up the FAT (✔ p. 4.4).

The software documentation (user's manual) that comes with your microcomputer tells you what commands to enter to format your diskettes. Alternatively, when you buy a new box of diskettes, the box may state that they are "formatted IBM" or "formatted Macintosh." This means that you can simply insert a diskette into the drive gate of your IBM or IBM-compatible (or Macintosh) microcomputer and use it immediately. It's just like plunking an audiotape into a standard tape recorder. (Note: If you ever put a formatted disk with data already written to it into the drive and reformat it, *all* data will be lost during the reformatting process.)

■ *Data capacity—sides and densities:* Not all diskettes hold the same amount of data. Diskettes are double-sided, called "DS" or "2," capable of storing data on both sides, but a diskette's capacity depends on its recording density. Recording density refers to the number of bits per inch that can be written onto the surface of the disk. Thus diskettes are either **high-density (HD)** or **extended density (ED).** A high-density 3½-inch disk can store 1.44 megabytes. Extended density diskettes can store 2.8 megabytes. (Note: You need an ED drive to use ED diskettes; an ED drive will also accept HD diskettes.)

■ *Write-protect features:* Diskettes have features to prevent someone from accidentally writing over—and thereby obliterating—data on the diskette or making changes to program files. To write-protect your diskette, you press a lever toward the edge of the diskette, uncovering a hole (which appears on the lower right side, viewed from the back). *(See Figure 4.7.)*

Figure 4.7 Write-protect features. For data to be written to this disk, a small piece of plastic must be closed over the tiny window on one side of the disk. To protect the disk from being written to, you must open the window (using the tip of a pen helps).

Writable

Write-protect window closed

Write-protected

Write-protect window open

Taking Care of Diskettes

There are a number of rules for taking care of diskettes. In general, they boil down to the following:

- *Don't touch diskette surfaces:* Don't touch anything visible through the protective case, such as the data access area on the disk surface.

- *Handle diskettes gently:* Don't try to bend them or put weights on them. (Try not to use them for coffee or soft-drink coasters. Moisture can seep underneath the sliding metal plate and damage the disk surface.)

- *Avoid risky physical environments:* Disks don't do well in sun or heat (such as in glove compartments or on top of steam radiators). They should not be placed near magnetic fields (including those created by nearby telephones or electric motors). They also should not be exposed to chemicals (such as cleaning solvents) or spilled coffee or alcohol.

    Most experts say that airport security systems will not damage disks. However, if you are unconvinced of this, hand your diskettes (and portable computer, if you wish) to a security guard before walking through the checkpoint.

    Many people also agree that it's OK to carry diskettes in your pocket or purse as long as the metal plate doesn't get pushed open and nothing is spilled on the diskettes.

What are tracks? sectors? What does formatting do?

- *Don't leave a diskette in the drive:* Take the diskette out of the drive when you're done. If you leave the diskette in the drive, the read/write head remains resting on the diskette surface.

Hard Disks

Hard disks have much greater storage capacities than diskettes. Hard disk drives can be internal, external, or use removable disks.

Comparing the use of diskettes to hard disks is like discovering the difference between moving your household in several trips in a small sports car and doing it all at once with a moving van. Whereas a high-density 3½-inch diskette holds 1.44 megabytes of data, a hard disk in a personal computer may hold up to 9 gigabytes. Indeed, at first with a hard disk you may feel you have more storage capacity than you'll ever need. However, after a few months you may worry that you don't have enough. This feeling may be intensified if you're using multimedia or graphics-oriented programs, because digital video and graphic-intensive data require immense amounts of storage.

Diskettes are made out of flexible material, which makes them "floppy." By contrast, **hard disks** are thin but rigid metal or glass platters covered with a substance that allows data to be held in the form of magnetized spots. Hard disks are also tightly sealed within an enclosed unit to prevent any foreign matter—dust or smoke, for example—from getting inside. Data may be recorded on both sides of the disk platters.

We'll now describe the following aspects of hard disk technology:

- Microcomputer internal hard disk drives
- Microcomputer hard disk variations
- Hard disk technology for large computer systems

Microcomputer Internal Hard Disk Drives

Magnetic bits on a disk surface, caught by a magnetic force microscope. The dark stripes are 0 bits; the bright stripes are 1 bits.

In microcomputers, hard disks are one or more platters sealed inside a hard disk drive that is built into the system unit and cannot be removed. This internal drive is installed in a drive bay, a slot or opening in the computer cabinet. From the outside of a microcomputer, a hard disk drive is not visible; it looks simply like part of the front panel on the system cabinet. Inside, however, are a disk or disks on a drive spindle, read/write heads mounted on an actuator (access) arm that moves back and forth, and power connections and circuitry. *(See Figure 4.8, opposite.)* The disks may be $5^{1}/_{4}$ inches in diameter, although today they are more often 1 to $3^{1}/_{2}$ inches. The operation is much the same as for a diskette drive, with the read/write heads locating specific pieces of data according to track and disk surface number. Whereas diskettes usually have 135 tracks per inch (TPI), hard disks have thousands; whereas an HD diskette may have 18 sectors, a hard disk may have up to 64.

Secondary storage systems that use several hard disks don't use the sector method to locate data. Rather they use what is known as the *cylinder method.* Because the access arms holding the read/write heads all move together, the read/write heads are always over the same track on each disk at the same time. All tracks with the same track number, lined up one above the other, thus form a cylinder. *(See Figure 4.9, below.)*

Figure 4.9 Cylinders

In a stack of disks, access arms slide in and out to specific tracks. They use the cylinder method to locate data—the same track numbers lined up vertically one above the other form a "cylinder."

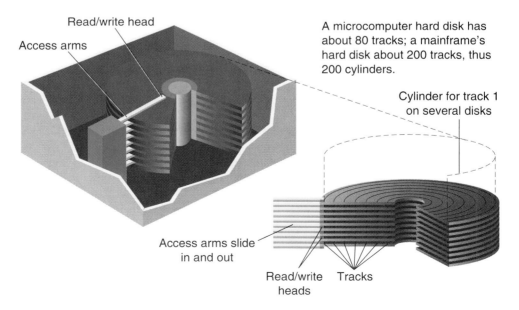

Read/write head

Access arms

A microcomputer hard disk has about 80 tracks; a mainframe's hard disk about 200 tracks, thus 200 cylinders.

Cylinder for track 1 on several disks

Access arms slide in and out

Read/write heads

Tracks

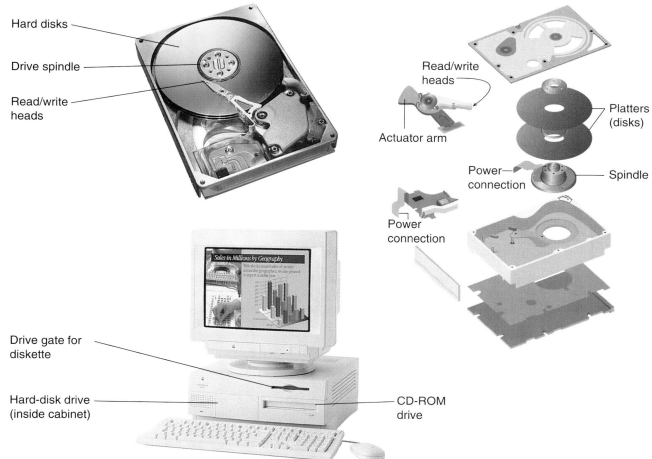

Hard disks

Drive spindle

Read/write heads

Read/write heads

Actuator arm

Platters (disks)

Power—connection

Spindle

Power connection

Drive gate for diskette

Hard-disk drive (inside cabinet)

CD-ROM drive

Figure 4.8 Internal microcomputer hard disk drive. (*Top*) Photo and cutaway view of drive. The hard disk drive is sealed inside the system cabinet and not accessible. The drive gate is for inserting a diskette. (*Bottom*) Disk drives keep shrinking. This 2.5-inch hard disk drive for portable computers is about the size of a cassette tape.

Forty years after inventing the world's first hard disk drive for computer storage, an IBM employee held the device's latest incarnation. The 2.5-inch hard disk drive for portable computers is about the size of a cassette tape and holds 320 times as much data as the 40-year-old model.

■ *Hard disk advantages—capacity and speed:* We mentioned that hard disks have a data storage capacity that is significantly greater than that of diskettes. Microcomputer hard disk drives now typically hold 2 gigabytes, and newer ones are in the 3–9 gigabyte range. As for speed, hard disks allow faster access to data than do diskettes because a hard disk spins several times faster than a diskette.

Speed is generally measured by *seek time, latency,* and *access time.* **Seek time** refers to the time it takes for the read/write head to move to the correct track, measured in *milliseconds,* or *ms* (1000th of a second). A fast hard disk drive may have a seek time of 8 ms. After the head reaches the correct track, it must wait for the disk to rotate so the head is positioned over the correct sector; this rotation time is called **latency,** which may be about 8 ms for a hard drive. If you add seek time to latency, you get the total **access time.** In advertisements for hard drives, these numbers are figured as averages.

- *Disadvantage—possible "head crash":* In principle a hard disk is quite a sensitive device. As opposed to the read/write head in a diskette drive, the read/write head in a hard disk drive does not actually touch the disk but rather rides on a cushion of air about 0.000001 inch thick. (It has been said that the read/write head flying over the hard disk surface is comparable to a jet plane flying 6 inches above the earth's surface.[3]) The disk is sealed from impurities within a container, and the whole apparatus is manufactured under sterile conditions. Otherwise, all it would take is a smoke particle, a human hair, or a fingerprint to cause what is called a *head crash.*

    A head crash happens when the surface of the read/write head or particles on its surface come into contact with the disk surface, causing the loss of some or all of the data on the disk. An incident of this sort could, of course, be a disaster if the data has not been backed up. There are firms that specialize in trying to retrieve (for a hefty price) data from crashed hard disks, though this cannot always be done.

    A head crash can also be caused by jarring the hard disk when it is in use, so caution should be exercised. In recent years, computer magazines have evaluated the durability of portable computers containing hard disks by submitting them to drop tests. Most of the newer machines are surprisingly hardy. However, with hard disks—whether in portable or in desktop computers—the possibility of disk failure always exists.

There are two common types of hard disk architectures used in microcomputers: EIDE and SCSI.

- *EIDE:* **Enhanced Integrated Drive Electronics,** or **EIDE,** refers to a type of hardware interface widely used to connect hard disks to a PC via a PCI bus (✔ p. 2.26). EIDE is popular because of its low cost, and it is increasingly being used to connect tape drives and CD-ROM drives. EIDE connects via a flat ribbon cable to an expansion board called a *host adapter,* which plugs into an expansion slot on the motherboard (✔ p. 2.20). With EIDE drives, the controller electronics are contained on a printed circuit board within the drive itself, so the adapter is a fairly simple circuit board. An inexpensive EIDE host adapter can control four hard drives (one of which may be a CD-ROM or optical disk drive), two diskette drives, two serial ports, a parallel port, and a game port (✔ p. 2.24). EIDE can attain data transfer rates up to 16.6 MB per second.

Does a microcomputer user need both a hard drive and a diskette drive? Why or why not?

- *SCSI:* **SCSI (small computer system interface,** ✔ pp. 2.24, 2.27) is the drive interface used on Mac computers and most high-end PCs, including multimedia workstations and network servers. SCSI allows the connection of eight to sixteen peripheral devices in a daisy chain hookup to a single expansion board. SCSI-2 can attain transfer rates of 20–40 MB per second.

Microcomputer Hard Disk Variations: Power and Portability

If you have an older microcomputer or one with limited capacity in its existing hard disk, some variations are available that can provide additional power or portability:

■ *Miniaturization:* Most hard disk drives nowadays are less than half the height of older drives ($1\frac{1}{2}$ inches versus $3\frac{1}{2}$ inches high) and so are called *half-height drives.* Thus, you could fit two disk drives into the bay in the system cabinet formerly occupied by one.

In addition, the diameter of the disks has been getting smaller. Instead of $3\frac{1}{2}$ inches, some platters are as small as 1 inch in diameter.

■ *External hard disk drives:* If you don't have room in the system unit for another internal hard disk but need additional storage, consider adding an external hard disk drive. Some detached external hard disk drives can store gigabytes of data. You can also attach several external hard drives via a SCSI interface.

■ *Removable disks:* **Hard disk cartridges,** or *removable hard disks,* consist of one or more platters enclosed along with read/write heads in a hard plastic case. The case is inserted into an external cartridge system connected to a microcomputer. A cartridge, which is removable and easily transported in a briefcase, may hold as much as 2 gigabytes of data. These cartridges are often used to transport huge files, such as desktop-publishing files with color and graphics and multimedia video segments. They are also frequently used for backing up data because, although they are more expensive, they are much faster than tape cartridges and hold much more data than diskettes. Removable magnetic disks and drives come in either SCSI or parallel configurations for Macs and PCs, respectively. Some popular hard disk cartridge systems are the Syquest, Zip, and Jaz drives. *(See Figure 4.10.)*

> **What uses could you find for hard disk cartridges?**

Figure 4.10 Removable hard disk cartridges and drives: Jaz, Zip, Syquest. Each cartridge has self-contained disks and read/write heads. The entire cartridge, which may contain as much as 2 gigabytes of data, may be removed for transporting or may be replaced by another cartridge.

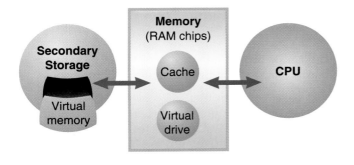

Memory
(RAM chips)

Secondary
Storage

Cache

CPU

Virtual
memory

Virtual
drive

Virtual Memory: Using Disk Space to Increase RAM

A type of hard drive space that mimics primary memory (RAM, ✔ p. 2.21) is **virtual memory.** When RAM space is limited, the use of virtual memory can let users run more software at once, if the computer's CPU and operating system are equipped to use it. The system does this by using some free disk space as an extension of RAM— that is, the computer *swaps* parts of the software program between the hard disk and RAM as needed. For example, when making up this book, we used the Mac PowerPC 9500's virtual memory function to be able to run QuarkXPress desktop-publishing software at the same time as Adobe PhotoShop, which was used to manipulate photos inserted on the book's pages. Note that virtual memory can make the computer run more slowly, as compared to cache memory (✔ p. 2.22), which makes the computer run faster.

Hard Disk Technology for Large Computer Systems

As a microcomputer user, you may regard secondary-storage technology for large computer systems as of only casual interest. However, this technology forms the backbone of the revolution in making information available to you over communications lines. The large databases offered by such organizations (at the time of this book's publication) as CompuServe, America Online, and Dialog, as well as the predicted movies-on-demand through cable and wireless networks and most Internet and World Wide Web locations, depend on secondary-storage technology.

Secondary storage devices for large computers consist of the following:

- *Removable packs:* A removable-pack hard disk system contains 6–20 hard disks, of $10\frac{1}{2}$- or 14-inch diameter aligned one above the other in a sealed unit. Capacity varies, with some packs ranging into the terabytes.

  These removable hard disk packs resemble a stack of phonograph records, except that there is space between disks to allow access arms to move in and out. Each access arm has two read/write heads—one reading the disk surface below, the other the disk surface above. However, only one of the read/write heads is activated at any given moment.

- *Fixed disk drives:* Fixed disk drives are high-speed, high-capacity disk drives that are housed (sealed) in their own cabinets. Although not removable or portable, they generally have greater storage capacity and are more reliable than removable packs and thus are now more common than removable packs. A single mainframe computer might have 20 to 100 such fixed disk drives attached to it.

- *RAID storage system:* A fixed disk drive sends data to the computer along a single path. A **RAID** storage system, which consists of two or more disk drives within a single cabinet or connected along a SCSI chain, sends data to the computer along several parallel paths simultaneously. Response time is thereby significantly improved. (*RAID* stands for *redundant array of inexpensive disks* that collectively act as a single storage system.)

RAID unit

The advantage of a RAID system is that it not only holds more data than a fixed disk drive within the same amount of space but also is more reliable because if one drive fails, others can take over.

A research group at the University of California at Berkeley has defined six RAID levels, each level using a different number of drives with different configurations applicable to various situations—such as for file servers, archival storage, multimedia development, and database servers.

Future Hard Disk Technology: The MR Head

Since its introduction in 1955, the magnetic storage industry has constantly increased the performance and capacity of hard disk drives to meet the demand for more and better storage. Applications like multimedia, video, audio, and graphical user interfaces, along with increasing program sizes, continue to drive the need for ever greater storage capacity.

The read/write head technology that has sustained the hard disk drive industry to date is based on the voltage produced when a permanent magnet (that is, the disk) moves past a wire-wrapped magnetic core (that is, the read/write head). Over the years, various improvements have been made to this arrangement to increase recording density; however, the ability to manufacture these heads cost-effectively is nearing its natural limit. Thus a new recording head technology is needed to allow disk storage technology to continue to provide increased storage capacity and performance. This new technology is the magnetoresistive (MR) read head (MRH).

In traditional read/write head technology, the head must alternately perform conflicting tasks of writing data on the disk as well as reading (retrieving) previously written data. MRH technology avoids this problem by separating the write and read functions into two physically distinct heads. This fundamental change in read/write technology will enable the disk drive industry to increase performance well into the 21st century.[4]

Optical Disks

Optical disks are removable disks on which data is written and read using laser technology. These disks store much more data than diskettes and sometimes more data than hard disks.

By now optical disk technology is well known to most people. An **optical disk** is a removable disk on which data is written and read through the use of laser beams—there is no mechanical arm, as with diskettes and hard disks. The most familiar form of optical disk is the one used in the music industry. A compact disk, or CD, is an audio disk using digital code that is like a miniature phonograph record. A CD holds up to 74 minutes (2 billion bits' worth) of high-fidelity stereo sound.

The optical disk technology that revolutionized the music business with music CDs is doing the same for secondary storage with computers. A single optical disk of the type called CD-ROM may hold 680 megabytes of data. This works out to 250,000 pages of text, or more than 7000 photos or graphics, or 19 hours of speech, or 74 minutes of video. Although some disks are used strictly for

Figure 4.11 Optical disks. (*Top*) Writing data: A high-powered laser beam records data by burning tiny pits onto the surface of the disk. (*Bottom*) Reading data: A low-powered laser beam reads data by reflecting smooth areas, which are inter-preted as 1 bits, and not reflecting pitted areas, which are interpreted as 0 bits.

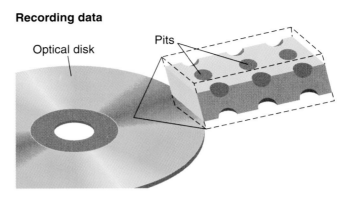

Recording data

Optical disk

Pits

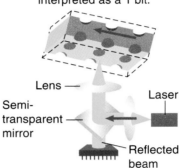
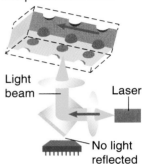

Reading data

Reading "1":
The laser beam reflects off the smooth surface, which is interpreted as a 1 bit.

Reading "0":
The laser beam enters a pit and is not reflected, which is interpreted as a 0 bit.

Lens

Semi-transparent mirror

Laser

Reflected beam

Light beam

Laser

No light reflected

digital data storage, many are used to distribute multimedia programs that combine text, visuals, and sound.

In the principal types of optical disk technology, a high-power laser beam is used to represent data by burning tiny pits into the surface of a hard-plastic disk. To read the data, a low-powered laser light scans the disk surface: Pitted areas are not reflected and are interpreted as 0 bits; smooth areas are reflected and are interpreted as 1 bits. (*See Figure 4.11.*) Because the pits are so tiny, a great deal more data can be represented than is possible in the same amount of space on a diskette and many hard disks.

The optical disk technology used with computers consists of these main types:

- CD-ROM disks

- CD-R disks

- Erasable disks (CD-E)

- DVD/DVD-ROM

CD-ROM Disks

For microcomputer users, the best-known type of optical disk is the CD-ROM. **CD-ROM,** which stands for **compact disk—read-only memory,** is an optical disk format that is used to hold software programs and data such as prerecorded text, graphics, and sound. Like music CDs, a CD-ROM is a read-only disk. *Read-only* means the disk's content is recorded at the time of manufacture and cannot be

Figure 4.12 Notebook computers with CD-ROM drives

written on or erased by the user, a feature that makes CD-ROMs excellent media for software distribution and copyrighted image catalogs.

Most microcomputers have built-in CD-ROM drives. *(See Figure 4.12.)* Users can also purchase external CD-ROM drives. The drives come either in a SCSI configuration for Macs or PCs, or in an EIDE configuration available only for PCs. In the former case, one also needs a SCSI adapter card; in the latter case, an EIDE-controller adapter card.

Whereas at one time a CD-ROM drive was only a single-speed drive, now there are four- (4x), six- (6x), eight- (8x), twelve- (12x), and sixteen-speed (16x) drives. A single-speed drive accessed data at 150 kilobytes per second (the equivalent of 50 typed pages). Therefore, a 12x drive accesses 1800 kilobytes of data per second. The faster the drive spins, the more quickly it can deliver data to the processor. CD-ROM drives used to handle only one disk at a time. Now, however, there are multidisk drives that can handle up to 100 disks. (Such drives are sometimes called *jukeboxes,* or *CD changers.*)

At present, CD-ROMs for desktop computers are a standard 120 millimeters in diameter, which is too bulky to fit in most notebook and handheld personal computers. These computers use 80-millimeter disks.

Clearly, CD-ROM has become an important medium. Among the uses are the following:

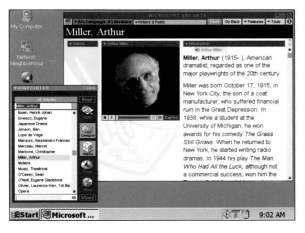

Encyclopedia entry

■ *Data storage:* Originally, computer makers thought that CD-ROM would be good for storing databases, documents, directories, and other archival information that would not need to be altered. Customers would be libraries and businesses.

In this vein, among the top-selling titles are road maps, typeface and illustration libraries for graphics professionals, and video and audio clips. Publishers are also mailing monthly "publications" of CD-ROMs on such subjects as medical literature, patents, and law.

■ *Encyclopedias:* The principal CD-ROM encyclopedias are The Grolier Multimedia Encyclopedia, Compton's New Century Encyclopedia, and Microsoft's Encarta.

Each packs the entire text of a traditional multivolume encyclopedia onto a single disk, accompanied by pictures, maps, animation, and snippets of audio and video.

■ *Catalogs:* Publishers have also discovered that CD-ROMs can be used as electronic catalogs, or even "megalogs." One, for instance, combines the catalogs of several companies. "A single disk now holds the equivalent of 7000 pages of information on almost 50,000 different products from salad-bar sneeze-guards to deep-fat fryers," noted one report.[5] Cinemania offers a multimedia catalog of movies available on videotape.

■ *Games:* As you might expect, CD-ROM has been a hugely successful medium for games. Early bestsellers on the CD-ROM hit parade included *Myst, 7th Guest, Battle Chess,* and *Kings Quest V.* The CD-ROM program called *Sherlock Holmes, Consulting Detective,* features three different murder mysteries to choose from. Each offers you the opportunity, with a Shakespearean actor playing Sherlock Holmes, to solve a murder with as few clues as possible.

■ *Edutainment:* Edutainment software consists of programs that look like games but actually teach in a way that feels like fun. An example for children aged 3–6 is *Yearn 2 Learn Peanuts,* which teaches math, geography, and reading. *Multimedia Beethoven: The Ninth Symphony,* an edutainment program for adults, plays the four movements of the symphony while the on-screen text provides a running commentary and allows you to stop and interact with the program. For adults there is, for example, Time Warner's *Body Voyage,* a CD-ROM package that allows Joseph Paul Jernigan—executed in 1993—to live again (all 15 gigabytes of him). With his permission, Jernigan was frozen and cut into 1878 1-millimeter slices, each of which was photographed and scanned into a computer. Thus *Body Voyage* teaches about the inner workings of the human body by allowing learners to take him apart and put him together again.

Name six ways CD-ROMs are used. How do you think you might use them?

■ *Magazines and books:* Several magazines, including *Newsweek* and *Business Week,* are publishing multimedia issues. Book publishers are constantly producing new CD-ROM titles.

■ *Movies:* As we describe shortly, using CD-ROMs for movies has some limitations. Nevertheless, the range of films available is increasing steadily.

CD-ROMs and Multimedia

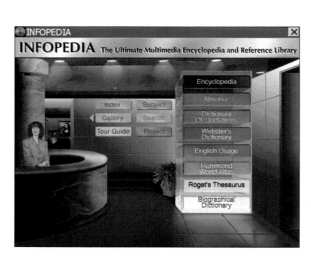

CD-ROMS have enabled the development of the multimedia business. However, as the use of CD-ROMs has burgeoned, so has the vocabulary, creating difficulty for consumers. Much of this confusion arises in conjunction with the words *interactive* and *multimedia.*

As we mentioned earlier (✔ p. 1.25), *interactive* means that the user controls the direction of a program or presentation on the storage medium. That is, there is back-and-forth interaction, as between a player and a video game. You could create an interactive production of your own on a regular 3½-inch diskette. However, because of its limited capacity, you would not be able to present full-motion video and high-quality audio. The best interactive storage media are those with high capacity, such as CD-ROMs.

Multimedia refers to technology that presents information in more than one medium, including text, graphics, animation, video, sound, and voice. As used by telephone, cable, broadcasting, and entertainment companies, *multimedia* also refers to the so-called Information Superhighway. On this avenue various kinds of information and entertainment will be delivered to your home through wired and wireless communication lines.

There are many different CD-ROM formats, some of which work on computers and some of which work only on TVs or special monitors. Most are not mutually compatible right now. The majority of non-game CD-ROM disks are available for Macintosh or for Windows- or DOS-based microcomputers. Among the variations on CD-ROM technology used for interactive and multimedia purposes are the following:

- *Game CD-ROMs:* Both Sega and 3DO offer video game machines that play their own types of CD-ROM disks. (Nintendo is sticking with cartridges for the moment.)

- *MPC:* The term *MPC* indicates that hardware or software meets the industry standard for connecting CD-ROM drives to IBM-compatible microcomputers and supporting multimedia input, processing, storage, and output requirements. An MPC machine is a multimedia personal computer that adheres to standards set by the

HOME MPC P166		HOME MPC P200	
Intel 166MHz Pentium processor 16MB EDO RAM 2.1GB EIDE hard drive 15" Micron 15FGx, .28dp (13.7" display)	**$1,599**	Intel 200MHz Pentium processor 32MB EDO RAM 3.1GB EIDE hard drive 17" Micron 17FGx, .26dp (15.8" display)	**$2,249**
With Intel 200MHz Pentium processor with MMX™ technology	add $300	With Intel 200MHz Pentium processor with MMX	add $100
With Intel 166MHz Pentium processor with MMX	add $100	With Intel 166MHz Pentium processor with MMX	subtract $100

Advertisements for MPC microcomputers

Multimedia PC (MPC) Marketing Council, a subsidiary of the Software Publishers Association. This organization consists of important hardware and software companies, including Intel, Microsoft, IBM, NEC, and Fujitsu. Current MPC recommendations for a multimedia microcomputer are called *Level 3 **minimum** requirements:* 8 MB RAM, 75 MHz Pentium (or equivalent) multimedia processor, 2-button mouse, 101-key keyboard, 540 MB hard disk, 8x CD-ROM drive, sound capabilities, video capabilities, and MIDI and joystick ports (in addition to regular ports).

CD-R Disks

CD-R, which stands for **compact disk—recordable,** is a CD format that allows users with CD-R drives to write data, only once, onto a specially manufactured disk that can then be read by a standard CD-ROM drive. One of the most interesting examples of CD-R technology is the Photo CD system. *(See Figure 4.13.)* Developed by Eastman Kodak, Photo CD is a technology that allows photographs taken with an ordinary 35-millimeter camera to be stored digitally on an optical disk. You can shoot up to 100 color photographs and take them to a local photo shop for processing. A week later you will receive back not only conventional negatives and snapshots but also the images on a CD-ROM disk. Depending on your equipment,

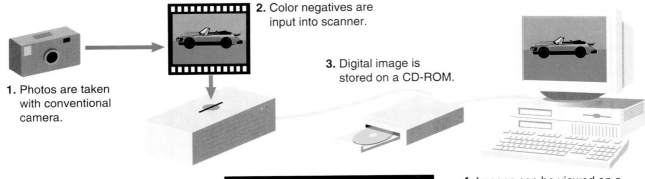

1. Photos are taken with conventional camera.

2. Color negatives are input into scanner.

3. Digital image is stored on a CD-ROM.

4. Images can be viewed on a television or computer screen.

Figure 4.13 Photo CD system

you can then view the disk using any compatible CD-ROM drive. The drive could be for an IBM PC or a Macintosh or one of Kodak's own Photo CD players, which attaches directly to a television set.

Photo CD is particularly significant for the impact it will have on the manipulation of photographs. With the right software, you can flip, crop, and rotate photos, incorporate them into desktop-publishing materials, and print them out on laser printers. Commercial photographers and graphics professionals can manipulate images at the level of pixels. Pixels, or picture elements, are the dots of color that make up a picture. For example, they can easily merge images from different sources, such as superimposing the heads of show-business figures in the places of the U.S. presidents on Mount Rushmore. "Because the image is digital," says one writer, "it can be taken apart pixel by pixel and put back together in many ways."[6] This helps photo professionals further their range, although at the same time it also presents a danger that photographs will be compromised in their credibility.

Erasable Optical Disks (CDE)

An **erasable,** or **rewritable, optical disk,** also called **CDE** or **CD-RW,** allows users to erase data so that the disk can be used over and over again. The most common type of erasable and rewritable optical disk is probably the *magneto-optical disk,* which uses aspects of both magnetic disk and optical disk technologies. Such disks are useful to people who need to save successive versions of large documents, handle databases, back up large amounts of data and information, or work in multimedia production or desktop publishing. These disks come in cartridges that are inserted into compatible external drives hooked up to the computer. Because these drives are so expensive, however, they are not yet widely used, even though they are much more durable than magnetic hard drives.

DVD-ROM: The "Digital Convergence" Disk

According to the various industries sponsoring it, DVD isn't an abbreviation for anything. (The letters used to stand for "digital video disk" and later, when its diverse possibilities became obvious, for "digital versatile disk.") But this is the designation that Sony/Philips (with its Multi Media CD) and Toshiba/Time Warner (with its Super Density disk) agreed to in late 1995, when they avoided a "format war" by joining forces to meld their two advanced disk designs into one. Suffice it to say that **DVD-ROM** is a silvery, 5-inch optically readable digital disk that looks like an audio compact disk but can store 4.7–17 gigabytes, allowing great data storage, studio-quality video images, and theater-like surround sound. *(See Figure 4.14.)* Actually, the home-entertainment version is called simply the DVD. The computer version of the DVD is called the DVD-ROM disk. It represents a new generation of high-density CD-ROM disks, with write-once and rewritable capabilities.

Manufacturers are aggressively developing DVD erasing/writing machines and DVD-compatible computers. All these devices should be able to play any CD-ROM or audio CD, finally producing a single player for any CD/DVD disk. DVD technology is expected to replace the VHS videotape now used in VCRs (video cassette recorders).

How does a DVD work? Like a CD or CD-ROM, the surface of a DVD contains microscopic pits, which represent the 0s and 1s of digital code that can be read by a laser. The pits on the DVD, however, are much smaller and closer together than those on a CD, allowing far more information to be represented there. Also, the technology uses a new generation of lasers, which allow a laser beam to focus on pits roughly half the size of those on current audio CDs. Another important development is that the DVD format allows for *two layers* of data-defining pits on each side of the disk. Finally, engineers have succeeded in squeezing more data into fewer pits, principally through data compression.

Besides being designed from the outset to work with the full range of electronic, television, and computer hardware, the major characteristics of the DVD are as follows:

■ *More storage capacity, faster data transfer:* A single-layer, single-sided disk will hold 4.7 gigabytes of information, or a library of 300-page novels or 7 hours of music. (This compares with 680 megabytes or 74 minutes of playing time on today's single-sided music CD.) Indeed, all ratings versions of a film (PG, PG-13, R, and so on) could be included. Parents could use a special password to protect children from selecting versions that are adult-only. A double-layer, double-sided DVD can hold 17 gigabytes of data.

Figure 4.14 DVD: new era of data storage. (a) This "super disk" can hold 4.7–17 gigabytes of information. (b) Recording on a DVD disk. (c) Comparative capacities of DVD, CD-ROM, and diskette.

(a)

(b) Inside a DVD disk

Four feature-length films can fit on a single DVD disk, which is CD-size but can hold about 25 times more information.

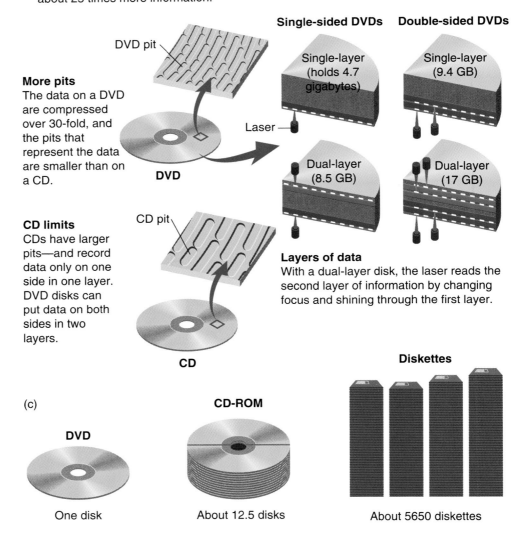

DVD pit

More pits
The data on a DVD are compressed over 30-fold, and the pits that represent the data are smaller than on a CD.

Laser

DVD

CD limits
CDs have larger pits—and record data only on one side in one layer. DVD disks can put data on both sides in two layers.

CD pit

CD

Single-sided DVDs

Single-layer (holds 4.7 gigabytes)

Dual-layer (8.5 GB)

Double-sided DVDs

Single-layer (9.4 GB)

Dual-layer (17 GB)

Layers of data
With a dual-layer disk, the laser reads the second layer of information by changing focus and shining through the first layer.

(c)

DVD

One disk

CD-ROM

About 12.5 disks

Diskettes

About 5650 diskettes

■ *Better audio:* "A Toshiba demonstration clip of the train wreck scene from *The Fugitive* put me right in the midst of squealing brakes and crunching metal," wrote an observer of a DVD prototype, "thanks to a 5.1-channel digital surround-sound specification."[7] The specification allows for six separate audio tracks. It also permits up to eight language translations, which means movie makers could put a number of languages on one disk. In time, there might be some new ultra-high-fidelity audio applications.

One important matter: DVD players will be backward compatible, able to play today's audio compact disks.

■ *Better video:* Picture quality can visibly surpass that currently delivered on videocassettes. In fact, the DVD is designed to offer the superb images found on the new digital satellite system (DSS). In its DVD-ROM form, it will deliver full-screen video that looks like television, rather than expanses of fuzzy blocks (called *pixelation*).

The increased capacity could allow viewers to choose variations in what's known as the "picture aspect-ratio" or screen size: wide-screen format for a wide-screen TV, letterbox format for a conventional TV, or a version cropped to fill a conventional TV screen. Viewers could also employ slow-motion, fast-forward, and freeze-frame features, as they do now on VCRs.

■ *DVD-ROM and recordable and rewritable capabilities:* Software publishers now employ so much space-eating video and animation in their programs that they are rapidly running out of room on standard 680-megabyte CD-ROM disks. Thus, they and computer makers decided they had to enter the DVD standards fray to push for a single DVD design that could be used for computer data storage as well as for movies and music. They also wanted the new drives to be able to read today's CD-ROM disks. The result is the DVD-ROM disk.

We are now entering one of those periods familiar to computer users in which new technology comes along that simultaneously delights and frustrates consumers. The delight, of course, will be that DVD-ROMs will store a lot more information and enable you to see movies and listen to music on your personal computer. (Movies such as *Blade Runner, Mars Attacks!, Casablanca, Doctor Zhivago,* and *Gone with the Wind* are already available for DVD players.) The frustration will be that many present kinds of hardware will soon become obsolete or irrelevant, and there will be lots of changes until everything shakes down.

What are three advantages of DVDs?

For instance, you won't be able to use a DVD-ROM drive to record DVD movies until Hollywood agrees on a technology to block copying or ensure that royalties from blank-disk sales flow back to content providers. For these reasons also, it will be some time before recordable DVD players appear for use with TVs.

The Importance of Backup

Don't lose your work! Back it up!

Even with the best of care, any disk can suddenly fail for reasons you can't understand. Many computer users have had the experience of being unable to retrieve data from a diskette that worked perfectly the day before, because some defect has damaged a track or sector. Hard disks can crash. Any computer system—large or small—can be hit by fire or flood.

Thus, users and companies should always be thinking about backup. As we've mentioned, backup is the name given to tapes, diskettes, or disks that store copies of programs and data stored elsewhere. The best protection if you're writing, say, a make-or-break research paper is to make two copies of your data. One copy may be on your hard disk, certainly, but duplicates should be on tape, diskettes, or removable hard disk cartridges or even recordable CD-ROMs, if available.

If you're backing up less than 10 MB, diskettes may work fine. If you're backing up more than that, tape or disk cartridges would be more efficient. If you work with files daily, you would be most secure if you backed up all your files every day. If you work with files only occasionally, you need to determine how often backup is needed. And remember to keep the backup media in a different place. If your computer system and your backup tapes are in the same structure and the place burns down, your backup is obviously worthless.

Some microcomputer software programs provide automatic backup. For example, with Colorado Scheduler, you insert your tape cartridge into the tape drive and click the mouse button on the Colorado Scheduler icon; the computer takes care of the rest. Almost all large computer systems have scheduled automatic backup—either of all files (*full backup*) or only those files that have changed since the last backup session (*incremental backup*).

Note that some storage media last longer than others. Tape will deteriorate within 5 to 15 years, depending on how it's stored. Hard disk cartridges such as Zip and Jaz have a shelf life of about 10 years, according to the manufacturers. MO drives are more expensive but also more durable. The life span of a CD-ROM disk is almost unlimited. Thus you need to determine how long you will need to archive your backup material before deciding on a storage medium. Also, be sure to have a timed backup strategy. For example, if you add and change data every day, set your backup software to back up those files every night. And you could keep two storage cartridges: a working one and one stored in a safe place. Then exchange the cartridges weekly.

What backup method would you use? Why?

Other Forms of Secondary Storage

Other types of secondary storage include flash memory and advanced storage technology.

The revolution in secondary-storage technology will probably continue throughout our lifetime and will have a profound effect on the way information is handled and business is conducted. In the next section we describe flash memory, a variation on conventional computer-memory chips that we mentioned in Chapter 2. Some noteworthy developments to which we should pay close attention involve advanced storage technology.

Flash-Memory Cards

Disk drives, whether for diskettes, hard disks, or CD-ROMs, all involve moving parts—and moving parts can break. Flash-memory cards, by contrast, are variations on conventional computer-memory chips, which have no moving parts. **Flash-memory,** or **flash RAM, cards** (✔ p. 2.23) consist of circuitry on credit-card-size cards that can be inserted into slots connecting to the motherboard. They can hold up to 100 megabytes of data.

A videotape produced for Intel Corp., which makes flash-memory cards, demonstrates their advantage, as one report makes clear: In it, engineers strap a memory card onto one electric paint shaker and a disk drive onto another. Each storage device is linked to a personal computer, running identical graphics programs. Then the engineers switch on the paint shakers. Immediately, the disk drive fails, its delicate recording heads smashed against its spinning metal platters. The flash-memory card takes the licking and keeps on computing.

Flash-memory cards are not infallible. Their circuits wear out after repeated use, limiting their life span. Still, unlike conventional computer memory (RAM), flash memory is *nonvolatile*. That is, it retains data even when the power is turned off.

As we described in Chapter 2, flash memory is only one of the options available with PCMCIA slots, which were designed primarily for small portable computers. PCMCIA slots in a computer's system cabinet allow users to insert credit-card-size peripherals (PC cards) measuring about 2.1 by 3.4 inches. Besides flash-memory cards, you can plug in modems, hard drives, and adapters for communicating over local area networks (LANs).

Advanced Storage Technology

Scientists keep finding new ways to put more and more data on storage media. IBM is working on development of an optical recording system capable of storing 350 million bits per square inch. The company said it expects to reach densities of 10 billion bits a square inch by the year 2000. Such densities would mean that a $3\frac{1}{2}$-inch disk drive could contain all the text of ten thousand 300-page novels.

In what has been called "the world's smallest Etch-a-Sketch," physicists at NEC Corp. in Tokyo used a sophisticated probe—a tool called a scanning tunneling microscope (STM)—to paint and erase tiny lines roughly 20 atoms thick. This development could someday lead to ultra-high-capacity storage devices for computer data.

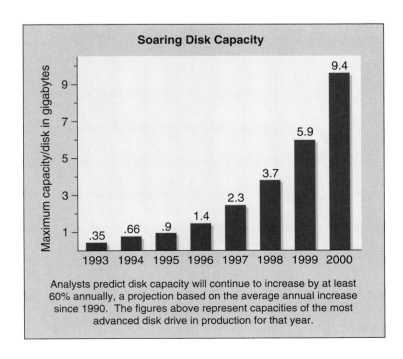

Soaring Disk Capacity

Analysts predict disk capacity will continue to increase by at least 60% annually, a projection based on the average annual increase since 1990. The figures above represent capacities of the most advanced disk drive in production for that year.

Finance and Banking Careers

The Omaha computer center for the credit card processor First Data Corporation is bigger than a football field. Most of it is a gigantic tape library of perhaps a quarter million reels of magnetic tape containing information on probably over 100 million credit cards. "You can walk blocks before bumping into a human being," says one report.[9]

Secondary storage has long been the backbone of finance and banking, but now careers in these institutions could become a lot more interesting as we move forward into the era of the cashless society—smart cards, electronic money, and Web banking.

"This is the beginning of the end of cash," says San Francisco secretary Valerie Baptiste, as she hands over her Mondex smart card—plastic embedded with a microchip containing stored-up funds like an electronic purse—to pay for her morning coffee and bagel. The cashier inserts the smart card into a machine that in less than five seconds deducts $2.15 from the stored value. Undergoing tests in several countries, Mondex-like cyber-cash systems come equipped with an electronic "wallet" with a modem that allows consumers to dial up their banks and refuel their smart cards while they're on the road.[10,11]

Smart cards are only one of several e-money experiments being pushed by banks. Citibank, for instance, is developing what it calls an Electronic Monetary System, which will allow customers to make payments electronically anywhere in the world. IBM, joined by 15 American and Canadian banks, has formed a partnership called Integrion, which will provide electronic bill paying, lending, and stock and bond trading to the banks' 60 million customers at the click of a mouse or touch of a telephone button.[12]

Six other banks are backing an electronic-payment system known as CyberCoin, which will allow Internet users to buy online goods and services with tiny prices—"micropayments," such as 25-cent transactions—from participating merchants. For instance, publishers could charge buyers as little as a quarter to buy an article or listen to a song online, a small transaction that until now has not been practical. "It allows you to buy things by the sip rather than the gulp," says futurist Paul Saffo.[13]

As mergers have forced banks to reduce their staff levels, causing the closing of branch banks and curtailing of some financial services, bankers have also looked to the Internet to further transform itself and reach more customers. More than 1000 banks have World Wide Web sites, offering services that include account access, funds transfer, bill payment, loan and credit card applications, and investments.

But, points out economics writer Julianne Malveaux, only a minority of American households presently have access to the Internet. "A disproportionate number of those who lack computer access are low-income, people of color, or both," she says. This suggests, then, the need to make such technological banking services more accessible. "If the Internet is perceived as so necessary that no family can manage banking or other key services without it," writes Malveaux, "what is being done to make it and the World Wide Web truly worldwide?"[14]

WHAT IT IS
WHAT IT DOES   WHY IT IS IMPORTANT

access time (LO 5, p. 4.16)   Seek time plus latency equals access time.

The faster a disk's access time, the faster data is retrieved.

ASCII files (LO 1, p. 4.4)   Text-only files (no formatting, such as boldface or italic, and no graphics).

This format is used to transfer documents between incompatible platforms, such as IBM and Macintosh. ASCII files may use the .TXT file name extension.

audio files (LO 1, p. 4.4)   Files that contain digitized sound.

.WAV and .MID (MIDI) files are audio files.

cartridge tape units (LO 3, p. 4.9)   Also called *tape streamers;* secondary storage used to back up data from a hard disk onto a tape cartridge.

Cartridge tape units are often used with microcomputers as a backup method and with larger systems for archival purposes.

CD-R (compact disk—recordable) (LO 6, p. 4.23)   CD format that allows users to write data only once onto a specially manufactured disk that can be read by a standard CD-ROM drive.

Home users can do their own recordings in CD format. CD-R can be used, for example, for recording photos and as a backup medium.

CD-ROM (compact disk—read-only memory) (LO 6, p. 4.20)   Optical-disk form of secondary storage that holds more data, including photographs, art sound, and video, than diskettes and some hard disks. Like music CDs, a CD-ROM is a read-only disk. CD-ROM disks will not play in a music CD player.

CD-ROM disks are used in multimedia, education, and entertainment.

data files (LO 1, p. 4.3)   Files that contain data, not programs.

Data files contain content that a user has created and stored using applications software programs. The program may add an extension, such as .DAT.

direct access storage (LO 3, p. 4.5)   Storage media that allow the computer direct access to a storage location without having to go through what's in front of it.

Direct access storage (disk) is much faster than sequential storage (tape).

disk drive (LO 4, p. 4.10)   Computer hardware device that holds, spins, reads from, and writes to magnetic or optical disks.

Users need disk drives in order to use their disks. Disk drives can be internal (built into the computer system cabinet) or external (connected to the computer by a cable).

diskette (LO 4, p. 4.9)   Also called *floppy disk;* secondary storage medium; removable round, flexible mylar disk that stores data as electromagnetic charges on a metal oxide film that coats the mylar plastic. Data is represented by the presence or absence of these electromagnetic charges, following standard patterns of data representation (such as ASCII). The diskette is contained in a plastic case to protect it from being touched by human hands. It is called "floppy" because the disk within the case is flexible, not rigid. The common diskette size is now 3½ inches.

Diskettes are used on all microcomputers.

document files (LO 1, p. 4.4)   Word-processed or desktop-publishing data files.

Document files, which may use the extension .DOC, are commonly created and used by many types of users.

DVD-ROM (LO 6, p. 4.25)   Five-inch optical disk that looks like a regular audio CD but can store 4.7 gigabytes of data on a side.

DVD-ROMs provide great storage capacity, studio-quality images, and theater-like surround sound.

EIDE (Enhanced Integrated Drive Electronics) (LO 5, p. 4.16)   Type of hardware interface widely used to connect hard disks to an IBM-type PC.

EIDE is popular because of its low cost, and it is increasingly being used to connect tape drives and CD-ROM drives to PCs.

erasable (rewritable) optical disk (CDE, CD-RW) (LO 6, p. 4.25)   Optical disk that allows users to erase data so that the disk can be used over and over again (as opposed to CD-ROMs, which can only be read). The most common type of erasable optical disk is probably the magnetic-optical disk, which uses aspects of both magnetic disk and optical disk technologies.

Such disks are useful to people who need to save successsive versions of large documents, handle enormous databases, back up large amounts of data and information, or work in multimedia production or desktop publishing.

executable file (LO 1, p. 4.3)   File that contains machine-language instructions.

Executable files, which may use the extension .EXE, contain the machine-language instructions the computer needs to run programs.

extended density (ED) diskette (LO 4, p. 4.12)   Diskette that can store 2.8 MB.

Newer microcomputers have ED drives that can accept ED diskettes along with HD diskettes.

flash-memory (flash RAM) cards (LO 8, p. 4.29)   Circuitry on credit-card-size cards (PC cards) that can be inserted into slots in the computer that connect to the motherboard.

Flash-memory cards are variations on conventional computer-memory chips; however, unlike standard RAM chips, flash memory is nonvolatile—it retains data even when the power is turned off. Flash memory can be used not only to simulate main memory but also to supplement or replace hard disk drives for permanent storage.

file allocation table (FAT) (LO 1, p. 4.4)   Function of the operating system that keeps track of where everything is stored on disk by maintaining a sort of indexed table with entries of locations for all file names.

FATs are needed for the computer system to find files.

formatting (initializing) (LO 4, p. 4.12)   Process by which users prepare diskettes so that the operating system can write information on them. This includes defining the tracks and sectors (the storage layout). Formatting is carried out by one or two simple computer commands.

Diskettes cannot be used until they have been formatted. Nowadays most diskettes are sold preformatted.

hard disk (LO 5, p. 4.13)   Secondary storage medium; rigid disk made out of metal and covered with a magnetic recording surface. Like diskettes and tape, it holds data in the form of magnetized spots. Hard disks are tightly sealed within an enclosed unit to prevent any foreign matter from getting inside. Data may be recorded on both sides of the disk platters.

Hard disks hold much more data than diskettes do. Nearly all microcomputers now use hard disks as their principal storage medium. Hard disk drives can be internal, external, or use removable disks.

hard disk cartridge (LO 5, p. 4.17)   One or more removable hard disk platters enclosed along with read/write heads in a hard plastic case. The case is inserted into an external cartridge system connected to the computer.

A hard disk cartridge, which is removable and easily transported in a briefcase, may hold gigabytes of data. Hard disk cartridges, such as Syquest, Zip, and Jaz, are often used for transporting large graphics files and for backing up data.

high-density (HD) diskette (LO 4, p. 4.12)   Diskette that can store 1.44 megabytes.

Most microcomputers use HD diskettes.

image files (LO 1, p. 4.4)   Files that contain digitized graphics.

Users working with graphics must learn how to use various types of graphics files, such as .EPS, .JPG, .TIF, .GIF, and .BMP.

latency (LO 5, p. 4.16)   The time it takes for the hard disk to rotate so the head is positioned over the correct sector.

Latency for a fast hard disk drive may be about 8 milliseconds.

magnetic tape (LO 3, p. 4.8)   Thin plastic tape coated with a substance that can be magnetized; data is represented by magnetized or nonmagnetized spots. Tape can store files only sequentially.

Tapes are used in reels, cartridges, and cassettes. Today "mag tape" is used mainly to provide backup, or duplicate storage, and for archiving .

optical disk (LO 6, p. 4.19)   Removable disk on which data is written and read through the use of laser beams.

Optical disks hold much more data than many magnetic disks and have helped enable the development of the multimedia industry.

program file (LO 1, p. 4.3)   File containing software instructions.

This term is used to differentiate program files from data files.

RAID (redundant array of inexpensive disks (LO 5, p. 4.18)   Storage system that consists of two or more disk drives within a single cabinet or connected along a SCSI chain that sends data to the computer along several parallel paths simultaneously. Response time is thereby significantly improved.

The advantage of a RAID system is that it not only holds more data than a fixed disk drive within the same amount of space but also is more reliable because if one drive fails, others can take over. RAID systems are commonly used for servers and multimedia systems.

read (LO 4, p.4.10)   Computer activity whereby data represented in the magnetized spots on the disk (or tape) are converted to electronic signals and transmitted to primary storage (RAM) in the computer.

Reading allows stored data and information to be transferred to a place where it can be manipulated.

SCSI (small computer system interface) (LO 5, p. 4.16) Peripheral-device interface used on Mac computers and some high-end PCs.

SCSI allows the connection of eight to sixteen peripheral devices connected in a daisy chain hookup to a single expansion board.

secondary storage (LO 1, p. 4.2) Consists of devices that store data and programs permanently on disk or tape.

Secondary storage is nonvolatile—that is, saved data and programs are permanent, or remain intact, when the power is turned off. Secondary storage is needed because computer users require far greater storage capacity than is available through primary storage (RAM).

sectors (LO 4, p. 4.11) On a diskette, eight or nine invisible wedge-shaped sections used by the computer for storage reference purposes.

When users save data from computer to diskette, it is distributed by tracks and sectors on the disk. That is, the systems software uses the point at which a sector intersects a track to reference the data location in order to spin the disk and position the read/write head.

seek time (LO 5, p. 4.15) The time it takes for the read/write head to move to the correct track, measured in *milliseconds,* or *ms* (1000th of a second).

Seek time varies in different hard disks. A fast hard disk may have a seek time of 8 milliseconds.

sequential storage (LO 3, p. 4.5) Data stored in sequence, such as alphabetically.

Sequential storage is the only type of storage provided by tape, which is used mostly for archiving and backup.

source program file (LO 1, p. 4.3) File containing high-level computer instructions.

These instructions must be translated into machine language in order for the processor to use them.

tracks (LO 4, p. 4.11) The rings on a diskette along which data is recorded. Each track is divided into eight or nine sectors.

See *sectors*.

video file (LO 1, p. 4.4) File that contains digitized video images.

.MPG and .AVI are common video file extensions.

virtual memory (LO 5, p. 4.18) Type of hard drive space that mimics primary memory (RAM).

When RAM space is limited, the use of virtual memory can let users run more software at once, if the computer's CPU and operating system are equipped to use it. The system does this by using some free disk space as an extension of RAM—that is, the computer swaps parts of the software program between the hard disk and RAM as needed. Virtual memory can make the computer run more slowly, as compared to cache memory, which makes the computer run faster.

write (LO 4, p. 4.10) Computer activity whereby data processed by the computer is recorded onto a disk (or tape).

Writing allows users to save data and information to secondary storage media.

1. A(n) _keyboard?_ is about 1 trillion bytes.

2. _Direct access_ is the data access method used by hard disks.

3. _Magnetic tape_, a secondary storage device, is most commonly used for backup and archiving information.

4. A(n) _cd-rom_ is a removable disk on which data is written and read through the use of laser beams.

5. _____ is the name given to a diskette (or tape) that is a duplicate or copy of data that is stored elsewhere.

SHORT-ANSWER QUESTIONS

1. What are the advantages of a hard disk over a diskette?

2. What kinds of secondary storage do large computer systems use?

3. What is the significance of the terms *track* and *sector*?

4. What is the difference between a program file and a data file?
   instructions   *rawdata*

5. What are some of the uses for CD-ROM technology?

MULTIPLE-CHOICE QUESTIONS

1. All diskettes must be _____ before they can store data.
   a. named
   b. saved
   c. retrieved
   d. formatted
   e. all the above

2. Which of the following is commonly used in microcomputers to speed up data retrieval?
   a. half-height drives
   b. disk caching
   c. EIDE
   d. SCSI
   e. all the above

3. Which of the following optical technologies can be used with the full range of electronic, television, and computer hardware?
   a. CD-ROM
   b. CD-R
   c. CD-RW
   d. DVD-ROM
   e. all the above

4. Which of the following is text-only with no formatting?
   a. program file
   b. data file
   c. document file
   d. ASCII file
   e. all the above

5. Which of the following file-management functions refers to copying a file from another disk or computer to your computer?
   a. upload
   b. download
   c. compress
   d. import
   e. none of the above

TRUE/FALSE QUESTIONS

1. Magnetic tape can handle only sequential data storage and retrieval. (true/false)

2. Hard disks may be affected by a head crash when particles on the read/write heads come into contact with the disk's surface. (true/false)

3. To use a diskette, you usually need a disk drive, but not always. (true/false)

4. One advantage of using diskettes is that they aren't susceptible to extreme temperatures. (true/false)

5. EIDE and SCSI are two common types of hard disk architecture. (true/false)

KNOWLEDGE IN ACTION

1. You want to purchase a hard disk for use with your microcomputer. Because you don't want to have to upgrade your secondary storage capacity in the near future, you are going to buy one with the highest storage capacity you can find. Use computer magazines or visit computer stores and find a hard disk you would like to buy. What is its capacity? How much does it cost? Who is the manufacturer? What are the system requirements? Is it an internal or an external drive? Can you install/connect this unit yourself? Why have you chosen this unit and this storage capacity?

2. What types of storage hardware are currently being used in the computer you use at school or at work? What is the storage capacity of these hardware devices? Would you recommend alternate storage hardware be used? Why or why not?

3. Do you think books published on CD-ROMs will ever replace printed books? Why or why not? Look up some recent articles on this topic and prepare a short report.

4. Sometimes users forget to back up their work, or their backup tape/diskettes are lost or destroyed. What can you do, then, if your hard disk crashes and you have forgotten to back up your work? Look in the Yellow Pages of your phone book under Computer Disaster Recovery or Data Recovery. Call up the services listed and find out what they do, how they do it, and what they charge. Give a short report on the topic.

5. What optical technologies do you think you will use in your planned career or profession? How do you expect to use this technology? Which optical technologies have you already used? For what?

WELCOME TO EARTH'S BIGGEST BOOKSTORE ......

Amazon.com

Now that you've come up with an idea for your Web business, it's time to consider the design of your site, where to store your site, and what hardware you'll need to get started. Keep in mind that initially you will run your business from a single computer. Perhaps after your business grows, you'll invest in additional processing power.

For anyone who has visited the Amazon.com site, it is obvious that careful planning went into its initial design and content. The site is very easy to navigate and makes you want to browse its "aisles." The Amazon.com Web site was rated by *Time* magazine as one of the "10 Best Websites of 1996." Let's look at some tips that will help you create a winning Web site for your online business.

PLANNING THE DESIGN OF YOUR SITE

No matter if you only have one employee (you) and your company headquarters is an arm's length from your refrigerator and sink full of dishes, customers will take you seriously if your site is professional in design and contains complete and accurate information. You can either create the site yourself or hire a Web consultant with graphics experience to assist you.

When planning the design of your site, first focus your attention on developing a clearly defined message. The text and graphics you choose to populate your site should all support your message. Amazon.com's message, emblazoned on the top of its home page, is clear: *Welcome to Earth's Biggest Bookstore*. The message tries to make you feel welcome to stay for a while as well as giving you the sense that you can find any book (on earth) that you choose. Amazon.com delivers on its message with numerous features and graphics. For example, you are welcomed to the site with the Win $1,000 of books, Browse, and Earn Money links, and

WELCOME TO EARTH'S BIGGEST BOOKSTORE ......

Amazon.com

2.5 MILLION TITLES | 1.5 MILLION BOOKS IN PRINT & 1 MILLION OUT-OF-PRINT BOOKS

Text Only

40% off the Amazon.com 500! ~ Browse our Miles of Aisles
Win $1,000 of books ~ Earn Money: Sell books from your Web site!

SEARCH BY
Author, Title, Subject
Keyword
ISBN
Advanced Query

First-Time Visitors Please Click Here

May 14th--New on Our Shelves

Into Thin Air, Jon Krakauer's chilling account of the ill-fated 1996 Mount Everest expedition, takes your breath away. Guaranteed can't-put-it-down

BUY BOOKS
Shopping Cart
Checkout

Book of the Day
Classic BOTD
Undiscovered BOTD
Science Fiction BOTD
Nonfiction BOTD
Mystery BOTD
Wacky BOTD
6 new books every day
for the next 1,000 years

SUPER ROOM
Computer & Internet

MILES OF AISLES
Business
Science Fiction

unless you don't understand the meaning of words like "2.5 million" or "Miles of Aisles," you know you have hit upon an enormous bookstore.

Your color scheme, or the collection of colors you use throughout your site, should also support your message. (Don't use psychedelic colors, for example, if your theme is traditional in nature.) Amazon.com uses predominantly black text on a white background, in keeping with how text usually appears on a printed page. To make things interesting, the site uses a few additional colors as well.

Consider asking a few people to review your color scheme before you actually implement it. You don't want customers to shop somewhere else simply because they were turned off by your choice of colors!

PLANNING YOUR HOME PAGE

The first page customers will see when they go to Yourname.com is your home page. Think of your home page as the online equivalent of a brochure or reception area where first impressions are all-important. As exemplified by the Amazon.com home page, your home page should make customers feel welcome and provide an entry point to the other pages of your site. And it should load fast. Web users are an impatient lot. If it takes more than 30 seconds before all the fancy graphics you've built into your home page appear on the screen, your customers will probably decide to shop somewhere else. This doesn't mean that your home page has to be boring—it's relatively simple to create fast-loading graphics (but these steps are beyond the scope of the current discussion). In general, you want your home page to:

■ *Make a good (and fast) first impression.* You can accomplish this with a well-thought-out theme and color scheme, and by including fast-loading graphics.

■ *Provide a means for navigating your site.* You can most easily accomplish this using a menu bar that provides links to the other areas (pages) of your site. Like Amazon.com, you will want to include the same navigation scheme on every page of your site.

■ *Highlight the latest news.* Users like to read "news" about your business. Consider including a navigation button that links to a list of press releases about you and your company, products, and services. Amazon.com, for example, includes the <u>About Our Store</u> and <u>Press Clips</u> links in the navigation bar.

■ *Provide a means for customers to contact you.* This can be accomplished with a navigation button or by including a link to your e-mail address at the bottom of the home page. Amazon.com includes a <u>Send Us E-mail</u> link on the navigation bar, which directs you to nine e-mail addresses including <u>orders@amazon.com</u>, <u>help@amazon.com</u>, <u>feedback@amazon.com</u>, and <u>marketing@amazon.com</u>.

PLANNING WHERE TO HOST YOUR SITE

An important decision to make when planning your Web site is where you will host your site, or store it. You can purchase your own computer to act as the server or rent space on another computer, either from your Internet access provider or from another company that specializes in renting out space for Web sites. You'll typically have more control over the operations of your Web site if you store your site on your own server computer.

However, if you're running your business from a single computer and are new to the Internet, we don't recommend that you run your own server computer. It might be simpler for you to rent space for your site from an access provider for $20 to $300 per month, depending on your needs. Customers will still be able to access your business 24 hours a day, 7 days a week, and you'll have full use of your desktop machine. Also, your provider will most likely use high-speed T1 or T3 connections so that your Web pages will flow to the Internet at swifter speeds than if they were originating from your computer. A note of caution: Beware of access providers that charge you per transaction, such as a nine-cent fee for credit card purchases, or for the number of "hits" your Web site generates.

Most of Amazon.com's computer and communications hardware is at a single location in the Seattle, Washington, area. A group of systems administrators and network managers, employees of Amazon.com, run the Web site. If the Web site experiences interrupted operation or problems with its transaction-processing systems, it is the responsibility of these individuals to fix them. Amazon.com leases space from two Internet access providers in order to obtain high-speed connections between its server computers and the Internet using multiple dedicated T1 lines.

CHOOSING THE RIGHT TOOLS

Before you embark on constructing a Web site, ensure that you have the right tools. First, if you're going to host your own site, you'll need a computer system on which you'll develop your Web site and support future business operations. Below we list some general system requirements for your computer.

Hard disk	1 GB or more
RAM	32 MB or more
Processor	133 MHz or more
Modem/hookup	56 kbps (kilobits per second) or more
Backup drive	Yes
Multimedia support	Yes

When you consider your computer system in terms of the everyday operation of your business, ensure that you have plenty of hard disk space for future software purchases and data inputs, including invoice data, personnel information, and general record keeping. You might also consider purchasing a laptop if you'll need to access your site from the road.

WHAT DO YOU THINK?

1. Map out on paper what you want to appear on your home page. What navigation links will you include? Describe the theme and color scheme that you will incorporate into your site. Feel free to search the Web for ideas and information to help when designing your site.

2. Will you host your site on your own server computer or on your access provider's computer? Describe the rationale for your decision. If you will be using an access provider, research the costs of doing business with an access provider in your area.

3. Describe the hardware that you think you'll need to run your business.
   a. Include as many categories as you think appropriate, and use computer publications and/or a visit to a computer store to help you determine prices for the various parts of your system. An excellent resource is the Guide to Computer Vendors site on the Web (www.ronin.com/SBA/). This site provides hundreds of links to hardware vendors and computer magazines. List reasons for your choices.
   b. What kind of backup device(s) will serve the backup needs of your business? Why?
   c. What is the overall cost of the hardware you want to purchase?

4. Does the hardware you chose in question 3 come with a maintenance contract? If so, what are the terms of the contract? Does it come with a technical support contract? Is there a charge? Is your hardware covered by a warranty? Make sure that the documentation that accompanies the hardware is clearly written and easy to use.

5. In what areas should your system have maximum upgrade capacity: Speed? Video capabilities? Communications? Secondary storage capacity? RAM? Why might these future upgrades be important?

CHAPTER 5

SYSTEM SOFTWARE
The Director

PREVIEW

When you have completed this chapter, you will be able to:

1. Define the various components of system software

2. Describe the three basic system software user interfaces

3. Define the word *platform* and discuss software compatibility issues

4. Name and describe some common operating systems

5. Explain why system software (and applications software) may no longer need to be installed on every personal computer

WHY IS THIS CHAPTER IMPORTANT?

"What we need," says Alan Robbins, a critic of machine interfaces, "is a science called *practology,* a way of thinking about machines that focuses on how things will actually be used."[1] *Interface* refers to the parts of a machine that humans manipulate—"the control panel," such as the volume and station-tuner knobs on an old radio, explains Robbins, a professor of visual communications. On a computer the interface, or *user interface,* consists of the controls you use for manipulating the software and hardware. One such area of contact is the mouse combined with on-screen menus. You use the mouse to make choices from the menus, or lists of options, shown on the display screen. Unfortunately, Robbins laments, a significant problem with many of today's machines—digital watches, VCRs, even stoves, as well as personal computers—is that the interface is often designed to accommodate the machine or some engineering ideas rather than the people actually using it.

Good interfaces are intuitive, like the twin knobs on an old radio, immediately usable by both novices and sophisticates. Bad interfaces force us to relearn the required behaviors every time, such as a software program with a bewildering array of menus and icons. Of course, you can prevail over a bad interface if you repeat the procedures often enough. "That's why you can become familiar with a befuddling word processor you use all the time," suggests Robbins, "but not with the cumbersome e-mail system you use intermittently."

In this chapter we embark on the first part of a discussion of software programs and the interfaces you can use to control them. When you get into hands-on use of software, you will find that some programs are relatively easy to use but some are not. When you encounter hard-to-use software, it's important to remember this: Don't always blame yourself for the difficulty. It should be the software designer's job to take your needs into account, not the other way around.

Two Basic Software Types: For the Computer and for the User

Software consists of the step-by-step instructions that tell the computer how to perform a task. Software is "soft" because you can't touch the instructions the way you can touch the computer equipment—the "hard" ware. There are two basic types of software: system software, for the computer, and applications software, for the user. Software consists of programs (instructions), not data. Thus software is "run," whereas data is "processed."

No such thing as software existed in the earliest computers. Instead, to change computer instructions, technicians actually had to rewire the equipment. Then in the 1950s, computer scientists began to use punched cards to store program instructions. In the mid-1950s, high-speed storage devices that were developed for ready retrieval eliminated the need for hand-wired control panels. Since that time, the sophistication of computer hardware and software has increased exponentially. Software is created by software programmers, who code instructions using special programming languages, such as C++. (This topic is covered in more detail in a later chapter.)

The appearance of the microcomputer in the late 1970s made computer hardware and software accessible to more people because they became more affordable, easier to use, and flexible enough to handle very specific job-related tasks. Because of this accessibility, a large pool of applications software has been created to satisfy almost any user's requirements. In other words, you do not have to be a technical specialist to use computer software to solve complicated and tedious problems. However, you will be entering the job race without your running shoes if you do not understand the uses of—and the differences among—types of system software and applications software.

To help you begin to understand the differences among types of software, let us repeat the definitions for applications and system software.

- **System software** "underlies" applications software; these programs start up the computer and function as the principal coordinator of all hardware components and applications software programs. Without system software loaded into the RAM [✔ pp. 2.12 and 2.15] of your computer, your hardware and applications software are useless.

- **Applications software** consists of computer programs designed to satisfy a user's specific needs. The task or problem may require, for example, computations for payroll processing, creation of animation, maintenance of different types of data in different types of files, designing a full-color magazine or a new artificial heart valve, or the preparation of forms and documents. Applications software communicates to system software all file management and resource requests (use of peripheral devices).

Every application works through "layers" in the computer to get to the hardware and perform the desired result. Think of the applications software layer as what the computer is doing and the system software as how the computer does it. Both system software and applications software must be purchased by the user (system software and some applications software are usually shipped with and included in the price of a microcomputer).

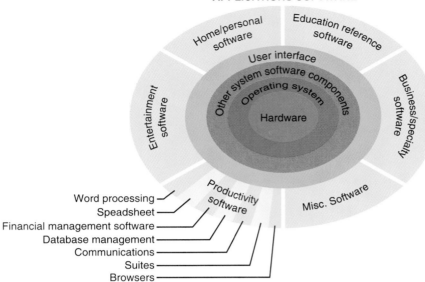

APPLICATIONS SOFTWARE

Home/personal software · Education reference software · User interface · Other system software components · Operating system · Hardware · Business/specialty software · Entertainment software · Productivity software · Misc. Software

Word processing
Spreadsheet
Financial management software
Database management
Communications
Suites
Browsers

For large computer systems, the choice of system software tends to be made by computer specialists and the hardware vendor, and the applications software is usually custom-written for the system; this type of software is called *custom software.* For microcomputer systems, most applications software is usually purchased at a store, direct from the manufacturer, or via mail order or online from a catalog. (There is much more applications software to choose from than system software.) Applications software purchased off the shelf is often referred to as *off-the-shelf,* or *packaged, software.* Microcomputer users generally receive system software along with the computer they purchase or use at work.

If you are a microcomputer user starting from scratch, you should choose your applications software first, after you identify your processing needs. Then choose compatible hardware models and system software that will allow you to use your applications software efficiently and to expand your system if necessary. By choosing your applications software first, you will ensure that all your processing requirements will be satisfied. You won't be forced to buy a software package that is your second choice simply because your first choice wasn't compatible with the hardware or system software already purchased.

When you go to work in an office, chances are that the computer hardware and system software will already be in operation; so if you have to choose anything, it will most likely be applications software to help you do your job. If you do find yourself in a position to choose applications software, make sure not only that it will satisfy the processing requirements of your job, but also that it is compatible with your company's hardware and system software.

System Software Components

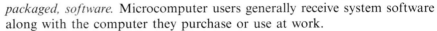
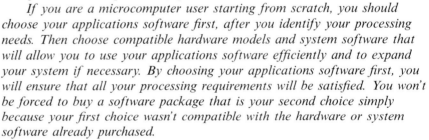

System software basically manages the computer's basic operations, allows the computer to run applications software, and allows the user to interact with the computer.

Without system software you won't be able to use any applications software. System software tells the computer how to interpret data and instructions; how to communicate with peripheral equipment like printers, keyboards, and disk drives; how to manage files; and how to use the hardware in general. Also, it allows you, the user, to interact with the computer. System software comprises a large number of instructions that can be grouped into the following categories (*not all types of system software include all these functions*):

1. Operating system and BIOS (basic input/output system)
2. Data management
3. TP monitor
4. Network operating system
5. Communications protocols
6. Messaging protocols
7. Drivers
8. Utility programs
9. Language translators

As a computer user, you will have to use system software, so it is important to understand the role it plays in the computer system.

Operating System: In Control

The **operating system (OS),** the most important system software component, consists of the master programs, called the **supervisor,** that manage the basic operations of the computer. These programs reside in RAM while the computer is on and provide resource management services of many kinds, handling such matters as running and storing programs and storing and processing data. The operating system allows you to concentrate on your own tasks or applications rather than on the complexities of managing the computer. It interprets the commands you give to run programs and allows you to interact with the programs while they are running.

The operating system is automatically loaded into main memory as soon as you turn on, or "boot," the computer. The term *booting* refers to the process of loading an operating system into a computer's main memory, usually from hard disk. *(See Figure 5.1.)* This loading is accomplished by a program (called the *bootstrap loader* or *boot routine*) that is stored permanently in the computer's electronic circuitry. When you turn on the machine, the program obtains the operating system from disk and loads it into memory. Other programs (called *diagnostic*

Figure 5.1 Booting process. When you turn on the computer, the processor (CPU) automatically begins executing the part of the operating system's start-up system located in ROM (1). These instructions help load the operating system from hard disk into RAM (2), and then they pass control to the OS.

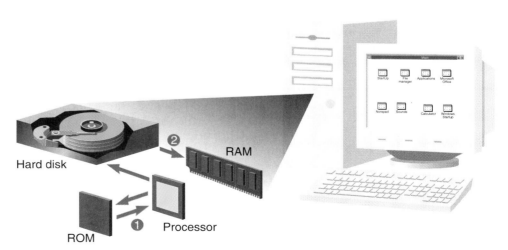

routines) also start up and test the main memory, the central processing unit, and other parts of the system to make sure they are running properly. As these programs are running, the display screen may show the message "Testing RAM" (main memory). Finally, other programs will be stored in main memory to help the computer interpret, for example, keyboard characters or transmit characters to the display screen or to a diskette.

The operating system performs file, task, and job management. File management involves, among other things, keeping track of file locations, erasing files, and loading files from disk to RAM. Task management involves the running of one or more programs on the computer at the same time. Job management involves managing units of work to be processed. That is, a job is a specified operation as simple as saving a document or as complex as organizing data into a document.

The operating system also includes **BIOS** (the **basic input/output system**), which manages the essential peripherals such as the keyboard, screen, disk drives, and parallel and serial ports (✔ p. 2.23). BIOS also manages some internal services

What happens when you boot your computer?

such as time and date. This is the part of the operating system that tests the computer upon booting via an autostart program. After running the autostart program, it loads the rest of the operating system and turns control over to it. BIOS is usually stored on a ROM chip (✔ p. 2.22) or a flash memory chip (✔ p. 2.23).

Data Management: Tracking Data

The **data management** component of system software keeps track of the data in secondary storage. Applications software doesn't know where the data is stored or how to get it. That "knowledge" is contained in the operating system's access method (✔ p. 4.5), or driver routines.

TP Monitor: Input Management

In large computer systems, the **TP monitor,** for *teleprocessing* or *transaction processing monitor,* distributes input from multiple terminals to the appropriate applications being run on the system.

Network Operating System: Traffic Management

The **network operating system** manages traffic and security between client workstations and file servers in a network (✔ p. 1.11).

Communications Protocols: Details for Data Transmission

Communications protocols comprise the set of rules, formats, and functions for sending data across a network. (This topic is covered in more detail in Chapter 7 on communications.)

Messaging Protocols: Details for E-Mail Transmission

Messaging protocols are the set rules, formats, and functions for sending, storing, and forwarding e-mail in a network.

Drivers: Peripheral Management

Most computer systems are configured with a variety of peripheral devices. So that the operating system does not need to load support for all types of existing peripherals every time the computer is turned on, it contains directions for device-specific software drivers. **Drivers** comprise software programs that support specific peripheral devices, such as printers, CD-ROM drives, and display adapter cards (✔ p. 3.26). The driver contains the detailed machine language (✔ p. 2.7) necessary to control each device. The operating system commands the driver, which in turn commands the peripheral devices.

Utility Programs: Helping Hands

Utility programs are generally used to support, enhance, or expand existing programs in a computer system. Many operating systems have utility programs built in for common purposes. Additional utility programs are available on separate diskettes. Examples of utility programs are:

■ *System diagnostics:* In addition to the basic diagnostic routines performed by BIOS, more sophisticated diagnostic programs can be provided in the form of a utility. A **diagnostic program** is one that compiles technical information about computer hardware, including peripherals, that can be used to diagnose almost any technical problem. Most diagnostic programs make a record of the computer's normal operational settings. Then, when a problem occurs, a new report is produced, and the problem can usually be resolved by finding discrepancies between the two reports. Note: You may need a computer technician to help you interpret the reports.

■ *Backup:* Suddenly your hard disk drive fails, and you have no more programs or files. Fortunately, we hope, you have used a **backup utility** to make a backup, or duplicate copy, of the information on your hard disk.

   Examples of backup utilities are Norton Backup from Symantec Corp. and Colorado Scheduler.

■ *Data recovery:* A **data recovery utility** is used to restore data that has been physically damaged or corrupted. Data can be damaged by viruses (see following), bad software, hardware failure, and power fluctuations that occur while being written/recorded.

This antivirus software screen is asking what drives the user wants to scan.

■ *Virus protection:* Few things can make your heart sink faster than the sudden failure of your hard disk. One exception may be the realization that your computer system has been invaded by a virus. A virus consists of hidden programming instructions that are buried within a program or data file (✔ p. 4.3). Sometimes they copy themselves to other programs, causing havoc. Sometimes the virus is merely a simple prank that pops up a message. Other times, however, it can destroy programs and data and wipe your hard disk clean. Viruses are spread when people exchange diskettes or download (make copies of) files from computer networks.

   Fortunately, antivirus software is available. **Antivirus software** is a utility program that scans hard disks, diskettes, and memory to detect viruses. Some utilities destroy the virus on the spot. Others notify you of possible viral behavior. Note that new viruses are constantly being developed. Thus you need the

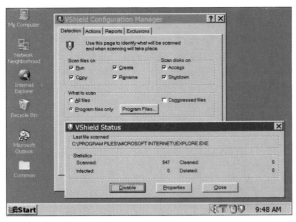

This antivirus software screen is displaying the file scanned.

type of antivirus software that can detect "unknown" viruses and that also offers frequent, free updates—which are usually available online, to be downloaded. Popular antivirus software utilities are Norton Antivirus, Dr. Solomon's Anti-Virus Toolkits, McAfee's VirusScan, and Webscan.

Note: Though it's a good idea to install an antivirus utility on your computer, virus risks are sometimes exaggerated. With few exceptions, if you don't boot your computer with a foreign diskette, directly run programs downloaded from a network, or use illegally copied program diskettes, your risk of virus infection is low. *(See Table 5.1.)*

■ *Data compression:* As you continue to store files on your hard disk, it will eventually fill up. You then have four choices. You can delete old files to make room for the new. You can buy a new hard disk with more capacity and transfer the old files and programs to it. You can install an additional hard disk. Or you can use a **data compression utility.** Data compression utilities remove redundant elements, gaps, and unnecessary data from a computer's storage space so fewer bits are required to store or transmit data.

With the increasing use of large graphic, sound, and video files, data compression is becoming an important issue—in regard both to storage space and time needed to transmit such large files over a network. Note, however, that as the use of sophisticated multimedia becomes common, compression/ decompression will be increasingly taken over by built-in hardware boards that specialize in this process. That will leave the main processor free to work on other things, and compression/decompression software utilities will become obsolete.

Table 5.1 **Prevention first**

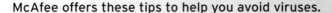

McAfee offers these tips to help you avoid viruses.

■ Never start your computer from an unknown diskette. Always make sure your diskette drive is empty before turning on or restarting your computer.

■ Run virus-scanning software on a new diskette before executing, installing, or copying its files into your system.

■ If you download or install software from a network server (including the Internet), bulletin board, or online service, always run scanning software on the directory you placed the new files in before executing them.

■ Create a start-up diskette containing the scan program. Make sure this disk is write-protected (✔ p. 4.12) so that it cannot become infected.

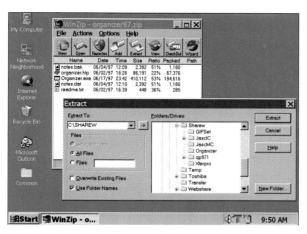

This screen is asking the user where the compressed files just downloaded should be stored after they are decompressed.

The following box lists the most common data compression formats.

Data Compression: Getting More from Less

Data-compression techniques can be divided into two major families: lossy and lossless. The trade-off between these two techniques is basically data quality versus storage space. Lossy data compression involves a certain loss of accuracy in exchange for a high degree of compression. This type of compression is often used for graphics files and digital voice files. Lossless compression involves techniques that generate an exact duplicate with a lower degree of compression. This is achieved by removing redundant data elements. Lossless compression is often used with database records, spreadsheets, and word processing files.

Several standards exist for compression, particularly of visual data. If you record and compress in one standard, you cannot play it back in another. The main reason for the lack of agreement is that different industries have different priorities. What will satisfy the users of still photographs, for example, will not work for users of moving images. Also keep in mind that some compression/decompression techniques—sometimes called *codecs*—require hardware involvement, along with the use of the software utility.

■ *Lossy compression utilities:* These compression schemes use ratios of 1:10 up to 1:50, meaning that the compressed files are about $\frac{1}{10}$ to $\frac{1}{50}$ of the original size.

   (1) JPEG ("jay-peg," Joint Photographers Experts Group): This is a compression program for still images. Motion-JPEG can be used for digital video storage and editing but not transmission. There are more than 30 types of JPEG programs, which can cause compatibility problems. (File extension [✔ p. 4.3] is .JPG.)

   (2) MPEG ("em-peg," Motion Pictures Experts Group): This is a compression program for storage, editing, and transmission of video images. MPEG keeps a complete, detailed image for the first frame (or key frame) of a video segment. For subsequent frames, only the information that changes is stored from frame to frame. Key frames with complete information (called *intra-coded frames,* or *I-frames*) are placed in regular intervals to maintain picture quality. The MPEG standard is supported by IBM, Apple, AT&T, and many other manufacturers and carriers. (File extension is .MPG.)

■ *Lossless compression utilities:* These compression schemes use a ratio of about 1:4 and are used for text files and graphics files. Most of these programs, along with decompression programs, can be downloaded free via the Internet.

NAME	FILE EXTENSION	MICROCOMPUTER TYPE (PLATFORM)
PKZIP/PKUNZIP (WINZIP)	.ZIP	PC
ARC	.ARC	PC
PAK	.PAK	PC
Windows Install	.xx$	PC
StuffIt	.SIT	Mac
PackIt	.PIT	Mac
DiskDoubler	.DD	Mac
Apple Link	.PKG	Mac
Self-Extracting	.SEA	Mac

Of course, other compression software programs exist, but the foregoing are some of the common ones.

To use one of these programs—say, PKZIP/UNZIP—on a file downloaded from a server on the Internet, you would do the following:

1. While online, designate the location (folder) on your hard disk where you want the downloaded file to be placed.

2. Download the file.

3. Go offline.

4. Load PKZIP/UNZIP, which has previously been installed on your hard disk, by double-clicking on its folder or icon.

5. After PKZIP/UNZIP is open, use its menu option to open the downloaded file into PKZIP/UNZIP.

6. Click on Extract, and designate the disk location (folder) where you want to save the decompressed file. (It can be the same place you put it when you downloaded it, or not.)

You can also "zip" (compress) the file again later.

Note that if you download a compressed multimedia file, you will need the appropriate software that supports the decompression and playback of sound and video to hear and view the presentation. *Multimedia utilities*, or *extensions*, may or may not include their own compression/decompression programs. Some multimedia utilities come packaged with the system software—QuickTime for the Mac and AVI (audio/video interleave) for Windows-equipped PCs.

■ *Memory management:* Different microcomputers have different types of memory, and different applications programs have different memory requirements. Memory-management utilities are programs that determine how to efficiently control and allocate memory resources. For example, *virtual memory* (✔ p. 4.18) implements the hardware and operating system to mimic actual memory (RAM) when this memory space is limited. This allows users to work with larger documents and run more software at once. When the processor needs information held in virtual memory addresses, it moves the information to RAM addresses and moves other information out of RAM and into virtual memory addresses in secondary storage, most commonly the hard disk. This process is called *swapping,* or *paging.* The use of virtual memory will affect performance a bit, but it provides the user with more flexibility.

■ *Defragmentation:* When a file is stored on a disk, the computer tries to put the elements of data next to one another. However, this is not always possible because previously stored data may be taking up locations that prevent this. Then, after the user has saved and deleted many files, there remain many scattered areas of stored data that are too small to be used productively. This is called *fragmentation.* It causes the computer to run slower than if all the data in a file were stored together in one location. Utility programs called **defraggers** are available to *defragment* the disk, thus rearranging the data so that the data units of each file are repositioned together (contiguously) in one location on the disk. (Note: You can also defragment a file by simply saving it under a different name onto a disk that has ample space available.)

Many other utilities exist, such as those for transferring files back and forth between a desktop microcomputer and a laptop and for "deinstalling" software programs on your hard disk. They are often offered by companies other than those making the operating system. Later the operating system developers may incorporate these features as part of a product. Note: Independent, or external, utilities must be compatible with your system software; check the software packaging and user documentation.

Language Translators

Why can't you run your computer without system software?

A **language translator** is software that translates a program written by a programmer in a language such as C++ into machine language (✔ p. 2.7), which the computer can understand. All system software and applications software must be turned into machine language for execution by the computer.

Other System Software Capabilities

A computer is required to perform many different jobs at once. In word processing, for example, it accepts input data, stores the data on a disk, and prints out a document—seemingly simultaneously. Some computers can also handle more than one program at the same time—word processing, spreadsheets, database management—displaying them in separate windows on the screen. Other computers can accommodate the needs of several different users at the same time. How does the computer keep everything straight? Among the ways operating systems manage operations more efficiently are multitasking, multiprogramming, time-sharing, and multiprocessing. Not all operating systems can do all these things.

■ *Multitasking—executing more than one program concurrently:* **Multitasking** is the execution of two or more programs by one user concurrently on the same computer with one central processor. You may be writing a report on your computer with one program while another program searches an online database for research material. How does the computer handle both programs at once?

The answer is that the operating system directs the processor to spend a predetermined amount of time executing the instructions for each program, one at a time. In essence, a small amount of each program is processed, and then the processor moves to the remaining programs, one at a time, processing small parts of each. This cycle is repeated until processing is complete. The processor speed is usually so fast that it may seem as if all the programs are being executed at the same time. However, the processor is still executing only one instruction at a time, no matter how it may appear to the user. Because processors work so much faster than peripheral devices, it can accomplish several processing tasks while waiting for, say, a printer to finish outputting a document.

Microcomputer users working on a system with multitasking capabilities will become familiar with the terms *foreground* and *background*. If, for example, your computer is printing out your psychology report while you are creating some graphs for your marine biology report, the printing will occur in the *background*—that is, the processor will allocate less time to it than to what is in the *foreground*—the current application you are working in. Background processing is non-interactive, low-priority processing; foreground processing is interactive, high-priority processing. With some operating systems you can specify the percentage of processor time spent on foreground and background applications.

- *Multiprogramming—a concurrent execution of different users' programs:* **Multiprogramming** is the execution of two or more programs on a multiuser operating system. As with multitasking, the processor spends a certain time executing each user's program, but it works so quickly, it seems as though all the programs are running at the same time. (Multiprogramming is essentially a multiple-user version of multitasking.)

- *Time-sharing—round-robin processing of programs for several users:* **Time-sharing** is a single large computer's processing of the tasks of several users at different stations in round-robin fashion. Time-sharing is used when several users are linked by a communications network to a single computer. The computer will first work on one user's task for a fraction of a second, then go on to the next user's task, and so on.

  How is this done? The answer is through *time slicing*. Computers operate so quickly that it is possible for them to alternately apportion slices of time (fractions of a second) to various tasks. Thus, the computer may rapidly switch back and forth among different tasks, just as a hairdresser or dentist works with several clients or patients concurrently. The users are generally unaware of the switching process.

  Multitasking and time-sharing differ slightly. With multitasking, the processor directs the programs to take turns accomplishing small tasks or events within the programs. These events may be making a calculation, searching for a record, printing out part of a document, and so on. Each event may take a different amount of time to accomplish. With time-sharing, the computer spends a fixed amount of time with each program before going on to the next one.

  Time-sharing is used by some companies' travel agents scattered around the country. The central computer allows the agents to make reservations at the same time. Time-sharing can also allow a research center's scientists and engineers to work on different projects at the same time.

- *Multiprocessing—simultaneous processing of two or more programs by multiple processors:* **Multiprocessing** is processing done by two or more computers or processors linked together to perform work simultaneously—that is, at precisely the same time. This can entail processing instructions from different programs or different instructions within the same program.

Multiprocessing goes beyond multitasking, which works with only one processor. In both cases, the processing should be so fast that, by spending a little bit of time working on each of several programs in turn, a number of programs can be run at the same time. With both multitasking and multiprocessing, the operating system keeps track of the status of each program so that it knows where it left off and where to continue processing. But the multiprocessing operating system is much more sophisticated than multitasking.

Multiprocessing can be done in several ways. One is by coprocessing, whereby the controlling processor works together with coprocessors (🖝 p. 2.12), each of which handles a particular task, such as display-screen graphics or high-speed mathematical calculations. Many microcomputer systems have coprocessing capabilities.

Another way to perform multiprocessing is by parallel processing (🖝 p. 2.12), whereby several full-fledged processors work together on the same tasks, sharing memory. Parallel processing is often used in large computer systems designed to keep running if one of the processors fails. These systems are called *fault-tolerant systems;* they have many processors and redundant components such as memory and input, output, and storage devices. Fault-tolerant systems are used, for example in airline reservation systems.

How do you think you might use multitasking?

System Software Interfaces

As we mentioned at the beginning of the chapter, the **user interface** controls the manner of interaction between the user and the operating system. The old type of interface is *command-driven. (See Figure 5.2.)* In this type of interface, the user must type in strings of characters to issue commands; the mouse cannot be used. The command-driven interface was replaced by the *menu-driven interface. (See*

Figure 5.2 Examples of command-driven (*top*), menu-driven (*middle*), and graphical user (*bottom*) interfaces

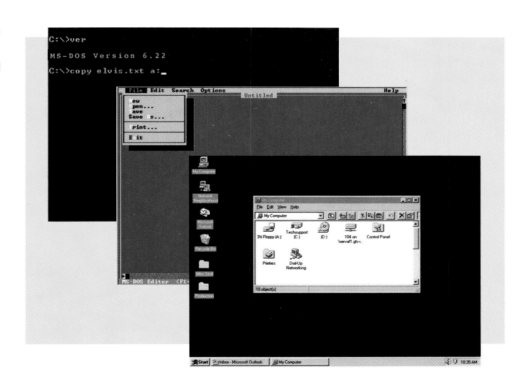

Figure 5.2.) In this case, the user is provided with menus—on-screen lists of options to choose from—that are used to issue commands. The mouse is used to click on choices. The menu-driven interface was greatly improved by the development of the **graphical user interface** (**GUI,** pronounced "gooey"). *(See Figure 5.2.)* The GUI was first developed by Xerox and then used by Apple in its first Macintosh machines. Later, the GUI was adopted by Microsoft for use in its PC system software called *Windows.* In addition to menus, GUIs use pictorial figures called *icons* to represent tasks, functions, and programs—for example, a trash can may represent a delete-file function.

Another feature of the GUI is the use of windows (lowercase "w"). **Windows** divide up the display screen into sections. Each window may show a different display, such as a word processing document in one and a spreadsheet in another.

Finally, the GUI permits liberal use both of the keyboard and the mouse. The mouse is used as a pointing device to move the cursor to a particular icon or place on the display screen. The function represented by the icon can be activated by pressing ("clicking") buttons on the mouse. Or, using the mouse, you can move ("drag") an image from one side of the screen to the other or change its size.

GUI has become the standard microcomputer system software interface. *(See Figure 5.3.)*

Common Operating Systems: Platforms

A computer platform is defined by its processor model and its operating system.

The type of processor used in a computer determines the type of machine language it uses. And the computer's operating system is created to work

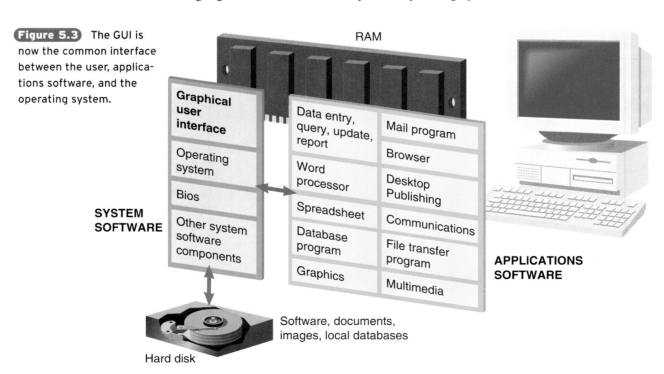

Figure 5.3 The GUI is now the common interface between the user, applications software, and the operating system.

RAM

Graphical user interface

Operating system

Bios

Other system software components

SYSTEM SOFTWARE

Data entry, query, update, report

Word processor

Spreadsheet

Database program

Graphics

Mail program

Browser

Desktop Publishing

Communications

File transfer program

Multimedia

APPLICATIONS SOFTWARE

Software, documents, images, local databases

Hard disk

with that particular type of machine language. Thus the processor model and the operating system determine the **platform**—that is, the type of computer architecture, or family, such as the IBM PC versus the Apple Macintosh. For the most part, software created for one type of platform will not run, without special arrangements, on other platforms. Once you understand the platform, you can begin to understand what the particular computer system is capable of and what types of tasks it can be used for. As a microcomputer user, you'll have to learn not only the applications software you want to use but also, to some degree, the operating system with which they work.

In this section, we describe the following microcomputer operating systems:

- DOS
- Windows 3.X
- Windows 95
- Windows NT
- OS/2
- Unix
- Macintosh Operating System (Mac OS)
- NetWare

DOS

DOS (in English, pronounced "dahss")—short for **Disk Operating System**—is the oldest commonly used microcomputer operating system. *(See Figure 5.4.)* It runs primarily on IBM and IBM-compatible microcomputers, such as Compaq, AST, Dell, and Gateway. IBM's version of DOS is called *PC-DOS*. Microsoft makes *MS-DOS* for IBM-compatibles. Microsoft launched its original version, MS-DOS 1.0, in 1981, and there have been several upgrades since then. MS-DOS 7.0 was issued in 1996.

What do the numbers mean? The number before the period refers to a *version*. The number after the period refers to a *release*, which has fewer refinements than a new version. The most recent versions are all backward compatible. *Backward compatible* means that users can run the same applications on the later versions of the operating system that they could run on earlier versions.

Figure 5.4 DOS 7.0 screen

```
07/03/97   12:20p    <DIR>         EZPHOTO
04/22/97   01:04p    <DIR>         COREL50
04/22/97   01:05p    <DIR>         Exchange
04/22/97   01:05p    <DIR>         MSOffice
04/22/97   01:05p    <DIR>         My Documents
04/22/97   01:05p    <DIR>         PM6
04/22/97   01:10p    <DIR>         WPWIN60
04/22/97   01:10p    <DIR>         util
04/22/97   01:10p    <DIR>         WPC20
04/22/97   01:11p    <DIR>         x
09/14/96   07:50p         218,112  PKWG32.DLL
04/22/97   01:11p    <DIR>         Acrobat3
06/20/97   10:32a    <DIR>         KPCMS
06/24/97   08:39a    <DIR>         PSFONTS
06/23/97   02:31p             43   AUTOEXEC.DOS
06/24/97   02:20p          1,181   WZT1
06/24/97   02:21p             26   WZT2
06/24/97   02:33p             26   WZT3
07/11/95   09:50a         92,870   COMMAND.COM
05/07/97   08:23a    <DIR>         fonts
06/20/97   12:35p              0   summary.dat
              57 File(s)     53,415,903 bytes
                            115,343,360 bytes free
```

Recent versions of DOS have expanded the range of the operating system. For example, version 4.0 changed MS-DOS from a command-driven interface to a menu-driven interface. Version 5.0 added a graphical interface. Version 6.0 added features that optimized the use of main memory. Version 7.0 added multitasking capabilities.

There are a great many old but still useful microcomputers running DOS, and a great many application programs have been written for it. Nevertheless, as a command-driven, single-user program, DOS is a fading product. Although satisfactory for many uses, it is being succeeded by other, more versatile operating systems.

Law Enforcement

"If you got clocked doing 85 mph on the Mass. Pike, now you can pay for it while doing 28,800 bps [bits per second] on the Internet," reports business writer Mark Maremont. In 1996 Massachusetts became the first state to allow motorists to pay speeding fines through the World Wide Web, using credit cards.[2]

This is a nice high-tech administrative convenience for reducing long lines at the motor vehicles department. But computers are finding even more important uses in law enforcement.

For instance, the Web is being used as a virtual post office wall to display wanted pictures of fugitives. The FBI has been posting its 10 "most wanted" on the Internet since 1995. Now other agencies and businesses, ranging from the Commodity Futures Trading Commission to Wells Fargo Bank, are using the Web to do the same thing.[3,4] On their days off, three San Jose, California, police officers have used a Web page, as well as a cable-TV show and a newspaper, to publicize more than 2000 fugitives and have helped police nab more than 200 suspects.[5] Also in San Jose, a 3-year-old who had been abducted was spotted in hours, rather than days, thanks to a system of computers, scanners, color printers, and modems that provided quick dissemination to the public of thousands of high-quality color photos of the missing boy.[6]

New York City reduced serious crime by 27% between 1993 and 1995 in part by using computerized crime-mapping software that enables beat cops to identify different kinds of crime clusters and trends and to fight them block by block. For example,

Detectives at Scotland Yard in England review computer fingerprint files.

maps revealed that police had been making drug arrests where they were easiest rather than where most citizens complained of drug sales, in hard-to-infiltrate public-housing complexes; vice cops were thereupon reassigned in more effective ways. Computerized crime mapping, says criminologist John Eck, "is probably the greatest technological innovation to hit policing in decades."[7]

As criminals become more computer-savvy, so must law-enforcement officials. "More and more evidence can be stuffed into a misidentified computer file, protected by an unknown password, or buried in an obscure file directory," says one report. "Police have found transactions detailing drug deals, child pornography, and even confessions on computers."[8] Robert Maez, of the Colorado Springs Police Department computer services unit, uses special software written by the U.S. Department of the Treasury to copy the contents of suspected hard disks so that they can be searched for information without the risk of altering the original evidence.

Computers are also being used to prevent as well as solve crimes. Instead of using alarm systems, for instance, drivers worried about car theft can install satellite-based tracking systems in their vehicles. With such a system mounted in her 1989 Porsche 928, high-school teacher Cheryl Lawton can call an operator at the security company's dispatch center any time she wants to know her car is where it's supposed to be. In a carjacking or other emergency, she can also hit a panic button that enables the operator to listen in on everything that's going on within the car, calling police, if necessary.[9]

Finally, computers are being used in police training. In her criminal investigation class at Solano Community College in Fairfield, California, Professor Sarah Nordin uses a computerized, interactive sleuthing game to allow students to practice what a real homicide investigation might be like. For instance, when students are convinced that a particular suspect in the game should be arrested, Nordin gathers the facts on the screen to see whether there is enough evidence to justify a search warrant. Bad news, says a fictional police investigator. "I tried. Judge says you didn't have enough probable cause."[10]

Windows 3.x

Microsoft's **Windows 3.x** is an operating *environment* that lays a graphical user interface shell around the MS-DOS and PC-DOS operating systems and extends DOS's capabilities. (Thus Windows 3.x is not a *true* operating system.) *(See Figure 5.5.)* There have been several releases of Windows version 3—3.0, 3.1, and 3.11. (Version 1 was released in 1985, and version 2 in 1988, but it wasn't until version 3 was released in 1990 that Windows really took off and created an industry tied to its graphical user interface and ability to manage large amounts of memory.)

Windows lets you display your work in *windows* on a *desktop*. As mentioned earlier, a window is a rectangular portion of the video display area with a title on top. With Windows, which supports multitasking, you can display several windows on a computer screen, each showing a different application, such as word processing or spreadsheet. (The number of windows you can display at one time depends on how much memory—RAM and virtual memory—your computer has. If you run out of memory, you will get an "Out of memory" message.) You can easily switch between the applications and move data between windows. (Each window can be enlarged, reduced, or "minimized" to an icon, which temporarily removes it from view.) Windows also supports multimedia, which DOS does not do.

Figure 5.5 Windows 3.x screen

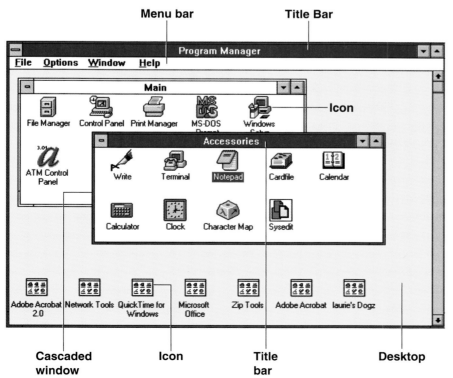

Windows 95

Windows 95 is the major upgrade designed to replace Windows 3.x. Windows 95 is a true multitasking operating system, not requiring the separate MS-DOS program. In Windows 95, the GUI is not a shell; instead it is integrated into the operating system. Like Windows 3.x, it uses windows

and a desktop. *(See Figure 5.6.)* Among the many features included in Windows 95 are support for e-mail, voice mail, fax transmission, and multimedia. It will run applications written for DOS and Windows 3.x, as well as those created for Windows 95.

During the Windows 95 development, Microsoft also worked with several hardware manufacturers to develop an industry-wide hardware standard to produce so-called *plug-and-play* products. Thus, users should be able to easily connect and use ("plug and play") hard disk drives, printers, and other peripheral equip-

Start button: Click for an easy way to start using the computer.

Microsoft Network: Click here to connect to the Microsoft Network, the company's online service.

My Briefcase: Allows you to synchronize files in two computers—say, an office PC and a laptop.

Recycle Bin: Allows you to dispose of files—or retrieve them later.

Network Neighborhood: If your PC is linked to a network of PCs, click here to get a glimpse of everything available on the network.

My Computer: Gives you a quick overview of all the files and programs installed in your PC.

Document: New multitasking capabilities allow people to smoothly run more than one program at once.

Multimedia: Windows 95 features sharper graphics and improved video capabilities.

Start menu: After clicking on the start button, a menu appears, giving you a quick way to handle common tasks. You can launch programs, call up documents, change system settings, get help, and shut down your PC.

Shortcuts: Allows you to immediately launch often-used files and programs.

Taskbar: Gives you a log of all programs your have opened. To switch programs, click on the buttons that appear in the taskbar.

Figure 5.6 Windows 95 screens

ment. This is a significant change from the dozen or so frustrating steps required to configure earlier IBM-style equipment running DOS and Windows 3.x programs, a difficulty not necessarily true of Macintoshes. Also, whereas file names in the DOS system had to be limited to eight characters plus a three-character extension following a period (for example, PSYCHRPT.NOV), file names under Windows 95 can be up to 255 characters in length (MY NOVEMBER PSYCHOLOGY REPORT).

To use Windows 95, a '486 or Pentium processor, 8–16 MB of RAM, and a 500 MB to 1 GB hard disk are recommended.

A slimmed-down version of Windows 95, called *Windows CE,* is used as an operating system in many handheld PCs.

Windows 97? 98? 99?

Will users still be running Windows 95 in 1998 and 1999? As of 1997, Microsoft is planning to call its new version *Windows 98.* It is supposed to include significant changes to the file management system, power management, Internet services, multimedia drivers, and other key components. A beta version of the future Windows operating system—at one point it was called Memphis—is being tested. No release date had been given for it as this book went to press. This updated Windows OS is also supposed to include drivers for most models of CD-ROM drives, DVD players, as well as SCSI and Traven tape drives; some animation built into menus and icons; automatic creation of an emergency start-up diskette; an automatic link to Microsoft's Web page for downloading additional drivers, utilities, and the like; and support (Point-to-Point Tunneling Protocol) for creating your own virtual private network across the Internet. In addition, it's supposed to allow you to plug in many more peripherals, including things like photocopiers, home surveillance systems, and even the coffee pot!

Windows NT

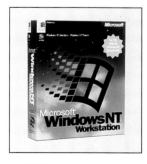

Whereas Windows 95 is basically consumer-oriented, Windows NT is business-oriented. *(See Figure 5.7.)* Unveiled by Microsoft in May 1993, **Windows NT,** for *New Technology,* is a multitasking, multiprocessing operating system with an integrated graphical user interface intended to support large networks of computers—that is, it is a *multiuser* system. Multiuser platforms support **workgroup** computing, situations in which LANs (local area networks, ✔ p. 1.14) are set up to allow users to share files, databases, and applications. Like Windows 95, Windows NT is a true operating system, interacting directly with the hardware. Windows NT is designed to run on workstations (✔ p. 1.14) or other powerful computer systems. It can run NT-specific applications as well as DOS and Windows 3.x/95 applications. It supports 2 GB of virtual memory for applications and 2 GB for its own use. Windows NT runs best on machines with high-end Pentium processors, 32 MB of RAM, and at least 3 GB of hard disk space.

There are two basic versions of Windows NT: Windows NT Server can support up to 32 processors; this version offers files server and print server capabilities, Internet services, office support, and database management. Windows NT Workstation supports 1–2 processors; this version supports computer graphics, computer-aided design, animation, multimedia, and group networking for up to ten users. In the long run, it is suggested, maintaining Windows 95 and Windows NT as separate operating systems will become a strain even for a company with the resources of Microsoft. That is why, then, the company will probably eventually merge the two.

Figure 5.7 Windows NT screen

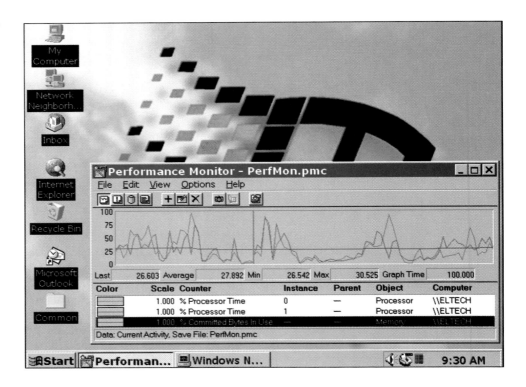

Ole! Ole!

OLE stands for *object linking and embedding.* Microsoft developed it to support documents that contain or reference other documents. OLE has now evolved into a base component of Microsoft's Windows 95 and Windows NT operating systems and has emerged as an industry standard. Basically, OLE allows one application to access the services and data of another. For example, OLE allows an object such as a video clip to be embedded in a text document, which is then called the *client application,* or *OLE container.* When the object is double-clicked, the application that created it, called the *OLE server,* is launched so that you can edit or play the object. The server application appears to run within the client application. An object can also be linked instead of embedded, in which case the OLE container does not physically hold the object but provides a pointer to it. If a change is made to the linked object, all documents that contain the same link are automatically updated the next time you open them.

OS/2

OS/2 (there is no OS/1) was initially released in April 1987 as IBM's contender for the next mainstream operating system. **OS/2**—for **Operating System/2**—is designed to run on many recent IBM and IBM-compatible microcomputers. Like Windows 95, OS/2 does not require DOS to run underneath it and has a graphical user interface, called the *Workplace Shell* (*WPS*), which uses icons resembling documents, folders, printers, and the like. OS/2 can also run most DOS, Windows, and OS/2 applications programs simultaneously. This means that users don't have to throw out their old applications to take advantage of new features. In addition, OS/2 was the first microcomputer operating system to take full advantage of the power of the Intel Pentium microprocessors. Lastly, this operating system is designed to connect everything from small handheld personal computers to large mainframes.

Unfortunately, because of an array of management and marketing disasters, IBM slipped far behind Microsoft in developing an installed base for OS/2. (In fact, IBM and Microsoft were once partners in developing OS/2. Then Microsoft abandoned it to put all its efforts into backing Windows and later Windows NT.)

In late 1994 IBM unveiled a souped-up version of OS/2 with the *Star Trek*–like name of Warp. But despite spending $2 billion on OS/2 in its long struggle against Windows—IBM even claimed that its operating system could run Windows better than Windows itself—the company failed to increase its market share.

Even though many experts rate OS/2 Warp more highly than Windows 95, developers of applications software abandoned it in droves in order to create new programs for the expected Microsoft blockbuster. As a result, in the summer of 1995—three weeks before Windows 95 was to be introduced—the chairman of IBM appeared to concede defeat for OS/2. Nevertheless, IBM continues to support its appoximately 10 million Warp users—the latest versions are OS/2 Warp 4.0 and OS/2 Warp Server. Upgrades are available online and can be downloaded from IBM's Web site. IBM also offers an OS/2-compatible version of the popular Web browser Netscape.

Unix

Unix was invented more than two decades ago by American Telephone & Telegraph, making it one of the oldest operating systems. *(See Figure 5.8.)* **Unix** is a multiuser, multitasking operating system with built-in networking capability and versions that can run on all kinds of computers. Because it can run with relatively simple modifications on different types of computers—from micros to minis to mainframes—Unix is called a *portable* operating system. The primary users of Unix are government agencies, universities, large corporations, and banks, which use the software for everything from airplane-parts design to currency trading to Web site management. Indeed, the developers of the Internet built it around Unix because of its ability to keep large systems with hundreds of processors churning out transactions for months or even years without fail. For that reason, companies such as PepsiCo's Taco Bell chain use Unix to link in-store cash registers to back-office servers for inventory control and labor scheduling. Red Roof Inn trusts Unix servers to run the daily operations of its 280 locations. Even the world's fastest system—a supercomputer at the U.S. Department of Energy's Sandia National Laboratory—is controlled by a variant of Unix. The supercomputer, which is used to simulate nuclear explosions and other situations, is powered by more than 9000 Pentium Pro microprocessors.[11]

For a long time, AT&T licensed Unix to scores of companies that made midsize computers and workstations. As a result, the operating system was modified and resold by several companies, producing several versions of Unix. Then Novell purchased the Unix trademark from AT&T. In order to promote standardized approaches to Unix, in 1993 Novell gave away the Unix brand name to an independent foundation and declared that it would be responsible for maintaining the Unix specifications. This foundation is made up of 75 software vendors, and they created a Unix standard in 1995.

Figure 5.8 Unix screen

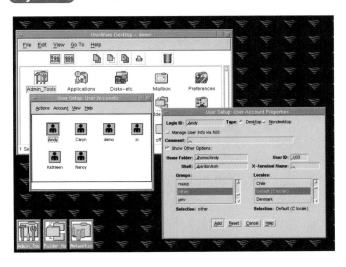

Will Unix endure? Rapid advances by Windows NT Server have convinced some industry analysts that it will overtake Unix. However, Unix vendors maintain that the Unix market is still healthy. They hang their hopes on the network computing movement and the emergence of the Internet as a computing environment. They believe that no other operating system is better suited for managing transactions conducted on large servers connected to the Internet than the operating system on which the "network of networks" was built.

In addition, hardware manufacturers such as Digital Equipment Corporation, Hewlett-Packard, and IBM are promoting convergence strategies that would lead to tools for uniting and managing Unix *and* NT devices on corporate networks. Microsoft also plans to make its Windows NT Server compatible with Unix by 1999 using San Francisco–based Softway's software interface that will put a Unix interface over the Windows architecture. The product will be called OpenNT.

Macintosh Operating System

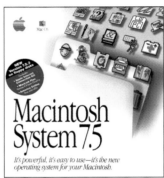

The Apple Macintosh has always had one outstanding feature: it is easy to use, and the easy-to-use interface has generated a strong legion of fans. In the past, however, because Apple kept its prices high and refused to license any cloning, Macs were expensive. Thus, picking a personal computer used to be a simple matter. As computer journalist David Kirkpatrick described it:

> If you wanted a friendly machine and could afford a premium price, you bought an Apple Macintosh. . . . If you needed lots of cheap computing power for complicated tasks, or didn't care so much about user-friendliness, you bought an IBM-style PC. There were dozens of brands to choose from. . . .[12]

Unfortunately, IBM-style and Macintosh microcomputers were designed around different microprocessors, so it was impossible to combine the best of both. IBM and IBM-compatible computers used microprocessors built by Intel. These were the Intel 80286 (called the '286 chip), 80386 ('386 chip), 80486 ('486 chip), and the Pentium, Pentium Pro, and Pentium MMX chips. Macintoshes were built around Motorola microprocessors—the 68000, 68020, 68030, and 68040 chips. Intel chips could not run Macintosh programs, and Motorola chips could not run DOS or Windows programs. In 1994, the PowerPC microprocessor was implemented in newer Macintoshes, part of a joint venture among Apple, IBM, and Motorola. PowerPC Macintoshes can read IBM-formatted diskettes, and many of the applications written for it can convert files created by Windows applications.

Because of price, and because in pre-PC times businesses were already comfortable with IBM equipment, DOS- and Windows-equipped microcomputers have ruled the day.

Still, the Mac, introduced in 1984, set the standard for icon-oriented graphical user interfaces and plug-and-play peripheral hook ups. Indeed, Macintosh system software is easy to use because Apple designed its hardware and software together, from the start. Until recently, the newest version of the **Macintosh operating system (Mac OS)** was *System 7.6,* which enables users to read MS-DOS and Windows files, even if they don't have the software to create such files. *(See Figure 5.9.)* In addition, System 7.6 has a feature called Apple Guide, which offers "active assistance." Active assistance helps users accomplish different tasks on the computer—for example, explaining how to share files with other users. (The Guide is similar to the "Wizard system" of Windows 95.) Apple released Mac OS 8.0 in July, 1997. This version is a little easier to use, faster, and more stable. It's also easier for Internet beginners to use. Further releases and updates called *Allegro, Sonata,* and *Rhapsody* are planned. Apple is also working on an alternative

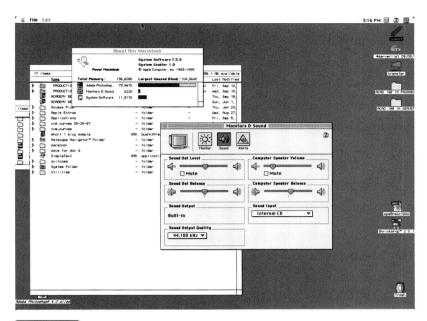

Figure 5.9 System 7.6
screen

operating system called *Be* for systems to be available from Power Computing, Motorola, Umax, and other hardware vendors. BeOS will support Unicode (✔ p. 2.5).

After almost a decade of Macintoshes costing more than comparable IBM-style personal computers, Apple cut its prices. The result was to bring Macs more into line with equipment from IBM, Compaq, Dell, and others (although Macs are still more expensive). In addition, Apple has been looking for ways to license its operating system to other computer makers without crippling its own hardware business. With this development, we may still see the appearance of Macintosh clones, more widespread applications, and further price drops.

With all the favorable publicity about ease of use for the Macintosh, is there a reason for not using it? Indeed there is: only about 7000 commercial applications packages have been written for Macs. By contrast, some 30,000 or more applications packages are available for DOS and Windows computers. However, its graphics capabilities still make the Macintosh a popular choice for people working in commercial art, desktop publishing, prepress operations, multimedia, and engineering design. Within large organizations it has also been an efficient machine for people for whom extensive training does not pay—whether temporary secretaries or senior executives. Those wanting to be able to sample a truly wide range of program offerings, however, may need to look elsewhere.

NetWare

A network needs **network operating system software (NOS)** to provide it with multiuser, multitasking capabilities. The operating system facilitates communications, resource sharing, and security, thereby providing the basic framework of the LAN. The NOS consists of modules that are distributed throughout the LAN environment. Some NOS modules reside in servers, while others reside in the clients. The client is generally an application—for example, a word processing program—that resides on a microcomputer hooked up to the network. The server is a multiport computer that contains large amounts of memory, allowing multiple clients to share the server's resources while still performing certain functions independently. Servers also manage the data.

Developed by Novell during the 1980s, *NetWare* has been the most popular operating system for orchestrating microcomputer-based LANs throughout a company or campus. The unveiling of NetWare 4.0 in March 1993 allowed organizations to extend the scope of their networks from less than 250 microcomputers connected to one file server to thousands of users connected to multiple servers.

Can you continue to use, say, MS-DOS on your office personal computer while it is hooked up to a LAN running NetWare? Indeed you can. NetWare provides a shell around your own operating system. If you want to work "off network" ("stand-alone"), you run the microcomputer's regular operating system—

DOS, OS/2, Mac OS, Unix, Windows. If you want to work "on network," you respond to another prompt and type in whatever password will admit you to the network.

One of the technologies NetWare offers that Windows NT does not is the NetWare Directory Services, which allows employees to access files and services on a corporate network no matter where they are, without searching mysterious lists of electronic addresses and without having to go through multiple requests for passwords and authorization. Novell plans to offer its directory services over the Internet, as well as through NetWare Connect Services, the private alternative to the Internet that it is developing with AT&T.

The long-term vision Novell has, according to its chairman, Robert Frankenberg, is to make possible a network for "connecting people with other people and the information they need, enabling them to act on it anytime, anyplace."[13] In this highly ambitious view, the network will extend beyond office networks of PCs, even beyond the global Internet. It envisions wireless networks linking automobiles, appliances, vending machines, electronic cash registers, factory automation, security systems and other nontraditional computing devices, as well as telephones, fax machines, and copiers. Novell has also developed ways to exchange information over ordinary electric power lines. With this, even standard electrical outlets could become NetWare connections.[14]

Which type(s) of system software do you think you will use? Why?

Whatever its plans, Novell has no illusions about the battle with Microsoft. Said Novell's director of product marketing, "If you underestimate the ocean, or you underestimate Microsoft, either way you are in great danger."[15]

Multimedia Support

Multimedia support programs now are major components of microcomputer operating systems. The two most widely used formats to store and play digitized video and audio are QuickTime, for the Mac, and AVI (audio/video interleave), for the PC. (Of course, you also need the appropriate hardware components: ✔ pp. 1.25, 3.20, 3.33, 4.22)

The Future: Is the Web Changing Everything?

Some future computers might be "network PCs," or "network computers," without their own operating systems and dominated by Web browsers and Java.

Nothing stands still. The major system software developers toil on the versions to come, those works in progress to which they have given fanciful code names such as Memphis and Cyberdog. However, almost without warning, the Internet and the World Wide Web have suddenly dramatically changed the picture.

Today personal computing is still complicated, representing conflicting standards. Could it be different tomorrow as more and more people join the trend toward networked computers and access to the World Wide Web?

As we've seen, there are different hardware and software standards, or "platforms." Developers of applications software, such as word processors or database managers, need to make different versions if they are to run on all the platforms. Networking complicates things even further. "Text, photos, sound files, video, and other kinds of data come in so many different formats that it's nearly impossible to maintain the software needed to use them," points out one writer. "Users must steer their own way through the complex, upgrade-crazy world of computing."[16]

Today microcomputer users who wish to access online data sources must provide not only their own computer, modem, and communications software but also their own operating system software and applications software. *(See Figure 5.10.)*

Could this change in the future?

Today you must take responsibility for making sure your computer system will be compatible with others you have to deal with. (For instance, if a Macintosh user sends you a file to run on your IBM PC, it's up to you to take the trouble to use special software that will translate the file so it will work on your system.) What if the responsibility for ensuring compatibility between different systems were left to online service providers?

In this future model, you would use your Web browser (✔ p. 1.25) to access the World Wide Web and take advantage of applications software anywhere on the network. *(See Figure 5.10, bottom.)* Whatever operating system ran on your computer would not matter. Applications software would become nearly disposable. You would download applications software and pay a few cents or a few dollars for each use. You would store frequently used software on your own computer. You would not need to worry about buying the right software, since it could be provided online whenever you needed to accomplish a task.

Figure 5.10 Online personal computing—today and tomorrow. (*Top*) Today users provide their own operating system software and their own applications software and are usually responsible for installing it on their personal computers. They are also responsible for any upgrades of hardware and software. Data can be input or downloaded from online sources. (*Bottom*) Tomorrow, according to this model, users would not have to worry about operating systems or even about having to acquire and install (and upgrade) their own applications software. Using a universal Web browser, they could download not only data but also different kinds of applications software from an online source.

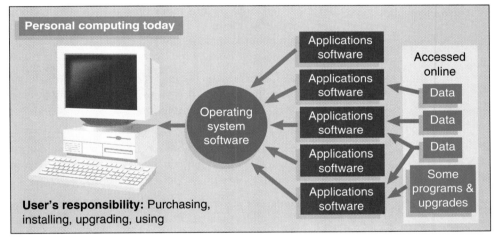

Personal computing today

Applications software / Applications software / Applications software / Applications software / Applications software

Operating system software

Accessed online — Data / Data / Data / Some programs & upgrades

User's responsibility: Purchasing, installing, upgrading, using

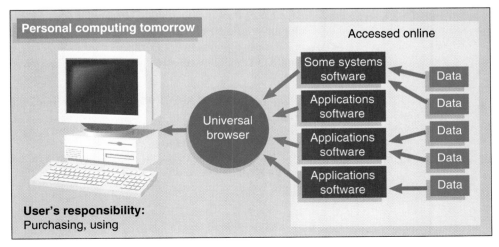

Personal computing tomorrow

Accessed online

Some systems software / Applications software / Applications software / Applications software

Universal browser

Data / Data / Data / Data / Data

User's responsibility: Purchasing, using

Bloatware or the Network Computer?

A new concept has entered the language, that of "bloatware." Bloatware is a colloquial name for software that is so crowded (bloated) with features that it requires a powerful microprocessor and enormous amounts of main memory and hard-disk storage capacity in order to run efficiently. In other words, the software application suffers from "featuritis." Bloatware, of course, fuels the movement toward upgrading, in which users must buy more and more powerful hardware to support the software.

Against this, engineers have proposed the idea of the "network computer" or "hollow PC" (p. 1.26). This view—which not everyone accepts—is that the expensive PCs with muscular microprocessors and operating systems would be replaced by network computers costing perhaps $500 or less. Also known as the *Internet PC,* the *network computer (NC)* would theoretically be a "hollowed out" computer, perhaps without even a hard disk, serving as a mere terminal or entry point to the online universe. The computer thus becomes a peripheral to the Internet, and remote servers would supply most software, processing, and information needs.

This concept of the stripped-down computer is also referred to as a *thin client.* The thin-client strategy is to replace existing desktop personal computers with a new generation of ultracheap computers. Thin clients are being developed by a consortium of, among others, IBM, Sun Microsystems, Netscape Communications, and Apple Computer according to a standard called the *NC Reference Profile.* Microsoft and Intel are sticking with their own versions of network PCs. Indeed, Microsoft has bought WebTV Networks with the plan of turning the WebTV (p. 1.25) into more than a home entertainment gadget by developing NT servers for them.

Some people in business and industry applaud the trend toward thin clients; critics, however, have raised such questions as the following:[17]

- *Would the browser really become the OS?* Would a Web browser become the operating system? Or will existing operating systems expand, as in the past, taking over browser functions?

- *Would communications functions really take over?* Would the communications functions described above become the entire computer, as proponents of the network PC contend? Or would they simply become part of the personal computer's existing repertoire of skills?

- *Would an NC really be easy to use?* Would a network computer really be user friendly? At present, features such as graphical user interfaces require lots of hardware and software.

- *Aren't high-speed connections required?* Even users equipped with the fastest modems would find downloading even small programs (applets) time-consuming. Doesn't the network computer ultimately depend on faster connections than are possible with the standard telephone lines and modems now in place?

- *Would an NC be reliable?* What if the communications channels go down? What if they're busy?

- *Doesn't the NC run counter to computing trends?* Most trends in computing have moved toward personal control and access, as from the mainframe to the microcomputer. Wouldn't a network computer that leaves most functions with online sources run counter to that trend?

What other potential problems can you foresee for the NC? Do you think you would enjoy using a network computer at home or at work? Why or why not?

■ *Would users go for it?* Would computer users really prefer scaled-down generic software that must be retrieved from the Internet each time it is used? Would a pay-per-use system tied to the Internet really be cheaper in the long run?

■ *What about mobile computer users?* According to Microsoft, users of all skill levels have embraced notebook computers with a passion. More than 30% of PCs sold in 1997 were mobile PCs. It would seem that the requirements of the notebook—local hard disk storage, local applications software, and so on—run counter to the direction the NC movement is taking.

■ *Will educational applications be adversely affected?* In the NC environment, educators in individual classrooms would have little choice of computer-based educational materials; they would have to use what was on the school's network.

The Jolt from Java

Thin clients will use new programming languages such as Java to download software code as needed and then execute it. What is Java? The arrival of Java in 1995 is a tale told in three acts:[18]

■ *Act I—the creation of HTML:* Perfected by researcher Tim Berners-Lee in Geneva, *HTML,* for *HyperText Markup Language,* lets people create graphical onscreen documents for the Internet that can easily be linked by words and pictures to other documents. Hypertext, which will be covered in more detail in Chapter 8, has been used to link documents on stand-alone personal computers. What is noteworthy about HTML is that it links documents wherever they are stored, including anywhere on the sprawling universe of the Internet.

Berners-Lee distributed HTML standards around the world via the Internet for free, and soon other researchers were creating and linking HTML documents. As one account explains, "Quickly it became apparent that HTML documents were an ideal medium for publishing and annotating scientific papers, research materials, reference works, and the like. These rich HTML documents collectively became a distinct domain within the Internet, a realm we now call the World Wide Web."[19]

■ *Act II—the appearance of Web browsers:* Very soon millions of HTML documents had appeared on the Web, but there was no easy way to locate them and view them. In 1993, Marc Andreeson and colleagues at the University of Illinois's National Center for Supercomputer Applications created the first Web browser software called *Mosaic.* The first version was for Sun workstations; later versions were developed for Macintoshes and Windows PCs. Andreeson went on to join with James Clark in founding *Netscape,* which makes a popular Web browser called *Netscape Navigator* (the newest version is called *Communicator*).

As both the number of Web sites and the number of viewers using browsers increased, people began to wish that Web pages would do more than just sit there. This was the problem for which Java was one solution.

■ *Act III—enter Java:* Java was written by ace programmer James Gosling for Sun Microsystems as part of an unsuccessful effort to develop equipment for interactive television. Java is a programming language that enables a Web page to deliver, along with the visual content, tiny application programs called *applets* (mini-applications) that, when downloaded, can make Web pages interactive.

"Applets," says one report, "can create dancing advertising, self-updating scoreboards, moving stock ticker marquees, even animated cartoons. . . . Think of Java applets as just-in-time software that you can simply throw away after each use. If you want to look at the same Web page again, the Internet will furnish a fresh copy of both the information and the applet."[20]

The significance of Java was that Sun wrote versions of it to run on all the major computers and then gave them away, so that anyone wanting to use applets to create "active content" (such as animated weather maps) on Web sites could use them. The result was a whole new style of computing that is built around the Internet.

Microsoft, accustomed to dominating the stand-alone computer market, found itself a bit behind in the turn toward the Internet era but quickly modified its business strategy. Among other developments, it included Java technology with its own Web browser, Internet Explorer.

Interestingly, when it agreed to make Java work with Windows 95 and Windows NT, Microsoft also agreed to give the rejiggered programming code back to Sun Microsystems, after which either company could license Java programming code to third parties. "This means that Sun will always own Microsoft's latest version of Java, and vice versa," said one report, "so the companies won't end up developing different, noncompatible forms of the language."[21]

Onward: Toward Compatibility

Future products will strive for compatibility and simplicity.

The push is on to make computing and communications products compatible. Customers are demanding that computer companies work together to create system software that is easy to use and very powerful. As technological capabilities increase, so will the demand for simplicity.

Whether compatibility and simplicity will be provided by a proprietary system like Windows 95 or Windows NT or by "open standards" of some sort of Web software, perhaps in the competition the best products will triumph.

Or perhaps the Japanese have the right idea with their TRON OS. It is being researched and developed as a common interface for all platforms and applications—from microwave oven, smart car, intelligent house to microcomputers and the largest supercomputer.[22]

WHAT IT IS
WHAT IT DOES   WHY IT IS IMPORTANT

antivirus software (LO 1, p. 5.7)
Software utility that scans hard disks, diskettes, and memory to detect viruses; some antivirus utilities also destroy viruses.

Computer users must find out what kind of antivirus software to install on their systems in order to protect them against damage and shutdown.

applications software (LO 1, p. 5.3)
Software that performs useful tasks for the user.

Applications software such as word processing, spreadsheet, database manager, graphics, and communications packages are commonly used tools for increasing people's productivity.

backup utility (LO 1, p. 5.7)   Operating system utility that makes a duplicate copy of contents of a disk.

Backing up is an essential function; users should back up all their work so that they don't lose it if original disks are destroyed.

BIOS (basic input/output system)
(LO 1, p. 5.6)   Part of the operating system that manages the essential peripherals such as the keyboard, screen, disk drives, and parallel and serial ports. It also manages some internal services such as time and date.

This is the part of the operating system that tests the computer upon booting via an autostart program.

communications protocols (LO 1, p. 5.6)   Set of rules, formats, and functions for sending data across a network.

Communications protocols handle the details for data transmission.

data compression utility (LO 1, p. 5.8)
Software utility that removes redundant elements, gaps, and unnecessary data from computer files so less space is required to store and transmit data.

Many of today's files, with graphics, sound, and video, require huge amounts of storage space; data compression utilities allow users to reduce the space they take up.

data management (LO 1, p. 5.6)   Part of system software that keeps track of the data in secondary storage.

Applications software doesn't know where the data is stored or how to get it. Data management programs take care of this.

data recovery utility (LO 1, p. 5.7)
System software utility used to restore data that has been physically damaged or corrupted on disk or tape.

Disks and tapes can be damaged by viruses, bad software, hardware failure, and power fluctuations that occur while data is being written/recorded.

defraggers (LO 1, p. 5.11)   Utility programs that rearrange the data on a disk so that the data units of each file are repositioned together in one location on the disk.

Fragmentation causes the computer to run slower than if all the data in a file were stored together in one location. Defraggers help fix this problem.

diagnostic program (LO 1, p. 5.7)   Program that compiles technical information about computer hardware, including peripherals, that can be used to diagnose almost any technical problem.

Most diagnostic programs make a record of the computer's normal operational settings. Then, when a problem occurs, a new report is produced, and the problem can usually be resolved by finding discrepancies between the two reports.

DOS (disk operating system) (LO 4, p. 5.15) Older command-driven microcomputer operating system that runs primarily on IBM and IBM-compatible microcomputers.

DOS used to be the most common microcomputer operating system. It is still used on many microcomputers, although it is being replaced by OSs with graphical user interfaces.

drivers (LO 1, p. 5.7)   Software programs that support specific peripheral devices.

Drivers are needed so that the computer's operating system can recognize and run peripheral hardware.

graphical user interface (LO 2, p. 5.14)   User interface that uses images to represent options. Some of these images take the form of icons, small pictorial figures that represent tasks, functions, and programs.

GUIs are easier to use than command-driven interfaces and menu-driven interfaces; they permit liberal use of the mouse as a pointing device to move the cursor to a particular icon or place on the display screen. The function represented by the icon can be activated by pressing ("clicking") buttons on the mouse.

language translator (LO 1, p. 5.11)   System software that translates a program written in a computer language (such as C++) into the language (machine language) that the computer can understand.

Without language translators, software programmers would have to write all programs in machine language (0s and 1s), which is difficult to work with.

Macintosh operating system (Mac OS) (LO 4, p. 5.22)   Systems software for the Macintosh.

Although Macs are not as common as PCs, many people believe they are easier to use. Macs are often used for graphics and desktop publishing.

messaging protocols (LO 1, p. 5.6)   Set of rules, formats, and functions for sending, storing, and forwarding e-mail in a network.

Messaging protocols handle details for e-mail transmission.

multiprocessing (LO 1, p. 5.12)   Operating system software feature that allows two or more computers or processors linked together to perform work simultaneously. (Whereas *concurrently* means "at almost the same time," *simultaneously* means "at precisely the same time.")

Multiprocessing is faster than multitasking and time-sharing. Microcomputer users may encounter an example of multiprocessing in specialized microprocessors called *coprocessors,* used for such specialized tasks as display screen graphics and high-speed mathematical calculations.

multiprogramming (LO 1, p. 5.12)   Operating system software feature that allows the execution of two or more programs on a *multiuser* system. Program execution occurs concurrently, not simultaneously.

See *multitasking.*

multitasking (LO 1, p. 5.11)   Operating system software feature that allows the execution of two or more programs concurrently on a single-user system.

Allows the computer to rapidly switch back and forth among different tasks. The user is generally unaware of the switching process and is able to use more than one application program at the same time.

network operating system (NOS) (LO 1, p. 5.23) Component of system software that manages traffic and security between client workstations and file servers in a network.

The network operating system is the traffic manager.

OLE (object linking and embedding) (LO 4, p. 5.20)   Program that allows one application to access the services and data of another.

Microsoft developed OLE to support documents that contain or reference other documents. OLE has now evolved into a basic component of Microsoft's Windows 95 and Windows NT operating systems and has emerged as an industry standard.

operating system (OS) (LO 1, p. 5.5)   Principal piece of system software in any computer system; consists of the master set of programs that manage the basic operations of the computer. The operating system remains in main memory until the computer is turned off.

These programs act as an interface between the user and the computer, handling such matters as running and storing programs and storing and processing data. The operating system allows users to concentrate on their own tasks or applications rather than on the complexities of managing the computer.

Operating System/2 (OS/2) (LO 4, p. 5.20)   Microcomputer operating system designed to run on many recent IBM and IBM-compatible microcomputers.

Like Windows 95, OS/2 does not require DOS to run underneath it, and it has an intetgrated graphical user interface. OS/2 can also run most DOS, Windows, and OS/2 applications programs simultaneously, which means users don't have to throw out their old applications to take advantage of new features. OS/2 is not used on as many microcomputers as Windows, for which many more applications programs have been written.

platform (LO 3, p. 5.15)   Refers to the particular hardware or software standard on which a computer system is based—for example, IBM platform or Macintosh platform.

Users need to be aware that, without special arrangements or software, different platforms are not compatible.

supervisor (LO 1, p. 5.5)   Central component of the operating system. It resides in main memory while the computer is on and directs other programs to perform tasks to support applications programs.

Were it not for the supervisor program, users would have to stop one task—for example, writing—and wait for another task to be completed—for example, printing a document.

system software (LO 1, p. 5.3)   Programs that start up the computer and function as the principal coordinator of all hardware components and applications software programs.

Applications software cannot run without system software.

time-sharing (LO 1, p. 5.12)   Operations system software feature whereby a single large computer processes the tasks of several users at different stations in round-robin fashion.

Time-sharing and multitasking differ slightly. With time-sharing, the computer spends a fixed amount of time with each program before going on to the next one. With multitasking the computer works on each program until it encounters a logical stopping point, as in waiting for more data to be input.

TP monitor (LO 1, p. 5.6)   Stands for *teleprocessing* or *transaction processing monitor;* system software component that distributes input from multiple terminals to the appropriate applications being run on the system.

Input management is handled with the TP monitor.

Unix (LO 4, p. 5.21)   Operating system originally developed by AT&T for multiple users, with built-in networking capability, the ability to run multiple tasks at one time, and versions that can run on all kinds of computers.

Because it can run with relatively simple modifications on many different kinds of computers, from micros to minis to mainframes, Unix is said to be a "portable" operating system. The main users of Unix are large corporations and banks that use the software for everything from designing airplane parts to currency trading. Unix was also used to build the Internet.

user interface (LO 2, p. 5.13)   Part of the operating system (or operating environment) that allows users to communicate, or interact, with it. There are three types of user interfaces: command-driven, menu-driven, and graphical. The last type is easiest to use.

User interfaces are necessary for users to be able to use a computer system.

utility programs (LO 1, p. 5.7)   System software generally used to support, enhance, or expand existing programs in a computer system.

Many operating systems have common utility programs built in. Other external utility programs are available separately. Examples of utilities are system diagnostics, data recovery, backup, virus protection, data compression/decompression, memory management, and defragmentation.

windows (LO 2, p. 5.14)   Feature of graphical user interfaces; causes the display screen to divide into sections. Each window is dedicated to a specific purpose.

Using the window feature, an operating system (or operating environment) can display several windows on a computer screen, each showing a different application program, such as word processing, spreadsheets, and graphics.

Windows 3.x (LO 4, p. 5.17)   Operating environment from Microsoft that places a graphical user interface shell around the MS-DOS/PC-DOS operating system.

The Windows operating environment made DOS easier to use; far more applications have been written for Windows than for DOS alone.

Windows 95 (LO 4, p. 5.17)   Successor to Windows 3.x; true operating system, with an integrated GUI, for IBM-style PCs.

Windows has become the most common system software used on microcomputers.

Windows NT (New Technology) (LO 4, p. 5.19) Operating system intended to support large networks of computers and high-end workstations.

Microsoft may eventually merge Windows 95 and Windows NT into one powerful operating system for microcomputers.

workgroup (LO 4, p. 5.19)   Situations in which LANs (local area networks) are set up to allow users to share files, databases, and applications.

Multiuser platforms support workgroup computing.

1. _Application_ _software_ is a collection of related programs designed to perform a specific task for the user.

2. A(n) _language_ _translator_ is software that translates a program written by a programmer into machine language.

3. _Communication_ protocols comprise the set of rules for sending data across a network.

4. Diagnostic programs compile technical information about your computer _hardware_, including peripherals.

5. JPEG and MPEG are two types of _compression_ _software_.

SHORT-ANSWER QUESTIONS

1. Why does a computer need system software?
2. What does the term *booting* mean?
3. What is the difference between multitasking and time-sharing?
4. What is a GUI?
5. What does the term *platform* refer to?

MULTIPLE-CHOICE QUESTIONS

1. Which of the following do you need in order to use a printer?
    a. messaging protocol
    b. TP monitor
    c. driver
    d. DBMS
    e. all the above

2. Which of the following would you use to restore data that has been physically damaged?
    a. diagnostic program
    b. data recovery utility
    c. backup utility
    d. antivirus software
    e. data compression utility

3. Which of the following allows Microsoft Windows users to easily share data between applications?
    a. GUI
    b. OLE
    c. OS/2
    d. NOS
    e. DOS

4. Which of the following provides a computer network with multiuser, multitasking capabilities?
   a. GUI
   b. OLE
   c. OS/2
   d. NOS
   e. DOS

5. Which of the following refers to the execution of two or more programs on a multiuser operating system?
   a. multiprocessing
   b. multitasking
   c. time-sharing
   d. multiprogramming
   e. all the above

TRUE/FALSE QUESTIONS

1. The operating system resides in RAM at all times when your computer is on. (true/false)

2. Applications software starts up the computer and functions as the principal coordinator of all hardware components. (true/false)

3. DOS is one of the oldest microcomputer operating systems. (true/false)

4. Multimedia support programs are now major components of microcomputer operating systems. (true/false)

5. A program that can defragment a disk is referred to as a *defragger*. (true/false)

KNOWLEDGE IN ACTION

1. If you have been using a particular microcomputer for two years and are planning to upgrade the version of system software you are using, what issues must you consider before you go ahead and buy the new version?

2. If your computer runs Windows 95, choose Settings, Control Panel from the Start menu to obtain information about your computer system. What are the current settings of your computer display (monitor)? Keyboard? Modem? Mouse? What other settings can you view in the Control Panel window?

3. Do you think the network computer will become a standard fixture in homes and businesses in the near future? If so, when? Research your answer on the Web and/or using current computer magazines.

4. What system software is used on the computer at your school, work, or home? Why was this software selected? Do you find this software easy to use? Would you prefer another type of system software or version upgrade? If so, why?

5. Locate someone who is using DOS and Windows 3.1. Why hasn't this person switched to Windows 95? Is the reason related to their existing hardware? Existing software? Other?

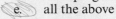

APPLICATIONS SOFTWARE

The User's Tools

6

PREVIEW

When you have completed this chapter, you will be able to:

1. Explain what applications software is and list its basic categories

2. Describe some features common to all types of applica-tions software

3. Describe the common software productivity tools

4. Describe some software specialty tools

5. Explain what software versions and releases are, and what software installation is

6. Describe the seriousness of software copyright violation

The "dirty little secret of computer buying," as one report puts it, is this: Getting the PC box, the hardware, is only the beginning. "Indeed, you may have agonized over the hardware for months," the writer states, "but it's your choice of software that will really determine the utility—or uselessness—of your new PC."[1]

There are thousands of programs to choose from—games alone number more than 2500—and some of them can make your life far easier and more productive than you might imagine. But others, unfortunately, don't even begin to live up to the magic promotional phrase "ease of use."

Even software programs advertised as "user friendly" are too complex for many people. Because of consumer frustration about software, "It's no surprise that computers are stuck at a relatively small percent of households," observes Jakob Nielsen, a distinguished fellow at SunSoft, a division of Sun Microsystems Inc.[2] That will no doubt change. Hardware and software manufacturers know that they will achieve growth and profits only by making their products as no-fuss as possible.

For you, however, there's no point in waiting. By setting your mind to learning software, you can begin to extend the range of your productivity. And when the software itself becomes better, so will you.

Applications Software Tools

There are five basic categories of applications software. Two of the main ones are productivity tools and business specialty tools. Many applications software packages share common features. To run, applications software packages must be compatible with the user's platform.

Computer software has become a multibillion-dollar industry. More than a thousand companies have entered the applications software industry, and they have developed a wide variety of products. As a result, the number of sources of applications software has grown. Applications software can be acquired directly from a software manufacturer or from the growing number of businesses that specialize in the sale and support of microcomputer hardware and software. Most independent and computer chain stores devote a substantial amount of shelf space to applications software programs; some businesses specialize in selling only software.

If you can't find off-the-shelf software to meet your needs, you can develop your own. If you don't know how to do it yourself, you can have the computer professionals within your own organization develop the software, or you can hire outside consultants to do it. Unfortunately, hiring a professional to write software for you can easily cost ten times more than off-the-shelf software.

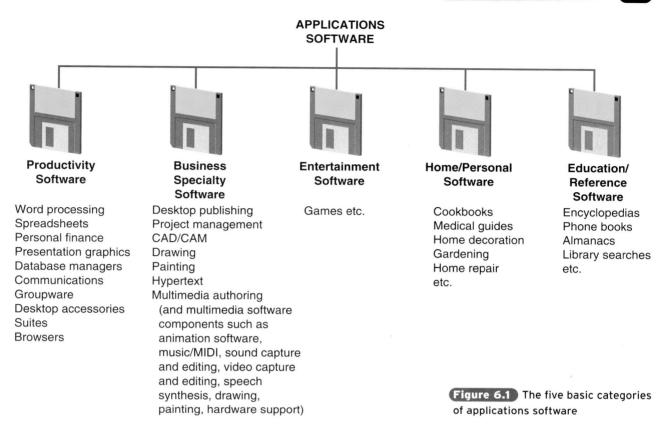

APPLICATIONS SOFTWARE

Productivity Software	Business Specialty Software	Entertainment Software	Home/Personal Software	Education/ Reference Software
Word processing	Desktop publishing	Games etc.	Cookbooks	Encyclopedias
Spreadsheets	Project management		Medical guides	Phone books
Personal finance	CAD/CAM		Home decoration	Almanacs
Presentation graphics	Drawing		Gardening	Library searches
Database managers	Painting		Home repair	etc.
Communications	Hypertext		etc.	
Groupware	Multimedia authoring			
Desktop accessories	(and multimedia software			
Suites	components such as			
Browsers	animation software,			
	music/MIDI, sound capture			
	and editing, video capture			
	and editing, speech			
	synthesis, drawing,			
	painting, hardware support)			

Figure 6.1 The five basic categories of applications software

Basically, there are five categories of applications software. *(See Figure 6.1.)* Most of the common applications software packages used today are *productivity tools.* Whatever your occupation, you will probably find it also has *specialty* software tools available to it. This is true whether your career is dairy farmer, building contractor, police officer, dance choreographer, or chef.

Many people will buy an applications software program just because it was recommended by a friend. They do not bother to evaluate whether the program offers all the features and processing capabilities necessary to meet their needs. It's much easier in the short run to simply take the friend's recommendation, but in the long run a lot of extra time and money may be spent. Knowing what software is available—and how to evaluate it—is vital to satisfy processing requirements.

■ *Productivity tools:* These are the programs found in most offices and probably all campuses. Their purpose is simply to make users more productive at performing general tasks. This category includes word processors, spreadsheets, financial management software, presentation graphics, database managers, communications programs, groupware, desktop accessories, software suites, and Web browsers.

It may still be possible to work in an office in some countries today without knowing any of these programs. However, that won't be the case in the 21st century.

■ *Specialty tools:* Knowledge of specialized programs is a necessity in some occupations and businesses (as desktop publishing is for people in publications work). You should have at least a nodding acquaintance with them because they are general enough to be used in many vocations and professions. Many specialty software tools exist today. Examples of some tools that fall into this category include desktop publishing, project management,

What is the difference
between software
productivity tools and
specialty tools?

computer-aided design/manufacturing software (CAD/CAM), drawing and painting programs, Web site creation, digital video editing, and multimedia authoring software.

Don't worry if you don't know all these terms; you will by the end of the chapter. However, before we discuss the different types of productivity and specialty software tools, we need to go over some of the features common to most kinds of applications software packages.

Common Features of Applications Software

Many applications software packages share similar features and functions, many of which are based on the system software's graphical user interface.

Although applications software packages differ in their use of specific commands and functions, most of them have some features in common:

- cursors
- scrolling
- windows
- menus
- Help screens and wizards
- icons
- buttons

- toolbars
- dialog boxes
- default values
- macros
- OLE
- clipboard
- tutorials and documentation

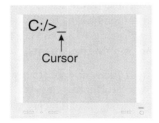

C:/>_
↑
Cursor

Windows

- *Cursor:* The **cursor,** also called the *insertion point,* is the movable symbol on the display screen that shows you where you may enter data next. You can move the cursor around using either the keyboard's directional arrow keys (✔ p. 3.5) or a mouse.

- *Scrolling:* **Scrolling** is the activity of moving quickly upward or downward through the text or other screen display. Normally a computer screen contains 20–22 lines of text. Using the directional arrow keys or a mouse, you can move ("scroll") through the display screen and into the text above and below. (Note: Sometimes what you are working on is too wide to fit on the screen. The term *panning* is used to describe the process of scrolling to the right and left.)

- *Windows:* As we mentioned in the last chapter in the section on GUIs (✔ p. 5.14), a **window** is a rectangular section of the display screen with a title bar on top. Each window may show a different display, such as a word processing document in one and a spreadsheet in another.

Scrolling

Menu bar

Icons

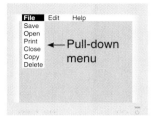

■ *Menu bar:* A **menu bar** is a row of menu options displayed across the top or the bottom of the screen. (Recall that a menu is a list of command options, or choices, ✔ p. 5.14.)

■ *Pull-down menu:* A **pull-down menu** is a list of command options, or choices, that is "pulled down" out of the menu bar. Pull-down menus can be opened by keystroke commands or by "clicking" (pressing) the mouse button while pointing to the title in the menu bar and then dragging the mouse pointer down. Some menus "pop up" from the menu bar and so are called **pop-up menus.**

File Edit Help
Save
Open
Print   ←—Pull-down
Close   menu
Copy
Delete

■ *Help menu and screens:* A **Help menu** offers a choice of *Help screens,* specific displayed explanations of how to perform various tasks, such as printing out a document. Having a set of Help screens is like having a built-in electronic instruction manual. Help features also include searchable topic indexes and online glossaries.

Help may also be available in the form of a **wizard.** In this case, the applications program leads you through a series of questions to determine exactly what you need help with. Then it leads you through the steps to accomplish your objective. The wizard appears as an icon or cartoon character you click on.

■ *Icons:* An **icon** is an on-screen pictorial representation of an object (file, program, disk, and so on) used in graphical user interfaces.

■ *Buttons:* A **button** is a simulated button on screen that is "pushed" by positioning the cursor on top of it and clicking the mouse. Pushing a button can execute a command. Buttons are usually identified by a small graphic.

\Button on Toolbar

■ *Toolbars:* A **toolbar** is a row of on-screen buttons, usually appearing immediately below the menu bar, used to activate a variety of functions of the applications program. Toolbars can often be customized and moved around on the screen.

■ *Dialog box:* A **dialog box** is a box that appears on the screen. It is used to collect information from the user and to display helpful messages.

■ *Default values:* **Default values** are the standard settings used by the computer when the user does not specifiy an alternative. For example, unless you specify particular margin widths in your page setup, the word processing program will use the manufacturer's default values.

■ *Macros:* A **macro** is a feature that allows you to use a single keystroke, command, or toolbar button to automatically issue a predetermined series of commands. Thus, you can consolidate several keystrokes or menu selections into only one or two keystrokes. Although many people have no need for macros, others who have been continually repeating complicated patterns of keystrokes find them quite useful.

■ *OLE:* Many software applications have the ability to integrate applications using **OLE** (object linking and embedding, ✔ p. 5.20). This feature enables you to embed an object created using one application (such as graphics) into another application (such as word processing). Changes made to the embedded object affect only the document that contains it. Objects can also be linked. In this case, changes made to the object are automatically made in

Dialog box

OLE

all the linked documents that contain it. Thus OLE facilitates the sharing and manipulating of information. An object may be a document, worksheet, chart, picture, or even a sound recording.

■ *Clipboard:* Many applications software programs allow you to copy an item from one document and then paste it into another document or application—or copy an item and place the copy in another part of the same document. The **clipboard** is the area where the copy is held before it is pasted. (The clipboard can hold only one item at a time.)

■ *Tutorials and documentation:* How are you going to learn a given software program? Most commercial packages come with tutorials.

A **tutorial** is an instruction book or program that takes you through a prescribed series of steps to help you learn the product.

Tutorials must be contrasted with documentation. **Documentation** is a user manual or reference manual that is a narrative and graphical description of a program. Documentation may be instructional, but features and functions are usually grouped by category for reference purposes. For example, in word processing documentation, all cut-and-paste features are grouped together so you can easily look them up if you have forgotten how to perform them. Documentation may come in booklet form or on diskette or CD-ROM; it may also be available online from the manufacturer.

> List and define six common features of applications software.

Compatibility Issues: What Goes with What?

As we mentioned in the last chapter (✔ p. 5.11), all system software and applications software must be turned into machine language for execution by the computer. Different computer families use different machine language coding. Thus each applications software program must be written to "talk" to the system software and its language translator. Applications software written, for example, for an IBM PC will not—without conversion—run on a Macintosh. This is why it's important for users to determine their applications software needs first—determine what they want the computer to do for them. Then select compatible hardware and system software. If you are going to be in a situation in which you will need to transfer files among different platforms, you will need to consider conversion options.

Some experts predict that sometime soon, compatibility will no longer be an issue, as the computer industry works toward universal standards and compatibility. However, this time has not yet come.

Now that we have taken a look at some of the features shared by many different types of applications software packages, let's briefly examine the most common types of productivity software tools. The next section will cover some common specialty tools.

Productivity Software Tools

Productivity software refers to software packages that are designed to help users accomplish general goals.

Let's get right to the point: What do most people use software for? The answer hasn't changed in a decade. If you don't count games, by far the most popular applications are (1) *word processing* and (2) *spreadsheets,* according to the Software Publishers Association. Moreover, studies show, most people use only a few basic features of these programs, and they use them for rather simple tasks. For example, 70% of all documents produced with word processing software are one-page letters, memos, or simple reports. And 70% of the time people use spreadsheets simply to add up numbers.[3]

This is important information. If you are this type of user, you may have no more need for fancy software and hardware than an ordinary commuter has for an expensive Italian race car. On the other hand, you may be in a profession in which you need to become a "power user," learning all the software features available in order to keep ahead in your career. Moreover, in this age of multimedia, you may wish to do far more than current software and hardware allow, in which case you need to be continually learning what computing and communications can do for you.

Let us now look at the various types and uses of productivity software for:

- Word processing
- Spreadsheet
- Personal finance
- Presentation graphics
- Database management
- Communications
- Group collaboration
- Desktop and personal information management
- Integrated applications
- Web browsing

Word Processing Software

One of the first typewriter users was Mark Twain. However, the typewriter, that long-lived machine, has gone to its reward. Indeed, if you have a manual typewriter, it is becoming as difficult to get it repaired as it is to find a blacksmith. What, then, is the alternative?—word processing.

Word processing software allows you to use computers to create, edit, store, and print documents. It enables the user to easily insert, delete, and move words, sentences, and paragraphs—without ever using an eraser. Word processing programs also offer a number of features for "dressing up" documents with variable margins, type sizes, and styles. The user can do all these manipulations on screen, in "wysiwyg" fashion, before printing out hardcopy. (*Wysiwyg* stands for "what you see is what you get," meaning that the screen displays documents exactly as they will look when printed.)

Word processing software also offers additional features, such as spelling checkers, as we shall describe.

Creating Documents

Creating a document means entering text, using the keyboard. As you type, *word wrap* automatically continues text on the next line when you reach the right margin. That is, the text "wraps around" to the next line.

Editing Documents

Editing is the act of making alterations in the content of your document. Some features of editing are *insert and delete; undelete; search and replace; cut, copy, and paste; spelling checker; grammar checker;* and *thesaurus.*

■ *Insert and delete: Inserting* is the act of adding to the document. You simply place the cursor wherever you want to add text and start typing; the existing characters will move aside.

　　Deleting is the act of removing text, usually using the Delete or Backspace keys.

　　The *Undelete,* or *Undo,* command allows you to change your mind and restore text that you have deleted. Some word processing programs offer as many as 100 layers of "undo," allowing users who delete several blocks of text, but then change their minds, to reinstate one or more of the blocks.

■ *Search and replace:* The *Search* command, or *Find* command, allows you to find any word, phrase, or number that exists in your document. The *Replace* command allows you to automatically replace it with something else.

■ *Cut, copy,* and *paste:* Typewriter users were accustomed to using scissors and glue to "cut and paste" to move a paragraph or block of text from one place to another in a manuscript. With word processing, you can easily select the portion of text you want to move and then use the *Cut* or *Copy* command to remove it or copy it. Then use the *Paste* command to insert it somewhere else.

■ *Spelling checker, grammar checker, thesaurus:* Many writers automatically run their completed documents through a *spelling checker,* which tests for incorrectly spelled words. (Some programs have an "Auto Correct" function that automatically fixes such common mistakes as transposed letters—"teh" instead of "the.") Another feature is a *grammar checker,* which flags poor grammar, wordiness, incomplete sentences, awkward phrases, and excessive use of the passive voice.

　　If you find yourself stuck for the right word while you're writing, you can call up an on-screen thesaurus, which will present you with the appropriate word or alternative words.

Formatting Documents

Formatting means determining the appearance of a document. *(See Figure 6.2.)* There are many choices here.

Figure 6.2 Word 97 screen, format pull-down menu. This menu offers many options for changing the formatting of a document. Any menu item with an arrowhead (▶) offers even more options.

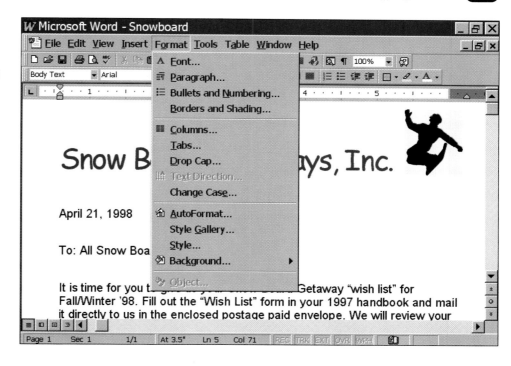

- *Type:* You can decide what *typeface* and *type size* you wish to use. A particular typeface and size is called a **font.** All variations of a particular typeface are called a *font family. (See Figure 6.3.)* You can specify whether the font should be <u>underlined,</u> *italic,* or **boldface.**

- *Spacing and columns:* You can choose whether you want the lines to be *single-spaced* or *double-spaced* (or something else). You can specify whether you want text to be *one column* (like this page), *two columns* (like many magazines and books), or *several columns* (like newspapers).

- *Margins and justification:* You can indicate the dimensions of the page borders, or *margins*—left, right, top, and bottom—around the text.

  You can specify whether the text should be *justified* or not. *Justify* means to align text evenly between left and right margins, as, for example, is done with most newspaper columns. *Ragged right* means to not align the text evenly on the right, as is done with many business letters (text is left-justified). *Ragged left* means the left side of the text is not evenly aligned (text is right-justified), and *centered* means that each line of text is centered on the page.

- *Pages, headers, footers:* You can indicate *page numbers* and *headers* or *footers.* A *header* is common text (such as a date or document name) that is printed at the top of every page. A *footer* is the same thing printed at the bottom of every page.

- *Other formatting:* You can specify *borders* or other decorative lines, *shading, tables,* and *footnotes.* You can even pull in ("import") *graphics* or drawings from files in other software programs.

It's worth noting that word processing programs (and indeed most forms of applications software) come from the manufacturer with default settings (✔ p. 6.5). Thus, for example, most word processing programs will automatically prepare a document single-spaced, justified, with 1-inch right and left margins unless you alter these default settings, which is easy to do.

This text is right- and left-justified. This style is often used in newspaper columns.

This text is left-justified and ragged right. This style is often used in business letters.

This text is right-justified and ragged left. This style is often used in ads and brochures.

This text is centered. This style is often used in headings.

Examples of fonts:

ABCDEFGHIJK   10-point Times Roman regular

ABCDEFGHIJK   14-point Ariel Bold

ABCDEFGHIJK   24-point Trump Medieval Italic

Type glossary:

Font	A character set in a particular size and type design (typeface)
Point	Unit of measurement of type size; 12 points equal 1 pica.
Pica	Unit of measurement of page elements, such as margin width; 6 picas equal 1 inch.
Leading	Unit of measurement between lines of type; for example, space (10 + 2 = 12) between lines. 10/12 lines would be closer together than 10/14 lines.

Type basics:

Many characteristics give fonts different looks—from the ornate to the plain, text-book style. Some fonts are more readable and better for reports and documents. Some are unique or formal and may be better for a logo or invitation.

But how do font designers give their fonts different looks? One of the most common ways to change a font is to add a *serif* or leave the font *sans serif* (without a serif). This serif is a little "foot" or "hat" added to the letters. Designers also can adjust some of the type characteristics, maybe making a loop a little wider, raising an ascender, or giving a jaunty lift to the ear on a *g*. They can change the *pitch* of letters, which is how much horizontal room they get. The pitch may be *fixed* or **monospaced**, meaning each letter gets the same amount of room, or it may be *proportional*, so that the spacing depends on the width of the particular character. Finally, they can give letters or numerals a different weight, which is the thickness, or a different style, such as straight up or italics.

To give you an idea of what designers have to play around with, here we've assembled a chart illustrating the names of all the parts of a typeface design.

f i tness
Monospaced type

fitness
Proportional type

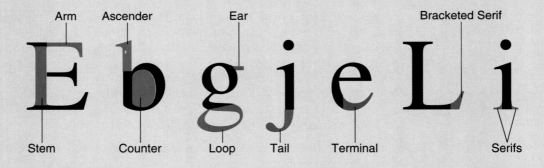

Arm   Ascender   Ear   Bracketed Serif

EbgjeLi

Stem   Counter   Loop   Tail   Terminal   Serifs

Figure 6.3 Font fundamentals

Printing Documents

Most word processing software gives you several options for printing. For example, you can print several copies of a document. You can print *individual pages* or a *range of pages.* You can even *preview* a document before printing it out. *Previewing* (print previewing) means viewing a document on screen to see what it will look like in printed form before it's printed. Whole pages are displayed in reduced size.

Some word processors even come close to desktop-publishing programs in enabling you to prepare professional-looking documents with different type faces

What do you plan to use word processing software for? Why?

and sizes. However, as we shall see later, desktop-publishing programs do far more.

Today, popular word processing programs are Microsoft Word for the PC, Word for the Mac, Corel WordPerfect for the PC, and WordPerfect for the Mac.

Spreadsheet Software

What is a spreadsheet? Traditionally, it was simply a grid of rows and columns, printed on special green paper, that was used by accountants and others to produce financial projections and reports. A person making up a spreadsheet often spent long days and weekends at the office penciling tiny numbers into countless tiny rectangles. When one figure changed, all the rest of the numbers on the spreadsheet had to be recomputed—and ultimately there might be wastebaskets full of jettisoned worksheets.

In the late 1970s, Daniel Bricklin was a student at the Harvard Business School. One day he was staring at columns of numbers on a blackboard when he got the idea for computerizing the spreadsheet. The result, VisiCalc, was the first of the electronic spreadsheets. An electronic **spreadsheet** allows users to create tables and financial schedules by entering data into rows and columns arranged as a grid on a display screen. *(See Figure 6.4.)*

The electronic spreadsheet quickly became the most popular small-business program. It has been held directly responsible for making the microcomputer a widely used business tool. Unfortunately for Bricklin, VisiCalc was shortly surpassed by Lotus 1-2-3, a sophisticated program that combines the spreadsheet with database and graphics programs. Today the principal spreadsheet programs are Microsoft Excel, Lotus 1-2-3, and Quattro Pro.

Principal Features

Spreadsheets include the following features:

■ *Columns, rows, and labels: Column headings* appear across the top ("A" is the name of the first column, "B" the second, and so on). *Row headings* appear

Figure 6.4 The Lotus 1-2-3 for Windows electronic spreadsheet is a computerized version of the traditional paper spreadsheet. The beauty of the electronic version, however, is its *recalculation* feature: when a number is changed, all related numbers on the spreadsheet are automatically recomputed.

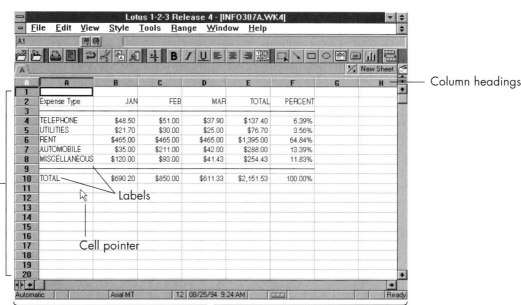

down the left side ("1" is the name of the first row, "2" the second, and so forth). Columns and rows relate to format. Labels, in contrast, relate to the contents of the spreadsheet. Labels are any descriptive text, such as APRIL, PHONE, or GROSS SALES.

■ *Cells, cell addresses, values, and spreadsheet cursor:* The place where a row and a column intersect is called a **cell,** and its position is called a **cell address.** For example, "A1" is the cell address for the top left cell, where column A and row 1 intersect. A number, date, or formula entered in a cell is called a *value.* The values are the actual numbers used in the spreadsheet—dollars, percentages, grade points, temperatures, or whatever. A *cell pointer,* or *spreadsheet cursor,* indicates where data is to be entered. The cell pointer can be moved around like a cursor in a word processing program.

■ *Formulas, functions, and recalculation:* Now we come to the reason the electronic spreadsheet has taken offices by storm. **Formulas** are instructions for calculations. For example, a formula might be SUM(A5:A15), meaning "Sum (add) all the numbers in the cells with cell addresses A5 through A15."

Functions are built-in formulas that perform common calculations. For instance, a function might average a range of numbers or round off a number to two decimal places. In the previous example, SUM is a built-in function.

After the values have been plugged into the spreadsheet, the formulas and functions can be used to calculate outcomes. What is revolutionary, however, is the way the spreadsheet can easily do recalculation. *Recalculation* is the process of recomputing values *automatically,* either as an ongoing process as data is being entered or afterward, with the press of a key. With this simple feature, the hours of mind-numbing work required to manually rework paper spreadsheets became a thing of the past.

The recalculation feature has opened up whole new possibilities for decision making. As a user, you can create a plan, put in formulas and numbers, and then ask yourself "What would happen if we change that detail?"—and immediately see the effect on the bottom line. This is called the *what if* function. You could use this if you're considering buying a new car. Any number of things can be varied: total price ($10,000? $15,000?), down payment ($2000? $3000?), interest rate on the car loan (7%? 8%?), or number of months to pay (36? 48?). You can keep changing the "what if" possibilities until you arrive at a monthly payment figure that you're comfortable with.

How might you use a spreadsheet in your chosen profession? In your personal life?

Spreadsheets can be linked with other spreadsheets. The feature of *dynamic linking* allows data in one spreadsheet to be linked to and automatically update data in another spreadsheet. Thus, the amount of data being manipulated can be enormous. For instance, Frank Austin, a computer consultant who developed a program for rehabilitating the sewers of Houston, says his average worksheets are a demanding 700 kilobytes to 1 megabyte, representing thousands of cells.[4]

Analytical Graphics: Creating Charts

A nice feature of spreadsheet packages is the ability to create analytical graphics. **Analytical graphics,** or *business graphics,* are graphical forms that make numerical data easier to analyze than when it is in the form of rows and columns of numbers, as in electronic spreadsheets. Whether viewed on a monitor or printed out, analytical graphics help make sales figures, economic trends, and the like easier to comprehend and analyze.

The principal examples of analytical graphics are *bar charts, line graphs,* and *pie charts. (See Figure 6.5.)* Quite often these charts can be displayed or printed out so that they look three-dimensional. Spreadsheets can even be linked to more exciting graphics, such as digitized maps.

Figure 6.5 Analytical graphics. Bar charts, line charts, and pie charts are used to display numerical data in graphical form.

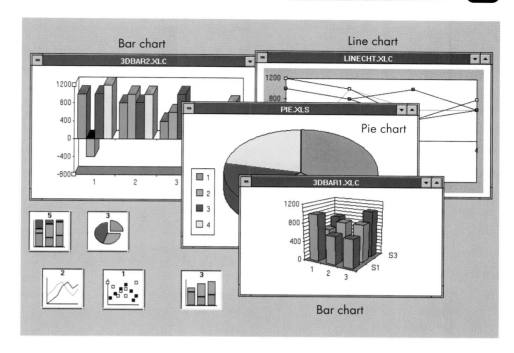

Personal Finance Software

Personal finance software lets you keep track of income and expenses, write checks, and plan financial goals. *(See Figure 6.6.)* Whether or not you learn how to use electronic spreadsheet programs, you'll probably find it useful to use personal finance software. Such programs don't promise to make you rich, but they can help you manage cash and investments, maybe even get you out of trouble.

Certainly that was the case for Nick Ryder. An airline pilot from Marietta, Georgia, Ryder credited the best-selling financial software Quicken with saving his marriage by keeping his finances afloat. When Ryder and his wife, Penny, were

Figure 6.6 M.Y.O.B. Accounting screen. Personal finance software allows users to write and print out checks.

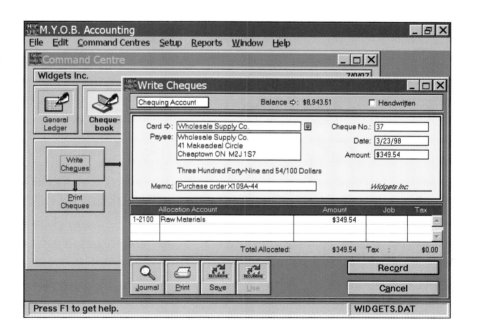

married, after many years of singlehood, they found themselves "deep into the credit-card hole." Despite two healthy paychecks, they never seemed to have enough money.

In 1991 the Ryders acquired Quicken and began entering everything into the program's various account categories: checking, credit cards, utility bills, all incidentals over a dollar. After a few months of tracking expenses, some patterns began to emerge. "We were spending way too much on eating out," Ryder said. "Day to day, it doesn't look like much, but it adds up." The incidentals category also turned up a shocking number of impulse buys—magazines, snacks—that were out of line. With the knowledge acquired from Quicken, the Ryders began to cut back on expenses and even saved enough to set up investment accounts—managed by Quicken.[5]

Many personal finance programs include a calendar and a calculator, but the principal features are the following.

- *Tracking of income and expenses:* The programs allow you to set up various account categories for recording income and expenses, including credit card expenses. (Some personal finance program developers even offer a Visa credit card that sends you monthly statements via your modem or a diskette for direct entry into your computer.)

- *Checkbook management:* All programs feature checkbook management, with an on-screen check writing form and check register that look like the ones in your checkbook. Checks can be purchased to use with your computer printer. Some programs even offer a nationwide electronic payment service (through BillPay USA or CheckFree) that lets you pay your regular bills automatically, even depositing funds electronically into the accounts of the people owed.

- *Reporting:* All programs compare your actual expenses with your budgeted expenses. Some will compare this year to last year.

- *Income tax:* All programs offer tax categories, for indicating types of income and expenses that are important when you're filing your tax return. Most personal finance programs are also able to interface with a tax-preparation program.

- *Other:* Some of the more versatile personal finance programs offer financial-planning, retirement-planning, and portfolio-management features. Quicken Deluxe also provides interactive tutorials and counseling sessions with leading financial consultants via a multimedia help system.

Quicken (there are versions for DOS, Windows, and Macintosh) seems to have generated a large following, but other personal finance programs exist as well. They include Kiplinger's CA-Simply Money, Managing Your Money, Microsoft Money, Simply Accounting, Peachtree, MYOB, and WinCheck. Some offer enough features that you could use them to manage a small business.

In addition, there are tax software programs, which provide virtually all the forms you need for filing income taxes. Tax programs make complex calculations, check for mistakes, and even unearth deductions you didn't know existed. (Principal tax programs are Andrew Tobias' TaxCut, Kiplinger TaxCut, TurboTax/MacInTax, Personal Tax Edge, and CA-Simply Tax.) Finally, there are investment software packages, such as StreetSmart from Charles Schwab and Online Xpress from Fidelity, as well as various retirement-planning programs.

Could you use personal finance software right now? What for?

Figure 6.7 Presentation graphics

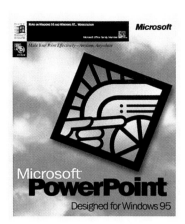 

Presentation Graphics

Computer graphics can be highly complicated, such as those used in special effects for movies (such as *Toy Story* and *Mission Impossible*). Here we are concerned with just one kind of graphics called presentation graphics.

Presentation graphics are part of *presentation software,* which uses graphics and data/information from other software tools to communicate or make a presentation to others, such as clients or supervisors. Presentations may make use of some analytical graphics—bar, line, and pie charts—but they usually look much more sophisticated, using, for instance, different texturing patterns (speckled, solid, cross-hatched), color, and three-dimensionality. *(See Figure 6.7.)* Examples of well-known presentation software packages are Microsoft PowerPoint, Aldus Persuasion, Lotus Freelance Graphics, and SPC Harvard Graphics.

In general, presentation graphics are output as 35-millimeter slides, which can be projected on a screen or displayed on a large monitor. Presentation software packages often come with slide sorters, which group together a dozen or so slides in miniature. The person making the presentation can use a mouse or keyboard to bring the slides up for viewing.

Some presentation software packages provide artwork called *clip art* that can be electronically cut and pasted into the graphics. These programs also allow you to use electronic painting and drawing tools for creating lines, rectangles, and just about any other shape. Depending on the system's capabilities, you can add text, animated sequences, and sound. With special equipment you can also output your presentations on transparencies and videotape.

Presentation software packages are also used in kiosks, multimedia training, and lectures. (A *kiosk* is a small, self-contained, booth-like structure. Multimedia kiosks dispense information via computer display.)

Database Management System Software

In its most general sense, a database is any electronically stored collection of data in a computer system. In its more specific sense, a *database* is a collection of interrelated files in a computer system. These computer-based files are organized according to their common elements, so that they can be retrieved easily. Sometimes called a *database manager* or *database management system (DBMS),* **database software** is a program that controls the structure of a database and access to the data. *(See Figure 6.8.)*

Figure 6.8 Microsoft Access screen. Database management software can manage huge amounts of data concerning all of a salesperson's contacts.

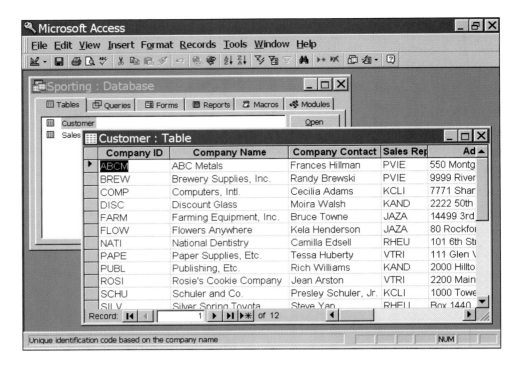

Benefits of Database Software

Because it can access several files at one time, database software is much better than the old file managers (also known as flat-file management systems) that used to dominate computing. A *file manager* is a software package that can access only one file at a time. With a file manager, you could call up a list of, say, all students at your college majoring in English. You could also call up a separate list of all students from Wisconsin. But you could not call up a list of English majors from Wisconsin, because the relevant data is kept in separate files. Database software allows you to do that.

Databases are a lot more interesting than they used to be. Once they included only text. Digital technology has added new kinds of information—not only documents but also pictures, sound, and animation. *(See Figure 6.9.)* It's likely, for

Figure 6.9 Graphical data. Database software increasingly is being used to store not only text but also graphics, sound, and animation.

instance, that your personnel record in a future company database will include a picture of you and perhaps even a clip of your voice. If you go looking for a house to buy, you will be able to view a real estate agent's database of video clips of homes and properties without leaving the realtor's office. Today the principal database programs are Microsoft Access, Microsoft Visual FoxPro, Paradox, and Claris Filemaker Pro. A multimedia program called Instant Database allows users to attach sound, motion, and graphics to forms. You can also attach these elements using OLE (✔ p. 6.6).

Databases have gotten easier to use, but they still can be difficult to design. Even so, the trend is toward making such programs easier for both database creators and database users.

Principal Features of Database Software

Some features of databases are as follows:

- *Organization of a database:* A database is organized—from smallest to largest items—into *fields, records,* and *files.*

  A **field** is a unit of data consisting of one piece of information, whether text, numbers, or media object (graphic, sound bite). Examples of a field are your name, your address, your driver's license number, *or* your photograph.

  A **record** is a collection of related fields. An example of a record would be your name *and* address *and* driver's license number *and* photograph.

  A **file** is a collection of related records. An example of a file could be one in your state's Department of Motor Vehicles. The file could include everyone who received a driver's license on the same day, including their names, addresses, and driver's license numbers.

  Database software allows records to be easily added, deleted, and revised.

- *Select and display:* The beauty of database software is that you can locate records in the file quickly. For example, your college may maintain several records about you—one at the registrar's, one in financial aid, one in the housing department, and so on. Any of these records can be called up on a computer display screen for viewing and updating. Thus, if you move, your address field will need to be changed in all databases. Each database is quickly corrected by finding your record. Once displayed, the address field can be changed. This field need be changed only once; it will automatically be updated in all files.

- *Sort:* With database software you can easily change the order of records in a file. Normally, records are entered into a database in the order they occur, such as by the date a person registered to attend college. However, all these records can be sorted in different ways. For example, they can be rearranged by state, by age, or by Social Security number.

- *Calculate and format:* Many database software programs contain built-in mathematical formulas. This feature can be used, for example, to find the grade-point averages for students in different majors or in different classes. Such information can then be organized into different formats and printed out.

In the career you are planning to enter, how do you think you might use database software?

- *Queries:* Database software allows you to query files and get answers—for example, "What are the grade-point averages of the students in Spanish 101?"

- *Reports:* Database software will also generate reports that sort and group data. You can publish these reports on paper or the Web, or simply view them on the screen.

Communications Software

Many microcomputer users feel they have all the productivity they need without ever having to hook up their machines to a telephone. One of the major themes of this book, however, is that having communications capabilities vastly extends your range. This great leap forward is made possible with communications software. Two types of communications software are *data communications software* and *electronic mail software.*

Data Communications Software

Data communications software manages the transmission of data between computers. For most microcomputer users this sending and receiving of data is by way of a modem and a telephone line. The modem translates the digital signals of the computer (✔ p. 1.6) into analog signals (✔ p. 1.7) that can travel over telephone lines to another modem, which translates the analog signals back to digital. When you buy a modem, you often get communications software with it. Popular microcomputer communications programs are QuickLink and Procomm Plus. If you subscribe to an online information service such as CompuServe or America Online, the company will provide you with its own communications software. (Online services and the Internet are covered in detail in Chapter 8.)

Data communications software gives you the following capabilities, among others:

- *Online connections:* You can connect to electronic bulletin board systems (BBSs) organized around special interests, to online services, and to the Internet. The software allows the microcomputer to operate in *terminal emulation mode*—that is, it allows the microcomputer to act like a terminal hooked up to a larger computer and thus gain access to it.

- *Use of financial services:* With communications software you can order discount merchandise, look up airline schedules and make reservations, follow the stock market, and even do some home banking and bill paying.

- *Automatic dialing services:* You can set your software to answer for you if someone tries to call your computer, to dial certain telephone numbers automatically, and to automatically redial after a certain time if a line is busy.

- *Remote access connections:* While traveling you can use your portable computer to exchange files via modem with your desktop computer at home.

- *File transfer:* Communications software allows users to *download* (copy to the user's disk) files from remote locations and *upload* (copy to a remote location's storage medium) files.

- *Fax support:* Communications software also allows users to fax messages and receive faxed messages directly from and to their microcomputers.

Electronic Mail Software

Do you currently use e-mail? Do you know what software you are using that supports it? What do you think you will use e-mail for in your job?

Electronic mail (e-mail) software enables users to send letters and documents from one computer to another. Many organizations have electronic mail systems, and each person is assigned a unique mailbox. If you were a sales representative, for example, such a mailbox would allow you to transmit a report you created on your word processor to a sales manager in another area. Or you could route the same message to a number of users on a distribution list. Popular e-mail software packages include Eudora, MS Exchange, and Pegasus Mail.

The "killer application" for the Internet is electronic mail. More people use e-mail than the Web. The principles of electronic communications are covered in detail in the next two chapters.

Groupware

Most microcomputer software is written for people working alone. **Groupware** is software that is used on a network and serves a group of users working together on the same project. Groupware improves productivity by keeping you continually notified about what your colleagues are thinking and doing, and vice versa. "Like e-mail," one writer points out, "groupware became possible when companies started linking PCs into networks. But while e-mail works fine for sending a message to a specific person or group—communicating one-to-one or one-to-many—groupware allows a new kind of communication: many-to-many."[6]

Groupware is essentially of four types:

■ *Basic groupware:* Exemplified by Lotus Notes, this kind of groupware uses an enormous database containing work records, memos, and notations and combines it with a messaging (e-mail) system. It is information-centered and allows people to do workgroup computing, focusing on the information being processed. Thus, a company like accounting giant Coopers & Lybrand uses Lotus Notes software to let co-workers organize and share financial and tax information. It can also be used to relay advice from outside specialists, speeding up audits and answers to complex questions from clients.[7]

  Groupware is more than just multiuser software, which allows users on a network to access the same data; groupware does this but also allows users to coordinate and keep track of an ongoing project.

■ *Workflow software:* Workflow software, exemplified by ActionWorkflow System and ProcessIt, helps workers understand and redesign the steps that make up a particular process—thus it is process-centered. It governs the tasks performed and coordinates the transfer of the information required to carry out the tasks. It also routes work automatically among employees and helps organizations reduce paper-jammed bureaucracies.

■ *Meeting software:* Examples of meeting software are Microsoft NetMeeting, Netscape's Collaborator, and Ventana's GroupSystems V, which allow people to have computer-linked meetings. With this software, people "talk," or communicate, with one another at the same time by typing on microcomputer keyboards. As one writer describes it, "Because people read faster than they speak, and don't have to wait for others to finish talking, the software can dramatically speed progress toward consensus."[8]

■ *Scheduling software:* Scheduling software such as Microsoft Outlook, Microsoft SchedulePlus, and Powercore's Network Scheduler 3 use a microcomputer network to coordinate co-workers' electronic datebooks or appointment calendars so they can figure out a time when they can all get together. (Note: Scheduling software is useful only if everyone uses it regularly and consistently—otherwise appointment information and the like will be missing.)

Groupware has changed the kind of behavior required for success in an organization. For one thing, it requires workers to take more responsibility. Ethically, of course, when you are contributing to a group project of any kind, you should try to do your best. However, when your contribution to the project is clearly visible to all, as happens with groupware, you *have* to do your best. In addition, using e-mail or groupware means you need to use good manners and be sensitive to others while you're online.

Desktop Accessories and PIMs

Pretend you are sitting at a desk in an old-fashioned office. You have a calendar, clock, calculator, Rolodex-type address file, and notepad. Most of these items could also be found on a student's desk. How would a computer and software improve on this arrangement? Many people find ready uses for types of software known as *desktop accessories* and *personal information managers (PIMs)*.

■ *Desktop accessories:* A **desktop accessory,** or *desktop organizer,* is a software package that provides an electronic version of tools or objects commonly found on a desktop: calendar, clock, card file, calculator, and notepad. *(See Figure 6.10.)*

   Some desktop-accessory programs come as standard equipment with some system software (such as with Microsoft Windows). Others, such as Borland's SideKick or Lotus Agenda, are available as separate programs to run in your computer's main memory at the same time you are running other software. Some are principally *scheduling and calendaring programs;* their main purpose is to enable you to do time and event scheduling.

   Suppose, for example, you are working on a word processing document and someone calls to schedule lunch next week. You can simply type a command that "pops up" your appointment calendar, type in the appointment, save the information, and then return to your interrupted work. Other features, such as a calculator keypad, a scratch pad for typing in notes to yourself, and a Rolodex-type address and phone directory (some with automatic telephone dialer), can be displayed on the screen when needed.

■ *Personal information managers:* A more sophisticated program is the **personal information manager (PIM),** a combination word processor, database, and desktop accessory program that organizes a variety of information. Examples of PIMs are Commence, Ecco, and Lotus Organizer. (PIMs are often integrated into e-mail and groupware products.)

   Lotus Organizer, for example, looks much like a paper datebook on the screen—down to simulated metal rings holding simulated paper pages. The program has screen images of section tabs labeled Calendar, To Do, Address, Notepad, Planner, and Anniversary. The Notepad section lets users enter long documents, including text and graphics, that can be called up at any time.

Do you think a PIM or a desktop accessory would be useful to you? How?

Figure 6.10 Desktop accessory. A daily schedule currently lies atop other tools.

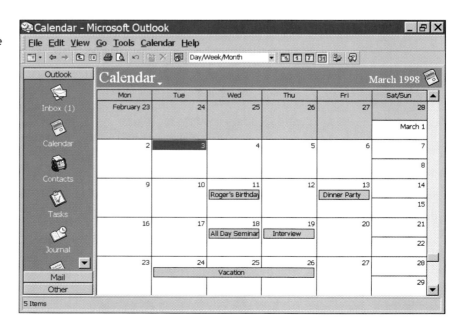

Integrated Software and Software Suites

What if you want to take data from one program and use it in another—say, call up data from a database and use it in a spreadsheet? You can try using separate software packages, but one may not be designed to accept data from the other. Two alternatives are the collections of software known as *integrated software* and *software suites.*

Integrated Software: "Works" Programs

Integrated software packages combine the features of several applications programs—such as word processing, spreadsheet, database, graphics, and communications—into one software package. These so-called "works" collections give good value because the entire bundle often sells for $100 or less. The principal representatives are AppleWorks, ClarisWorks, Lotus Works, Microsoft Works, and PerfectWorks.

Some of these "works" programs have "assistants" that help you accomplish various tasks. Thus, Microsoft's Works for Windows 95 helps you create new documents using any of 39 "task wizards." The wizards lead you through the process of creating a letter, for example, that permits you to customize as many features as you want.

Integrated software packages are less powerful than separate programs used alone, such as a word processing or spreadsheet program used by itself. But that may be fine, because single-purpose programs may be more complicated and demand more computer resources than necessary. You may have no need, for instance, for a word processor that will create an index. Moreover, Microsoft Word takes up about 20 megabytes on your hard disk, whereas Microsoft Works takes only 7 megabytes.

Despite these advantages, system software such as Windows makes the advantage of sharing information in integrated programs redundant, since the user can easily shift between applications programs that are *completely different.* In addition, integrated programs are largely being replaced in the Windows environment by software suites, as we discuss next.

Software Suites: "Office" Programs

Software suites, or simply *suites,* are applications—like spreadsheet, word processing, graphics, communications, and groupware—that are bundled together and sold for a fraction of what the programs would cost if bought individually.

"Bundled" and "unbundled" are jargon words frequently encountered in software and hardware merchandising. *Bundled* means that components of a system are sold together for a single price. *Unbundled* means that a system has separate prices for each component.

The principal suites, sometimes called "office" programs, are Office from Microsoft, SmartSuite from Lotus, and Perfect Office from Corel. Microsoft's Office 97 consists of programs that separately would cost perhaps $1500 but as a suite cost roughly $500 to $600.

Although cost is what makes suites attractive to many corporate customers, they have other benefits as well. Software makers have tried to integrate the "look and feel" of the separate programs within the suites to make them easier to use. "The applications mesh more smoothly in the package form," says one writer, "and the level of integration is increasing. More and more, they use the same commands and similar icons in the spreadsheet, word processor, graphics, and other applications, making them easier to use and reducing the training time."[9]

A trade-off, however, is that such packages require a lot of hard-disk storage capacity. Microsoft Office 97, for instance, comes on 24 or more floppy disks or 1 CD-ROM and may occupy 180 megabytes of hard disk space.

Software for the "Digital Office"

Do you use a "works" or an "office" program? If so, which parts of it do you use most?

Software suites are probably only a way station to something else. The push is on to link *everything*—to achieve the complete "digital office." For instance, Microsoft is spearheading a standard, using infrared technology, by which microcomputers are integrated with other office technologies. This union will include printers, fax machines, photocopiers, and telephones. Microsoft is working in partnership with more than 60 companies in the computer, office machinery, and telecommunications industries to establish connectivity and common linkages.

Web Browsers

The Internet, that network of millions of interconnected networks, "is just a morass of data, dribbling out of [computers] around the world," says one writer. "It is unfathomably chaotic, mixing items of great value with cyber-trash." This is why browser software have caught people's imaginations, he states. "A browser cuts a path through the tangled growth and even creates a form of memory, so each path can be retraced."[10]

We cover the Internet in detail in Chapter 8. Here let us consider briefly just a part of it, one that you may find particularly useful.

The World Wide Web

The most exciting part of the Internet is probably that fast-growing region or subset of it known as the World Wide Web. The *World Wide Web,* or simply *the Web,* consists of hundreds of thousands of intricately interlinked sites called *home pages* set up for on-screen viewing in the form of colorful magazine-style "pages" with text, images, and sound.

To be connected to the World Wide Web, you need a modem and an automatic setup with an online service or Internet access provider (described in Chapter 8), who often provides the browser software for exploring the Web. (The reverse is also true: If you buy some Web browsers, they will help you find an access provider.) A **Web browser,** or simply *browser,* is software that enables you to "browse through" and view Web sites. You can move from page to page by clicking on or selecting a hyperlink—either underlined text or a graphic—or by typing in the address of the destination page.

There are a great many browsers, including some unsophisticated ones offered by Internet access providers and some by the large commercial online services such as America Online, CompuServe, and Prodigy. However, the recent battle royal to find the "killer app" (killer application) browser, the one that would bring a flood of new users to the Web, has been between Netscape, which produces Navigator and Communicator, and Microsoft, which offers Microsoft Explorer.

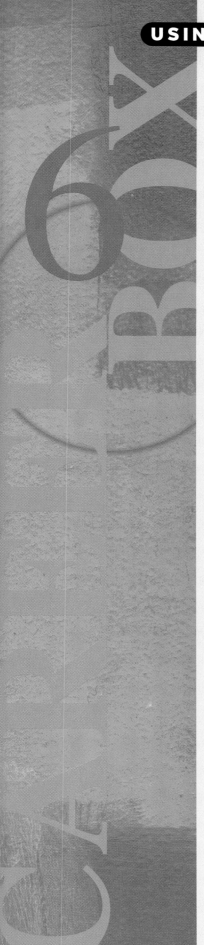

Transportation

In the 1980s, in Ohio, Steve Roberts built several bicycles with enough computer equipment on board to enable him to stay connected to cyberspace and make a living writing about his adventures during four years of pedaling around the United States. The latest version, "Behemoth," had 105 gears, four computers, a satellite Internet link, a cellular modem, a ham radio, and a stereo. A shorthand keyboard embedded in the handlebars allowed Roberts to write while pedaling.[11]

Is "Behemoth" a forerunner of our transportation future? Who knows? But it suggests how the use of high technology is possible in any of the vehicles we have for getting around.

Consider trucking. "These days, some truckers are more inclined to sport white collars than tank tops," says one article. "Once (and still) lumped as rednecks and high-school dropouts, they are now fluent with computers, satellites, and fax machines—all of which can be found in the cabs of their 18-wheelers."[12]

Truckers may now be required to carry laptops with which they keep in touch via satellite with headquarters, or the trucks themselves may carry onboard computers that relay their positions to company dispatchers. The home office can also monitor trucks' engine performance and give customers information about the status of the cargos. In addition, drivers may now have to take on tasks previously never dreamed of. These include faxing sales invoices, hounding late-paying customers, and training people to whom they deliver high-tech office equipment.

Race-car teams have taken technology even further. The Newman-Haas Grand Prix racing team—run by actor Paul Newman and racing veteran Carl Haas—is one of the most advanced. Before a car even goes onto the track, engineers run a computerized image of the vehicle through dozens of simulated races in a Chicago computer lab, using 3-D software. "We can literally predict how a car will perform under 20 different scenarios without using the car or driver," says one automotive engineer. During time trials a laptop computer with sophisticated software is placed in a real car, and its data is downloaded later to a workstation with 3-D color graphics, enabling engineers to make alterations to the car to improve its speed. "If you don't know computers, you have a serious disadvantage racing competitively," says the engineer.[13]

When you're out on the highway yourself, there are many ways that computer technology makes driving easier. In the San Francisco Bay area, for instance, a customized telephone traffic and transit service called Trav-Info allows callers to dial up information about up-to-the-minute traffic conditions on 37 different freeways, eight bridges, and major roads. Information is fed to a kind of "freeway war room" in Oakland from closed-circuit television cameras, freeway tow-truck patrols, the California Highway Patrol computer-assisted dispatch system, and sensors embedded in the roadway that can measure the speed and density of traffic.[14] In northern Nevada, sensors in the pavement that detect changing weather conditions enable dispatchers to notify snowplow crews exactly when and where to plow and salt snowy or icy roads.[15]

In certain areas of the country, some new cars—Acura, BMW, Cadillac, Lincoln, Oldsmobile—can be bought with computer-based navigation and communications systems that tell you how to get where you want to go and can even make reservations for your arrival. These systems rely on global positioning satellites that relay information to a dashboard video screen that shows directions.[16]

Some new car-navigation systems also use voice-recognition technology. "You simply spell out one word in the street or landmark you plan to drive to," says one description, "and the system audibly presents you with a choice of possible destinations" that contain the word.[17]

These and other technologies may presage a time when, as one report suggests, you could be "driving down the freeway at 100 mph in pouring rain, 12 feet behind the car in front of you—and your hands off the steering wheel."[18] You would be protected by collision-avoidance radar and automatic brakes and be guided by satellite-linked computer systems to your exit, where you would then take over manual operation of the car.[19]

Transportation experts say widespread application of such "auto-robotics" is years away, and in any case what use is any of this if you don't own a car? But bus riders may soon find things getting easier, too. Combining satellite tracking that pinpoints a bus's position with technology used in pagers, developers of the NextBus Information System have found a way to eliminate the frustration of riders waiting too long or showing up at the stop just as the bus drives by.

With a credit-card-size electronic device called "BusTracker," which issues speaker sounds with increasing urgency as a bus approaches, users would not even have to leave their front doors until the last minute. The device would also relay information from passenger load sensors about whether the bus was too full. "I think it would be absolutely fabulous!" says one transit board member. "Riders really want to know what they are getting into before they get to the bus stop."[20]

Specialty Applications Software Tools

Specialty applications software tools allow people in many specialized businesses and professions to accomplish very sophisticated and creative tasks with the computer.

After learning some of the productivity software just described, you may wish to extend your range by becoming familiar with more specialized programs. For example, you might first learn word processing and then move on to desktop publishing, the technology used to prepare much of today's printed information. Or you may want to move beyond presentation graphics and learn how to prepare animation and special effects. Let us consider the following examples of these specialized tools, although these are but a handful of the thousands of programs available:

- Desktop-publishing programs
- Project management programs
- Computer-aided design and manufacturing
- Drawing and painting programs
- Hypertext and Web site management
- Multimedia authoring software

Desktop-Publishing Software

Not everyone can set up a successful desktop-publishing business, because many complex layouts require experience, skill, and knowledge of graphic design and of typography. Indeed, use of these programs by nonprofessional users can lead to rather unprofessional-looking results. Nevertheless, the availability of microcomputers and reasonably inexpensive software has opened up a career area formerly reserved for professional typographers, compositors, and printers. **Desktop publishing,** abbreviated *DTP,* involves using a microcomputer and mouse, scanner, laser or ink-jet printer, and DTP software for mixing text and graphics to produce high-quality printed output for commercial printing. *(See Figure 6.11.)* Often the printer is used primarily to get an advance look before the completed job is sent to an imagesetter for even higher quality output. (Imagesetters generate images directly onto film, which is then given to the printer for platemaking and printing.) Professional desktop-publishing programs are QuarkXPress and PageMaker. Microsoft Publisher is a "low-end," consumer-oriented DTP package. Some word processing programs, such as Word and WordPerfect, have many DTP features but at nowhere near the level of sophistication of the aforementioned packages.

Desktop-publishing software has the following characteristics:

■ *Mix of text with graphics:* Unlike traditional word processing programs, desktop-publishing software allows you to manage and merge precisely typographically aligned text with graphics. Indeed, while laying out a page on screen, you can make the text flow, liquid-like, around graphics such as photographs. Among many other things, you can make art drop behind text or text drop out from (print white in) art. You can make text columns uneven and art bleed out into the margin. You can resize art, silhouette it, change the colors, change the texture, flip it upside down, and make it look like a photo negative.

■ *Varied type and layout styles:* As do word processing programs, DTP programs provide a variety of fonts. Additional fonts can be purchased on disk or downloaded online. You can also create all kinds of rules, borders, columns, and page numbering styles. A *style sheet* in the DTP program enables you to choose and record the settings that determine the appearance of the pages and save document templates, or master documents, that can be used repeatedly. This may include defining size and typestyle of text and headings, numbers of columns of type on a page, and width of lines and boxes.

■ *Use of files from other programs:* It's not usually efficient to do word processing, drawing, and painting within the DTP software. Thus, text is usually composed on a word processor, such as Word or WordPerfect, artwork is created with drawing and painting software, such as Adobe Illustrator or CorelDRAW, and photographs are scanned in using a scanner and then manipulated and stored using Adobe PhotoShop or other photo-manipulation or imaging software. Prefabricated art may also be obtained from disks containing clip art, or "canned" images that can be used to illustrate DTP documents. The DTP program is used to integrate all these files. On the display screen you can look at your work one page or two facing pages at a time (in reduced size). Then you can see it again after it is printed out.

What is the basic function of DTP software?

An example of the use of QuarkXPress to combine Word, Adobe Illustrator, and Photoshop files is this book: it was laid out electronically by one of the authors. The Quark files and the art files were then sent to a prepress house for certain refinements, color separation, and film imposition. Then the book went to the printer. (It could just as easily have been output electronically using Adobe's Portable Document Format [PDF] or placed on the Web.)

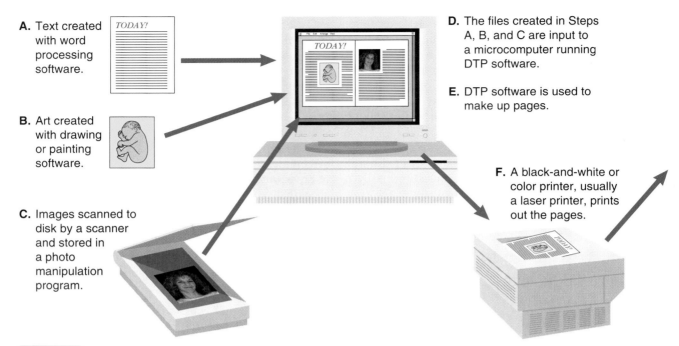

A. Text created with word processing software.

B. Art created with drawing or painting software.

C. Images scanned to disk by a scanner and stored in a photo manipulation program.

D. The files created in Steps A, B, and C are input to a microcomputer running DTP software.

E. DTP software is used to make up pages.

F. A black-and-white or color printer, usually a laser printer, prints out the pages.

Figure 6.11 How DTP uses other files. Text is composed on a word processor, graphics are drawn with drawing and painting programs, and photographs and other artwork are scanned in with a scanner and manipulated with appropriate software. Data from these files is integrated using desktop-publishing software, then printed out on a laser printer or sent to an imagesetter. *(continues on next two pages)*

Project Management Software

A desktop accessory/PIM can help you schedule your appointments and do some planning. That is, it can help you to manage your own life. But what if you need to manage the lives of others to accomplish a full-blown project, such as steering a political campaign or handling a nationwide road tour for a band? Strictly defined, a *project* is a one-time operation consisting of several tasks that must be completed during a stated period of time. The project can be small, such as an advertising campaign for an in-house advertising department, or large, such as construction of an office tower or a jetliner.

Project management software is a program used to plan, schedule, and control resources—people, costs, and equipment—required to complete a project on time. For instance, the associate producer on a feature film might use such software to keep track of the locations, cast and crew, materials, dollars, and schedules needed to complete the picture on time and within budget. The software would show the scheduled beginning and ending dates for a particular task, called a *milestone*—such as shooting all scenes on a certain set—and then the date that task was actually completed. Examples of project management software are Harvard Project Manager, Microsoft Project for Windows, Project Scheduler 4, SuperProject, and Time Line.

> If someone asked you to pick a project right now in which you had to use project management software, what kind of project would you choose?

Two important tools available in project management software are Gantt charts and PERT charts. *(See Figure 6.12.)* A *Gantt chart* uses lines and bars to indicate the duration of a series of tasks. The time scale may range from minutes to years. The Gantt chart allows you to see whether tasks are being completed on schedule. A *PERT chart* (Program Evaluation Review Technique) shows not only timing but also relationships among the tasks of a project. The relationships are represented by lines that connect boxes describing the tasks.

Even project management software has evolved into new forms. For example, a program called ManagePro for Windows is designed to manage not only goals and tasks but also the people charged with achieving them. "I use it to track projects, due dates,

G. If you plan to print on a printing press, the page layout file may be sent to a service bureau, which loads the file onto a micro-computer or workstation.

H. At the service, images may be rescanned at a higher resolution.

I. If the document is in full color, color separation software produces four electronic files for each page; each representing the amount of cyan, magenta, yellow, and black that will go on the page.

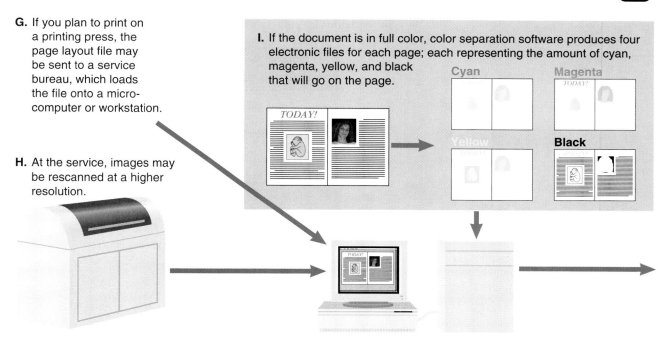

and the people who are responsible," says the director of management information systems at a Lake Tahoe, Nevada, timeshare condominium resort. "And then you can get your reports out either on project information, showing progress on all the steps, or a completely different view, showing all the steps that have to be taken by a given individual."[21]

Computer-Aided Design (CAD) and Manufacturing (CAM)

Computers have long been used in engineering design. **Computer-aided design (CAD)** programs are software programs for the design of products and structures. CAD programs, which are now available for microcomputers, help architects design buildings and work spaces and engineers design cars, planes, electronic

Figure 6.12 Project management software. *(Left)* Gantt chart from Microsoft Project for Windows. *(Right)* PERT chart from Microsoft Project for Windows.

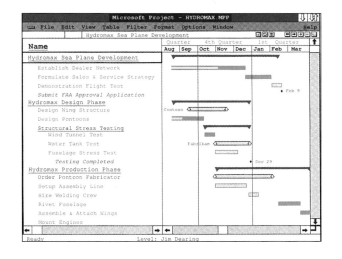

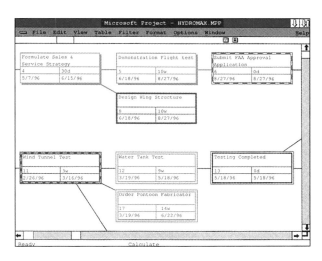

J. The electronic files are input to an imagesetter, which produces four negatives for each page (one for each color).

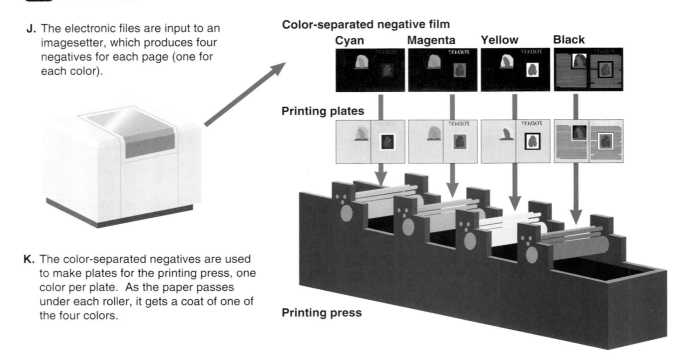

Color-separated negative film
Cyan   Magenta   Yellow   Black

Printing plates

Printing press

K. The color-separated negatives are used to make plates for the printing press, one color per plate. As the paper passes under each roller, it gets a coat of one of the four colors.

devices, roadways, bridges, and subdivisions. One advantage of CAD software is that the product can be drawn in three dimensions and then rotated on the screen so the designer can see all sides. *(See Figure 6.13)*

Examples of CAD programs for beginners are Autosketch, CorelCAD, Easy-CAD2 (Learn CAD Now), and TurboCAD. One CAD program, Parametric, allows engineers to do "what if" overhauls of designs, much as users of electronic spreadsheets can easily change financial data. This feature can dramatically cut design time. For instance, using Parametric, Motorola was able to design its Micro Tac personal cellular telephone in 9 months instead of the usual 18.[22] Yet not all CAD programs are used by technical types; a version is available now, for example, that a relatively unskilled person can use to design an office. Other programs are available for designing homes. These programs include "libraries" of options such as cabinetry, furniture, fixtures, and, in the landscaping programs, trees, shrubs, and vegetables.

A variant on CAD is *CADD,* for *computer-aided design and drafting,* software that helps people do drafting. CADD programs include symbols (points, circles,

Figure 6.13 CAD. (*Left*) Screens from Autodesk CAD system. (*Right*) CAD screen of an automobile brake assembly. The designer can draw in three dimensions and rotate the figures on the screen.

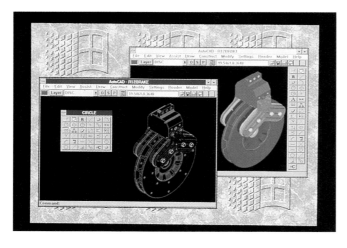

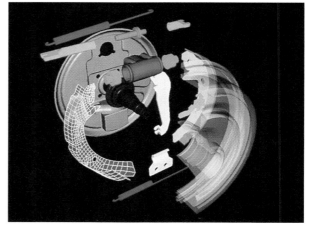

straight lines, and arcs) that help the user put together graphic elements, such as the floor plan of a house. An example is Autodesk's AutoCAD.

CAD/CAM—for **computer-aided design/computer-aided manufacturing**—software allows CAD product designs to be input into an automated manufacturing system that makes the products. For example, CAD and its companion CAM brought a whirlwind of enhanced creativity and efficiency to the fashion industry. Some CAD systems, says one writer, allow designers to electronically drape digitally generated mannequins in flowing gowns or tailored suits that don't exist, or twist imaginary threads into yarns, yarns into weaves, weaves into sweaters without once touching needle to garment.[23] The designs and specifications are then input into CAM systems that enable robot pattern-cutters to automatically cut thousands of patterns from fabric, with only minimal waste. Whereas previously the fashion industry worked about a year in advance of delivery, CAD/CAM has cut that time to 8 months—a competitive edge for a field that feeds on fads.

Drawing and Painting Software

It may be no surprise to learn that commercial artists and fine artists are abandoning the paintbox and pen-and-ink for software versions of palettes, brushes, and pens. The surprise, however, is that an artist can use mouse and pen-like stylus to create computer-generated art as good as that achievable with conventional artist's tools. More surprising, even *nonartists* can be made to look good with these programs.

There are two types of computer art programs: drawing and painting.

■ *Drawing programs:* A **drawing program** is graphics software that allows users to design and illustrate objects and products. CAD and drawing programs are similar. However, CAD programs provide precise dimensioning and positioning of the elements being drawn, so they can be transferred later to CAM programs. Also, CAD programs lack the special effects for illustrations that come with drawing programs.[24]

A program named Sketcher, for example, is described as having 12 different "paper" textures from which to choose, mimicking a range of surfaces from plain paper to canvas. There are even more choices in pencils, chalks, air brushes, pens, felt pens, markers, charcoals, and a variety of brush types. Drawing with a charcoal-like tool "is just like drawing with real paper and charcoal, except neater."[25] Other drawing programs are CorelDRAW, Adobe Illustrator, and Macromedia Freehand.

■ *Painting programs:* Whereas drawing programs are generally vector-based programs, painting programs are raster-based color (*see box at the end of chapter*). **Painting programs** are graphics programs that allow users to simulate painting on screen. A mouse or a tablet stylus is used to simulate a paintbrush. The program allows you to select "brush" sizes and shapes, as well as colors from a color palette.

The difficulty with using painting programs is that a powerful computer system is needed because color images take up so much main memory and disk storage space. In addition, these programs require sophisticated color printers of the sort found in specialized print shops called *service bureaus*.

What's the difference between drawing and painting software?

How can nonartists be made to look good with these programs? Consider the "Auto van Gogh" feature offered by a painting program called Painter, into which you feed your scanned photograph or other digital image. With a few clicks of a mouse, you can have that scanned photo rendered in Vincent van Gogh's

Figure 6.14 Morphed illustration in PowerGoo

style of multicolored brush strokes. Other programs such as Kai's PowerGoo can be used to "morph" (alter) scanned-in or created illustrations. *(See Figure 6.14.)*

Hypertext and Web Site Management

Hypertext is a concept that allows users to have fast and flexible access to information in large documents, constructing associations among data items as needed. Database managers have made the retrieval and organization of facts infinitely easier than was possible in the old index-card and file-cabinet days. Hypertext goes beyond the restrictive search-and-retrieval methods of traditional database systems and encourages people to follow their natural train of thought as they discover information. That is, hypertext works the way people think, allowing them to link facts into sequences of information in ways that resemble those that people use to obtain new knowledge. The term *hypertext* was coined by computer visionary Ted Nelson, who is still working on an advanced version that he calls Xanadu, named after Kublai Khan's legendary pleasure dome.

Hypertext is often used in Help systems, a staple of many programs. Help systems allow users to query the software for help or additional information on how a program or system works. Another well-known example of the use of hypertext is that found in HyperCard, introduced for the Apple Macintosh in 1987. Since then other companies have introduced similar products, such as Super-Card from Silicon Beach Software. HyperCard is based on the concept of *cards* and *stacks* of cards—just like notecards, only they are electronic. A card is a screenful of data that makes up a single record; cards are organized into related files called stacks. On each card there may be one or more *buttons,* which, when clicked on by a mouse, can pull up another card or stack. By clicking buttons, you can make your way through the cards and stacks to find information or discover connections between ideas. *(See Figure 6.15.)*

Recently, hypertext has come into its own as a means of accessing Web sites. The hidden codes of hypertext allow users to use a mouse to click on an underlined or highlighted word, phrase, or graphic to automatically access a related site. As we will discuss in detail elsewhere (Chapter 8), *hypertext markup language (HTML)* is the language in which Web pages are written and linked; *hypertext transfer protocol (HTTP)* is how information is sent over the Web.

Multimedia Authoring Software

Multimedia authoring software enables creators to combine not only text and graphics but animation, video, voice, and sound effects as well. A multimedia system is not just a single technology or software application but instead a combination of hardware and software that incorporates multiple media within a desktop computer system. In previous chapters you learned what hardware is necessary to play multimedia presentations. When you buy a multimedia item on CD-ROM, it basically needs to be compatible with your system to run. However, who puts those complicated multimedia presentations together? Project managers; creative directors; content and subject matter experts; writers, editors, and researchers; graphic designers; photographers; image processing specialists; sound designers; musicians; voice talent; audio engineers; animators; and video professionals, to name a few. These people work with various types

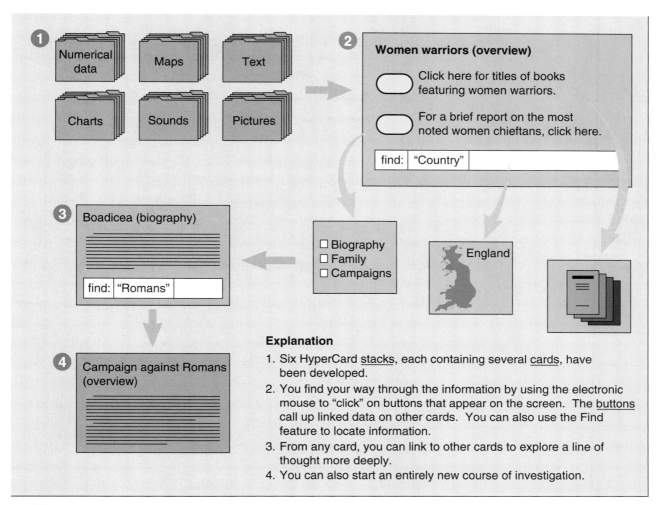

1

Numerical data

Maps

Text

Charts

Sounds

Pictures

2 Women warriors (overview)

Click here for titles of books featuring women warriors.

For a brief report on the most noted women chieftans, click here.

find: "Country"

3 Boadicea (biography)

find: "Romans"

☐ Biography
☐ Family
☐ Campaigns

England

4 Campaign against Romans (overview)

Explanation

1. Six HyperCard <u>stacks</u>, each containing several <u>cards</u>, have been developed.

2. You find your way through the information by using the electronic mouse to "click" on buttons that appear on the screen. The <u>buttons</u> call up linked data on other cards. You can also use the Find feature to locate information.

3. From any card, you can link to other cards to explore a line of thought more deeply.

4. You can also start an entirely new course of investigation.

Figure 6.15 Hypertext: How HyperCard works. The subject here is women warriors.

of software programs, depending on their specialties. Then multimedia authoring software is used to synchronize the parts of the whole and ready the product for distribution.

Because people tend to remember much more of what they hear *and* see—as opposed to what they only hear or only see—multimedia has become a useful tool in many areas: information management, training, interactive learning, electronic publishing, entertainment, and communications, to name a few. For example, Atlanta won the bid for the 1996 Olympics on the strength of a multimedia presentation that put the Olympic committee "inside" the stadium, which had yet to be built.[26] Multimedia uses are covered in detail in a later chapter. However, here we list a few basic things you can do.[27]

■ Browse through an encyclopedia and check out animations on everything from the circulatory system to an atomic nucleus during fission.

■ Explore the intimate details of a musical selection, moving from discussions of the historical period to explanations of the themes, to pictures of the composer, to a game that tests your knowledge of music.

■ Build a business presentation that includes sound effects, music, still pictures, animation, video, and text.

■ Explore your creative musical interests, even recording and editing music on your PC.

■ Add sounds to files or tasks.

■ Hold up a part for a complex machine in front of a video camera and have the video appear on someone else's computer far, far away while you explain how to install the part.

■ Explore the topography of the Atlantic Ocean for a geology paper.

■ Create 3-D and sound effects.

■ Create animated birthday cards for your friends who have computers.

■ Call up a map of the country you're visiting next week and, with the click of a mouse, look up sights to see.

■ Capture a video image from your wedding videotape.

■ Record your thoughts about a letter, and insert the recording right into the document for later review.

■ Explore medical terminology, using pictures and animations to help out with the hard parts.

■ Look up the history of the word *set* (all 150 or so pages) in the *Oxford English Dictionary* on CD-ROM.

■ Make a sale using life-like animation of your product in use on your color portable computer in your client's office.

■ Learn a new language by interacting with the written and spoken words.

Professionals who develop multimedia projects have special hardware needs—such as equipment to record and copy their own CD-ROMS and/or DVDs, particular types of sound boards and audio controllers, video boards, compression/decompression-compatible hardware, graphics cards and accelerators, microphones, music synthesizers, projection options, and so forth. And, as mentioned, they need authoring software. Some of the common authoring tools, which differ in levels of sophistication and authoring method, are Microsoft Powerpoint and Hypercard for the Mac (presentation-graphics level), Macromedia Authorware and Macromedia Director, AimTech IconAuthor, Asymetrix Toolbook, and Action! for Macintosh and Windows. Basically, authoring tools allow the creator to sequence and time the occurrence of events, determining which previously created graphics, sound, text, and video files come into action when. The software also allows the creator to determine the type and level of user interaction. For example, does each event require the user to answer a question with a keyboarded "yes" or "no" before the program can proceed?

Multimedia creation on a simple level—such as creating presentation graphics with Microsoft PowerPoint for a business or educational presentation—is accessible to many users. However, multimedia on the most sophisticated

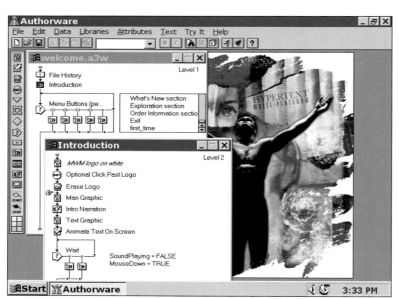

This Authorware screen shows a chain of icons, each of which represents an occurrence in a multimedia presentation.

level, using Director or Toolbook, for instance, requires quite a bit of knowledge and training.

Installing and Updating Applications Software

Software manufacturers produce updated versions of software packages called *releases* and *versions*. All software must be installed before it can be used.

Installing Applications Software

You can buy a videotape, CD-ROM, or audiotape, insert it into its player, and view or listen to it by simply pressing a button. This is not the case with applications software. To use it in your microcomputer, you must first *install* it. Installation means copying and usually decompressing (✔ p. 5.9) program files from a CD-ROM or other medium to your hard disk. Directions for installing come with the instructions (documentation) accompanying applications software. Additional advice is available, usually through a toll-free 800 number, from the software manufacturer.

The installation program may also ask you to specify what kind of microcomputer and monitor you are using, whether you are using a hard disk, and so on. Once you have completed the installation procedure, which takes 5–30 minutes, the application program will store most of your responses in a special file (.INI) on the disk. This file is referred to by the applications program every time you load the software. (More and more applications programs get this information from the system software. Therefore, the user need not specify the hardware; in this case, there is no need to store the information in an .INI file.)

Applications Software Versions and Releases

We have previously mentioned that, every year or so, software developers find ways to enhance their products and put forth a new *version* or new *release.* To recap:

- *Version:* A *version* is a major upgrade in a software product. Versions are usually indicated by numbers such as 1.0, 2.0, 3.0, and so forth. The higher the number preceding the decimal point, the more recent the version.

- *Release:* A *release* is a minor upgrade. Releases are usually indicated by a change in the number after the decimal point—3.0, then 3.1, then perhaps 3.11, then 3.2, and so on.

Mindful that many users are wise to this system and so may avoid a new "X.0" version on the theory that not all the bugs have been worked out yet, some software developers have departed from this system. Microsoft, for instance, decided to call its new operating system, launched in 1995, "Windows 95" (✔ p. 5.17) instead of "Windows 4.0."

Most software products are upward compatible (or "forward compatible"). *Upward compatible* means that documents created with earlier versions of the

What's the difference between a software version and a release? software can be processed successfully on later versions. Thus, you can use the new version of a word processing program, for instance, to get into and revise the file of a term paper you wrote on an earlier version of that program. However, downward-compatible ("backward-compatible") software is less common. *Downward compatible* means that applications developed for a new version of a software product can be run on older versions. For example, if you can run your new word processing program on your old operating system then the new package is downward compatible.

Although we cover most of the ethical and societal issues related to computerization in Chapter 14, before we close this chapter on applications software we do need to raise the ethical issues of copying intellectual property, including software.

Ethics and Intellectual Property Rights: When Can You Copy?

Intellectual property consists of the products of the human mind. Such property can be protected by copyright, the exclusive legal right that prohibits copying it without the permission of the copyright holder.

Information technology has presented legislators and lawyers—and you—with some new ethical questions regarding rights to intellectual property. **Intellectual property** consists of the products, tangible or intangible, of the human mind. There are three methods of protecting intellectual property. They are *patents* (as for an invention), *trade secrets* (as for a formula or method of doing business), and *copyrights* (as for a song or a book).

What Is a Copyright?

Of principal interest to us is copyright protection. A **copyright** is the exclusive legal right that prohibits copying of intellectual property without the permission of the copyright holder. Copyright law protects books, articles, pamphlets, music, art, drawings, movies—and, yes, computer software. Copyright protects the *expression* of an idea but not the idea itself. Thus, others may copy your idea for, say, a new shoot-'em-up videogame but not your particular variant of it. Copyright protection is automatic and lasts a minimum of 50 years; you do not have to register your idea with the government (as you do with a patent) in order to receive protection.

These matters are important because digital technology has made the act of copying far easier and more convenient than in the past. Copying a book on a photocopier might take hours, so people felt they might as well buy the book. Copying a software program onto another floppy disk, however, might take just seconds.

Digitization threatens to compound the problem. For example, current copyright law doesn't specifically protect copyright material online. Says one article:

> Copyright experts say laws haven't kept pace with technology, especially digitization, the process of converting any data—sound, video, text—into a series of ones and zeros that are then transmitted over computer net-

works. Using this technology, it's possible to create an infinite number of copies of a book, a record, or a movie and distribute them to millions of people around the world at very little cost. Unlike photocopies of books or pirated audiotapes, the digital copies are virtually identical to the original.[28]

Piracy, Plagiarism, and Ownership of Images and Sounds

Three copyright-related matters deserve our attention: software and network piracy, plagiarism, and ownership of images and sounds.

- *Software and network piracy:* It may be hard to think of yourself as a pirate (no sword or eyepatch) when all you've done is make a copy of some commercial software for a friend. However, from an ethical standpoint, an act of piracy is like shoplifting the product off a store shelf—even if it's for a friend.

  Piracy is theft or unauthorized distribution or use. A type of piracy is to appropriate a computer design or program. This is the kind that Apple Computer claimed in a suit (since rejected) against Microsoft and Hewlett-Packard alleging that items in Apple's interface, such as icons and windows, had been copied.

  Software piracy is the unauthorized copying of copyrighted software. One way is to copy a program from one floppy disk to another. Another is to download a program from a network and make a copy of it.

  Network piracy is using electronic networks to distribute unauthorized copyrighted materials in digitized form. Record companies, for example, have protested the practice of computer users' sending unauthorized copies of digital recordings over the Internet.[29]

  The easy rationalization is to say that "I'm just a poor student, and making this one copy or downloading only one digital recording isn't going to cause any harm." But it is the single act of software piracy multiplied millions of times that is causing the software publishers a billion-dollar problem. They point out that the loss of revenue cuts into their budget for offering customer support, upgrading products, and compensating their creative people. Piracy also means that software prices are less likely to come down; if anything, they are more likely to go up.

  In time, anti-copying technology may be developed that, when coupled with laws making the disabling of such technology a crime, will reduce the piracy problem. Regardless, publishers, broadcasters, movie studios, and authors must be persuaded to take chances on developing online and multimedia versions of their intellectual products. Such information providers need to be able to cover their costs and make a reasonable return. If not, says one writer, the Information Superhighway will remain "empty of traffic because no one wants to put anything on the road."[30]

- *Plagiarism:* **Plagiarism** is the expropriation of another writer's text, findings, or interpretations and presenting it as one's own. Information technology puts a new face on plagiarism in two ways. On the one hand, it offers plagiarists new opportunities to go far afield for unauthorized copying. On the other hand, the technology offers new ways to catch people who steal other people's material.

  Electronic online journals are not limited by the number of pages, and so they can publish papers that attract a small number of readers. In recent years, there has been an explosion in the number of such journals and of their academic and scientific papers. This proliferation may make it harder to detect when a work has been plagiarized, since few readers will know if a similar paper has been published elsewhere.[31]

Yet information technology may also be used to identify plagiarism. Scientists have used computers to search different documents for identical passages of text. In 1990, two "fraud busters" at the National Institutes of Health alleged after a computer-based analysis that a prominent historian and biographer had committed plagiarism in his books. The ensuing uproar shook the academic community for four years. The historian, who said the technique turned up only the repetition of stock phrases, was later exonerated in a scholarly investigation.[32]

■ *Ownership of images and sounds:* Computers, scanners, digital cameras, and the like make it possible to alter images and sounds to be almost anything you want. What does this mean for the original copyright holders? An unauthorized sound snippet of James Brown's famous howl can be electronically transformed by digital sampling into the background music for dozens of rap recordings.[33] Images can be appropriated by scanning them into a computer system, then altered or placed in a new context.

The line between artistic license and infringement of copyright is not always clear-cut. In 1993, a federal appeals court in New York upheld a ruling against artist Jeff Koons for producing ceramic art of some puppies. It turned out that the puppies were identical to those that had appeared in a postcard photograph copyrighted by a California photographer.[34] But what would have been the judgment if Koons had scanned in the postcard, changed the colors, and rearranged the order of the puppies to produce a new postcard?

In any event, to avoid lawsuits for violating copyright, a growing number of artists who have recycled material have taken steps to protect themselves. This usually involves paying flat fees or a percentage of their royalties to the original copyright holders.

These are the general issues you need to consider when you're thinking about how to use someone else's intellectual property in the Digital Age. Now let's see how software fits in.

Public Domain Software, Freeware, and Shareware

No doubt most of the applications programs you will study in conjunction with this book will be commercial software packages, with brand names such as Microsoft Word or Lotus 1-2-3. However, there are a number of software products—many available over communications lines from the Internet—that are available to you as *public domain software, freeware,* or *shareware.*[35]

■ *Public domain software:* **Public domain software** is software that is not protected by copyright and thus may be duplicated by anyone at will. Public domain programs have been donated to the public by their creators. They are often available through sites on the Internet (or electronic bulletin boards) or through computer users groups. A users group is a club, or group, of computer users who share interests and trade information about computer systems.

You can duplicate public domain software without fear of legal prosecution. (Beware: Downloading software through the Internet may introduce viruses [✔ p. 5.7] when you run the programs.)

■ *Freeware:* **Freeware** is software that is available free of charge. Freeware is usually distributed through the Internet or computer users groups.

Why would any software creator let the product go for free? Sometimes developers want to see how users respond so they can make improvements in a later version. Sometimes it is to further some scholarly purpose, such as to create a standard for software on which people are apt to agree because there is no need to pay for it.

Freeware developers often retain all rights to their programs, so that technically you are not supposed to duplicate and distribute it further. Still, there is no problem about your making several copies for your own use.

■ *Shareware:* **Shareware** is copyrighted software that is distributed free of charge but requires users to make a contribution in order to receive technical help, documentation, or upgrades. Shareware, too, is distributed primarily by communications connections such as the Internet. An example of shareware is WinZip, a program for decompressing/compressing computer files, which you can obtain from the Internet.

Is there any problem about making copies of shareware for your friends? Actually, the developer is hoping you will do just that. That's the way the program gets distributed to a lot of people—some of whom, the software creator hopes, will make a "contribution" or pay a "registration fee" for advice or upgrades.

Though copying shareware is permissible, because it is copyrighted you cannot use it as the basis for developing your own program in order to compete with the developer.

What types of software do you use? Are any public domain? freeware? shareware?

Proprietary Software and Types of Licenses

Proprietary software is software whose rights are owned by an individual or business, usually a software developer. The ownership is protected by the copyright, and the owner expects you to buy a copy in order to use it. The software cannot legally be used or copied without permission.

Software manufacturers don't sell you the software so much as sell you a license to become an authorized user of it. What's the difference? In paying for a **software license,** you sign a contract in which you agree not to make copies of the software to give away or for resale. That is, you have bought only the company's permission to use the software and not the software itself. This legal nicety allows the company to retain its rights to the program and limits the way its customers can use it.[36] The small print in the licensing agreement allows you to make one copy (backup copy or archival copy) for your own use.

There are several type of licenses:

■ *Shrink-wrap licenses:* **Shrink-wrap licenses** are printed licenses inserted into software packages and visible through the clear plastic wrap or printed directly on the plastic wrap. The use of shrink-wrap licenses eliminates the need for a written signature, since buyers know they are entering into a binding contract by merely opening the package. Each shrink-wrap license is for a single system.

■ *Single-user licenses:* A **single-user license** limits the use of the software in a network to one user at a time.

■ *Multiple-user licenses:* A **multiple-user license** allows more than one person in a network to use the software. Each user is assigned a license, and only these people may use the software.

■ *Concurrent-use license:* A **concurrent-use license** allows a specified number of software copies to be used at the same time. If, for example, the concurrent-use license is for 10 users, any 10 users in the company may use the software at the same time.

■ *Site licenses:* A **site license** permits a customer to make as many copies of a software product as necessary for use just within a given facility, such as a college computer lab or a particular business.

What's the difference between a shrink-wrap license and a site license?

The Software Police

Industry organizations such as the Software Publishers Association (hotline for reporting illegal copying: 800-388-7478) are going after software pirates large and small. Commercial software piracy is now a felony, punishable by up to five years in prison and fines of up to $250,000 for anyone convicted of stealing at least ten copies of a program or more than $2500 worth of software. Campus administrators are getting tougher with offenders and are turning them over to police.

SOFTWARE EXTRA: Vector Graphics Versus Raster Graphics

A *vector* is a line calculated in either two dimensions or three dimensions and defined by its endpoints, which are *x-y* coordinates on a grid. Thus pictures are represented as points, lines, arcs, and other geometric figures.

In *raster graphics,* the picture image is created using a complex series of dots, or pixels (✔ p. 3.27). Raster graphics are often called *bit-mapped graphics.*

Understanding these two methods and how they function in today's graphics systems is necessary for mastering computer graphics. When you create an image on the computer, if you don't know which method is used, you will become aware of it when you try to manipulate the image. Drawing programs create vector graphics; painting programs and scanning produce raster graphics.

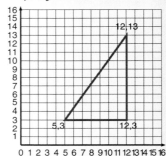

In vector graphics, you can manipulate parts of the whole in ways not possible with raster graphics. For example, sizes of vector-graphic images can be changed without adversely affecting the graphic quality. And individual parts of a graphic can be rotated or easily made to disappear behind or overprint other parts of the graphic. However, vector-graphics programs have trouble with, for instance, lots of tiny squiggles, since they try to view each squiggle as made up of many tiny arcs. In addition, these programs do not store the color of each pixel as you are working. Instead, they store a memo about a geometric shape and the color of the entire shape. Vector graphics are best for high-contrast art such as logos, weather maps, architectural drawings, and bright-colored charts. Also, many word processing programs include basic drawing programs for creating simple illustrations to insert in text documents.

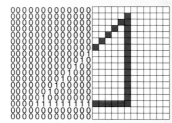

Because raster-graphics programs remember the color of each pixel, the colors of all the pixels are stored in RAM while you're painting. Thus you need lots of RAM if your screen is large and if you are using lots of colors. Raster graphics are good for representing continuous ranges of colors with soft edges, such as impressionist paintings and photographs. However, enlarging and reducing a raster-graphic image too much can make dots ungainly or too fine to reproduce well. Also, raster graphics take up more storage space than vector graphics.

Software programs exist that convert vector graphics to raster graphics, and vice versa, and that allow both types of graphics to be used in the same document. Common vector-graphic file extensions (✔ p. 4.4) are .EPS (encapsulated PostScript), .DCS (desktop color separator), and .WMF (Windows meta file). Common raster-graphic file extensions are .TIF (tagged image file format), .BMP (bitmap), and .GIF (graphics interchange format).

WHAT IT IS
WHAT IT DOES
WHY IT IS IMPORTANT

analytical graphics (LO 3, p. 6.12)
Also called *business graphics;* graphical forms representing numeric data. The principal examples are bar charts, line graphs, and pie charts.

Numeric data is easier to analyze in graphical form than in the form of rows and columns of numbers, as in electronic spreadsheets.

button (LO 2, p. 6.5)   Simulated on-screen button (kind of icon) that is activated ("pushed") by a mouse click (or other pointing device) to issue a command.

Buttons make it easier for users to enter commands.

cell (LO 3, p. 6.12)   In an electronic spreadsheet, the rectangle where a row and a column intersect.

The cell is the smallest working unit in a spreadsheet. Data and formulas are entered into the cells.

cell address (LO 3, p. 6.12)   In an electronic spreadsheet, the position of a cell—for example, "A1," where column A and row 1 intersect.

Cell addresses provide location references for spreadsheet users.

clipboard (LO 2, p. 6.6)   Area where cut or copied material is held before it is pasted.

The clipboard allows you to copy or cut an item from one document and then paste it into another part of the same document, another document, or another application.

computer-aided design/computer-aided manufacturing (CAD/CAM) (LO 4, p. 6.27)   Applications software that allows products designed with CAD to be input into a computer-based manufacturing system (CAM) that makes the products.

CAD/CAM systems have greatly enhanced creativity and efficiency in many industries.

concurrent-use license (LO 6, p. 6.37) Allows a specified number of software copies to be used at the same time.

If, for example, the concurrent-use license is for 10 users, *any* 10 users in the company may use the software at the same time.

copyright (LO 6, p. 6.34)   Body of law that prohibits copying of intellectual property without the permission of the copyright holder.

Copyright law aims to prevent people from taking credit for and profiting unfairly from other people's work.

cursor (LO 2, p. 6.4)   Also called the *insertion point;* the movable symbol on the display screen that shows the user where data may be entered next. The cursor is moved around with the keyboard's directional arrow keys or a mouse.

All applications software packages use cursors to show users their current work location on the screen.

database software (LO 3, p. 6.15)   Applications software for maintaining a database. It controls the structure of a database and access to the data.

Database manager software allows users to organize and manage huge amounts of data.

data communications software (LO 3, p. 6.18) Applications software that manages the transmission of data between computers.

Communications software is required to transmit data in a communications system.

default values (LO 2, p. 6.5)   Settings automatically used by a program unless the user specifies otherwise, thereby overriding them.

Users need to know how to change default settings in order to customize their documents.

desktop accessory (LO 3, p. 6.20)   Also called *desktop organizer;* software package that provides electronic counterparts of tools or objects commonly found on a desktop: calendar, clock, card file, calculator, and notepad.

Desktop accessories help users to streamline their daily activities.

desktop publishing (DTP) (LO 4, p. 6.25) Applications software that, along with a microcomputer, mouse, scanner, and printer, is used to mix text and graphics, including photos, to produce high-quality printer output. Some word processing programs also have many DTP features. Text is usually composed first on a word processor, artwork is created with drawing and painting software, and photographs are scanned in using a scanner. Prefabricated clip art and photos may also be obtained from disks (CD-ROM and/or floppy) containing clip art.

Desktop publishing has reduced the number of steps, the time, and the money required to produce professional-looking printed projects.

dialog box (LO 2 , p. 6.5)   In a graphical user interface, a box that appears on the screen and is used to collect information from the user and display helpful messages.

Dialog boxes make software easier to use.

documentation (LO 2, p. 6.6)   User's manual or reference manual that is a narrative and graphical description of a program. Documentation may be instructional, but usually features and functions are grouped by category.

Documentation helps users learn software commands and use of function keys, solve problems, and find information about system specifications.

drawing program (LO 4, p. 6.29)   Applications software that allows users to design and illustrate objects and products.

Drawing programs are vector-based and are best used for geometric-shape-based, straightforward illustrations.

electronic mail (e-mail) software (LO 3, p. 6.18) Software that enables computer users to send letters and documents from one computer to another.

E-mail allows businesses and organizations to quickly and easily send messages to employees and outside people without resorting to paper messages.

field (LO 3, p. 6.17)   Unit of data consisting of one piece of information, whether text, numbers, or media object (sound bite, graphic).

Examples of a field are your name, your address, your driver's license number, *or* your photo.

file (LO 3, p. 6.17)   Collection of related records.

An example of a file could be one in your state's Department of Motor Vehicles. This file would include everyone who received a driver's license on the same day, including their names, addresses, and driver's license numbers.

font (LO 3, p. 6.9)   A particular typeface and size.

formatting (LO 3, p. 6.8)   Determining the appearance of a document.

formula (LO 3, p. 6.12)   In an electronic spreadsheet, instruction for calculations that are entered into designated cells. For example, a formula might be SUM(A5:A15), meaning "Sum (add) all the numbers in the cells with cell addresses A5 through A15."

freeware (LO 6, p. 6.36)   Software that is available free of charge.

groupware (LO 3, p. 6.19)   Applications software that is used on a network and serves a group of users working together on the same project.

Help menu (LO 2, p. 6.5)   Applications software feature that offers instructions for using software features; includes Help screens, searchable indexes, and online glossaries.

hypertext (LO 4, p. 6.30)   Applications software concept that allows users to link information in large documents, constructing associations among data items as needed.

icon (LO 2, p. 6.5)   Small pictorial figure that represents a task, function, program, file, or disk. The function or object represented by the icon can be activated by clicking on it.

integrated software package (LO 3, p. 6.21)   Applications software that combines several applications programs into one package—usually electronic spreadsheet, word processing, database management, graphics, and communications.

intellectual property (LO 6, p. 6.34)   Consists of the products, tangible or intangible, of the human mind.

macro (LO 2, p. 6.5)   Software feature that allows a single keystroke, command, or toolbar button to be used to automatically issue a predetermined series of commands.

menu bar (LO 2, p. 6.5)   A row of menu options displayed across the top or bottom of the screen.

Once the font is set, you can make headings or emphasized words stand out by adding bold, italic, or underlined styles.

There are many ways to format a document, including using different typefaces, boldface, italics, variable spacing, columns, and margins. The document's format should match the needs of its users.

The use of formulas enables spreadsheet users to change data in one cell and have all the cells linked to it by formulas automatically recalculate their values.

Freeware is usually distributed through the Internet. Users can make copies for their own use but are not free to make unlimited copies.

Groupware improves productivity by keeping users continually notified about what colleagues are thinking and doing, and vice versa.

Help menus provide a built-in electronic instruction manual.

Hypertext goes beyond the restrictive search-and-retrieval methods of traditional database systems and encourages people to follow their natural train of thought as they discover information. Hypertext is used to link Web pages.

The use of icons has simplified the use of software.

Integrated software packages offer greater flexibility than separate single-purpose programs.

Such property can be protected by copyright, the exclusive legal right that prohibits copying without the permission of the copyright holder.

Macros increase productivity by consolidating several command keystrokes into one or two.

Menu bars make software easier for people to use.

multimedia authoring software (LO 4, p. 6.30) Special applications software that enables creators to combine not only text and graphics but also animation, video, music, voice, and sound effects, as well as a measure of user interaction, into multimedia productions.

Because people tend to remember much more of what they both hear and see, multimedia has become a useful tool in many areas, including education, professional training and simulation, and entertainment.

multiple-user license (LO 6, p. 6.37) Allows more than one person in a network to use the software.

Each user is assigned a license, and only these people may use the software.

network piracy (LO 6, p. 6.35) The use of electronic networks for unauthorized distribution of copyrighted materials in digitized form.

If piracy is not controlled, people may not want to let their intellectual property and copyrighted material be dealt with in digital form.

OLE (object linking and embedding) (LO 2, p. 6.5) Enables user to embed an object created using one application (such as graphics) into another application (such as word processing).

OLE facilitates the sharing and manipulating of information.

painting program (LO 4, p. 6.29) Raster-graphics program that allows the user to simulate painting, in color, on the screen.

Painting programs are good for art with soft edges and many colors.

personal finance software (LO 3, p. 6.13) Applications software that helps users track income and expenses, write checks, and plan financial goals.

Personal finance software can help people manage their money more effectively.

personal information manager (PIM) (LO 3, p. 6.20) Combined word processor, database, and desktop accessory software to organize information.

PIMs offer an electronic version of an appointment calendar, to-do list, address book, notepad, and similar daily office tools, all in one place.

plagiarism (LO 6, p. 6.35) Expropriation of another writer's text, findings, or interpretations and presenting them as one's own.

Information technology offers plagiarists new opportunities to go far afield for unauthorized copying, yet it also offers new ways to catch these people.

pop-up menu (LO 2, p. 6.5) A menu that "pops up" from the menu bar.

Pop-up menus make programs easier for people to use.

presentation graphics (LO 3, p. 6.15) Graphical forms used to communicate or make a presentation of data to others, such as clients or supervisors.

Presentation graphics programs, part of presentation software packages, may make use of analytical graphics but look much more sophisticated, using texturing patterns, complex color, and dimensionality.

project management software (LO 4, p. 6.26) Applications software used to plan, schedule, and control the resources—people, costs, and equipment—required to complete a project on time.

Project management software increases the ease and speed of planning and managing complex projects.

proprietary software (LO 6, p. 6.37) Software whose rights are owned by an individual or business.

Ownership of propriety software is protected by copyright. This type of software must be purchased to be used. Copying is restricted.

public domain software (LO 6, p. 6.36) Software that is not protected by copyright and thus may be duplicated by anyone at will.

Public domain software offers lots of software options to users who may not be able to afford a lot of commercial software. Users may download such software from the Internet for free and make as many copies as they wish.

pull-down menu (LO 2, p. 6.5)   A list of command options, or choices, that is "pulled down" out of the menu bar.

Like other menu-based and GUI features, pull-down menus make software easier to use.

record (LO 3, p. 6.17)   Collection of related fields.

An example of a record would be your name *and* address *and* driver's license number *and* photograph.

scrolling (LO 2, p. 6.4)   The activity of moving quickly upward or downward through text or other screen display, using directional arrow keys or mouse.

Normally a computer screen displays only 20–22 lines of text. Scrolling enables users to view an entire document, no matter how long.

shareware (LO 6, p. 6.37)   Copyrighted software that is distributed free of charge, usually over the Internet, but that requires users to make a contribution in order to receive technical help, documentation, or upgrades.

Along with public domain software and freeware, shareware offers yet another inexpensive way to obtain new software.

shrink-wrap license (LO 6, p. 6.37)   Printed licenses inserted into software packages and visible through the clear plastic wrap.

The use of shrink-wrap licenses eliminates the need for a written signature, since buyers know they are entering a binding contract by opening the package.

single-user license (LO 6, p. 6.37)   Limits the use of the software in a network to one user at a time.

Only one person is licensed to use the software.

site license (LO 6, p. 6.37)   License that permits a customer to make multiple copies of a software product for use only within a given facility.

Site licenses eliminate the need to buy many copies of one software package for use in, for example, an office or a computer lab.

software license (LO 6, p. 6.37)   Contract by which users agree not to make copies of proprietary software to give away or to sell.

Software manufacturers don't sell people software so much as licenses to become authorized users of the software.

software piracy (LO 6, p. 6.35)   Unauthorized copying of copyrighted software—for example, copying a program onto a diskette for a friend.

Software piracy represents a serious loss of income to software manufacturers and is a contributor to high prices of new programs.

software suite (LO 3, p. 6.21)   Several applications software packages—like spreadsheet, word processing, graphics, communications, and groupware—bundled together and sold for a fraction of what the programs would cost if bought individually.

Software suites can save users a lot of money.

spreadsheet (LO 3, p. 6.11)   Also called *electronic spreadsheet;* applications software that simulates a paper worksheet and allows users to create tables and financial schedules by entering data and/or formulas into rows and columns displayed as a grid on a screen. If data is changed in one cell, values in other cells specified in the spreadsheet will automatically recalculate.

The electronic spreadsheet has become such a popular small-business applications program that it has been held directly responsible for making the microcomputer a widely used business tool.

toolbar (LO 2, p. 6.5)   A row of on-screen buttons used to activate a variety of functions of the applications program.

Toolbars can often be customized and moved around on the screen.

tutorial (LO 2, p. 6.6)   Instruction book or program that takes users through a prescribed series of steps to help them learn the product.

Tutorials, which accompany applications software packages as booklets or on disk, enable users to practice new software in a graduated fashion, thereby saving them the time they would have used trying to teach themselves. Tutorials may also be available online via the Internet.

Web browser (LO 3, p. 6.22)   Software that enables people to view Web sites on their computers.

Without browser software, users cannot use the part of the Internet called the World Wide Web.

window (LO 2, p. 6.4)   Feature of graphical user interfaces; rectangle that appears on the screen and displays information from a particular part of a program.

Using the windows feature, you can display several windows on a computer screen, each showing a different application program such as word processing, spreadsheets, and graphics, or showing different files within the same application.

wizard (LO 2, p. 6.5)   Feature of applications programs that leads you through a series of questions to determine exactly what you need help with.

If the user doesn't know what kind of help is needed, the wizard can often figure it out.

word processing software (LO 3, p. 6.8)   Applications software that enables users to create, edit, revise, store, and print documents.

Word processing software allows a person to use a computer to easily create, change, and produce attractive documents such as letters, memos, reports, and manuscripts.

SELF-TEST EXERCISES

1. ___word___ ___processing___ software allows you to create and edit documents.
2. A(n) ___DBMS___ is a collection of interrelated files in a computer system.
3. New applications software must be ___installed___ by the user before it can be used.
4. ___Scroll___ is the activity of moving quickly upward or downward through the text or other screen display.
5. Workflow software, meeting software, and scheduling software are all considered ___groupware___.

SHORT-ANSWER QUESTIONS

1. What type of software do you need before you can send data from one computer to another?
2. What is a desktop accessory?
3. What is the difference between integrated software and a software suite?
4. What do the abbreviations CAD and CAM mean?
5. What is the purpose of multimedia authoring software?

MULTIPLE-CHOICE QUESTIONS

1. Which of the following types of software should you use to manage a large amount of data?
   a. word processing
   b. electronic spreadsheet
   c. database management
   d. financial management
   e. all the above

2. Which of the following do you need in order to surf the Web?
   a. communications software
   b. computer
   c. browser
   d. modem
   e. all the above

3. Which of the following is used when text is copied from one application to another?
   a. clipboard
   b. word processing software
   c. documentation
   d. dialog box
   e. all the above

4. Which of the following includes applications that are bundled together?
   a. integrated software
   b. word processing software
   c. electronic spreadsheet software
   d. communications software
   e. none of the above

5. Gantt and PERT charts are used by
   _____.
   a. desktop publishing software
   b. multimedia authoring software
   c. project management software
   d. drawing programs
   e. painting programs

TRUE/FALSE QUESTIONS

1. Word processing and database management are the two most popular software applications. (true/false)

2. Electronic spreadsheet software enables you to perform "what if" calculations. (true/false)

3. A spreadsheet is composed of fields, records, and files. (true/false)

4. Hypertext software enables users to design and illustrate objects and products. (true/false)

5. You can access the World Wide Web using multimedia authoring software. (true/false)

KNOWLEDGE IN ACTION

1. Attend a meeting of a computer users group in your area. What is the overall purpose of the group? Software support? Hardware support? How is support available? Does it cost money to be a member? How many members are there? How does the group get new members? If you were looking to join a user group, would you be interested in joining this group? Why/why not?

2. Research what is meant by the phrase *digital office*. What would a digital office look like? How is this different from today's offices? Describe Microsoft's efforts as they relate to the digital office. What other companies are involved in digital-office technologies? Perform your research using the Web and current computer periodicals.

3. What is your opinion about the issue of free speech on an electronic network? Research some recent legal decisions in various countries, as well as some articles on the topic, and then give a short report about what you think. Should the contents of messages be censored? If so, under what conditions?

4. Prepare a short report about how you would use an electronic spreadsheet to organize and manage your personal finances and to project outcomes of changes. What column headings (labels) would you use? Row headings? What formula relationships would you want to establish among which cells? (For example, if your tuition increased by $2000, how would that affect the monthly amount set aside to buy a car or take a trip?)

5. Picture yourself in your future job. What types of current applications software do you see yourself using? What are you producing with this software? What kinds of new applications software would you invent to help you do your job better?

WELCOME TO EARTH'S BIGGEST BOOKSTORE . . . . . .

Amazon.com

Imagine if someone pointed you in the direction of a pile of four-by-fours and construction tools and said "Build something." There's no saying what you would come up with. The possibilities are almost as varied when you consider options for constructing a Web-based system for presenting your products and supporting financial transactions.

The degree to which you make it easy for customers to find out about your products, make selections, and provide payment information will directly affect the success of your online business. Amazon.com has been very successful in these areas. As one Amazon.com customer commented, "Your site is dangerous. I could easily spend half my salary here. I love bookstores and libraries, but frankly, I find more of the titles I want on your site, and they're so easy to order, and the interface is so friendly that I think this new vice is going to corrupt me permanently."

CREATING AN ONLINE CATALOG

How you present your product(s) can be determined to a large extent by how many products you sell. If you sell just a few products, a simple table that lists the name, description and price for each product you sell might work just fine. A more interesting approach would be to use graphical representations of your products that are linked to pages containing more detailed information. With this approach, users selectively reveal more information about the products they're interested in. Let's look at how you might obtain more information about the book entitled *Overdrive,* by James Wallace, as featured on Amazon.com's home page on May 15, 1997.

Step 1:
One method you can use to find out more about *Overdrive* is to click the book's cover graphic. (Note: Another method would be to click the <u>Overdrive</u> link.)

<u>Romance</u>
<u>Children's Books</u>
<u>And Many More . . .</u>

LISTS
<u>Titles in the News</u>
<u>Bestsellers</u>
<u>Award Winners</u>
<u>Amazon.com 500</u>
<u>Hot 20</u>
<u>Mystery 50</u>
<u>Literary 50</u>
<u>Computer 50</u>
<u>Business 50</u>
<u>Science Fiction 50</u>

journal . . . .

amazon.com

Amazon.com Journal: Oops. Your billion-dollar software company missed the biggest trend to hit computing since the PC. What to do? If you're Bill Gates, you shift into <u>*Overdrive*</u>... Were badly conceived charts responsible for the *Challenger* disaster? Edward Tufte thinks so. We talk with the information design wizard about his latest work, <u>*Visual Explanations*</u>... Media mogul Mike Bloomberg chats with Amazon.com about empire

Step 2:
After clicking the graphic, the following screen appears. Click the <u>Article, interview, and excerpt</u> link.

Welcome to the Amazon.com Journal. Here you'll find
articles, author interviews, and reading lists--all about books
we think will interest you. Below are highlights of current
articles; at the bottom of the page are links to all our past
articles and interviews. Happy reading!

CONTENTS

James Wallace's *Overdrive*
How Microsoft was blindsided by the
Internet--and then raced to dominate
it. Wallace, a prize-winning
investigative reporter, delivers choice
revelations.
Article, interview, and excerpt
Buy your copy now

Step 3:
Additional informational links exist on this screen.
For example, to see an excerpt from the book, click
the excerpt link.

The Drive to Dominate

In *Overdrive*, veteran journalist
James Wallace recounts round
one of Microsoft vs. the Internet

Opening Gates

Read our exclusive
interview with James
Wallace.

Sample an excerpt
from *Overdrive*.

Check out James
Wallace's previous
book on Gates and
Microsoft, *Hard...*

Step 4:
An excerpt of the book appears.

Go to *Overdrive* article

From James Wallace's *Overdrive: Bill Gates and the Race to Control Cyberspace*

It was all very hush-hush. No one was supposed
to know that the very pregnant woman who
quietly checked into Bellevue's Overlake
Hospital under an assumed name in late April
1996 was the wife of the richest person in the
world. William Henry Gates III was about to
become a father, and this was one event that he
did not want the world to know about.

Step 5:
After reading the entire excerpt, you may decide to
purchase the book by clicking the "Buy *Overdrive*
now!" link.

But he changed his tune when he finally became a father. A few
months after his daughter Jennifer was born, he told a *New York
Times* reporter that it had been "much more of a thrill then I
expected. I thought, 'Well, when the kid starts talking, we'll do
things together.' But even a kid who doesn't talk has little triumphs
and a personality." Gates would later joke at a Microsoft sales
conference that there was something besides Netscape keeping him
up at night.

From *Overdrive: Bill Gates and the Race to Control Cyberspace*, © 1997
by James Wallace. Used by permission of John Wiley & Sons, Inc.

Go to *Overdrive* article

Buy *Overdrive* now!

Step 6:
Details such as price, page length, and availability
now appear on the screen. At this point, you can
put the book in your shopping cart by clicking the
"Add this Book to your Shopping Cart" button.

Cyberspace

by James Wallace

Hardcover, 256 pages
List: $24.95 -- **Amazon.com Price: $17.47** -- Yo
Published by John Wiley & Sons
Publication date: May 1,1997
Dimensions (in inches): 9.54 x 6.48 x 1.15
ISBN: 0471180416

Availability: This item usually shipped within 2-3 days.

| Add this Book to your Shopping Cart |

If you sell many products, consider building a
search capability into your site or organizing your
products into categories. Amazon.com has done
both. With Amazon.com's search tools, for example,
you can locate a book based on its title, subject,
author, keyword, publication date, or ISBN (International Standard Book Number). If you want to
find out what books are available in a broader topic
area, such as the topic of starting a Web-based
business, you might be better off browsing through
Amazon.com's categories and subcategories until
you target a book of interest.

TAKING ORDERS AND COLLECTING PAYMENT

A common method for taking orders is to simply
include contact information, such as your business
address, phone number, fax number, and e-mail
address, at the bottom of every page in your site.

Customers can then use one of these contact points to obtain additional information about your products or to place an order. This method works well if your online catalog contains a few products.

If your online catalog contains many products, consider automating your transaction processing system using Web shopping carts and interactive forms. A customer can easily add products to or take products out of a virtual shopping cart prior to making the actual decision to purchase. Next we show an Amazon.com shopping cart that contains two books and how you would go about buying them.

Step 1:
To purchase the contents of your shopping cart, click the "Proceed to Checkout" button.

Items in your shopping cart:

> **Proceed to Checkout**

Quantity:

Available in 2-3 days:

1   *Overdrive : Bill Gates and the Race to Control Cyberspace*; James Wallace; Hardcover;

List: $24.95 -- **Amazon.com Price: $17.47 -- You Save: $7.48(30%)**

1   *Training a Tiger : A Father's Account of How to Raise*

Step 2:
Click the secure server link so that your credit card information is encrypted before being sent over the Internet. If you receive an error message, you can submit your order using the standard server and then phone Amazon.com to provide credit card details.

Before we begin....

We'd like to use the Netscape Secure Commerce Server to satisfy your request. The Netscape Secure Commerce Server works with most browsers, including Internet Explorer. It encrypts information, keeping it private and protected. This technology makes it safe to transmit your complete credit card number over the Internet.

Use the secure server.

If you get an error message when you try to use the secure server, it may be because you've run into a firewall. Ask your system administrator to reconfigure it. (You can say that the port for Secure HTTP, 443, needs to be opened up.)

Step 3:
Use the interactive form to fill in e-mail, shipping, and payment information.

Completing Your Order is

We encourage you to enter your credit card number online (why this is safe). Howev also have the option of phoning us with the number after completing the order form have any problems or questions, see the bottom of the page for details on our toll-f (800) customer support number.

1. Welcome.

Please enter your e-mail address: yourname@yourname.com
Please **double check** your e-mail address; one small typo and we won't be your order.

⦿ I am a first-time customer. (You will be asked to create a password late
○ I am a returning customer, and my password is [   ]

Interactive forms, like the one shown in Step 3, can be quite useful when collecting customer data. For example, if you incorporate error-checking into the form's input windows, it becomes possible to alert your customer if information was omitted or entered incorrectly. Radio buttons, check boxes, pull-down menus, and default values in different areas of your form work to narrow customer responses. Input windows that hide text as it is being typed, with asterisks (*) or other characters, are useful when you need customers to type in a secret code or password.

Customers using Amazon.com's automatic transaction processing system only need to provide payment and shipping information the first time they make a purchase. This information is then stored on one of Amazon.com's secure server computers. Thereafter, the customer simply types in a password to recall the previously entered information. After the form is processed, the system automatically notifies the customer (within 15 minutes) via e-mail that the order was received.

SECURITY CONCERNS

Some of your customers may not feel comfortable about providing financial details, such as credit card numbers, over the Internet. To make customers feel more comfortable, consider giving them options such as talking to someone in order to complete the order.

Additional methods for collecting payment involve personal checks, purchase orders, membership systems, and electronic money. But as Web authors David Cook and Deborah Sellers put it

". . . [E]ither trust the human or the machine. And many users who would balk at entering their number via the Internet would easily use their cordless or cellular phone, both of which are extremely open to eavesdropping."[1] Software-based commerce servers are available that attempt to make the Internet secure for credit card transactions. Amazon.com, for example, uses Netscape's Secure Commerce Server for all of its credit card transactions, but also provides customers with the option of placing an order over the phone. In 1996, Jeff Bezos said: "When we first started a year ago, 50% of the people were typing their credit card number in and 50% were phoning it in, and now it's more like 80 percent typing and 20 percent phoning. So I think finally perception is starting to catch up with reality."[2]

TRACKING INVENTORY

Now that your customer's job of providing order and payment information is done, you must do your part by shipping the product quickly, and ideally, providing the customer with an e-mail notice describing the status of the order (that is, when it was shipped). Keeping good track of inventory through the use of a database application that is constantly updated with order information will help you chart current inventory levels, so that you can replenish inventory when necessary. These steps will ensure that you have product in stock, your orders are shipped promptly, and customer relations remain strong.

CHOOSING SOFTWARE

Much of the software you'll need to create your Web site is available for free on the Internet. For starters, you'll need a software tool called an *HTML (hypertext markup language) editor* that you will use to build your Web site and a graphics program that will let you work with a broad range of graphics files. If this topic is starting to sound a bit technical, remember that your expert Web consultant can take care of creating your site for you. In this Episode, continue to focus on "what" you want to do, not "how" you're going to do it.

Below we provide some general software recommendations for gaining access to the Internet and using some of its features. Your access provider can provide you with most of this software.

- *Internet connection software*—This type of software is necessary for you to establish a connec-

tion between your computer and the Internet. This software may already be built into your computer's system software.

- *Web browser software*—Browser software enables you to view your Web site.

- *E-mail software*—With e-mail software, you can receive and send electronic messages to anyone on the Internet.

- *Usenet software*—With Usenet software, you can read, post, and reply to messages in the many thousands of newsgroups on the Internet. Usenet provides an excellent means for you to advertise your business to people with a specific interest in your product.

- *FTP (File Transfer Protocol)*—This software provides your primary means of sending and receiving files when you're not using the Web. You would use FTP, for example, to update your Web site if it is located remotely on your provider's computer.

Keep in mind that as you continue to develop your business, you'll come up with additional software requirements.

WHAT DO YOU THINK?

1. Describe the specific features of the Yourname.com online catalog. Why have you chosen this method to present your products?

2. How do you plan to take customer orders at Yourname.com? Why? If you plan to use an interactive order form, provide an example of how you want your form to look (using pen and paper or design software), and then describe the rationale behind the specific features of your form.

3. How have you decided to collect payment from your customers? Why?

4. What software do you think you will need to start business? Feel free to expand on the discussion presented in this Episode. For example, will you need inventory software? Tax software?

5. How do you plan to keep track of inventory? If you will be using a database management system, what fields will you include in your inventory database?

CHAPTER 7

COMMUNICATIONS TECHNOLOGY

Starting Along the Information Superhighway

PREVIEW

After reading this chapter, you should be able to:

1. Explain the basic communications principles of analog and digital signals, modems, communications software, and protocols

2. Identify and explain the various communications channels, both wired and wireless

3. List and discuss the factors affecting communications among devices

4. Discuss the three main types of networks

5. Describe the five basic types of local area networks

WHY IS THIS CHAPTER IMPORTANT?

"Computers and communications: These are the parents of the Information Age," says one writer. "When they meet, the fireworks begin."[1] What is meant by "fireworks"? Maybe it is that portable information and technologies are changing conventional meanings of time and space. Says one expert, "the physical locations we traditionally associate with work, leisure, and similar pursuits are rapidly becoming meaningless."[2]

The students who live in the Computer Science House, a drab brick dormitory at Rochester Institute of Technology in upstate New York, exemplify this blurring of traditional boundaries between work and leisure, isolation and availability.[3] The 64 CSH residents spend most of their time hunched over computer keyboards, linked electronically to people down the hall and around the world.

One of them is sophomore Tom Frazier, whose jeans have a special pocket for his cellular phone. Frazier keeps up with his girlfriend across the state via cell phone, pager, and the Internet and gets wake-up calls for classes from an alarm on his pager, which also acts as his pocket watch. Another, Matt "Soup" Campbell, hands in homework assignments electronically and instructs his computer to send reminder e-mail messages ("Don't forget the meeting!") to his pager hours before he is supposed to be somewhere. Unlike Frazier, however, Campbell refuses to date via the Internet. "I believe in people interaction," he says, "and sometimes I wonder if we're getting away from that."

Through communications and connectivity, computers, telephones, and wireless devices are being linked by invisible networks everywhere. In this chapter we describe the basics of communications technology. In the next chapter we describe some of the things you can do with this technology.

Using Computers to Communicate: Technological Basics

To communicate online through a microcomputer, users need a modem to send and receive computer-generated messages over telephone lines. A modem may be external to the computer or internal and may have various transmission speeds.

Communications, or **telecommunications,** refers to the transfer of data (*communications*) from a transmitter—also called a sender or a source—to a receiver—also called a sink—across a distance (*tele,* from ancient Greek, meaning "far off").

Some form of electromagnetic energy—electricity, radio waves, or light—is used to represent the data or code, which is transmitted through a physical medium—for example, wire, cable, or the atmosphere. Additionally, some number of intermediate devices are often involved to set up a path for the data transfer and to maintain adequate signal strength.[4] The data transmitted can be voice, text, video, images, sound, or a combination of these (multimedia).

Recall from Chapter 1 (✔ p. 1.6) that data is transmitted by two types of signals, each requiring different kinds of communications technology. The two types of signals are *analog* and *digital*. *(See Figure 7.1 for a review.)* In a way they resemble analog and digital watches. An analog watch shows time as a continuum. A digital watch shows time as discrete numeric values.

Analog Signals: Continuous Waves

Telephones, radios, and televisions—the older forms of communications technology—were designed to work with an analog signal. An **analog signal** is a continuous electrical signal in the form of a wave called a *carrier wave.*

Two characteristics of analog carrier waves that can be altered are frequency and amplitude.

■ *Frequency:* **Frequency** is the number of times a wave repeats during a specific time interval—that is, how many times it completes a *cycle* in a second.

■ *Amplitude:* **Amplitude** is the height of a wave within a given period of time. Amplitude is actually the strength or volume—the loudness—of a signal.

Both frequency and amplitude can be modified by making adjustments to the wave. Indeed, it is by such adjustments that an analog signal can be made to express a digital signal, as we shall explain.

Digital Signals: Discrete Bursts

You have learned that a *digital signal* uses on/off or present/absent electrical pulses in discontinuous, or discrete, bursts, rather than a continuous wave. This two-state kind of signal represents the two-state binary language of 0s and 1s that computers use. That is, the presence of an electrical pulse can represent a 1 bit, its absence a 0 bit.

Actually, the transmission of data as discrete (digital) signals is not as new as you might think. In the mid-1880s, Samuel Morse developed the Morse code, which on paper consisted of a series of dots and dashes. Thus the letter V, for

Figure 7.1 Analog and digital signals. An analog signal represents a continuous electrical signal in the form of a wave. A digital signal is discontinuous, expressed as discrete bursts in on/off electrical pulses.

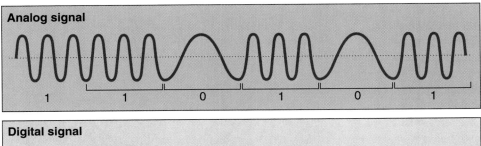

Analog signal

1   1   0   1   0   1

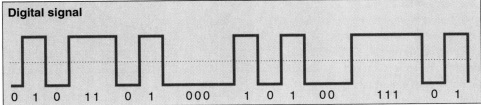

Digital signal

0 1 0   11   0   1   000   1 0 1   00   111   0   1

example, consisted of three dots and a dash (. . . –). However, the actual transmission of this character via telegraph wires and telegraphing equipment consisted of three short signals ("taps") and one long signal, each signal being separated by a pause.

The Modem: The Great Translator

Digital signals are better—that is, faster and more accurate—at transmitting computer data. However, many of our present communications lines, such as telephone and microwave, are still analog. To get around this problem, we need a **modem**—short for *mo*dulate/*dem*odulate—to convert digital signals into analog form (a process known as *modulation*) to send over phone lines. A receiving modem at the other end of the phone line then converts the analog signal back to a digital signal (a process known as *demodulation*). *(See Figure 7.2.)*

Modulation/demodulation does not actually change the wave form of an analog signal into the on/off form of the digital signal. Rather, it changes the form of the wave. For instance, the frequency might be changed. A normal wave cycle within a given period of time might represent a 1, but more frequent wave cycles with a given period might represent a 0. Or, the amplitude might be changed. A loud sound might represent a 1 bit, a soft sound might represent a 0 bit. That is, a wave with normal height (amplitude) might signify a 1, a wave with smaller height a 0. *(See Figure 7.3.)* The wave itself does not assume the boxy on/off shape represented by the true digital signal.

From this we can see that modems are a compromise. They cannot transmit digital signals in a way that delivers their full benefits. As a consequence, communications companies have been developing alternatives, such as the Integrated Services Digital Network (ISDN) and cable modems, discussed shortly.

Figure 7.2 How modems work. A sending modem translates digital signals into analog waves for transmission over phone lines. A receiving modem translates the analog signals back into digital signals.

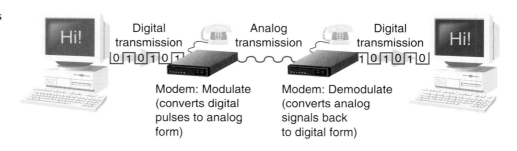

Digital transmission 0 1 0 1 0 1   Analog transmission   Digital transmission 1 0 1 0 1 0

Modem: Modulate (converts digital pulses to analog form)

Modem: Demodulate (converts analog signals back to digital form)

Figure 7.3 Modifying an analog signal. A modem may modify an analog signal to carry the on/off digital signals of a computer in two ways. (*Top*) The frequency of wave cycles is altered so that a normal wave represents a 1 and a more frequent wave within a given period represents a 0. (*Bottom*) The amplitude (height) of a wave is altered so that a wave of normal height represents a 1 and a wave of lesser height represents a 0.

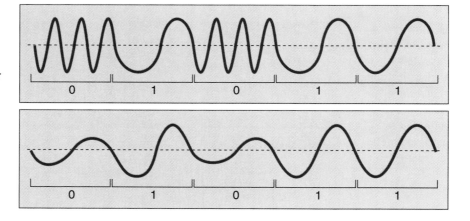

Choosing a Modem

Two criteria for choosing a modem are whether you want an internal or external one, and what transmission speed you wish:

■ *External versus internal:* Modems are either internal or external. *(See Figure 7.4.)* An external modem is a box that is separate from the computer. The box may be large or it may be portable, pocket size. A cable connects the modem to a port in the back of the computer. A second line connects the modem to a standard telephone jack. There is also a power cord that plugs into a standard AC wall socket. The advantage of the external modem is that it can be used with different computers. Thus, if you buy a new microcomputer, you will probably be able to use your old external modem.

An internal modem is a circuit board that plugs into a slot inside the system cabinet or that is integrated into the motherboard (✔ p. 2.20). Nowadays most new microcomputers come with an internal modem already installed. Advantages of the internal modem are that it doesn't take up extra space on your desk and doesn't have a separate power cord.

For laptop computers, you can also purchase modems on PC cards (✔ p. 2.27).

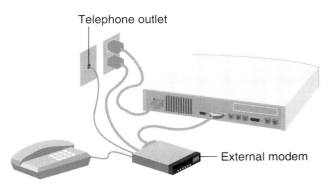
Telephone outlet

External modem

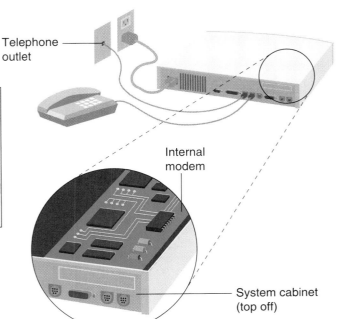
Telephone outlet

Internal modem

System cabinet
(top off)

Figure 7.4 External versus internal modems. An external modem is a box that is outside the computer. An internal modem is a circuit board installed in an expansion slot inside the system cabinet

■ *Transmission speed:* Because most modems use standard telephone lines, users are charged the usual rates by phone companies, whether local or long-distance. Users are also often charged by online services for time spent online. Accordingly, *transmission speed*—the speed at which modems transmit data—becomes an important consideration. The faster the modem, the less time you need to spend on the telephone line.

With older modems, users talked about *baud rate,* the speed at which data is transmitted, measured by the number of times per second the signal being transmitted changed. At these lower speeds, one bit was usually transmitted with each signal change per second—thus the baud rate could be the same as the bits-per-second (bps) rate. Baud rate applied to very slow speeds (such as 300 bps, the speed of a modem 15 years ago). At speeds above 2400 bps, more than 1 bit is transmitted with each signal change; thus today users refer to **bits per second (bps)** or, more likely, **kilobits per second (Kbps)** to express data transmission speeds. A 28,800-bps modem, for example, is a 28.8-Kbps modem.

Modems transmit at 1200, 2400, and 4800 bps (slow and not worth using anymore), 9600 and 14,400 bps (moderately fast), and 28,800, 33,600 and 56,000 bps (high-speed). A ten-page single-spaced letter can be transmitted by a 2400-bps modem in $2\frac{1}{2}$ minutes. It can be transmitted by a 9600-bps modem in 38 seconds, by a 28,800-bps modem in about 10 seconds, and by a 56,000-bps modem in about 5 seconds. (Currently there are two incompatible types of 56-Kbps modems; however, a single standard is expected to evolve shortly. Since the maximum theoretical speed limit of data transmission over ordinary phone lines is 60 Kbps, this modem will likely be the last of its type.)

Why do you need a modem? How can its data-transmission speed affect you?

Noisy phone lines may reduce a modem's efficiency. The next generation will probably consist of modem-type hardware using ISDN (integrated services digital network), ADSL (asymmetric digital subscriber line), or cable-TV circuits. Cable modems operate up to 1000 times faster than a 14.4-Kbps modem. (We will discuss these possible upcoming improvements to the traditional modem later in the chapter.)

Communications Software

To communicate via modem, your microcomputer requires communications software. *Communications software,* as we mentioned in Chapter 6 (✔ p. 6.18), manages the transmission of data between computers. Macintosh users have Smartcom; Windows users have Smartcom, Crosstalk, Wincom, CommWorks, Telix, Crosstalk, Procomm Plus, and HyperTerminal; OS/2 Warp users have HyperAccess. Often the software comes on diskettes bundled with the modem. Also, communications software may be embedded in the computer's system software.

Besides establishing connections between computers, communications software may perform other functions:

■ *Error correction:* Static on telephone lines can introduce errors into data transmission, or "noise." Noise is an extraneous signal that causes distortion in the data signal. Noise can be caused by power line spikes, poorly fitting electrical contacts, or strong electrical/magnetic signals coming from nearby power lines or equipment such as air conditioners and X-ray machines. Although such "noise" may not affect voice transmission very much, it can garble high-speed data transmission. When acquiring a modem and its accompanying software, you should inquire whether it incorporates error-correction features.

■ *Data compression:* As we mentioned in Chapter 5 (✔ p. 5.9), data compression reduces the volume of data in a message, thereby reducing the amount of time required to send data from one modem to another. The communications software does this by replacing repeating patterns with symbols that indicate what the pattern is and how often it is repeated. When the compressed message reaches the receiver, the symbols are then replaced and the full message is restored. With text and graphics, a message may be compressed to as much as one-tenth of its original size.

■ *Remote control:* Remote-control software allows you to control a microcomputer from another microcomputer in a different location, perhaps even thousands of miles away. One part of the program is in the machine in front of you, the other in the remote machine. Such software is useful for travelers who want to use their home machines from afar. It's also helpful for technicians trying to assist users with support problems. Examples of remote-control software for microcomputers are Carbon Copy, Commute, Norton PCAnywhere, and Timbuktu/Remote.

What are five functions of communications software?

■ *Terminal emulation:* Mainframes and minicomputers are designed to be accessed by terminals, not by microcomputers, which have a different operating system. Terminal emulation software allows you to use your microcomputer to simulate a mainframe or minicomputer terminal. That is, the software tricks the large computer into acting as if it is communicating with a terminal. (Some system software, such as Windows 95, includes terminal emulation software.)

ISDN, Cable Modems, ADSL, and Dishes: Faster, Faster, Faster!

Users who find themselves banging the table in frustration as their 28.8-Kbps modem takes 25 minutes to transmit a 1-minute low-quality video from a Web site are about to get some relief. Probably the three most immediate contenders to standard phone modems are *ISDN, cable modems,* and *ADSL.*

■ *ISDN lines:* **ISDN** stands for **Integrated Services Digital Network,** which consists of hardware and software that allow voice, video, and data to be communicated as digital signals over traditional copper-wire telephone lines. Capable of transmitting up to 128 Kbps, ISDN lines are up to five times faster than conventional phone modems.

Provided by many telephone companies, ISDN is not cheap, costing perhaps two or three times as much as regular monthly phone service. Installation could also cost $300 or more if you need a phone technician to wire your house and install the software in your PC; and you need to purchase a special ISDN connector box or adapter card, to which you connect your microcomputer, fax machine, analog modem, and telephone. Nevertheless, with the number of people now working at home and/or surfing the Internet, demand has pushed ISDN orders off the charts. Forecasts are for 7 million U.S. installations by 2000, from the current 450,000 lines today.

Even so, ISDN's time may have come and gone. The reason: cable modem and other technologies threaten to render it obsolete.

■ *Cable modems:* Cable companies say that a cable modem can carry digital data more than 1000 times faster than plain old telephone system (POTS) lines, and they've found that usage shoots up when the service is connected. (This speed is 30–43 Mbps, compared to a standard 28.8- or 33.6-Kbps modem.) "Some nights I can't get off the thing," said biology professor Grant

A **cable modem** could transmit all 857 pages of Melville's *Moby Dick* in about two seconds.

In the same time, a high-speed **ISDN phone line** could move 10 pages.

And a **28.8 modem**, the most common way of accessing the Internet today, wouldn't get past page 3.

Balkema, after a cable company installed cable modems at Boston College. "I've started some nights at around 10 and stayed up until 2 A.M. It's—dare I say?—addictive."[5]

A **cable modem** is a modem that connects a personal computer to a cable-TV system that offers online services. The gadgets are still not in common use, and it will probably be awhile before internationally standardized cable modems go on sale. The reason? So far probably 90% of U.S. cable subscribers are served by networks that don't permit much in the way of two-way data communications. "The vast majority of today's . . . cable systems can deliver a river of data downstream," says one writer, "but only a cocktail straw's worth back the other way."[6] Nevertheless, Forrester Research Inc. predicts about 6.8 million American homes will have cable modems by 2000.[7]

■ *ADSL:* Most of the people using the Internet today are connected to it by 14.4-Kbps modems, which transmit data at the rate of 14,400 bits per second, or 14.4 kilobits. However, about 25% of current Internet surfers use a 28.8-kilobit modem, which effectively doubles the bandwidth (range of frequencies) available to 14.4 modem users. In 1995, a new but not universally adopted modem standard called v.34 bis became available. This type of modem offers data transmission speeds of about 33.6 kilobits (33,600 bits) per second.

Even 33.6 Kbps, however, is not fast enough for Internet mavens, and it is still not fast enough to smoothly transmit real-time video. For this reason telephone companies are working hard to simplify ISDN installation and to lay fiber-optic cable. Cable companies hope to provide two-way data transmission options via cable modems and either cable or wireless systems in one to two years. And a new technology is on the way: ADSL (asymmetric digital subscriber line). ADSL, which should be available in about two years, was developed by Bellcore Labs, the biggest research consortium in the United States, jointly owned by the seven regional Bell operating companies.

At an average speed of 1.5 megabits per second (Mbps), ADSL technology—which uses regular phone lines—can send 25% more data each second than one diskette can hold. This high transmission speed is needed to transmit good-quality video images with enough frames per second to make motion appear smooth. Recent test adapters have even reached 6.14 Mbps when downloading test files. Of course, as with ISDN and cable transmission, the PC user fortunate enough to obtain ADSL access will have to pay for add-on hardware and software—for example, a router between the ADSL adapter and the user's PC.

Hardware	Speed	Installation Cost	Local Use Cost
ISDN	128 Kbps	$199–$700	0–$0.36 per minute
Cable	30–43 Mbps	$300–$500	$35–$40 per month projected
ADSL	640 Kbps (upload)– 6.14 Mbps (download)	$300–$500	About $100 per month projected

■ *Dishes:* Satellite dishes offer yet another improvement in data transmission speed. Hughes Network Systems offers a 36-inch satellite dish called the Convergence Antenna that transmits 15 times faster than a standard high-speed modem. Instead of, for example, connecting to the Internet through telephone lines, users subscribe to Hughes's satellite Internet service, called DirecPC.

Thus a 90-second animation clip that normally takes an hour to download arrives in less than two minutes. This service is expensive, however—about $650 for the antenna and about $150 a month for unlimited access. (We discuss satellites in more detail later in the chapter.)

Communications Channels: The Conduits of Communications

A channel is the path over which information travels. Various channels occupy various radio-wave bands on the electromagnetic spectrum. The various types of wired channels included twisted-pair wire, coaxial cable, and fiber-optic cable. Two principal types of wireless channels are microwave and satellite systems.

If you are of a certain age, you may recall when two-way individual communications were accomplished mainly in two ways. They were carried by (1) a telephone wire or (2) a wireless method such as shortwave radio. Today there are many kinds of communications channels, although they are still wired or wireless. A **communications channel** is the path—the physical medium—over which data travels in a telecommunications system from its source to its destination. (Channels are also called *links, lines,* or *media.*) The basis for all telecommunications channels, both wired and wireless, is the electromagnetic spectrum.

The Electromagnetic Spectrum

Telephone signals, radar waves, and the invisible commands from a garage-door opener all represent different waves on what is called the *electromagnetic spectrum.* The **electromagnetic spectrum** consists of fields of electrical energy and magnetic energy, which travel in waves. *(See Figure 7.5, next page.)*

All radio signals, light rays, X rays, and radioactivity radiate an energy that looks like rippling waves. The waves vary according to two characteristics, frequency and wavelength:

- *Frequency:* As we've seen, *frequency* is the number of times a wave repeats (makes a cycle) in a second. Frequency is measured in **hertz (Hz),** with 1 Hz equal to 1 cycle per second. One thousand hertz is called a *kilohertz (KHz),* 1 million hertz is called a *megahertz (MHz),* and 1 billion hertz is called a *gigahertz (GHz).*

  Ranges of frequencies are called **bands** or **bandwidths.** The bandwidth is the difference between the lowest and highest frequencies transmitted. Thus, for example, cellular phones operate in the 800–900 megahertz bandwidth. The wider the bandwidth, the faster data can be transmitted.

- *Wavelength:* Waves also vary according to their length—their *wavelength.* We hear references to wavelength in "shortwave radio" and "microwave oven."

  At the low end of the spectrum, the waves are of low frequency and of long wavelength (such as domestic electricity). At the high end, the waves are of high frequency and short wavelength (such as cosmic rays).

The electromagnetic spectrum can be represented in terms of appliances and machines. We could start on the left, at the low-frequency end, with video display

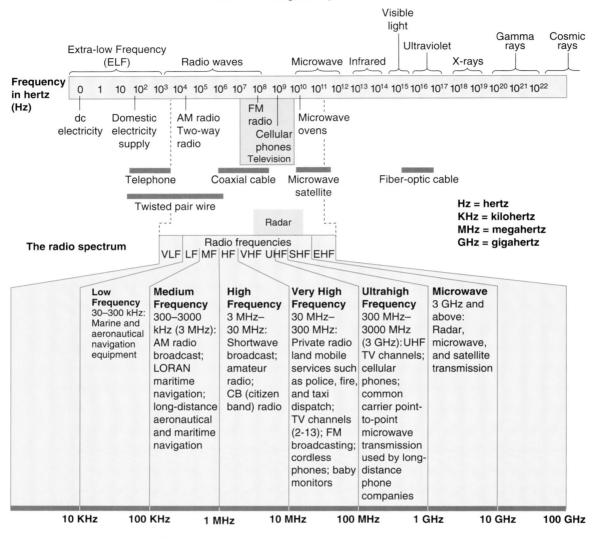

Figure 7.5 The electro-magnetic spectrum

The electromagnetic spectrum

Hz = hertz
KHz = kilohertz
MHz = megahertz
GHz = gigahertz

Frequencies for wireless data communications

Cellular	Private land mobile	Narrowband PCS	Industrial	Common carrier paging	Point-to-multipoint Point-to-point	PCS	Industrial
824–849 MHz 869–894 MHz	896–901 MHz 930–931 MHz Includes RF packet radio services	901–902 MHz 930–931 MHz	902–928 MHz Unlicensed commercial use such as cordless phones and LANs	931–932 MHz Includes national paging services	932–935 MHz 941–944 MHz	1850–1970 MHz 2130–2150 MHz 2180–2200 MHz	2400–2483.5 MHz Unlicensed commercial use such as LANs

terminals and hair dryers. We would then range up through AM (amplitude modulation) and FM (frequency modulation) radios, shortwave radios, UHF and VHF television, and cellular phones. Next we would proceed through radar, microwave ovens, infrared "nightscope" binoculars, and ultraviolet-light tanning machines. Finally, we would go through X-ray machines and end up with gamma-ray machines for food irradiation at the high-frequency end. The part of the spectrum of interest to us is that area in the middle. This is the portion that is regulated by the government for communications purposes.

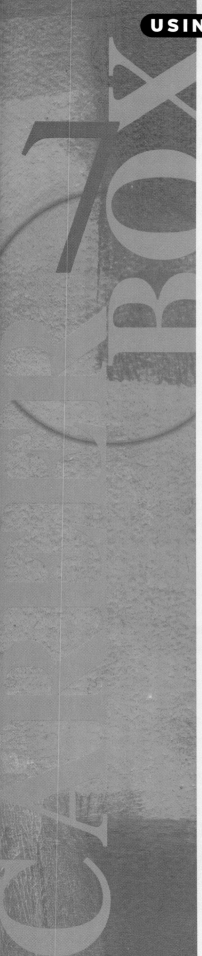

Education Careers

Stuck for a topic for a research paper? Word processing software and electronic spell-checkers and dictionaries are great tools for student writers, but they won't unblock a writer's block. Maybe you need something to help you brainstorm ideas. Maybe you need Paradigm Online Writing Assistant.

Developed by Chuck Guilford, an English professor at Boise State University in Idaho, Paradigm is a World Wide Web site (*http://www.idbsu.edu/ english/cguilfor/paradigm/*) that offers exercises to stimulate creative juices. "While style and grammar are important considerations for writers," says Guilford, "I want Paradigm to emphasize larger conceptual issues, such as discovering, exploring, and shaping ideas."[8]

Computer high-tech tools have long been in use in higher education, and in recent years they have been finding their way into college classrooms. *The 1996 Campus Computing Survey,* for instance, which studied 660 college campuses, found that 25% of the courses surveyed used electronic mail as part of their instruction. About 28% used computerized presentation slides and handouts, 15% used computer simulations or exercises, and 11% used multimedia.[9]

In 24% of cases, courses were held in computer classrooms. Some instructors object that banks of bulky desktop machines wall them off from the students, turning classrooms into "silicon sweatshops." Stanford University, however, has developed a new style of classroom in which computers are both omnipresent and invisible. Freshman students enrolled in a class on expository writing, for instance, come into the classroom, grab Apple Powerbook laptop computers off a library cart, flop into a circle of bean-bag chairs, then plug the computers into floor sockets concealed by blue carpeting. "One student read an essay to the class, while the text scrolled down on a back-lit screen so bright there was no need to dim the lights or shut out the view . . . ," says an account of one class meeting.[10]

The advantage of the Stanford setup is that it allows the instructor to interact with students more casually and gives them greater freedom to share ideas. "They lose some of their self-consciousness," says an English instructor. "It really fosters a sense of community." The room could become a model for what could happen in colleges across the country.

Many schools are already becoming cyberspace campuses. The University of Southern California, for instance, teamed up with a multimedia company to develop a course on film that is taught over the Internet.[11] Students enrolled in the course receive course materials on videotapes and CD-ROMs, complete with clips from Hollywood movies. They interact with each other and with instructors over the Internet. Across the country, New York's New School for Social Research offers more than 90 courses on the Internet and even tries to mimic some of the attractions on its campus in Manhattan's Greenwich Village. "On-line students," reports one writer, "can view art exhibitions, visit a 'music cafe,' or participate in debates concerning politics, the death penalty, and other topics."[12] Duke University offers a way to obtain a master's degree in business administration in which students need only spend 11 weeks of the 19-month program on campus; the rest of their education is obtained online.[13] The most ambitious idea is the Western Governors University, being developed by 13 states, which will ultimately deliver degrees through "distance learning"—education through computers or cable TV—anywhere in the world.[14]

Certain bands are assigned by the Federal Communications Commission (FCC) for certain purposes—that is, to be controlled by different types of media equipment. Some frequencies traditionally used by railroads, electric utilities, and police and fire departments have in recent times been opened up for new uses. These new applications include personal telephones, mobile data services, and satellite message services. We explain these further in the next few pages.

Let us now look more closely at the various types of channels:

- Twisted-pair wire
- Coaxial cable
- Fiber-optic cable
- Microwave and satellite systems
- Other wireless communications
- The next generation of wireless communications

What are "bandwidths"? What are the most commonly used bandwidths?

Twisted-Pair Wire

Figure 7.6 Three types of wired communications channels. *(Top left)* Twisted-pair wire. This type does not protect well against electrical interference. *(Top right)* Coaxial cable. This type is shielded against electrical interference. It also can carry more data than twisted-pair wire. *(Bottom right)* When coaxial cable is bundled together, as here, it can carry more than 40,000 conversations at once. *(Bottom left)* Fiber-optic cable. Thin glass strands transmit pulsating light instead of electricity. These strands can carry computer and voice data over long distances.

The telephone line that runs from your house to the pole outside, or underground, is probably twisted-pair wire. **Twisted-pair wire** consists of two strands of insulated copper wire, twisted around each other. They are then covered in another layer of plastic insulation. *(See Figure 7.6.)* The two major types of twisted pair wire are unshielded (UTP) and shielded (STP). STP is wrapped in a metal sheath for added protection against external influence. UTP is pliable and doesn't take up as much room in ductwork as STP and other types of cable.

Because so much of the world is already served by twisted-pair wire (the "plain old telephone system," or POTS), it will no doubt continue to be used for years, both for voice messages and for modem-transmitted computer data. However, because twisted pair has a relatively small bandwidth, it can be slow, and it also does not protect well against electrical interference. It is still used to connect parts of a LAN over short distances, but it will certainly be superseded by better communications channels, wired or wireless.

Coaxial Cable

Coaxial cable, commonly called "co-ax," consists of insulated copper wire wrapped in a solid or braided metal shield, then in an external cover. Co-ax is widely used for cable television and to connect parts of a LAN over longer distances. The extra insulation makes coaxial cable much better at resisting noise than twisted-pair wiring. Moreover, because it has a greater bandwidth, it can carry voice and data at a faster rate (up to about 200 Mbps, compared to 16–100 Mbps for twisted-pair wire). Often many coaxial cables will be bundled together.

Fiber-Optic Cable

A **fiber-optic cable** consists of hundreds or thousands of thin strands of glass that transmit not electricity but rather pulsating beams of light. These strands, each as thin as a human hair, can transmit billions of pulses per second, each "on" pulse representing one bit. When bundled together, fiber-optic strands in a cable 0.12 inch thick can support a quarter- to a half-million voice conversations at the same time. Moreover, unlike electrical signals, light pulses are not affected by random electromagnetic interference in the environment. Thus, they have much lower error rates than normal telephone wire and cable. In addition, fiber-optic cable is lighter and more durable than twisted-wire and coaxial cable.

What does "POTS" stand for? What are some of its limitations? Why do coaxial cable and fiber-optic cable offer improvements?

The main drawbacks until now have been cost and the material's inability to bend around tight corners. In mid-1995, however, new material was announced—called *graded-index plastic optical fiber*—that was cheaper, lighter, and more flexible than glass fibers. The plastic flexible fiber is said to handle loops and curves with ease and thus will be better than glass for curb-to-home wiring.

Microwave and Satellite Systems

Wired forms of communications, which require physical connection between sender and receiver, will not disappear any time soon, if ever. For one thing, fiber-optic cables can transmit data communications 10,000 times faster than microwave and satellite systems can. Moreover, they are resistant to illegal data theft.

Still, some of the most exciting developments are in wireless communications. After all, there are many situations in which it is difficult to run physical wires.

■ *Microwave systems:* **Microwave systems** transmit voice and data through the atmosphere as high-frequency radio waves. Microwave systems transmit microwaves, of course. *Microwaves* are the electromagnetic waves that vibrate at 1 gigahertz (1 billion hertz) per second or higher. These frequencies are used not only to operate microwave ovens but also to transmit messages between ground-based earth stations and satellite communications systems.

Nowadays you see dish- or horn-shaped microwave antennas nearly everywhere—on towers, buildings, and hilltops. *(See Figure 7.7.)* Why, you might wonder, do people have to interfere with nature by putting a microwave dish on top of a mountain? The reason is that microwaves cannot bend around corners or around the earth's curvature; they are *line-of-sight.* Line-of-sight means that there must be an unobstructed view between transmitter and receiver. Thus, microwave stations need to be placed within 25–30 miles of each other, with no obstructions in between. The size of the dish varies with the distance (perhaps 2–4 feet in diameter for short distances, 10 feet or more for long distances). A string of microwave relay stations will each receive incoming messages, boost the signal strength, and relay the signals to the next station.

Figure 7.7 Microwave systems. Microwaves cannot bend around corners or around the curvature of the earth. Therefore, microwave antennas must be in "line of sight" of each other—that is, unobstructed. Microwave dishes and relay towers are usually situated atop high places, such as mountains or tall buildings, so that signals can be beamed over uneven terrain.

Microwave relay station

Line-of-sight signal

More than half of today's telephone system uses dish microwave transmission. However, the airwaves are becoming so saturated with microwave signals that future needs will have to be satisfied by other channels, such as satellite systems.

■ *Satellite systems:* To avoid some of the limitations of microwave earth stations, communications companies have added microwave "sky stations"—communications satellites. **Communications satellites** are microwave relay stations in orbit around the earth. Traditionally, the orbit has been 22,300 miles above the earth, although newer systems will be much lower. Because they travel at the same speed as the earth, they appear to an observer on the ground to be stationary in space—that is, they are *geostationary.* Consequently, microwave earth stations are always able to beam signals to a fixed location above. The orbiting satellite has solar-powered receivers and transmitters (transponders) that receive the signals, amplify them, and retransmit them to another earth station. *(See Figure 7.8.)* The satellite contains many communications channels and receives both analog and digital signals from earth stations. (Note that it can take more than one satellite to get a message delivered, and the extra relay can slow the delivery process down.)

> **What are some of the benefits of microwave and satellite communications?**

To transmit a signal from a ground station to a satellite is called *uplinking.* The signal is then *downlinked* to, for example, a TV station.

Other Wireless Communications

Of course, mobile wireless communications have been around for some time. The Detroit Police Department started using two-way car radios in 1921. Mobile telephones were introduced in 1946. Today, however, we are witnessing an explosion in mobile wireless use that is making worldwide changes.

There are essentially four ways to move information through the air long-distance on radio frequencies: (1) via *one-way communications,* as typified by the satellite navigation system known as GPS and by pagers, and via *two-way communications,* which are classified as (2) analog cellular phones, (3) packet radio, and (4) CDPD. (Other wireless methods operate at short distances.)

■ *One-way communications—the Global Positioning System (GPS):* A $10 billion infrastructure developed by the military in the mid-1980s, **GPS,** for

Figure 7.8
Communications satellite

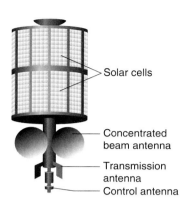

Solar cells

Concentrated
beam antenna

Transmission
antenna

Control antenna

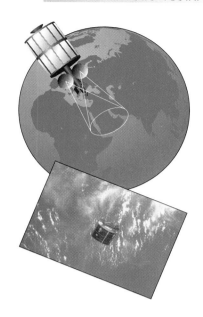

Global Positioning System, consists of a series of 24 earth-orbiting satellites that continuously transmit timed radio signals that can be used to identify earth locations. A GPS receiver—handheld or mounted in a vehicle, plane, or boat—can pick up transmissions from any four satellites, interpret the information from each, and calculate to within a few hundred feet or less the receiver's longitude, latitude, and altitude. The accuracy of GPSs is expected to improve to plus or minus a few feet.

The system is used by the military to tell military units exactly where they are, but it is also being used for civilian purposes such as tracking trucks and taxis, locating stolen cars, orienting hikers, and aiding in surveying, and it has become standard safety equipment on boats. The makers of the film *Forrest Gump* used a GPS device to track the sun and time their sunrise and sunset shots so they didn't get shadows. Some GPS receivers include map software for finding your way around, as with the Guidestar system available with some rental cars in cities such as Miami, Los Angeles, and New York.

■ *One-way communications—pagers:* In a Clearwater, Florida, child-care center, if one child bites another or otherwise misbehaves, the head of the center can instantly alert the parents. He or she need only dial the number of the pager that parents are given as part of the child-care service.[15]

Once stereotyped as devices for doctors and drug dealers, pagers are now consumer items. Commonly known as *beepers,* for the sound they make when activated, *pagers* are simple radio receivers that receive data sent from a special radio transmitter. Often the pager has its own telephone number. When the number is dialed from a phone, the call goes by way of the transmitter straight to the designated pager. Paging services include SkyTel (MTel), PageNet, and EMBARC (Motorola).

Today's pagers are available in pocket sizes and designer colors (including Bimini blue and neon green). Some sell for as little as $29.95, with monthly service charges as low as $8. Pagers also do more than beep, transmitting full-blown alphanumeric text (such as four-line, 80-character messages) and other data. Newer ones are mini-answering machines, capable of relaying digitized voice messages.[16]

Pagers are very efficient for transmitting one-way information—emergency messages, news, prices, stock quotations, mortgage rates,

What can you imagine using a GPS system for?

delivery-route assignments, even sports news and scores[17]—at low cost to single or multiple receivers. Recently some companies have introduced what is called *two-way paging* or *enhanced paging*. This technology allows customers to send a preprogrammed acknowledgment ("Will be late—stuck in traffic") after they have received a message. Eventually, paging companies hope, these two-way devices will evolve into full-fledged handheld communicators.

■ *Two-way communications—analog cellular: Analog cellular phones* are designed primarily for communicating at 824–894 MHz by voice through a system of ground-area cells. Each *cell* is hexagonal in shape, usually 8 miles or less in diameter, and is served by a transmitter-receiving tower. Calls are directed between cells by a mobile telephone switching office (MTSO). Movement between cells requires that calls be handed off by the MTSO. *(See Figure 7.9.)*

Handing off voice calls between cells poses only minimal problems. However, handing off data transmission (where every bit counts), with the inevitable gaps and pauses as one moves from one cell to another, is much more difficult. In the long run, data transmissions will probably have to be handled by the technology we discuss next, packet radio.

■ *Two-way communications—packet radio: Pocket-radio-based communications* use a nationwide system of radio towers that send data to handheld computers. Packet radio is the basis for services such as RAM Mobile Data and Ardis. The advantage of packet-radio transmission is that the wireless com-

Figure 7.9 Cellular connections

Calling from a cellular phone:
When you dial a call on a cellular phone, whether on the street or in a car, the call moves as radio waves to the transmitting-receiving tower that serves that particular cell. The call then moves by wire or microwaves to the mobile telephone switching office (MTSO), which directs the call from there on—generally to a regular local phone exchange, after which it becomes a conventional phone call.

Receiving a call on a cellular phone:
The MTSO transmits the number dialed to all the cells it services. Once it finds the phone, it directs the call to it through the nearest transmitting-receiving tower.

On the move:
When you make calls to or from phones while on the move, as in a moving car, the MTSO's computers sense when a phone's signal is becoming weaker. The computers then figure out which adjacent cell to "hand-off" the call to and find an open frequency in that new cell to switch to.

1. A call originates from a mobile cellular phone.
2. The call wirelessly finds the nearest cellular tower using its FM tuner to make a connection.
3. The tower sends the signal to a Mobile Telephone Switching Office (MTSO) using traditional telephone network land lines.
4. The MTSO routes the call over the telephone network to a land-based phone or initiates a search for the recipient on the cellular network.
5. The MTSO sends the recipient's phone number to all its towers, which broadcast the number via radio frequency.
6. The recipient's phone "hears" the broadcast and establishes a connection with the nearest tower. A voice line is established via the tower by the MTSO.

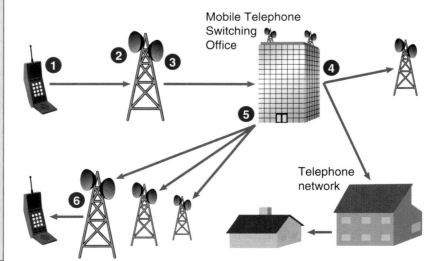

Nokia wireless phone with a PC card modem that is inserted in a slot on the side of the notebook computer.

puter identifies itself to the local base station, which can transmit over as many as 16 separate radio channels. Packet switching encapsulates the data in "envelopes," which ensures that the information arrives intact.

Packet-radio data networks are useful for mobile workers who need to communicate frequently with a corporate database. For example, National Car Rental System sends workers with handheld terminals to prowl parking lots, recording the location of rental cars and noting the latest scratches and dents. They can thereby easily check a customer's claim that a car was already damaged or find out quickly when one is stolen.

- *Two-way communications—CDPD:* Short for *Cellular Digital Packet Data,* CDPD places messages in packets, or digital electronic "envelopes," and sends them through underused radio channels or between pauses in cellular phone conversations. CDPD is thus an enhancement to today's analog cellular phone systems, allowing packets of data to "hop" between temporarily free voice channels. As a result, a user carrying a CDPD device could have access to both voice and data. One problem with CDPD so far, however, is that it has limited coverage.

The Next Generation of Wireless Communications

Other kinds of wireless data services are on the way, promising to offer us lots of choices. The following are a few such developments:

- *Digital cellular phone:* Cellular telephone companies are trying to rectify the problem of faulty data transmission by switching from analog to digital. *Digital cellular phone* networks turn your voice message into digital bits, which are sent through the airwaves, then decoded back into your voice by the cellular handset. Unlike analog cellular phones, digital phones can handle short e-mail messages, paging, and some headline news items in addition to voice transmission. But currently these extra features won't work if the user is traveling outside the digital network service area. And you'll be able to make and receive nondigital phone calls only if your handset is equipped to function both in digital and analog modes.

    Despite advances in wireless technology, American cell phones remain useless outside North America. Travelers wishing to use cell phones abroad have to rent temporary units. But a recent move by the World Trade Organization (WTO) will change that by standardizing worldwide telecommunications systems. The agreement, set to be implemented by 69 nations over the next eight to nine years, provides a framework for an eventual global system that will be low in cost, high in quality, and extremely efficient.

    A digital cell phone costs two or three times more than an analog one ($300 and up), but the monthly bill may be less, especially for heavy users. Digital phone networks promise clearer sound, although some consumers don't agree. They also offer more privacy (*see box on next page*).

- *Personal communications services:* Personal communications services *(PCS)* are digital wireless services that use a new band of frequencies (1850–1990 MHz) and transmitter-receivers in thousands of microcells. PCS systems operate at high frequencies, where the spectrum isn't crowded. The microcells are smaller than the cells of today's cellular phone systems.

Eavesdropping[18]

Forget about glass tumblers pressed up against the wall. Eavesdropping has gone high tech. Millions of Americans—including John and Alice Martin, the Florida couple who say they taped the infamous conversation between [U.S. House Speaker] Newt Gingrich and other GOP leaders [in December 1996]—now snoop with "scanners," computerized radio receivers that surf the airwaves and pluck out transmissions. The machine, usually no bigger than a shoe box, has spawned a whole community complete with newsletters. Most people tune to police, fire, ambulance, and weather channels. Though it's illegal, some scanner users listen in on cellular phone calls. Others tap into their neighbor's cordless phone calls. "I'm not Mr. Paranoid," says Harold Ort, editor of *Popular Communications* magazine and an avid scanner. "But always assume someone is listening."

Scanners occasionally catch extraordinary moments: astronauts describing the stars from space, police officers detailing high-speed chases, ambulance attendants outlining a patient's condition, airline pilots reporting equipment failure. "Some of what you hear knocks your socks off," says Ort.

The wireless Nokia 9000 Communicator phones, faxes, e-mails, logs on to the Internet, and downloads files from a PC. The phone splits open to reveal a keyboard and a display screen. (Actor Val Kilmer used it in *The Saint*.)

The first commercial test area for PCS was the Washington, D.C./Baltimore area, where a system called Sprint Spectrum offered a combination of wireless telephone, paging, and voice-mail services.[19] Walter Mossberg, who regularly writes for the *Wall Street Journal* about personal computing, said in early 1996 that the Sprint PCS phone he tested was "superior in nearly every respect to a cellular phone, with better call quality and greater security."[20] He found digital PCS calls had much less static and fading, even while in a car or inside most buildings.

Note that users of digital cellular phones and PCS phones must investigate where their phones will and will not work. There are three distinct digital wireless technologies, and equipment that works with one technology won't work on the others. Thus units that operate on AT&T Wireless network won't work in a Sprint network area, and vice versa. Many of the PCS networks won't be fully operational until 1998–2005.

■ *Specialized mobile radio:* Specialized mobile radio (SMR) is a two-way radio voice-dispatching service used by taxis and trucks that is being converted to digital. Nextel Communications is building a nationwide SMR network, putting itself in direct competition with cellular phone services.

■ *Satellite-based systems:* More than half the people in the world, mostly in underdeveloped countries, live more than 2 hours from the nearest telephone. (China has only about four telephone lines for every 100 people.) These people, along with business travelers and corporations needing speedy data transmission, will probably demand more than wire-line or cellular service can deliver. As a result, the race is on to build constellations of satellites. "Almost three dozen programs—totaling more than 1500 satellites—are in the works," says one reporter. "That's almost five times the number of commercial communications satellites launched since the first, AT&T's Telstar, in 1962."[21]

Projects include Globalstar and Iridium (both scheduled to begin service in 1998); Astrolink, Odyssey, Spaceway, and Voicespan (beginning in 2000); and the giant $9 billion Teledesic (backed by Microsoft's Bill Gates and cellular phone pioneer Craig McCaw, and projected to comprise a staggering 840

Geostationary Earth orbit (GEO)

SPACEWAY

Subscribers access service with $1,000 terminal, 26-inch dish antenna.

Satellites: 8
Orbits: Geostationary, 22,300 miles above equator
Operational in: First global region in 1999, rest in 2000
Cost: $3 billion
Speed: 16 kilobits per second

to 6 megabits per second
Applications: ordinary fixed telephone service in developing areas, fax, videoconferencing, data, broadband multimedia, such as from Internet
Investor: Hughes Electronics

Medium-Earth orbit (MEO)

ICO GLOBAL COMMUNICATIONS

A London-based private offshoot of INMARSAT, ICO has 47 telecommunications investors and COMSAT, Hughes.

Satellites: 10
Orbits: Inclined 45 degrees to equator, 6,434 miles up
Operational in: 2000
Cost: $3.7 billion

Applications: Hand-held dual-mode mobile phones that talk to satellites and cellular systems; phones for cars, ships, aircraft; fixed phones in developing areas

ODYSSEY

Founded by TRW Inc. and Teleglobe Inc. to offer worldwide mobile phone service

Satellites: 12
Orbits: Inclined 50 degrees to equator, 6,434 miles up
Operational in: 2001
Cost: $3.2 billion

Applications: Hand-held dual mode phones, other personal communications services, largely in developing nations

Low-Earth orbit (LEO)

GLOBALSTAR

A simple, beefy system for worldwide mobile and fixed-phone service

Satellites: 48
Orbits: Inclined 52 degrees to equator, 763 miles up
Operational in: Fall 1998 (partial), full in 1999
Cost: $2.5 billion

Applications: Hand-held dual-mode phones, fixed ordinary phones, paging, low-speed data
Partners: Loral Space & Communications, Qualcomm Inc.

IRIDIUM

Designed so business travelers can call anywhere from anywhere

Satellites: 66
Orbits: Near polar orbit at 421.5 miles up
Operational in: Sept. 1998
Cost: $5 billion
Applications: Hand-held dual-

mode phones, paging, low-speed data, fax
Investors: Motorola, Raytheon, Lockheed Martin, Sprint, Khrunichev State Research, 12 others

ORBCOMM

95-pound minisatellites to provide message services for industry, outdoors enthusiasts

Satellites: 28
Orbits: Inclined 45 and 70 degrees to equator, 480 miles up
Operational in: 1997
Cost: $330 million
Applications: Data messages

from individuals; tracking of barges, truck trailers; remote monitoring of industrial installations, oil wells
Partners: Orbital Sciences Corp., Teleglobe Inc.

TELEDESIC

"Internet in the Sky" aims to make broadband multimedia connections anywhere just like fiber-optic cables.

Satellites: 840
Orbits: Near polar orbits, 420 miles up
Operational in: 2002
Cost: $9 billion
Applications: Broadband

multimedia for corporate intranets, Internet, videoconferencing, up to 28 megabits per second
Investors: Bill Gates, Craig McCaw

---

satellites, going online by 2002).[22] Some will operate as "geosynchronous" satellites 22,300 miles above a fixed point on earth, thus covering broad swaths of ground but being handicapped by an inherent half-second signal delay from sender to receiver. Other satellite networks are planned for "medium-earth orbit," about 5000–10,000 miles up, and "low-earth orbit," only 400–700 miles from earth. Among other things, these would offer wireless phone, messaging, paging, and related services, as well as satellite-to-home TV signals.[23]

Already GM Hughes Electronics (along with U.S. Satellite Broadcasting Co.) offers the 200-channel DirecTV service, which digitally beams television programs to the 1.25 million consumers who have already purchased pizza-size receiving dishes.[24] The market for digital video users is expected to grow to 20 million by 2000.

Clearly, we are very near the time when voices, images, and information can be transmitted to any place on earth. Says C. Michael Armstrong, chairman of Hughes, these advances already are revolutionizing "how we talk to each other and how we relate to each other." He adds, as an understatement: "It's a societal change."[25]

The future of satellite operations

Factors Affecting Communications Among Devices

Many factors govern the way data is transmitted and how fast it moves.

Having gotten a good look at the kinds of communication channels available and on the horizon, we can take a brief look at other factors that affect data transmission. The whole topic of communications technology is quite complicated and very technical. However, in this age of communicating via computers, you need to be familiar with some of the other basic factors that affect data transmission, including the following:

■ Transmission rate—frequency and bandwidth

■ Line configurations—point-to-point versus multipoint

■ Serial versus parallel transmission

■ Direction of transmission—simplex, half-duplex, and full-duplex

■ Transmission mode—asynchronous versus synchronous

■ Packet switching

■ Multiplexing

■ Protocols

Transmission Rate: Higher Frequency, Wider Bandwidth, More Data

Transmission rate is a function of two variables: frequency and bandwidth.

■ *Frequency:* The amount of data that can be transmitted on a channel depends on the wave frequency—the cycles of waves per second. Frequency is expressed in hertz: 1 cycle per second equals 1 hertz. The more cycles per second, the more data that can be sent through that channel.

■ *Bandwidth:* As we mentioned earlier, bandwidth is the difference between the highest and lowest frequencies—that is, the range of frequencies. Data may be sent not just on one frequency but on several frequencies within a particular bandwidth, all at the same time. Thus, the greater the bandwidth of a channel, the more frequencies it has available and hence the more data that can can be sent through that channel. The rate of speed of data through the channel is expressed in bits per second (bps).

Why is bandwidth an important factor in data transmission?

A twisted-pair telephone wire of 4000 hertz might send only 1 kilobyte of data in a second. A coaxial cable of 100 megahertz might send 10 megabytes. And a fiber-optic cable of 200 trillion hertz might send 1 gigabyte.

Line Configurations: Point-to-Point and Multipoint

There are two principal line configurations, or ways of connecting communications lines: point-to-point and multipoint.

- *Point-to-point:* A *point-to-point line* directly connects the sending and receiving devices, such as a terminal with a central computer. This arrangement is appropriate for a private line whose sole purpose is to keep data secure by transmitting it from one device to another. A point-to-point line may be public or private (leased). As an improvement to its telephone service, in 1958 Bell Labs developed the T1 line, which uses special signaling techniques and multiplexers to increase the capacity of existing copper long-distance lines. The T1 line can carry 24 signals on a single set of twisted copper wires. Since long-distance calls are now handled mostly by microwave, satellite, and fiber-optic systems, T1 lines—although expensive—are now often used as leased (private, or dedicated) point-to-point lines for high-speed data transmission between offices or schools and, for example, companies that provide access to the Internet. *(See Figure 7.10.)*

- *Multipoint:* A *multipoint line* is a single line that interconnects several communications devices to one computer. Often on a multipoint line only one communications device, such as a terminal, can transmit at any given time. (In rural areas with a number of telephone subscribers connected to a single copper telephone line, this type of connection was called a *party line.*)

Serial and Parallel Transmission

Data is transmitted in two ways: serially and in parallel.

- *Serial data transmission:* In **serial data transmission,** bits are transmitted sequentially, one after the other. *(See Figure 7.11.)* This arrangement resembles cars proceeding down a one-lane road.

  Serial transmission is the way most data flows over a twisted-pair telephone line. Serial transmission is found in communications lines, modems, and most mice. The plug-in board for a microcomputer modem usually has a serial port.

Figure 7.10 Three schools in Palo Alto, California, share T1 access to the Internet over a wide area network that uses the local cable TV system as its high-speed backbone.

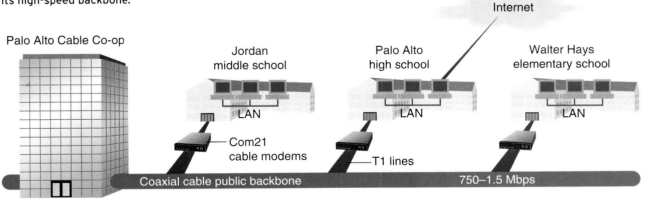

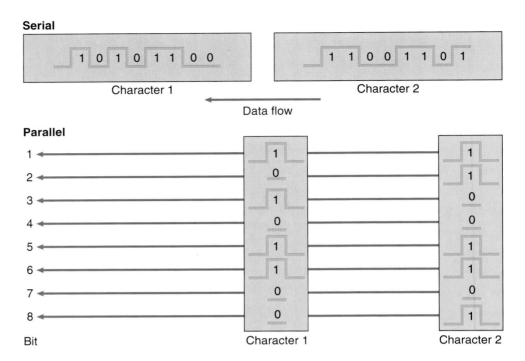

Figure 7.11 Serial and parallel data transmission

- *Parallel data transmission:* In **parallel data transmission,** bits are transmitted through separate lines simultaneously. The arrangement resembles cars moving in separate lanes at the same speed on a multilane freeway.

  Parallel lines move information faster than serial lines do, but they are efficient for up to only 15 feet. Thus, parallel lines are used, for example, to transmit data from a PC's processor to a printer.

  Parallel transmission may also be used within a company's facility, for terminal-to-main-computer data transmission.

Direction of Transmission Flow: Simplex, Half-Duplex, and Full-Duplex

When two computers are in communication, data can flow in three ways: simplex, half-duplex, or full-duplex. These are fancy terms for easily understood processes. (*See Figure 7.12.*)

- *Simplex transmission:* In **simplex transmission,** data can travel in only one direction. An example is a traditional television broadcast, in which the signal is sent from the transmitter to your TV antenna. There is no return signal. Some computerized data collection devices also work this way (such as seismograph sensors that measure earthquakes).

- *Half-duplex transmission:* In **half-duplex transmission,** data travels in both directions but only in one direction at a time. This arrangement resembles traffic on a one-lane bridge; the separate streams of cars must take turns. Half-duplex transmission is seen with CB or marine radios, in which both parties must take turns talking. This is the most common mode of data transmission used today.

- *Full-duplex transmission:* In **full-duplex transmission,** data is transmitted back and forth at the same time. This arrangement resembles automobile traffic on

Figure 7.12

Transmission directions.
Simplex, half-duplex, and
full-duplex.

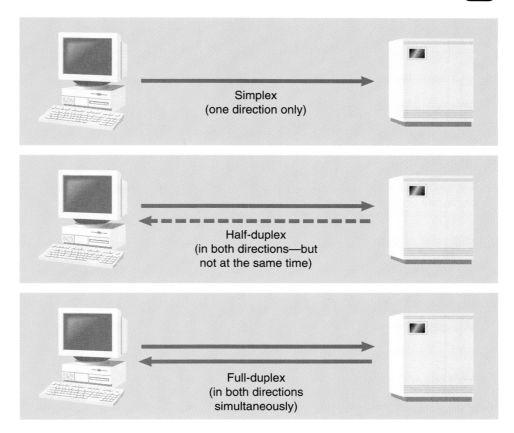

Figure 7.12

Transmission directions. Simplex, half-duplex, and full-duplex.

Simplex
(one direction only)

Half-duplex
(in both directions—but
not at the same time)

Full-duplex
(in both directions
simultaneously)

a two-way street. An example is two people on the telephone talking and listening simultaneously. Full-duplex transmission is sometimes used in large computer systems. It is also available for some new microcomputer modems and software to support truly interactive collaboration using products like Microsoft NetMeeting.

Transmission Mode: Asynchronous Versus Synchronous

Suppose your computer sends the word CONGRATULATIONS! to someone as bits and bytes over a communications line. How does the receiving equipment know where one byte (or character) ends and another begins? This matter is resolved through either *asynchronous transmission* or *synchronous transmission. (See Figure 7.13.)*

■ *Asynchronous transmission:* This method, used with most microcomputers, is also called *start-stop transmission. (Asynchronous* comes from the ancient Greek word meaning "not timed.") In **asynchronous transmission** data is sent one byte (or character) at a time. Each string of bits making up the byte is bracketed, or marked off, with special control bits. That is, a "start" bit represents the beginning of a character, and a "stop" bit represents its end.

Most microcomputers use asynchronous transmission—at only one byte at a time, with start and top pulses, this is a relatively slow method. As a result, asynchronous transmission is not used when great amounts of data must be sent rapidly. Its advantage is that the data can be transmitted whenever it is convenient for the sender.

Asynchronous transmission

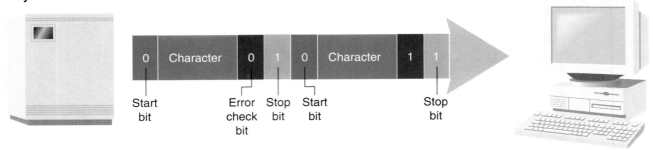

Synchronous transmission

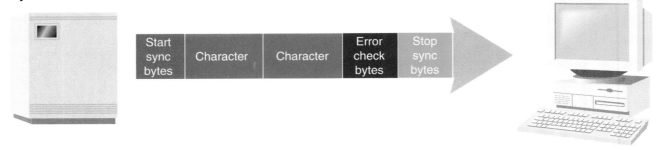

Figure 7.13 Transmission modes. There are two ways that devices receiving data transmissions can determine the beginning and ends of strings of bits (bytes, or characters). *(Top)* Asynchronous transmission. Each character is preceded by a "start" bit and followed by a "stop" bit. *(Bottom)* Synchronous transmission. Messages are sent in blocks, with start and stop patterns of bits, called *synch bytes*, before and after the blocks. The synch bytes synchronize the timing of the internal clocks between sending and receiving devices.

■ *Synchronous transmission:* Instead of using start and stop bits, **synchronous transmission** sends data in blocks (*synchronous* = "timed"). Start and stop bit patterns, called *synch bytes*, are transmitted at the beginning and end of the blocks. These start and end bit patterns synchronize internal clocks in the sending and receiving devices so that they are in time with each other.

This method is rarely used with microcomputers because it is more complicated and more expensive than asynchronous transmission. (However, some microcomputer modems will convert the asynchronous signals from the computer's serial port into synchronous signals on the transmission line.) It also requires careful timing between sending and receiving equipment. It is appropriate for large computer systems that need to transmit great quantities of data quickly.

Packet Switching: Getting More Data on a Network

A **packet** is a fixed-length block of data for transmission. The packet also contains instructions about the destination of the packet. **Packet switching** is a technique used in wide area networks for dividing electronic messages into packets for transmission over a network to their destination through the most expedient routes. (A wide area network, discussed shortly, is a communications network that covers a wide geographical area, such as a state or a country.) The benefit of packet switching is that it can handle high-volume traffic in a network. It also allows more users to share a network, thereby offering cost savings. The method is particularly appropriate for sending messages long distances, such as across the country. Accordingly, it is used in large networks such as Telenet, Tymnet, and AT&T's Accunet.

Here's how packet switching works: A sending computer breaks an electronic message apart into packets. The various packets are sent through a communications network—often by different routes, at different speeds, and sandwiched in between packets from other messages. Once the packets arrive at their destination, the receiving computer reassembles the packets into proper sequence to complete the message. Packet switching is suitable for data, but not real-time voice and video, transmission.

Packet switching is contrasted with *circuit switching,* by which the transmitter has full use of the circuit until all the data has been transmitted and the circuit is terminated. Circuit switching is used by the telephone company for its voice networks to guarantee steady, consistent service for telephone conversations. A newer technology, called *asynchronous transfer mode,* or *ATM,* combines the efficiency of packet switching with some aspects of circuit switching, thus enabling it to handle both data and real-time voice and video. ATM is designed to run on high-bandwidth fiber-optic cables.

Multiplexing: Enhancing Communications Efficiencies

Communications lines nearly always have far greater capacity than a single microcomputer or terminal can use. Because operating such lines is expensive, it's more efficient if several communications devices can share a line at the same time. This is the rationale for multiplexing. **Multiplexing** is the transmission of multiple signals over a single communications channel.

Three types of devices are used to achieve multiplexing—*multiplexers, concentrators,* and *front-end processors:*

■ *Multiplexers:* A **multiplexer** is a device that merges several low-speed transmissions into one high-speed transmission. *(See Figure 7.14.)* Depending on the model, 32 or more devices may share a single communications line. Messages

Figure 7.14 How multiplexing works. With sending and receiving multiplexers, several low-speed transmissions may share a high-speed line.

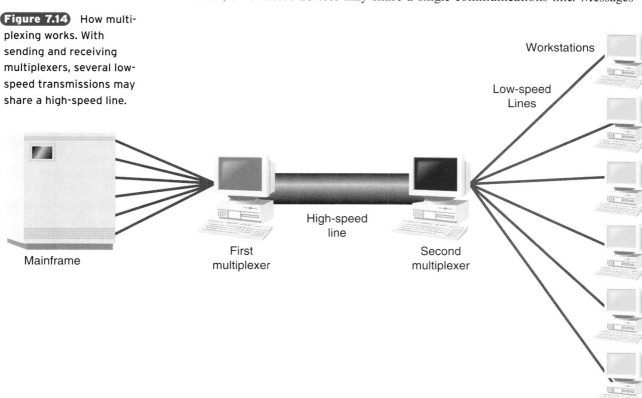

Workstations

Low-speed
Lines

Mainframe

First
multiplexer

High-speed
line

Second
multiplexer

What are multiplexers

used for?

sent by a multiplexer must be received by a multiplexer of the same type. The receiving multiplexer sorts out the individual messages and directs them to the proper recipient.

■ *Concentrators:* Like a multiplexer, a concentrator is a piece of hardware that enables several devices to share a single communications line. However, unlike a multiplexer, a **concentrator** collects data in a temporary storage area. In other words, unlike a multiplexer, which spreads the signals back out again on the receiving end, the concentrator has a receiving computer to perform that function.

■ *Front-end processors:* The most sophisticated of these communications-management devices is the front-end processor, a computer that handles communications for mainframes. A **front-end processor** is a smaller computer that is connected to a larger computer and assists with communications functions. It transmits and receives messages over the communications channels, corrects errors, and relieves the larger computer of routine computational tasks. Sometimes the term *front-end processor* is used synonymously with the term *communications controller,* although this latter device is usually less sophisticated. (A communications controller handles communications between a computer and peripheral devices such as terminals and printers.) In a local area network, the functions of a front-end processor are performed by a *network adapter.* This is simply a printed circuit board inserted into a workstation or server (✔ p. 1.14).

Protocols: The Rules of Data Transmission

All of the foregoing information in this section may seem unduly technical for an ordinary computer user. Fortunately, when you sit down to send a message through a telecommunications system, you won't usually have to think about these details. Experts will already have taken care of them for you in sets of rules called *protocols.*

The word *protocol* is used in the military and in diplomacy to express rules of precedence, rank, manners, and other matters of correctness. (An example would be the protocol for who will precede whom into a formal reception.) Here, however, a **protocol,** or *communications protocol,* is a set of conventions governing the exchange of data between hardware and/or software components in a communications network.

Protocols are built into the hardware or software you are using. The protocol in your communications software, for example, will specify how receiver devices will acknowledge sending devices, a matter called *handshaking.* Handshaking establishes the fact that the circuit is available and operational. It also establishes the level of device compatibility and the speed of transmission. Protocols will also specify the type of electrical connections used, the timing of message exchanges, error-detection techniques, and so on—protocol functions called *line discipline.*

In the past, not all hardware and software developers subscribed to the same protocols. As a result, many kinds of equipment and programs have not been able to work with one another. In recent years, more developers have agreed to subscribe to a standard of protocols called OSI, short for Open Systems Interconnection. Backed by the International Standards Organization, **OSI** is an international standard that defines seven layers of protocols, or software responsibilities, for worldwide computer communications. *(See Figure 7.15.)* We provide some information about some specific protocols in the next chapter.

Now that we have covered the basic principles of communications technology, we turn to one of the main uses of that technology: networks.

Figure 7.15 OSI. The seven layers of the ISO standard for worldwide communications that defines a framework for implementing protocols.

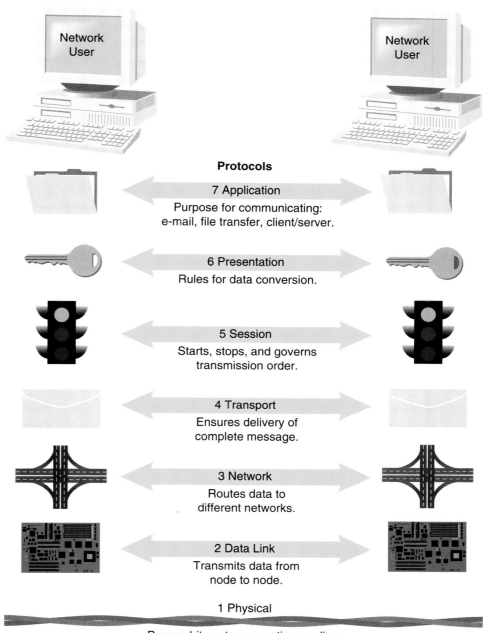

Protocols

7 Application
Purpose for communicating:
e-mail, file transfer, client/server.

6 Presentation
Rules for data conversion.

5 Session
Starts, stops, and governs
transmission order.

4 Transport
Ensures delivery of
complete message.

3 Network
Routes data to
different networks.

2 Data Link
Transmits data from
node to node.

1 Physical

Passes bits onto connecting medium.

Communications Networks

Communications channels and hardware may be used in different layouts or networks, varying in size from large to small. Networks allow users to share peripheral devices, programs, and data; to have better communications; to have more secure information; and to have access to databases.

Whether wired, wireless, or both, all the channels we've described can be used singly or in mix-and-match fashion to form networks. A **network,** or *communications network,* is a system of interconnected computers, telephones, or other communications devices that can communicate with one another and share applications and data. It is the tying together of so many communications devices in so many ways that is changing the world we live in.

A network requires a network operating system—NOS—to manage network resources. It may be a completely self-contained operating system, such as NetWare (✔ p. 5.23), or it may require an existing operating system in order to function—for example, LAN Manager requires OS/2 (✔ p. 5.20), and LANtastic requires DOS (✔ p. 5.15).

Here we will consider the following aspects of networks:

■ Types of networks—wide area, metropolitan area, and local

■ Some network features

■ Advantages of networks

Types of Networks: Wide Area, Metropolitan Area, and Local

Networks are categorized principally in the following three sizes:

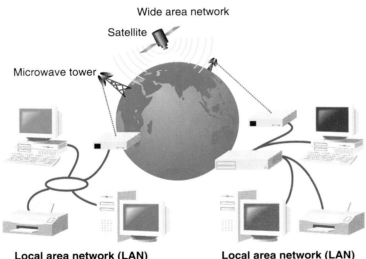

Wide area network

Satellite

Microwave tower

Local area network (LAN)   **Local area network (LAN)**

A wide area network connects local area networks

■ *Wide area network:* A **wide area network (WAN)** is a communications network that covers a wide geographical area, such as a state or a country. Some examples of computer WANs are Tymnet, Telenet, Uninet, and Accunet. The Internet links together hundreds of computer WANs. Of course, most telephone systems—long-distance, regional Bells, and local—are WANs.

■ *Metropolitan area network:* A **metropolitan area network (MAN)** is a communications network covering a geographic area the size of a city or suburb. The purpose of a MAN is often to avoid long-distance telephone charges. Cellular phone systems are often MANs.

■ *Local network:* A **local network** is a privately owned communications network that serves users within a confined geographical area. The range is usually within a mile—perhaps one office, one building, or a group of buildings close together, as a college campus. Local networks are of two types: private branch exchanges (PBXs) and local area networks (LANs), as we discuss shortly.

All these networks may consist of various combinations of computers, storage devices, and communications devices.

What's the difference between a WAN and a LAN?

Some Features: Hosts and Nodes; Downloading and Uploading

Many computer networks, particularly large ones, are served by a host computer. A **host computer,** or simply a *host,* is the main computer—the central computer that controls the network. On a local area network, some of the functions of the host may be performed by a computer called a server. A **server** is a computer shared by several users in a network.

A **node** is simply a device that is attached to a network. A node may be a microcomputer, terminal, storage device, or some peripheral device.

As a network user you can download and upload files. **Download** means that you retrieve files from another computer and store them in your computer. **Upload** means that you send files from your computer to another computer.

Advantages of Networks

The following advantages are particularly true for LANs, although they apply to MANs and WANs as well.

■ *Sharing of peripheral devices:* Laser printers, disk drives, and scanners are examples of peripheral devices—that is, hardware that is connected to a computer. Any newly introduced piece of hardware is often quite expensive, as was the case with laser or color printers. To justify their purchase, companies want them to be shared by many users. Usually the best way to do this is to connect the peripheral device to a network serving several computer users.

■ *Sharing of programs and data:* In most organizations, people use the same software and need access to the same information. It could be expensive for a company to buy one copy of, say, a word processing program for each employee. Rather, the company will usually buy a network version of that program that will serve many employees.

Organizations also save a great deal of money by letting all employees have access to the same data on a shared storage device. This way the organization avoids such problems as some employees updating customer addresses on their own separate machines while other employees remain ignorant of such changes.

Finally, network-linked employees can, using groupware (✔ p. 6.19), work together online on shared projects.

■ *Better communications:* One of the greatest features of networks is electronic mail, as we have seen. With e-mail everyone on a network can easily keep others posted about important information. Thus, the company eliminates the delays encountered with standard interoffice mail delivery or telephone tag.

■ *Security of information:* Before networks became commonplace, an individual employee might be the only one with a particular piece of information, stored in his or her desktop computer. If the employee was dismissed—or if a fire or flood demolished the office—no one else in the company might have any knowledge of that information. Today such data would be backed up or duplicated on a networked storage device shared by others.

How do you think networks might be used in your planned career area?

■ *Access to databases:* Networks also enable users to tap into numerous databases, whether the private databases of a company or the public databases of online services.

Local Networks

Local networks may be private branch exchanges (PBXs) or local area networks (LANs). LANs may be client-server or peer-to-peer and include components such as network cabling, network interface cards, operating system, other shared devices, and bridges and gateways. The topology, or shape, of a network may take five forms.

Although large networks are useful, many organizations need to have a local network—an in-house network—to tie together their own equipment. Here let's consider the following aspects of local networks:

- Types of local networks—PBXs and LANs

- Types of LANs—client-server and peer-to-peer

- Components of a LAN

- Topology of LANs—star, ring, bus, hybrid, and FDDI

- Impact of LANs

Types of Local Networks: PBXs and LANs

The most common types of local networks are PBXs and LANs.

- *Private branch exchange (PBX):* A **private branch exchange (PBX)** is a private or leased telephone switching system that connects telephone extensions in-house. It also connects them to the outside telephone system.

    A public telephone system consists of "public branch exchanges"—thousands of switching stations that direct calls to different branches of the network. A private branch exchange is essentially the old-fashioned company switchboard. You call in from the outside, the switchboard operator says "How may I direct your call?" and you are connected to the extension of the person you wish to talk to.

    Newer PBXs can handle not only analog telephones but also digital equipment, including computers. However, because older PBXs use existing telephone lines, they may not be able to handle the volumes of electronic messages found in some of today's organizations. These companies may be better served by LANs.

- *Local area network (LAN):* PBXs may share existing phone lines with the telephone system. Local area networks usually require installation of their own communication channels, whether wired or wireless. **Local area networks (LANs)** (pronounced "lans") are local networks consisting of a communications link, network operating system, microcomputers or workstations, servers, and other shared hardware. Such shared hardware might include printers, scanners, and storage devices. Unlike larger networks, LANs do not use a host computer.

Name some places where your phone call goes through a PBX.

Types of LANs: Client-Server and Peer-to-Peer

Local area networks are of two principal types: client-server and peer-to-peer. *(See Figure 7.16.)*

■   *Client-server LANs:* A **client-server LAN** consists of requesting microcomputers, called *clients,* and supplying devices that provide a service, called *servers.* The server is a computer that manages shared information or devices, such as laser printers. One piece of the NOS resides in each client machine and

Figure 7.16 Two types of LANs: client-server and peer-to-peer. (*Top*) Client-server LAN. Individual microcomputer users, or "clients," share the services of a centralized computer called a *server.* In this case, the server is a file server, in which users share files of data and some programs. (*Bottom*) Peer-to-peer LAN. Computers share equally with one another without having to rely on a central server.

Client/server LAN

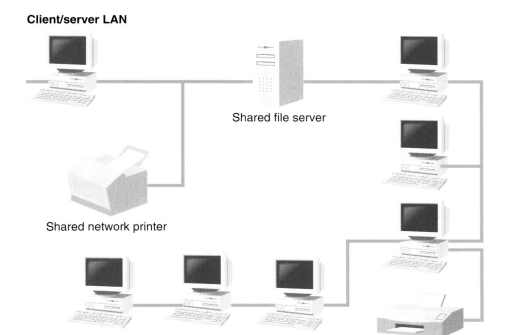

Shared file server

Shared network printer

Local printer

Peer-to-peer LAN

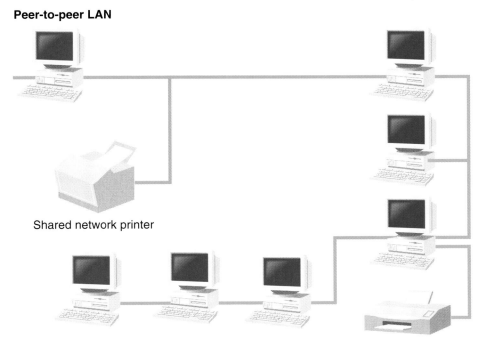

Shared network printer

Local printer

another resides in each server. The NOS allows the remote drives on the servers to be accessed as if they were local drives on the client machine. The server microcomputer is usually a powerful one, with a lot of RAM and secondary storage capacity. Client-server networks, such as those run under Novell's NetWare operating system, are the most common type of LAN.

Another example of a client/server hookup is a user's microcomputer at home connected to America Online (AOL). The user uses the GUI (✔ p. 5.14) and browser software (✔ p. 6.22) on his or her *client* machine. When initiating an Internet session, that software runs with software installed on AOL's communications *server.* That way the two devices communicate effectively without requiring that the Internet communications software be downloaded from the server to the client as part of every Internet session.

There may be different servers for managing different tasks—files and programs, databases, printers. The one you may hear about most often is the file server. A **file server** is a computer that stores the programs and data files shared by users on a LAN. It acts like a disk drive but is in a remote location. (Any files stored on client machines cannot be accessed by other clients.)

A *database server* is a computer in a LAN that stores data. Unlike a file server, it does not store programs. A *print server* is a computer in a LAN that controls one or more printers. It stores the print-image output from all the microcomputers on the system. It then feeds the output to one or more printers one document at a time. *Fax servers* are dedicated to managing fax transmissions, and *mail servers* manage e-mail.

- *Peer-to-peer:* The word *peer* denotes one who is equal in standing with another (as in the phrases "peer pressure" or "jury of one's peers"). A **peer-to-peer LAN** is one in which all microcomputers on the network communicate directly with one another without relying on a server—that is, the NOS allows each station to be both client and server. Thus files stored on one peer machine can be accessed by other peer machines. Peer-to-peer networks are less expensive than client-server networks and work effectively for up to 25 computers. Beyond that they slow down under heavy use. Thus, they are appropriate for networking in small groups, as for workgroup computing. Software used includes LANtastic by Artisoft, Localtalk by Apple, and Windows for Workgroups by Microsoft.

Many LANs mix elements from both client-server and peer-to-peer models.

Components of a LAN

Local area networks are made up of several standard components. *(See Figure 7.17.)*

- *Connection or cabling system:* LANs do not use the telephone network. Instead, they use some other cabling or connection system, either wired or wireless. Wired connections may be twisted-pair wiring, coaxial cable, or fiber-optic cable. Wireless connections may be infrared or radio-wave transmission. Wireless networks are especially useful if computers are portable and are moved often. However, they are subject to interference.

- *Microcomputers with interface cards:* Two or more microcomputers are required, along with network interface cards. A **network interface card,** inserted into an expansion slot (✔ p. 2.25) in a microcomputer, enables the computer to send and receive messages on the LAN. The interface card can also exist in a separate box, which can serve a number of devices.

- *Network operating system:* As we mentioned earlier, the network operating system software manages the activity of the network—it provides it with

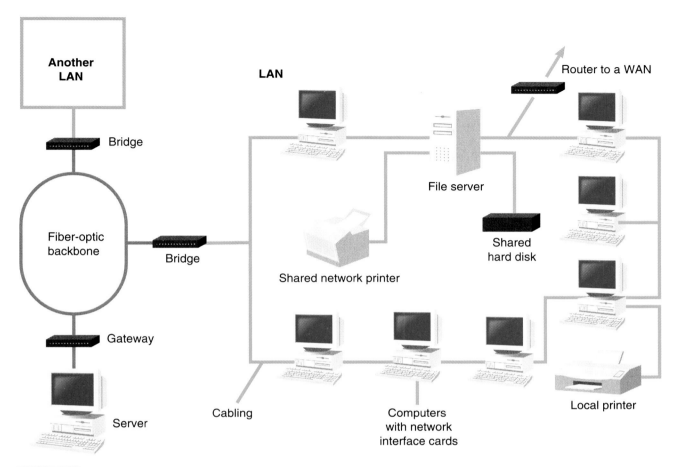

Figure 7.17 Components of a typical LAN

multiuser, multitasking (✔ p. 5.11) capabilities. Depending on the type of network, the operating system software may be stored on a server, on each microcomputer on the network, or a combination of both.

In addition to supporting multitasking and multiuser access, LAN operating systems provide for recognition of users based on passwords, user IDs, and terminal IDs.

Examples of network operating systems are Novell's NetWare, Microsoft's LAN Manager, and IBM's PC LAN. As mentioned in Chapter 5, you can also establish peer-to-peer networking using Microsoft Windows for Workgroups, Windows 95, and Windows NT.

- *Other shared devices:* Printers, fax machines, scanners, storage devices, and other peripherals may be added to the network as necessary and shared by all users.

- *Bridges, routers, and gateways:* A LAN may stand alone, but it may also connect to other networks, either similar or different in technology. Hardware and software combinations are used as interfaces to make these connections.

  A **bridge** is an interface used to connect the same types of networks. Bridges operate at the bottom two levels of the OSI protocol model, providing physical layer and data link layer connectivity. Bridges extend the physical reach of a LAN, passing traffic from one LAN segment to another based on the address of the packet. They also have buffers that can store messages to forward later in case of traffic congestion.

What kinds of LANS does your school use?

A **router** is a highly intelligent device that supports connectivity between both like and unlike LANs and between LANs and WANs/MANs. Routers operate at the bottom three of the OSI model's seven layers of protocol. The router software enables the router to view the network as a whole; bridges, in contrast, view the network only on a link-by-link basis.

Bridges are protocol independent; routers are protocol dependent. Bridges are faster than routers because they do not have to deal with protocol reading. Gateways are the slowest of the three. Network designers determine which types of bridges, gateways, and routers to use depending on what types of networks and e-mail systems they are connecting, how fast things need to work, and how much everything is going to cost.

A **gateway** performs all functions of bridges and routers, including protocol conversion at all seven layers of the OSI model. For example, an online information service such as CompuServe acts as a gateway, via servers, for your microcomputer's connection to the Internet (a WAN). A gateway supplies entrances to dissimilar networks by tearing down a packet of information from one network and restructuring it for a different network's protocol format. Gateway software generally resides in a midsize or mainframe computer.

Topology of LANs

Networks can be laid out in different ways. The physical layout, or shape, of a network is called a *topology.* The five basic topologies are *star, ring, bus, hybrid,* and *FDDI.*

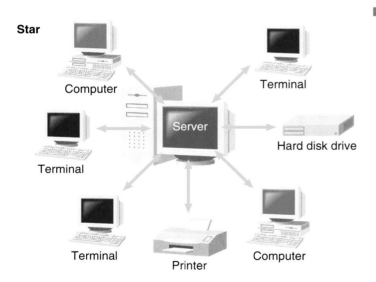

Star

Computer

Terminal

Server

Hard disk drive

Terminal

Terminal

Printer

Computer

■ *Star network:* A **star network** is one in which all microcomputers and other communications devices are connected to a central *hub,* such as a file server or host computer, via UTP (unshielded twisted pair) or STP (shielded twisted pair). Some intelligent hubs can provide switching, bridging, and routing capabilities. Electronic messages are sent through the central hub to their destinations at rates of 1–100 Mbps. The central hub monitors the flow of traffic. A PBX system is an example of a star network.

The advantage of a star network is that the hub prevents collisions between messages. Moreover, if a connection is broken between any communications device and the hub, the rest of the devices on the network will continue operating. The primary disadvantage is that a hub failure is catastrophic.

■ *Ring network:* A **ring network** is one in which all microcomputers and other communications devices are connected in a continuous loop. Electronic messages are passed around the ring in one direction, with each node serving as a repeater, until they reach the right destination. There is no central host computer or server. Rings generally are co-ax or fiber with transmission speeds of 100+ Mbps. An example of a ring network is IBM's Token Ring Network, in which a bit pattern (called a "token") determines which user on the network can send information.

Ring

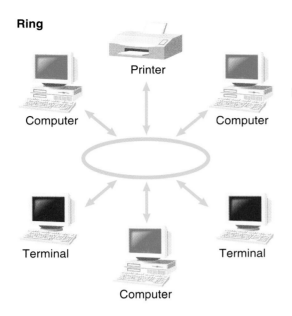

The advantage of a ring network is that messages flow in only one direction. Thus, there is no danger of collisions. The disadvantage is that the failure of a single node can compromise the entire network.

■ *Bus network:* The bus network works like a bus system at rush hour, with various buses pausing in different bus zones to pick up passengers. In a **bus network,** all communications devices are connected to a common channel using co-ax, STP, or UTP. There is no central computer or server, and data transmission is bidirectional at a rate of about 1–10 Mbps. Each communications device transmits electronic messages to other devices. If some of those messages collide, the device waits and tries to retransmit.

An example of a bus network is Xerox's Ethernet. LAN technology was first developed at the Xerox Research Center in Palo Alto, California. That concept, originally known as the Altos Aloha Network, became known as *ethernet,* from *luminiferous ether,* the mythological omnipresent passive medium once thought to support

the transmission of electromagnetic energy through a vacuum.

When Xerox standardized the technology in 1979, they officially named it Ethernet, which quickly became the LAN standard. It is still a very popular LAN configuration.

The advantage of a bus network is that it may be organized as a client-server or peer-to-peer network. The disadvantage is that extra circuitry and software are needed to avoid collisions between data. Also, if the bus itself is compromised, the entire network is compromised.

Bus

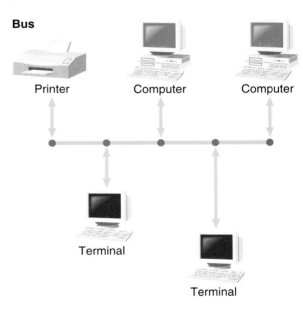

■ *Hybrid network:* **Hybrid networks** are combinations of star, ring, and bus networks. For example, a small college campus might use a bus network to connect buildings and star and ring networks within certain buildings.

■ *FDDI network:* A newer and higher-speed—and more costly—network is FDDI (pronounced "fiddy"), short for Fiber Distributed Data Interface. Capable of transmitting 100–200 Mbps, a **FDDI network** uses fiber-optic cable with a duplex token ring topology. The FDDI network is being used for such high-tech purposes as electronic imaging, high-resolution graphics, and digital video.

F D D I

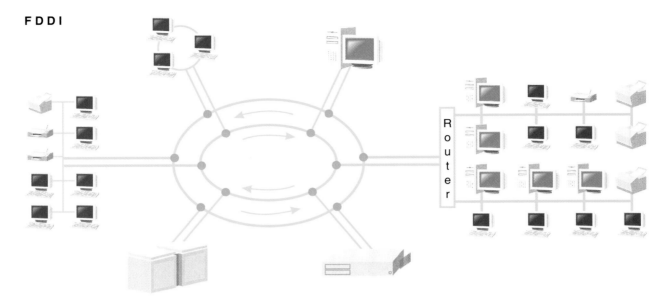

In addition to the high cost of this type of network configuration, the fragility of the fiber-optic cable is a disadvantage. Should the primary ring fail, the network can continue operating via the secondary cable ring, which is typically located in the same cable sheath as the primary ring. However, if there are problems on both rings, the network will fail.

The Impact of LANs

Sales of mainframes and midsize computers have been falling for some time. This is largely because companies have discovered that LANs can take their place for many functions, and at considerably less expense. This situation reflects a trend known as *downsizing.* Still, a LAN, like a mainframe, requires a skilled support staff. Moreover, LANs have neither the great storage capacity nor the security that mainframes have, so they are not useful for some applications.

What's Next?

At Duke University in North Carolina and at the University of California at Santa Cruz, the campuses have been equipped with wireless networking, so that students can access them from anywhere. "I use it a lot," says Thao Vo, majoring in computer engineering at Santa Cruz. "Instead of going to the library to Xerox solutions to homework, I'd do it from home."

In late 1995, the Federal Communications Commission also opened up virgin territory on the electromagnetic spectrum, a section known as *millimeter waves,* those situated above 40 gigahertz. These open up possibilities not only for wireless campuses—so that phones, pagers, and other communications devices could be easily connected—but also for "smart homes," with appliances, heating and cooling, and security controlled by wireless systems. There could also be "smart cars," with radar systems to alert drivers to potential collisions.

Clearly, more roads will be added in cyberspace.

WHAT IT IS
WHAT IT DOES

WHY IT IS IMPORTANT

amplitude (LO 1, p. 7.3)   In analog transmission, the height of a wave within a given period of time.

Amplitude refers to strength or volume—the loudness of a signal.

analog signal (LO 1, p. 7.3)   Continuous electrical signal in the form of a wave. The wave is called a *carrier wave.* Two characteristics of analog carrier waves that can be altered are frequency and amplitude. Computers cannot process analog signals.

Analog signals are used to convey voices and sounds over wire telephone lines, as well as in radio and TV broadcasting. Computers, however, use digital signals, which must be converted to analog signals in order to be transmitted over telephone wires.

asynchronous transmission (LO 3, p. 7.23)   Also called *start-stop transmission;* data is sent one byte (character) at a time. Each string of bits making up the byte is bracketed with special control bits; a "start" bit represents the beginning of a character, and a "stop" bit represents it end.

This method of communications is used with most microcomputers. Its advantage is that data can be transmitted whenever convenient for the sender. Its drawback is that transmitting only one byte at a time makes it a relatively slow method that cannot be used when great amounts of data must be sent rapidly.

bands (bandwidths) (LO 2, p. 7.9)   Ranges of frequencies. The bandwidth is the difference between the lowest and highest frequencies transmitted.

Different telecommunications systems use different bandwidths for different purposes. The wider the bandwidth, the faster data can be transmitted.

bits per second (bps) (LO 1, p. 7.6)   Measurement of data transmission speeds. Modems transmit at 1200 and 2400 bps (slow), 4800 and 9600 bps (moderately fast), and 14,400, 28,800, 33,600, and 56,000 bps (high-speed).

The faster the modem, the less time online and therefore the less expense.

bridge (LO 5, p. 7.33)   Interface that enables similar networks to communicate.

Smaller networks (local area networks) can be joined together to create larger area networks.

bus network (LO 5, p. 7.35)   Type of network in which all communications devices are connected to a common channel, with no central server. Each communications device transmits electronic messages to other devices. If some of those messages collide, the device waits and tries to retransmit.

The advantage of a bus network is that it may be organized as a client-server or peer-to-peer network. The disadvantage is that extra circuitry and software are needed to avoid collisions between data. Also, if a connection is broken, the entire network may stop working.

cable modem (LO 1, p. 7.8)   Modem that connects a PC to a cable-TV system that offers online services, as well as TV.

Cable modems transmit data faster than standard modems.

client-server LAN (LO 5, p. 7.31)   Type of local area network (LAN); it consists of requesting microcomputers, called *clients,* and supplying devices that provide a service, called *servers.* The server is a computer that manages shared information or devices, such as laser printers.

Client-server networks are the most common type of LAN. Compare with *peer-to-peer LAN.*

coaxial cable (LO 2, p. 7.13)   Type of communications channel; commonly called *co-ax,* it consists of insulated copper wire wrapped in a solid or braided metal shield, then in an external cover.

Coaxial cable is much better at resisting noise than twisted-pair wiring. Moreover, it can carry voice and data at a faster rate.

communications (LO 1, p. 7.2)   Also called *telecommunications;* the electronic transfer of information from one location to another. Also refers to electromagnetic devices and systems for communicating data.

Communications systems have helped to expand human communication beyond face-to-face meetings to electronic connections sometimes called the *global village.*

communications channel (LO 2, p. 7.9)   The path—the physical medium—over which data travels in a telecommunications system from its source to its destination.

Today there are many kinds of communications channels, wired and wireless.

communications satellites (LO 2, p. 7.14)   Microwave relay stations that orbit, most at an altitude of 22,300 miles above the equator. Because they travel at the same speed as the earth, thus appearing stationary in space, microwave earth stations can beam signals to a fixed location above. The satellite has solar-powered receivers and transmitters (transponders) that receive the signals, amplify them, and retransmit them to another earth station.

An orbiting satellite contains many communications channels and receives both analog and digital signals from ground microwave stations anywhere on earth.

concentrator (LO 3, p. 7.26)   Hardware that allows several devices to share a single communications line. It collects data in a temporary storage area, then forwards the data when enough has been accumulated.

Concentrators enable data to be sent more economically.

download (LO 4, p. 7.29)   To retrieve files online from another computer and store them in one's own microcomputer. Compare with *upload.*

Downloading enables users of online systems to quickly scan file names and then save the files for later reading; this reduces the time spent online and charges for it.

electromagnetic spectrum (LO 2, p. 7.9)   All the fields of electrical energy and magnetic energy, which travel in waves. This includes all radio signals, light rays, X rays, and radioactivity.

The part of the electromagnetic spectrum of particular interest is the area in the middle, which is used for communications purposes. Various frequencies are assigned by the federal government for different purposes.

FDDI network (LO 5, p. 7.35)   Short for Fiber Distributed Data Interface; a type of local area network that uses fiber-optic cable with a dual counter-rotating ring topology.

The FDDI network is being used for such high-tech purposes as electronic imaging, high-resolution graphics, and digital video.

fiber-optic cable (LO 2, p. 7.13)   Type of communications channel consisting of hundreds or thousands of thin strands of glass that transmit pulsating beams of light. These strands, each as thin as a human hair, can transmit billions of pulses per second, each "on" pulse representing 1 bit.

When bundled together, fiber-optic strands in a cable 0.12 inches thick can support a quarter- to a half-million simultaneous voice conversations. Moreover, unlike electrical signals, light pulses are not affected by random electromagnetic interference in the environment and thus have much lower error rates than telephone wire and cable.

file server (LO , p. 7.32)   Type of computer used on a local area network (LAN) that acts like a disk drive and stores the programs and data files shared by users of the LAN.

A file server enables users of a LAN to all have access to the same programs and data.

frequency (LO 1, p. 7.3)   Number of times a radio wave repeats during a specific time interval—that is, how many times it completes a cycle in a second; 1 Hz = 1 cycle per second.

The higher the frequency—that is, the more cycles per second—the more data can be sent through a channel.

front-end processor (LO 3, p. 7.26)   Smaller computer that is connected to a larger computer to assist it with communications functions.

The front-end processor transmits and receives messages over the communications channels, corrects errors, and relieves the larger computer of routine tasks.

full-duplex transmission (LO 3, p. 7.23)   Type of data transmission in which data is transmitted back and forth at the same time, unlike simplex and half-duplex.

Full-duplex is frequently used between computers in large computer systems.

gateway (LO 5, p. 7.34)   Interface that enables dissimilar networks to communicate with one another.

With a gateway, a local area network may be connected to a larger network, such as a wide area network.

Global Positioning System (GPS) (LO 2, p. 7.15)   Consists of a series of 24 earth-orbiting satellites that continuously transmit timed radio signals that can be used to identify earth locations.

A GPS receiver—handheld or mounted in a vehicle, plane, or boat—can pick up transmissions from any four satellites, interpret the information from each, and calculate to within a few hundred feet or less the receiver's longitude, latitude, and altitude.

half-duplex transmission (LO 3, p. 7.22)   Type of data transmission in which data travels in both directions but only in one direction at a time, as with CB or marine radios; both parties must take turns talking.

Half-duplex is a common transmission method with microcomputers, as when logging onto an electronic bulletin board system.

hertz (Hz) (LO 2, p. 7.9)   Provides a measure of the frequency of electrical vibrations (cycles) per second.

One million hertz equals 1 megahertz (MHz). Bandwidths are defined according to megahertz and gigahertz ranges.

host computer (LO 4, p. 7.28)   The central computer that controls a network. On a local area network, the host's functions may be performed by a computer called a *server*.

The host is responsible for managing the entire network.

hybrid network (LO 5, p. 7.35)   Type of local area network (LAN) that combines star, ring, and bus networks.

A hybrid network can link different types of LANs. For example, a small college campus might use a bus network to connect buildings and star and ring networks within certain buildings.

Integrated Services Digital Network (ISDN) (LO 1, p. 7.7)   Hardware and software system standard for transmitting voice, video, and data simultaneously as digital signals over traditional telephone lines.

The main benefit of ISDN is speed. It allows people to send digital data much faster than most modems can now deliver on the analog voice network.

kilobits per second (Kbps) (LO 1, p. 7.6)   Thousand bits per second, a measure of data transmission speed.

See *bits per second (bps)*.

local area network (LAN) (LO 4, p. 7.30)   Network that serves users within a confined geographical area; consists of a communications link, network operating system, microcomputers or workstations, servers, and other shared hardware such as printers or storage devices. LANs are of two principal types: client-server and peer-to-peer.

LANs have replaced large computers for many functions and are considerably less expensive. However, LANs have neither the great storage capacity nor the security of mainframes.

local network (LO 4, p. 7.28)   Privately owned communications network that serves users within a confined geographical area. The range is usually within a mile.

Local networks are of two types: private branch exchanges (PBXs) and local area networks (LANs).

metropolitan area network (MAN) (LO 4, p. 7.28)   Communications network that covers a geographic area the size of a city or a suburb.

The purpose of a MAN is often to avoid long-distance telephone charges. Cellular phone systems are often MANs.

microwave systems (LO 2, p. 7.13)   Communications systems that transmit voice and data through the atmosphere as super-high-frequency radio waves. Microwaves are electromagnetic waves that vibrate at 1 billion hertz per second or higher.

Microwave frequencies are used to transmit messages between ground-based earth stations and satellite communications systems. More than half of today's telephone system uses microwave transmission.

modem (LO 1, p. 7.4)   Short for *mo*dulater/*dem*odulater; device that converts digital signals into a representation of analog form (modulation) to send over phone lines; a receiving modem then converts the analog signal back to a digital signal (demodulation).

A modem enables users to transmit data from one computer to another by using standard telephone lines instead of special communication lines such as fiber-optic or cable.

multiplexer (LO 3, p. 7.25)   Device that merges several low-speed transmissions into one high-speed transmission. Depending on the model, 32 or more devices may share a single communications line.

High-speed multiplexers using high-speed digital lines can carry as many messages, both voice and data, as 24 analog telephone lines.

multiplexing (LO 3, p. 7.25)   The transmission of multiple signals over a single communications channel.

Multiplexing allows several communications devices to share one line at the same time. Three types of devices are used to achieve multiplexing—*multiplexers, concentrators,* and *front-end processors.*

network (LO 4, p. 7.28)   Also called *communications network;* a system of interconnected computers, telephones, or other communications devices that can communicate with one another and share applications and data.

Networks allow users to share peripheral devices, programs, and data and to have access to databases.

network interface card (LO 5, p. 7.32)   Circuit board inserted into an expansion slot in a micro-computer that enables it to send and receive messages on a local area network.

Without a network interface card, a microcomputer cannot be used to communicate on a LAN.

node (LO 4, p. 7.29)   Any device that is attached to a network.

A node may be a microcomputer, terminal, storage device, or some peripheral device, any of which enhance the usefulness of the network.

OSI (Open Systems Interconnection) (LO 3, p. 7.26)   International standard that defines seven layers of protocols, or software responsibilities, for worldwide computer communications.

In the past, not all hardware and software developers subscribed to the same protocols. As a result, many kinds of equipment and programs have not been able to work with one another.

packet (LO 3, p. 7.24)   Fixed-length block of data for transmission. The packet also contains instructions about the destination of the packet.

By creating data in the form of packets, a transmission system can deliver the data more efficiently and economically, as in packet switching.

packet switching (LO 3, p. 7.24)   Technique for dividing electronic messages into packets—fixed-length blocks of data—for transmission over a network to their destination through the most expedient route. A sending computer breaks an electronic message apart into packets, which are sent through a communications network—via different routes and speeds—to a receiving computer, which reassembles them into proper sequence to complete the message.

The benefit of packet switching is that it can handle high-volume traffic in a network. It also allows more users to share a network, thereby offering cost savings.

parallel data transmission (LO 3, p. 7.22) Method of transmitting data in which bits are sent through separate lines simultaneously.

Unlike serial lines, parallel lines move information fast, but they are efficient for only up to 15 feet. Thus, parallel lines are used, for example, to transmit data from a computer's CPU to a printer.

peer-to-peer LAN (LO 5, p. 7.32)   Type of local area network (LAN); all microcomputers on the network communicate directly with one another without relying on a server.

Peer-to-peer networks are less expensive than client-server networks and work effectively for up to 25 computers. Thus, they are appropriate for networking in small groups.

private branch exchange (PBX) (LO 5, p. 7.30) Private or leased telephone switching system that connects telephone extensions in-house as well as to the outside telephone system.

Newer PBXs can handle not only analog telephones but also digital equipment, including computers.

protocol (LO 3, p. 7.26)   Set of conventions governing the exchange of data between hardware and/or software components in a communications network.

Protocol specify how receiver devices acknowledge sending devices, along with the type of connections used, the timing of message exchanges, error-detection techniques, etc.

ring network (LO 5, p. 7.34)   Type of local area network (LAN) in which all communications devices are connected in a continuous loop and messages are passed around the ring until they reach the right destination. There is no central server.

The advantage of a ring network is that messages flow in only one direction, so there is no danger of collisions. The disadvantage is that if a connection is broken, the entire network stops working.

router (LO 5, p. 7.34)   Highly intelligent device that supports connectivity between both like and unlike LANs and between LANs and WANs/MANs. Routers operate at the bottom three layers of the OSI model.

The router software enables the router to view the network as a whole; bridges, in contrast, view the network only on a link-by-link basis.

serial data transmission (LO 3, p. 7.21)   Method of data transmission in which bits are sent sequentially, one after the other, through one line.

Serial transmission is found in communications lines, modems, and mice.

server (LO 4, p. 7.29)   Computer shared by several users in a network.

With servers, users on a LAN can share several devices, as well as data.

simplex transmission (LO 3, p. 7.22)   Type of transmission in which data travels in only one direction; there is no return signal.

Some computerized data collection devices, such as seismograph sensors that measure earthquakes, use simplex transmission.

star network (LO 5, p. 7.34)   Type of local area network in which all microcomputers and other communications devices are connected to a central hub, such as a file server. Electronic messages are routed through the central hub to their destinations. The central hub monitors the flow of traffic.

The advantage of a star network is that the hub prevents collisions between messages. Moreover, if a connection is broken between any communications device and the hub, the rest of the devices on the network will continue operating.

synchronous transmission (LO 3, p. 7.24)   Type of transmission in which data is sent in blocks. Start and stop bit patterns, called *synch bytes,* are transmitted at the beginning and end of the blocks. These start and end bit patterns synchronize internal clocks in the sending and receiving devices so that they are in time with each other.

Synchronous transmission is rarely used with microcomputers because it is more complicated and more expensive than asynchronous transmission. It is appropriate for computer systems that need to transmit great quantities of data quickly.

twisted-pair wire (LO 2, p. 7.12)   Type of communications channel consisting of two strands of insulated copper wire, twisted around each other.

Twisted-pair wire has been the most common channel or medium used for telephone systems. It is relatively slow and does not protect well against electrical interference.

upload (LO 4, p. 7.29)   To send files from a user's microcomputer to another computer. Compare with *download.*

Uploading allows microcomputer users to easily exchange files with each other over networks.

wide area network (WAN) (LO 4, p. 7.28)   Communications network that covers a wide geographical area, such as a state or a country.

The Internet links together hundreds of computer WANs. Most telephone systems are WANs.

SELF-TEST EXERCISES

1. A(n) _____ converts digital signals into analog signals for transmission over phone lines.

2. A(n) _____ is a one-way communications device that receives data from a special radio transmitter.

3. _____ transmission sends data in both directions simultaneously, similar to two trains passing in opposite directions on side-by-side tracks.

4. A(n) _____ _____ network is a communications network that covers a wide geographical area, such as a state or a country.

5. _____ cable transmits data as pulses of light rather than as electricity.

SHORT-ANSWER QUESTIONS

1. Why is speed an important consideration when selecting a modem?
2. What is meant by the term *protocol* as it relates to communicating between two computers?
3. What is meant by the terms *upload* and *download*?
4. What is a hybrid network?
5. When talking about communications, what is the significance of the electromagnetic spectrum?

MULTIPLE-CHOICE QUESTIONS

1. Which of the following functions does communications software perform?
   a. error correction
   b. data compression
   c. remote control
   d. terminal emulation
   e. all the above

2. Which of the following offers the fastest data transmission speed?
   a. ISDN
   b. cable modem
   c. ADSL
   d. satellite dish
   e. telephone modem

3. Which of the following best describes the telephone line that is used in most homes today?
   a. twisted-pair wire
   b. coaxial cable
   c. fiber-optic cable
   d. modem cable
   e. none of the above

4. Which of the following isn't used to perform multiplexing?
   a. multiplexer
   b. packet switcher
   c. concentrator
   d. front-end processor
   e. all the above

5. Which of the following do local area networks enable?
   a. sharing of peripheral devices
   b. sharing of programs and data
   c. better communications
   d. access to databases
   e. all the above

TRUE/FALSE QUESTIONS

1. Frequency and amplitude are two characteristics of analog carrier waves. (true/false)

2. The current limitation of cable modems is that they don't provide much online interactivity. (true/false)

3. You must purchase special hardware and software before you can use ISDN technology. (true/false)

4. All communications channels are either wired or wireless. (true/false)

5. Parallel transmission is faster than serial transmission. (true/false)

KNOWLEDGE IN ACTION

1. Are the computers at your school or work connected to a network? If so, what are the characteristics of the network? What advantages does the network provide in terms of hardware and software support? What types of computers are connected to the network (microcomputers, minicomputers, and/or mainframes)? Specifically, what software/hardware is allowing the network to function?

2. Using current articles, publications, and/or the Web, research the history of cable modems, how they are being used today, and what you think the future holds for them. Do you think you will use a cable modem in the future? Present your findings in a paper or a 15-minute discussion.

3. Find out more about ADSL. When did Bellcore Labs begin developing it? When will it become available? How will ADSL be sold to the public? Who will most likely use ADSL technology? What are its current limitations? What do you think the future holds for ADSL? Perform your research using current articles, publications, and/or the Web.

4. Describe in more detail the FCC's role in regulating the communications industry. What happens when frequencies are opened up for new communications services? Who gets to use these frequencies?

5. Of the different technologies discussed in this chapter, which do you think will have the biggest impact on you? Why? Do you think that some of the topics presented here aren't relevant? Why? Why not?

USES OF COMMUNICATIONS TECHNOLOGY

Telecommuting, Online Resources, and the Internet

PREVIEW

After reading this chapter, you should be able to:

1. Discuss examples of telephone-related services

2. Describe videoconferencing and picture phones

3. Explain what online information services offer and how to connect with them

4. Explain what the Internet is and how to connect with it

5. Describe the World Wide Web and how to move around it

6. Name some of the problems involved with use of the Internet and the Web

7. Explain how communications technology supports shared resources, including intranets and extranets

8. Describe how telecommuting is done

WHY IS THIS CHAPTER IMPORTANT?

"On the 21st-century Internet, as in the 19th-century American West," says former *Time* magazine journalist Kurt Andersen, "the mavericks and cranks drawn to the frontier will not be wiped out, and their romantic sensibility will inform the spirit of the place, but the rude settlements and wild behavior are being overshadowed by more traditional, trustworthy modes."[1]

In our time the Internet is a "hyper-democratic media world," in which speculation, rumor, and pseudoinformation seem to have equal footing with reliable news and scientific facts. As in the 19th century, before the arrival of mass-circulation magazines and wire services, and then later with centralized radio and television networks, the Internet represents a collection of "media" that are scattered and local even as they are linked internationally.

But that is changing. "The once-untamed territory is becoming rapidly civilized . . . ," says Andersen. "Each year on the Net is equal to about a decade in 19th-century-frontier terms: the rise of Internet news groups and bulletin boards is analogous to the half century after Lewis and Clark; the beginning of the World Wide Web, in the early 1990s, can be compared to the discovery of gold in California; and the present cybermoment [1997] is equivalent to, say, 1880." Users of the Internet are now demanding reliable filters that can help them separate the bogus and the bunk from the mostly accurate. In the next century, these will no doubt fall into place.

This chapter describes the Internet, of course, but it is also concerned with the much wider world of communications—the uses of everything from fax machines to virtual offices.

The Practical Uses of Communications and Connectivity

Users can use communications technology for *many* purposes. For example, they can use telephone-related services, such as fax, voice mail, and e-mail. They can do teleconferencing and videoconferencing. They can share resources through workgroup computing and Electronic Data Interchange. They can make their work portable, with telecommuting, mobile workplaces, and virtual offices. They can use online information services for research, e-mail, games, travel services, and teleshopping. They can connect with the Internet and the Web for almost any activity imaginable.

Twenty-two-year-old shipping clerk Neal Berry (online moniker: Shylent Cat) had enough money to buy a Toshiba laptop, a cellular phone, and a connection to an electronic bulletin board. But he couldn't afford an apartment in pricey Novato, California, so he lived in a tent near the freeway, hunkered on a mattress rescued from a trash bin. Though homeless, he spent his evenings happily tapping on his laptop, communicating with the online world. "I made more friends in a month [electronically]," he said, "than I had all year in Novato."[2]

Clearly, communications is extending into every nook and cranny of civilization—the "plumbing of cyberspace," as it has been called. The term *cyberspace* was coined by William Gibson in his novel *Neuromancer.* In that book it refers to a futuristic computer network that people use by plugging their brains into it. Today *cyberspace* has come to mean the computer online world and the Internet in particular, but it is also used to refer to the whole wired and wireless world of communications in general.

The television set is an instrument of communications, but it is a low-skill tool. That is, the many people of a mass audience receive one-way communications from a few communicators. This is why television (like AM/FM radio, newspapers, and music CDs) is called one of the *mass media.* Telephone systems are not mass media, since they involve two-way communications of many to many. But they, too, are low-skill communications tools. By contrast, linkages of microcomputers have allowed a few people with a fairly high level of skill to achieve two-way communication with a few others. The ability to connect devices by communications lines to other devices and sources of information is known as *connectivity* (✔ p. 1.5). Traditionally, computers have offered greater varieties of connectivity than have other communications devices.

Tools of Communications and Connectivity

What kinds of options do communications and connectivity give you? Let us consider the possibilities. We will take them in order, more or less, from simpler to more complex activities. *(See Figure 8.1.)* They include:

- Telephone-related communications services: fax messages, voice mail, and e-mail

- Video/voice communication: videoconferencing and picture phones

- Online information services

- The Internet and the World Wide Web

- Shared resources: workgroup computing, Electronic Data Interchange (EDI), intranets and extranets

- Portable work—telecommuting and virtual offices

Figure 8.1 The world of connectivity. Wired or wireless communications links offer several options for information and communications.

World of Connectivity

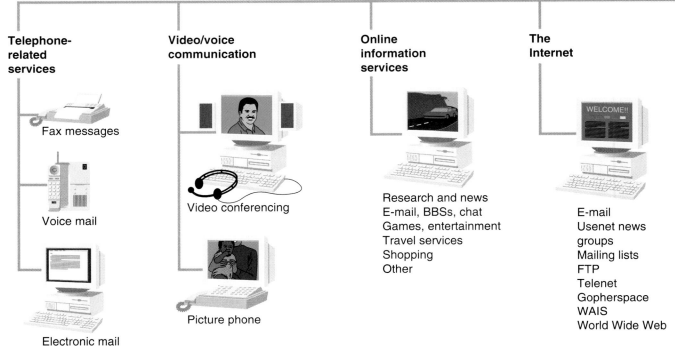

Telephone-related services

Fax messages

Voice mail

Electronic mail

Video/voice communication

Video conferencing

Picture phone

Online information services

Research and news
E-mail, BBSs, chat
Games, entertainment
Travel services
Shopping
Other

The Internet

E-mail
Usenet news groups
Mailing lists
FTP
Telenet
Gopherspace
WAIS
World Wide Web

Telephone-Related Communications Services

Telephone-related communications include fax, voice mail, and e-mail.

Phone systems and computer systems have begun to fuse together. Services available through telephone connections, whether the conventional wired kind or the wireless cellular-phone type, include *fax message, voice mail,* and *e-mail.*

Fax Messages

Asking "What is your fax number?" is about as common a question in the work world today as asking for someone's telephone number. Indeed, the majority of business cards include a telephone number, a fax number, and an e-mail address. Recall from Chapter 3, in the section on scanners (✔ p. 3.13), that **fax** stands for "facsimile transmission" or reproduction. A fax may be sent by dedicated fax machine, which scans paper documents, or by fax modem, a circuit board inside the computer.

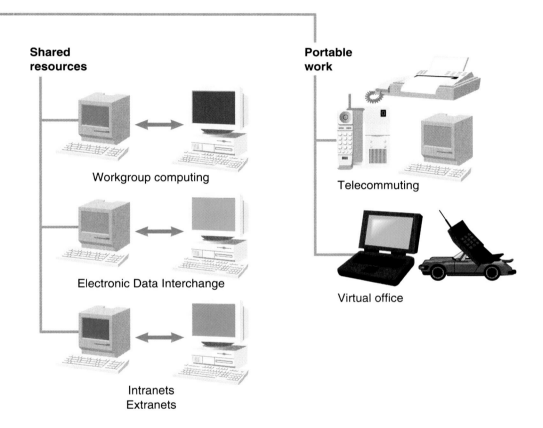

Shared resources

Workgroup computing

Electronic Data Interchange

Intranets
Extranets

Portable work

Telecommuting

Virtual office

Some hotels now offer a service in which you can read fax messages sent to you on your hotel room's television set.

Voice Mail

Like a sophisticated telephone answering machine, **voice mail** digitizes incoming voice messages and stores them in the recipient's "voice mailbox" in digitized form. It then converts the digitized versions back to voice messages when they are retrieved by dialing in from any phone or via newer micro- and notebook computers.

Voice mail systems also allow callers to deliver the same message to many people within an organization by pressing a single key. They can forward calls to the recipient's home or hotel. They allow the person checking messages to speed through them or to slow them down. He or she can save some messages and erase others and can dictate replies that the system will send out.

You don't even need to have a fixed address to use voice mail. Carl Hygrant, a homeless person in New York, found that the technology helped him get work. Earlier, when he put down on his resume the phone number of the Bronx shelter that was his temporary home, prospective employers would lose interest when they called. After a telephone company launched an experimental voice mail program for homeless people, he landed a job.[3]

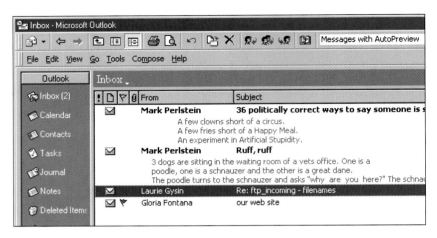

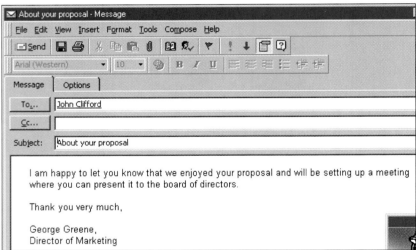

E-Mail

"E-mail is so clearly superior to paper mail for so many purposes," writes *New York Times* computer writer Peter Lewis, "that most people who try it cannot imagine going back to working without it."[4] Says another writer, e-mail "occupies a psychological space all its own: It's almost as immediate as a phone call, but if you need to, you can think about what you're going to say for days and reply when it's convenient."[5]

As previously discussed (✔ p. 6.18), **e-mail,** or **electronic mail,** links computers by wired or wireless connections and allows users, through their keyboards, to post messages and to read responses on their display screens. With e-mail software, you use preset computer options to dial the e-mail system's telephone number, type in the recipient's "mailbox" number or name, usually an *alias,* and then type in the message to be stored in the recipient's mailbox (actually a file stored on the computer system's server), and click on the "Send" button. To gain access to your own mailbox, you dial the e-mail sys-

tem's telephone number and type in the number of your mailbox and your *password,* a secret word or numbers that limit access. You may then read the list of senders and topics, read the messages, print them out, delete them, send copies to other people, or download (transfer) them to your hard disk. With some e-mail services, you simply connect to the service and then choose the "Get Mail" or "Create Mail" menu option. (Note: If you are on a proprietary e-mail system such as one on a company network, you do not need to dial any outside telephone numbers; you would just indicate the mailbox numbers.)

If you're part of a company, university, or other large organization, you may get e-mail services as part of an established network. Otherwise you can sign up with a commercial online service (America Online, CompuServe, Microsoft Network), e-mail service (such as MCI Mail), or Internet access provider (such as Pipeline USA, Mindspring).

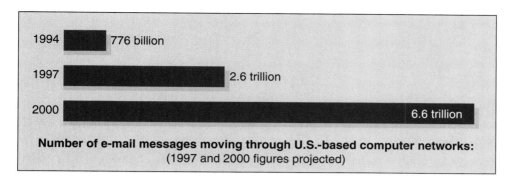

1994	776 billion
1997	2.6 trillion
2000	6.6 trillion

Number of e-mail messages moving through U.S.-based computer networks:
(1997 and 2000 figures projected)

E-mail has both advantages and disadvantages:[6-9]

- *Advantages of e-mail:* Like voice mail, it helps people avoid playing phone tag or coping with paper and stamps. A message can be as simple as a birthday greeting or as complex and lengthy as a report with supporting documents and links to additional online services (including attached video and sound files). It can be quicker than a fax message and more organized than a voice mail message. By reading the list of senders and topics displayed on the screen you can quickly decide which messages are important. Also, e-mail software automatically creates an archive of all sent and received messages. Sending an e-mail message usually costs as little as a local phone call or less but it can go across several time zones and be read at any time. Indeed, some e-mail messages are now received as voice mail by the software and can be played back as such.

- *Disadvantages of e-mail:* Nevertheless there are some problems: You might have to sort through scores or even hundreds of messages a day, a form of junk mail brought about by the ease with which anyone can send duplicate copies of a message to many people. Your messages are far from private and may be read by e-mail system operators and others (such as your employer); thus, experts recommend you think of e-mail as a postcard rather than a private letter. Mail that travels via the Internet often takes a circuitous route, bouncing around various computers in the country, until one of them recognizes the address and delivers the message. Thus, although a lot of messages may go through in a minute's time, others may be hung up because of system overload, taking hours and even days. Last, users should not let their e-mail pile up; all those messages may be taking up space on some system's server. (Some systems will automatically delete messages left on the server longer than the time limit allows.)

If you use e-mail, to whom do you send messages? For what purposes do you think you'll use e-mail in your job?

The e-mail boom is only just beginning. The U.S. Postal Service has begun to offer e-mail with features of first-class mail, including "postmarks" and return receipts. Telephone companies are offering phones with small screens for displaying e-mail sent through their e-mail centers. And in some cases, you can already hear your e-mail via telephone. Octel Communications and Microsoft have introduced technology that combines voice mail and e-mail functions. This hardware-and-software product will, for example, allow you to listen to a computerized voice read your e-mail via a car phone on your way to work. You could also phone in messages to the e-mail center, which will then transfer the messages as e-mail to their recipients.

Video/Voice Communication: Videoconferencing and Picture Phones

Videoconferencing is the use of television, sound, and computer technology to enable people in different locations to see, hear, and talk with one another. Videoconferencing could lead to V-mail, or video mail, which allows video messages to be sent, stored, and retrieved like e-mail. The picture phone is a telephone with a TV-like screen and a built-in camera that allow you to see the person you're calling and vice versa.

Figure 8.2 Video/voice communication. *(Top)* Videoconferencing, or face-to-face communication via desktop computer. *(Bottom)* A picture phone.

Want to have a meeting with people on the other side of the country or the world but don't want the hassle of travel? You may have heard of or participated in a *conference call,* also known as *audio teleconferencing,* a meeting in which people in different geographical locations talk on the telephone. (Audio conferencing is also used in distance education.) A variation on this meeting format is e-mail-type *computer conferencing,* sometimes called *chat sessions.* Computer conferencing is a keyboard conference among several users at microcomputers or terminals linked through a computer network. (Because a computer-conference meeting need not take place in "real time," it may go on all day or several days—another example of how information technology is changing conventional notions of time and space.) Now we have video/voice communication, specifically *videoconferencing* and *picture phones. (See Figure 8.2.)*

Videoconferencing and V-Mail

Videoconferencing, also called *teleconferencing,* is the use of television video and sound technology as well as computers to enable people in different locations to see, hear, and talk with one another. At one time, videoconferencing consisted of people meeting in separate conference rooms that were specially equipped with television cameras. Now videoconferencing software and equipment can be installed on microcomputers, with a camera and microphone to capture the person speaking and a monitor and speakers for the person being spoken to.

Although videoconferencing is being done, it is still problematic. The audio- and video-capturing abilities of today's computers are very sophisticated; however, traditional phone lines handle only voice transmission well (✔ p. 7.12). If you can't afford to spend thousands of dollars on a special dedicated line, you will have to live with the less-than-optimal quality of videoconferencing over regular phone lines. And even in this case, the more you spend, the better the quality will be. For instance, relatively inexpensive ($150) CineVideo from CINECOM comes with a black-and-white camera and microphone. More expensive systems, such as Sony Electronics' TriniCom 500, run on ISDN lines and cost around $2000. The high-end systems that run on dedicated lines such as a T1 can cost in the tens of thousands of dollars.

The requirements for a videoconference over phone lines are a camera, a way to get video on your computer (usually via a video capture card), a modem, a sound card, videoconferencing software, a microphone, and speakers.

A relatively new development is an initiative to deliver *v-mail,* or *video mail,* video messages that are sent, stored, and retrieved like e-mail. One version would use the Proshare Windows-based videoconferencing product, Oracle's Media Server—a computer storage system developed for movies-on-demand technologies—and ISDN telephone lines (✔ p. 7.7).

Picture Phones

The **picture phone** is a telephone with a TV-like screen and a built-in camera that allows you to see the person you're calling, and vice versa. An example is AT&T's VideoPhone.

The idea of the picture phone has been around since 1964, when AT&T showed its Picturephone at the New York World's Fair. However, as with videoconferencing, the main difficulty is that the standard copper wire in what the industry calls POTS—for "plain old telephone service"— has been unable to communicate images very rapidly. Thus, present-day picture phones convey a series of jerky, freeze-frame or stop-action still images of the faces of the communicating parties. However, ISDN lines and fiber-optic cables, rapidly being installed in many places, can transmit more visual information. Moreover, new software such as FlashWare and IP/TV from Precept Software can compress images quickly, delivering video as well as audio images in real time even over old-fashioned copper wires.

The 1996 Telecommunications Act (which President Clinton signed using a digitizing pen and tablet) permits more competition in telephone service; thus we will probably see a real free-for-all in the phone business, which could speed up the delivery of picture phones. Already the telcos (telephone companies) are getting competition from unexpected quarters. Many cable companies are jumping into the phone business. Technology such as CU-SeeMe software, developed at Cornell University in 1994, is allowing video/voice communication on the Internet. In 1995, a California company called Connectix Inc. unveiled a video phone for under $200 for use with ISDN lines. Even power companies may get into the act: In 1996, San Diego Gas and Electric, which, like other utilities, has long been putting fiber-optic lines along its main power lines, offered its customers a low-cost phone with a screen for displaying text, which could evolve into a picture phone. In Vancouver, British Columbia, new condominiums are wired with fiber-optic cable with video-phone capabilities.

Do you think you would use a picture phone? Why or why not?

Online Information Services

For a monthly fee, commercial companies called *online information services* provide software that hooks up users' computers and modems over phone lines with facilities that provide e-mail, research, shopping, financial services, and Internet connections, among a host of other services.

An **online information service** provides access to all kinds of databases and electronic meeting places, for a fee, to subscribers equipped with telephone-linked microcomputers. Says one writer:

Online services are those interactive news and information retrieval sources that can make your computer behave more like a telephone; or a TV set; or a newspaper; or a video arcade, a stock brokerage firm, a bank, a travel agency, a weather bureau, a department store, a grocery store, a florist, a set of encyclopedias, a library, a bulletin board, and more.[10]

There are several online services, but those with the most subscribers are considered the most mainstream. They are *America Online* (*AOL*), with more than 8 million subscribers; *CompuServe,* with about 5½ million users; *Microsoft Network,* with about 2 million subscribers; and *Prodigy,* with about 1 million users. Some other online services have been merged into other enterprises (Delphi), are considered special interest (GEnie, oriented toward games), or have redefined their missions (eWorld). Still others (Dialog, Dow Jones News/Retrieval, Nexis, Lexis) may principally be considered huge collections of databases rather than "department-store"-like online services.

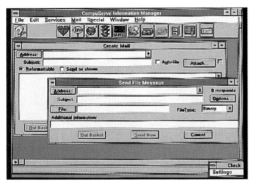

There are also some small services that measure their membership in the hundreds rather than the millions. Examples are The WELL and Women's Wire in the San Francisco Bay area and ECHO (East Coast Hang Out) in New York. The San Francisco-based Institute for Global Communications operates four online services to link people and organizations working on issues of peace and justice: PeaceNet, EcoNet, ConflictNet, and LaborNet. "Many of these small online communities have a cult-like following," says an analyst at Simba Information, a Connecticut market research firm, "and the users log on more often than they do to more general online services."[11]

Getting Access

To gain access to online services, you need a microcomputer and a modem. To download and print out online materials, you need a hard disk (or CD-E, ✔ p. 4.25) and a printer. Finally, you need communications software, so your computer can communicate via modem and interact with distant computers that have modems. America Online, CompuServe, and other mainstream services provide subscribers with their own software, but you can also buy communications programs separately, such as ProComm Plus.

Opening an account with an online service requires a credit card, and billing policies resemble those used by cable-TV and telephone companies. As with cable TV, you may be charged a fee for basic service, with additional fees for specialized services. In addition, the online service may charge for the time you spend on the line. (Many of the services charge $19.95 per month for unlimited use of general services; CompuServe charges $9.95 per month for the first 5 hours and $2.95 per hour thereafter, but these amounts can change at any time.) Finally, you will also be charged by your telephone company for your time on the line, just as when making a regular phone call. However, most information services offer local access numbers. Thus, unless you live in a rural area, you will not be paying long-distance phone charges. All told, the typical user may pay $20–40 a month to use an online service. (Note: Obsessive users can run up much larger bills, as can users of non-general services, such as research using proprietary—that is, privately owned—databases like Knowledge Index and Data Quest.)

Offerings of Online Services

Although the Internet offers the same information as online services, many users still prefer online services because the information is "packaged." The services charge for their organization and filtering of the information and for providing a user-friendly forum for accessing the information.

What kinds of things could you use an online service for? Here are some (not all) of the options:

■ *People connections—e-mail, bulletin boards, chat rooms:* Online services can provide a community through which you can connect with people with kindred interests (without identifying yourself, if you prefer). The primary means for making people connections are via e-mail, bulletin boards, and "chat rooms."

E-mail is the same as we described earlier.

Bulletin boards, or *message boards,* allow you to post new messages and answer posted messages on any of thousands of special topics. A **bulletin board system,** or **BBS,** is a centralized information source and message-switching system for a particular computer-linked interest group. There are perhaps 100,000 BBSs operating in the United States, covering just about every topic you can imagine, from bird watching to socialism. Some BBSs are mostly file libraries, offering games, software, and data files that may be downloaded (transferred) to users' personal computers.

All the major online services operate bulletin boards. However, some BBSs are operated by small, independent groups. For example, Katie and Gene Hamilton of St. Michaels on Maryland's Eastern Shore had renovated 13 houses and written numerous books and newspaper columns about home repair when in 1991 they decided to start their BBS called HouseNet. The Hamiltons are *sysops,* or system operators, of an electronic bulletin board system. Operated in the midst of perpetual remodeling chaos and consisting of a few modems and personal computers, HouseNet dispenses advice about home repair. It also offers software programs on such matters as how to estimate materials or design a new deck.[12] Small BBSs are generally run by individuals, often out of their homes, and like the Hamiltons' HouseNet, are oriented toward a particular subject. Although such BBSs are generally friendly, the limited phone lines and resources can strain the systems, so busy signals may be common.

(Note that you cannot use an information service's software to access some of the small independent BBSs; for this, you need standard communications software like that included in Windows 3.1 and Windows 95.)

Chat rooms are discussion areas in which you may join with others in a real-time "conversation," typed in through your keyboard. The topic may be general or specific, and the collective chat-room conversation scrolls on the screen.

■ *Research and news:* The only restriction on the amount of research you can do online is the limit on whatever credit card you are charging your time to if you are not using a free database. Depending on the online service, you can avail yourself of several free encyclopedias, such as *Compton's Interactive Encyclopedia* and *Grolier Academic American Encyclopedia.* Many online services also offer access to databases (not usually free) of unabridged text from newspapers, journals, and magazines. Indeed, the information resources available online are mind-boggling, impossible to describe in this short space.

■ *Games, entertainment, and clubs:* Online computer games are extremely popular. In single-player games, you play against the computer. In multiplayer games, you play against others, whether someone in your household or someone overseas.

Other entertainments include cartoons, sound clips, pictures of showbusiness celebrities, and reviews of movies and CDs. You can also join online clubs with others who share your interests, whether science fiction, punk rock, or cooking.

■ *Travel services:* Online services use Eaasy Sabre or Travelshopper, streamlined versions of the reservations systems travel agents use. You can search for flights and book reservations through the computer and have tickets sent to you by FedEx. Or you can go online with an American Express travel agent who will help you plan your trip. You can also refer to weather maps, which show regions of interest. In addition, you can review hotel directories, such as the ABC Worldwide Hotel Guide, and restaurant guides, such as the Zagat Restaurant Directory.

■ *Downloading:* Many users download freeware, shareware (✔ p. 6.36), and commercial demonstration programs from online hosts. They can also download software updates, called *patches.*

■ *Shopping:* If you can't stand parking hassles, limited store hours, and checkout lines, online services may provide a shopping alternative. CompuServe, for instance, offers 24-hour shopping with its Electronic Mall. This feature lists products from more than 100 retail stores, discount wholesalers, specialty shops, and catalog companies. You can scan through listings of merchandise, order something on a credit card with a few keystrokes, and have the goods delivered by UPS or U.S. mail.

In some cities it's even possible to order groceries through online services. Peapod Inc. is an online grocery service serving 10,000 households in the Chicago and San Francisco areas. Peapod offers more than 18,000 items, from laundry detergent to lettuce, available in Jewel/Osco in Chicago or Safeway in San Francisco. Users can shop by brand name, category, or store aisle, and they can use coupons. Specially trained Peapod shoppers handle each order, even selecting the best produce available. The orders are then delivered in temperature-controlled containers.[13]

How might online services change the way you work and play?

■ *Financial management:* Online services also offer access to investment brokerages so that you can invest money and keep tabs on your portfolio and on the stock market. You can even manage your portfolio yourself if you want to.

Will Online Services Survive the Internet?

Many experts and users believe that the Internet and particularly the World Wide Web threaten to swamp the online services. As the Net and the Web have become easier to navigate, as we will discuss shortly, online services have begun to lose customers and content providers—even as they have added arrangements for accessing the Internet through them. Indeed, many of the services offered by information services are now directly accessible through the Internet. However, users may benefit from the user-friendly interface provided by the information service's software.

"Right now, the services thrive because they seem the most painless route to the Internet," wrote *Newsweek's* technology writer Steven Levy in early 1996. "But within a year or two, new heavyweight players, notably telephone and cable companies, will offer easy-to-install, lightning-fast Internet connections at five or 10 bucks a month for unlimited Web surfing, e-mail, and everything else."[14] Actually, Levy was off by about a year: Within days, Pacific Bell, AT&T, and cable-TV giant Tele-Communications Inc. announced they were launching Internet access services.[15,16]

Still, the online services have a lot to offer. One survey, for instance, found that *half* the people on the Net got there through commercial services, which suggests they still may be among the easiest ways to get to the Web.[17] In addition, the online services package information so that you can more quickly and easily find what you're looking for. It's also easier to conduct a live "chat" session on an online service than it is on the Web, and it is easier for parents to exert control over the kinds of materials their children may view.

The Internet

The Internet is the world's biggest network. It can be accessed in various ways and can hook you up with virtually any resource imaginable. However, it is not necessarily easy to use without some knowledge and experience.

Where Did the Internet Come From?

Called "the mother of all networks," the **Internet,** or simply "the Net," is an international network connecting more than 140,000 smaller networks in more than 170 countries. These networks are formed by educational, commercial, nonprofit, government, and military entities. According to Dataquest research services 82 million computers were hooked up to the Internet in 1997; they predict 163 million computers in 200 countries to be hooked up by 2000.

To connect with the Internet, you need pretty much the same things you need to connect with online information services: a computer, modem and telephone line (or other network connection), and appropriate software.

Created by the U.S. Department of Defense in 1969 (under the name ARPAnet—ARPA was the department's Advanced Research Project Agency), the Internet was built to serve two purposes. The first was to share research among military, industry, and university sources. The second was to provide a system for sustaining communication among military units in the event of nuclear attack. Thus, the system was designed to allow many routes among many computers, so that a message could arrive at its destination by many possible ways, not just a single path. This original network system was largely based on the Unix operating system (p. 5.21).

With the many different kinds of computers being connected, engineers had to find a way for the computers to speak the same language. The solution developed was *TCP/IP,* the Unix communications protocol standard since 1983 and the heart of the Internet. **TCP/IP,** for Transmission Control Protocol/Internet Protocol, is the standardized set of computer protocols (p. 7.26) that allow different computers on different networks, using different operating systems, to communicate with each other efficiently—thus making the Internet appear to the user to operate as a single network. TCP/IP breaks data and messages into packets of information of about 1500 characters each, gives them a destination, and formats them with error-protection bits. Each packet travels via the fastest route possible. On the Internet, this route may change in seconds. Thus the last packet sent may arrive first at the destination. For this reason, TCP/IP is needed to reassemble the packets into their original order. (For detailed histories of the Internet try these sites: Hobbe's Internet Timeline—*http://info.isoc.org/guest/zakon/Internet/History/ HIT.html;* History of the Internet—*http://www.Internetvalley.com/intval.html;* NetHistory—*http://www.geocities.com/SiliconValley/2260.)*

As an aside: On the Internet's global computer links, communication is about 90% in English, about 5% in French, 2% in Spanish, and 3% in other languages.[18]

Connecting to the Internet

There are three basic ways to connect your microcomputer with the Internet. The first is through a dedicated connection:

■ *Through school or work:* Universities, colleges, and most large businesses have dedicated, high-speed phone lines that provide a direct connection to the Internet. If you're a student, this may be the best deal, because the connection is free or low cost. However, if you live off-campus and want to get this Internet connection from home, you probably won't be able to do so. To use a direct connection, your microcomputer must have TCP/IP software and be connected to the local area network that has the direct-line connection to the Internet.

The next two types of connections are called "dial-up" connections:

■ *Through online information services:* As mentioned, subscribing to a commercial online information service, which provides you with its own communications software, may not be the cheapest way to connect to the Internet, but it may be the easiest. In this case, the online service acts as a "gateway" to the Internet. However, such services may not offer access to all aspects of the Internet.

■ *Through Internet service providers (ISPs):* To obtain complete access to the Internet through a dial-up connection, you use an ISP. **Internet service providers (ISPs)** are local or national companies that provide unlimited public access to the Internet and World Wide Web for a flat, monthly fee. Essentially an ISP is a small network that connects to the high-speed communications links that make up the Internet's backbone—the major supercomputer sites and educational and research foundations within the United States and

Figure 8.3 From your room to the world. The backbones and major arteries of the Internet are run by a group of larger network providers, often called *network providers* (*NSPs*). Users connect to local ISPs via modems, ISDN adapters, or other means (such as a school network). Local ISPs in turn connect to NSPs like, in the United States, UUnet's Alternet, IBM's Advantis, and those offered by AGIS, AT&T, MCI, and Sprint. ISPs connect to NSPs by lines leased from local telephone companies.

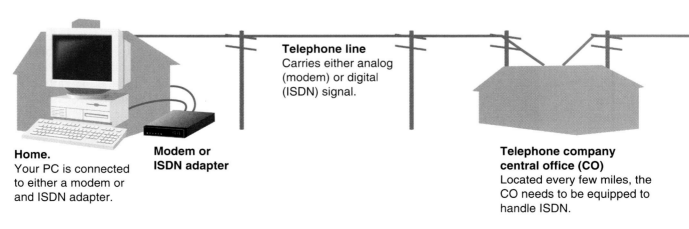

Telephone line
Carries either analog (modem) or digital (ISDN) signal.

Home.
Your PC is connected to either a modem or and ISDN adapter.

Modem or ISDN adapter

Telephone company central office (CO)
Located every few miles, the CO needs to be equipped to handle ISDN.

throughout the world. Forrester Research Inc. predicts that ISPs could claim as many as 32 million online subscribers in the U.S. by 2000 versus 12.7 million for commercial online services.[19] Once you have contacted an ISP and paid the required fee, the ISP will provide you with information about phone numbers for connections and about how to set up your computer and modem to dial into their network of servers. This will require dealing with some system software settings, using a user name ("userID") and a password, and typing in some other specified configuration information. Once the first connection is made, your computer will usually save the settings and other information and provide you with a shortcut method of connecting to the ISP in the future. Once you are connected to the ISP, if you are an experienced user, you can type in Unix-based commands or use specifically designed software to navigate around the Internet. Or, if you are not an experienced Internet user, you can launch your browser software (such as Netscape) by clicking on its icon, and then use the browser's graphical user interface (✔ p. 5.14) and menus to move around the part of the Internet called the "Web" (discussed in more detail shortly).

So far, most ISPs have been small and limited in geographic coverage; the largest national company has been Netcom Online Communication Services Inc. of San Jose, Calif. Other established national ISPs are MindSpring Enterprises, Inc., UUnet Technologies, and BBN Corporation. Competitors are MCI Internet, AT&T WorldNet, and Pacific Bell Internet (all from telephone companies); and Tele-Communication Inc.'s @Home (from the cable-TV giant and pronounced "At Home"). Clearly, this is an area of fierce competition, but the presence of the phone and cable-TV companies in particular could help expand the mass market for Internet services.

You can ask someone who is already connected to the Internet to access the worldwide list of ISPs at *http://www.thelist.com.* At this site, you can view pricing data and a description of supported features for each provider in your area.

Figure 8.3 shows a basic Internet connection.

Browser icons that appear on the user's desktop screen

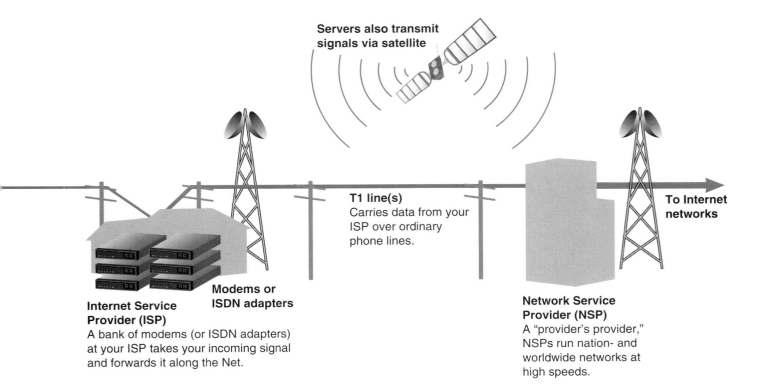

Servers also transmit signals via satellite

T1 line(s)
Carries data from your ISP over ordinary phone lines.

To Internet networks

Internet Service Provider (ISP)
A bank of modems (or ISDN adapters) at your ISP takes your incoming signal and forwards it along the Net.

Modems or ISDN adapters

Network Service Provider (NSP)
A "provider's provider," NSPs run nation- and worldwide networks at high speeds.

TIPS FOR CHOOSING AN ISP

■ *Is the ISP connection a local call?* Some ISPs are local, some are national. Be sure to select an ISP in your local calling area, or the telephone company will charge you by the minute for your ISP connection. To find out if your ISP is local, call the phone company's directory assistance operator, and provide the prefix of your modem's phone number and the prefix of the ISP's number. The operator can tell you if the call to the ISP is free.

■ *How much will it cost?* Ask about setup charges, and ask if the ISP will waive those charges if you use the setup features of your operating system, such as Windows 95. (A microcomputer's OS uses a protocol called *PPP* [point-to-point protocol] to access an ISP or other online resource via serial lines.) Ask what the fee is per month for how many hours. Ask what software is included when you join. Also ask what Web page services the ISP provides—can it design a page for you? Store the page you design? How much do these Web services cost? If you install a Web page on the ISP's server, can you send files to it, for example to update it, via standard file transfer protocol?

■ *How good is the service?* Ask how long the ISP has been in business, how fast it has been growing, what the peak periods are, and how frequently busy signals occur. (Before you sign up with an ISP, dial its local access number from your home phone at various times to see how often you get a busy signal.) Ask if customer service (a help line or online help site) is available evenings and weekends as well as during business hours. Is it toll-free? Ask about the ratio of subscribers to ISP modems. If the ISP's modems are all in use, you will get a busy signal when you dial in. A ratio of 15 or 20 subscribers to every 1 modem probably means frequent busy signals (a 10-to-1 ratio is better). Also, review the technical capabilities of your provider (for example, do they offer ISDN support?). You may have all the latest equipment, but if your provider doesn't support that, you will find yourself getting very frustrated very fast.

■ *What e-mail software does it offer?* Can you access your e-mail through another ISP?

Once you're on the Net, how do you get where you want to go? That topic is next.

Internet Addresses

To send and receive e-mail using the Internet, you need an Internet address. When Internet e-mail became fashionable, such addresses began to appear on business cards just as fax numbers did a couple of years earlier. For a while, news magazines such as *Time* and *Newsweek* even printed the Net addresses of writers of e-mail letters—until one complained that it exposed them to cranks (like publicizing someone's private postal mail address in a national magazine).

In the **Domain Name System (DNS),** the Internet's addressing scheme developed in 1984, an Internet address (domain name) usually has two sections, reading left to right from the specific to the general. Consider the following address:

INTERNET IMPROVEMENTS COMING UP!

In the United States the Federal Communications Commission (FCC) has cleared the way for telephone, television, and data services, including Internet access, to be delivered via a fledgling wireless technology called *LMDS (local multipoint distribution service)*. This service resembles cellular phone service, but to receive it, users will need a small receiver dish in or near a window. The FCC is currently licensing companies to produce this service.

Another attempt to improve the Internet involves what is called *Internet II,* a zippier information highway for universities. In October of 1996 computing authorities at 34 research universities and several representatives of technology companies agreed to help create a national network for higher education that will be up to 100 times faster than the Internet. This Internet II involves large financial commitments from participating schools—$25,000 up front and $500,000 a year for three years. These participants will join forces in various regions to build extremely high-speed regional networks. Each of these shared pieces of the Internet II infrastructure would be known as a "gigpop," which stands for "gigbit capacity point of presence." A gigbit network connection can offer speeds hundreds of times as fast as today's typical Internet connection. A "point of presence" refers to a local or nearby site at which a process is taking place, like getting information via telephone without incurring long-distance charges.

Yet another way some people are trying to avoid the traffic jams on the Internet is via *vBNS (very high speed backbone network service)*, a scientists-only computer network established in 1995 by the U.S. National Science Foundaton that exchanges data at very high speeds—21,000 times that of the average modem. The network will be able to transmit the entire contents of the U.S. Library of Congress twice a day, which would take an entire month on the current Internet. Although the general public may never have access to vBNS, telecommunications companies are already using ideas from the vBNS to ease congestion on the Internet. For example, MCI Telecommunications is using a vBNS routing technology on its Internet service. Experts predict that the Internet could be upgraded to run as fast as the vBNS by 2002–2012, letting average consumers download a high-quality, 2-hour movie in seconds. In the meantime, we will have to hope for common ISDN connections, cable modems, and fiber-optic connections.

president@whitehouse.gov.us

The first section, the *userID,* tells "who" is at the address—in this case, *president* is the recipient. The second section, after the @ ("at") symbol, tells "where" the address is—*location* (which may have more than one part), *top-level domain,* and *country* (if required, such as *us* for the United States, *ca* for Canada, *cx* for Christmas Island, and *se* for Sweden)—in this case, *whitehouse.gov.us.* Components of the second part of the address are separated by periods (called "dots"). *(See Figure 8.4.)* Sometimes an underscore (_) is used between a recipient's first-name initials and last name, such as *s_claus@northpole.org.*

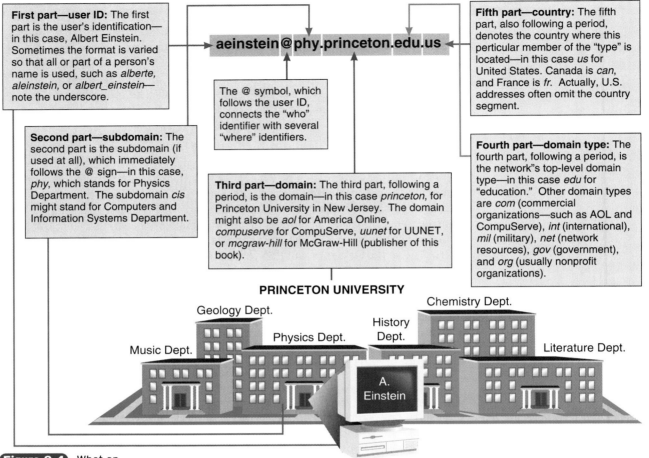

First part—user ID: The first part is the user's identification—in this case, Albert Einstein. Sometimes the format is varied so that all or part of a person's name is used, such as *alberte, aleinstein,* or *albert_einstein*—note the underscore.

Second part—subdomain: The second part is the subdomain (if used at all), which immediately follows the @ sign—in this case, *phy*, which stands for Physics Department. The subdomain *cis* might stand for Computers and Information Systems Department.

The @ symbol, which follows the user ID, connects the "who" identifier with several "where" identifiers.

Third part—domain: The third part, following a period, is the domain—in this case *princeton*, for Princeton University in New Jersey. The domain might also be *aol* for America Online, *compuserve* for CompuServe, *uunet* for UUNET, or *mcgraw-hill* for McGraw-Hill (publisher of this book).

Fifth part—country: The fifth part, also following a period, denotes the country where this perticular member of the "type" is located—in this case *us* for United States. Canada is *can*, and France is *fr*. Actually, U.S. addresses often omit the country segment.

Fourth part—domain type: The fourth part, following a period, is the network"s top-level domain type—in this case *edu* for "education." Other domain types are *com* (commercial organizations—such as AOL and CompuServe), *int* (international), *mil* (military), *net* (network resources), *gov* (government), and *org* (usually nonprofit organizations).

aeinstein@phy.princeton.edu.us

PRINCETON UNIVERSITY

Geology Dept.

Chemistry Dept.

Physics Dept.

History Dept.

Music Dept.

Literature Dept.

A. Einstein

Figure 8.4 What an Internet address means. How an e-mail message might find its way across the Internet to a hypothetical address for Albert Einstein in the Physics Department of Princeton University.

Currently there are six top-level domain types:

- *.com* = commercial organizations
- *.edu* = educational and research organizations
- *.gov* = government organizations
- *.mil* = military organizations
- *.net* = gateway or host network
- *.org* = nonprofit or miscellaneous organizations

Another example of an address is that of the Free Software Foundation,

gnu@prep.ai.mit.edu

where *gnu* is the recipient, *prep.ai.mit* are the components of the location, and *edu* indicates the top-level domain, or type of organization. An individual's e-mail address via an online information service might be

jimbob@compuserve.com

Who has the authority to assign new domain names? Since 1993, Network Solutions, Inc. has held the National Science Foundation contract to register domain names and issue new ones. Their approximately 45 employees register about 85,000 names a month—more than 1 million names to date. Users pay

$100 to register a name for the first two years and $50 per year after that. However, Network Solutions' contract expires in March 1998, and several groups are battling for control of the naming system. Among them is the Internet Ad Hoc Coalition, a part of the Internet Society. This group advocates introducing up to 28 new top-level domain registries such as:

- *.firm* = business
- *.store* = shopping
- *.web* = Web-related activities
- *.arts* = culture/entertainment

- *.rec* = recreation
- *.info* = information services
- *.nom* = individual/personal
- *.xxx* = x-rated adult material

Other groups that may get involved in the naming system are the U.S. Federal Communications Commission, the Commercial Internet Exchange, and the World Intellectual Property Organization in Geneva, Switzerland.

Features of and Tools for Navigating the Internet

The principal features of the Internet are e-mail, discussion groups, file transfer, remote access, and information searches (*see Figure 8.5*):

Figure 8.5

What's available through the Internet

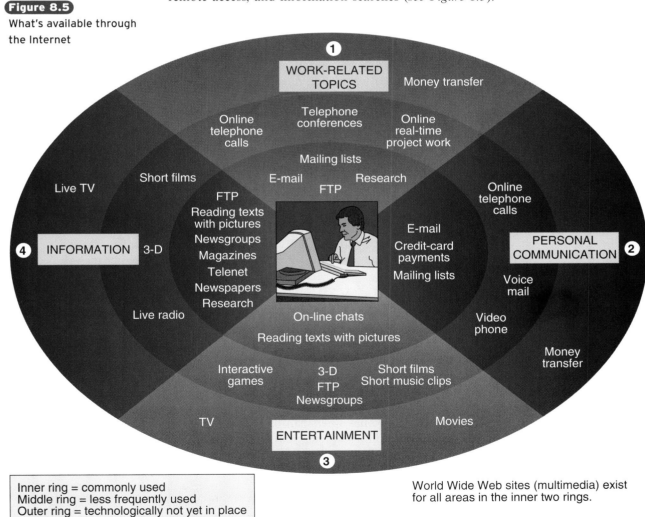

Inner ring = commonly used
Middle ring = less frequently used
Outer ring = technologically not yet in place

World Wide Web sites (multimedia) exist for all areas in the inner two rings.

■ *E-mail:* The World Wide Web is getting all the headlines, but, as we have mentioned, for many people the main attraction of the Internet is electronic mail. Foremost among the Internet e-mail programs is Qualcomm's Eudora software, which is also used by many educational institutions on the Internet. Eudora Light is free and comes bundled with other Internet products. (Note that if you are using an information service such as CompuServe to connect to the Internet, you would use the service's e-mail system; thus you would not need separate e-mail software.)

■ *Usenet newsgroups—electronic discussion groups:* One of the Internet's most interesting features goes under the name *usenet,* short for user network, which is essentially a giant, dispersed bulletin board. **Usenet newsgroups** are electronic discussion groups that focus on a specific topic, the equivalents of CompuServe's or AOL's "forums." They are one of the most lively and heavily trafficked areas of the Net. Usenetters exchange e-mail and messages ("news"). "Users post questions, answers, general information, and FAQ files on usenet," says one online specialist. "The flow of messages, or 'articles,' is phenomenal, and you can get easily hooked."[20] A **FAQ** (pronounced "fack"), for **Frequently Asked Questions,** is a file that lays out the basics for a newsgroup's discussion. It's always best to read a newsgroup's FAQ before joining the discussion or posting (asking) questions.

There are more than 15,000 usenet newsgroup forums and they cover hundreds of topics. Examples are *rec.arts.startrek.info, soc.culture.african. american* and *misc.jobs.offered.* The first part, in these examples, is the recipient group—*rec* for recreation, *soc* for social issues, *comp* for computers, *biz* for business, *sci* for science, *misc* for miscellaneous. The next part is the subject—for example, *rec.food.cooking.* The category called *alt* newsgroups offers more free-form topics (one might say "alternative" lifestyles), such as *alt.rock-n-roll.metal* or *alt.internet.services.*

■ *Mailing lists—e-mail-based discussion groups:* Combining e-mail and newsgroups, mailing lists—called *listservs*—allow you to subscribe (generally free) to an e-mail mailing list on a particular subject or subjects. The mailing-list sponsor then sends the identical message to everyone on that list. Thus the newsgroup listserv messages automatically appear in your mailbox—you do not have to access the newsgroup. There are more than 3000 electronic mailing-list discussion groups. (Subscribers to mailing lists need to check and download/delete mail almost every day; otherwise their mailboxes will become "full.")

■ *FTP—for copying all the free files you want:* Many Net users enjoy "FTPing" —cruising the system and checking into some of the tens of thousands of so-called FTP sites offering interesting free files to copy (download). **FTP,** for **File Transfer Protocol,** is a method whereby you can connect to a remote computer called an *FTP site* and transfer publicly available files to your microcomputer's hard disk. The free files offered cover nearly anything that can be stored on a computer: software, games, photos, maps, art, music, books, statistics. Some 2000-plus FTP sites (so-called *anonymous FTP sites*) are open to anyone; others can be accessed only by knowing a password. You can also use FTP to upload your files to an FTP site. (Not all FTP files are free to download.)

If you know an FTP file's name or partial name, you can use an Internet software utility called **Archie** (ARCHIvE) to help find the file. There are more than 30 computer systems throughout the Internet that maintain Archie servers, which keep catalogs of files available for downloading from FTP sites.

The Archie servers periodically update their lists. Once you find a file's location, you can use the FTP feature to download it using your e-mail address and a sign-in name. Many other FTP programs exist. Many ISPs and information services, as well as Web browsers, offer FTP programs to their users.

■ *Telnet—to connect to remote computers:* **Telnet** is a terminal emulation protocol that allows you to use an Internet account to connect (log on) to remote computers as if you were directly connected to those computers instead of, for example, through your ISP site. Once you are logged on, everything you see on the screen and everything you can do is controlled by programs running on the host system. This feature, which allows microcomputers to communicate successfully with mainframes, is especially useful for perusing large databases and library card catalogs. There are perhaps 1000 Telnet-accessible library catalogs, and a few thousand more Internet sites around the world have Telnet interfaces. (Telnet is a text-only means of communication.) Telnet programs are also usually provided by ISPs and information services, as well as some operating systems.

■ *Gopherspace, including Veronica and Jughead—the easy menu system:* Several software tools exist to help sift through the staggering amount of information on the Internet, but one of the most important is Gopher. **Gopher,** one of the older Internet protocols along with Telnet and FTP, is a uniform system of menus, or series of lists, that allows users to easily search for and retrieve files stored on different computers. Why is it called "Gopher"? Because the first gopher was developed at the home of the Golden Gophers, the University of Minnesota, and it helps you "go fer" the files you seek. There are thousands of Gopher servers hooked up to the Internet—"Gopherspace."

A classic running joke on the Internet is the use of puns on cartoon character names, such as those in the "Archie" comics. It started with ARCHIE, and then the developers of a search application for Gopherspace concocted *Veronica* (for Very Easy Rodent-Oriented Net-wide Index to Computerized Archives). Veronica is a tool to help you search a large collection of Gopher menus for the keyword you specify. Jughead does the same thing but just for the Gopher menu at the particular site you are currently visiting. (Jughead was developed at the University of Utah by Rhett "Jonzy" Jones and stands for Jonzy's Universal Gopher Hierarchy Excavation And Display.) "Think of Veronica as a good general Gopherspace search tool," advises one writer, "and Jughead as the tool of choice for deep burrowing of a local system.[21]

■ *WAIS—ways of searching by content:* Pronounced "ways" ("wayz"), **WAIS,** for **Wide Area Information Server,** is a database on the Internet that contains Internet databases by content, using specific words or phrases rather indexes of documents that reside on the Internet. It facilitates searching other than sorting through a hierarchy of menus. Unfortunately, WAIS is offered only by certain information sites (servers) and so can be applied to only a limited number of files.

What are the main purposes you think you will use the Internet for?

One last feature of the Internet remains to be discussed—perhaps for most general users, the most important one: the World Wide Web.

World Wide Web

The Web is one component of the Internet; however, because it's graphics-based, it's much easier to use than many of the tools used to navigate the Internet.

The Internet itself is not designed for sound and video. So why are we reading about multimedia on the Internet? The answer lies with the fastest-growing part of the Internet—many times larger than any online service—the World Wide Web. This is the most graphically inviting and easily navigable section of the Internet. The **World Wide Web,** or simply "the Web," consists of an interconnected (hyperlinked) system of sites—servers all over the world that can store information in multimedia form—sounds, photos, video, as well as text. The system is called the "Web" because the screens you see in rapid sequence from various files may be on different computers all over the world.

Note three distinctive features:

1. The Web subsumes Internet information systems such as Gopher and FTP. These resources can still be accessed through the Web, but the Web provides a wealth of additional capabilities not previously offered by these more restricted connection methods.

2. Whereas Archie, Gopher, and WAIS deal with text, the Web provides information in *multimedia* form—graphics, video, and audio as well as text.

3. Whereas Gopher is a menu-based approach to accessing Net resources, the Web uses a hypertext format. **Hypertext** (✔ p. 6.30) is a system in which documents scattered across many Internet sites are directly linked, so that a word or phrase in one document becomes a connection to a document in a different place. The format, or language, used for files on the Web is called **Hypertext Markup Language (HTML),** a subset of *Standard Generalized Markup Language,* or *SGML,* created by the International Standards Organization (ISO) in New York. SGML defines formatting in a text document. The protocol for transferring HTML files is **Hypertext Transfer Protocol (HTTP).** (Web software was developed in 1990 by Tim Berners-Lee at CERN, in Geneva, Switzerland. CERN stands for *Centre European pour la Recherche Nucleaire.*) When you use your mouse to point-and-click on a hypertext link (a highlighted or underlined word or phrase), it may become a doorway to another place within the same document or to another document on a computer thousands of miles away. For example, one writer states:

> When you surf the Web, you don't care where the documents actually reside. Instead, you simply move from one document to another, by clicking your mouse on the corresponding links. During one of my last Web tours, I started with a document that discussed Microsoft. Within the document I found a link [underlined word] to the Comdex computer convention held each fall in Las Vegas. As I viewed information about this year's Comdex, I encountered a list of shows playing on the Las Vegas strip, one of which featured Elvis impersonators. As I read a description of the show, I noticed a link to Graceland, on which I clicked my mouse and soon found myself on a tour of Presley's Memphis home.[22]

ADDING ON TO YOUR WEB BROWSER

Add-ons are programs that can be attached to your Web browser, giving it additional capabilities. Many of these add-ons are free, or at least free for a trial period, and can be easily downloaded from the Web and installed into your browser. Generally, they have capabilities in two major areas: multimedia and utility. Multimedia expansions can give your browser the ability to run video and animation and to listen to audio files. Utilities have a wide range, from allowing you to tell the time in a foreign city to spell checking your e-mail to checking stock fluctuations.

Netscape's Navigator and Communicator call add-ons *plug-ins;* Microsoft's Internet Explorer calls them *ActiveX controls.* (ActiveX is a Microsoft technology geared toward creating a seamless desktop browser environment.) Some add-ons are compatible with only one browser; others will run on any browser.

Note that Navigator/Communicator and Internet Explorer already come equipped with one particularly interesting add-on: *telephony,* a way to make use of the Internet for inexpensive long-distance calls. If two users have the same software, they can communicate orally with microcomputer microphones and speakers and have to pay only their local dial-up connection charge. That means users can call anyone in the world and talk as long as they like for the ISP monthly charge. Netscape's add-on is called *CoolTalk;* Microsoft's is called *NetMeeting.*

The places you might visit on the Web are called *Web sites,* and the estimated number of such sites throughout the world ranges up to 1,250,000. More specifically, a **Web site** is a file or files stored on a computer (Web server). For example, the Parents Place Web site (*http://www.parentsplace.com*) is a resource run by mothers and fathers that includes links to related sites, such as the Computer Museum Guide to the Best Software for Kids and the National Parenting Center.

Information on a Web site is stored on "pages." The **home page** is the main page or first screen you see when you access a Web site, but there are often other pages or screens. "Web site" and "home page" tend to be used interchangeably, although a site may have many pages. (Some sites are simply abandoned because their creators have not updated or deleted them, the online equivalent of space-age debris orbiting the earth.)

To access a Web site (home page), you use Web browser software (✔ p. 6.22) and the site's address, called a *URL* (*Universal Resource Locater*). A **Web browser** is graphical user interface software that translates HTML documents and allows you to view Web pages on your computer screen. The main Web browsers are Netscape Navigator, Netscape Communicator, and Microsoft Internet Explorer. Others include HotJava and Mosaic. With the browser you can browse (search through) the Web. When you connect with a particular Web site, the screen full of information (the home page) is sent to you. You can easily skip from one page to another by using your mouse to click on the hypertext/hypermedia links.

To locate a Web site, you type in its address, or **URL,** for **Uniform Resource Locator.** Often it looks something like this: *http://www.blah.blah.html* (*http* stands for "Hypertext Transfer Protocol," *www* for "World Wide Web," and *html* for "Hypertext Markup Language.") In many cases you can omit the *http://* and just start with *www.* Note that in URLs, as well as in domain-type Internet addresses, lowercase and capital letters should be typed in as such—this relates to the

Figure 8.6 Common examples of Web page components and hyperlinks (underlined items that will take you to new Web pages.

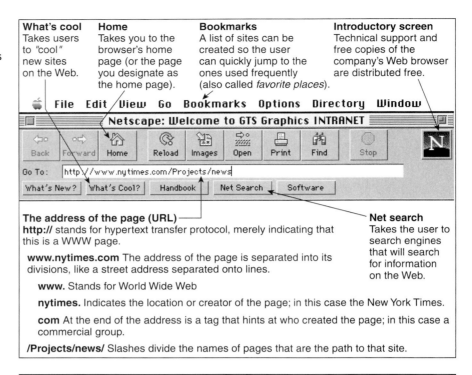

What's cool Takes users to *"cool"* new sites on the Web.

Home Takes you to the browser's home page (or the page you designate as the home page).

Bookmarks A list of sites can be created so the user can quickly jump to the ones used frequently (also called *favorite places*).

Introductory screen Technical support and free copies of the company's Web browser are distributed free.

The address of the page (URL)
http:// stands for hypertext transfer protocol, merely indicating that this is a WWW page.

www.nytimes.com The address of the page is separated into its divisions, like a street address separated onto lines.

www. Stands for World Wide Web

nytimes. Indicates the location or creator of the page; in this case the New York Times.

com At the end of the address is a tag that hints at who created the page; in this case a commercial group.

/Projects/news/ Slashes divide the names of pages that are the path to that site.

Net search Takes the user to search engines that will search for information on the Web.

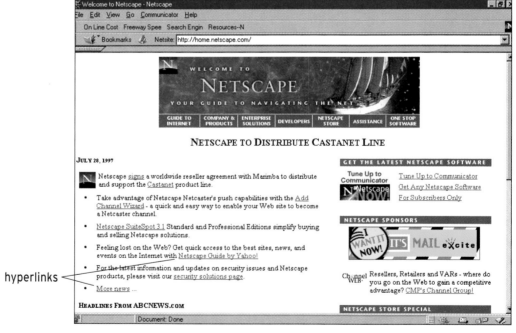

hyperlinks

underlying Unix structure of the Internet. Also, URLs *do* change; if you get a "cannot locate server" message, try using a search engine to locate the site at its new address.

The figure above illustrates the various components of Web pages and URLs. *(See Figure 8.6.)*

Note that anyone can have a home page. Professional Web page designers can do it for you, or you can do it yourself using a menu-driven program included with your Web browser software (such as with Netscape) or using a stand-alone Web-page design software package such as PageMill. Once your home page is designed, complete with links, you can either let it reside on your hard disk—in which case you will have to leave your computer and your modem turned on all the time, tying up your equipment and allowing only one user access at a time—or you can rent space on your ISP's server. In the latter case, after you have designed your page(s), your ISP will give you directions about how to send your page file to their server by modem. (The ISP will charge you according to how many megabytes of space your file takes up on their server.)

What Can You Find on the Web?

It's hard to conceive how much information is available on the Web. To obtain many of the services also offered by online information services you can access the URLs of, for example, travel agents, financial investment groups, restaurant guides, mail-order shopping sites, free software download sites, and so on. You can also read online versions of newspapers and magazines (called *e-zines*). (Note that heavy-duty database research will still require some Archie-type and FTP Internet navigation or the use of an information service's connection to research databases.) But there are *many* more places to go.

But how do you find these places? First, several books are available, updated every year, that list the URLs of hundreds of popular Web sites—for example, *1001 Really Cool Web Sites* from Jamsa Press. Sites listed include Best of the Web Award Recipients (*http://wings.buffalo.edu/contest/awards/*), Library of Congress Cultural Exhibits (*http://lcweb.loc.gov/homepage/exhibits.html*), The Nine Planets: A Multimedia Tour of the Solar System (*http://seds.lpl.arizona.edu/billa/tnp*), Stock Market Data from MIT (*http://www.ai.mit.edu/stocks*), and Physicians for Social Responsibility (*http://www.pst.org:8000/*).

Second, you can use a Web search engine or directory to locate the URLs of sites on topics that interest you. **Search engines** find Web pages on their own; **directories** are created by people submitting Web sites to a group that classifies and indexes them. Search engines use software *spiders* (indexers) to "crawl" around the Web and build indexes based on what they find.

Web browsers allow you to quickly use search engines and directories by clicking the NET SEARCH button and then clicking on the icon of the engine/directory you want to use. Web browsers also allow you to type in the directories' URLs, for example, under the "Open location" option on the "File" menu.

Some popular engines and directories are the following:

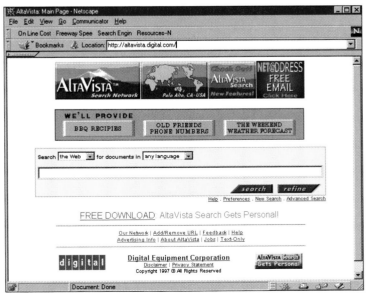

- *AltaVista:* The most popular search engine on the Web is Digital's AltaVista site: *www.altavista.digital.com.*

- *Excite NetSearch* (*http://www.excite.com/*) differs from other Web index services in that it returns not only a list of sites and articles in which the keywords you specified appear but also a list of relevant pages based on "concept" by analyzing words in a document. In addition, it ranks the documents as to how well they fit your original search criteria.

- *InfoSeek* (*http:www.infoseek.com/*) ranks results according to relevance to your search criteria. InfoSeek also searches more than the Web, indexing Usenet newsgroups and several non-Internet databases.

■ *Lycos* (*http://www.lycos.com/*) offers a list of interesting Web sites called A2Z, which indicates the most popular pages on the Web, as measured by the number of hypertext links, or "hits," from other Web sites pointing to them.

■ *Yahoo!* (*http://www.yahoo.com/*) is one of the most popular Web directories and lists not only Web pages but also Usenet newsgroups, Gophers, and FTP sites. Among other things, it features a weekly list of "cool sites" and headline news from the wire service Reuters.

■ *Magellan* (*http://www.mckinley.com/*) offers detailed overviews of many Web sites and brief descriptions of another 1 million sites.

■ *Argus/University of Michigan Subject-Oriented Clearinghouse* (*http://www.lib.umich.edu/chhome.html*) is a directory of directories. It provides a list of subject-specific directories on topics ranging from arts and entertainment to social science and social issues. For example, if you're interested in art, you would see it lists *World Wide Arts Resources* (*http://www.concourse.com/wwar/default.html*), which has links to many museums and galleries and an index of more than 2000 artists. (Besides material on the Web, Argus also lists information in FTP servers and Gopher sites.)

You can also purchase Web search utilities, software tools you can install on your microcomputer that orchestrate simultaneous, intelligent queries in multiple Web search engines. Examples are Quarterdeck WebCompass, ForeFront Group WebSeeker, Symantec Internet FastFind, Tympani NetAttaché, and Iconovex EchoSearch.

Specialized search engines also exist on the net. For instance, Catch Up (*www.manageable.com*) searches for shareware; NewsMonger (*www.techsmith.com*) searches newsgroups; ICQ (*www.mirabillis.com*) sees who is live on the Net at any moment.

Tips for Searching

Here are some rules that will help improve your chances for locating the information you want:[23,24]

■ *Read the instructions!* Every search site has an online search manual. Read it.

■ *Make your keywords specific:* The more narrow or distinctive you can make your keywords, the more targeted will be your search. Say *drag racing* or *stock-car racing* rather than *auto racing,* for example. Also try to do more than one pass and try spelling variations: *drag racing, dragracing, drag-racing.* In addition, think of synonyms, and write down related key terms as they come to mind.

■ *Use AND, OR, and NOT:* Use connectors as a way of making your keyword requests even more specific. For example, if you were looking for a 1996 Mustang convertible, you could search on the three terms "1996," "Mustang," and "convertible." However, since you want all three together, try linking them with a connector: "Mustang AND convertible AND 1996." You can also sharpen the keyword request by using the word NOT for exclusion—for example, "Mustang NOT horse."

■ *Don't bother with "natural language" queries:* Some search engines will let you do *natural language queries,* which means you can ask questions as you might in conversation. For example, you could ask, "Who was the Indianapolis 500 winner in 1996?" You'll probably get better results by entering "Indianapolis 500 AND race AND winner AND 1996."

■ *Use more than one search engine:* Many users find surprisingly little overlap in the results from a single query performed on several different search engines. So to make sure that you've got the best results, be sure to try your search with numerous sites.

■ *Use quotes when you want two words to appear next to each other:* If you don't want words to be separated, use quotes: for instance, type in: wine AND "cakebread cellars." This way the search engine won't look for separate entries for *cakebread* and *cellars.*

What can you imagine using a search engine for?

All these search tools are constantly adding new features, such as easier interfaces. But whichever you end up using, you'll find that they can turn the Web from a playground or novelty into a source of real value.

Speed of Web Data Transfer: How to Get Old Fast

The aggrativingly long time it currently takes to transfer graphic information from a Web page to your screen, or to download a video or sound clip, may cause you to visually age. Recall from Chapter 7 (✔ p. 7.6) that many Web users find them-selves banging the table in frustration as their 28.8-Kbps modem takes 25 minutes to transmit a 1-minute low-quality video from a Web site. This situation will prob-ably not change radically in the near future, unless you are lucky enough to be hooked up to the Internet via a high-speed dedicated T1 or T3 line, ISDN, ADSL, or a cable modem. So, it's best to have something to do while you're waiting for data to transfer or download. Also, make sure you have the compression/decompression utilities (✔ pp. 5.9–5.10) installed on your hard disk that are needed to open downloaded compressed files.

Marketing and Business on the Web: If You Build It, Will They Come?

Many people are now putting their businesses online. To do this, one needs to develop a Web site—that is, design a series of Web pages and online order forms, if necessary, determine any hyperlinks, and either hire space on a Web server that runs 24 hours a day or purchase an in-house Web server. All this costs money, of course. Added to the cost of this initial investment is the cost of setting up neces-sary support structures, such as inventory and inventory-control procedures, accounting procedures, paperwork needs, warehousing, etc. Some businesses don't turn a profit for quite a while; for this reason, they often use the Web site to supple-ment an existing business.

Bob Nelson of Phoenix, Ari-zona, for example, supplements his consulting business with a 15-page Web business site that helps small retailers survive chain-store

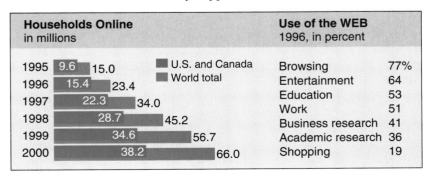

Households Online in millions		Use of the WEB 1996, in percent	
1995	9.6 / 15.0	Browsing	77%
1996	15.4 / 23.4	Entertainment	64
1997	22.3 / 34.0	Education	53
1998	28.7 / 45.2	Work	51
1999	34.6 / 56.7	Business research	41
2000	38.2 / 66.0	Academic research	36
	■ U.S. and Canada ■ World total	Shopping	19

COOKIES AND . . . BILK?

Internet *cookies* are data files created and sent to a user's computer by Web servers. They record what pages you've visited at a Web site and keep track of your online purchases, electronic transactions, and other information. When you revisit the Web site, the browser will automatically look for the cookie on your hard disk. When it finds the cookie, the browser sends the information stored in the cookie to the Web server. While cookies can help Web server administrators build profiles of visitors and can save a user's password to a particular site, critics say that they can also invade privacy—for example, revealing users' behavior to direct marketers without the users' knowledge.

Users have the option of simply deleting cookies from their hard disks or purchasing a utility such as Pretty Good Privacy's PGPcoookie.cutter, which blocks cookies.

competition (*www.retailing.com*). Through his site, he sells a system called "Power Retailing." "It's been a major investment in time, a small investment in money," he says, and it's brought in some new clients.[25] With two colleagues, Charlotte Buchanan runs GlamOrama, a Seattle-based apparel store. They took their boutique online (*www.glamorama.com*) and broke even within 6 months. At their site you can buy some of the "kewlest toys and gifts around" from a catalog of more than 150 items.[26] Jim and Audri Lanford offer a free *e*-zine called *Internet Scambusters* (*www.scambusters.com*) from which they have gotten new subscribers to their $197-a-year Internet business newsletter, *NETrageous.*[27] *Scambusters* is a newsletter that exposes online scams. *NETrageous* offers interviews and stories about proven business techniques of Internet entrepreneurs.

How do you think Internet/Web use would change if people had to pay a fee each time they accessed something?

If you want to build a business Web site, first check out some of the books and magazine articles with tips from experienced builders—such as how to choose your domain name, why to avoid changing your domain name, and using graphics sparingly if you want to attract customers from around the world. (Transatlantic phone lines, for example, are frequently busy, and European clients don't appreciate having to spend a lot of time downloading graphics.)

If you spend any time on the Web, you can't help noticing that advertisements are everywhere. This is another way for people to earn money online. If you have a Web site, you can offer advertising space to clients who pay for the use of that space.

Life After Browsers: Push/Pull

Some Internet experts predict that like telegrams and postcards, we'll always have Web pages, but that the Internet's center of activity is moving to a post-HTML environment where Web browsers will no longer be used. This does not mean that Web pages will disappear; they'll continue to proliferate, perhaps to 1 billion Web pages by the year 2000. However, Web browsers will probably become ubiquitous —that is, invisible, submerged inside other programs.

Currently Web information is displayed on a two-dimensional hypertext page. Users navigate the pages by clicking on hypertext links and by using directories and search engines to find what they want. The new form of navigation involves "push media," whereby content is automatically "pushed" to the user, according to his or her preferences, perhaps in 3-D form and over communications devices

NETIQUETTE

As we have mentioned, many online bulletin boards and other online sites have a set of FAQs—Frequently Asked Questions—that newcomers, or "newbies," are expected to become familiar with. Most FAQs offer *netiquette*—or "net etiquette"—guides to appropriate behavior while online. Examples of netiquette blunders are typing with the CAPS LOCK key on—the Net equivalent of yelling—discussing subjects not appropriate to the situation, using inappropriate language, repeating points made earlier, and improper use of the software. *Spamming*, or sending unsolicited e-mail, is especially irksome; a *spam* includes chain letters, advertising, and junk mail. Something that helps smooth communicating in the online culture is the use of *emoticons*, keyboard-produced pictorial representations of expressions:

:-) = happy face	\<g\> = grin
:-(= sorrow or frown	BTW = by the way
:-O = shock	IMHO = in my humble opinion
:-/ = sarcasm	FYI = for your information
;-) = wink	

other than the computer—phones and pagers, for example. In other words, push programs proactively deliver information to users, who no longer have to brave cyberspace to seek it out. Several types of push-media programs are available: BackWeb, Ifusion, InCommon, Intermind, Marimba, PointCast, and Wayfarer are examples. With PointCast, when your computer is idle, the program uses the Web to push news bits of your choice and advertising onto your screen in a slow parade. Netscape has a push-media Internet interface, code-named Constellation, in the works; Microsoft is releasing Active Desktop. With these interfaces, you won't have to launch anything to get the Internet/Web information you want. Instead, the content launches itself from the level of the operating system, and the content will move by you in an ongoing stream.

Push technology can notify you of updates to your favorite Web sites, advise you of a tornado alert, let you know about your stock performance, or let you know that your software has been updated while you were at lunch. In each case, your client software and its server counterpart have negotiated delivery based on what you asked for during the initial setup phase.

Critics of push technology warn that it is really a *pull* technology: Although a server delivers the information to the desktop, the transaction is actually initiated by a software agent in the client, which means that content and software updates have the potential "to stack up at your Internet gateway like planes on the runway during the holiday rush."[28]

Net Loss?

Lately many media articles have been hyping the Internet and the Web as magic information and educational resources that will almost instantly make us the best-informed and educated people in history. However, many experts view this hype as optimistic and naive at best and damaging at worst.

Although a later chapter in this book focuses on matters of ethics, privacy, and security, we believe a quick discussion here of some of the downside issues related to use of the Internet and the Web is in order. Although you may not agree with some of the concerns, they are still worth considering.

An initial problem of obtaining information from the Internet and the Web is that it is often impossible to know where the information has come from, who has paid for it, and whether it is reliable. And how does one know if the creators of the source of information or the Web page are who they say they are? For example, you might be preparing a research paper on the Holocaust and access a Web site with related information actually run by people who are Holocaust "revisionists"—that is, they don't believe the Holocaust occurred. If these people don't identify themselves as such, how will you know how to evaluate the information they offer?

And, in spite of the many conveniences offered by the Internet and the Web, many people are concerned about the adverse effect current modes of information presentation may have on the educational levels and critical-thinking abilities of young people. Whereas the pre-TV and pre-computer generations learned to think linearly—that is, in an inductive/deductive fashion, building new learning on directly related educational foundations—many younger people are more used to the information-bite atmosphere of entertainment-related presentations of information, which seems to engender shorter attention spans and a lessened ability to "think things through." Clearly much of the information presented on the Web is oriented this way. What disadvantages could be associated with this? The following concerns, among others, have been raised:[29]

■ *The Internet isn't a library. It's a television.* The Internet is less like a giant library than it is like a television. You may recall that, in the United States, Channel One television was introduced in some classrooms in 1990. Although it was initially criticized for introducing commercialism into the classroom, it now reaches about 40% of the homerooms in public schools. Allowing Channel One into classrooms enables school districts to pay for some educational materials and supplies that government no longer pays for. Is the educational use of the Internet and the Web like using Channel One? Not really. In fact, it's more problematic. First, Channel One's educational programming can be screened by teachers and local school boards before it is shown, and requests for changes can be made. Second, the company that controls Channel One can be held accountable for its contents. Thus using the Internet in the classroom and for educational purposes is more like using a super television that can be turned on at any time and tuned in to any of 100,000 unrestricted channels, only a tiny fraction of which are dedicated to educational programming—and even many of those include commercials. (For some excellent articles on the use of the Internet in education, visit *http://sunsite.unc.edu/ horizon/mono.*)

■ *The Internet isn't about education. It's about marketing.* Many people feel that the Internet erases the already blurry line between education and corporate marketing. That is, many presentations ignore the traditional division of editorial content and advertising that has been maintained in quality print publications.

■ *Kids want to use the Internet for entertainment.* Are the behavior patterns that dictate how kids use the Web already established? It may be too late to establish the Web as a primarily educational medium. Kids already know how to use the Web—for games and entertainment. And is it this mindset that discourages the ability and/or willingness to stick to one train of thought and research a topic to learn about it thoroughly?

■ *Other reliable high-tech resources exist that are better for educational uses than the Internet.* For example, there are thousands of educational CD-ROM software packages available—most in multimedia format.

What about the dehumanizing aspects of substituting online time for real-life time? As Clifford Stoll, physicist, astronomer, and author of *Silicon Snake Oil: Second Thoughts on the Information Highway,* said:[30]

> The future of cyberspace? . . . Everyone says, "It's amazing," and I go, "yawn." I'm a physicist, so I don't predict the future. Lots of people in computers think because you use the World Wide Web you suddenly are a futurist who understands what tomorrow's society will be like. I cannot imagine my life 50 years from now being spent online. Indeed, I hope my life 10 or 20 years from now will be spent with relatives, friends, and neighbors. I hope I'll spend more time in coffee shops and less time on the Net. . . . I've been on the Internet since 1975. I'm not afraid of computers. I don't feel our problem is fear of computers. Quite the opposite. I feel our problem is a blind love affair with the Internet. Some day soon, we'll wake up and say, "Oh my god. Look at all the time I've wasted online." Is this not obvious? To me, talk about a virtual community, and artificial neighborhood, and artificial life—come on. For me, real warmth, love, and compassion come from real people, real neighborhoods, real life and real friends and real family.

What is your opinion of people who spend most of their time surfing the Web?

Now that we have covered the Internet and the Web, it's time to close the chapter with a discussion of how communications technology supports the use of shared resources and telecommuting.

Shared Resources: Workgroup Computing, EDI, and Intranets and Extranets

Workgroup computing enables teams of co-workers to use networked microcomputers to share information and cooperate on projects. Electronic data interchange (EDI) is the direct electronic exchange of standard business documents between organizations' computer systems. Intranets and extranets are special-purpose spin-offs of Internet and Web technologies.

When they were first brought into the workplace, microcomputers were used simply as another personal-productivity tool, like typewriters or calculators. Gradually, however, companies began to link a handful of microcomputers together on a network, usually to share an expensive piece of hardware, such as a laser printer. Then employees found that networks allowed them to share files and databases as well. Networking using common software also allowed users to buy equipment from different manufacturers—a mix of workstations from both Sun Microsystems and Hewlett-Packard, for example. The possibilities for sharing resources have led to workgroup computing.

Workgroup Computing and Groupware

Workgroup computing, also called *collaborative computing,* enables teams of coworkers to use networks of microcomputers to share information and cooperate on projects. Workgroup computing is made possible not only by networks and microcomputers but also by *groupware* (✔ p. 6.19). You'll recall that groupware is software that allows two or more people on a network to work on the same information at the same time.

In general, groupware permits office workers to collaborate with colleagues and tap into company information through computer networks. It also enables them to link up with crucial contacts outside their organization—a customer in Nashville, a supplier in Hong Kong, for example.

The best-known groupware is Lotus Notes. Notes has been compared to jazz music. "Like jazz, Notes carries a free-wheeling, improvisational quality," says one writer. "For example, it lets individuals tailor their main menu of options, giving them more control over what information they can retrieve and what programs they can run. It also lets companies easily customize programs."[31] Among its advantages, Notes can run on a variety of operating systems and allows users to send e-mail via several online services. It also lets users create and store all kinds of data—text, audio, video, pictures—on common databases. Notes 4.0 lets users create documents that can be displayed on the Web and use a built-in browser to surf the Web. In addition, Notes has the advantages of offering better security and the ability to synchronize multiple kinds of databases.

Electronic Data Interchange

Paper handling is the bane of organizations. Paper must be transmitted, filed, and stored. It takes up much of people's time and requires the felling of considerable numbers of trees. Is there a way to accomplish the same business tasks without using paper?

One answer lies in business-to-business transactions conducted via a computer network. **Electronic data interchange (EDI)** is the direct electronic exchange between organizations' computer systems of standard business documents, such as purchase orders, invoices, and shipping documents. For example, Wal-Mart has electronic ties to major suppliers like Procter & Gamble, allowing both companies to track the progress of an order or other document through the supplier company's computer system.

To use EDI, organizations wishing to exchange transaction documents must have compatible computer systems, or else go through an intermediary. For example, more than 500 colleges are now testing or using EDI to send transcripts and other educational records to do away with standard paper handling and its costs. Software organizations are urging that such schools adopt a standardized format (called SPEEDE/EXPRESS) as a common language to facilitate the task.[32]

Intranets and Extranets

It had to happen: First, businesses found that they could use the World Wide Web to get information to customers, suppliers, or investors. FedEx, for example, saved millions by putting up a server in 1994 that enabled customers to click through Web pages to trace their parcels, instead of having FedEx customer-service agents do it. It was a short step from that to companies starting to use the same technology inside—in internal Internet-like networks called *intranets*. **Intranets** are internal corporate networks that use the infrastructure and standards of the Internet and the World Wide Web. "The Web, it turns out, is an inexpensive yet powerful alternative to other forms of internal communications, including conventional computer setups," says one writer. "Because Web browsers run on any type of computer, the same electronic information can be viewed by any employee."[33] Thus, intranets connect all the types of computers, be they PCs, Macs, or workstations.

One of the greatest considerations of an intranet is security—making sure that sensitive company data accessible on intranets is protected from the outside world. The means for doing this is security software called *firewalls*. A **firewall** is a security program that connects the intranet to external networks, such as the Internet. It blocks unauthorized traffic from entering the intranet and can also prevent unauthorized employees from accessing the intranet.

Taking intranet technology a few steps further, extranets may change forever the way business is conducted. Whereas intranets are internal systems, designed to connect the members of a specific group or single company, **extranets** are extended intranets connecting not only internal personnel but also select customers, suppliers, and other strategic offices. As intranets do, extranets offer security and controlled access. By using extranets, large companies can, for example, save millions in telephone charges for fax documents.

Ford Motor Co. has already introduced an extranet that connects more than 15,000 Ford dealers worldwide. Called FocalPt, the network supports sales and servicing of cars, with the aim of providing support to Ford customers during the entire life of their cars.

Portable Work: Telecommuting, and Virtual Offices

Working at home with computer and communications connections between office and home is called *telecommuting*. The virtual office is a nonpermanent and mobile office run with computer and communications technology.

"In a country that has been moaning about low productivity and searching for new ways to increase it," observed futurist Alvin Toffler, "the single most anti-productive thing we do is ship millions of workers back and forth across the landscape every morning and evening."[34]

Toffler was referring, of course, to the great American phenomenon of physically commuting to and from work. More than 108 million Americans commute to work by car and another 6 million by public transportation. Information technology has responded to the cry of "Move the work instead of the workers!" Computers and communications tools have led to telecommuting and telework centers, the mobile workplace, and the virtual office and "hoteling."

Telecommuting and Telework Centers

Working at home with telecommunications between office and home is called **telecommuting.** Many companies, particularly high-technology ones, are encouraging telecommuting because they have found it boosts morale and improves productivity. The reasons for telecommuting are quite varied. One may be to eliminate the daily drive, reducing traffic congestion, energy consumption, and air pollution. Another may be to take advantage of the skills of homebound workers with physical disabilities (especially since the passage of the Americans with Disabilities Act). Parents with young children, as well as "lone eagles" who prefer to live in resort areas or other desirable locations, are other typical telecommuter profiles.

Another term for telecommuting is *telework.* However, telework includes not only those who work at least part time from home but also those who work at remote or satellite offices, removed from organizations' main offices. Such satellite offices are sometimes called *telework centers.* An example of a telework center is the Riverside Telecommuting Center, in Riverside, California, supported by several companies and local governments. The center provides office space that helps employees who live in the area avoid lengthy commutes to downtown Los Angeles. However, these days an office can be virtually anywhere.

The Virtual Office

The term *virtual office* borrows from "virtual reality" (artificial reality that projects the user into a computer-generated three-dimensional space). The **virtual office** is a nonpermanent and mobile office run with computer and communications technology. Employees work not in a central office but from their homes, cars, and other new work sites. They use pocket pagers, portable computers, fax machines, and various phone and network services to conduct business.

Could you stand not having a permanent office at all? Here's how one variant, called *hoteling,* would work: You call ahead to book a room and speak to the concierge. However, your "hotel" isn't a Hilton, and the "concierge" isn't a hotel employee who handles reservations, luggage, and local tours. Rather, the organization is Ernst & Young, an accounting and management consulting firm. The concierge is an administrator who handles scheduling of available office cubicles—of which there is only one for every three workers.

Hoteling works for Ernst & Young because its auditors and management consultants spend 50–90% of their time in the field, in the offices of clients. When they need to return to their local E&Y office, they call a few hours in advance. The concierge consults a computerized scheduling program and determines which

cubicles are available on the days requested. He or she chooses one and puts the proper nameplate on the office wall. The concierge then punches a few codes into the phone to program its number and voice mail. When employees come in, they pick up personal effects and files from lockers. They then take them to the cubicles they will use for a few days or weeks.

What makes hoteling possible, of course, is computer and communications technology. Computers handle the cubicle scheduling and reprogramming of phones. They also allow employees to carry their work around with them stored on the hard drives of their laptops. Cellular phones, fax machines, and e-mail permit employees to stay in touch with supervisors and co-workers.

So-called blue-collar workers are also now working out of virtual offices. For example, truckers may now be required to carry laptops with which they keep in touch via satellite with headquarters. They may also have to take on tasks previously never dreamed of. These include faxing sales invoices, hounding late-paying customers, and training people to whom they deliver high-tech office equipment.

Other workers—field service representatives, salespeople, and roving executives—also find that to stay competitive they must bring office technology with them. For instance, Bob Spoer of San Francisco, who started a telecommunications firm that needs constant tending, takes a cell phone to baseball games and on ski lifts ("I actually get some good reception up there").[35] Many people, however, find that technology creates an electronic leash. "I get 20 beeps on a weekend," said Peter Hart, then a supervisor at a California chip manufacturer—before he changed jobs because pagers, cell phones, and e-mail were taking over his life.[36]

Would you like to telecommute in your job? Why or why not?

As we stated elsewhere, information technology is blurring time and space, eroding the barriers between work and private life. Some people thrive on it, but others hate it.

Job Searches

The digital revolution is changing everything it touches, and the job market is no exception. Until recently several large, all-purpose Web sites have assisted people in finding internships and jobs and helped companies fill job vacancies. Now, however, job-related sites have mushroomed, and there are many additional sites relating to specific jobs and professions, such as accounting, medicine, engineering, and law. Some of these sites charge fees; others don't. Here are a few.

www.jobtrak.com/jobguide	The Riley Guide to Internet Job Searching
www.jobweb.org/occhandb.htm	The Occupational Outlook Handbook
www.collegegrad.com/	College Grad Job Hunter
www.occ.com	Online Career Center
www.ajb.dni.us	America's Job Bank
www.careermosaic.com	Career Mosaic
www.develop.mainquad.com	The Main Quad
www.monster.com	The Monster Board
www.careermag.com/news/indes.html	Career Magazine Jobline Database
http://classifieds.yahoo.com	Yahoo!Classifieds
www.bizwomen.com/	Bizwomen
www.4work.com	4Work
www.cweb.com/	CareerWEB
www.espan.com	E-Span Interactive Employment Network
www.financialjobs.com	Accounting-related jobs
www.healthsearchusa.com	Jobs in the health industry
www.engineeringjobs.com	Engineering jobs
www.attorneysatwork.com	Jobs in the field of law

You can also go to the Web sites of individual companies to see if they are hiring. Don't forget: The rules of creating a good resume still apply, even if it's in electronic form, ready to be e-mailed or faxed.

For a report on predicted needs for people to work in information technology fields, go to http://www.itaa.org for an electronic copy of "Help Wanted: The IT Workforce Gap at the Dawn of a New Century," issued by the Information Technology Association of America.

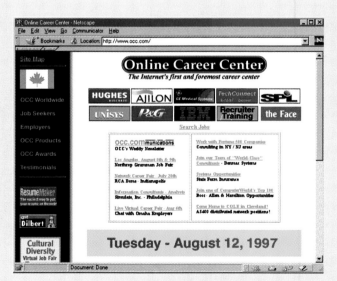

WHAT IT IS
WHAT IT DOES

WHY IT IS IMPORTANT

Archie (LO 4, p. 8.20)   Internet software utility that helps locate files.

Short for ARCHIvE; there are more than 30 computer systems throughout the Internet that maintain Archie servers, which keep catalogs of files available for downloading from FTP sites.

bulletin board system (BBS) (LO 3, p. 8.11)   Centralized information source and message-switching system for a particular computer-linked interest group. A BBS may be operated by an online service or an individual (called a *sysop,* for system operator).

The subjects of discussion on BBSs are practically limitless, enabling people with all kinds of special interests to "chat" with each other and to post notices.

directories (LO 5, p. 8.25)   Lists of Web sites classified by topic. Yahoo! and Lycos are popular examples.

See *search engine.*

Domain Name System (DNS) (LO 4, p. 8.16)   Addressing system for the Internet that uses six top-level domain designations: *.com, .edu, .gov, .mil, .net, .org.* An address—for example, *president@whitehouse.gov.us*—proceeds from the specific to the general.

A domain name is necessary for sending and receiving e-mail and for accomplishing many other activities on the Internet.

electronic data interchange (EDI) (LO 7, p. 8.32)   System of direct electronic exchange between organizations' computer systems of standard business documents, such as purchase orders, invoices, and shipping documents.

EDI allows the companies involved to do away with standard paper handling and its costs.

electronic mail (e-mail) (LO 1, p. 8.6) System in which computer users, linked by wired or wireless communications lines, use their keyboards to post messages and to read responses on their display screens.

E-mail allows users to send messages to recipients' "mailboxes"—files stored on the computer system. It is a much faster way of transmitting written messages than traditional mail services.

extranet (LO 7, p. 8.33)   Extended intranet that uses Internet and Web technology to connect not only internal personnel in a company but also select customers, suppliers, and other strategic offices.

Extranets allow companies network security and controlled access and save millions in telephone charges for fax documents.

FAQ (Frequently Asked Questions) (LO 4, p. 8.20)   Refers to the file that contains basic information about a newsgroup on the Internet.

FAQ files provide users with information they need to decide if a particular newsgroup is right for them.

fax (LO 1, p. 8.4)   Stands for *facsimile transmission* or reproduction; a message sent by dedicated fax machine or by fax modem.

A fax message may transmit a copy of text and/or graphics for the price of a telephone call.

firewall (LO 7, p. 8.33)   Software used in corporate networks (intranets and extranets) to prevent unauthorized people from accessing the network.

Firewalls are necessary to protect an organization's network against theft and corruption.

FTP (file transfer protocol) (LO 4, p. 8.20)   Feature of the Internet whereby users can connect their PCs to remote computers and transfer (download) publicly available files.

FTP enables users to copy free files of software, games, photos, music, and so on.

Gopher (LO 4, p. 8.21)   Internet program that allows users to use a system of menus to browse through and retrieve files stored on different computers.

Gophers can simplify Internet searches.

home page (LO 5, p. 8.23)   The first page (main page)—that is, the first screen—seen upon accessing a Web site.

The home page provides a menu or explanation of the topics available on that Web site.

hypertext (LO 5, p. 8.22)   A system in which documents scattered across many Internet sites are directly linked, so that a word or phrase in one document becomes a connection to a document in a different place.

Hypertext links many documents by topics.

Hypertext Markup Language (HTML) (LO 5, p. 8.22)   The format, or language, used for formatting files on the Web.

Programmers and users use HTML code to format Web programs and documents.

Hypertext Transfer Protocol (HTTP) (LO 5, p. 8.22)   The protocol for transferring HTML files on the Web.

See *Hypertext Markup Language.*

Internet (LO 4, p. 8.13)   International network composed of more than 140,000 smaller networks. Created as ARPAnet in 1969 by the U.S. Department of Defense, the Internet was designed to share research among military, industry, and university sources and to sustain communication in the event of nuclear attack.

Today the Internet is essentially a self-governing and noncommercial community offering both scholars and the public such features as information gathering, electronic mail, and discussion and newsgroups.

Internet service provider (ISP) (LO 4, p. 8.14)   Local or national company that provides unlimited public access to the Internet and the Web for a flat fee.

Unless they are connected to the Internet through an online information service or a direct network connection, microcomputer users need an ISP to connect to the Internet.

intranet (LO 7, p. 8.33)   Internal corporate network that uses the infrastructure and standards of the Internet and the World Wide Web.

Intranets can connect all types of computers and provide information in multimedia form.

online information service (LO 3, p. 8.9)   Company that provides access to databases, electronic meeting places, and the Internet to subscribers equipped with telephone-linked microcomputers—for example, CompuServe and America Online.

Online information services offer user-friendly access to a wealth of services, from electronic mail to home shopping to video games to enormous research facilities to discussion groups.

picture phone (LO 2, p. 8.9)   Telephone with a TV-like screen and a built-in camera that allow you to see the person you're calling, and vice versa.

As technology advances with ISDN lines and fiber-optic cables, picture phones may become the mainstream form of long-distance communicating.

search engine (LO 5, p. 8.25)   Software program that finds Web pages for users based on the users' search terms and topics.

Search engines, along with directories, allow users to find Web sites of interest to them.

TCP/IP (Transmission Control Protocol/Internet Protocol) (LO 4, p. 8.13)   Standardized set of guidelines (protocols) that allow computers on different networks to communicate with one another efficiently.

Unix-based TCP/IP is the standard protocol of the Internet.

telecommuting (LO 8, p. 8.34)   Way of working at home and communicating ("commuting") with the office by phone, fax, and computer.

Telecommuting can help ease traffic and the stress of commuting by car and extend employment opportunities to more people, such as those who need or want to stay at home.

Telnet (LO 4, p. 8.21)   Internet feature that allows users to connect (log on) to remote computers as if they were directly connected to those computers.

With Telnet, users can peruse large databases and library card catalogs.

URL (Uniform Resource Locator) (LO 5, p. 8.23)   Address that points to a specific resource on the Web.

Addresses are necessary to distinguish among Web sites.

usenet newsgroups (LO 4, p. 8.20)   Electronic discussion groups of people that focus on a specific topic.

Usenet newsgroups are one of the most lively and heavily trafficked areas of the Net.

videoconferencing (LO 2, p. 8.8)   Also called *teleconferencing;* form of conferencing using video cameras and monitors that allow people at different locations to see, hear, and talk with one another.

Videoconferencing allows people in different locations around the world to meet personally and share presentations.

virtual office (LO 8, p. 8.34)   A nonpermanent and mobile office run with computer and communications technology.

Employees work not in a central office but from their homes, cars, and customers' offices. They use pocket pagers, portable computers, fax machines, and various phone and network services to conduct business.

voice mail (LO 1, p. 8.5)   System in which incoming voice messages are stored in a recipient's "voice mailbox" in digitized form. The system converts the digitized versions back to voice messages when they are retrieved. With voice mail, callers can direct calls within an office using buttons on their Touch-Tone phone.

Voice mail enables callers to deliver the same message to many people, to forward calls, to save or erase messages, and to dictate replies.

WAIS (Wide Area Information Server) (LO 4, p. 8.21)   Database on the Internet that contains indexes for searching other Internet databases by subject, using specific words or phrases.

WAIS provides one of several tools to simplify searching Internet databases.

Web browser (LO 5, p. 8.23)   Graphical user interface software used to browse through multimedia Web sites.

Users can't surf the Web without a browser.

Web site (LO 5, p. 8.23)   Filee stored on a computer (Web server) as part of the World Wide Web.

Each Web site focuses on a particular topic. The information on a site is stored on "pages." The starting page is called the *home page.*

workgroup computing (LO 7, p. 8.32)   Also called *collaborative computing;* technology that enables teams of co-workers to use networks of microcomputers to share information and cooperate on projects. Workgroup computing is made possible not only by networks and microcomputers but also by groupware.

Workgroup computing permits office workers to collaborate with colleagues, suppliers, and customers and to tap into company information through computer networks.

World Wide Web (LO 5, p. 8.22)   Interconnected (hyperlinked) system of sites on the Internet that store information in multimedia form.

Web software allows users to view information that includes not just text but graphics, animation, video, and sound. The types of information available on the Web are limitless.

SELF-TEST EXERCISES

1. The _____ is the most extensive network in the world.

2. _____ is an Internet feature that lets you connect to a remote computer and download files to your computer's hard disk.

3. _____ _____ enables teams of co-workers to collaborate on projects via a network of microcomputers. The software component is referred to as *groupware*.

4. Internal corporate networks that use the infrastructure and standards of the Internet and the World Wide Web are called _____.

5. _____ refers to working at home with telecommunications between office and home.

SHORT-ANSWER QUESTIONS

1. List three ways you can connect your microcomputer to the Internet.
2. What is an Internet service provider?
3. What are the principal features of the Internet?
4. What is a firewall?

MULTIPLE-CHOICE QUESTIONS

1. Which of the following enables different computers running different operating systems to communicate with each other?
   a.   modems
   b.   Internet service provider
   c.   TCP/IP software
   d.   FTP
   e.   all the above

2. Which of the following would you use to search for and retrieve files stored on different computers?
   a.   FTP
   b.   Gopher
   c.   HTTP
   d.   HTML
   e.   all the above

3. Which of the following would you use to format files for the Web?
   a.   FTP
   b.   Gopher
   c.   HTTP
   d.   HTML
   e.   all the above

4. Which of the following has the most potential to reduce paper handling?
   a. EDI
   b. intranets
   c. HTML
   d. Veronica
   e. all the above

5. Which of the following addresses might you use to connect to a nonprofit organization?
   a. *clifford@mindspring.com*
   b. *jimbob@compuserve.com*
   c. *susanh@universe.org*
   d. *help@volunteer.mil*
   e. all the above

TRUE/FALSE QUESTIONS

1. Because of technological limitations, the Web will never support 3-D. (true/false)

2. The term *cyberspace* refers to the World Wide Web, but not to most of the other features of the Internet. (true/false)

3. A picture phone has already been developed. (true/false)

4. With a direct connection to the Internet, you don't need to use a modem. (true/false)

5. Using a commercial online service, you can send e-mail, access bulletin board systems, and download shareware. (true/false)

KNOWLEDGE IN ACTION

1. You need to purchase a computer to use at home to perform business-related (school-related) tasks. You want to be able to communicate with the network at work (school) and the Internet. Include the following in a report:

   ■ Description of the hardware and software used at work (school).

   ■ Description of the types of tasks you will want to perform at home.

   ■ Name of the computer system you would buy. (Include a detailed description of the computer system, such as the RAM capacity, secondary storage capacity, and modem speed.)

   ■ The communications software you would need to purchase or obtain.

   ■ The cost estimate for the system and for the online and telephone charges.

2. In an effort to reduce new construction costs, some rapidly expanding companies are allowing more and more employees to telecommute several days a week. Offices are shared by several telecommuting employees. One employee will use the office two or three days a week, and another employee will use the same office other days of the week. What advantages does the company gain from this type of arrangement? What advantages do these employees have over the traditional work environment? What are some of the disadvantages to both the company and the employees? Do you think employees' productivity will decline from telecommuting and/or sharing office space with other telecommuting employees? If so, why?

3. What do you think the future holds for commercial online services? Research your response using current magazines and periodicals and/or on the Internet.

4. Explore the state-of-the-art of v-mail (video mail). What software and hardware is required? What companies currently have v-mail products and when were they released? What are the current limitations of v-mail?

5. "Distance learning," or "distance education," uses electronic links to extend college campuses to people who otherwise would not be able to take college courses. Is your school or someone you know involved in distance learning? If so, research the system's components and uses. What hardware and software do students need in order to communicate with the instructor and classmates?

WELCOME TO EARTH'S BIGGEST BOOKSTORE . . . . . .

Amazon.com

When you think of traffic, the first thought that comes to mind probably isn't a happy one. But when it comes to your Web site, traffic, and lots of it, is a good thing. It means that you've been successful in advertising your site and that customers find value in your products. If you receive a lot of repeat traffic, it means that customers enjoyed the experience and convenience of shopping at your site. With your site construction efforts well underway, let's focus on ways to advertise your site and encourage repeat visits.

Amazon.com began in December 1995, and in its first year of business the number of average daily visits to its site was 2200. By March 1997, the number of daily visits had grown to approximately 80,000, with repeat customers accounting for 40% of Amazon.com's orders. This impressive growth record is due in large part to Amazon.com's discounted pricing, which provides customers with the initial inspiration to visit the site. To help encourage repeat visits, Amazon.com offers customers engaging content and personalized services. In this Episode, we look at some general strategies for promoting traffic to your site and review the Amazon.com formula for success in more detail.

ESTABLISHING A WEB PRESENCE

Once your site is up and running, make sure to list it on all the major search engines and directories. Most customers will use a search engine or directory to begin a search for a specific product or service on the Internet. You can do this yourself by loading your browser and then going to the search engine or list that you want your address added to. Look on the top or bottom of the home page for directions on submitting your address (www.yourname.com) to the list. For example, to add your site to the Yahoo search engine, go to the site (http://www.yahoo.com) and then click the How to Include Your Site link, located on the bottom of the first page. Some sites are dedicated to promoting your site for free. For example, by filling out a single form at the Submit-it site (http://www.submit-it.com), your Web site is automatically listed on a number of search engines. The over 200 search engines and directories on the Internet have also given rise to companies such as WebPromote (http://www.webpromote.com), which generate revenue by assisting businesses with this important step of establishing a Web presence.

Another way to generate traffic to your site is to join an electronic mall such as the Internet Mall (http://www.internet-mall.com). For a $24 annual fee, the Internet Mall will include a description of your business and a link to your Web site. The Internet Mall contains links to more than 26,000 other online stores. Also, consider advertising to Usenet newsgroups with a direct interest in your product. (Note: Don't advertise to newsgroups who have little or no interest. This action, known as *spamming,* will guarantee that you receive a lot of e-mail telling you never to do it again.)

At some point, you may become curious about what sites have links to your Web site. One way to obtain this information is to use the AltaVista search engine (http://www.altavista.com) and then type "link: yourname.com" into the search field. A list of every site that references your site will appear.

GETTING YOUR SITE BOOKMARKED

The ability to bookmark a Web address is a feature of your browser that enables you to go quickly to the bookmarked address, such as www.yourname.com, without having to type it in. The process of using a bookmark is similar in concept to using the speed-dial function on your telephone or executing a macro. It stands to reason that customers will only bookmark your Web address if you provide compelling content and incentives for users to want to revisit your site. Amazon.com's engaging content and personalized services have factored greatly into its high percentage of repeat customers. At the Amazon.com site, you have access to author interviews, entertaining editorial content, and synopses. You also have the opportunity to post reviews, discuss your favorite books with other customers, and provide feedback to authors. In short, Amazon.com's dynamic content is worth checking out every once in a while.

Amazon.com also offers a free personalized service called *Eyes*. For each of your favorite authors and/or subjects, you submit an online form to Amazon.com. The Eyes automated search agent will display a list of published books that match your search criteria as well as send you an e-mail message when books that match your criteria are about to be published. Let's look at how you might use the Eyes service if your favorite author is Bill Gates.

Step 1:
After clicking the Eyes link in the navigation bar, this search screen will appear. This is where you type in your search criteria. To continue, click the Search Now button.

Search Now	Clear the Form

Author: Gates, Bill

○ *Exact Name* ◉ *Last Name, First Name* ○ *Start of Last Name*

Title:

○ *Exact Start of Title* ◉ *Title Word(s)* ○ *Start(s) of Title Word(s)*

Subject:

○ *Exact Subject* ○ *Start of Subject* ◉ *Subject Word(s)*

Step 2:
Your search results, a list of published books written by Bill Gates, appear on the screen. To request that Amazon.com notify you when new books by Bill Gates are released, click the Sign up link.

Your Search Results

You searched for: **the author(s) are like "Gates, Bill"**

Eyes **Personal Notification Service:** Sign up to be notified whenever new books are released in which the author(s) are like "Gates, Bill".

7 items shown. Click on title for more details.

Camino Al Futura - The Road Ahead; Bill Gates; Hardcover; $22.50

The Road Ahead; Bill Gates; Rick Adamson (Narrator); Audio Cassette; $14.35; *Read more about this title...*

Step 3:
After clicking the Sign up link, type in your e-mail address and then click the Sign Up button to initiate the service.

Amazon.com Personal Notification Service

We can automatically send you e-mail announcements whenever new books are released that match the following criteria:

the author(s) are like "Gates, Bill"

Make sure your correct e-mail address is entered below. This is where we'll send you announcements of new books.

Your e-mail address:

yourname@yourname.com

Sign Up

If you have questions about this service, then perhaps some further information can help.

"I am excited about your 'Eyes' program. Living in a small, fairly isolated town in North Carolina it is extremely difficult to get new books when they are released," said one enthusiastic customer. Amazon.com's *Editors* service, performed by human experts in more than 50 subjects, studies advance reviews and galleys to find books that might be interesting to customers. Both of these services are free. Amazon.com also holds regular contests that serve to encourage repeat visits.

ADVERTISING YOUR SITE

Some sites, such as Yahoo!, are visited by thousands of visitors a day. These sites often generate additional revenue through *banner advertising,* whereby you pay a fee (as much as $5000) to include your own banner ad on the top and bottom of the highly trafficked page. A banner ad typically contains a graphic that is linked to your site. By clicking the graphic, the user becomes a potential customer. As of this writing, Amazon.com includes banners on seven highly trafficked sites including Yahoo! (see below), Excite, and CNN.

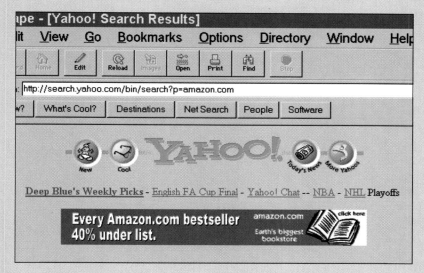

GATHERING CUSTOMER INFORMATION

The more information you have about your customers, such as their specific areas of interest, the better off you will be when trying to target their needs in the future. The question now is how do you get Sam and Suzie Surfer to take a moment to provide information to you about themselves without annoying them? One method is to give the customer the option of filling out a customer survey. Perhaps include a humorous graphic on a Web page that links to a customer survey form. Make sure to ask customers for their e-mail address and if they would be open to receiving periodic information about your latest products and promotions.

Amazon.com collects information about you when you purchase products and sign up for one or more of its personalized services. In the future, Amazon.com plans to add "collaborative filtering" to its list of personalized services. This new service will collect data from customers with similar tastes and interests and then provide targeted reading suggestions.

LISTENING TO YOUR CUSTOMERS

By including e-mail addresses so that customers can contact you with questions, comments, or complaints, you improve the chances that customers will want to do business with you in the future. Standard e-mail addresses include info@yourname.com for general inquiries, webmaster@yourname.com for Web site inquiries, and sales@yourname.com for inquiries about products and services. Consider including contact links on the bottom of your home page or on a separate Contacts page that your customer can easily navigate to. In Episode 2, we described Amazon.com's Send Us E-Mail link, which appears on every page of the site and provides nine additional e-mail links. Remember also that by replying promptly to messages, your customers will know that their concerns are important to you.

SITE SECURITY CONSIDERATIONS

Many security options are available to ensure that your Web site is secure from hackers, sometimes called *Internet graffiti artists,* who have enough knowledge about the Internet to access or change the files at your Web site. Make sure to talk with your access provider or system administrator to ensure that not just anybody has access privileges to your Web files. Also, consider weekly changes for the password you use to access your Web site.

WHAT DO YOU THINK?

1. Use Amazon.com's Eyes service to locate some books that deal with the general topic of "Web business." Describe the procedure you used and include a printout of your search results.

2. What specific features are you going to include at your site in order to inspire customers to visit again?

3. How do think you will establish a market presence? Describe the process you will follow.

4. How will you advertise your site? Will you advertise on highly trafficked sites using a banner? Why/why not?

5. What method(s) will you use to gather demographic information about your customers? How will you use this information to your advantage in the future? Will your use of this information also be beneficial to your customers?

6. What contact information do you plan to include at your site? Why?

7. What procedures do you plan to follow in order to protect your site from unwanted visitors? Feel free to research your response using current computer publications and by performing a search for this topic on the Internet.

INFORMATION SYSTEMS ANALYSIS AND DESIGN

The Systems Development Life Cycle

PREVIEW

When you have completed this chapter, you will be able to:

1. Describe the role of the user in the systems development life cycle, and explain why some systems fail

2. Identify six phases of a systems development life cycle and describe the basic functions of each phase

3. List some techniques for gathering and analyzing data describing the current system

4. Describe some software tools systems analysts use in the analysis, design, and development of information systems

5. Describe four basic approaches to implementing a new computer-based information system

WHY IS THIS CHAPTER IMPORTANT?

No matter what your position in an organization, you will undoubtedly come in contact with a systems development life cycle (SDLC)—the process of setting up a business system, or an information system. The user always has a definite role in this systems approach to solving problems. But first, what *is* a "system"?

We know that a system does not have to include computers. For example, suppose you are managing a fleet of delivery trucks for a small family-owned business. When the drivers need to refuel their trucks, they come into the head office and borrow one of a number of gasoline credit cards. These cards are simply kept in an office desk drawer. You suspect that the reason fuel bills are so high is that drivers are also filling up their personal cars and charging the gas to the company. (A better idea would be to open an account with one local gas station. You could then direct the gasoline seller to bill you only for filling the company's trucks.)

Is this a system? It certainly is. A **system** is defined as a collection of related components that interact to perform a task in order to accomplish a goal. When information technology is used, an organization has a computer-based information system consisting of hardware, software, data/information, procedures, people, and communications setups (✔ p. 1.4). *(See Figure 9.1 for a review.)* These work together to provide management with information for running the organization.

A system may not work very well, but it is nevertheless a system. The point of systems analysis and design is to ascertain how a system works and then take steps to make it better. Often people apply a systems approach to defining, describing, and solving a problem or meeting an objective—for example, systems analysis and design principles are often used in producing multimedia CD-ROMs.

From time to time, organizations need to change their information systems. The reasons may be new marketing opportunities, changes in government regulations, introduction of new technology, merger with another company, or other changes. The company may be as big as a cable-TV company trying to set up a billing system for movies-on-demand. Or it may be as small as a two-person graphic design business trying to change its invoice and payment system. When change is needed, the time is ripe for applying the principles of systems analysis and design.

The extent to which your job brings you in contact with your company's **systems development life cycle (SDLC)**—the formal process by which organizations build systems—will vary depending on a number of factors. These factors can include the size of the organization, your job description, your relevant experience, and your educational background. In large companies the SDLC is usually a formal process with clearly defined standards and procedures. Although the technical aspects of each phase of the cycle will undoubtedly be handled by information specialists, users will always interface with these specialists.

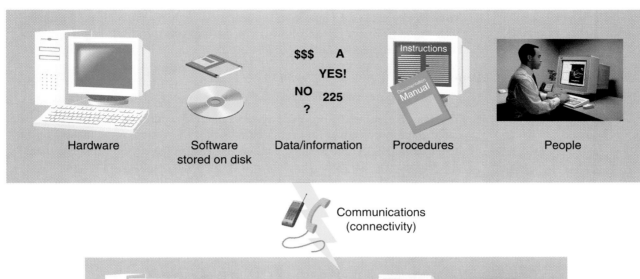

Figure 9.1 Review of components of a computer-based information system

User Participation in Systems Development: Helping to Avoid System Failure

Knowledge of systems analysis and design helps you explain your present job, improve personal productivity, and lessen risk of a project's failure. It also helps you take a systematic approach to solving problems in whatever job area you end up in.

Many general users of computers, upon being acquainted with the subjects of analyzing and developing information systems, assume they will have little to do with these areas. However, this is not true in many businesses and professional situations. For example:

■ It may be necessary for you to explain how the current system works in your department: the manual procedures you use or what you do to support an existing computer-based system, as well as the current business terminology and purpose of the system.

■ You could easily find yourself in a meeting discussing the nature of problems with the current system and how it can be improved. Indeed, in progressive companies, management may *require* employee input in developing new systems through a process called *JAD* (*joint applications development*), which uses highly organized, intensive workshops to bring together system owners, users, analysts, and designers to jointly define and design systems.

■ You may be required to provide systems analysts and designers with the departmental objectives and requirements that the system must meet. For instance, if you expect to have the new system produce useful reports, then you should plan to assist the information specialists in designing how these reports should look and what information or data they should contain.

■ You may often be involved in the approval of projects and budgets as a member of a special steering committee (a directing, or managing, committee that determines the order in which business will be taken up).

■ As the development of a new system nears completion, you will probably help evaluate and test it to ensure that it works as expected.

■ You may have to help prepare some of the documentation that is accumulated during the entire process of system development.

■ You will attend briefings and training sessions to learn how the new system will affect your job and what its new operating procedures will be.

■ And last, but certainly not least, you will end up using the new system. This may involve preparing data for input, processing data, or using information produced by the system.

The importance of user input should not be underrated. Indeed, sometimes systems fail because the components and the functions of the system are not clearly defined in terms of user objectives and are not controlled tightly enough. In these situations, user requirements are not met, or user input was disregarded. Other reasons why systems fail include:

■ *Lack of communication:* Sometimes failures can be traced to a breakdown in communications among users, management, and information specialists. Vague definitions of the project and of project goals can be included here.

■ *Continuation of a project that should have been canceled:* Often it's tempting to not cancel a project because of the investment already made (called *sunk costs*). Analysts should reevaluate the project—including costs and schedules—at various phases to determine if it remains feasible—in other words, multiple feasibility checkpoints should be established throughout the development process. Superficial project reviews and status reports can cause disaster.

■ *The failure of two or more portions of the new system to fit together properly* (called *systems integration*): This often results when major portions of the systems are worked on by different groups of technical specialists who do not communicate well or who have different priorities and objectives.

■ *Politics:* Generating a project environment with political maneuvering, manipulation of participants, and hidden motives can defeat the chances for successful outcome.

■ *Lack of management support:* Lack of support from management is usually infectious: lower-level employees, as well as outside consultants, may lose confidence in and enthusiasm for the project, and their work may suffer.

■ *Technological incompetence:* Of course, there is always the chance that the skills of the people working on the project are not up to the challenge. The "Peter principle" may also come into play here, whereby a technical systems engineer is inappropriately promoted to manage a project component. Although the engineer was competent at the previous job level, he or she may be incompetent as a manager. (The Peter principle is named after the author who wrote the book of the same name.)

■ *Major changes in available technology in the middle of a project:* New generations of software and hardware may cause a project to be abandoned and the SDLC to be started all over again.

■ *Lack of user training:* As we will discuss later in the chapter, user training is essential for the success and acceptance of a new system.

Responses to systems failure vary. Project leaders may be fired. Usually the systems requirements are reassessed, and the highest-priority requirements are identified to be satisfied by a smaller system that can be more easily controlled.

In most large companies, a great deal of money is allocated for information processing functions (hardware, software, and staff support). In such companies, a systems development project that costs more than $1 million is not uncommon. Hundreds, even thousands, of individual tasks may need to be performed as part of the development effort. These tasks may involve many people within an organization, often in several different organizational units. This multiplicity of effort can lead to conflicting objectives and result in a project that is difficult to coordinate. If the process of developing a system bogs down, the final product can be delayed, and the final cost can be more than double the original estimate. To avoid such difficulties, the SDLC—along with project management software (✔ p. 6.26) and other software tools to be discussed—is used as a guideline to direct and administer the activities and to control the financial resources expended. In other words, following a structured procedure brings order to the development process. In a small company the amount of money spent on project development may not be much; however, following the steps of the SDLC is no less significant. Some—but by no means all—risks of ignoring these steps include the following:

■ *The new system does not meet the users' needs.* Inaccurate or incomplete information gathered by systems analysts and designers may result in the development of software that does not do what the users need.

■ *Unnecessary hardware or too much hardware is acquired.* If personal computers and printers are sitting idle most of the time, then probably far too much money has been invested without a clear definition of how much processing power is needed.

Have you participated in a project that failed? Why did it fail? Based on what you know now, what might you have done to help the project succeed?

■ *Insufficient hardware may be acquired.* For example, users may have to wait in line to use printers, or the system may have inadequate storage capacity.

■ *Software may be inadequately tested and thus may not perform as expected.* Users tend to rely heavily on the accuracy and the completeness of the information provided by the computer. However, if software is not adequately tested before it is given to users, undetected programming logic errors may produce inaccurate or incomplete information.

WHEN SYSTEMS DON'T WORK . . .

Some complex technological projects put enormous demands on software writers. Examples are programming for Star-Wars-type missile defense or for huge video servers to handle movies on demand through cable-TV systems. However, consider the trials and tribulations of software contractors for the Denver International Airport (DIA) who were charged with launching an automated baggage-handling system.

When it opened on February 28, 1995, the first major U.S. airport to be built in 20 years, DIA was 16 months behind schedule and nearly $3 billion over early cost estimates. Moreover, it was far from the high-tech marvel Denver officials guaranteed would generate jobs for 100 years without spending local tax dollars.

What went wrong? Although government investigators dug into allegations of shoddy workmanship, favoritism in awarding contracts, and attempts to influence city officials, there was also the problem with the computerized baggage system.

As designed, the $193 million underground system was suppose to consist of 4000 computer-guided carts, whizzing 1400 pieces of bar-coded luggage a minute along 22 miles of little tracks at speeds up to 19 miles an hour. The goal was that passengers would virtually never have to wait at baggage-claim sections.

In early tests, however, the system was a designer's nightmare. Carts crashed into one another, bending rails and disgorging clothes from suitcases. Others were knocked off the rails, jammed, or mysteriously failed to appear when summoned. (Legal battles currently rage over why the baggage project was allowed to proceed even though some people insisted early on that it wouldn't work.)

The main culprit seemed to be software bugs, although the larger challenge was the task of automating an airport's baggage system, something never done before. In the end, DIA had to spend an extra $57 million to install a conventional baggage system as backup.

When the airport opened, the new system was used to handle only outbound bags. Arriving bags were moved by the backup system of old-fashioned tugs and carts.

Denver isn't alone. Virtually every U.S. government agency is struggling with outdated technology, but nowhere are the stakes higher or the problem more apparent than at the Internal Revenue Service. The IRS is still trying to salvage a multibillion-dollar attempt to overhaul its computer system and eliminate paperwork. When planning began in 1988, the modernization was expected to have been completed by 2000 at a cost of $8 billion. But most officials agree that the IRS proceeded with a poorly conceived plan and inadequate in-house computer expertise and then was unable to manage the original goals, much less incorporate newer technology. Now the cost has ballooned to more than $20 billion, with no completion date in sight. Although problems with the new system have yet to become noticeable to all taxpayers, officials say that unless the modernization is completed soon, the day will come when continued use of computers designed in the 1960s will result in embarrassing and costly breakdowns. And, while IRS employees can now call up taxpayer accounts on computer screens, they cannot immediately post changes, like agreements resulting from telephone conversations. These changes must be made in batches, by a data-entry clerk. In addition, many IRS computers cannot communicate with one another, meaning that the agency must still take magnetic tapes by plane and truck between offices.

Under congressional legislation enacted in the fall of 1996, the IRS must cut all but 150 of its 2016 jobs on the modernization project and turn over the work to private contractors.

Then there is the case of the U.S. Defense Department's mapping system. This effort, begun in 1982 to improve existing technology for crafting military maps, ended a decade later in an obsolete computer system. This mapping system cost at least $2.6 billion and was designed to meet the military threat from the Soviet Union. However, building it took so long that the Cold War ended before the system was completed. At its worst, the mapping system was riddled with an estimated 82,000 software defects. In the middle of 1996, Defense Department officials said they had abolished the mapping agency and handed over its operations to a new organization.

The problems encountered with the mapping system seem to exemplify some of the pitfalls that have plagued the federal government's information technology projects for at least the last 20 years: overly ambitious goals were set, accountability was not clear, the timetable was unrealistic, inside critics were ignored, and technological competency was lacking in some areas.

Systems Development Life Cycle (SDLC)

The six phases of systems analysis and design are known as the *systems development life cycle* (*SDLC*). The six phases are (1) preliminary investigation, (2) systems analysis, (3) systems design, (4) systems development, (5) systems implementation, and (6) systems maintenance.

Different organizations may refer to the systems development life cycle by different names—such as *applications development cycle, systems development cycle,* or *structured development life cycle*—or, indeed, sometimes by no name at all. However, the general objectives remain the same. The number of steps necessary to complete the cycle may also vary from one company to another, depending on the level of detail necessary to effectively administer and control the development of systems. One way to look at systems development is to divide it into six phases *(see Figure 9.2):*

- Phase 1: *Preliminary investigation*
- Phase 2: *Systems analysis*
- Phase 3: *Systems design*
- Phase 4: *Systems development*

Figure 9.2 (*Below and top of next page*) The systems development life cycle. An SDLC typically includes six phases.

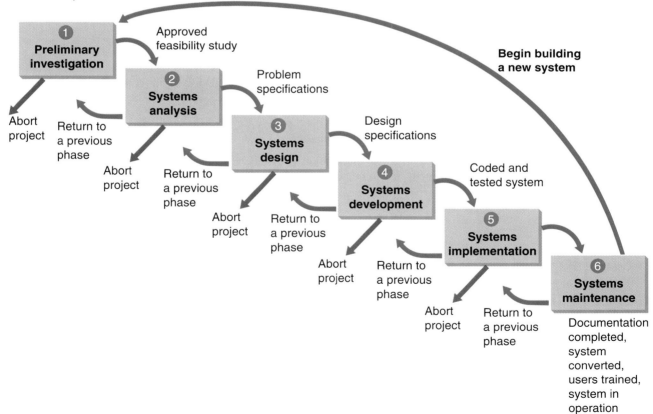

SDLC PHASES	BUILDING A NEW FACTORY	CREATING A NEW INFORMATION SYSTEM
	The SDLC of a building versus the SDLC of an information system.	
1	**Preliminary investigation** Management determines the existing building is too small; analyst (architect) does initial study to determine preliminary costs and constraints of new building.	Management determines there is a problem with the existing information system; systems analyst does initial study to determine preliminary costs and constraints.
2	**Systems analysis** Architect investigates the problems with the existing building and the requirements for the new building.	Analyst investigates the problems in the existing system and the requirements for the new system.
3	**Systems design** Architect creates detailed drawings of the proposed new building.	Analyst creates detailed diagrams, charts, models, and prototypes of components of the proposed new system.
4	**Systems development** The contractor, monitored by the architect, builds the factory. Building inspectors examine the factory for quality and safety.	The programmers, monitored by the analysts, build the system. Testers test the systems for quality.
5	**Systems implementation** Machinery and people are moved into the new factory, and production begins.	Data, people, and procedures are converted from the old system to the new; final documentation is compiled; users are trained; the new system is put into operation.
6	**Systems maintenance** The factory must be maintained and repaired by the maintenance crew until the day when it's determined to be obsolete, at which point the SDCL begins again for a new building.	The information system must be maintained, repaired, and enhanced by analysts and maintenance programmers until it is suspected to be obsolete. Then the SDLC begins again for a new system.

- *Phase 5: Systems implementation*

- *Phase 6: Systems maintenance; when the system becomes obsolete, a planning stage is then entered to start the SDLC over again and develop a new system*

Are Phases Clearly Distinct from One Another? Not Always

Keep in mind that, although we speak of six separate SDLC phases, one phase does not necessarily have to be completed before the next one is started. In other words, the phases often overlap; some activities in all phases are interrelated and interdependent and called *cross-life-cycle activities*. These activities include fact-finding, documentation and presentation, estimation and measurement, feasibility analysis, project management, and process management.[1]

- *Fact-finding:* Information gathering/data collection—using research, meetings, interviews, questionnaires, sampling, and so forth—about systems, requirements, and preferences

- *Documentation:* Recording facts and specifications for a system

■ *Presentation:* Formally packaging documentation for review by users and managers

■ *Estimation:* Approximating the time, effort, cost, and benefits of developing systems

■ *Measurement:* Measuring and analyzing developer productivity and quality (perhaps including costs)

■ *Feasibility:* Analyzing how beneficial the development of the system would be to the organization

■ *Project management:* Ongoing activity by which the system analyst plans, delegates, directs, and controls progress to develop an acceptable system within the allotted time and budget

■ *Process management:* Ongoing activity that establishes standards for activities, methods, tools, and products of the SDLC

Who Participates? Basically, Everyone

To get a systems development project going, sometimes all it takes is a single individual who believes that something badly needs changing. An employee may influence a supervisor. A customer or supplier may get the attention of someone in higher management. Top management on its own may decide to take a look at a system that seems to be inefficient. A steering committee may be formed to decide which of many possible projects should be worked on.

Participants in the project are of three types:

■ *Users:* As mentioned, the system under discussion should always be developed in consultation with users, whether floor sweepers, research scientists, or customers, internal users, telecommuting users, or external users (such as those using electronic data interchange, ✔ p. 8.32). Indeed, inadequate user involvement in analysis and design can be a major cause of system failure or lack of its acceptance. Many systems that work are never fully adopted by users.

■ *Management:* Managers within the organization should also be consulted about the system.

■ *Technical staff:* Members (called *IS technicians*) of the company's information systems department, consisting of systems analysts and software programmers, need to be involved. For one thing, they may well have to carry out and execute the project. Even if they don't, they may have to work with outside IS people contracted to do the job.

The computer professional generally in charge of the SDLC is the head **systems analyst,** also called a *systems engineer* or a *project leader. (See Figure 9.3.)* This person, who is a member of the information systems department—or perhaps from an outside consulting firm—studies the information and communication needs of an organization and determines what changes are required to deliver better information to people who need it, when they need it. "Better" information means information that is **c**omplete, **a**ccurate, **r**elevant, and **t**imely ("CART"). The systems analyst achieves this goal through the problem-solving method of systems analysis and design—the "systems approach." Large and complex projects usually require the services of several systems analysts specializing in different areas of information systems—such as databases, software programming, client-server programming, personal computing (also called *end-user computing*), and networks/telecommunications.

Figure 9.3 The systems analyst acts as a facilitator. The job description for a typical systems analyst provides an example of some of the many tasks the analyst must perform and the people and departments he or she must serve.

JOB DESCRIPTION:

The systems analyst gathers and analyzes information about current systems and any new requirements for any new systems. He or she uses that information to plan modifications to existing systems or to design new systems. The analyst introduces the specifications through formal presentations and documentation. The analyst supervises the coding and testing of new programs, site preparation, documentation and training, conversion, and maintenance.

DUTIES:
- Apply fact-gathering techniques to study current systems and develop requirements for proposed information systems.
- Develop solutions to business system problems.
- Design procedures for data collection and processing.
- Use structured diagramming and documentation methods to illustrate and define both existing and proposed information systems.
- Estimate requirements for time and resources, and estimate benefits.
- Perform cost-benefit analysis on any proposed system solution.
- Supervise site preparation.
- Choose hardware and software.
- Use prototyping techniques to develop abbreviated systems quickly during analysis and design.
- Evaluate system designs for quality and ease of maintenance.
- Design input forms, output reports, and display formats.
- Incorporate security measures into a system design.
- Supervise coding, testing, and quality control.
- Supervise user documentation and training.
- Oversee conversion to new system.
- Supervise maintenance and change control after the system is in operation.
- Establish system development standards.
- Keep current with developments in the field of computer technology.

EXPERIENCE AND SKILLS:
- Bachelor's degree in computer science, information science, accounting, statistics, or business. Graduate degree is desirable.
- Experience as a programmer.
- Training in systems analysis and design.
- Experience or training in business systems.
- Effective verbal and written communications skills.
- Experience or training in management skills.

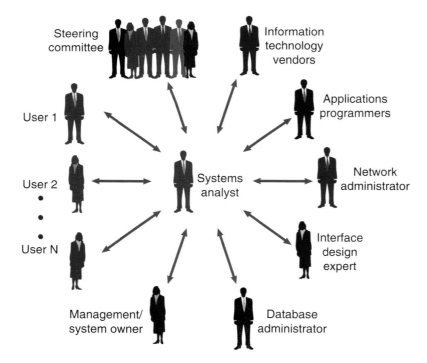

Occasionally steering committees are formed to help decide how to get started. Steering committees determine which systems development projects to work on first. A steering committee is a group of individuals from each department in an organization. It may hear reports from experts about the advantages, disadvantages, and costs of a particular project. The committee must then decide whether it is in the organization's interest to implement the project. If it decides to go ahead, the systems development life cycle proceeds.

All the detailed processes and tools used in the SDLC phases cannot be covered in one chapter of an introductory text. However, in the following sections, we provide the basic principles of the SDLC.

The First Phase: Conduct a Preliminary Investigation

In the first phase, preliminary investigation, a systems analyst conducts a preliminary analysis, determining the organization's objectives and the nature and scope of the problems. The analyst then proposes some possible solutions, comparing costs and benefits. Finally, he or she submits a preliminary plan to top management.

The objective of **Phase 1, preliminary investigation,** is to conduct a preliminary analysis, propose alternative solutions, describe costs and benefits, and submit a preliminary plan with recommendations. *(See Figure 9.4.)* This phase of preliminary investigation is often called a *feasibility study.*

If you are doing a systems analysis and design, it is safe, even preferable, to assume that you know nothing about the problem at hand. In this first phase, it is your job mainly to ask questions, do research, and try to come up with a preliminary plan. During this process a systems analyst trained in JAD (✔ p. 9.4) may run a 3- to 5-day workshop (often called a *focus group*) to replace months of traditional interviews and follow-up meetings.

1. Conduct the Preliminary Study

In this step, you need to find out what the organization's objectives are and the nature and scope of the problems under study.

■ *Determine the organization's objectives:* Even if a problem pertains to only a small segment of the organization, you cannot study it in isolation. You need to find out what the objectives of the organization itself are. Then you need to see how the problem being studied fits in with them.

Figure 9.4 Phase 1

1. Conduct preliminary analysis. This includes stating the objectives, defining nature and scope of the problem.
2. Propose alternative solutions: leave system alone, make it more efficient, or build a new system.
3. Describe costs and benefits of each solution.
4. Submit a preliminary plan with recommendations.

To define the objectives of the organization, you can do the following:

(1) Read internal documents about the organization. These can include original corporate charters, prospectuses, annual reports, and procedures manuals.

(2) Read external documents about the organization. These can include news articles, accounts in the business press, reports by securities analysts, audits by independent accounting firms, and similar documents. You should also read reports on the competition (as in trade magazines, investors services' newsletters, and annual reports).

(3) Interview important executives within the company. Within the particular area you are concerned with, you can also interview key users. Some of this may be done face to face. However, if you're dealing with people over a wide geographical area you may spend a lot of time on the phone or using e-mail.

From these sources, you can find out what the organization is supposed to be doing and, to some extent, how well it is doing it. Also, you must try to understand the "corporate culture," the set of shared attitudes, values, goals, and practices that characterize the company.

Note that systems analysis does not focus only on information technology; a method called *business process redesign* (*BPR*) is used to apply systems analysis principles to the goal of dramatically changing and improving the fundamental business processes of an organization, *independent of information technology.* The interest in BPR was driven by the discovery that most current information systems and applications have merely automated existing inefficient business processes. BPR analysis focuses almost entirely on noncomputer processes. Each process is studied and analyzed for bottlenecks, value returned, and opportunities for elimination or streamlining. Thereafter, one examines how information technology might best be applied to the improved business processes.[2] In this chapter, however, we *are* focusing on computer-based information systems.

■ *Determine the nature and scope of the problems:* You may already have a sense of the nature and scope of a problem. This may derive from the very fact that you have been asked to do a systems analysis and design project. However, with a fuller understanding of the goals of the organization, you can now take a closer look at the specifics. Is too much time being wasted on paperwork? on waiting for materials? on nonessential tasks? How pervasive is the problem within the organization? outside of it? What people are most affected? And so on. Your reading and your interviews should give you a sense of the character of the problem.

2. Propose Alternative Solutions

In delving into the organization's objectives and the specific problems, you may have already discovered some solutions. Other possible solutions can come from interviewing people inside the organization, clients or customers affected by it, suppliers, and consultants. You can also study what competitors are doing. With this data, you then have three choices. You can leave the system as is, improve it, or develop a new system.

■ *Leave the system as is:* Perhaps the problem really isn't bad enough to take the measures and spend the money required to get rid of it. This is often the case. Some paper-based or nontechnological systems may work best that way.

■ *Improve the system:* Maybe changing a few key elements in the system—upgrading to a new computer or new software, or doing a bit of employee retraining, for example—will do the trick. Efficiencies might be introduced over several months, if the problem is not serious.

■ *Develop a new system:* If the existing system is truly harmful to the organization, radical changes may be warranted. A new system would not mean just tinkering around the edges, introducing a new piece of hardware or software. It could mean changes in every part and at every level.

3. Describe Costs and Benefits

Whichever of the three alternatives is chosen, it will have costs and benefits. In this step, you need to indicate what these are.

The changes or absence of changes will have a price tag, of course, and you need to indicate what it is. Costs may depend on benefits, which may offer savings. All kinds of benefits may be derived. A process may be speeded up, streamlined through elimination of unnecessary steps, or combined with other processes. Input errors or redundant output may be reduced. Systems and subsystems may be better integrated. Users may be happier with the system. Customers or suppliers may interact better with the system. Security may be improved. Costs may be cut.

4. Submit a Preliminary Plan

Now you need to wrap up all your findings in a written report. The readers of this report will be the executives (probably top managers) who are in a position to decide in which direction to proceed—make no changes, change a little, or change a lot—and how much money to allow the project. You should describe the potential solutions, costs, and benefits and indicate your recommendations. If management approves the feasibility study, then the systems analysis phase can begin.

In your planned career, what activities in Phase 1 do you see yourself participating in?

The Second Phase: Do a Detailed Analysis of the System

In the second phase, systems analysis, a systems analyst gathers data. Next he or she analyzes the data, using various tools. Finally, the analyst writes a report.

The objective of **Phase 2, systems analysis,** is to gather data, analyze the data, and write a report. *(See Figure 9.5.)* Systems analysis describes *what* a system should do to meet the needs of users. Systems design—the next phase—specifies *how* the system will accommodate the objective.[3]

Figure 9.5 Phase 2

1. Gather data, using tools of written documents, interviews, questionnaires, observations, and sampling.
2. Analyze the data, using CASE tools, data flow diagrams, systems flowcharts, connectivity diagrams, grid charts, and decision tables.
3. Write a report.

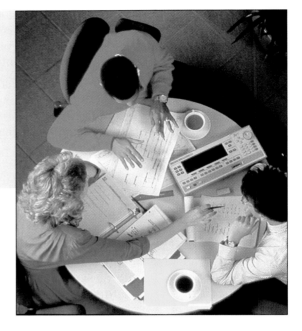

In this second phase of the SDLC, you will follow the course that management has indicated after having read your Phase 1 feasibility report. We are assuming that they have directed you to perform Phase 2—to do a careful analysis or study of the existing system in order to understand how the new system you proposed would differ. This analysis will also consider how people's positions and tasks will have to change if the new system is put into effect. In general, it involves a detailed study of:[4]

- The information needs of the organization and all users

- The activities, resources, and products of any present information systems

- The information systems capabilities required to meet the established information needs and user needs

1. Gather Data

In gathering data, there are a handful of tools that systems analysts use, most of them not terribly technical. They include written documents, interviews, questionnaires, observation, and sampling.

- *Written documents:* A great deal of what you need is probably available in the form of written documents: reports, forms, manuals, memos, business plans, policy statements, and so on. Documents are a good place to start because they at least tell you how things are or are supposed to be. These tools will also provide leads on people and areas to pursue further.

   One document of particular value is the organization chart. *(See Figure 9.6.)* An organization chart shows levels of management and formal lines of authority.

- *Interviews:* Interviews with managers, workers, clients, suppliers, and competitors will also give you insights. Interviews may be structured or unstructured.

   —*Structured interviews* include only questions you have planned and written out in advance. By sticking with this script and not asking other questions, you can then ask people identical questions and compare their answers.

Figure 9.6 Organization chart

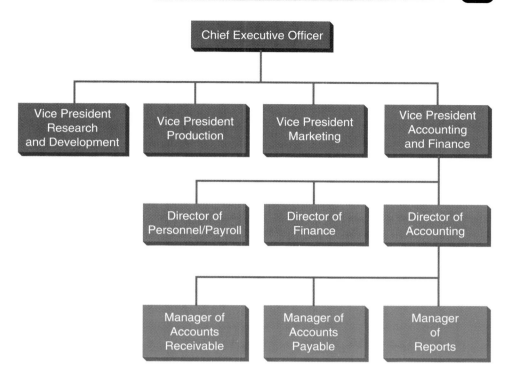

—*Unstructured interviews* also include questions prepared in advance, but you can vary from the line of questions and pursue other subjects if it seems productive.

Again, JAD sessions may be used.

■ *Questionnaires:* Questionnaires are useful for getting information from large groups of people when you can't get around to interviewing everyone. Questionnaires may also yield more information because respondents can be anonymous. In addition, this tool is convenient, is inexpensive, and yields a lot of data. However, people may not return their forms, results can be ambiguous, and with anonymous questionnaires you'll have no opportunity to follow up.

■ *Observation:* No doubt you've sat in a coffee shop or on a park bench and just done "people watching." This can be a tool for analysis, too. Through observation you can see how people interact with one another and how paper moves through an organization. Observation can be nonparticipant or participant. If you are a *nonparticipant* observer, and people know they are being watched, they may falsify their behavior in some way. If you are a *participant* observer, you may gain more insights by experiencing the conflicts and responsibilities of the people you are working with.

■ *Sampling:* If your data-gathering phase involves a large number of people or a large number of events, it may simplify things to study just a sample. That is, you can do a sampling of the work of 5 people instead of 100, or 20 instances of a particular transaction instead of 500.

2. Analyze the Data

Once the data is gathered, you need to come to grips with it and analyze it. Many analytical tools, or modeling tools, are available. Modeling tools enable a systems analyst to present graphic (pictorial) representations of a system. Examples are

CASE tools, data flow diagrams, systems flowcharts, connectivity diagrams, grid charts, decision tables, and object-oriented analysis.

■ *CASE tools:* CASE (computer-aided software engineering) tools—software programs that automate many activities in the SDLC—are also used to analyze various aspects of a system. We cover these tools in more detail in the next section.

■ *Data flow diagrams:* A **data flow diagram (DFD),** also called a *process model,* graphically shows the flow of data through a system—that is, the essential processes of a system along with inputs, outputs, and files. *(See Figure 9.7, right.)* CASE tools may be used to assist in diagramming activities.

   In analyzing the current system and preparing data flow diagrams, the systems analyst must also prepare a data dictionary, which is then used and expanded during all remaining phases of the systems development life cycle. A **data dictionary** defines all the elements of data that make up the data flow. Among other things, it records what each data element is by name, how long it is (how many characters), where it is used (files in which it will be found), as well as any numerical values assigned to it. This information is usually entered into a data dictionary software program.

■ *Systems flowcharts:* Another tool is the **systems flowchart,** also called the *system flow diagram. (See Figure 9.8, page 18.)* A systems flowchart diagrams the major inputs, outputs, and processes of a system. In some cases a systems flowchart can be used in place of a DFD; in other cases, it is a useful supplement.[5]

■ *Connectivity diagrams:* A **connectivity diagram** is used to map network connections of people, data, and activities at various locations. *(See Figure 9.9, page 19.)* Because connectivity diagrams are concerned with communications networks, we may expect to see these in increasing use.

■ *Grid charts:* A **grid chart** shows the relationship between data on input documents and data on output documents. *(See Figure 9.10, page 19.)*

■ *Decision tables:* A **decision table** shows the decision rules that apply when certain conditions occur and what actions to take. That is, a decision table provides a model of a simple, structured decision-making case. It shows which conditions must take place in order for which actions to occur. *(See Figure 9.11, page 20.)*

■ *Object-oriented analysis (OOA):* For the past 30 years, most systems development strategies have deliberately separated concerns of data from those of processes. Although most systems analysis and design methods have attempted to combine data and process models, the results have been less than fully successful. Object technologies and techniques attempt to eliminate the separation of concerns about data and process. Instead data and processes that act on the data are combined, or *encapsulated,* into things called *objects*—"building blocks" made of software routines. The only way to create, delete, change, or use the data in an object (called *properties*) is through one of its encapsulated processes (called *methods*). The systems and software development strategy is changed to focus on the "assembly" of the system from a library of reusable objects. Of course, the objects must be defined, designed, and constructed. An analyst using OOA techniques studies existing objects to see if they can be reused or adapted for new uses and defines new and modified objects that will be combined with existing objects into a useful business computing application.[6]

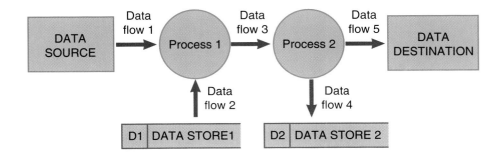

Explanation of standard data flow diagram symbols

Terminator Symbols (entity name)
(person or organization outside the
system boundaries)

Data Store Symbol

Process Symbol

Data Flow Symbol
(inputs and outputs)

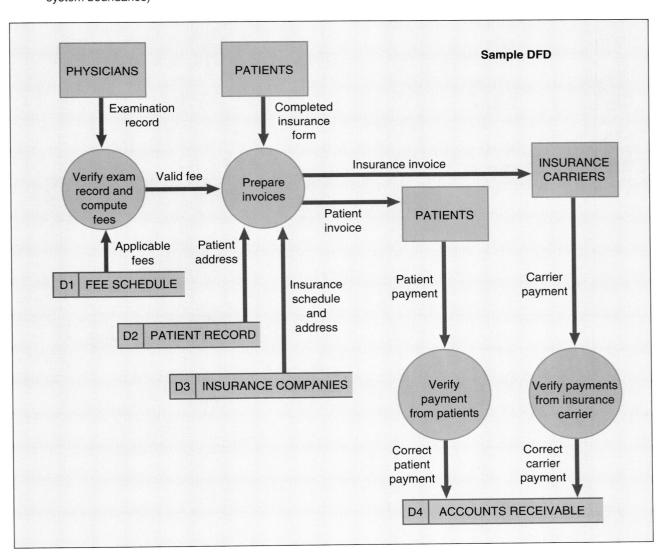

Figure 9.7 Data flow diagram

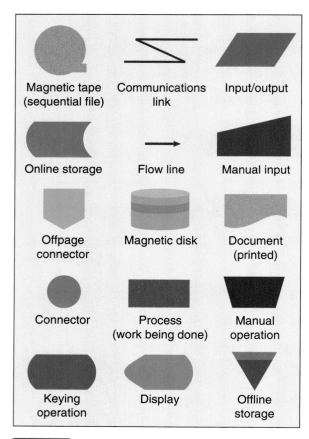

Figure 9.8 System flow diagram

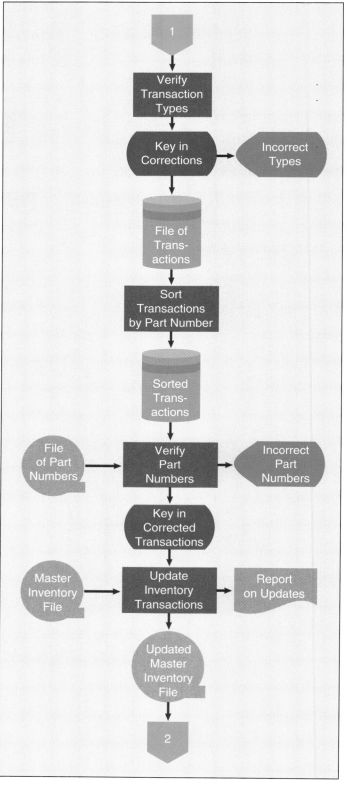

Figure 9.9 Connectivity diagram

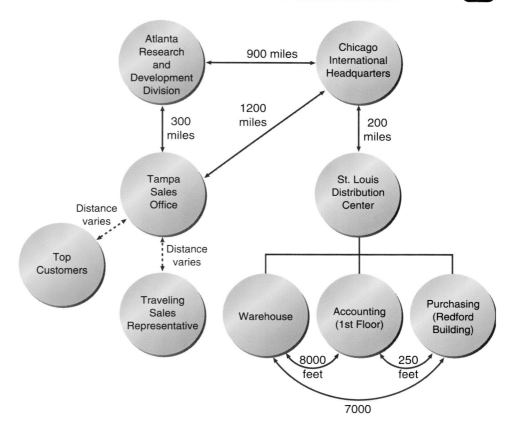

Figure 9.10 Grid chart

Forms (input)	Reports (output)		
	Report A	**Report B**	**Report C**
Form 1	✓	✓	
Form 2			✓
Form 3	✓	✓	

3. Write a Report

Once you have completed the analysis, you need to document this phase. This report to management should have three parts. First, it should explain how the existing system works. Second, it should explain the problems with the existing system. Finally, it should describe the requirements for the new system and make recommendations on what to do next.

If you worked in a large company, what aspects of Phase 2 might make you, as a general user of the system, nervous?

At this point, not a lot of money will have been spent on the systems analysis and design project. If the costs of going forward seem to be prohibitive, this is a good time for the managers reading the report to call a halt. Otherwise, you will be called on to move to Phase 3.

	1	2	3	4	5	6	7	8	9	10	11	12
Invoice Amount	<100	<100	<100	<100	100-1000	100-1000	100-1000	100-1000	>1000	>1000	>1000	>1000
Invoice Age	10 or less	10 or less	>10	>10	10 or less	10 or less	>10	>10	10 or less	10 or less	>10	>10
Payment Discount	Y	N	Y	N	Y	N	Y	N	Y	N	Y	N
Authorize Payment	X	X	X	X	X		X	X				
Set Invoice Aside						X						
Put Invoice on CRR									X	X	X	X

Key

<100 = less than $100	10 or less = less than or equal to 10 days
100 – 1000 = $100 to $1000 inclusive	>10 = greater than 10 days
>1000 = greater than $1000	Y = yes
CRR = cash requirements report	N = no

Figure 9.11 Decision table

The Third Phase: Design the System

The objective of **Phase 3, systems design,** is to do a preliminary design and then a detail design, and write a report. *(See Figure 9.12.)* In this third phase of the SDLC, you will essentially create a "rough draft" and then a "detail draft" of the proposed information system.

1. Do a Preliminary Design

A preliminary design describes the general functional capabilities of a proposed information system. It reviews the system requirements and then considers major components of the system. Usually several alternative systems (called *candidates*) are considered, and the costs and the benefits of each are evaluated.

Some tools that may be used in the preliminary design and the detail design are the following:

Figure 9.12 Phase 3

1. Do a preliminary design, using CASE tools, prototyping tools, and project management software, among others.
2. Do a detail design, defining requirements for output, input, storage, and processing and system controls and backup.
3. Write a report.

■ *CASE tools:* As we mentioned earlier, **CASE** (for **computer-aided software engineering**) **tools** are software programs that automate various activities of the SDLC in several phases. *(See Figure 9.13.)* This technology is intended to speed up the process of developing systems and to improve the quality of the resulting systems.[7] Examples of such programs are Excelerator, Iconix, System Architect, and Powerbuilder.

CASE tools may be used at almost any stage of the systems development life cycle, not just design. So-called *front-end CASE tools,* or *upper-CASE tools,* are used during the first three phases—preliminary investigation, systems analysis, systems design—to help with early analysis and design. So-called *back-end CASE tools,* or *lower-CASE tools,* are used during the later stages—systems development and implementation—to help in coding and

Figure 9.13 Iconix offers many CASE tools. This screen is from one of their banking system tools. It shows a model for an ATM transaction. The purchaser of the CASE tool would enter details relative to the particular situation.

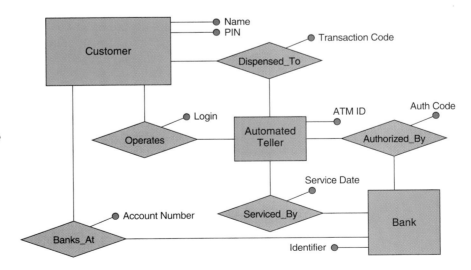

testing, for instance. (There is some overlap between front-end and back-end CASE tools because analysts have never reached agreement on exactly when systems design ends and when system development begins.[8])

CASE tools can be used for many functions. Among them are these:[9]

—*Diagramming:* Drawing diagrams of system components and models, which can be linked to other components.

—*Prototyping:* **Prototyping** refers to using workstations, CASE tools, and other software applications to build working models (experimental versions) of system components—such as inputs, outputs, and various programs—so that they can be quickly tested and evaluated. Thus a **prototype** is a limited working system developed to test out design concepts. A prototype allows users to find out immediately how a change in the system might benefit them. Then the prototype can be refined and included in the final working system. For example, a systems analyst might develop a menu as a possible screen display, which users could try out. The menu can then be redesigned or fine-tuned, if necessary. Prototyping is also often used to build user interfaces (✔ p. 5.13).

—*Reporting:* Reports can be extracted from the CASE tool's database.

—*Managing quality:* CASE tools can analyze models, descriptions, and prototypes for consistency, completeness, and conformance to rules.

—*Supporting decisions:* Some CASE tools help systems analysts estimate and analyze feasibility.

—*Organizing documentation:* CASE tools can assemble, organize, and report information for review by system owners, users, and designers.

—*Generating code:* Some applications software code, or significant portions of the application, can be automatically generated.

—*Testing:* CASE tools help the system designers and developers test databases and application programs.

■ *Project management software:* As we described in Chapter 6 (✔ p. 6.26), project management software consists of programs used to plan, schedule, and control the people, costs, and resources required to complete a project on time. Project management software often uses Gantt charts and PERT charts.

A *Gantt chart* uses lines and bars to indicate the duration (of time) of a series of tasks. The time scale may range from minutes to years. The Gantt chart allows you to see whether tasks are being completed on schedule. A *PERT* (*Program Evaluation Review Technique*) *chart* shows not only timing but also relationships (dependencies) among the tasks of a project, some of which must be completed before others can begin. The relationships are indicated by arrows joining numbered circles that represent events. Elapsed time is indicated alongside the arrows.

2. Do a Detail Design

A detail design describes how a proposed information system will deliver the general capabilities described in the preliminary design. The detail design usually considers the following parts of the system, in this order: output requirements, input requirements, storage requirements, processing and networking requirements, and system controls and backup.

■ *Output requirements:* What do you want the system to produce? That is the first requirement to determine. In this first step, the systems analyst determines what media the output will be—whether hardcopy and/or softcopy. He or she will also design the appearance or format of the output, such as headings, columns, menus, and the like.

- *Input requirements:* Once you know the output, you can determine the inputs. Here, too, you must define the type of input, such as keyboard or source data entry (✔ p. 3.11). You must determine in what form data will be input and how it will be checked for accuracy. You also need to figure what volume of data the system can be allowed to take in.

- *Storage requirements:* Using the data dictionary as a guide, you need to define the files and databases in the information system. How will the files be organized? What kind of storage devices will be used? How will they interface with other storage devices inside and outside of the organization? What will be the volume of database activity?

- *Processing and networking requirements:* What kind of computer or computers will be used to handle the processing? What kind of operating system and applications software will be used? Will the computer or computers be tied to others in a network? Exactly what operations will be performed on the input data to achieve the desired output information? What kinds of user interface are desired?

- *System controls and backup:* Finally, you need to think about matters of security, privacy, and data accuracy. You need to prevent unauthorized users from breaking into the system, for example, and snooping in people's private files. You need to have auditing procedures and set up specifications for testing the new system (Phase 4). You need to institute automatic ways of backing up information and storing it elsewhere in case the system fails or is destroyed.

In what ways do you think prototyping might be useful in your planned career?

3. Write a Report

All the work of the preliminary and detail designs will end up in a large, detailed report. When you hand over this report to senior management, you will probably also make some sort of presentation or speech.

The Fourth Phase: Develop the System

The fourth phase, systems development, consists of acquiring software and hardware and then testing the system.

In **Phase 4, systems development,** the systems analyst or others in the organization acquire the software, acquire the hardware, and then test the system. *(See Figure 9.14.)* This phase begins once management has accepted the report containing the design and has "greenlighted" the way to development. Depending on the size of the project, this is the phase that will probably involve the organization in spending substantial sums of money. It could also involve spending a lot of time. However, at the end you should have a workable system.

Figure 9.14 Phase 4

1. Acquire software.
2. Acquire hardware.
3. Test the system.

1. Acquire Software

During the design stage, the systems analyst may have had to address what is called the "make-or-buy" decision, but that decision certainly cannot be avoided now. In the make-or-buy decision, you decide whether you have to create a program—have it custom-written—or buy it, meaning simply purchase an existing software package. Sometimes programmers decide they can buy an existing program and modify it rather than write it from scratch.

If you decide to create a new program, then the question is whether to use the organization's own staff programmers or hire outside contract programmers (*outsource* it). Whichever way you go, the task could take many months. (Programming is an entire subject unto itself, and we address it in Chapter 10.)

2. Acquire Hardware

Once the software has been chosen, the hardware to run it must be acquired or upgraded. It's possible your new system will not require obtaining any new hardware. It's also possible that the new hardware will cost millions of dollars and involve many items: microcomputers, minicomputers, mainframes, monitors, modems, and many other devices. The organization may find it's better to lease rather than to buy some equipment, especially since chip capability has traditionally doubled about every 18 months. (The doubling of raw computing power every 18 months is known as Moore's law, a formula postulated years ago by Intel cofounder Gordon Moore.)

3. Test the System

With the software and hardware acquired, you can now start testing the system. Testing is usually done in stages called *unit testing;* then system testing is done. (If CASE tools have been used throughout the SDLC, testing is minimized because any automatically generated program code is more likely to be error free than if no CASE tools were used.[10])

■ *Unit testing:* In **unit testing,** individual parts of the program are tested, using test (made-up, or sample) data. If the program is written as a collaborative effort by multiple programmers, each part of the program is tested separately.

■ *System testing:* In **system testing,** the parts are linked together, and test data is used to see if the parts work together. At this point, actual organization data

Which systems development tools might you be interested in learning to use? Why?

may also be used to test the system. The system is also tested with erroneous and massive amounts of data to see if it can be made to fail ("crash").

At the end of this long process, the organization will have a workable information system, one ready for the implementation phase. (*Figure 9.15* summarizes the tools used in phases 2–4.)

The Fifth Phase: Implement the System

The fifth phase, systems implementation, consists of converting the hardware, software, and files to the new system, compiling final documentation, and training the users.

Whether the new information system involves a few handheld computers, an elaborate telecommunications network, or expensive mainframes, **Phase 5, systems implementation,** will involve some close coordination to make the system not just workable but successful. *(See Figure 9.16.)*

Figure 9.15 Summary of tools used in Phases 2–4

Phase 2	Phase 3	Phase 4
CASE tools	CASE tools and	CASE tools
Data flow diagrams	prototyping	Programming
System flowcharts	Project management	languages
Connectivity diagrams	software	
Grid charts		
Decision tables		
Object-oriented analysis		

Figure 9.16 Phase 5

1. Convert hardware, software, and files through one of four types of conversions: direct, parallel, phased, or pilot.
2. Compile final documentation.
3. Train the users.

1. Convert to the New System

Conversion, the process of converting from an old information system to a new one, involves converting hardware, software, and files.

■ *Hardware conversion* may be as simple as taking away an old PC and plunking a new one down in its place. Or it may involve acquiring new buildings and putting in elaborate wiring, climate-control, and security systems.

■ *Software conversion* means making sure the applications that worked on the old equipment also work on the new.

■ *File,* or *data, conversion* means converting the old files to new ones without loss of accuracy. For example, can the paper contents from the manila folders in the personnel department be input to the system with a scanner? Or do they have to be keyed in manually, with the consequent risk of errors being introduced?

There are four strategies for handling conversion: direct, parallel, phased, and pilot. *(See Figure 9.17.)*

■ *Direct approach:* **Direct,** or **"plunge," implementation** means the user simply stops using the old system and starts using the new one. The risk of this method should be evident: What if the new system doesn't work? If the old system has truly been discontinued, there is nothing to fall back on.

■ *Parallel approach:* **Parallel implementation** means that the old and new systems are operated side by side until the new system has shown it is reliable, at which time the old system is discontinued. Obviously there are benefits in taking this cautious approach. If the new system fails, the organization can switch back to the old one. The difficulty of this method is the expense of paying for the equipment and people to keep two systems going at the same time.

■ *Phased approach:* **Phased implementation** means that parts of the new system are phased in separately—either at different times (parallel) or all at once in groups (direct).

■ *Pilot approach:* **Pilot implementation** means that the entire system is tried out but only by some users. Once the reliability has been proved, the system is implemented with the rest of the intended users. The pilot approach still has its risks, since all of the users in a particular group are taken off the old system. However, the risks are confined to only a small part of the organization.

In general, the phased and pilot approaches are the most favored methods. Phased is best for large organizations in which people are performing different jobs. Pilot is best for organizations in which all people are performing the same task (such as order takers at a direct-mail house).

2. Compile Final Documentation

Developing good documentation is an ongoing process during all phases of the SDLC. Examples include manuals of operating procedures and sample data-entry display screen, forms, and reports.[11] Of course, if CASE tools have been used, much of the documentation will have been automatically generated and updated during the SDLC. *(See Figure 9.18.)*

Figure 9.17 Four strategies for converting to a new system are direct, parallel, phased, and pilot.

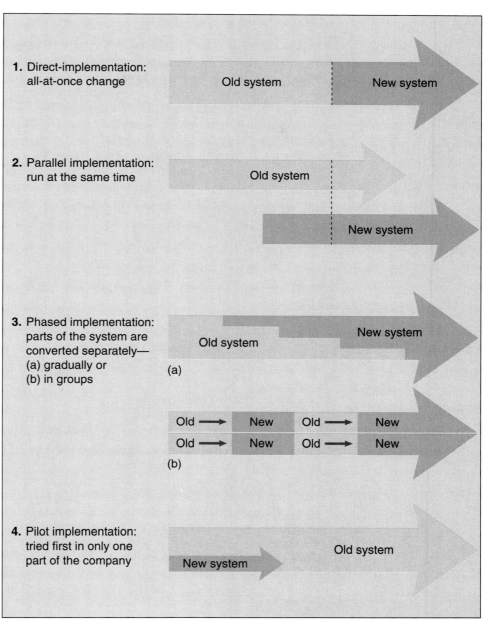

1. Direct-implementation: all-at-once change

Old system | New system

2. Parallel implementation: run at the same time

Old system

New system

3. Phased implementation: parts of the system are converted separately—
(a) gradually or
(b) in groups

(a)

Old system | New system

Old → New | Old → New
Old → New | Old → New

(b)

4. Pilot implementation: tried first in only one part of the company

New system | Old system

Figure 9.18 What documentation includes

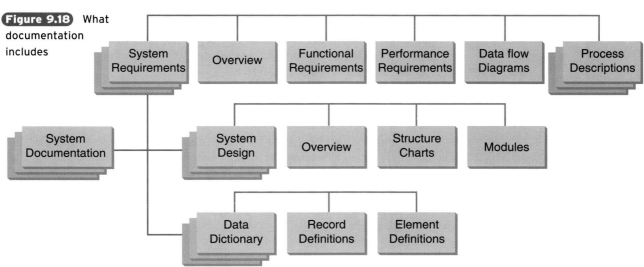

System Requirements | Overview | Functional Requirements | Performance Requirements | Data flow Diagrams | Process Descriptions

System Documentation

System Design | Overview | Structure Charts | Modules

Data Dictionary | Record Definitions | Element Definitions

3. Train the Users

Back in the beginning of this book (Chapter 1), we pointed out that people are one of the important elements in a computer-based information system. You wouldn't know this, however, to see the way some organizations have neglected their role when implementing a new computer system. An information system, however, is no better than its users. Hence, training is essential.

Training is done with a variety of tools. They run from documentation (instruction manuals) to videotapes to live classes to one-on-one, side-by-side teacher-student training. Sometimes training is conducted by the organization's own staff; at other times it is contracted out. Some companies build interactive multimedia presentations and electronic performance support systems (EDSS) to train and support users.

If you had to learn to use a new system, which training method would you prefer?

The Sixth Phase: Maintain the System

The last phase, systems maintenance, adjusts and improves the system through system audits and periodic evaluations.

Phase 6, systems maintenance, adjusts and improves the system by having system audits and periodic evaluations and by making changes based on new conditions.

Even with the conversion accomplished and the users trained, the system won't just run itself. There is a sixth—and never-ending—phase in which the information system must be monitored to ensure that it is successful. Maintenance includes not only keeping the machinery running but also updating and upgrading the system to keep pace with new products, services, customers, government regulations, and other requirements.

Two tools that are sometimes considered part of the maintenance phase are auditing and evaluation.

- *Auditing:* Auditing means an independent review of an organization's information system to see if all records and systems are as they should be. Often a systems analyst will design an audit trail. An audit trail helps independent auditors trace the record of a transaction from its output back through all processing and storage to its source.

- *Evaluation:* Auditing, which is usually done by an accountant, is one form of evaluation. Other evaluations may be done by the head systems analyst or outside systems analysts. Evaluations may also be done by a user or client who is able to compare the workings of the system against some preset criteria.

The sixth phase is to keep the system running through system audits and periodic evaluations.

Once the system is old enough to present new problems, the SDLC is started all over again to design and develop a replacement. In large corporations, a typical SDLC can be measured in years, not months or weeks.

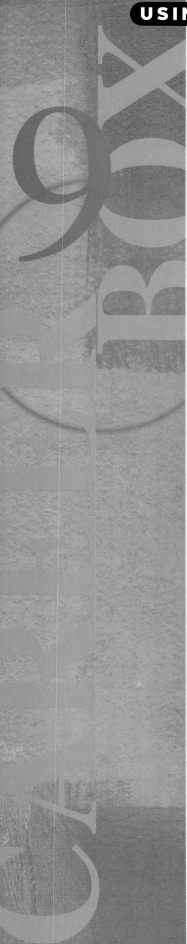

Sales and Marketing Careers

In the old days, "you could earn a good living" as a salesperson if you could talk and read a price list, says Ted Urpens, the head of sales training for Caradon Everest, a British manufacturer of replacement windows. Now sales representatives not only need to be better educated and more knowledgeable about their customers' businesses but also must be comfortable with computer technology.

Caradon Everest, for example, equips its sales staff with laptops containing software that "configures" customized windows and calculates the prices on the spot, a process that was once handled by the company's technical people and that took a week. "The company can also load on product images for multimedia presentations and training programs," says one account. "Using a digital camera, pictures of the customer's house can be loaded into the computer, which can superimpose the company's windows and print out a color preview."[12]

Future Caradon Everest reps will have to be even more technologically savvy. There will be more product options available, Urpens says, which will require that reps know computers well enough to put together comprehensible presentations. Salespeople will become more like consultants, trying to define customer problems and find solutions, rather than just sell ready-made products.

Other companies are also fast catching on to the importance of information technology in marketing. An Atlanta company called The Mattress Firm, for instance, acquired some "geographical information systems," or GIS, software called MapLinx that plots drop-off points for a driver's most efficient delivery of mattresses to customers. However, MapLinx also depicts sales by neighborhood, showing owner Darin Lewin where his mattresses are selling well and thus where he should spend money to market them. "It's like shooting a rifle instead of a shotgun," says Lewin. "We can pinpoint our customer."[13]

As might be expected, the Internet and World Wide Web are also becoming popular marketing tools. Lou Ann Hammond's four-person company, Car-List Inc. of San Francisco, uses telecommunications links to provide customers with access to a database describing features, prices, and availability of new and used cars at selected dealerships and among individual sellers.[14] A similar service, Auto-By-Tel in Irvine, California, which is free to consumers, slashes the cost of marketing cars to as low as $25 per car—as compared to the average of $425 and three to five salespeople required to market a car the old-fashioned way. "At traditional dealerships you talk to lots of people," says president Peter Ellis. "Through Auto-By-Tel, you're already predisposed to buying so all the dealer does is write up the contract."[15]

Although they account for less than 2% of sales, there are an estimated 10,000 online retail-shopping sites selling everything from books to beer.[16] "People are browsing and buying," says an executive for QVC, the company known principally for its home-shopping TV channel but which also operates a Web site. He credits success to the convenience that online shopping offers to buyers strapped for time.

WHAT IT IS / WHAT IT DOES

WHY IT IS IMPORTANT

computer-aided software engineering (CASE) tools (LO 4, p. 9.21) Software that provides computer-automated means of designing and changing systems.

CASE tools may be used in almost any phase of the SDLC, not just design. So-called *front-end CASE tools* are used during the first three phases—preliminary analysis, systems analysis, systems design—to help with the early analysis and design. So-called *back-end CASE tools* are used during two later phases—systems development and implementation—to help in coding and testing, for instance.

connectivity diagram (LO 3, p. 9.16) Modeling tool used to map network connections of people, data, and activities of various locations.

Because connectivity diagrams are concerned with communications networks, their use is increasing.

data dictionary (LO 3, p. 9.16) Record of all the elements of data that make up the data flow in a system.

In analyzing a current system and preparing data flow diagrams, systems analysts must prepare a data dictionary, which is used and expanded during subsequent phases of the SDLC.

data flow diagram (DFD) (LO 3, p. 9.16) Modeling tool that graphically shows the flow of data through a system.

A DFD diagrams the processes that change data into information.

decision table (LO 3, p. 9.16) Modeling tool that shows the decision rules that apply when certain conditions occur and what actions to take.

A decision table provides a model of a simple, structured decision-making case. It shows which conditions must take place in order for which actions to occur.

direct implementation (LO 5, p. 9.26) Method of system conversion; the users simply stop using the old system and start using the new one.

The risk of this method is that there is nothing to fall back on if the old system has been discontinued.

grid chart (LO 3, p. 9.16) Modeling tool that shows the relationship between data on input documents and data on output documents.

Grid charts are used in the systems design phase of the SDLC.

parallel implementation (LO 5, p. 9.26) Method of system conversion whereby the old and new systems are operated side by side until the new system has shown it is reliable.

If the new system fails, the organization can switch back to the old one. The difficulty is the expense of paying for equipment and people to operate two systems simultaneously.

phased implementation (LO 5, p. 9.26)   Method of system conversion whereby parts of the new system are phased in gradually, perhaps over several months, or all at once, in groups.

This conversion strategy is prudent, though it can be expensive.

pilot implementation (LO 5, p. 9.26)   Method of system conversion whereby the entire system is tried out by only some users. Once the reliability has been proved, the system is implemented with the rest of the intended users.

The pilot approach has risks, since all the users of a particular group are taken off the old system. However, the risks are confined to only a small part of the organization.

preliminary investigation (LO 2, p. 9.11)   Phase 1 of the SDLC; the purpose is to conduct a preliminary analysis (determine the organization's objectives, determine the nature and scope of the problem), propose alternative solutions (leave the system as is, improve the efficiency of the system, or develop a new system), describe costs and benefits, and submit a preliminary plan with recommendations.

The preliminary investigation lays the groundwork for the other phases of the SDLC.

prototype (LO 3, p. 9.22)   Limited working system developed to test out design concepts.

A prototype allows users to find out immediately how a change in the system might benefit them. Then the prototype can be refined and included in the final working system.

prototyping (LO 4, p. 9.22)   Involves building a model or experimental version of all or part of a system so that it can be quickly tested and evaluated.

Prototyping is part of the preliminary design stage of Phase 3 of the SDLC.

system (LO 1, p. 9.2)   Collection of related components that interact to perform a task in order to accomplish a goal.

The point of systems analysis and design is to ascertain how a system works and then take steps to make it better.

systems analysis (LO 2, p. 9.13)   Phase 2 of the SDLC; the purpose is to gather data (using written documents, interviews, questionnaires, observation, and sampling), analyze the data, and write a report.

The results of systems analysis will determine whether the system should be redesigned.

systems analyst (LO 2, p. 9.9)   Information specialist who performs systems analysis, design, and implementation.

The systems analyst studies the information and communications needs of an organization to determine how to deliver information that is more accurate, timely, and useful. The systems analyst achieves this goal through the problem-solving method of systems analysis and design.

systems design (LO 2, p. 9.20)   Phase 3 of the SDLC; the purpose is to do a preliminary design and then a detail design, and write a report.

Systems design is one of the most crucial phases of the SDLC.

systems development (LO 2, p. 9.23)   Phase 4 of the SDLC; hardware and software for the new system are acquired and tested. The fourth phase begins once management has approved the way to development.

This phase may involve the organization in investing substantial time and money.

systems development life cycle (SDLC) (LO 1, p. 9.2)   Six-phase process that many organizations follow during systems analysis and design: (1) *preliminary investigation;* (2) *systems analysis;* (3) *systems design;* (4) *systems development;* (5) *systems implementation;* (6) *systems maintenance.* Phases often overlap, and a new one may start before the old one is finished. After the first four phases, management must decide whether to proceed to the next phase. User input and review is a critical part of each phase.

The SDLC is a comprehensive tool for solving organizational problems, particularly those relating to the flow of computer-based information.

systems flowchart (LO 3, p. 9.16)   Modeling tool that uses many symbols to diagram the input, processing, and output of data in a system as well the interaction of all the parts in a system.

A systems flowchart graphically depicts the major inputs, outputs, and processes of a system.

systems implementation (LO 2, p. 9.25)   Phase 5 of the SDLC; consists of converting the hardware, software, and files to the new system and training the users.

This phase involves putting design ideas into operation.

systems maintenance (LO 2, p. 9.28)   Phase 6 of the SDLC; consists of adjusting and improving the system through system audits and periodic evaluations.

Systems won't run themselves; they must be maintained.

system testing (LO 2, p. 9.24)   Part of Phase 4 of the SDLC; the parts of a new program are linked together, and test (sample) data is used to see if the parts work together.

Test data may consist of actual data used within the organization. Also, erroneous and massive amounts of data may be used to see if the system can be made to fail.

unit testing (LO 2, p. 9.24)   Part of Phase 4 of the SDLC; individual parts of a new program are tested, using test (sample) data.

If the program is written as a collaborative effort by multiple programmers, each part of the program is tested separately. See *system testing*.

1. A _____ is a collection of related components that interact to perform a task in order to accomplish a goal.

2. _____ _____ is when the old system is halted on a given date and the new system is activated.

3. The modeling tool used by the systems analyst to focus on the flow of data through a system is called a(n) _____ _____ _____.

4. The situation in which the old system and the new system are running at the same time for a specified period is called _____ implementation.

5. The process of building a small, simple model of a new information system is called _____.

SHORT-ANSWER QUESTIONS

1. What are CASE tools used for?
2. List the six phases of the SDLC.
3. What is the purpose of joint applications development (JAD)?
4. What is the purpose of the systems development phase of the SDLC?
5. What is the difference between a structured and unstructured interview?

MULTIPLE-CHOICE QUESTIONS

1. Which of the following isn't used to gather data in the second phase of the SDLC?
   a. written documents
   b. structured interviews
   c. questionnaires
   d. connectivity diagrams
   e. observation

2. Which of the following describes the method of trying out a new system on a few users?
   a. direct approach
   b. parallel approach
   c. phased approach
   d. pilot approach
   e. none of the above

3. In which phase of the SDLC are Gantt charts and PERT charts used?
   a. Phase 1
   b. Phase 2
   c. Phase 3
   d. Phase 4
   e. Phase 5

4. Which of the following is used to indicate the timing of and relationships among the tasks of a project?
   a. data flow diagram
   b. data dictionary
   c. PERT chart
   d. connectivity diagram
   e. all the above

5. In the sixth phase of the SDLC, systems maintewnance, _____ is used to review an organization's information system to see if all records and systems are as they should be.
   a. auditing
   b. evaluation
   c. unit testing
   d. system testing
   e. all the above

TRUE/FALSE QUESTIONS

1. Users are rarely involved in systems development. (true/false)

2. During the system testing phase of the SDLC, the system is often fed erroneous data. (true/false)

3. Software and hardware are acquired in the systems development phase of the SDLC. (true/false)

4. Gantt charts are used to automate various activities in the SDLC. (true/false)

5. Data dictionaries are used to define the elements of data that make up a data flow diagram. (true/false)

KNOWLEDGE IN ACTION

1. Design a system that would handle the input, processing, and output of a simple form of your choice. Use a data flow diagram to illustrate the system.

2. Interview a student majoring in computer science who plans to become a systems analyst. Why is this person interested in this field? What does he or she hope to accomplish in it? What courses must be taken to satisfy the requirements for becoming an analyst? What major changes in systems design and analysis does this person forecast for the next five years?

3. Using current newspaper publications, such as the *Wall Street Journal,* identify a company that has decided on a change of strategy. For example, in 1997, McDonald's decided to build fewer restaurants than in 1996. Obviously, the management at McDonald's analyzed its current system before arriving at this decision. By applying as many aspects of the SDLC as possible, describe why you think the company you've chosen has decided on a change of direction.

4. Using the Internet or current publications, identify a company that develops computer-aided software engineering (CASE) tools. In a few paragraphs, describe what this company's CASE tools are used for.

SOFTWARE PROGRAMMING AND LANGUAGES

Where Your Software Comes From

10

PREVIEW

When you have completed this chapter you will be able to:

1. Explain what a program is.

2. Explain the five steps in traditional programming.

3. Discuss the concepts of structured program design.

4. Identify and give examples of the five generations of programming languages.

5. Distinguish among assembler, compiler, and interpreter.

6. Identify some traditional programming languages.

7. Explain object-oriented and visual programming.

8. Briefly describe HTML, VRML, and Java.

WHY IS THIS CHAPTER IMPORTANT?

"We live in a society that is enlarging the boundaries of knowledge at an unprecedented rate," says James Randi, a debunker of pseudoscience and author, "and we cannot keep up with more than a small portion of what is made available to us." Devoted to exposing the truth behind paranormal phenomena, Randi deplores the uncritical thinking he sees on every hand—people basing their lives on horoscopes, numerology, and similar nonsense. To mix the data available to our senses "with childish notions of magic and fantasy is to cripple our perception of the world around us," he says. "We must reach for the truth, not for the ghosts of dead absurdities."[1]

In other words, we must learn to liberate ourselves from certain mind-sets and learn to think critically. By the time we are grown, our minds have become "set" in various patterns of thinking that affect the way we respond to new situations and new ideas. These mind-sets are the result of our personal experiences and the various social environments in which we grew up. Such mind-sets determine what ideas we think are important and, conversely, what ideas we ignore.

"Because we can't pay attention to all the events that occur around us," points out one book on clear thinking, "our minds filter out some observations and facts and let others through to our conscious awareness."[2] Herein lies the danger: "As a result we see and hear what we subconsciously want to, and pay little attention to facts or observations that have already been rejected as unimportant."

Having mind-sets makes life comfortable. However, as the same writers point out, "Familiar relationships and events become so commonplace that we expect them to continue forever. Then we find ourselves completely unprepared to accept changes that are necessary, even when they stare us in the face."[3]

To break past mind-sets, we need to learn to think critically. Critical thinking is sorting out conflicting claims, weighing the evidence for them, letting go of personal biases, and arriving at reasonable views. Critical thinking means actively seeking to understand, analyze, and evaluate information in order to solve specific problems. It is very much a feature of the problem-solving process of the systems development life cycle (SDLC) (✔ p. 9.2) in general and of programming in particular.

Critical thinking is simply clear thinking, an attribute that can be developed. "Before making important choices," says one writer, clear thinkers "try to clear emotion, bias, trivia and preconceived notions out of the way so they can concentrate on the information essential to making the right decision."[4] All it takes is practice.

Programming: A Five-Step Procedure

Traditional programming is a five-step procedure for producing a program—a list of instructions—for the computer. The actual program coding is done in step 3 using a programming language.

People often think of programming as simply typing words and numbers into a computer. This is part of it, but only a small part. Basically, programming is a method of solving a problem; that is, it uses **algorithms,** each a set of ordered steps for solving a problem. (*Algorithm* essentially means the same thing as *logic*.)

What a Program Is

To see how programming works, consider what a program is. A program is a list of instructions that the computer must follow in order to process data into information. The instructions consist of statements written in a programming language, such as BASIC. **Programming,** also called *software engineering,* is a multistep process for creating that list of instructions. Only one of those steps (the step called *coding*) consists of sitting at the keyboard typing in code.

Traditionally, the steps of the program development cycle are as follows. *(See Figure 10.1.)* These steps are used for the development of programs using traditional programming languages. Newer approaches to creating programs—discussed later in the chapter—may adapt these steps to their particular needs.

1. Clarify the programming needs

2. Design the program

3. Code the program

4. Test the program

5. Document and maintain the program

Recall that program development constitutes Phase 4.1 of the systems development life cycle (✔ p. 9.24).

The First Step: Clarify the Programming Needs

This step requires performing six mini-steps. They include clarifying objectives, output, input, and processing tasks, then studying their feasibility and documenting them. Let us consider these six mini-steps.

1. Clarify Objectives and Users

You solve problems all the time. A problem might be deciding whether to take a required science course this term or next. Or you might try to solve the problem of grouping classes so you can fit in a job. In such cases you are specifying your objectives. Programming works the same way. You need to write a statement of the objectives you are trying to accomplish—the problem you are trying to solve. If the problem is that your company's systems analysts (✔ p. 9.9) have designed a new computer-based payroll processing system and brought it to you as the programmer, you need to clarify the programming needs.

You also need to make sure you know who the users of the program will be. Will they be people inside the company, outside, or both? What kind of skills will they bring?

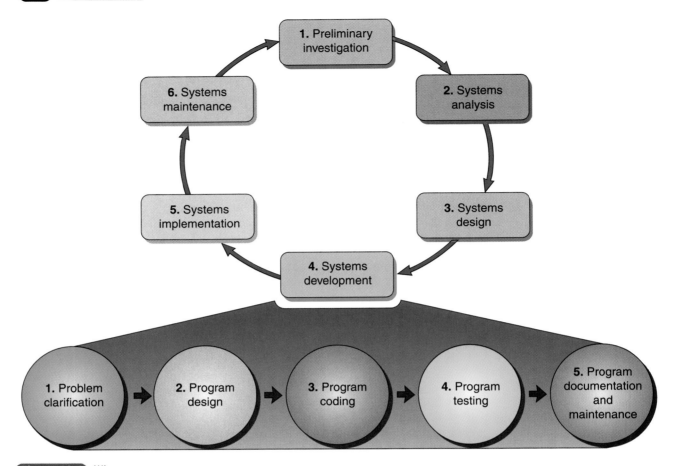

Figure 10.1 Where programming fits in the systems development life cycle. The fourth phase of the six-phase systems development life cycle has a five-step procedure of its own. These five steps are the traditional problem-solving process called *programming.*

2. Clarify Desired Outputs

Make sure you understand the outputs—what the system designers want to get out of the system—before you study the inputs. For example, what kind of hard-copy is wanted? What information should the outputs include? This step may require several meetings with systems designers and users to make sure you're creating what they want.

3. Clarify Desired Inputs

Once you know the kind of outputs required, you can then think about input. What kind of input data is needed? What form should it appear in? What is its source?

4. Clarify the Desired Processing

Here you make sure you understand the processing tasks that must occur in order for input data to be processed into output data.

5. Double-check the Feasibility of Implementing the Program

Is the kind of program you're supposed to create feasible within the present bud-get? Will it require hiring a lot more staff? Will it take too long to accomplish?

Sometimes programmers decide they can buy an existing program and modify it rather than write it from scratch.

6. Document the Analysis

Throughout this first step on program clarification, programmers must document everything they do. This includes writing objective specifications of the entire process being described.

The Second Step: Design the Program

Assuming the decision is to make, or custom-write, the program, you then move on to design the solution specified by systems analysts. In the program-design step, the software is designed in three mini-steps. First, the program logic is determined through a top-down approach and modularization, using a hierarchy chart. Then it is designed in detailed form, either in narrative form, using pseudocode, or graphically, using flowcharts. Finally, the design is tested with a structured walkthrough.

It used to be that programmers took a kind of seat-of-the-pants approach to programming. Programming was considered an art, not a science. Today, however, most programmers use a design approach called *structured programming*. **Structured programming** takes a top-down approach that breaks programs into modular forms. It also uses standard logic tools called *control structures* (sequential, selection, case, and iteration). The point of structured programming is to make programs more efficient (with fewer lines of code) and better organized (more readable), and to have better notations so that they have clear and correct descriptions.

The three mini-steps of program design are as follows.

1. Determine the Program Logic, Using Top-Down Approach

Logically laying out the program is like outlining a lengthy term paper before you proceed to write it. **Top-down program design** proceeds by identifying the top element, or module, of a program and then breaking it down in hierarchical fashion to the lowest level of detail. The top-down program design is used to identify the program's processing steps, or modules. After the program is designed, the actual coding proceeds from the bottom up, using the modular approach.

The concept of modularization is important. The beauty of modularization is that an entire program can be more easily developed because the parts can be developed and tested separately.

A module is a processing step of a program. Each module is made up of logically related program statements. (Sometimes a module is called a *subprogram* or *subroutine*.) An example of a module might be a programming instruction that simply says "Open a file, find a record, and show it on the display screen." It is best if each module has only a single function, just as an English paragraph should have a single, complete thought. This rule limits the module's size and complexity.

Top-down program design can be represented graphically in a hierarchy chart. A hierarchy chart, or structure chart, illustrates the overall purpose of the program, identifying all the modules needed to achieve that purpose and the relationships among them. *(See Figure 10.2.)* The program must move in sequence from one module to the next until all have been processed. There must be three principal modules corresponding to the three principal computing operations—input, processing, and output. (In Figure 10.2 they are "Read input," "Calculate pay," and "Generate output.")

2. Design Details, Using Pseudocode and/or Flow~

Once the essential logic of the program has been determ~
top-down programming and hierarchy charts, you ca~

Figure 10.2 A hierarchy chart. This represents a top-down design for a payroll program. Here the modules, or processing steps, are represented from the highest level of the program down to details. The three principal computing operations—input, processing, and output—are represented by the modules in the second layer: "Read input," "Calculate pay," and "Generate output." Before tasks at the top of the chart can be performed, all the ones below must be performed. Each module represents a logical processing step.

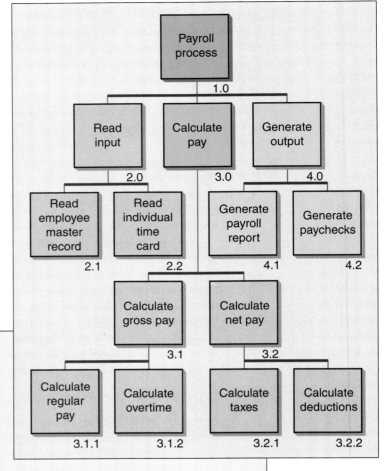

1. Each module must be of manageable size—have fewer than 50 program instructions.

2. Each module should be independent and have a single function.

3. The functions of input and output are clearly defined in separate modules.

4. Each module has a single entry point (execution of the program module always starts at the same place) and a single exit point (control always leaves the module at the same place).

5. If one module refers to or transfers control to another module, the latter module returns control to the point from which it was "called" by the first module.

There are two ways to show details—write them and draw them; that is, use pseudocode and flowcharts. Most projects use both methods.

■ *Pseudocode:* **Pseudocode** is a method of designing a program using normal human-language statements to describe the logic and processing flow. *(See Figure 10.3.)* Pseudocode is like an outline or summary form of the program you will write. Sometimes pseudocode is used simply to express the purpose of a particular programming module in somewhat general terms. With the use of such terms as IF, THEN, or ELSE, however, the pseudocode follows the rules of control structures, an important aspect of structured programming, as we shall explain.

■ *Program flowcharts:* A **program flowchart** is a chart that graphically presents the detailed series of steps (algorithms, or logical flow) needed to solve a programming problem. The flowchart uses standard symbols—called ANSI symbols, after the American National Standards Institute, which developed them. *(See Figure 10.4, page 10.8.)*

The symbols at the left of the drawing might seem clear enough. But how do you know how to express the logic of a program? How do you know how to reason it out so it will really work? The answer is to use control structures as explained next.

When you're trying to determine the logic behind something, you use words like "if" and "then" and "else." (For example, without actually using these exact words, you might reason something like this: "If she comes over, then we'll go out to a movie, else I'll just stay in and watch TV.") Control structures make use of the same words. A **control structure,** or *logic structure,* is a structure that controls the logical sequence in which computer program instructions are executed. In structured program design, three basic control structures are used to form the logic of a program: sequence, selection, and iteration (or loop). *(See Figure 10.5.)* (Additional variations of these three basic structures are also used.) These are the tools with which you can write structured programs and take a lot of the guess-work out of programming.

One thing that all three control structures have in common is one entry and one exit. (Modules, as noted in Figure 10.2, rule 4, also have only one entry and one exit.) The control structure is entered at a single point and exited at another single point. This helps simplify the logic so that it is easier for others following in a programmer's footsteps to make sense of the program. (In the days before this requirement was instituted, programmers could have all kinds of variations, leading to the kind of incomprehensible program known as *spaghetti code.*)

Let us consider the three control structures:

■ In the **sequence control structure,** one program statement follows another in logical order. In the example shown in Figure 10.5, there are two green boxes ("statement" and "statement"). One box could say "Open file," the other "Read a record." There are no decisions to make, no choices between "yes" or "no." The boxes logically follow one another in sequential order.

■ The **selection control structure**—also known as an *IF-THEN-ELSE struc-ture*—is a structure that represents choice. It offers two or more paths to fol-low when a decision must be made by a program. An example of a selection structure is as follows:

Figure 10.3 Pseudocode If a list of payroll tasks looks like this:

> Read name, hourly rate, hours worked
> Calculate gross pay and net pay
> Write name, gross pay and net pay
> Write name, gross pay, net pay

The pseudocode would look like this:

> READ name, hourly rate, hours worked
> Gross pay = hourly rate times hours worked
> Net pay = Gross pay minus 15
> WRITE name, Gross pay, Net pay

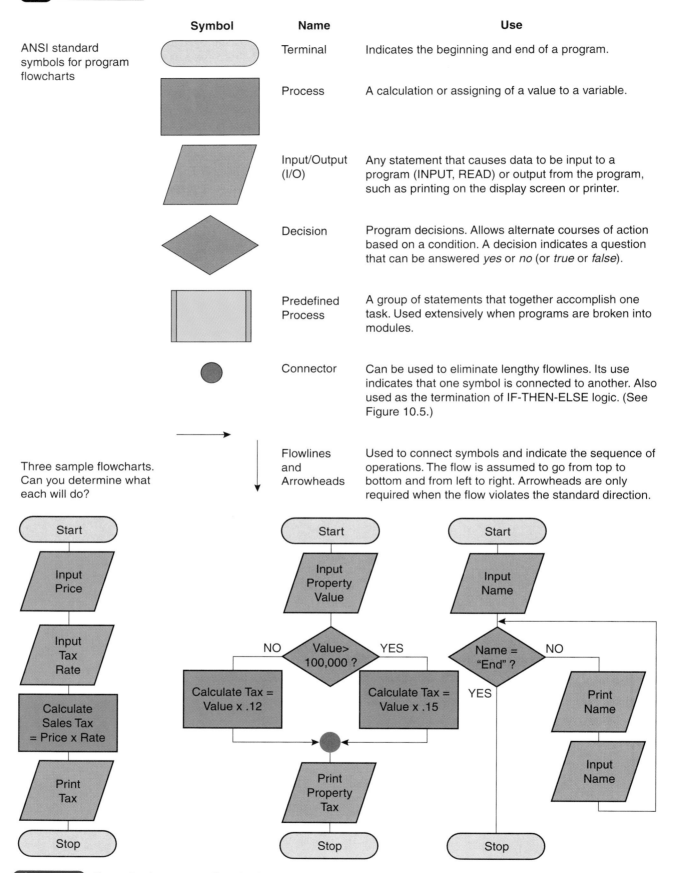

Symbol	Name	Use
	Terminal	Indicates the beginning and end of a program.
	Process	A calculation or assigning of a value to a variable.
	Input/Output (I/O)	Any statement that causes data to be input to a program (INPUT, READ) or output from the program, such as printing on the display screen or printer.
	Decision	Program decisions. Allows alternate courses of action based on a condition. A decision indicates a question that can be answered *yes* or *no* (or *true* or *false*).
	Predefined Process	A group of statements that together accomplish one task. Used extensively when programs are broken into modules.
	Connector	Can be used to eliminate lengthy flowlines. Its use indicates that one symbol is connected to another. Also used as the termination of IF-THEN-ELSE logic. (See Figure 10.5.)
	Flowlines and Arrowheads	Used to connect symbols and indicate the sequence of operations. The flow is assumed to go from top to bottom and from left to right. Arrowheads are only required when the flow violates the standard direction.

ANSI standard symbols for program flowcharts

Three sample flowcharts. Can you determine what each will do?

Figure 10.4 Example of a program flowchart and explanation of flowchart symbols

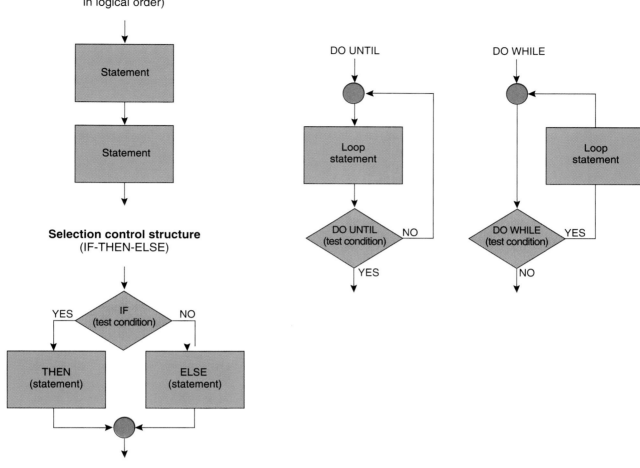

Sequence control structure
(one program statement follows another in logical order)

Statement

Statement

Selection control structure
(IF-THEN-ELSE)

YES — IF (test condition) — NO

THEN (statement)

ELSE (statement)

Iteration control structures:
DO UNTIL and DO WHILE

DO UNTIL

Loop statement

DO UNTIL (test condition) — NO

YES

DO WHILE

Loop statement

DO WHILE (test condition) — YES

NO

Variation on selection: the case control structure
(more than a single yes-or-no decision)

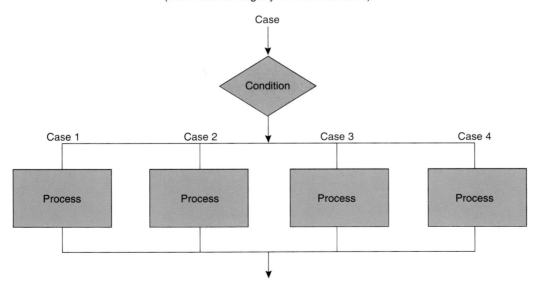

Case

Condition

Case 1

Case 2

Case 3

Case 4

Process

Process

Process

Process

Figure 10.5 The three control structures. The three structures used in structured program design to form the logic of a program are *sequence*, *selection*, and *iteration* (*loop*).

IF a worker's hours in a week exceed 40
THEN overtime hours equal the number of hours exceeding 40
ELSE the worker has no overtime hours.

A variation on the usual selection control structure is the case control structure. This offers more than a single yes-or-no decision. The case structure allows several alternatives, or "cases," to be presented. ("IF Case 1 occurs, THEN do thus-and-so. IF Case 2 occurs, THEN follow an alternative course. . . . " And so on.) The case control structure saves the programmer the trouble of having to indicate a lot of separate IF-THEN-ELSE conditions.

■ The **iteration,** or **loop, control structure** is a structure in which a process may be repeated as long as a certain condition remains true. There are two types of iteration structures—DO UNTIL and DO WHILE. An example of a DO UNTIL structure is as follows:

DO read in employee records UNTIL there are no more employee records.

An example of a DO WHILE structure is as follows:

DO read in employee records WHILE—that is, as long as—there continue to be employee records.

What seems to be the difference between the two iteration structures? It is simply this: if there are several statements that need to be repeated, you need to decide when to stop repeating them. You can decide to stop them at the beginning of the loop, using the DO WHILE structure. Or you can decide to stop them at the end of the loop, using the DO UNTIL structure. The DO UNTIL iteration means that the loop statements will be executed at least once. This is because the iteration statements are executed before the program checks whether to stop.

3. Do a Structured Walkthrough

No doubt you've had the experience, after having read over your research paper or project several times, of being surprised when a friend (or instructor) pointed out some things you missed. The same thing happens to programmers.

In the **structured walkthrough,** a programmer leads other people in the development team through a segment of code. The structured walkthrough is actually an established part of the design phase. It consists of a formal review process in which others—fellow programmers, systems analysts, and perhaps users—scrutinize ("walk through") the programmer's work. They review the parts of the program for errors, omissions, and duplications in processing tasks. Because the whole program is still on paper at this point, these matters are easier to correct now than they will be later. Some programmers get very nervous before a structured walkthrough, treating it as some sort of test of their competence. Others see it as merely a cooperative endeavor.

The Third Step: Code the Program

Once the design has been developed and reviewed in a walkthrough, the actual writing of the program begins. Writing the program is called **coding.** Coding is what many people think of when they think of programming, although it is only one of the five steps. Coding consists of translating the logic requirements from pseudocode or flowcharts into a programming language—the letters, numbers, and symbols arranged according to syntax rules (language rules) that make up the program.

1. Select the Appropriate Programming Language

A **programming language** is a language used to write instructions for the computer. Examples of well-known programming languages are COBOL, C, and BASIC. These languages are called "high-level languages," as we explain in a few pages.

Not all languages are appropriate for all uses. Some have strengths in mathematical and statistical processing, whereas others are more appropriate for database management. Thus, the language needs to be chosen based on such considerations as what purpose the program is designed to serve and what languages are already being used in the organization or field you are in.

2. Follow the Syntax

For a program to work, you have to follow the **syntax,** the rules of a programming language that specify how words and symbols are put together. Programming languages have their own grammar just as human languages do. But computers are probably a lot less forgiving if you use these rules incorrectly.

The Fourth Step: Test the Program

Program testing involves running various tests, such as desk-checking and debugging, and then running actual (real) data to make sure the program works.

The first two principal activities are desk-checking and debugging, called *alpha testing.*

1. Perform Desk-Checking

Desk-checking is simply reading through, or checking, the program to make sure that it's free of errors and that the logic works. In other words, desk-checking is sort of like proofreading. This step should be taken before the program is actually run on a computer.

2. Debug the Program

Once the program has been desk-checked, further errors, or "bugs," will doubtless surface. *(See Figure 10.6.)* To **debug** means to detect, locate, and remove all errors in a computer program. Mistakes may be syntax errors or logic errors. **Syntax errors** are caused by typographical errors and incorrect use of the programming language. **Logic errors** are caused by incorrect use of control structures. Debugging utility programs sometimes called *diagnostics* exist to check program syntax and display syntax-error messages. Diagnostic programs thus help identify and solve problems.

Figure 10.6 The first actual case of a "bug" being found in a computer dates from 1945, when a moth was discovered lodged in the wiring of the Mark I computer. The moth disrupted the execution of the program.

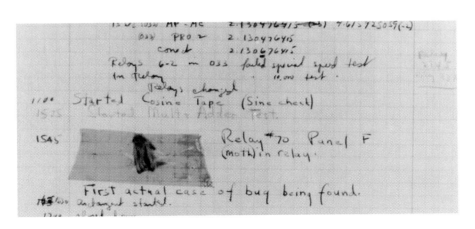

3. Run Real Data

After desk-checking and debugging, the program may run fine—in the laboratory. However, it then needs to be tested with real data, called *beta testing*. Indeed, it is even mandatory to test it with bad data—data that is faulty, incomplete, or in overwhelming quantities—to see if you can make the system crash. Many users, after all, may be far more heavy-handed, ignorant, and careless than programmers have anticipated.

The testing process may take several trials using different test data before the programming team is satisfied the program can be released. Even then, some bugs may remain, but there comes a point at which the pursuit of errors becomes uneconomical. This is one reason many users are nervous about using the first version (version 1.0) of a commercial software package.

The Fifth Step: Document and Maintain the Program

Preparing the program documentation is the fifth step in programming. The resulting **documentation** consists of written, graphic, and electronic descriptions of what a program is and how to use it. Documentation is not just an end-stage process of programming. It has been (or should have been) going on throughout all previous programming steps. Documentation is needed for people who will be using or involved with the program in the future.

Documentation should be prepared for different kinds of readers—users, operators, and programmers.

1. Prepare User Documentation

When you buy a commercial software package, such as a spreadsheet, you usually get a printed, on-disk, or online manual with it. This is user documentation. Programmers need to write documentation to help nonprogrammers use the software.

2. Prepare Operator Documentation

The people who run large computers are called *computer operators*. Because they are not always programmers, they need to be told what to do when the program malfunctions. The operator documentation gives them this information.

3. Prepare Programmer Documentation

Long after the original programming team has disbanded, the program may still be in use. If, as often happens, one-fifth of the programming staff leaves every year, after 5 years there could be a whole new group of programmers who know nothing about the software. Program documentation helps train these newcomers and enables them to maintain the existing system.

4. Maintain the Program

A word about maintenance: Maintenance is any activity designed to keep programs in working condition, error-free, and up to date. Maintenance includes adjustments, replacements, repairs, measurements, tests, and so on. Modern organizations are changing so rapidly—in products, marketing strategies, accounting systems, and so on—that these changes are bound to be reflected in their computer systems. Thus, maintenance is an important matter, and documentation must be available to help programmers make adjustments in existing systems.

The five steps of the programming process and their substeps are summarized in Figure 10.7.

Figure 10.7 Summary of the traditional programming steps

Step	Activities
Step 1: Problem definition	1. Specify program objectives and program users. 2. Specify output requirements. 3. Specify input requirements. 4. Specify processing requirements. 5. Study feasibility of implementing program. 6. Document the analysis.
Step 2: Program design	1. Determine program logic through top-down approach and modularization, using hierarchy chart. 2. Design details using pseudocode and/or using flowcharts, preferably using control structures. 3. Test design with structured walkthrough.
Step 3: Program coding	1. Select the appropriate high-level programming language. 2. Code the program in that language, following the syntax carefully.
Step 4: Program testing	1. Desk-check the program to discover errors. 2. Run the program and debut it (alpha testing). 3. Run real-world data (beta-testing).
Step 5: Program documentation and maintenance	1. Write user documentation. 2. Write operator documentation. 3. Write programmer documentation. 4. Maintain the program.

Five Generations of Programming Languages

Languages are said to have evolved in "generations," or levels, from machine language to natural languages.

As we've said, a programming language is a set of rules that tells the computer what operations to perform. Programmers, in fact, use these languages to create other kinds of software. Many programming languages have been written, some with colorful names (SNOBOL, HEARSAY, DOCTOR, ACTORS, JOVIAL). Each is suited to solving particular kinds of problems. What is it that all these languages have in common? Simply this: ultimately they must be reduced to digital form—a 1 or 0, electricity on or off—because that is all the computer can work with.

To begin to see how this works, it's important to understand that there are five levels or generations of programming languages, ranging from low-level to high-level. The five generations of programming languages start at the lowest level with (1) machine language. They range up through (2) assembly language, (3) high-level languages, and (4) very-high-level languages. At the highest level are (5) natural languages. Programming languages are said to be *lower level* when they are closer to the language that the computer itself uses—the 1s and 0s. They are called *higher level* when they are closer to the language people use—more like English, for example.

Beginning in 1945, programming languages have evolved over the years, with later generations gradually coming into greater use with programmers. The births of the generations are as follows. *(See Figure 10.8.)*

- First generation, 1945—Machine language

- Second generation, mid-1950s—Assembly language

- Third generation, early 1960s—High-level languages: COBOL, C, BASIC, and Ada

- Fourth generation, early 1970s—Very-high-level languages: NOMAD and FOCUS

- Fifth generation, early 1980s—Natural languages

Let us consider these five generations.

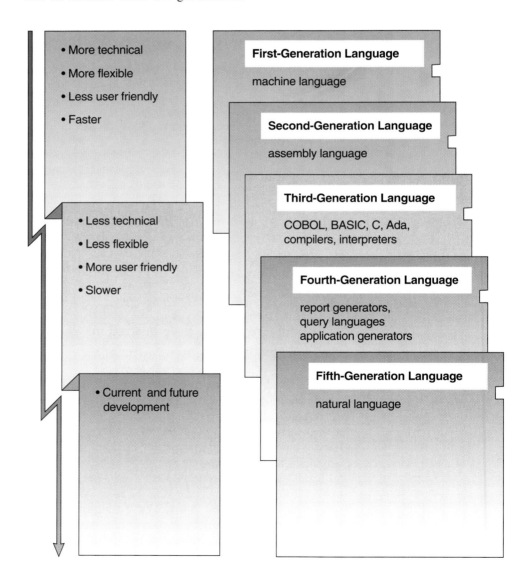

Figure 10.8 The five generations of programming languages

First Generation: Machine Language

The lowest level of language, **machine language** is the basic language of the computer, representing data as 1s and 0s (✔ p. 2.7). *(See Figure 10.9.)* Machine language programs varied from computer to computer; that is, they were machine dependent.

These binary digits, which correspond to the on and off electrical states of the computer, clearly are not convenient for people to read and use. Believe it or not, though, programmers did work with these mind-numbing digits. When the next generation of programming languages came along, assembly language, there must have been great sighs of relief.

Second Generation: Assembly Language

Assembly language is a low-level language that allows a programmer to use abbreviations or easily remembered words instead of numbers. *(Refer to Figure 10.9 again.)* For example, the letters MP could be used to represent the instruction MULTIPLY, and STO to represent STORE.

As you might expect, a programmer can write instructions in assembly language faster than in machine language. Nevertheless, it is still not an easy language to learn, and it is so tedious to use that mistakes are frequent. Moreover, assembly language has the same drawback as machine language in that it varies from computer to computer—it is machine dependent.

We now need to introduce the concept of language translator. Because a computer can execute programs only in machine language, a translator or converter is needed if the program is written in any other language. A **language translator** is a type of system software (✔ p. 5.3) that translates a program written in a second or higher-generation language into machine language.

Language translators are of three types:

- Assemblers

- Compilers

- Interpreters

An assembler, or assembler program, is a program that translates the assembly-language program into machine language. We describe compilers and interpreters in the next section.

Figure 10.9 (*Top*) Machine language is all binary 0s and 1s—very difficult for people to work with. (*Middle*) Assembly language uses abbreviations for major instructions (such as MP for MULTIPLY). This is easier for people to use, but still quite difficult. (*Bottom*) Third-generation languages use English words that can be understood by people.

First generation
Machine language

```
11110010 01110011 1101 001000010000 0111 000000101011
11110010 01110011 1101 001000011000 0111 000000101111
11111100 01010010 1101 001000010010 1101 001000011101
11110000 01000101 1101 001000010011 0000 000000111110
11110011 01000011 0111 000001010000 1101 001000010100
10010110 11110000 0111 000001010100
```

Second generation
Assembly language

```
         PACK  210(8,13),02B(4,7)
         PACK  218(8,13),02F(4,7)
         MP    212(6,13),21D(3,13)
         SRP   213(5,13),03E(0),5
         UNPK  050(5,7),214(4,13)
```

Third generation   `OI    054(7),X'F0'`
COBOL

`MULTIPLY HOURS-WORKED BY PAY-RATE GIVING GROSS-PAY ROUNDED`

Third Generation: High-Level Languages

A high-level language is an English-like language, such as COBOL and BASIC. *(Refer again to Figure 10.9.)* A high-level language allows users to write in a familiar notation, rather than numbers or abbreviations. Most high-level languages are not machine dependent—they can be used on more than one kind of computer.

As we mentioned, assembly language requires an assembler as a language translator. The translator for high-level languages is, depending on the language, either a compiler or an interpreter.

Figure 10.10 Compiler. This language translator converts the high-level language (source code) into machine language (object code) before the computer can execute the program.

Source Code
(high-level language)

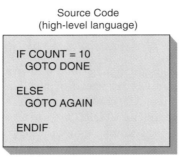

IF COUNT = 10
   GOTO DONE

ELSE
   GOTO AGAIN

ENDIF

Language translator
program

100101010010100001010100
101010100101010010010110
101001010100010100100010

Object Code
(machine langue)

■ *Compiler—execute later.* A **compiler** is language translator software that converts the entire program of a high-level language into machine language before the computer executes the program. The programming instructions of a high-level language are called the *source code.* The compiler translates it into machine language, which in this case is called the *object code.* The significance of this distinction is that the object code can be saved. Thus, it can be executed later—as many times as desired, without recompiling—rather than run right away. *(See Figure 10.10.)*

Examples of high-level languages using compilers are C and COBOL.

■ *Interpreter—execute immediately:* An **interpreter** is a language translator that converts each high-level language statement into machine language and executes it immediately, statement by statement. No object code is saved, as with the compiler. Therefore, interpreted code generally runs more slowly than compiled code. However, code can be tested line by line.

An example of a high-level language using an interpreter is BASIC.

What's the difference between a compiler and an interpreter? Why are they important?

Third-generation, high-level languages are also known as *procedural languages.* That is, programs set forth precise procedures, or series of instructions, meaning that the programmer has to follow a proper order of actions to solve a problem. To do that, the programmer has to have a detailed knowledge of programming and the computer it will run on. For example, say you want to take a taxi to a theater showing a particular movie. If you tell the taxi driver precisely how to get to the theater, that's procedural. You have to know how to get there yourself, and you will probably get there efficiently. However, if you simply tell the taxi driver to "take me to see movie X," then you're saying only what you want, which is nonprocedural. In this case, you may not get to the theater in an efficient manner.

The fourth generation of languages are nonprocedural languages, as we shall explain.

Fourth Generation: Very-High-Level Languages

A **very-high-level language** is often called a *4GL,* for *4th-generation language.* 4GLs are much more user-oriented and allow programmers to develop programs with fewer commands compared with third-generation languages, although 4GLs require more computing power. 4GLs are called *nonprocedural* because programmers and even users can write programs that need only tell the computer what they want done, not all the procedures for doing it. That is, they do not have to specify all the programming logic or otherwise tell the computer how the task should be carried out. This saves programmers a lot of time because they do not need to write as many lines of code as they do with procedural languages. 4GLs are also called *RAD (rapid application development) tools.*

Fourth-generation languages consist of report generators, query languages, application generators, and interactive database management system programs. Some 4GLs are tools for end-users, some are tools for programmers.

■ *Report generators:* A *report generator,* also called a *report writer,* is a program for end-users that is used to produce a report. The report may be a printout or a screen display. It may show all or part of a database file. You can specify the format in advance—columns, headings, and so on—and the report generator will then produce data in that format.

Report generators were the precursor to today's query languages.

■ *Query languages:* A *query language* is an easy-to-use language for retrieving data from a database management system. The query may be expressed in the form of a sentence or near-English command. Or the query may be obtained from choices on a menu.

Examples of query languages are SQL (for structured query language) and Intellect.

■ *Application generators:* An *application generator* is a programmer's tool that generates applications programs from descriptions of the problem rather than by traditional programming. The benefit is that the programmer does not need to specify how the data should be processed. The application generator is able to do this because it consists of modules preprogrammed to accomplish various tasks.

Programmers use application generators to help them create parts of other programs. For example, the software is used to construct on-screen menus or types of input and output screen formats. NOMAD and FOCUS, two database management systems, include application generators.

4GLs may not entirely replace third-generation languages because they are usually focused on specific tasks and hence offer fewer options. Still, they improve productivity because programs are easy to write.

Fifth Generation: Natural Languages

Natural languages are of two types. The first are ordinary human languages: English, Spanish, and so on. The second are programming languages that use human language to give people a more natural connection with computers. Some of the query languages mentioned above under 4GLs might seem pretty close to human communication, but natural languages try to be even closer.

With 4GLs, you can type in some rather routine inquiries. An example of a request in FOCUS might be:

SUM SHIPMENTS BY STATE BY DATE.

Natural languages allow questions or commands to be framed in a more conversational way or in alternative forms. For example, with a natural language, you might be able to state:

I WANT THE SHIPMENTS OF PERSONAL DIGITAL ASSISTANTS FOR ALABAMA AND MISSISSIPPI BROKEN DOWN BY CITY FOR JANUARY AND FEBRUARY. ALSO, I NEED JANUARY AND FEBRUARY SHIPMENTS LISTED BY CITIES FOR PERSONAL COMMUNICATORS SHIPPED TO WISCONSIN AND MINNESOTA.

Natural languages are part of the field of study known as *artificial intelligence* (discussed in detail in Chapter 13). Artificial intelligence (AI) is a group of related technologies that attempt to develop machines to emulate human-like qualities, such as learning, reasoning, communicating, seeing, and hearing.

The dates of the principal programming languages are shown in the accompanying two-page timeline. *(See Figure 10.11.)*

Traditional Programming Languages

Major third-generation programming languages used today are COBOL, C, BASIC, and Ada.

Many of the older, traditional high-level (third-generation) programming languages are being replaced in the mainstream by more modern programming tools, as we will discuss shortly. However, there are still a sizable number of older computer-based information systems maintained whose code was created using traditional languages. Thus there is a need for programmers familiar with some of these languages as well as with newer languages. Following are a few important traditional languages.

COBOL: The Language of Business

Figure 10.11 Timeline for development of programming languages and formatting tools

Formally adopted in 1960, **COBOL** (for **CO**mmon **B**usiness **O**riented **L**anguage) has been the most frequently used business language for large computers. *(See*

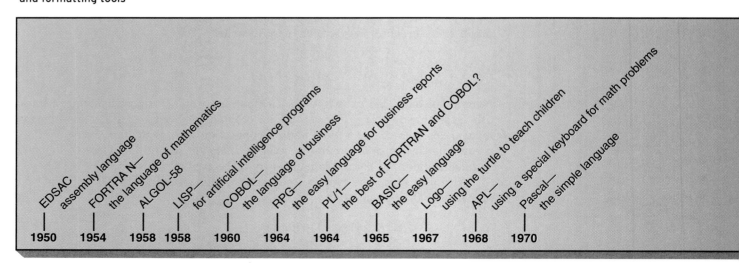

Figure 10.12, page 20.) Its most significant attribute is that it is extremely readable. For example, a COBOL line might read:

MULTIPLY HOURLY-RATE BY HOURS-WORKED GIVING GROSS-PAY

First standardized in 1968 by the American National Standards Institute (ANSI), the language has been revised several times.

Writing a COBOL program resembles writing an outline for a research paper. The program contains four divisions—Identification, Environment, Data, and Procedure. The divisions in turn are broken into sections, which are divided into paragraphs, which are further divided into sections. The Identification Division identifies the name of the program and the author (programmer) and perhaps some other helpful comments. The Environment Division describes the computer on which the program will be compiled and executed. The Data Division describes what data will be processed. The Procedure Division describes the actual processing procedures.

As do all programming languages, COBOL has both advantages and disadvantages.

■ *Advantages:* (1) It is machine independent. (2) Its English-like statements are easy to understand, even for a nonprogrammer. (3) It can handle many files, records, and fields. (4) It easily handles input/output operations.

■ *Disadvantages:* (1) Because it is so readable, it is wordy. Thus, even simple programs are lengthy, and programmer productivity is slowed. (2) It cannot handle mathematical processing as well as some other languages.

C: For Portability and Scientific Use

"C" is the language's entire name, and it does not "stand for" anything. Developed at Bell Laboratories, **C** is a general-purpose, compiled language that works well for microcomputers and is portable among many computers. *(Refer back to Figure 10.12.)* It is widely used for writing operating systems and utilities. C is also the programming language used most commonly in commercial software development, including games, robotics, and graphics. It is now considered a necessary language for programmers to know.

Here are the advantages and disadvantages of C:

■ *Advantages:* (1) C works well with microcomputers. (2) It has a high degree of portability—it can be run without change on a variety of computers. (3) It is

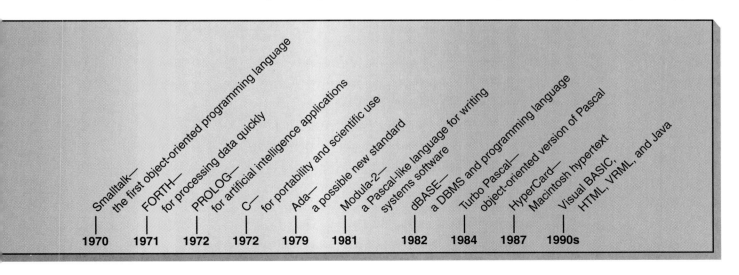

Figure 10.12

Comparison of third-generation language code. This shows how four languages handle the same statement.

COBOL

```
OPEN-INVOICE-FILE.
      OPEN I-O INVOICE FILE.

READ-INVOICE-PROCESS.
      PERFORM READ-NEXT-REC THROUGH READ-NEXT-REC-EXIT UNTIL END-OF-FILE.
      STOP RUN.

READ-NEXT-REC.
      READ INVOICE-REC
           INVALID KEY
                 DISPLAY 'ERROR READING INVOICE FILE'
                 MOVE 'Y' TO EOF-FLAG
                 GOTO READ-NEXT-REC-EXIT.
      IF INVOICE-AMT > 500
           COMPUTE INVOICE-AMT = INVOICE-AMT - (INVOICE-AMT * .07)
           REWRITE INVOICE-REC.

READ-NEXT-REC-EXIT.
      EXIT.
```

C

```
if (invoice_amount>500.00)

    DISCOUNT=0.07*invoice_amount;

else

    discount=0.00;

invoice_amount=invoice_amount-discount;
```

BASIC

```
10   REM  This Program Calculates a Discount Based on the Invoice Amount
20   REM        If Invoice Amount is Greater Than 500, Discount is 7%
30   REM        Otherwise Discount is 0
40   REM
50   INPUT "What is the Invoice Amount"; INV.AMT
60   IF INV.AMT A> 500 THEN LET DISCOUNT = .07 ELSE LET DISCOUNT = 0
70   REM        Display results
80   PRINT "Original Amt", "Discount", "Amt after Discount"
90   PRINT INV.AMT, INV.AMT * DISCOUNT, INV.AMT - INV.AMT * DISCOUNT
100  END
```

Ada

```
if INVOICE_AMOUNT>500.00 then

    DISCOUNT:=0.07*INVOICE_AMOUNT

else

    DISCOUNT:=0.00

endif;

INVOICE_AMOUNT:=INVOICE_AMOUNT-DISCOUNT
```

fast and efficient. (4) It enables the programmer to manipulate individual bits in main memory.

■ *Disadvantages:* (1) C is considered difficult to learn. (2) Because of its conciseness, the code can be difficult to follow. (3) It is not suited to applications that require a lot of report formatting.

BASIC: The Easy Language

BASIC was developed by John Kemeny and Thomas Kurtz in 1965 for use in training their students at Dartmouth College. By the late 1960s, it was widely used in academic settings on all kinds of computers, from mainframes to PCs. Now its use has extended to business.

BASIC (for **Beginner's All-purpose Symbolic Instruction Code**) has been the most popular microcomputer language and is considered the easiest programming language to learn. *(Refer again to Figure 10.12.)* Although it is available in compiler form, the interpreter form is more popular with first-time and casual users. This is because it is interactive, meaning that user and computer can communicate with each other during the writing and running of the program.

The advantages and disadvantages of BASIC are as follows:

■ *Advantage:* BASIC is very easy to use.

■ *Disadvantages:* (1) Its processing speed is relatively slow, although compiler versions are faster than interpreter versions. (2) There is no one version of BASIC, although in 1987 ANSI adopted a new standard that eliminated portability problems.

One of the current evolutions of BASIC is Visual BASIC, covered shortly.

Ada: A Possible New Standard

Ada is an extremely powerful structured programming language designed by the U.S. Department of Defense to ensure portability of programs from one application to another. *(Refer back to Figure 10.12.)* Ada was named for Countess Ada Lovelace, considered the world's "first programmer." Its primary use is scientific, including missile guidance systems. However, it has also been used in commercial applications.

The pluses and minuses of Ada are these:

■ *Advantages:* (1) Ada is a structured language, with a modular design. This means pieces of a large program can be written and tested separately. (2) It has more input and output capability than Pascal, which might make it more favorable to industry.

■ *Disadvantages:* (1) The amount of memory required hinders its use on microcomputers. (2) It has a high level of complexity and difficulty. (3) Business users already have so much invested in COBOL and C that they have little motivation to switch over to Ada.

Other Programming Languages

Several other high-level languages exist that, though not as popular or as famous as the foregoing, are well known enough that you may encounter them. Some of them are special-purpose languages.

■ *LISP—for artificial intelligence programs:* LISP (for LISt Processor) is a third-generation language used principally to construct artificial intelligence programs. Developed at the Massachusetts Institute of Technology in 1958 by mathematician John McCarthy, LISP is used to write expert systems and natural language programs. Expert systems are programs that are imbued with knowledge by a human expert; the programs can walk you through a problem and help solve it.

■ *Logo—using the turtle to teach children:* Logo was developed at MIT in 1967 by Seymour Papert, using a dialect of LISP. Logo is a third-generation language designed primarily to teach children problem-solving and programming skills. At the basis of Logo is a triangular pointer, called a "turtle," which responds to a few simple commands such as forward, left, and right. The pointer produces similar movements on the screen, enabling users to draw geometric patterns and pictures on screen. Because of its highly interactive nature, Logo is used not only by children but also to produce graphics reports in business.

■ *APL—using a special keyboard for math problems:* APL was designed in 1968 by Kenneth Iverson for use on IBM mainframes. APL (for A Programming Language) is a third-generation language that uses a special keyboard with special symbols to enable users to solve complex mathematical problems in a single step. The special keyboard is required because the APL symbols are not part of the familiar ASCII (✔ p. 2.4) character set. Though hard to read, this mathematically oriented and scientific language is still found on a variety of computers.

■ *FORTH—for processing data quickly:* FORTH was created in 1971 by Charles Moore. FORTH (for FOuRTH-generation language) is actually a third-generation language designed for real-time control tasks, as well as business and graphics applications. The program is used on all kinds of computers, from PCs to mainframes, and runs very fast because it requires less memory than other programs. Because it runs so fast, it is used in applications that must process data quickly. Thus, it is used to process data acquired from sensors and instruments, as well as in arcade game programs and robotics.

■ *PROLOG—for artificial intelligence applications:* Invented in 1972 by Alan Colmerauer of France, PROLOG did not receive much attention until 1979, when a newer version appeared. PROLOG (for PROgramming LOGic) is used for developing artificial intelligence applications, such as natural language programs and expert systems.

Object-Oriented and Visual Programming

Object-oriented programming (OOP) is a programming method that combines data and instructions for processing that data into a self-sufficient "object," or block of preassembled programming code, that can be used in other programs. Visual programming takes OOP a step farther by using icons—pictorial representation of objects.

Consider how it was for the computer pioneers, programming in machine language or assembly language. Novices putting together programs in BASIC can breathe a collective sigh of relief that they weren't around at the dawn of the

Can you imagine yourself becoming a programmer? If so, what types of problems would you like to work on?

Computer Age. Even some of the simpler third-generation languages represent a challenge, because they are *procedure oriented,* forcing the user (programmer) to follow a predetermined path from step A to step B, and so on. Fortunately, two new developments have made things easier—object-oriented programming and visual programming. These types of programming are *event driven*—that is, they respond to input from the user or other programs at unregulated times and thus are driven by user (programmer) choices.

Object-Oriented Programming: Block by Block

Imagine you're programming in a traditional third-generation language, such as BASIC, creating your coded instructions one line at a time. As you work on some segment of the program (such as how to compute overtime pay), you may think, "I'll bet some other programmer has already written something like this. Wish I had it. It would save a lot of time."

Fortunately, a kind of recycling technique now exists. This is object-oriented programming, which is rapidly replacing structured programming.

> The popularity of OOP will continue to increase as the backlog of yet unwritten programs rises at large businesses and software houses. Today, applications are becoming larger and more complex. As the size and complexity of applications increase, so does the number of person-years required to complete a project. The result is that projects will be either stretched out over years and completed by the traditional small teams (impractical), or more programmers will be added to projects, along with the associated problems of coordination and integration. One of the few proven methodologies for handling this increase in complexity is object-oriented programming.[5]

The following four steps briefly describe OOP (pronounced "oop," as in "oops!"):

1. *What OOP is:* **Object-oriented programming (OOP)** is a programming method that combines data and instructions for processing that data into a self-sufficient "object" that can be used in other programs. The important thing here is the object.

2. *What an "object" is:* An **object** is a block of preassembled programming code that is a self-contained module. The module contains, or encapsulates (✔ p. 9.16), both (1) a chunk of data and (2) the processing instructions that may be called on to be performed on that data. In a banking system, some objects might be "ATM and "account." In a flight simulation system, an aircraft is an object composed of subordinate objects like "rudder" and "engine."

3. *When an object's data is to be processed—sending the message:* Once the object becomes part of a program, the processing instructions may or may not be activated. That happens only when a "message" is sent. A message is an alert sent to the object when an operation involving that object needs to be performed.

4. *How the object's data is processed—the methods:* The message need only identify the operation. How it is actually to be performed is embedded within the processing instructions that are part of the object. These instructions about the operations to be performed on data within the object are called the methods.

Conventional Programs

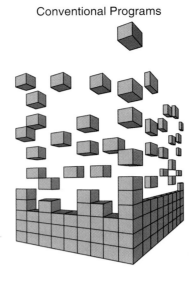

Object-Oriented Programs

Figure 10.13

Conventional versus object-oriented programs. (*Top*) When building conventional programs, programmers write every line of code from scratch. (*Bottom*) With object-oriented programs, programmers can use blocks, or "objects," of preassembled modules containing data and the associated processing instructions.

Once you've written a block of program code (that computes overtime pay, for example), it can be reused in any number of programs. Thus, unlike with traditional programming, with OOP you don't have to start from scratch—that is, reinvent the wheel—each time. *(See Figure 10.13.)* An object can be used repeatedly in different applications and by different programmers, thereby speeding up development time and lowering costs.

Programmers of the past 20 years were like the master crafts[people] of 200 years ago. They made all the components of a program and made them to fit together into a whole. That's like a carpenter who builds a desk by planing all the panels and forging the iron handles and even the wood screws. That's the paradigm [model] that we've been working under with procedural languages. But as OOP takes off, we will have reusable objects that can be purchased and simply plugged in or customized to fit virtually every need. With OOP the programmer is freed from the need to create every detail and instead can concentrate on what the application is going to do and what benefits it is going to provide to the user. Because of OOP we're going to see a tremendous flowering of creativity and productivity among programmers, just like we did in the 1800s, when the availability of standardized parts like wood screws gave birth to a virtual explosion of productivity and new inventions.[6]

Three Important Concepts of OOP

Object-oriented programming involves three important concepts, which go under the jaw-breaking names of encapsulation, inheritance, and polymorphism. Actually, these terms are not as fearsome as they look:

- *Encapsulation:* Encapsulation means an object contains (encapsulates) both (1) data and (2) the instructions for processing it, as we have seen. Once an object has been created, it can be reused in other programs. An object's uses can also be extended through concepts of class and inheritance.

- *Inheritance:* Once you have created an object, you can use it as the foundation for similar objects that have the same behavior and characteristics. All objects that are derived from or related to one another are said to form a class. Each class contains specific instructions (methods) that are unique to that group.

    Classes can be arranged in hierarchies—classes and subclasses. Inheritance is the method of passing down traits of an object from classes to subclasses in the hierarchy. Thus, new objects can be created by inheriting traits from existing classes.

    Writer Alan Freedman gives this example: "The object MACINTOSH could be one instance of the class PERSONAL COMPUTER, which could inherit properties from the class COMPUTER SYSTEMS."[7] If you were to add a new computer, such as COMPAQ, you would need to enter only what makes it different from other computers. The general characteristics of personal computers could be inherited.

- *Polymorphism:* Polymorphism means "many shapes." In object-oriented programming, polymorphism means that a message (generalized request) produces different results based on the object that it is sent to. Polymorphism has important uses. It allows a programmer to create procedures for objects whose exact type is not known in advance but will be at the time the program is actually run on the computer. Freedman gives this example: "A screen cursor may change its shape from an arrow to a line depending on the program mode." The processing instructions "to move the cursor on screen in response to mouse movement would be written for 'cursor,' and polymorphism would allow that cursor to be whatever shape is required at runtime." It would also allow a new cursor shape to be easily integrated into the program.

Examples of OOP Languages

Some examples of object-oriented programming languages are Smalltalk, C++, and Hypertalk.

■ *Smalltalk—the first OOP language:* Smalltalk was invented by computer scientist Alan Kay in 1970 at Xerox Corporation's Palo Alto Research Center in California. Smalltalk, the first OOP language, uses a keyboard for entering text, but all other tasks are performed with a mouse.

■ *C++—more than C:* The plus signs in C++ stand for "more than C" because it combines the traditional C programming language with object-oriented capability. C++ was created by Bjarne Stroustrup. With C++, programmers can write standard code in C without the object-oriented features, use object-oriented features, or do a mixture of both.

■ *Hypertalk—the language for HyperCard:* HyperCard (✔ p. 6.30), the software introduced for the Apple Macintosh in 1987, is based on the concept of cards and stacks of cards—just like notecards, only they are electronic. A card is a screenful of data that makes up a single record; cards are organized into related files called stacks. Using a mouse, you can make your way through the cards and stacks to find information or discover connections between ideas. HyperCard is not precisely an object-oriented programming language, but a language called Hypertalk is. Hypertalk, which uses OOP principles, is the language used in the HyperCard program to manipulate HyperCard stacks.

Distributed Object Technology[8]

Clearly, OOP is a useful advancement in programming technology. But things get more interesting when objects can communicate across a network—this is called *distributed object computing.*

Without distribution, objects are reusable only within the context of a given programming language. Thus changing an aspect of an object isn't the end of the maintenance story; you still need to install the revised object on every computer on which it's being used.

In a distributed object system, objects that support important parts of a business are centralized on network application servers, making it relatively easy to implement changes that will ripple across many applications. For example, a bank might have several applications at many locations that rely on the "account" object. If that object includes the code for assigning new account numbers and the bank needs to change that procedure, it can implement the change in just one place.

Ultimately, given a set of standardized objects and a consistent model of how they interact, distributed objects should make every computer system in the world compatible with every other system. Businesses would be able to form a partnership one day and integrate the supporting computer systems the next.

In many ways, the Internet is perfectly suited to this vision. Like any two objects, any two computers on the Internet communicate by sending messages encoded in protocols (✔ p. 7.26) that both understand. Unfortunately, however, the Web was designed for sharing documents, not objects. For example, when you fill out a form on a Web page and click on the Submit button, your browser sends the input as one long coded string of text—not objects.

Do you think it would be advantageous for you to learn a programming language?

Distributed object technology can make the Web stronger and more flexible while the Web, in turn, can boost the use of distributed object systems. Rather than working with text-based HTML forms, applications designers can use technologies like Java to create program components that download to the Web browser.

Visual Programming

Essentially, visual programming takes OOP to the next level. It does so by borrowing the object orientation of OOP languages but exercising it in a graphical or visual way. Thus **visual programming** is a method of creating programs by using icons that represent common programming routines. The programmer makes connections between objects by drawing, pointing, and clicking on diagrams and icons and by interacting with flowcharts. The goal of visual programming is to make programming easier for programmers and more accessible to nonprogrammers. It enables users to think more about solving the problem than about handling the programming language.

With one example, ObjectVision (from Borland), the user doesn't employ a programming language but simply connects icons and diagrams on screen. Visual BASIC offers another visual environment for program construction for Windows applications, allowing you to build various components using buttons, scroll bars, and menus. Microsoft Visual Studio 97 is an integrated development system for Windows and the Internet.

HTML, VRML, and Java

These formats and languages are used for Web pages.

As we mentioned in Chapter 8, the Internet connects thousands of data and information sites around the world. Many of these sites are text-based only; that is, the user sees no graphics, animation, or video, and hears no sound. One method for building multimedia on the World Wide Web is to use programming languages and standards for defining documents such as HTML, VRML, and Java.

■ *HTML:* **HTML (Hypertext Markup Language)** (✔ p. 8.22) is a type of code that embeds simple commands within standard ASCII text documents to provide an integrated, two-dimensional display of text and graphics. It was developed as a subset of SGML (Standard Generalized Markup Language), most commonly used to define text-formatting and page layout in the electronic publishing industry. In other words, a document created in any word processor and stored in ASCII format can become a Web page with the addition of a few HTML commands. *(See Figure 10.14.)* One of the main features of HTML is its ability to insert hypertext links into a document. Hypertext links enable you to display another Web document simply by clicking on a link area (usually underlined or highlighted) on the current screen. One document may contain links to many other related documents. The related documents may be on the same server as the first document, or they may be on a computer halfway around the world. A link may be a word, a group of words, or

Figure 10.14 Examples of HTML code

Every Web page has a fundamental design to it. All need to have this basic structure:

```
<html>
<head>
<title>The Home Page Title</title>
</head>
<body>

The text to appear on the Web page.

</body>
</html>
```

Each tag is enclosed in '<' and '>' as '<command>', with no spaces between the command and its enclosing less-than and greater-than signs. Most of the commands come in pairs. For instance, the body section is started with '<body>' and finished with the command and a leading slash in '</body>'. To make words appear in italics, you'll use the commands '<i>' and '</i>'. Thus, a line of HTML written with

```
The speed of the new processor is '<i>' really
'</i>' amazing!
```

will appear on the browser as

The speed of the new processor is *really* amazing!

As you can see, the HTML source of the page looks very flat compared to what the user will see.
Other types of text formatting you can use include:

- `<b>... </b>`
  Make the text be in bold.
- `<u>... </u>`
  Underline the text.
- `<tt>... </tt>`
  Present the text in a typewriter font.

- `<em>... </em>`
  Show the text for emphasis.
- `<strong>... </string>`
  Provide more emphasis than `<em>`.

You can show section headings with different character sizes. This makes it possible to clearly display sections and subsections. The tags vary in size from `<H1>`, the largest, through `<H6>` for the smallest. Each is closed out with `</H1>` through `</H6>`. The most common use of these tags is to present the Web page separated by topic:

```
<h1>Hardware</h1>              <h1>Software</h1>
<h3>Processors</h3>            <h3>Word Processing</h3>
<h3>Disk Cartridges</h3>       <h3>Spreadsheets</h3>
```

The result would be like:

Hardware
Processors
Disk Cartridges

Software
Word Processing
Spreadsheets

a picture. Most commercial applications software packages, such as Microsoft Word, can save documents in HTML format.

Various HTML editors and filters—commercial HTML packages—also exist to help people who do not want to learn everything about HTML to create their own Web pages by choosing menu options and filling out templates—examples are Adobe's PageMill, Soft Quad's Hot Metal Pro, and

Microsoft's FrontPage Editor. Recent releases of Netscape and Microsoft Internet Explorer (browsers) also allow users to easily create their own Web pages. (Note that users generally need an Internet service provider, ✔ p. 8.14, to act as a server to store their Web pages.)

■ *VRML:* **VRML (Virtual Reality Markup Language)** is a type of programming language used to create three-dimensional Web pages. For example, Planet 9 Studios (*http://www.planet9.com*) has created a number of virtual cities one can tour. An architecture and landscaping firm in Philadelphia (*http://www. mrabsi.com/contents_top_nj.html*) uses VRML to market its products by developing interactive 3-D environments that can be walked through. The Geosphere Project (*http://www.infolane.com/geosphere*) offers a virtual control center for accessing a global library of earth-resource management visualizations (such as rain forest destruction, animal extinction patterns, and so on).

VRML (rhymes with "thermal") is not an extension of HTML; thus, HTML Web browsers cannot interpret it. That is, users need a VRML browser plug-in (✔ p. 8.23)—for example, Netscape's Live3D—to receive VRML Web pages. If they are not on a large computer system, they also need a high-end microcomputer such as a Power Macintosh or a Pentium-based PC. Like HTML, VRML is a document-centered ASCII language. Unlike HTML, it tells the computer how to create 3-D worlds. VRML pages can also be linked to other VRML pages.

Even though VRML's designers wanted to let nonprogrammers create their own virtual spaces quickly and painlessly, it's not as simple to describe a 3-D scene as it is to describe a page in HTML. However, many existing modeling and CAD (✔ p. 6.27) tools now offer VRML support, and new VRML-centered software tools are arriving (such as Virtual Home Space Builder).

■ *Java:* **Java** is a relatively recent OOP programming language from Sun Microsystems. It allows programmers to build applications that run on any kind of operating system. And applications and software upgrades written in Java can be downloaded off the Internet. If the use of Java becomes widespread, the Web will be transformed from the information-delivering medium it is today into a completely interactive computing environment. You will be able to treat the Web as a giant hard disk loaded with a never-ending supply of software applications. However, Java is not compatible with most existing microprocessors, such as those from Intel and Motorola. For this reason, users need to use a small "interpreter" program to be able to use Java applications (called *applets*). They also need a recent-version operating system and a Java-capable browser in order to view Java special effects. Microcomputers are now available with special Java chips designed to run Java software directly.

Java is a major departure from the HTML coding that makes up most Web pages. It is an interpreted programming environment, and the language is object-oriented and comparable to C++.

In addition to Java development programs available for programmers, Java toolkits are available to give nonprogrammers the ability to add multimedia effects to their Web pages. Examples are ActionLine, Activator Pro, AppletAce, and Mojo. They can be used by anyone who understands multimedia file formats and is willing to experiment with menu options. Each program produces applets that can be viewed by any Java-equipped browser. In all cases, the bottom line is motion and sound, which, before the advent of Java-based tools, were available on the Web only via plug-in viewer/players.[9]

The Future

What do object-oriented, visual, and Internet programming imply for the future? Will tomorrow's programmer look less like a writer typing out words and more like an electrician wiring together circuit components, as one magazine suggests?[10] What does this mean for the five-step programming model we have described?

Some institutions are now teaching only object-oriented design techniques, which allow the design and ongoing improvement of working program models. Here programming stages overlap and repeatedly flow through analysis, design, coding, and testing stages. Thus, users can test out new parts of programs and even entire programs as they go along. They need not wait until the end of the process to find out if what they said they wanted is what they really wanted.

OLDER COMPUTER PROGRAMMERS GO BACK TO FIX THE FUTURE

Several years ago, Donald Fowler's employer in Gaithersburg, Maryland, coaxed him into early retirement, telling him that his skill in programming mainframe computers was a thing of the past. He eventually moved to Florida to vegetate on the beach and play golf. Not too soon thereafter, however, a software firm came begging for his help in reprogramming old mainframes so the machines would believe that there will be a year 2000. (Most computers log years by the final two digits—for example, "98" and "99." So, lacking human intuition, they may treat 2000 as 1900 or reject it completely as an invalid date.) It turns out that many people did not expect older computers and computer systems to hang around this long.

Now Fowler spends weekdays in an office tapping away on a computer and earning a salary that would make young programmers in Silicon Valley envious.

Fowler's rehabilitation is not unique. Faced with a shortage of young programmers fluent in the languages used in older systems, companies are increasingly turning to gray-haired veterans. The job: help fix what many experts are calling the world's biggest computer problem. Come January 1, 2000, millions of large computer systems worldwide will either grind to a halt or start spewing out wildly erroneous data if they are not fixed first.

Solving the year 2000 problem, in many cases, requires a large amount of grunt work, such as poring over thousands or more lines of code in a program to look for and change certain commands, which are often written in COBOL or Fortran, the Greek and Latin of the computer world.

It is estimated that 500,000 to 700,000 additional programmers are still needed to work in the United States alone to handle date conversion. In England, a law has been adopted forcing British companies to correct the so-called Millennium Bug, which could snarl almost any aspect of modern life, including communications, credit card transactions, banking, payrolls, air traffic movements, and nuclear power plant cooling. Library books overdue by one day on January 1, 2000 could be a century overdue. Your insurance policies could be canceled. The interest on your credit cards could finance the national debt. Your driver's license expired before you were born. If you were born in 1925 and at age 75 in the year 2000 were expecting Social Security benefits, that system's computer, thinking it's 1900, would calculate your age to be −25 and thus deny those benefits!

Professional Sports Careers

Say you're a diehard Miami Dolphins football fan who lives in Houston. The local TV and radio stations don't broadcast Dolphin games, and you rarely get the chance to see your team in action.

Luckily for you, the National Football League operates an Internet site *(NFL.com)* that enables you to track every play of every game in progress and gain access to the same statistics being fed to the sportswriters in the press box. Or later you can go to the Web site Dolphins End-Zone, administered by the team *(http://204. 254.173.2/dolphins)*, which, as one writer says, allows you to "read postgame reports and injury updates on the Miami team, [and] inquire about tickets. . . ."[11]

The NFL is not the only sports organization to use high technology to reach out to fans and customers and to sell tickets and merchandise. Also offering World Wide Web sites are the National Basketball Association *(www.nba.com)*, Major League Baseball *(http:www.majorleague baseball.com)*, and the National Hockey League *(http:www.nhl.com)*.

The high-technology heart of professional sports may be secondary storage hardware, wherein reside the databases with their vast compilations of statistics. However, computers are present in many other ways as well.

"Armed with notebook computers, fax modems, and specialized software," says one report on professional basketball, "the teams compile scouting reports, analyze statistics, and create models to predict what players and teams might do in specific game situations. In a matter of minutes and a few keystrokes, the machines permit coaches to do work that used to take hours of laborious sorting through statistics sheets and play diagrams."[12]

The NFL has borrowed the same technology that physicians use for sonograms to produce still-image photos from video films. Whereas at one time coaches on the sidelines used runners (or even nylon cord and shower-curtain hooks) to convey Polaroid photos of game movements taken from the booth high above the field, today they rely on sophisticated video printers to spit out almost instantaneous images to enable them to evaluate formations and plays.

"It's a good coaching tool," says Tom Donahoe, director of football operations for the Pittsburgh Steelers. "The game happens so fast. Sometimes, the picture verifies what you saw. Sometimes, it shows you something else."[13]

WHAT IT IS
WHAT IT DOES
WHY IT IS IMPORTANT

Ada (LO 6, p. 10.21)   Powerful third-generation, structured programming language designed by U.S. Defense Department to ensure portability of programs from one application to another.

Originally intended to be a standard language for weapons systems, Ada has been used successfully in commercial applications.

algorithm (LO 1, p. 10.3)   Set of ordered steps for solving a problem.

Algorithms are used in programming to solve problems.

BASIC (Beginner's All-purpose Symbolic Instruction Code) (LO 6, p. 10.21)   Developed in 1965, a popular microcomputer language that is easy to learn.

The interpreter form of BASIC is popular with first-time and casual users because it is interactive—user and computer can communicate during the writing and running of a program.

C (LO 6, p. 10.19)   General-purpose, compiled language that works well for microcomputers and is portable among many computers.

C is widely used for writing operating systems and utilities and is also the programming language used most commonly in commercial software development, including games, robotics, and graphics. It is now considered a necessary language for programmers to know.

COBOL (COmmon Business Oriented Language) (LO 6, p. 10.18)   High-level programming language of business. First standardized in 1968, the language has been revised several times.

COBOL has been the most frequently used business language for large computers.

coding (LO 2, p. 10.10)   Writing the program. Coding consists of translating the logic requirements from pseudocode, flowcharts, and the like into a programming language—letters, numbers, and symbols that make up the code.

Coding is what many people think of when they think of programming, although it is only one of the five steps.

compiler (LO 5, p. 10.16)   Language translator that converts the entire program of a high-level language (called the *source code*) into machine language (called the *object code*) for execution later. Examples of compiler languages: C and COBOL.

Unlike other language translators (assemblers and interpreters), a compiler program allows the object code to be saved and executed later rather than run right away. The advantage of a compiler is that, once the object code has been obtained, the program executes faster than when an interpreter is used.

control structure (LO 3, p. 10.7)   Also called *logic structure;* in structured program design, it controls the logical sequence in which computer program

One thing that all three control structures have in common is one entry and one exit. The control structure is entered at a single point and exited at

instructions are executed. Three basic control structures are used to form the logic of a program: sequence, selection, and iteration (or loop).

debugging (LO 2, p. 10.11)   Part of program testing; the detection and removal of syntax and logic errors in a program.

desk-checking (LO 2, p. 10.11)   Form of program testing; the detection and removal of syntax and logic errors in a program.

documentation (LO 2, p. 10.12)   Written, graphic, and electronic descriptions of a program and how to use it; supposed to be done during all programming steps.

HTML (Hypertext Markup Language) (LO 8, p. 10.26)   Type of code that embeds commands within standard ASCII text documents to provide an integrated, two-dimensional display of text and graphics. Hypertext is used to link the displays.

interpreter (LO 5, p. 10.16)   Language translator that converts each high-level language statement into machine language and executes it immediately, statement by statement. An example of a high-level language using an interpreter is BASIC.

iteration control structure (LO 3, p. 10.10)   Also known as *loop structure;* one of the control structures used in structured programming. A process is repeated as long as a certain condition remains true; the programmer can stop repeating the repetition at the *beginning* of the loop, using the DO WHILE iteration structure, or at the *end* of the loop, using the DO UNTIL iteration structure (which means the loop statements will be executed at least once.)

Java (LO 8, p. 10.28)   New type of programming language used to create any conceivable type of software applications that will work on the Internet.

language translator (LO 5, p. 10.15)   Type of system software that translates a program written in a second- or higher-generation language into machine language. Language translators are of three types: (1) assemblers, (2) compilers, and (3) interpreters.

logic errors (LO 2, p. 10.11)   Programming errors caused by not using control structures correctly.

machine language (LO 4, p. 10.15)   Lowest level of programming language; the language of the computer, representing data as 1s and 0s. Most

another single point. This helps simplify the logic so that it is easier for others following in a programmer's footsteps to make sense of the program.

Debugging may take several trials using different data before the programming team is satisfied the program can be released. Even then, some errors may remain, because trying to remove all of them may be uneconomical.

Desk-checking should be done before the program is actually run on a computer.

Documentation is needed for all people who will be using or involved with the program in the future—users, operators, and programmers.

HTML is used to create Web pages.

When a compiler is used, no object code is saved. The advantage of an interpreter is that programs are easier to develop.

Iteration control structures help programmers write better-organized programs.

Java may be able to transform the Internet from just an information-delivering medium into a completely interactive computing environment.

Because a computer can execute programs only in machine language, a translator is needed if the program is written in any other language.

If a program has logic errors, it will not run correctly or perhaps not run at all.

Machine language, which corresponds to the on and off electrical states of the computer, is not convenient for people to use. Assembly language

machine language programs vary from computer to computer—they are machine-dependent. All software programs must be translated into machine language by a compiler, an interpreter, or an assembler.

natural languages (LO 4, p. 10.17)   Fifth-generation programming languages that use human language to give people a more natural connection with computers.

Natural languages are part of the field of study known as artificial intelligence.

object (LO 7, p. 10.23)   In object-oriented programming, block of preassembled programming code that is a self-contained module. The module contains (encapsulates) both (1) a chunk of data and (2) the processing instructions that may be called on to be performed on that data. Once the object becomes part of a program, the processing instructions may be activated only when a "message" is sent.

The object can be reused and interchanged among programs, thus making the programming process easier, more flexible and efficient, and faster.

object-oriented programming (OOP) (LO 7, p. 10.23)   Programming method in which data and the instructions for processing that data are combined into a self-sufficient object—a piece of software that can be used in more than one program. Examples of OOP languages: Smalltalk, C++, and Hypertalk.

Objects can be reused and interchanged among programs, producing greater flexibility and efficiency than is possible with traditional programming methods.

program flowchart (LO 3, p. 10.6)   Structured programming tool for designing a program in graphical (chart) form; it uses standard symbols called ANSI symbols.

The program flowchart graphically presents the detailed series of steps needed to solve a programming problem.

programming (LO 2, p. 10.3)   Five-step process for creating software instructions: (1) clarify the problem; (2) design a solution; (3) write (code) the program; (4) test the program; (5) document the program.

Programming is Phase 4.1 in the systems development life cycle.

programming language (LO 4, p. 10.11)   Set of words and symbols that allow programmers to tell the computer what operations to follow. The five levels (generations) of programming languages are (1) machine language, (2) assembly language, (3) high-level (procedural) languages (COBOL, C, BASIC, Ada, etc.), (4) very-high-level (nonprocedural) languages (NOMAD, FOCUS, etc.), and (5) natural languages.

Not all programming languages are appropriate for all uses. Thus, a language must be chosen to suit the purpose of the program and to be compatible with other languages being used.

pseudocode (LO 3, p. 10.6)   Structured programming tool for designing a program in narrative form using normal human-language statements to describe the logic and processing flow. Using pseudocode is like doing an outline or summary form of the program to be written.

By using such terms as IF, THEN, or ELSE, pseudocode follows the rules of control structures, an important aspect of structured programming.

selection control structure (LO 3, p. 10.7)   Also known as an *IF-THEN-ELSE structure;* one of three

Selection control structures help programmers write better-organized programs.

basic control structures used in structured programming. It offers two paths to follow when a decision must be made by a program.

sequence control structure (LO 3, p. 10.7) One of three basic control structures used in structured programming, whereby each program statement follows another in logical order. There are no decisions to make.

structured programming (LO 3, p. 10.5) Method of programming that takes a top-down approach, breaking programs into modular forms and using standard logic tools called *control structures* (sequence; selection; iteration [loop]).

structured walkthrough (LO 2, p. 10.10) Program review process that is part of the design phase of the programming process; a programmer leads other development team members in reviewing a segment of code to scrutinize the programmer's work.

syntax (LO 2, p. 10.11) "Grammar" rules of a programming language that specify how words and symbols are put together.

syntax errors (LO 2, p. 10.11) Programming errors caused by typographical errors and incorrect use of the programming language.

top-down program design (LO 3, p. 10.5) Method of program design; a programmer identifies the top or principal processing step, or module, of a program and then breaks it down in hierarchical fashion into smaller processing steps. The design can be represented in a top-down hierarchy chart.

very-high-level languages (LO 4, p. 10.17) Also known as *nonprocedural languages* and *fourth-generation languages (4GLs);* more user-oriented than third-generation languages, 4GLs require fewer commands. 4GLs consist of report generators, query languages, and applications generators. Some 4GLs are tools for end-users, some are tools for programmers.

visual programming (LO 7, p. 10.26) Method of creating programs whereby the programmer makes connections between objects by drawing, pointing, and clicking on diagrams and icons. Programming is made easier because the object orientation of object-oriented programming is used in a graphical or visual way.

VRML (Virtual Reality Markup Language) (LO 8, p. 10.28) Type of programming language used to create three-dimensional (3-D) Web pages.

Sequence control structures help programmers write better-organized programs.

Structured programming techniques help programmers make programs more efficient (with fewer lines of code), write better-organized programs, and use standard notations with clear, correct descriptions.

The structured walkthrough helps programmers find errors, omissions, and duplications, which are easy to correct because the program is still on paper.

Each programming language has its own syntax, just as human languages do.

If a program has syntax errors, it will not run correctly or perhaps not run at all.

Top-down program design enables an entire program to be more easily developed because the parts can be developed and tested separately.

Programmers can write programs that need only tell the computer what they want done, not all the procedures for doing it, which saves them the time and labor of having to write many lines of code.

Visual programming enables users to think more about the problem solving than about handling the programming language.

VRML expands the information-delivering capabilities of the Web.

SELF-TEST EXERCISES

1. Machine language is a _____-generation language.

2. Fifth-generation languages are often called _____ languages.

3. _____ programming takes a top-down approach that breaks programs into modular forms.

4. In the _____ control structure, one program statement follows another in logical order.

5. A _____ language is a language used to write instructions for the computer.

SHORT-ANSWER QUESTIONS

1. What is natural language?

2. How do third-generation languages differ from first- and second-generation languages?

3. What is visual programming?

4. What were the reasons behind the development of high-level programming languages?

5. Why is documentation important during program development?

MULTIPLE-CHOICE QUESTIONS

1. _____ is a relatively simple high-level language that was developed to help students learn programming.
   a. BASIC
   b. COBOL
   c. C
   d. ADA
   e. all the above

2. Query languages, report generators, and application generators are examples of _____-generation languages.
   a. first
   b. second
   c. third
   d. fourth
   e. fifth

3. Which of the following is used to design a program using English-like statements?
   a. pseudocode
   b. program flowcharts
   c. control structures
   d. structured talkthroughs
   e. none of the above

4. Which of the following control structures use DO UNTIL?
   a. sequence
   b. selection
   c. iteration (loop)
   d. pseudocode
   e. none of the above

5. Assemblers, compilers, and interpreters are types of _____ _____.
   a. programming languages
   b. language translators
   c. alpha testers
   d. application generators
   e. all the above

TRUE/FALSE QUESTIONS

1. The rules for using a programming language are called *syntax*. (true/false)

2. A query allows the user to easily retrieve information from a database using English-like statements. (true/false)

3. Objects found in an object-oriented program can be reused in other programs. (true/false)

4. It is correct to refer to programming as *software engineering*. (true/false)

5. A syntax error can be caused by a simple typographical error. (true/false)

KNOWLEDGE IN ACTION

1. Suppose you're in charge of creating a Web site that will be used by the other students in your class to access assignment information, a list of suggested reading materials, relevant Web addresses, and other course information. How might you implement HTML, JAVA, and VRML to create this site?

2. Some experts think that before long we will have only one superapplication to run on our computers instead of several separate applications packages. However, people in the computer industry are commonly overoptimistic about the speed at which new developments will occur. What do you think will be the obstacles to achieving a superapplication?

3. Visit the computer laboratory at your school.
   a. Identify which high-level languages are available.
   b. Determine if each language processor identified is a compiler or an interpreter.
   c. Determine if the language processors are available for microcomputers, larger computers, or both.
   d. Identify any microcomputer-based electronic spreadsheet software and database management system software. Have any applications been created with these tools that are used in the lab or by the lab staff?

4. Interview several students who are majoring in computer science and studying to become programmers. What languages do they plan to master? Why? What kinds of jobs do they expect to get? What kinds of future developments do they anticipate in the field of software programming?

5. Check the yellow pages in your phone book, and contact a company that develops custom-designed software. What languages do they use to write the software? Does this company follow the five stages of software development described in this book, or does it use another set of stages? If another set of software-development stages is used, what are its characteristics?

INFORMATION MANAGEMENT

Who Needs to Know What, and When?

PREVIEW

After reading this chapter, you should be able to:

1. Identify traditional organizational departments, tasks, and levels of managers and the types of information needed by different managers and workers

2. Define and distinguish among several types of management information systems: TPS, MIS, DSS, EIS, ES, and OAS

3. Give some examples of how computers are used at different management levels

4. Describe the major future direction of information management

"We're experiencing the beginning of what is perhaps the most radical redefinition of the workplace since the Industrial Revolution, with some tremendous benefits involved," says a longtime proponent of flexible work arrangements. "Yet the early signs are that corporations are as likely as not to mess this up."

The speaker, a management consultant, was referring to the changes, a trickle now turning into a tidal wave, brought about by the "mobile office"—also called the virtual office (✔ p. 8.34).[1] Part of the redefinition of the workplace comes with handing employees laptop computers with modems, portable phones, and beepers and telling them to work from their homes, cars, or customers' offices—virtually anywhere. Part of it involves the use of a grab bag of electronic information organizers, personal communicators, personal digital assistants, and similar gadgets that help free people from a fixed office.

"Flex-time" shift hours and voluntary part-time telecommuting programs have been around for a few years. Unlike those slight alterations to traditional worklife, however, the virtual office and its high-tech tools are forcing some profound changes in the way people work. Many people, of course, like the flexibility of a mobile office. However, others resent having to work at home or being unable to limit their work hours. One computer-company vice president worries about getting her staff to stop sending faxes to each other in the middle of the night. Some employees may work 90 hours a week and still feel as if they are falling short. In great part, this is because people's skills have not kept pace with technological trends.[2] At some point, a constant-work lifestyle becomes counterproductive.

Trends Forcing Change in the Workplace

The trends of automation, downsizing and outsourcing, total quality management, and employee empowerment, among others, have forced organizations to give considerable thought to reengineering. Reengineering is the search for and implementation of radical change in business processes to achieve breakthrough results.

The virtual office is only one of several trends in recent years that are affecting the way we work. Others, most of which have been under way for some time, have also had a profound effect. They include, but are not limited to, the following:

- Automation
- Downsizing and outsourcing
- Total quality management
- Employee empowerment
- Reengineering

The Virtual Office

As we mentioned earlier, the virtual office is essentially a mobile office. Using integrated computer and communications technologies, corporations will increasingly be defined not by concrete walls or physical space but by collaborative networks linking hundreds, thousands, even tens of thousands of people together. Widely scattered workers can operate as individuals or as if they were all at company headquarters. Such "road warriors" break the time and space barriers of the organization, operating anytime, anywhere.

Automation

When John Diebold wrote his prophetic book *Automation* in the 1950s, the computer was nearly new. Yet Diebold predicted that computers would make many changes. First, he suggested, they would change how we do our jobs. Second, he thought, they would change the kind of work we do.[3] He was right, of course, on both counts. In the 1950s and 1960s, computers changed how factory work, for instance, was done. In the 1970s and 1980s, factory work itself began to decline as Western nations went from manufacturing economies to information economies.

Diebold's third prediction was that the technologies would change the world in which we work. "This is the beginning of the next great development in computers and automation," he says, "which has already begun in the 1990s."

Downsizing and Outsourcing

The word *downsizing* has two meanings. First, it means the movement in the 1980s from mainframe-based computer systems to systems linking smaller computers in networks. Second, downsizing means reducing the size of an organization by eliminating workers and consolidating and/or eliminating operations.

As a result of automation, economic considerations, and the drive for increased profitability, in recent years many companies have had to downsize their staffs—lay off employees. In the process, they have, in business jargon, "flattened the hierarchy," reducing the levels and numbers of middle managers. Of course, much of the company's work still remains, forcing the rest of the staff to take up the slack. For instance, the secretary may be gone, but the secretarial work remains. The lower-level and middle-level managers found that with personal computers they could accomplish much of this work.

Downsizing has also led to another development: outsourcing. *Outsourcing* is the contracting with outside businesses or services to perform the work once done by in-house departments. The outside specialized contractors, whether janitors or computer-system managers, often can do the work more cheaply and efficiently.

Hospital information systems now frequently use computers to record patients' statistics.

Total Quality Management

Total quality management (*TQM*) is managing with an organization-wide commitment to continuous work improvement and satisfaction of customer needs. The group that probably benefited most from TQM principles was the American automobile makers, who had been devastated by better-made foreign imports. However, much of the rest of U.S. industry would probably also have been shut out of competition in the global economy without the quality strides made in the last few years.

In many cases, unfortunately, the push for quality became principally a matter of pursuing the narrow statistical benchmarks favored by TQM experts. This put considerable stress on employees, with no appreciable payoff in customer satisfaction or profitability. For example, originally FedEx pursued speed over accuracy in its sorting operation. However, it found the number of misdirected packages soared as workers scrambled to meet deadlines.[4] Now companies are looking for a better return on quality-management efforts.

Employee Empowerment

Empowerment means giving employees the authority to act and make decisions on their own. The old style of management was to give lower-level managers and employees only the information they "needed" to know, which minimized their power to make decisions. As a result, truly good work could not be achieved because of the attitude "If it's not part of my job, I don't do it." Today's philosophy is that information should be spread widely, not closely held by top managers, to enable employees lower down in the organization to do their jobs better. Indeed, the availability of networks and groupware (✔ p. 6.19) has enabled the development of task-oriented teams of workers who no longer depend on individual managers for all decisions in order to achieve company goals.

Reengineering

Trends such as the foregoing force—or should force—organizations to face basic realities. Sometimes the organization has to actually reengineer—rethink and redesign itself or key parts of it. *Reengineering* is the search for and implementation of radical change in business processes to achieve breakthrough results. Reengineering, also known as *process innovation* and *core process redesign,* is not just fixing up what already exists. Says one description:

> Reengineers start from the future and work backward, as if unconstrained by existing methods, people, or departments. In effect they ask, "If we were a new company, how would we run this place?" Then, with a meat ax and sandpaper, they conform the company to their vision.[5]

Reengineering works best with big processes that really matter, such as new-product development or customer service. Thus, candidates for this procedure include companies experiencing big shifts in their definition, markets, or competition. Examples are information technology companies—computer makers, cable-TV providers, local and long-distance phone companies, and publishers—which are wrestling with technological and regulatory change. Expensive software systems are available to help companies reengineer and standardize their information systems to give employees the data they need when they need it.

To understand how to bring about change in an organization, we need to understand how organizations work—how they need, organize, and use information.

Organizations: Departments, Tasks, Management Levels, and Types of Information

Common departments in an organization are research and development, production, marketing, accounting and finance, and human resources. The traditional tasks of managers have been planning, organizing, staffing, supervising (leading), and controlling (including budgeting).

Consider any sizable organization you are familiar with. Its purpose is to perform a service or deliver a product. If it's nonprofit, for example, it may deliver the service of educating students or the product of food for famine victims. If it's profit-oriented, it may, for example, sell the service of fixing computers or the product of computers themselves.

Information—whether computer-based or not—has to flow within an organization in a way that will help managers, and the organization, achieve their goals. To this end, business organizations are often structured with five departments.

Departments: R&D, Production, Marketing, Accounting, Human Resources

Depending on the services or products they provide, most companies have departments that perform five functions: research and development (R&D), production, marketing, accounting and finance, and human resources (personnel).

- *Research and development:* The research and development (R&D) department does two things: (1) It conducts basic research, relating discoveries to the organization's current or new products. (2) It does product development and tests and modifies new products or services created by researchers. Special software programs are available to aid in these functions.

- *Production:* The production department makes the product or provides the service. In a manufacturing company, it takes the raw materials and has people or machinery turn them into finished goods. In many cases, this department uses CAD/CAM software and workstations (✔ p. 1.14), as well as robotics. *(See Figure 11.1.)* In another type of company, this department might manage the purchasing, handle the inventories, and control the flow of goods and services.

Figure 11.1 Examples of computer-based information systems in production

Computer-Aided Design
Create, simulate, and evaluate models of products and manufacturing processes.

Computer-Aided Manufacturing
Use computers and robots to fabricate, assemble, and package products.

Factory Management
Plan and control production runs, coordinate incoming orders and raw material requests, oversee cost, and quality assurance programs.

Quality Management
Evaluate product and process specifications, test incoming materials and outgoing products, test production processes in progress, and design quality assurance programs.

Logistics
Purchase and receive materials, control and distribute materials, and control inventory and shipping of products.

Maintenance
Monitor and adjust machinery and processes, perform diagnostics, and do corrective and preventive maintenance.

■ *Marketing:* The marketing department oversees advertising, promotion, and sales. *(See Figure 11.2.)* The people in this department plan, price, advertise, promote, package, and distribute the services or goods to customers or clients. The sales reps may use laptop computers, cell phones, wireless e-mail, and faxes in their work while on the road.

■ *Accounting and finance:* The accounting and finance department handles all financial matters. It handles cash management, pays bills, issues paychecks, records payments, makes investments, and compiles financial statements and reports. It also produces financial budgets and forecasts financial performance after receiving information from the other departments.

■ *Human resources:* This department finds and hires people and administers sick leave and retirement matters. It is also concerned with compensation levels, professional development, employee relations, and government regulations.

Figure 11.2 Examples of computer-based information systems in marketing

Sales Management
Plan, monitor, and support the performance of salespeople and sales of products and services.

Sales Force Automation
Automate the recording and reporting of sales activity by salespeople and the communications and sales support from sales management.

Product Management
Plan, monitor, and support the performance of products, product lines, and brands.

Advertising and Promotion
Help select media and promotional methods and control and evaluate advertising and promotion results.

Sales Forecasting
Produce short- and long-range sales forecasts.

Market Research
Collect and analyze internal and external data on market variables, developments, and trends.

Marketing Management
Develop marketing strategies and plans based on corporate goals and market research and sales activity data, and monitor and support marketing activities.

Whatever the organization—grocery store, computer maker, law firm, hospital, or university—it is likely to have departments corresponding to these. Each department has managers and employees. Although office automation brought about by computers, networks, and groupware has given employees more decision-making power than they used to have, managers in these departments still perform five basic functions.

Management Tasks: Five Functions

Certain specific duties are associated with being a manager. Management is about overseeing resources, including the tasks of planning, organizing, staffing, supervising, and controlling business activities. These five functions, considered the classic tasks of management, are defined as follows:

- *Planning*—setting objectives, both long-term and short-term, and developing strategies for achieving them. Whatever you do in planning lays the groundwork for the other four tasks.

- *Organizing*—making orderly arrangements of resources, such as people and materials.

- *Staffing*—selecting, training, and developing people. In some cases, it may be done by specialists, such as those in the personnel department.

- *Supervising* (*leading*)—directing, guiding, and motivating employees to work toward achieving the organization's goals.

- *Controlling*—monitoring the organization's progress and adapting methods toward achieving its goals.

All managers perform all these tasks, to some degree, as part of their jobs. However, the level of responsibility regarding these tasks varies with the level of the manager, as we discuss next. A manager may also be responsible for maintaining an image within the company or within the community.

Management Levels: Three Levels, Three Kinds of Decisions

How do managers carry out the tasks just described? They do it by making decisions on the basis of the information available to them. A manager's daily job is to decide on the best course of action, based on the facts known at the time.

For each of the five departments there are three traditional levels of management—top, middle, and lower. These levels are reflected in the organization chart. An organization chart is a schematic drawing showing the hierarchy of formal relationships among an organization's employees. (*See Figure 11.3.*)

Managers on each of the three levels have different kinds of responsibility and are therefore required to make different kinds of decisions.

- *Top managers—strategic decisions:* The chief executive officer (CEO) or president is the very top manager. However, for our purposes, "top management" refers to the vice presidents, one of whom heads each of the departments.

  Top managers are concerned with long-range planning and external market forces. Their job is to make strategic decisions. Strategic decisions are complex decisions rarely based on predetermined routine procedures, involving the subjective judgment of the decision maker. Strategic means that of the five management tasks (planning, organizing, staffing, supervising, controlling), top managers are principally concerned with planning.

Figure 11.3 Management levels and responsibilities. (*Left*) An organization generally has five departments: research and development, production, marketing, accounting and finance, and human resources. This organization chart shows the management hierarchy for just one department, accounting and finance. Three levels of management are shown—top, middle, and lower. (*Right*) The entire organization can also be represented as a pyramid, with the five departments and three levels of management as shown. Top managers are responsible for strategic decisions, middle management for tactical decisions, and lower management for operational decisions. Office automation is changing the flow of information in many organizations, thus "flattening" the pyramid, because not all information continues to flow through traditional hierarchical channels.

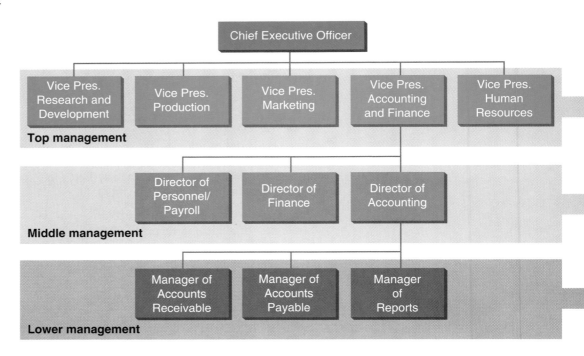

Besides CEO, president, and vice president, typical titles found at the top management level are treasurer, director, controller (chief accounting officer), and senior partner. Examples of strategic decisions are how growth should be financed and what new markets should be tackled first. Other strategic decisions are deciding the company's 5-year goals, evaluating future financial resources, and deciding how to react to competitors' actions.

An AT&T vice president of marketing might have to make strategic decisions about promotional campaigns to sell a new paging service. The top manager who runs an electronics store might have to make strategic decisions about stocking a new line of paging devices.

■ *Middle managers—tactical decisions:* Middle-level managers implement the goals of the organization. Their job is to oversee the supervisors and to make tactical decisions. A tactical decision is a decision that must be made without a base of clearly defined informational procedures, perhaps requiring detailed analysis and computations. Tactical means that of the five management tasks, middle managers deal principally with organizing and staffing. They also deal with shorter-term goals than top managers do.

Examples of middle managers are plant manager, division manager, sales manager, branch manager, and director of personnel. An example of a tactical decision is deciding how many units of a specific product should be kept in inventory. Another is whether or not to purchase a larger computer system.

The director of sales, who reports to the vice president of marketing for AT&T, sets sales goals for district sales managers throughout the country. They in turn feed him or her weekly and monthly sales reports.

■ *Lower or supervisory managers—operational decisions:* Lower-level managers, or supervisory managers, manage or monitor nonmanagement employees. Their job is to make operational decisions. An operational decision is a predictable decision that can be made by following a well-defined set of routine procedures. Operational means these managers focus principally on supervis-

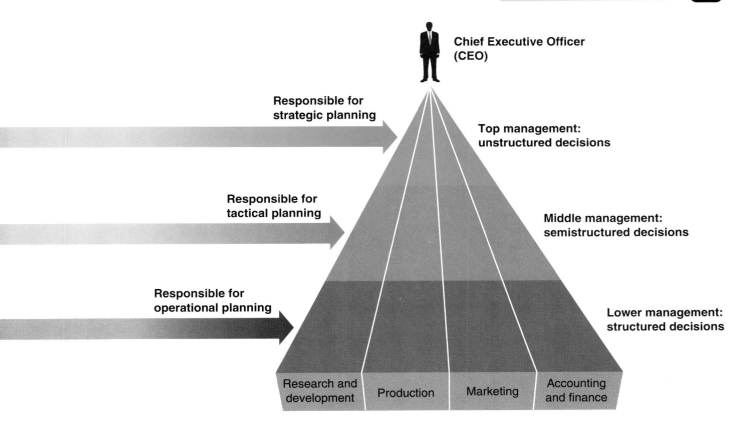

ing (leading) and controlling. They monitor day-to-day events and, if necessary, take corrective action.

An example of a supervisory manager is a warehouse manager in charge of inventory restocking. An example of an operational decision is one in which the manager must choose whether or not to restock inventory. (The guideline on when to restock may be determined at the level above.)

A district sales manager for AT&T would monitor the promised sales and orders for pagers coming in from the sales representatives. When sales begin to drop off, the supervisor would need to take immediate action.

Types of Information: Unstructured, Semistructured, and Structured

Figure 11.4 Examples of decisions by the type of decision structures and by level of management

To make the appropriate decisions—strategic, tactical, operational—the different levels of managers need the right kind of information: unstructured, semistructured, and structured. *(See above right and see Figure 11.4.)*

Decision Structure	Operational Management	Tactical Management	Strategic Management
Unstructured	Cash management	Work group reorganization	New business planning
		Work group performance analysis	Company reorganization
Semistructured	Credit management	Employee performance appraisal	Product planning
	Production scheduling	Capital budgeting	Mergers and aquisitions
	Daily work assignment	Program budgeting	Site location
Structured	Inventory control	Program control	

In general, all information to support intelligent decision making at all three levels must be correct—that is, accurate. It must also be complete, including all relevant data, yet concise, including only relevant data. It must be cost-effective, meaning efficiently obtained, yet understandable. It must be current, meaning timely, yet also time-sensitive, based on historical, current, or future information needs. This shows that information has three distinct properties:

1. Level of summarization

2. Degree of accuracy

3. Timeliness

These properties may vary in the degree to which they are structured or unstructured, depending on the level of management and type of decision making required. Structured information is detailed, current, concerned with past events; requires highly accurate, nonsubjective data; records a narrow range of facts; and covers an organization's internal activities. Unstructured information is the opposite. Unstructured information is summarized, less current, concerned with future events; requires subjective data; records a broad range of facts; and covers activities outside as well as inside an organization. Semistructured information includes some structured information and some unstructured information.

Consider, for example, what information the three levels of management might deal with in a food-supply business *(see Figure 11.5)*.

Now that we've covered some basic concepts about how organizations are structured and what kinds of information are needed at different levels of management, we need to examine what types of management information systems provide the information.

Management Information Systems

Six basic types of computer-based information systems provide information for decision making.

Figure 11.5 Areas covered by the three management levels in a food-supply business

Top managers (executives) make strategic decisions using unstructured information, as we have seen. Middle managers make tactical decisions using semistructured information. Lower-level managers make operational decisions using struc-

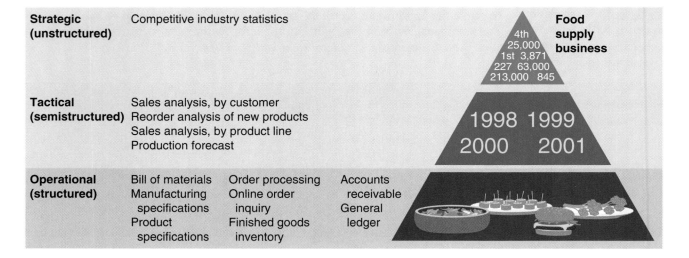

Strategic (unstructured)	Competitive industry statistics			Food supply business
Tactical (semistructured)	Sales analysis, by customer Reorder analysis of new products Sales analysis, by product line Production forecast			
Operational (structured)	Bill of materials Manufacturing specifications Product specifications	Order processing Online order inquiry Finished goods inventory	Accounts receivable General ledger	

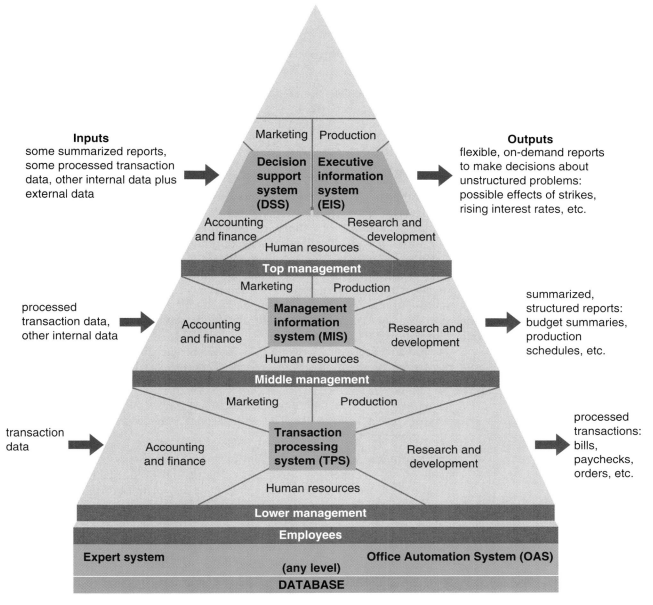

Inputs
some summarized reports, some processed transaction data, other internal data plus external data

Outputs
flexible, on-demand reports to make decisions about unstructured problems: possible effects of strikes, rising interest rates, etc.

Marketing | Production

Decision support system (DSS) | **Executive information system (EIS)**

Accounting and finance | Research and development

Human resources

Top management

Marketing | Production

Accounting and finance | **Management information system (MIS)** | Research and development

Human resources

Middle management

processed transaction data, other internal data

summarized, structured reports: budget summaries, production schedules, etc.

Marketing | Production

Accounting and finance | **Transaction processing system (TPS)** | Research and development

Human resources

Lower management

transaction data

processed transactions: bills, paychecks, orders, etc.

Employees

Expert system | **Office Automation System (OAS)**
(any level)
DATABASE

Figure 11.6 Six information systems for three levels of management. The pyramid shows the following: (1) The three levels of management: top, middle, and lower. (2) The five departments for each level: research and development, production, marketing, accounting and finance, and human resources. (3) The kinds of computer-based information systems corresponding to each management level. (4) The kind of data input for each level, and the kind of information output.

tured information. The purpose of a computer-based information system is to provide managers (and various categories of employees) with the appropriate kind of information to help them make decisions.

Here we describe the following types of computer-based information systems, corresponding to the three management layers and their requirements. Note that we are taking this material from the bottom up because the higher levels build on the lower levels. *(See Figure 11.6.)*

- For lower managers: Transaction processing systems (TPSs)

- For middle managers: Management information systems (MISs)

- For top managers: Decision support systems (DSSs) and executive information systems (EISs)

- For all levels including nonmanagement: Expert systems (ESs) and office automation systems (OASs)

Transaction Processing Systems: To Support Operational Decisions

In most organizations, particularly business organizations, most of what goes on takes the form of transactions. A **transaction** is a recorded event having to do with routine business activities. This includes everything concerning the product or service in which the organization is engaged: production, distribution, sales, orders. It also includes materials purchased, employees hired, taxes paid, and so on. Today in most organizations, the bulk of such transactions are recorded in a computer-based information system. These systems tend to have clearly defined inputs and outputs, and there is an emphasis on efficiency and accuracy. Transaction processing systems record data but do little in the way of converting data into information.[6]

A **transaction processing system (TPS)** is a computer-based information system that keeps track of the transactions needed to conduct business.

Some features of a TPS are as follows:

- *Input and output:* The inputs to the system are transaction data: bills, orders, inventory levels, and the like. The output consists of processed transactions: bills, paychecks, and so on.

- *For lower managers:* Because the TPS deals with day-to-day matters, it is principally of use to supervisory managers. That is, the TPS helps in making operational decisions. Such systems are not usually helpful to middle or top managers.

- *Produces detail reports:* A lower-level manager typically will receive information in the form of detail reports. A detail report contains specific information about routine activities. An example might be the information needed to decide whether to restock inventory.

- *One TPS for each department:* Each department or functional area of an organization—Research and Development, Production, Marketing, Accounting and Finance, and Human Resources—usually has its own TPS. For example, the Accounting and Finance TPS handles order processing, accounts receivable, inventory and purchasing, accounts payable, and payroll.

- *Basis for MIS and DSS:* The database of transactions stored in a TPS is used to support management information systems and decision support systems.

Management Information Systems: To Support Tactical Decisions

A **management information system (MIS)** is a computer-based information system that uses data recorded by TPSs as input into programs that produce routine reports as output.

Features of an MIS are as follows:

■ *Input and output:* Inputs consist of processed transaction data, such as bills, orders, and paychecks, plus other internal data. Outputs consist of summarized, structured reports: budget summaries, production schedules, and the like.

■ *For middle managers:* A MIS is intended principally to assist middle managers. That is, it helps them with tactical decisions. It enables them to spot trends and get an overview of current business activities.

■ *Draws from all departments:* The MIS draws from all five departments or functional areas, not just one.

■ *Produces several kinds of reports:* Managers at this level usually receive information in the form of several kinds of reports: summary, exception, periodic, on-demand.
   —*Summary reports* show totals and trends. An example would be a report showing total sales by office, by product, by salesperson, or as total overall sales.
   —*Exception reports* show out-of-the-ordinary data. An example would be an inventory report that lists only those items that number fewer than 10 in stock.
   —*Periodic reports* are produced on a regular schedule. These may be daily, weekly, monthly, quarterly, or annually. They may contain sales figures, income statements, or balance sheets. Such reports are usually produced on paper, such as computer printouts.
   —*On-demand reports* produce information in response to an unscheduled demand. A director of finance might order an on-demand credit-background report on a new customer who wants to place a large order. On-demand reports are often produced on a terminal or microcomputer screen rather than on paper.

Decision Support Systems: To Support Strategic Decisions

A **decision support system (DSS)** is an interactive, computer-based information system that provides a flexible tool for analysis and helps managers focus on the future. To reach the DSS level of sophistication in information technology, an organization must have established a transaction processing system and a management information system.

Some features of a DSS are as follows:

■ *Input and output:* Inputs consist of some summarized reports, some processed transaction data, and other internal data. They also include data that is external to that produced by the organization. This external data may be produced by trade associations, marketing research firms, the U.S. Bureau of the Census, and other government agencies.
   The outputs are flexible, on-demand reports with which a top manager can make decisions about unstructured problems.

■ *Mainly for top managers:* A DSS is intended principally to assist top managers, although it is now being used by other managers, too. Its purpose is to help them make strategic decisions—decisions about unstructured problems, often unexpected and nonrecurring. These problems may involve the effect of events and trends outside the organization. Examples are rising interest rates or a possible strike in an important materials-supplying industry.

■ *Produces analytic models:* The key attribute of a DSS is that it uses models. A model is a mathematical representation of a real system. The models use a DSS database, which draws on the TPS and MIS files, as well as external data such as stock reports, government reports, national and international news. The system is accessed through DSS software.

The model allows the manager to do a simulation—play a "what if" game—to reach decisions. Thus, the manager can simulate an aspect of the organization's environment in order to decide how to react to a change in conditions affecting it. By changing the hypothetical inputs to the model— number of workers available, distance to markets, or whatever—the manager can see how the model's outputs are affected.

Components of a DSS

Figure 11.7 illustrates the components of a DSS:[7]

■ *Hardware:* Personal workstations provide the primary resource for a DSS. They can be used on a stand-alone basis. However, they are typically connected by wide area or local area networks (✔ pp. 7.28–7.36) to other computer systems for access to other DSS software and resources.

■ *Software:* DSS software packages (DSS generators) contain software modules to manage DSS databases, decision modules, and interaction (dialogue) between user and system.

■ *Data resources:* A DSS database contains data and information extracted from the database of the organization, external databases, and managers' personal databases. It includes summarized data and information most needed by managers.

■ *Model resources:* The model base includes a library of mathematical models and analytical techniques stored as programs, subroutines, spreadsheets, and command files.

■ *People resources:* A DSS can be used by managers or their staff specialists to explore decision alternatives. DSSs can also be developed by such end users. However, the development of large or complex DSSs is typically left to information systems specialists.

Examples of DSS Applications

Many DSSs are developed to support the types of decisions faced by specific industries, such as the airline and real estate industries. Here are three examples:[8]

■ *Airline DSS:* The American Analytical Information Management System (AAIMS) is a decision support system used in the airline industry. It was developed by American Airlines but is used by other airlines, aircraft manufacturers, airline financial analysts, consultants, and associations. AAIMS sup-

Figure 11.7 Components of a DSS

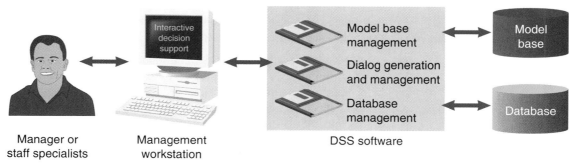

Manager or staff specialists   Management workstation   DSS software

ports a variety of airline decisions by analyzing data collected on airline aircraft utilization, seating capacity and utilization, and traffic statistics. For example, it produces forecasts of airline market share, revenue, and profitability. Thus, AAIMS helps airline management make decisions on aircraft assignments, route requests, ticket classifications, pricing, and so on.

Another successful DSS for American Airlines is its *yield management system*. This DSS helps managers and analysts decide how much to overbook and how to set prices for each seat so that a plane is filled and profits are maximized. American's yield management system deals with more than 250 decision variables. The system is estimated to generate up to 5% of American Airline's revenues.

■ *Real estate DSS:* RealPlan is a DSS used in the real estate industry to do complex analyses of investments in commercial real estate. For example, investing in commercial real estate properties typically involves highly detailed income, expense, and cash flow projections. RealPlan easily performs such analyses, even for properties with multiple units, lease terms, rents, and cost-of-living adjustments. Since RealPlan can also make forecasts of property values up to 40 years into the future, it helps decision makers not only with acquisition decisions but with real estate improvement and divestment decisions as well.

■ *Geographic DSS:* Geographic information systems (GISs) are a special category of DSS that integrate computer graphics and geographic databases with other DSS features. *(See Figure 11.8.)* A geographic information system is a DSS that constructs and displays maps and other graphics that support decisions affecting the geographic distribution of people and other resources. Many companies use GIS technology to choose new store locations, optimize distribution routes, and analyze the demographics of target audiences. For example, companies like Levi Strauss, Arby's, Consolidated Rail, and FedEx use GISs to integrate maps, graphics, and other geographic data with business data from spreadsheets and statistical packages. GIS software is also available for microcomputers—for example, MapInfo and Atlas GIS. The use of GISs

Figure 11.8 Geographic DSS (GIS) screen. Using MapInfo technology, insurance underwriters can set rates and examine potential financial liability in the event of a natural disaster. Here, policyholders who live on earthquake fault lines are visualized and analyzed.

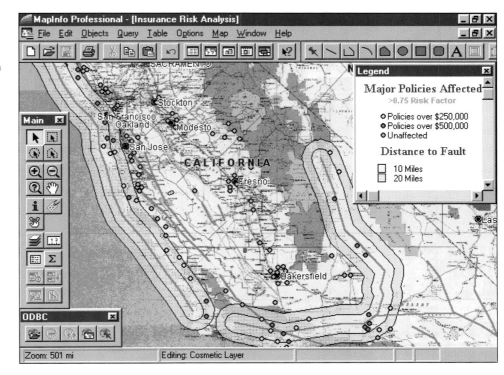

for decision support should accelerate the use of mapping capabilities that have been integrated in the latest versions of spreadsheet packages such as Lotus 1-2-3 and Microsoft Excel.

As communications becomes a more important component of an information system, so does a kind of DSS called *group decision support systems.* A group decision support system (GDSS) enables teams of co-workers to use networks of microcomputers to share information and cooperate on projects. A group decision support system is also called *workgroup computing* and is facilitated by groupware (✔ p. 6.19). By sharing ideas, workers can build consensus and arrive at decisions collaboratively. GDSSs are being found in fields ranging from banking and insurance to architectural design and newspaper publishing.

Executive Information Systems

An **executive information system (EIS)** is an easy-to-use DSS made especially for top managers; it specifically supports strategic decision making. *(See Figure 11.9.)* An EIS is also called an *executive support system* (*ESS*). It draws on data not only from systems internal to the organization but also from those outside. An EIS might allow senior executives to call up predefined reports from their personal computers, whether desktops or laptops. They might, for instance, call up sales figures in many forms—by region, by week, by fiscal year, by projected increases. The EIS includes capabilities for analyzing data and doing "what if" scenarios. EISs also have the capability to browse through information on all aspects of the organization and then zero in on areas the manager believes require attention.[9]

Figure 11.9 EIS. (*Top*) Components of an EIS. (*Bottom left*) This Comshare EIS, called *Commander Decision,* can easily calculate averages, variances, ratios, and summaries. (*Bottom right*) It can also generate exception reports, among other things.

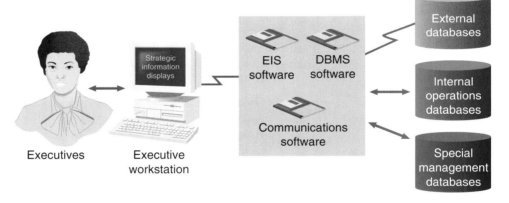

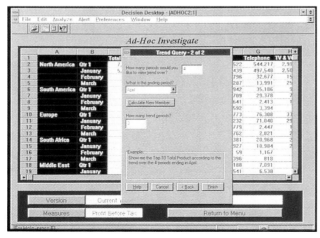

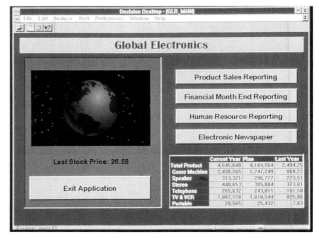

Expert Systems

An **expert system (ES),** or *knowledge system,* is a set of interactive computer programs that helps users solve problems that would otherwise require the assistance of a human expert. Expert systems are used by both management and nonmanagement personnel to solve specific problems, such as how to reduce production costs, improve workers' productivity, or reduce environmental impact.

Expert systems simulate the reasoning process of experts in certain well-defined areas. That is, professionals called *knowledge engineers* interview the expert or experts and determine the rules and knowledge that must go into the system.

USING AN EXPERT SYSTEM IN JOURNALISM

Journalist Steve Weinberg, former executive director of Investigative Reporters and Editors, agreed to provide his knowledge of investigative journalism as the basis for Muckraker, an expert system for journalists. The following excerpt explains how he was interviewed about his knowledge by an authority on expert systems.

It was Louanna Furbee . . . who worked hardest in the early stages to puzzle out the underlying logic (if any, I worried) of how I worked on the investigation. She explained that, after interviewing me, she would try to reduce what I had said into concepts. She would write each concept separately on an index card, then ask me to sort the cards into groupings. From these groupings, she hoped to sketch a tree of knowledge, which the computer programmers could then translate into electronic impulses [using a programming language].

When I viewed the tree a week later, I was amazed how Furbee had managed to translate my words into a graphic that would be the basis of a computer program. She had sketched 57 connected branches. The main trunks were "paper trails" and "people trails," a distinction I had made when she interviewed me. (When conducting an investigation. I almost always consult paper first, then find the people to help explain the paper.)

On the "paper trail" trunk, Furbee sketched my distinctions between primary-source documents and secondary-source documents. She also captured my thinking about how the type of subject (Is the story primarily about an individual, an institution, or an issue?) determines which documents I will seek first. . . .

On the "people" trunk, Furbee focused on the two main problems I had found of most concern to journalists: getting in the door and, once inside, conducting the interview successfully. She worked in branches reflecting my thinking on when to request an interview by letter or telegram rather than by telephone, on dealing with secretaries and other potential bars to access, on how to bring an off-the-record source back on the record.

Using her tree, the rest of the expert system's team began to imprint my thinking onto a computer disk. . . .

When the system was unveiled, the first screen after the title read: "Muckraker's purpose is to provide advice on following the paper trail and interviewing sources. After a series of questions, Muckraker will make a recommendation. Use Muckraker to help plan your investigation."

—Steve Weinberg, "Steve's Brain," *Columbia Journalism Review*

Programs incorporate not only surface knowledge ("textbook knowledge") but also deep knowledge ("tricks of the trade"). What, exactly, is this latter kind of knowledge? "An expert in some activity has by definition reduced the world's complexity by his or her specialization," say some authorities. One result is that "much of the knowledge lies outside direct conscious awareness."[10] Expert systems exist in many areas. MYCIN helps diagnose infectious diseases. PROSPECTOR assesses geological data to locate mineral deposits. DENDRAL identifies chemical compounds. Home-Safe-Home evaluates the residential environment of an elderly person. Business Insight helps businesses find the best strategies for marketing a product. REBES (Residential Burglary Expert System) helps detectives investigate crime scenes. CARES (Computer Assisted Risk Evaluation System) helps social workers assess families for risk of child abuse. CLUES (Countryside Loan Underwriting System) evaluates home-mortgage-loan applications. Muckraker (*see previous page*) assists journalists with investigative reporting. Crush takes a body of expert advice and combines it with worksheets reflecting a user's business situation to come up with a customized strategy to beat out competitors.

Office Automation Systems

Office automation systems (OASs) are those that combine various technologies to reduce the manual labor required in operating an efficient office environment. These technologies include voice mail, e-mail, scheduling software, desktop publishing, word processing, fax, and so on. OASs are used throughout all levels of an organization. The backbone of office automation is a network—perhaps a LAN (✔ p. 7.30), an intranet over a LAN, or an extranet (✔ p. 8.33). All office functions, including dictation, typing, filing, copying, fax, Telex, microfilm and records management, telephone calls and telephone switchboard operations, are candidates for integration.

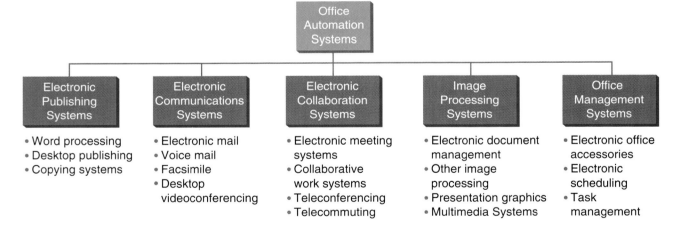

The Future: Going Sideways

Rigid, top-down corporate hierarchies are being rejected by more and more companies.

As we described in the beginning of this chapter, things are changing rapidly in the business and organizational worlds. Networks and new technologies are flattening the traditional pyramid-shaped hierarchical structure of management levels and sending information of many types in a more lateral (horizontal) manner than was previously the case. (*See Figure 11.10.*)

Figure 11.10 The traditional pyramid-shaped hierarchical structure of management levels is changing.

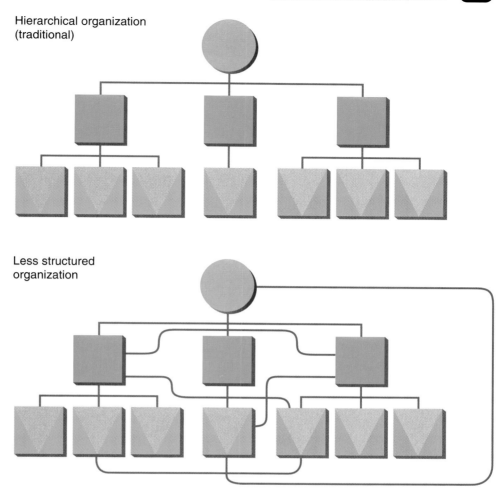

Hierarchical organization (traditional)

Less structured organization

Says Frances Hesselbein, president and chief executive officer of the Peter F. Drucker Foundation for Nonprofit Management, "I think today most organizations, whether public, private or nonprofit, are really trying to manage well. They're trying to reduce the rigidity of the old hierarchy." Hesselbein thinks organizations retain the old hierarchy of top-down management at their peril. She prefers "circular management," which places the leader in the center of the organizational chart and managers at various points along three concentric circles around that center. That way, she says, "People functions move easily across the organization. . . ." It gives all members of the organization the freedom to do their best work.

"Almost every company inherited the old hierarchy where rank equaled responsibility, and it doesn't work in today's world," Hesselbein says. Instead people are trying to use new technologies to allow more fluid structures that release people to be more creative and productive. "When you have an energetic, highly motivated workforce, performance and morale just soar. You don't get magnificent performance from dispirited workers who feel they are not appreciated."

WHAT HAPPENS WHEN THE RIGHT INFORMATION DOESN'T GET TO THE RIGHT PERSON AT THE RIGHT TIME?

The efficient management of information can be critical to all of us . . . not just managers. Here are a few examples of what can go wrong when information is not managed properly.

■ Months before ValuJet flight 592 crashed in 1996, the Federal Aviation Administration had the safety data it later used to ground the airline. But much of it was stored in warehouses out of sight of the FAA's key decision makers.

■ In Saudi Arabia, U.S. authorities wanted to widen the security zone around the towers housing the U.S. troops, but the Saudis turned down the request. Defense Secretary William Perry didn't learn about the denial until four days after a terrorist bombing killed 19 Americans.

■ In April of 1996, Ford recalled 8.7 million cars and trucks to replace potentially faulty ignition switches after more than 1000 cars and trucks caught fire. Yet long before the recall, more than 4000 documents detailing the fires' frequency and suspected cause lay buried in thousands of pages of files at the national Highway Traffic Safety Administration.

■ A sharp rise in arson incidents at African-American churches in the South was not detected until February 1996, partly because the system for collecting fire data is haphazard. In each case, critically important information was collected but not organized or analyzed in a way to give it meaning.

■ On June 21, 1996, Manhattan Bagel stock fell 46% after it reported its West Coast unit had been supplying incorrect financial information. The president said he hadn't known.

The dire need to unearth information and convert it into knowledge and appropriate action has spawned a cutting-edge field known as *knowledge management*. Knowledge management is technology driven, using computers to help analyze data, pinpoint trends, flag the unusual, and sort the important from the mundane. Finally, it must result in getting critical data to decision makers. But Larry Prusak, author of two books on managing information, warns that technology is not the ultimate answer because most information is gray, not black and white, and requires a human brain to decipher it. The real problem, Prusak says, is getting the CEO's attention.

Real Estate Careers

You've walked through the house that's for sale and you want to buy it. Now what?

First you might want to check out whether it's overpriced for the neighborhood. That used to mean going through the county recorder or a real-estate office to get detailed information about comparable properties. Realtors have long had access to multiple-listing databases that contain information about properties in their area.

Now, however, even home buyers and homeowners can go to an Internet site (*http://www.recomps.com*) established by Stewart Title of Orange County, California, and dial into a national database that allows them to compare recent sale prices of similar homes in the same neighborhood. Says Gregg Shuler, president of Stewart Title, "in addition to sales price data, detailed information is provided on square footage, lot size, number of bedrooms and bathrooms, taxes, and special amenities, such as a swimming pool, spa, and remodeling." The data search will cover as many as 30 comparable homes sold in a neighborhood during the past 12 months.[11]

If you want to know where some of those comparable properties are located, you can go to the Web site for MapBlast (*http://www.mapblast.com*). MapBlast allows you to produce a detailed map from almost any street address in the United States.[12]

Normally it takes a month or more to arrange the financing and sign closing papers for a home purchase. But now there are ways to speed this up. St. Petersburg, Florida-based CREDCO offers one-stop-investigation shopping that provides residential mortgage credit reports, assesses a borrower's credit risk, and gives consumers a personal credit report.[13] And Alltel Information Systems and Data Track Systems formed a combined network that allows buyers to reduce the time for loan qualifying and closing from a month to a few days. With the real-estate agent, appraiser, bank, and insurer associated with the sale all on the same secure network, there is no need for the time-consuming process of printing, faxing, or express-mailing hard-copy forms and documents.

Finally, if you want to remodel your less-than-desirable new domicile or see how it might look with various kinds of floor, wall, and fabric coverings or furnishings and appliances, you can obtain three-dimensional models from a CD-ROM called *Visual Home* from the Palo Alto, California, company Books That Work. "Simply download these models and materials onto your PC," says one report, "and 'see' how a new appliance or cabinet will fit into your existing home—before it arrives on the delivery truck."[14]

WHAT IT IS
WHAT IT DOES

WHY IT IS IMPORTANT

decision support system (DSS) (LOs 2, 3, p. 11.13)   An interactive, computer-based information system (integrated hardware and software) that provides a flexible tool for analysis and helps managers focus on the future.

To reach the DSS level of sophistication in information technology, an organization must have established a transaction processing system and a management information system.

executive information system (EIS) (LOs 2, 3, p. 11.16)   Easy-to-use DSS made especially for top managers; it specifically supports strategic decision making.

An EIS draws on data internal and external to the organization. It allows senior executives to call up predefined reports from their personal computers, such as sales figures by region, by week, by fiscal year, and by projected increases. The EIS includes capabilities for analyzing data and doing "what if" scenarios. With an EIS a manager can browse through information on all aspects of the organization and then zero in on areas requiring attention.

expert system (ES) (LOs 2, 3, p. 11.17)   Also called *knowledge system;* a set of interactive computer programs that helps users solve problems that would otherwise require the assistance of a human expert.

Expert systems are used by both management and nonmanagement personnel to solve specific problems, such as how to reduce production costs, improve workers' productivity, or reduce environmental impact.

management information system (MIS) (LOs 2, 3, p. 11.12)   Computer-based information system that uses data recorded by TPSs as input into programs that produce routine reports as output.

An MIS principally assists middle managers, helping them make *tactical* decisions—spotting trends and getting an overview of current business activities.

office automation systems (OASs) (LOs 2, 3, p. 11.18)   Systems that combine various technologies to reduce the manual labor required in operating an efficient office environment. These technologies include voice mail, e-mail, scheduling software, desktop publishing, word processing, fax, and so on.

OASs are used throughout all levels of an organization.

transaction (LOs 2, 3, p. 11.12)   A recorded event having to do with routine business activities. This includes everything concerning the product or service in which the organization is engaged: production, distribution, sales, orders. It also includes materials purchased, employees hired, taxes paid, and so on.

transaction processing system (TPS) (LOs 2, 3, p. 11.12)   Computer-based information system that keeps track of the transactions needed to conduct business. Inputs are transaction data (for example, bills, orders, inventory levels, production output). Outputs are processed transactions (for example, bills, paychecks). Each functional area of an organization—Research and Development, Production, Marketing, Accounting and Finance, and Human Resources—usually has its own TPS.

Today in most organizations, the bulk of such transactions are recorded in a computer-based information system. These systems tend to have clearly defined inputs and outputs, and there is an emphasis on efficiency and accuracy. TPSs record data but do little in the way of converting data into information.

The TPS helps supervisory managers in making *operational decisions.* The database of transactions stored in a TPS is used to support a management information system and a decision support system.

1. Middle managers make _____ decisions.

2. A(n) _____ _____ system is one that combines various technologies to reduce the manual labor required in operating an efficient office environment.

3. _____ refers to the transition from mainframe-based computer systems to linking smaller computers in networks.

4. Information has three properties that vary in importance depending on the decision and the decision maker. They are:

   a. _____

   b. _____

   c. _____

5. A report that shows out-of-the-ordinary data is a(n) _____ report.

SHORT-ANSWER QUESTIONS

1. What is an expert system?
2. What is a decision support system?
3. What is an executive information system?
4. What is the difference between structured information and semistructured information, and which type of information is easier to manage from a computer-based data processing standpoint?
5. What five departments exist in most companies?

MULTIPLE-CHOICE QUESTIONS

1. Which of the following isn't a trend that is part of the reengineering of the workplace?
   a. downsizing and outsourcing
   b. total quality management
   c. reengineering
   d. employee empowerment
   e. increased salaries

2. Which of the following is used to support the making of tactical decisions?
   a. transaction processing system
   b. management information system
   c. decision support system
   d. executive information system
   e. all the above

3. Which of the following is considered a classic function of management?
   a. planning
   b. organizing
   c. staffing
   d. controlling
   e. all the above

4. Which of the following is used to support all levels of management (including nonmanagement)?
   a. transaction processing system
   b. management information system
   c. decision support system
   d. expert system
   e. none of the above

CHAPTER 12

FILES AND DATABASES

Organizing and Maintaining Digital Data

PREVIEW

When you have completed this chapter, you will be able to:

1. Explain the importance of database administration within an organization

2. Describe the parts of the data hierarchy, including key fields

3. Distinguish batch from real-time processing, and online from offline storage

4. Explain the best uses for sequential, direct, and indexed sequential access storage

5. Describe the difference between file management systems and database management systems

6. Identify the advantages and the disadvantages of the four database models and of database management systems in general

7. Explain how a data warehouse is set up and what tools are used to sift through it

8. Describe some ways database users can invade people's privacy and some methods and laws used to prevent such invasions

WHY

WHY IS THIS CHAPTER IMPORTANT?

"We want to capture the entire human experience throughout history." So states Corbis Corp. chief executive officer Doug Rowan.[1] Corbis was formed in 1989 by software billionaire Bill Gates to acquire digital rights to fine art and photographic images that can be viewed electronically in everything from electronic books to computerized wall hangings.

In 1995 Corbis acquired the Bettmann Archive of 17 million photographs for scanning into its digital database. Its founder, Dr. Otto Bettmann, called his famous collection a "visual story of the world," and indeed many of the images are unique. They include tintypes of black Civil War soldiers, the 1937 crash of the *Hindenburg* dirigible, John F. Kennedy Jr. saluting the casket of his assassinated father. A few Bettmann images can be viewed electronically at no charge on Corbis's World Wide Web site: *http://www.corbis.com/@@/ 50Gjud5NsUF9/exhibit/bysubject.html.*

However, when Rowan says Corbis wants to capture all of human experience, he means not just photos and art works from the likes of the National Gallery in London and the State Hermitage Museum in St. Petersburg, Russia, for which Corbis also owns digital imaging rites. "Film, video, audio," he says. "We are interested in those fields too."[2]

Are there any ethical problems with one company having in its database the exclusive digital rights to our visual and audio history? Like many museums and libraries (such as the Library of Congress), by converting the images and texts of the past into digital form and making them available to people who could never travel to, say, London or St. Petersburg, Corbis joins a trend toward democratizing art and scholarship by converting the images and texts of the past into digital form and making them available to more people.

However, when Gates acquired the Bettmann images, for example, the move put their future use "into the hands of an aggressive businessman who, unlike Dr. Bettmann, is planning his own publishing ventures," points out one reporter. "While Mr. Gates's initial plans will make Bettmann images more widely accessible, this savvy competitor now ultimately controls who can use them—and who can't."[3] Adds Paul Saffo, of the nonprofit Institute for the Future, "The cultural issue raised by the Bettmann purchase is whether we're seeing history sold to the highest bidder or we'll eventually see history made more accessible to the public as a result."[4] Curators of art museums and families of famous persons are afraid that the rights to art works will slip away for less than they are worth or that the images will be pirated or used in silly ways in advertising. (For example, one of Fred Astair's children sent an angry letter to several publications after a well-known film clip of his dancing father was used in a vacuum cleaner ad on TV.)

All forms of information technology are affecting our social and business institutions in significant ways. However, as the Corbis example suggests, the arrival of databases promises to stand some of them on their heads. Databases are not just an interesting new way to computerize filing systems. Databases are collections of related files, which, as we shall see, makes them usable in ways that traditional filing systems (even computerized ones) are not.

All Databases Great and Small

A database is a set of related files that is created and managed by a database management system (DBMS). Database and file structures are determined by the software; the hardware deals with bits and bytes. Organizations usually appoint a database administrator to manage the database and related activities.

A database may be small, contained entirely within your own personal computer. Or it may be massive, like those of Corbis, available online through computer and telephone connections. *(See Figure 12.1.)* Such online databases are of special interest to us in this book because they offer us phenomenal resources that until recently were unavailable to most ordinary computer users.

Microcomputer users can set up their personal databases using popular database management software like that we discussed earlier (✔ p. 6.15). Examples are Paradox, FileMaker Pro, Access, FoxPro, and dBASE. *(See Figure 12.2.)* Such programs are used, for example, by graduate students to conduct research, by salespeople to keep track of clients, by purchasing agents to monitor orders, and by coaches to keep watch on other teams and players.

Figure 12.1 Small (personal), medium-size, and large databases: examples

Type	Example	Typical number of users	Typical size of database
Personal	Mary Richards House Painting	1	< 10 MB
Medium-size (workgroup)	Seaview Yacht Sales	25 or less	< 100 MB
Large organizational	Automobile Licensing and Registration	100s	> 1 trillion bytes

Figure 12.2 Software for personal databases. These popular microcomputer database packages are available in computer stores.

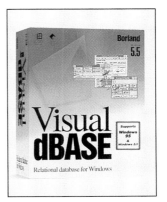

Some databases are so large that they cannot possibly be stored in a microcomputer. Some of these can be accessed by going online through a microcomputer or other computer. Such databases, sometimes called *information utilities,* represent enormous compilations of data, any part of which is available, for a fee, to the public.

Examples of well-known information utilities—more commonly known as *online services* (✔ p. 8.9)—are America Online, CompuServe, and Prodigy. As we described in Chapter 8, these offer access to news, weather, travel information, home shopping services, reference works, and a great deal more. Some public-access databases are specialized, such as Lexis, which gives lawyers access to local, state, and federal laws.

Other public-access databases are online archives like those of "virtual art museums," such as the Smithsonian's National Museum of American Art, which has put images from its collections online since 1993, and the National Gallery of Art in Washington, D.C. The Library of Congress also is involved in an ambitious plan to digitize some of its 104 million items—books, manuscripts, drawings, photographs—for access online.

Other types of databases are collections of records shared or distributed throughout a company or other organization. Generally, the records are available only to employees or selected individuals and not to outsiders.

For example, many university libraries have been transforming drawers of catalog cards into electronic databases for use by their students and faculty. Libraries at Yale, Johns Hopkins, and other universities have contracted with a Virginia company called The Electronic Scriptorium, which employs monks and nuns at six monasteries to convert card catalogs to an electronic system. *(See Figure 12.3.)*

Figure 12.3 Building a library database. Father Patrick Creeden enters data into a computer at the Monastery of the Holy Cross in Chicago.

"CHICAGO–Father Thomas Baxter stands in his habit, holding a computer printout. Later today, he'll review the Scriptures in his cell here at the Monastery of the Holy Cross of Jerusalem, but this morning he's carefully proofreading a library's computerized records.

He and two other monks in this community of five are modern-day scribes, using computers to participate in an age-old monastic tradition: preserving knowledge. In this case, they're helping university and public libraries transform drawers of catalogue cards into electronic databases.

Father Baxter is pointing at a line of text highlighted in yellow, indicating a discrepancy between two data fields. One of his jobs as prior, or leader, of the monastery is to look for typographical errors, call them to the attention of the brother responsible for them, and remind him to concentrate more closely on his work.

This monastery is part of an effort to bring religious communities back into the information business. A company calling itself The Electronic Scriptorium—referring to the room where monks would use quills and ink to copy intricate manuscripts long ago—is matching up monastic communities with libraries and others in need of complex data-entry work. The partnerships benefit the monasteries and convents, which need flexible jobs to support themselves, and the libraries, which need their records entered accurately."

–Jeffrey R. Young, "Modern-Day-Monastery," *Chronicle of Higher Education*

A private database may be *shared* or *distributed.* A **shared database** is shared by users of one company or organization in one location. Shared databases can be found in local area networks (✔ p. 7.30). The company owns the database, which is often stored on a minicomputer or mainframe. Users are linked to the database through terminals or microcomputer workstations.

How do you think you could use an online database?

A **distributed database** is one that is stored on different computers in different locations connected by a client-server network (✔ p. 7.31). For example, sales figures for a chain of discount stores might be located in computers at the various stores, but they would also be available to executives in regional offices or at corporate headquarters. An employee using the database would not know where the data is coming from. However, all employees still use the same commands to access and use the database.

One thing that large databases have in common is that they must be professionally managed. This is done by database managers.

The Database Administrator

Technically, a single user's personal database must also be managed. Often personal database administration is informal. For example. each individual follows simple procedures for backing up his or her database, keeping minimal records for documentation.[5] However, the information in a large database—such as a corporation's patents, formulas, advertising strategies, and sales information—is the organization's lifeblood and much more difficult to manage. Professionals, then, need to manage all activities related to the database. These people are the *database administrators (DBAs),* people who coordinate all related activities and needs for an organization's database. The responsibilities include, among others, the following:

■ *Database design, implementation, and operation:* At the beginning, the DBA helps determine the design of the database. Later he or she determines how space will be used on secondary storage devices, how files and records may be added and deleted, and how changes are documented. (A change in the database structure may cause an error that is not revealed for months, and without proper documentation of the change, diagnosing the problem may be next to impossible. Today, CASE tools [computer-aided systems engineering, ✔ p. 9.21] can be used to document database design.)[6]

■ *Coordination with users:* The DBA determines user access privileges; sets standards, guidelines, and control procedures; assists in establishing priorities for requests; and adjudicates conflicting user needs.

■ *System security:* The DBA sets up and monitors a system for preventing unauthorized access to the database.

■ *Backup and recovery:* Because loss of data or a crash in the database could vitally affect the organization, the DBA needs to make sure the system is regularly backed up. He or she also needs to develop plans for recovering data or operations should a failure occur.

■ *Performance monitoring:* The database administrator compiles and analyzes statistics concerning the database's performance and identifies problem areas. The DBA monitors the system to make sure it is serving users appropriately. A standard complaint is that the system is too slow, usually because too many users are trying to access it.

As an example of a case of performance monitoring, on a recent Super Bowl Sunday, the National Football League's Web site scored 6 million "hits"—a measure of the number of transmissions of text, video, graphics, or audio files. Expecting heavy traffic, managers of the site had used five servers, but network problems still affected visitors, and many reported long waits or just being turned away.[7] Although the Super Bowl is a once-a-year event, it will be the job of the database manager in charge of the site to make sure things run more smoothly the next time.

The Data Storage Hierarchy and the Key Field

Data in storage is organized as a hierarchy: bits, bytes, fields, records, and files, which are the basic elements of a database. The key field is used to uniquely identify a record.

How does a database actually work? To understand this, first we need to consider how stored data is structured—the *data storage hierarchy* and the concept of *key field.* We then need to discuss *file management systems,* and finally *database management systems.*

The Data Storage Hierarchy

Data can be grouped into a hierarchy of categories, each increasingly more complex. The **data storage hierarchy** consists of the levels of data stored in a computer file: bits, bytes (characters), fields, records, files, and databases. *(See Figure 12.4.)*

Computers, we have said, are based on the principle that electricity may be "on" or "off," or "high-voltage" or "low-voltage," or "present" or "absent," or of some similar two-state system. Thus, individual items of data are represented by 0 for off and 1 for on. A 0 or 1 is called a *bit.* A unit of 8 bits is called a *byte;* it may be used to represent a character, digit, or other value, such as A, ?, or 3. Bits and bytes are the building blocks for representing data, whether it is being processed, stored, or telecommunicated. Bits and bytes are what the computer hardware deals with, but most users need not be concerned with them. They will, however, be dealing with characters, fields, records, files, and databases.

- *Character:* A **character** may be—but is not necessarily—the same as a byte. A character is a single letter, number, or special character such as ; or $ or %.

- *Field:* A **field** is a unit of data consisting of one or more characters. An example of a field is your name, date of birth, or Social Security number.
  Note: One reason the Social Security number is often used in computing—for good or for ill—is that, perhaps unlike your name, it is a *distinctive* (unique) field. Thus, it can be used to easily locate information about you. Such a field is called a *key field.* More on this below.

- *Record:* A **record** is a collection of related fields. An example of a record would be your name *and* date of birth *and* Social Security number.

- *File:* A **file** is a collection of related records. An example of a file is collected data on everyone employed in the same department of a company, including all names, addresses, and Social Security numbers.

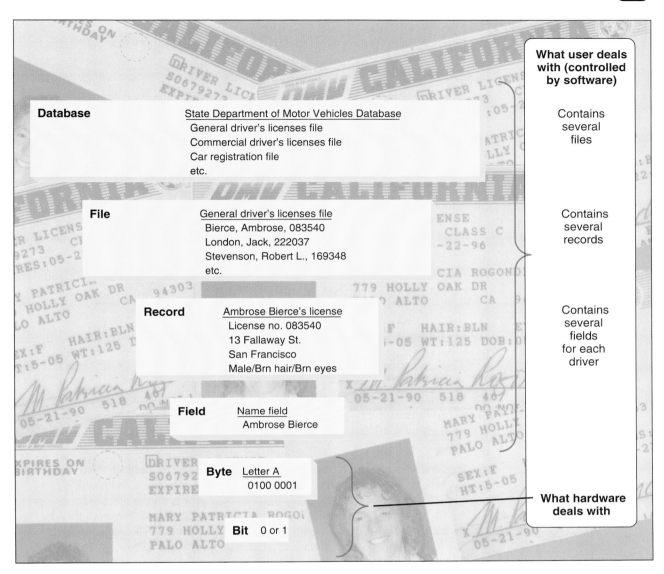

Figure 12.4 Data storage hierarchy: how data is organized. Bits are organized into bytes, bytes into fields, fields into records, records into files. Related files may be organized into a database.

■ *Database:* A **database** is a collection of interrelated files. A company database might include files on all past and current employees in all departments. There would be various files for each employee: payroll, retirement benefits, sales quotas and achievements (if in sales), and so on.

The Key Field

An important concept in data organization is that of the *key field*. A **key field** contains unique data used to identify a record so that it can be easily retrieved and processed. The key field is often an automatically generated identification number, Social Security number, customer account number, or the like. As mentioned, the primary characteristic of the key field is that it is *unique*. Thus, numbers are clearly preferable to names as key fields because there are many people with common names like James Johnson, Susan Williams, Ann Wong, or Roberto Sanchez, whose records might be confused.

File Handling: Basic Concepts

Before databases existed there were files. To understand database management, therefore, we first need to understand file management.

Types of Files: Program and Data Files

There are many kinds of files, but, as described in Chapter 4 (✔ p. 4.3), the principal division is between program files and data files.

■ *Program files:* **Program files** are files containing software instructions. In a word processing program, for example, you may see files listed (with names such as SETUP.EXE) that perform specific functions associated with installing the program. These files are part of the software package.

■ *Data files:* **Data files** are files that contain data. Often you will create and name these files yourself, such as DOCUMENT.1 or Psychology Report.

Two Types of Data Files: Master and Transaction

Among the several types of data files two are commonly used to update data in large systems: a master file and a transaction file.

■ *Master file:* The **master file** is a data file containing relatively permanent records that are generally updated periodically. An example of a master file would be the address-label file for all students currently enrolled at your college.

■ *Transaction file:* The **transaction file** is a temporary holding file that holds all changes to be made to the master file: additions, deletions, revisions. For example, in the case of the address labels for your college, a transaction file would hold new names and addresses to be added (because over time new students enroll) and names and addresses to be deleted (because students leave). It would also hold revised names and addresses (because students change their names or move). Each month or so, the master file would be *updated* with the changes called for in the transaction file.

Batch Versus Online Processing

Data may be taken from secondary storage (✔ p. 4.2) and processed in either of two ways: (1) "later," via *batch processing,* or (2) "right now," via *online (real-time) processing.*

■ *Batch processing:* In **batch processing,** data is collected over several days or weeks and then processed all at one time, as a "batch," against a master file. Thus, if users need to make some request of the system, they must wait until the batch has been processed. Batch processing is less expensive than real-time processing and is suitable for work in which immediate answers to queries are not needed.

An example of batch processing is that done by banks for balancing checking accounts. When you deposit a check in the morning, the bank will make a record of it. However, it will not compute your account balance until the end of the day, after all checks have been processed in a batch.

■ *Online processing:* **Online processing,** also called *real-time processing,* means entering transactions into a computer system as they take place and updating the master files as the transactions occur. For example, when you use your ATM card to withdraw cash from an automated teller machine, the system automatically computes your account balance then and there. Airline reservation systems also use online processing.

Offline Versus Online Storage

Whether it's on magnetic tape or on some form of disk, data may be stored either offline or online.

■ *Offline:* **Offline storage** means that data is not directly accessible for processing until the tape or disk has been loaded onto an input device. That is, the storage is not under the direct control of the central processing unit.

■ *Online:* **Online storage** means that stored data is directly accessible for processing. That is, storage is under the direct control of the central processing unit. You need not wait for a tape or disk to be loaded onto an input device.

For processing to be online, the storage must be online and fast. Generally, this means storage on disk rather than magnetic tape. With tape, it is not possible to go instantly to the record on the tape you are looking for (✔ p. 4.5); instead, the read/write head has to search through all the records that precede it, which takes time. With disk, however, the system can go directly and quickly to the record—just as a CD player can go directly to a particular spot on a music CD.

File Organization: Three Methods

To quickly review some material from Chapter 4 (✔ p. 4.5), tape storage falls in the category of sequential access storage. *Sequential access storage* means that information is stored in sequence, such as alphabetically. Thus, you would have to search a tape past all the information from A to J, say, before you got to K. This process may require running several inches or feet off a reel of tape, which, as we said, takes time.

Disk storage, by contrast, generally falls into the category of direct access storage (although data *can* be stored sequentially). *Direct access storage* means that the system can go directly to the required information. Because you can directly access information, retrieving data is much faster with magnetic or optical disk than it is with magnetic tape.

From these two fundamental forms, computer scientists devised three methods of organizing files for secondary storage: *sequential, direct,* and *indexed-sequential.*

■ *Sequential file organization:* Sequential file organization stores records in sequence, one after the other. This is the only method that can be used with magnetic tape. Records can be retrieved only in the sequence in which they were stored. The method can also be used with disk.

  For example, if you are looking for employee record 8888, the computer will have to start with record 0001, then go past 0002, 0003, and so on, until it finally comes to record 8888.

  Sequential file organization is useful, for example, when a large portion of the records needs to be accessed, as when a mail-order house is sending out catalogs to all names on a mailing list. The method also is less expensive than other methods because it uses magnetic tape, which is cheaper than magnetic or optical disk.

The disadvantage of sequential file organization is that records must be ordered in a particular way and so searching for data is slow.

■ *Direct file organization:* Instead of storing records in sequence, direct file organization, or *random file organization,* stores records in no particular sequence. A record is retrieved according to its key field, or unique element of data. This method of file organization is used with disk storage. It is ideal for applications such as airline reservations systems and computerized directory-assistance operations. In these cases, records need to be retrieved only one at a time, and there is no fixed pattern to the requests for records.

A mathematical formula, called a *hashing algorithm,* is used to produce a unique number that will identify the record's physical location on the disk. (For example, one hashing algorithm divides the record's key field number by the prime number closest to that of the total number of records stored.)

Direct file organization is much faster than sequential file organization for finding a specific record. However, because the method requires hard-disk or optical-disk storage, it is more expensive than magnetic tape. Moreover, it is not as efficient as sequential file organization for listing large numbers of records.

■ *Indexed-sequential file organization:* A compromise was developed between the preceding two methods. Indexed-sequential file organization, or simply *indexed file organization,* stores records in sequential order. However, the file in which the records are stored contains an index that lists each record by its key field and identifies its physical location on the disk. The method requires magnetic or optical disk.

For example, a company could index certain ranges of employee identification numbers—0000 to 1000, 1001 to 2000, and so on. For the computer to find the record with the key field 8888, it would go first to the index. The index would give the location of the range in which the key field appears (for example, 8001 to 9000). The computer would then search sequentially (from 8001) to find the key field 8888.

This method is slower than direct file organization because of the necessity of having to do an index search. The index-sequential method is best when large batches of transactions occasionally must be updated, yet users want frequent, rapid access to records. For example, bank customers and tellers want to have up-to-the-minute information about checking accounts, but every month the bank must update bank statements to send to customers.

An illustration of the three file organization methods is shown in Figure 4.1 on page 4.6.

File Management Systems

Files may be retrieved through a file management system, one file at a time. Disadvantages of a file management system are data redundancy, lack of data integrity, and lack of program independence.

In the 1950s, when commercial use of computers was just beginning, magnetic tape was the storage medium and records and files were stored sequentially. In order to work with these files, a user needed a file management system. A **file management system,** or *file manager,* is software for creating, retrieving, and manipulating files, one file at a time. Traditionally, a large organization such as a university would have different files for different purposes. For you as a student, for example, there might be one file for course grades, another for student records, and a third for tuition billing. Each file would be used independently to produce its own separate reports. *(See Figure 12.5.)* If you changed your address, someone had to make the change separately in each file.

Disadvantages of File Management Systems

File management systems worked well enough for the time, but they had several disadvantages:

- *Data redundancy: Data redundancy* means that the same data fields appear in many different files and often in different formats. Thus, separate files tend to repeat some of the same data over and over. A student's course grades file and tuition billing file would both contain similar data (name, address, telephone number). When data fields are repeated in different files, they waste storage space and create headaches when a field must be updated that is common to all files.

- *Lack of data integrity: Data integrity* means that data is accurate, consistent, and up to date. However, when the same data fields (a student's address and phone number, for example) must be changed in different files, some files may be missed or mistakes will be made. The result is that some reports will be produced with erroneous information.

- *Lack of program independence:* With file management systems, different files were often written by different programmers using different file formats. Thus, the files were not *program independent.* The arrangement meant more time was required to maintain files. It also prevented a programmer from writing a single program that would access all the data in multiple files.

As computers became more and more important in daily life, the frustrations of working with separate, redundant files lacking data integrity and program independence began to be overwhelming. Fortunately, magnetic disks and then optical disks began to supplant magnetic tape as the most popular medium of secondary storage, leading to new possibilities for managing data, which we discuss next.

Figure 12.5 File management system. In the traditional file management system, some of the same data elements, such as addresses, were repeated in different files. Information was not shared among files.

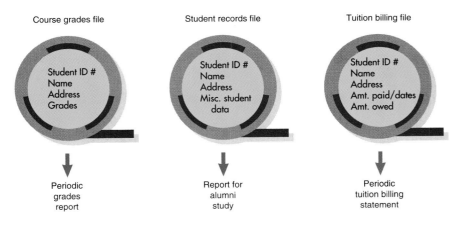

Course grades file

Student records file

Tuition billing file

Student ID #
Name
Address
Grades

Student ID #
Name
Address
Misc. student data

Student ID #
Name
Address
Amt. paid/dates
Amt. owed

Periodic grades report

Report for alumni study

Periodic tuition billing statement

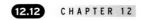

Database Management Systems

Database management systems are an improvement over file management systems. They use DBMS software to control the structure of the database and access to the data.

When magnetic tape began to be replaced by disk, sequential access storage began to be replaced by direct access storage. The result was a new technology and new software: the database management system.

As mentioned, a *database* is a collection of many related files. More specifically, the files are usually *integrated,* meaning that the file records are logically related, or cross-referenced, to one another. Thus, even though all data elements on a topic are kept in records in different files, they can easily be organized and retrieved with simple requests.

The software for manipulating databases is **database management system (DBMS software),** or a *database manager,* a program that controls the structure of a database and access to the data. With a DBMS, then, a large organization such as a university might still have different files for different purposes. If you were a student, you might have the same files as existed in a file management system (one for course grades, another for student records, and a third for tuition billing). However, in the database management system, data elements are integrated (cross-referenced) and shared among different files. *(See Figure 12.6.)* Thus, if you changed your address, the address change would automatically be reflected in the different files.

Advantages and Disadvantages of a DBMS

The advantages of databases and DBMSs are as follows:

- *Reduced data redundancy:* Instead of some of the same data fields being repeated in different files, in a database the information appears just once. The single biggest advantage of a database is that the same information is available to different users. Moreover, reduced redundancy lowers the expense of storage media and hardware because more data can be stored on the media.

- *Improved data integrity:* Reduced redundancy increases the chances of data integrity—data that is accurate, consistent, and up to date—because each updating change is made in only one place.

Figure 12.6 Database management system. In the database management system, data elements are integrated and information is shared among different files. Information updated in one file will automatically be updated in other files.

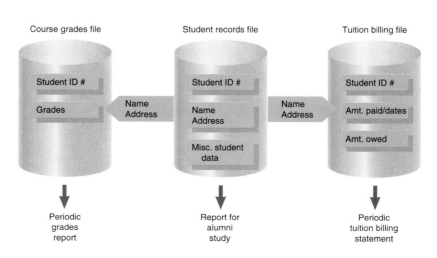

■ *More program independence:* With a database management system, the program and the file formats are the same, so that one programmer or even several programmers can spend less time maintaining files.

■ *Increased user productivity:* Database management systems are fairly easy to use, so that users can get their requests for information answered without having to resort to technical manipulations. In addition, users don't have to wait for a computer professional to provide what they need.

■ *Increased security:* Although various departments may share data in common, access to specific information can be limited to selected users. Thus, through the use of passwords, a student's financial, medical, and grade information in a university database is made available only to those who have a legitimate need to know.

Although there are clear advantages to having databases, there are still some disadvantages:

■ *Cost issues:* Installing and maintaining a database is expensive, particularly in a large organization. In addition, there are costs associated with training people to use it correctly.

■ *Data vulnerability issues:* Although databases can be structured to restrict access, it's always possible unauthorized users will get past the safeguards. And when they do, they may have access to *all* the files, not just a few. In addition, if a database is destroyed by fire, earthquake, theft, or hardware or software problem, it could be fatal to an organization's business activities—unless steps have been taken to regularly make backup copies of the files and store them elsewhere.

What kind of databases do you think you will use in your planned profession/career?

■ *Privacy issues:* Databases may hold information that they should not and be used for unintended purposes, perhaps intruding on people's privacy. Medical data, for instance, may be used inappropriately in evaluating an employee for a job promotion. (Privacy and other ethical issues are discussed later in this chapter.)

Types of Database Organization

Types of database organization are hierarchical, network, relational, and object-oriented.

Just as files can be organized in different ways (sequentially or directly, for example), so can databases. The four most common arrangements for database management systems are *hierarchical, network, relational,* and *object-oriented.* Except for personal microcomputer databases, the installation and maintenance of each of the four types of databases require a database administrator trained in its structure.

Hierarchical Database

In a **hierarchical database,** fields or records are arranged in related groups resembling a family tree, with lower-level records subordinate to higher-level records. *(See Figure 12.7.)* A lower-level record is called a *child,* and a higher-level record is called a *parent.* The parent record at the top of the database is called the *root record.*

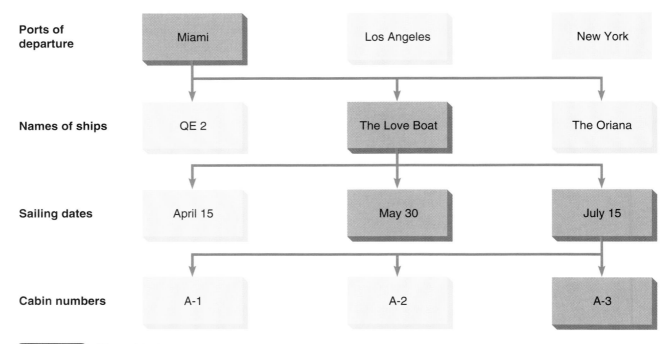

Ports of departure	Miami	Los Angeles	New York
Names of ships	QE 2	The Love Boat	The Oriana
Sailing dates	April 15	May 30	July 15
Cabin numbers	A-1	A-2	A-3

Figure 12.7 Hierarchical database: example of a cruise ship reservation system. Records are arranged in related groups resembling a family tree, with "child" records subordinate to "parent" records. Cabin numbers (A-1, A-2, A-3) are children of the parent July 15. Sailing dates (April 15, May 30, July 15) are children of the parent The Love Boat. The parent at the top, Miami, is called the "root record."

Unlike families in real life, a parent in a hierarchical database may have more than one child, but a child always has only *one* parent. This is called a *one-to-many relationship.* To find a particular record, you have to start at the top with a parent and trace down the chart to the child.

Hierarchical DBMSs are the oldest of the four forms of database organization and are still used in some reservations systems. Accessing or updating data is very fast because the relationships have been predefined. However, because the structure must be defined in advance, it is quite rigid. There may be only one parent per child and no relationships among the child records. Moreover, adding new fields to database records requires that the entire database be redefined.

Network Database

A **network database** is similar to a hierarchical DBMS, but each child record can have more than one parent record. *(See Figure 12.8.)* Thus, a child record, which in network database terminology is called a *member,* may be reached through more than one parent, called an *owner.*

This arrangement is more flexible than the hierarchical one because different relationships may be established between different branches of data. However, it still requires that the structure be defined in advance. Moreover, there are limits to the number of links that can be made among records.

Network and hierarchical databases are commonly used in large computer systems.

Relational Database

More flexible than hierarchical and network database models, the **relational database** relates, or connects, data in different files through the use of a key field, or common data element. *(See Figure 12.9.)* In this arrangement there are no access paths down through a hierarchy. Instead, data elements are stored in different tables made up of rows and columns. In database terminology, the tables are

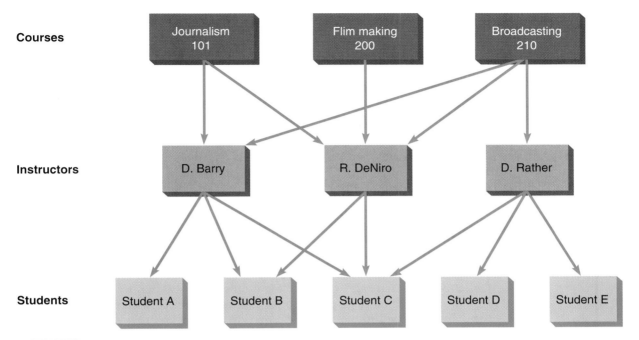

Figure 12.8 Network database: example of a college class scheduling system. This is similar to a hierarchical database, but each child, or "member," record can have more than one parent, or "owner." For example, Student B's owners are instructors D. Barry and R. DeNiro. Owner Broadcasting 210 has three members—D. Barry, R. DeNiro, and D. Rather.

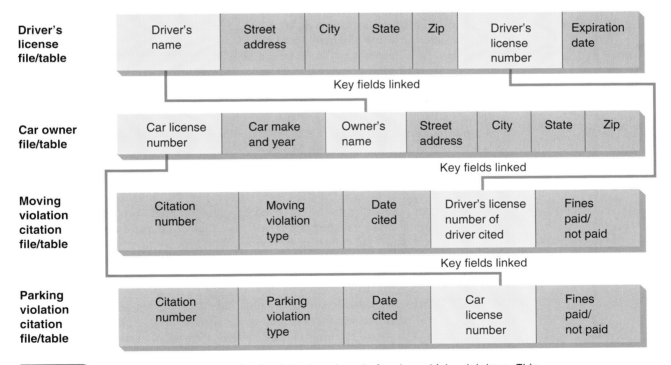

Figure 12.9 Relational database: example of a state department of motor vehicles database. This kind of database relates, or connects, data in different files through the use of a key field, or common data element. The relational database does not require predefined relationships.

called *relations* (files), the rows are called *tuples* (records), and the columns are called *attributes* (fields).

Within a table, a row resembles a record—for example, a car license-plate number, which is one field, and the car owner's name and address, which is another field. All related tables must have a key field that uniquely identifies each row. Thus, another table might have a row consisting of a driver's license number, the key field, and any traffic violations (such as speeding) attributed to the license holder. Another table would have the driver's license number and the bearer's name and address.

The advantage of relational databases is that the user does not have to be aware of any "structure." Thus, they can be used with little training. Moreover, entries can easily be added, deleted, or modified. A disadvantage is that some searches can be time-consuming. Nevertheless, the relational model has become popular for *microcomputer* DBMSs, such as Paradox and Access.

Object-Oriented Database (OODBMS)

Object-oriented databases can handle not only numerical and text data but any type of data, including graphics, audio, and video. Object-oriented databases, then, are important in the new world of video servers and new businesses related to technological convergence and storage of data in multimedia form, such as those that deliver multimedia information through the Web.

In the late 1980s, the graphical user interface (GUI, ✔ p. 5.14) for IBM-type microcomputers, with its support for windows, icons, mouse, and pointers, became increasingly common. Object-oriented programming languages (✔ p. 10.23) are invaluable to the development of GUIs, which further enhanced the popularity of object orientation. As these languages matured, object orientation found its way into the realm of database design.[8]

An **object-oriented database management system (OODBMS)** uses objects (✔ p. 10.23) as elements within database files. An **object** consists of data in the form of (1) text, sound, video, and pictures and (2) instructions (algorithms) on the action to be taken on the data. A hierarchical or network database would contain only numerical and text data about a student—identification number, name, address, and so on. By contrast, an object-oriented database might also contain multimedia—the student's photograph, a "sound bite" of his or her voice, and even a short piece of video. Moreover, the object would store operations, called *methods,* programs that objects use to process themselves—for example, how to calculate the student's grade-point average and how to display or print the student's record. Objects interact by sending messages to one another.

In the data hierarchy discussed at the beginning of this chapter, an object would be approximately at the level of a record, but of course an object contains more types of data than a record, as well as some processing instructions, which a traditional record or tuple does not. (Some relational databases can handle sound, graphics, and video as well as alphanumeric text, but its components do not include processing instructions.)

For a variety of reasons, object-oriented databases are not yet commonly used in more traditional businesses. This type of database is very expensive to develop, and most organizations have millions or billions of bytes of data already organized in relational databases. Thus these companies are unwilling to bear the cost and risk required to convert their databases to an OODBMS format.[9] However, database experts predict that this situation will change in some areas in which the multimedia capabilities of OODBMSs will be of great benefit to users—such as:[10]

■ *Medical information systems:* In addition to text-based data elements, databases could include images such as X rays, CAT scans, and MRI (magnetic resonance imaging) scans, electrocardiogram recordings, and photographs.

■ *Engineering information systems:* Databases could contain blueprints, sketches, diagrams, photos, and illustrations.

■ *Geographic databases:* Maps of all kinds, as well as aerial and satellite photographs, could be stored, coordinated, and analyzed.

■ *Training and education:* These databases could include video clips demonstrating how thing work, how to repair things, how to assemble things, and how to perform certain operations.

Features of a DBMS

Features of a database management system include (1) data dictionary, (2) utilities, (3) query language, (4) report generator, (5) access security, and (6) system recovery.

A database management system may have a number of components, including the following. *(See Figure 12.10.)*

Data Dictionary

Some databases have a **data dictionary,** in itself a small database that stores the data definitions—descriptions of the structure of data used in the database. This includes the name, type, source, and authorization for access for each data element. The data dictionary may monitor the data being entered to make sure it conforms to the rules defined during data definition, such as field name, field size, type of data (text, numeric, date, and so on). It also indicates which application programs use that data so that when a change in data structure is planned, a list of affected programs can be generated.[11]

Utilities

DBMS utilities are programs that allow you to maintain the database by creating, editing, and deleting data, records, and files. The utilities allow you to establish

Figure 12.10 Some important features of a database management system

Component	Description
Data dictionary	Describes files and fields of data
Utilities	Help maintain the database by creating, editing, and monitoring data input
Query language	Enables users to make queries to a database and retrieve selected records
Report generator	Enables nonexperts to create readable, attractive on-screen or hardcopy reports of records
Access security	Specifies user access privileges
Data recover	Enables contents of database to be recovered after system failure

what is acceptable input data, to monitor the types of data being input, and to adjust display screens for data input.

Query Language

Also known as a *data manipulation language,* a **query language** is an easy-to-use computer language for making queries to a database and for retrieving selected records, based on the particular criteria and format indicated. Query languages were developed to provide a user interface to the database that does not require typing in traditional programming commands in a procedural language (✔ p. 10.16). Typically, the query is in the form of a sentence or near-English command, using such basic words as SELECT, DELETE, and MODIFY. There are several different query languages, each with its own vocabulary and procedures. One of the most popular is *Structured Query Language,* or *SQL* (pronounced "see quill").

Originally developed by IBM for its mainframes, SQL is a relational database search standard recognized by the American National Standards Institute. Software designers use this standard to design database query interfaces with which users conduct data searches. Thus SQL is the data access language used by many commercial DBMS products, including ORACLE, SYBASE, dBASE, Paradox, and Microsoft Access.[12] An example of a SQL-based query is as follows:

```
SELECT   PRODUCT-NUMBER, PRODUCT-NAME
FROM     PRODUCT
WHERE    PRICE < 100.00
```

This query selects all records in the PRODUCT file for products that cost less than $100.00 and displays the selected records according to product number and name—for example, like this:

```
A-34      MIRROR
C-50      CHAIR
D-168     TABLE
```

Another popular query language is *query by example,* whereby a user will seek information in a database by describing a procedure for finding it. In query by example (QBE), the user asks for information in a database by using a sample record to define the qualifications he or she wants for selected records.

For example, a university's database of student-loan records of its students all over the United States and the amounts they owe might have the column headings (field names) NAME, ADDRESS, CITY, STATE, ZIP, AMOUNT OWED. When you use the QBE method, the database would display an empty record with these column headings. You would then type in the search conditions that you want in the appropriate columns.

Thus, if you wanted to find all Beverly Hills, California, students with a loan balance due of $3000 or more, you would type *BEVERLY HILLS* under the CITY column, *CA* under the STATE column, and *>=3000* ("greater than or equal to $3000") in the AMOUNT OWED column.

Some newer DBMSs, such as Symantec's Q&A, use natural language (✔ p. 10.17) interfaces, which allow users even more flexibility and convenience in conducting database searches. With this type of interface, users can make queries in the normal form of any spoken language—in this case, English. An example would be "how many sales reps sold more than 1 million dollars of sniglets in South Dakota in January?" This query could be typed in to the computer or, if a voice-recognition system has been installed, simply spoken.

Report Generator

A **report generator** is a program users may employ to produce an on-screen or printed-out document from all or part of a database. You can specify the format of the report in advance—row headings, column headings, page headers, and so on. With a report generator, even nonexperts can create attractive, readable reports on short notice.

Access Security

At one point in the Michael Douglas/Demi Moore movie *Disclosure,* Douglas's character, the beleagured division head suddenly at odds with his company, types SHOW PRIVILEGES into his desktop computer, which is tied to the corporate network. To his consternation, the system responds by showing him downgraded from PRIOR USER LEVEL: 5 to CURRENT USER LEVEL: 0, shutting him out of files to which he formerly had access.

This is an example of the use of *access security,* a feature allowing database administrators to specify different access privileges for different users of a DBMS. For instance, one kind of user might be allowed only to retrieve (view) data whereas another might have the right to update data and delete records. The purpose of this security feature, of course, is to protect the database from unauthorized access and sabotage.

Physical security is also important. *Isolation* is a preventive strategy that involves procedures to insulate the physical database from destruction. For example, one organization keeps backup copies of important databases on removable magnetic disks, stored in a guarded vault. To gain access to the vault, employees need a badge with an encoded personal voice print.[13] Many companies are building total backup computer centers, which contain duplicate databases and documentation.

System Recovery

Database management systems should have *system recovery* features that enable the DBA to recover contents of the database in the event of a hardware or software failure and allow business functions to continue. Performing a recovery may be very difficult. It is impossible to simply fix the problem and resume processing where it was interrupted. Even if no data is lost during a failure (which assumes that all types of memory are nonvolatile [✔ p. 1.11]—an unrealistic assumption), the timing and scheduling of computer processing are too complex to be accurately re-created. It is simply not possible to roll back the clock and put all the electrons in the same configuration they were in at the time of failure. Thus four approaches are possible: *mirroring, reprocessing, rollforward,* and *rollback.*[14]

In database *mirroring,* frequent simultaneous copying of the database is done to maintain two or more complete copies of the database online but in different locations. Mirroring is an expensive backup strategy but is necessary when recovery is needed very quickly, say in seconds or minutes, as with an airline reservation system's database.

In *reprocessing,* the DBA goes back to a known point of database activity (before the failure) and reprocesses the workload from there. To make reprocessing an available option, periodic database copies (called *database saves*) must be made and records kept of all the transactions made since each save. Then, when there is a failure, the database can be restored from the save, and all the transactions made since that save can be re-entered and reprocessed. This type of recovery can be very time-consuming, and the processing of new transactions must be delayed until the database recovery is completed.

Rollforward, also called *forward recovery,* is somewhat similar to reprocessing in that it involves recreating the current database using a previous database state—a recent copy of the database. However, in this case, transactions made since the last save are not re-entered and reprocessed entirely all over again. Instead, the lost data is recovered using a more sophisticated version of a transaction log that contains what are called *after-image records* and that includes some processing information.

Rollback, or *backward recovery,* in contrast, is used to *undo* unwanted changes to the database. This is done, for example, when some failure interrupts a half-completed transaction.

New Approaches: Mining, Warehouses, and "Siftware"

Data mining is the computer-assisted process of sifting through and analyzing vast amounts of data in order to extract meaning and discover new knowledge. The data is then sent to a special database called a *data warehouse.* "Siftware" tools are used to perform data mining.

New approaches are being taken with databases that are almost unimaginably large-scale, involving records of millions of households and thousands of terabytes of data. Some of these activities require the use of so-called *massively parallel database computers* costing $1 million or more. "These machines gang together scores or even hundreds of the fastest microprocessors around," says one description, "giving them the oomph to respond in minutes to complex database queries."[15]

The efforts of which we speak go under the name *data mining.* Let us see what this is.

Data Mining: What It Is, What It's Used For

Data mining (DM), also called *knowledge discovery,* is the computer-assisted process of sifting through and analyzing vast amounts of data in order to extract meaning and discover new knowledge. The purpose of DM is to describe past trends and predict future trends. Although the definition seems simple enough, data mining has overwhelmed traditional query-and-report methods of organizing and analyzing data, such as those previously described in this chapter. The result has been the need for "data warehouses" and for new software tools, as we shall discuss.

Data mining has come about because companies find that, in today's fierce competitive business environment, they need to turn the gazillions of bytes of raw data at their disposal to new uses for further profitability. However, nonprofit institutions have also found DM methods useful, as in the pursuit of scientific and medical discoveries. For example:[16]

■ *Marketing:* Marketers uses DM tools (such as one called Spotlight) to mine point-of-sale databases of retail stores, which contain facts (such as prices, quantities sold, dates of sale) for thousands of products in hundreds of geographic areas. By understanding customer preferences and buying patterns, marketers hope to target consumers' individual needs.

■ *Health:* A coach in the U.S. Gymnastics Federation is using a DM system (called IDIS) to discover what long-term factors contribute to an athlete's performance, so as to know what problems to treat early on. A Los Angeles hospital is using the same tool to see what subtle factors affect success and failure in back surgery. Another system helps health-care organizations pinpoint groups whose costs are likely to increase in the near future, so that medical interventions can be taken.

■ *Science:* DM techniques are being employed to find new patterns in genetic data, molecular structures, global climate changes, and more. For instance, one DM tool (called SKICAT) is being used to catalog more than 50 million galaxies, which will be reduced to a 3-terabye galaxy catalog.

Clearly, short-term payoffs can be dramatic. One telephone company, for instance, mined its existing billing data to identify 10,000 supposedly "residential" customers who spent more than $1000 a month on their phone bills. When it looked more closely, the company found these customers were really small businesses trying to avoid paying the more expensive business rates for their telephone service.[17]

However, the payoffs in the long term could be truly astonishing. Sifting medical-research data or subatomic-particle information may reveal new treatments for diseases or new insights into the nature of the universe.[18]

Preparing Data for the Data Warehouse

The data mining begins with acquiring data and preparing it for what is known as the "data warehouse." *(See Figure 12.11.)* This takes the following steps.

1. *Data sources:* Data may come from a number of sources: (1) point-of-sale transactions in files (flat files) managed by file management systems on mainframes, (2) databases of all kinds, and (3) other—for example, news articles transmitted over news wires or online sources such as the Internet. To the mix may also be added (4) data from existing data warehouses.

2. *Data fusion and cleansing:* Data from diverse sources, whether from inside the company (internal data) or purchased from outside the company (external data), must be fused together, then put through a process known as *data cleansing* or *scrubbing.*

   Even if the data comes from just one source, such as the company's mainframe, the data may be of poor quality, full of errors and inconsistencies. Therefore, for data mining to produce accurate results, the source data has to be *"scrubbed"*—that is, cleaned of errors and checked for consistency of formats.

3. *Data and meta-data:* Out of the cleansing process come both the cleaned-up data and a variation of it called *meta-data.* Meta-data shows the origins of the data, the transformations it has undergone, and summary information about it, which makes it more useful than the unintegrated, unsummarized data. The meta-data also describes the contents of the data warehouse.

4. *The data warehouse:* Both the data and the meta-data are sent to the data warehouse. A *data warehouse* is a special database of cleaned-up data and meta-data. It is a replica, or close reproduction, of a mainframe's data. The data warehouse is stored using disk storage technology such as RAID

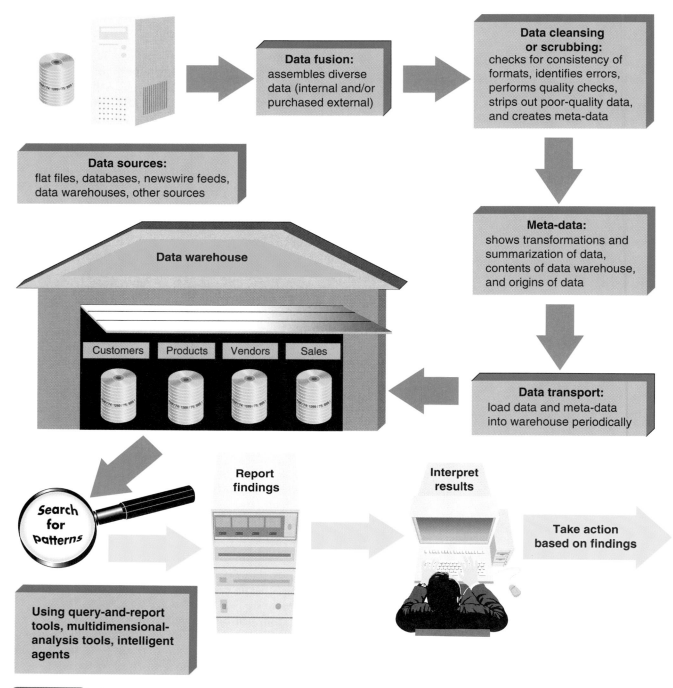

Figure 12.11 The data-mining process

(redundant arrays of independent disks, ✔ p. 4.18). Small data warehouses may hold 100 gigabytes of data or less. Once 500 gigabytes are reached, *massively parallel processing (MPP)* computers (✔ p. 2.12) are needed. Projections call for large data warehouses holding hundreds of terabytes fairly soon. Data warehouses commonly support organizations' decision support systems and executive information systems (✔ p. 11.16).

"Siftware" for Finding and Analyzing

Three kinds of software, or "siftware," tools are used to perform data mining—that is, to do finding and analyzing tasks. They are *query-and-reporting tools, multidimensional-analysis (MDA) tools,* and *intelligent agents.*[19]

▪ *Query-and-reporting tools: Query-and-reporting tools* (examples are Focus Reporter and Esperant) require a database structure and work well with relational databases. They may have graphical interfaces. Their best use is for specific questions to verify hypotheses.

　　For example, if a company decides to mine its database to find customers most likely to respond to a mail-order promotion, it might use a query-and-reporting tool and construct a query (using SQL): "How many credit-card customers who made purchases of over $100 on sporting goods in August have at least $2000 of available credit?"[20]

▪ *Multidimensional-analysis tools: Multidimensional-analysis (MDA) tools* (examples are Essbase and Lightship) can do "data surfing" to explore all dimensions of a particular subset of data. In one writer's example, "The idea [with MDA] is to load a multidimensional server with data that is likely to be combined. Imagine all the possible ways of analyzing clothing sales: by brand name, size, color, location, advertising, and so on."[21] Using MDA tools, you can analyze this multidimensional database from all points of view.

▪ *Intelligent agents:* An *intelligent agent* is a computer program that roams through networks performing complex work tasks for people. There are several kinds of intelligent agents, such as those used to prioritize e-mail messages for individuals. However, the kind we are concerned with here (such as DataEngine and Data/Logic) are those used as data-mining tools.

　　Intelligent agents are best used for turning up unsuspected relationships and patterns. "These patterns may be so nonobvious as to appear almost nonsensical," says one writer, "such as that people who have bought scuba gear are good candidates for taking Australian vacations."[22]

Is data about you finding its way into data warehouses? No doubt it is. Gathering data isn't difficult. You participate in probably hundreds of transactions a year, recorded in point-of-sale terminals (✔ p. 3.34), teller machines, credit-card files, and 1-800 telemarketing responses. Sooner or later, some of the records of your past activities will be used, most likely by marketing companies, to try to influence you.

The Ethics of Using Databases: Concerns About Accuracy and Privacy

Databases may contain inaccuracies or be incomplete. They also may endanger privacy—in the areas of finances, health, employment, and commerce.

"The corrections move by bicycle while the stories move at the speed of light," says Richard Lamm, a former governor of Colorado.

　　Lamm was lamenting that he was quoted out of context by a Denver newspaper in a speech he made in 1994. Yet even years afterward—long after the paper had run a correction—he still saw the error repeated in later newspaper articles.[23]

How do such mistakes get perpetuated? The answer, suggests journalist Christopher Feola, is the Misinformation Explosion. "Fueled by the growing popularity of both commercial and in-house computerized news databases," he says, "journalists have found it that much easier to repeat errors or rely on the same tired anecdotes and experts."[24]

If news reporters—who are supposed to be trained in careful handling of the facts—can continue to repeat inaccuracies found in databases, what about those without training who have access to computerized facts? How can you be sure that databases with essential information about you—medical, credit, school, employment, and so on—are accurate and, equally important, are secure in guarding your privacy? We examine the topics of *accuracy and completeness* and of *privacy* in this section.

Matters of Accuracy and Completeness

Databases—including public databases such as Nexis, Lexis, Dialog, and Dow Jones News/Retrieval—can provide you with *more* facts and *faster* facts but not always *better* facts. Penny Williams, professor of broadcast journalism at Buffalo State College in New York and formerly a television anchor and reporter, suggests there are five limitations to bear in mind when using databases for research:[25]

■ *You can't get the whole story:* For some purposes, databases are only a foot in the door. There may be many facts or aspects to the topic you are looking into that are not in a database. Reporters, for instance, find a database is a starting point, but it may take old-fashioned shoe leather to get the rest of the story.

■ *It's not the gospel:* Just because you see something on a computer screen doesn't mean it's accurate. Numbers, names, and facts may need to be verified in other ways.

■ *Know the boundaries:* One database service doesn't have it all. For example, you can find full text articles from the *New York Times* on Lexis/Nexis, from the *Wall Street Journal* on Dow Jones News/Retrieval, and from the *San Jose Mercury News* on America Online, but no service carries all three.

■ *Find the right words:* You have to know which key words (search words) to use when searching a database for a topic. As Lynn Davis, a professional researcher with ABC News, points out, in searching for stories on guns the key word "can be guns, it can be firearms, it can be handguns, it can be pistols, it can be assault weapons. If you don't cover your bases, you might miss something."[26]

■ *History is limited:* Most public databases, Davis says, have information going back to 1980, and a few into the 1970s, but this poses problems if you're trying to research something that happened or was written about earlier.

Matters of Privacy

Privacy is the right of people to not reveal information about themselves. Who you vote for in a voting booth and what you say in a letter sent through the U.S. mail are private matters. However, the ease with which databases and communications lines may pull together and disseminate information has put privacy under extreme pressure.

As you've no doubt discovered, it's no trick at all to get your name on all kinds of mailing lists. Theo Theoklitas, for instance, has received applications for credit cards, invitations to join video clubs, and notification of his finalist status in Ed McMahon's $10 million sweepstakes. Theo is a 6-year-old black cat who's been getting mail ever since his owner sent in an application for a rebate on cat food.[27] A whole industry has grown up of professional information gatherers and sellers, who collect personal data and sell it to fund-raisers, direct marketers, and others.

How easy is it to find out about you or anyone else? Using his home computer, journalist Jeffrey Rothfeder once obtained Dan Quayle's credit report. (He bought his clothes mainly at Sears.) All Rothfeder had to do was pay an information seller $50 and type in the former vice president's name. He also found out from another data seller where anchorman Dan Rather shops. "This seller warmed to me quickly," Rothfeder said. "As a bonus, I was sent Vanna White's home phone number for free."[28] In an even worse case of invasion of privacy, a California man, obsessed with a woman he had once known, was able to hatch intricate schemes of harassment—from within a maximum-security prison. He filed post office change-of-address forms so her mail was forwarded to him in prison and obtained a credit report on her. He even sent the IRS forged power-of-attorney forms so he could get her tax returns.[29]

In the 1970s, the U.S. Department of Health, Education, and Welfare developed a set of five Fair Information Practices. These rules have since been adopted by a number of public and private organizations. The practices also led to the enactment of a number of laws to protect individuals from invasion of privacy. Perhaps the most important law is the Federal Privacy Act, or Privacy Act of 1974. The *Privacy Act of 1974* prohibits secret personnel files from being kept on individuals by government agencies or their contractors. It gives individuals the right to see their records, to see how the data is used, and to correct errors. Another significant piece of legislation was the Freedom of Information Act, passed in 1970. The *Freedom of Information Act* allows ordinary citizens to have access to data gathered about them by federal agencies. Most privacy laws regulate only the behavior of government agencies or government contractors. For example, the *Computer Matching and Privacy Protection Act* of 1988 prevents the government from comparing certain records to try to find a match. This law does not affect most private companies.

Of particular concern for privacy are the areas of finances, health, employment, commerce, and communications:

■ *Finances:* Banking and credit are two private industries for which there are federal privacy laws on the books. The *Fair Credit Reporting Act of 1970* allows you to have access to and gives you the right to challenge your credit records. If you have been denied credit, this access must be given to you free of charge. The *Right to Financial Privacy Act of 1978* sets restrictions on federal agencies that want to search customer records in banks.

In the past, credit bureaus have been severely criticized for disseminating errors and for having reports that were difficult for ordinary readers to understand. Although it may still not be easy to clear up a mistake, the industry has a dispute-resolution process that should make dealing with them less complicated. The major credit bureaus are Experian, Equifax, and Trans Union.

■ *Health:* No federal laws protect medical records in the United States (except those related to treatment for drug and alcohol abuse and psychiatric care, or records in the custody of the federal government). Of course, insurance companies can get a look at your medical data, but so can others that you might not suspect. Getting a divorce or suing an employer for wrongful dismissal? A lawyer might subpoena your medical records in hopes of using, say, a drinking problem or medical care for depression against you. When employers have information about personal health, they often use them in making employment-related decisions, according to one study.[30]

Your best strategy is to not routinely fill out medical questionnaires or histories. You should also not tell any business more than it needs to know about your health. You can ask your doctor to release only the minimum amount of information that can be released. Finally, ask for a copy of your medical records if you have doubts about the information your doctor or hospital has on you.[31]

■ *Employment:* Private employers are the least regulated by privacy legislation. If you apply for a job, for instance, a background-checking service may verify your educational background and employment history. It may also take a look at your credit, driving violations, workers' compensation claims, and criminal record if any.

Cellular phones, global positioning systems, and "active badges" (clip-on ID cards readable by infrared sensors throughout a building) can tell your employer where you are. Software that counts keystrokes or tracks sales can monitor your productivity. E-mail memos may be read not only by the recipient but perhaps by your boss, if company policy allows.

■ *Commerce:* As we've seen, marketers of all kinds would like to get to know you. For example, Virginia Sullivan, a retired school teacher, weighed the junk mail she received every month. She found after 11 months that she had received about 98 pounds' worth. Sullivan also noticed that the junk mail companies seemed to know personal details of her private life, such as her age, buying habits, and favorite charities.

"We constantly betray secrets about ourselves," says Erik Larson, author of *The Naked Consumer,* "and these secrets are systematically collected by the marketers' intelligence network."[32] Larson has a number of suggestions for avoiding putting yourself on mailing lists in the first place.

With few exceptions, the law does not prohibit companies from gathering information about you for one purpose and using it without your permission for another.[33] This information is culled from both public information sources, such as driver's license records, and commercial transactions, such as warranty cards. One exception is the Video Privacy Protection Act of 1988. The *Video Privacy Protection Act* prevents retailers from disclosing a person's video rental records without their consent or a court order.

"Somewhere along the way," Larson points out, "the data keepers made the arbitrary decision that everyone is automatically on their lists unless they ask to be taken off."[34] Why not have a law that keeps consumers off all lists unless they ask to be included? Congress has considered this approach, but lobbyists for direct marketing companies object that it would put them out of business.[35]

Privacy concerns don't stop with the use or misuse of information in databases; it also extends to privacy in communications. Although the government is constrained by several laws on acquiring and disseminating information, and listening in on private conversations, privacy advocates still worry. In recent times, the government has tried to impose new technologies that would enable law-enforcement agents to gather a wealth of personal information. Proponents have urged that Americans must be willing to give up some personal privacy in exchange for safety and security. We discuss this matter in Chapter 14.

What are your biggest concerns regarding your own privacy and the use of databases?

Information Brokering, Philanthropy, Job Hunting

Information Brokering

When Cynthia Schoenbrun was laid off as a research administrator from a computer software company, she found something even better. She used her own personal computer to link up with people she knew in Russia and become part of a new field known as *information brokering.*

What is an information broker? "Part librarian, part private eye, and part computer nerd," one writer explains, "an information broker searches for everything written and published on a given subject, be it an obscure corner of the biomedical market or the whereabouts of a German engineering expert."[36] Schoenbrun, for instance, searches computer databases and her network of contacts to find business and investment information about Russia and other former countries of the Soviet Union. She then sells this information to clients.

The majority of information brokers, who are mainly in one- or two-person firms, are people who have seen a chance to own a business without making a heavy investment. Among other advantages, the profession gives people a lot of flexibility in setting their own hours.

One need not become an information broker, however, to benefit from being able to search a database. Doctors, lawyers, and other professionals are turning to databases in order to keep up with the information explosion within their fields. In the new world of computers and communications, everyone should at least know the rudiments of this skill.

Philanthropy[37]

Each December in Yellow Springs, Ohio, sacks of sugar and flour are distributed to all widows living there. The tradition started in 1894, when Wheeling Gaunt, a former slave, bequeathed 9 acres of land to the village with the stipulation that the "poor worthy widows" in town be given 25 pounds of flour every Christmas. Yellow Springs was a stop on the Underground Railroad that helped Mr. Gaunt find freedom in the North.

Further back than anyone can remember, the village council ruled that all local widows should receive the gift, lest there be any embarrassment over who was poor and who was worthy. In the 1950s, the council changed the allotment to 10 pounds of flour and 10 pounds of sugar. . . . Other than that, the tradition has continued, unabated, for more than a century.

This year, 110 widows are on the list. "We call ahead to make sure they're home," says John Campbell, who has served on the public-works crew that makes the deliveries. It's not a bad assignment, says village administrative assistant Lina Verdon, since many widows later thank the crew with home-baked cookies. . . .

Ms. Verdon keeps a database of widows, updating it by reading obituaries in the local newspaper and by word of mouth. "This is a small enough town," she says, "so we maintain an up-to-date list."

Job Hunting

Several organizations maintain job-related databases accessible via the Internet and the Web. The databases are designed to help people match their talents and education with job opportunities. Here are a few:

■ The Business Job Finder (*http://www.cob.ohio-state.edu/dept/fin/osujobs.htm*)—Designed to help recent college graduates get started on careers in the business world.

■ Chancellor and Chancellor, Inc. (*http://www.chancellor.com*)—A brokerage firm offering placement services for computer technology professionals.

■ Dick Williams and Associates (*http://www.netrep.com/home/dwa*)—Specializes in high-technology recruiting.

■ Casting Online (*http://hookomo.aloha.net/wrap/*)—One-stop cybercasting site for the performing arts industry.

You can find other sites by using Web search engines such as Yahoo!, Lycos, InfoSeek, and Magellan. Try keywords (✔ p. 8.26) such as "careers," "jobs," "employment," and "resumes."

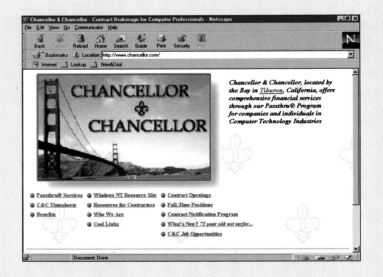

WHAT IT IS
WHAT IT DOES

WHY IT IS IMPORTANT

batch processing (LO 3, p. 12.8) Method of processing whereby data is collected over several days or weeks and then processed all at one time, as a "batch."

With batch processing, if users need to make a request of the system, they must wait until the batch has been processed. Batch processing is less expensive than online processing and is suitable for work in which immediate answers to queries are not needed.

character (LO 2, p. 12.6) May be—but is not necessarily—the same as a byte (8 bits); a single letter, number, or special character such as ; or $, or %.

Characters (bytes) are at the lowest level of the data hierarchy.

data dictionary (LO 6, p. 12.17) Small database that stores data definitions and descriptions of database structure. It also monitors new entries to the database as well as user access to the database.

The data dictionary monitors the data being entered to make sure it conforms to the rules defined during data definition. The data dictionary may also help protect the security of the database by indicating who has the right to gain access to it.

data file (LO 3, p. 12.8) File that contains data.

This term is used to differentiate data files from program files.

data storage hierarchy (LO 2, p. 12.6) Defines the levels of data stored in a computer database; bits, bytes, fields, records, and files.

Bits and bytes are what the computer hardware deals with, so users need not be concerned with them. They will, however, deal with characters, fields, records, files, and databases.

database (LO 2, p. 12.7) Collection of related files in a computer system.

Business and organizations build databases to help them keep track of and manage their affairs. In addition, users with online connections to database services have enormous research resources at their disposal.

database management system (DBMS) (LO 5, p. 12.12) Also called *database manager;* software that controls the structure of a database and access to the data. It allows users to manipulate more than one file at a time (as opposed to file managers).

This software enables: sharing of data (same information is available to different users); economy of files (several departments can use one file instead of each individually maintaining its own files, thus reducing data redundancy, which in turn reduces the expense of storage media and hardware); data integrity (changes made in the files in other departments); security (access to specific information can be limited to selected users).

DBMS utilities (LO 6, p. 12.17)   Programs that allow the maintenance of databases by creating, editing, and deleting data, records, and files.

DBMS utilities allow people to establish what is acceptable input data, to monitor the types of data being input, and to adjust display screens for data input.

distributed database (LO 1, p. 12.5)   Geographically dispersed database (located in more than one physical location). Users are connected to it through a client-server network.

Data need not be centralized in one location.

field (LO 2, p. 12.6)   Unit of data consisting of one or more characters (bytes). An example of a field is your name, your date of birth, or your Social Security number.

A collection of fields make up a record. Also see *key field.*

file (LO 2, p. 12.6)   Collection of related records.

A collection of related files makes up a database.

file management system (LO 5, p. 12.10)   Also called *file manager;* software for creating, retrieving, and manipulating files, one file at a time.

In the 1950s, magnetic tape was the storage medium and records and files were stored sequentially. File managers were created to work with these files. Today, however, database managers are more common.

hierarchical database (LO 6, p. 12.13)   Oldest one of four common arrangements for database management systems; fields or records are arranged in related groups resembling a family tree, with "child" records subordinate to "parent" records. A parent may have more than one child, but a child always has only one parent. To find a particular record, one starts at the top with a parent and traces down the chart to the child.

Hierarchical DBMSs work well when the data elements have an intrinsic one-to-many relationship, as might happen with a reservations system. The difficulty, however, is that the structure must be defined in advanced and is quite rigid.

key field (LO 2, p. 12.7)   Field that contains unique data used to identify a record so that it can be easily retrieved and processed. The key field is often an identification number, Social Security number, customer account number, or the like. The primary characteristic of the key field is that it is *unique.*

Key fields are needed to identify and retrieve specific records in a database.

master file (LO 3, p. 12.8)   Data file containing relatively permanent records that are generally updated periodically.

Master files contain relatively permanent information used for reference purposes. Master files are updated through the use of transaction files.

network database (LO 6, p. 12.14)   One of four common arrangements for database management systems; it is similar to a hierarchical DBMS, but each child record can have more than one parent record. Thus, a child record may be reached through more than one parent.

This arrangement is more flexible than the hierarchical one. However, it still requires that the structure be defined in advance. Moreover, there are limits to the number of links that can be made among records.

object (LO 6, p. 12.16)   In an OODBMS, consists of data in the form of (1) text, sound, video, and pictures and (2) instructions (algorithms) on the action to be taken on the data.

See *object-oriented database management system.*

object-oriented database management system (OODBMS) (LO 6, p. 12.16)   Database structure that uses objects as elements within database files. An object consists of (1) text, sound, video, and pictures and (2) instructions on the action to be taken on the data.

In addition to textual data, an object-oriented database can store, for example, a person's photo, "sound bites" of her voice, and a video clip.

offline storage (LO 3, p. 12.9)   Refers to data that is not directly accessible for processing until a tape or disk has been loaded onto an input device.

The storage medium and data are not under the immediate, direct control of the central processing unit.

online processing (LO 3, p. 12.9)   Also called *real-time processing;* means entering transactions into a computer system as they take place and updating the master files as the transactions occur; requires direct access storage.

Online processing gives users accurate information from an ATM machine or an airline reservations system, for example.

online storage (LO 3, p. 12.9)   Refers to stored data that is directly accessible for processing.

Storage is under the immediate, direct control of the central processing unit; users need not wait for a tape or disk to be loaded onto an input device before they can access stored data.

program file (LO 3, p. 12.8)   File containing software instructions.

This term is used to differentiate program files from data files.

query language (LO 6, p. 12.18)   Easy-to-use computer language for making queries to a database and retrieving selected records.

Query languages make it easier for users to deal with databases.

record (LO 2, p. 12.6)   Collection of related fields. An example of a record would be your name *and* date of birth *and* Social Security number.

Related records make up a file.

relational database (LO 6, p. 12.14)   One of four common arrangements for database management systems; relates, or connects, data in different files through the use of a key field, or common data element. In this arrangement there are no access paths down through a hierarchy. Instead, data elements are stored in different tables made up of rows are called *tuples,* and the columns are called *attributes.* Within a table, a row resembles a record. All related tables must have a key field that uniquely identifies each row.

A relational database is more flexible than hierarchical or network databases. The advantage of relational databases is that the user does not have to be aware of any "structure." Thus, they can be used with little training. Moreover, entries can easily be added, deleted, or modified. A disadvantage is that some searches can be time-consuming. Nevertheless, the relational model has become popular for microcomputer DBMSs.

report generator (LO 6, p. 12.19)   Program that database management program users can employ to produce on-screen or printed-out documents from all or part of a database.

Report generators allow users to produce finished-looking reports without much fuss.

shared database (LO 1, p. 12.5)   Database shared by users in one company or organization in one location.

Shared databases give all users in one organization access to the same information.

transaction file (LO 3, p. 12.8)   Temporary data file that holds all changes to be made to the master file: additions, deletions, revisions.

The transaction file is used to periodically update the master file.

1. According to the data storage hierarchy, databases are composed of:

   a. _____   d. _____

   b. _____   e. _____

   c. _____

2. An individual piece of data within a record is called a(n) _____.

3. A special file in the DBMS called the _____ _____ maintains descriptions of the structure of data used in the database.

4. A(n) _____ is a collection of related files that are created and managed by a _____ management system.

5. A(n) _____ _____ coordinates all related activities and needs for an organization's database.

1. What is the difference between batch and online processing?

2. What are the main disadvantages of traditional file management systems?

3. What is a query language?

4. What is meant by the term *data mining*?

1. Which of the following is a disadvantage of database management systems?
   a. cost issues
   b. data redundancy
   c. lack of program independence
   d. lack of data integrity
   e. all the above

2. Which of the following database organizations should you choose if you need to store photos along with methods for processing them?
   a. hierarchy
   b. network
   c. relational
   d. object-oriented
   e. none of the above

3. In the event of a hardware or software failure, which of the following approaches might you use to recover lost data?
   a. mirroring
   b. reprocessing
   c. rollforward
   d. rollback
   e. all the above

CHAPTER 13

TRENDS IN COMPUTING

Multimedia and Developments in Information Technology

PREVIEW

When you have completed this chapter, you will be able to:

1. Discuss current and future applications for multimedia

2. Define artificial intelligence and give a few examples of how it is used

3. Describe how robots are used

4. Define natural language and fuzzy logic

5. Describe what an expert system is

6. Explain what neural networks and genetic algorithms are

7. Explain what the Turing test is

8. Define virtual reality and describe a few of its applications

9. Explain what intelligent agents, avatars, and information filtering are used for

WHY IS THIS CHAPTER IMPORTANT?

Few inventions have changed the world as profoundly—and rapidly—as the microprocessor, born at Intel Corporation in November 1971. Today the world's chip population has swollen to 350 billion, including 15 billion microprocessors.[1] That's more than two silicon brains for every person on earth[2]—and as profound as the changes have been that they have caused, the silicon age is just dawning.

Experts predict that by 2011, one chip will be crammed with the power of 250 Pentium Pros.[3] The implications of such power growth are staggering. Perhaps we will have autonomously intelligent machines: tell them what to do, and they'll figure out how to do it. Multimedia will be combined with virtual reality to create environments that *become* reality. These technologies represent a few of the cutting-edge aspects of computerization, the topic of this chapter. How do you think *you* will be using computers in 2011?

Multimedia as Part of Your World

Although the applications for desktop multimedia are numerous, three distinct areas have made the industry worth billions of dollars annually. This section describes the primary uses of multimedia in business, education, and entertainment and the steps in creating multimedia for each of these fields.

In the chapters on processing, input, output, storage, and software, we discussed the system requirements for users wishing to take advantage of multimedia offerings. In the following sections we review some of that information and go into more detail about what people are using multimedia for, and how they create it.

Business and Industry

The increased use of multimedia technology by corporate America can be largely attributed to easy-to-use presentation software (✔ p. 6.15) like Microsoft Power-Point. Together with decreasing costs for presentation hardware, such as LCD projection panels and notebook computers, this software lets novice computer users design and build professional-looking on-screen presentations in less time than it would take to print overhead acetates. With more advanced multimedia authoring software, corporations are creating in-house advertising and promotional programs for display using kiosks at trade shows and during product

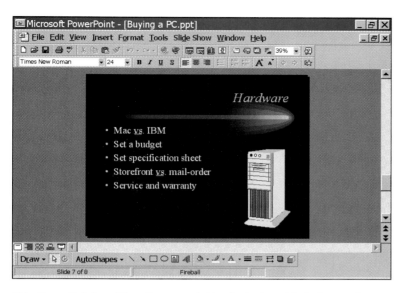

This PowerPoint multimedia presentation is designed to help people choose computer hardware.

demonstrations. (A **kiosk** is a small, self-contained structure such as a newsstand or a ticket booth, designed to serve a large number of people. Unattended multimedia kiosks dispense information via computer screens. Keyboards and touch screens are used for input.) Other common uses for multimedia in business include interactive product catalogs, annual reports, safety manuals, employee handbooks, and electronic performance support systems (EPSS).

Education and Training

The education and training industry is by far the most active area in multimedia. The benefits of multimedia technology in providing flexibility for students and in enhancing learning are well documented. Most people agree that "learners retain about 20% of what they hear; 40% of what they see and hear; and 75% of what they see, hear, and do."[4] For younger children, multimedia programs provide teachers with an exciting new tool for stimulating class discussions, conducting student research, and promoting teamwork. For older learners, the interactive nature of multimedia promotes active participation and affords user control over the pace and flow of delivery. Educational multimedia, also called *courseware,* allows adult learners to determine when and where they want to access training, whether at home, work, or school. Other multimedia resources related to education include multimedia reference material, electronic textbooks and course supplements, online lecture notes, interactive testing, and virtual simulations.

Kiosks at a computer technology show dispense product information to attendees.

Entertainment and Games

Although educational courseware is the most established multimedia product, the entertainment and games industry has provided the greatest examples of commercial success. Software development companies such as Electronic Arts and Id Software have achieved huge financial returns and recognition for games like *Doom, 7th Guest,* and *Myst.* Multimedia CD-ROMs in glossy packaging are now commonplace on the shelves of your local software store. But aside from these video-arcade-like programs, there are several excellent educational/entertainment (edutainment) titles available. The Random House/Broderbund Living Book series produces such

Many multimedia titles exist for children, such as this learn-to-read program.

popular children's titles as *Arthur's Teacher Trouble, Just Grandma and Me,* and *The Tortoise and the Hare.* Not only do these titles help children learn to read, they promote computer literacy at a very young age.

The Multimedia Computer

Shopping for a new computer is one of those enlightening experiences that you can complain about to your friends. In 1993, most multimedia computer systems were sold in pieces that you had to assemble yourself on the living room floor. Today, thankfully, almost every retail computer system that is sold is multimedia-capable. To help consumers identify a minimum system configuration for playing back multimedia on Intel-based and similar computers, the Multimedia PC Marketing Council publishes a set of minimum standards known as **MPC classifications.** The *minimum* MPC Level 3 standard, for example, recommends the following hardware:

1. Pentium (or equivalent) 75 MHz CPU
2. 8 MB of RAM
3. 540 MB hard disk
4. 3.5-inch, high-density floppy disk drive
5. 4X CD-ROM drive with 600 Kbps data transfer
6. 16-bit wavetable sound card with MIDI playback and speakers
7. VGA graphics card with 8-bit (256) colors
8. MPEG video playback
9. 101-key keyboard and two-button mouse
10. I/O ports for MIDI, serial, parallel, and joystick

The precise equipment that you need for multimedia will depend on your level of involvement. To experiment with the technology, you need only purchase a personal computer capable of playing back multimedia. Creating multimedia content requires a more advanced system configuration. You will require specialized input hardware devices, such as a flatbed scanner and video capture card, to create the individual media elements. To output a completed production to CD-ROM requires that you have access to a removable storage device (to send to a service bureau for mastering a CD) or your own CD-ROM recordable unit.

> What subjects are you studying now that you think would be easier to learn through the use of multimedia?

Creating Multimedia

Development of multimedia is a complex process, and not many of us will become deeply involved in it. However, to give you an idea of what that process is like, the following pages give you a brief overview.

The multimedia production process, similar to video and film production, consists of the following stages: pre-production, production, and post-production. In the *pre-production* stage, the program objectives, design, and details are worked out through audience analysis, script writing, and storyboarding (visually mapping out the sequence of and links among information on bulletin-type boards). *Production* entails gathering content, either by acquiring another's content through copyright and licensing arrangements or by creating your own media elements. *Post-production* is the process by which the media elements are combined to meet the overall design and program objectives.

Within these stages, there are nine specific steps that you should complete from start to finish.

1. *Develop the project specification,* which includes the statement of purpose, audience analysis, concept treatment, and content requirements.

2. *Plan and budget your production,* which results in a production calendar, resource schedule, financial budget, and summary of equipment and staff requirements.

3. *Prepare a treatment and storyboard,* which provides a written script and visual outline for the entire production.

4. *Design the user interface* to finalize the look and feel of the production.

5. *Prepare a prototype or working model,* which lets you test interface features, concept implementations, and audience assumptions.

6. *Acquire the content* by converting, purchasing, or producing media elements.

7. *Author and program* the title (the project being created) to assemble the media elements and build in interactivity.

8. *Test and evaluate* the title to ensure consistency, accuracy, and audience acceptance.

9. *Prepare the title for distribution,* which typically results in a CD-ROM master complete with an installation or setup program and user documentation.

Acquiring Content

Let's review our definition of multimedia: *multimedia* is any combination of text, images, illustrations, animation, sound, and video for the purpose of communicating information electronically. Therein lie the media elements to be considered when assembling a multimedia production. In the simplest terms, you have three choices for acquiring media: *convert, purchase,* or *produce.* Since multimedia titles are often derived from existing print materials or video programs, you can use a scanner, video capture card, or other hardware device to convert media to a digital form. Before doing so, however, ensure that you have written permission to manipulate and use the material that you want to convert. If you decide to purchase the content from a professional media service, you will spend most of your time browsing image catalogs and sound libraries, not to mention reading copyright and licensing statements. If you decide to produce original content, you must then determine whether to create it yourself or hire a writer, artist, animator, musician, or video producer. Although it can be expensive to hire a professional, creating your own media gives you complete control over the production quality, copyright, and deliverables.

In larger multimedia productions, the producer will establish a database management system to catalog and track the digitized media elements. This database will typically contain the following information for each element:

- File name and version control number

- Description of contents, usage, and location in the final production

- File format and specifications, such as color-depth, resolution, track length, or sampling rate (✔ p. 3.16)

- Copyright, licensing, and royalty information, if required

- Media service vendor's name and address, if required

- Author, developer, or person responsible for acquiring the media

This media database is an extremely important resource that is shared among all team members. It allows the producer (and peers) to manage the deadlines and deliverables for media content production. Because the database is centrally located on a networked file server, the entire library of media elements can be backed up regularly for safekeeping. Furthermore, the database provides an excellent reusable resource for new productions. (This database is likely to be an object-oriented database management system—OODBMS, ✔ p. 12.16.)

Text

Text is the primary media element for communicating information in a multimedia production. However, people do not enjoy reading from the computer screen. Therefore, you must make text more appealing by limiting passages to less than 40 words, selecting easy-to-read typefaces, and "erring" on the side of a larger-sized font. Also, ensure that you proofread your on-screen text very carefully to avoid grammatical and spelling mistakes. Most authoring software tools allow you to enter text directly, import text from an editor or word processor, or scan text using a scanner and optical character recognition (OCR) software.

Graphics

There are two types of graphics that you normally include in a multimedia production. *Draw, or vector-based, graphics* (✔ p. 6.38) are created using an illustration program, such as Adobe Illustrator or CorelDRAW. Vector graphics are stored as a set of instructions for drawing lines on an invisible screen grid. These files are much smaller than bit-mapped graphics, but they cannot reproduce the quality necessary for displaying photo-realistic images. *Bit-mapped, or raster-based, graphics* (✔ p. 6.38) are created by scanning images and using paint programs, such as Adobe Photoshop or Paint Shop Pro. A bit-mapped image can contain millions of pixels (✔ p. 3.27), which is the smallest unit a computer can display on a monitor. These pixels contain color information that must travel from the storage medium (hard disk or CD-ROM) through memory to the processor, back to memory, and finally to the video card. The larger or more colorful the bit-mapped image, the more storage space is required, and the longer it takes to display on the screen.

Sound

Audio is often the forgotten element in a multimedia production. We get so distracted with the appearance of the screens that we forget to set the ambience and tone using background music, sound effects, and voice narration. Used effectively, sound can enhance the audience's enjoyment of your production. Used ineffectively, sound can elicit reactions opposite to those desired and distract focus from other, more important content.

Using the sound card in a computer, you record sounds by performing a process called *sampling.* Sampling lets you determine how much information you want to digitize or capture, which also directly affects the file size once the

SAMPLING FREQUENCY RATE			
Bits/Sample	**11.025 kHz**	**22.05kHz**	**44.1 kHz**
8 bits	Lowest quality	Good quality	Very good quality
16 bits	Good quality	Very good quality	Excellent quality

recorded information is saved to a disk. The higher the rate of sampling, the more information must be stored, and the higher the quality of the recorded sound. (For example, a sampling rate of 44.1 kHz means that 44,100 samples are taken every second. If each sample contains 16 bits of information, a sound file can become very large very fast.) Most audio-editing software tools let you record at radio-quality (best for voice narration) or at CD-quality (best for audio recording.) For commercial multimedia productions, hire a musician to produce original MIDI (Musical Instrument Digital Interface, ✔ p. 3.16) compositions for your background music and then purchase a sound effects CD-ROM library from a professional media service.

Animation

Animation in a multimedia production can be as simple as an icon bouncing around the screen or as complex as a virtual walkthrough of ancient Greece. Most authoring tools let you animate drawn and text objects, but you will need animation software, such as Autodesk's Animator Pro or LightWave 3D, for more complex sequences. Animation software can produce either a digitized movie file or a series of bit-mapped images that you can later assemble like a *flipbook* (a book that contains a gradually changing image over a series of pages). You create animation similarly to creating a bit-mapped graphic, using a scanner and paint software. Because this is an extremely detail-oriented and time-consuming process, multimedia producers commonly hire a professional animator or contract out their requirements.

Video

Video is an exciting component of multimedia. To retain the attention of your audience, nothing seems to be more effective than sound and motion. In the past few years, digital video on the personal computer has exploded in popularity, in large part because of hardware improvements with accelerated graphics cards and video capture boards (✔ p. 3.17). In fact, many of the leading editing solutions for professional video producers are currently based on the personal computer platform. However, incorporating video into your multimedia production still requires compromises.

You digitize video using a video capture card or professional media service. Depending on the original quality of the video and the equipment used during the digitizing process, you may create some very large files. Digital video requires more storage space and processing power than any other form of media. For example, a 10-second video clip that will play back using one-quarter of the screen requires about 68 MB of storage space. You can reduce the storage requirements using compression technologies (✔ p. 5.9) and by decreasing the frame output size, the color depth, or the frames per second (fps) display rate. You can also enhance your video clips with voice-overs, music and sound effects, animated titles, and scene transitions using video-editing software such as Adobe Premiere.

Do you remember what the MPC minimum requirements are?

The Authoring Process

Today's popular authoring programs simplify the task of multimedia development by providing a user-friendly environment for placing and presenting digital media. Within the typical authoring environment, you will find design templates, pre-built component libraries, and media catalogs. The existence of these elements allows you to spend more time designing the user interface and flow of the multimedia title, rather than having to write and debug lines of code. To get the desired interactivity from your title, however, you will most likely attach some procedural code to objects like graphics, buttons, and menus.

Several multimedia authoring and presentation programs offer a click-and-drag model for creating multimedia titles. In reality, the development of a commercial multimedia title is much more intense, closely resembling the model for applications software development. Although the click-and-drag technique may be used for creating electronic slide presentations and for prototyping a production, most developers adopt sophisticated authoring and programming tools to get the performance and interactivity desired by end-users.

Selecting a multimedia authoring software is much more involved than determining which word processor or electronic spreadsheet to use. Unlike word processors that contain basically the same features, one authoring tool can differ dramatically from the next. One way to categorize authoring software is by the output that is created. Some authoring tools are geared toward developing *linear slide-based presentations,* while other tools are better for creating *interactive presentations* or *computer-based training* (*CBT*) *programs.* Not surprisingly, most of the authoring software currently available lets you develop and deliver content via the World Wide Web.

A second categorization method separates authoring tools based on which of three metaphors best fits the project: timeline, flowchart, or book. Multimedia presentation software uses a slide-show or timeline format, but authoring software for CBT development follows either an icon-based flowchart or a book and page metaphor. The *timeline* metaphor provides a videographer's perspective to multimedia production. Although your design is linear, you can add several navigational aids, including hypertext links, for moving randomly through a project. Using the *flowchart* metaphor, you place icons (symbols and arrows) onto a flow line to show the sequence or progression of events. These icons can represent various functions. For instance, one icon may display a background graphic or video clip, and another may process a conditional programming loop. Lastly, in the *book* metaphor, you populate a book (project) with pages (screens). To the page, you add media objects, navigational elements, and event-driven programming scripts.

When you must select multimedia authoring software, make sure that you consider its portability, performance, productivity, and extensibility. The importance that you place on each of these issues is determined by the production objectives. To help you analyze your choices for a multimedia authoring software, we've provided some basic starting questions:

- *Portability*
  Is the authoring environment cross-platform?
  Is the authoring runtime module cross-platform?

- *Performance*
  How responsive is the authoring environment?
  How responsive are the runtime module and the completed production?

■ *Productivity*
How easily can I reuse scripts and programming modules?
How easily can I organize and access media catalogs?
How fast can I produce a prototype?
How fast can I complete a production?

■ *Extensibility*
How important is database access?
What programming tools or options are available?
Can I access external programs and dynamic link libraries?

Multimedia Presentation Software

Presentation software allows you to create multimedia slide-shows, animated business presentations, and informational kiosk applications. Software in this category uses a slide-based, *timeline* metaphor for sequencing a multimedia presentation. This linear format is supplemented by outlining and sorting tools, which allow you to easily rearrange and navigate the slides in your presentation. You can also specify hyperlinks for jumping directly to a specific slide. Some of the more advanced multimedia features that you can incorporate include path animation, object and slide transitions, background music, and video clips. In addition to the program files, most presentation software packages also include clip art media, bit-mapped images, sound and video clips, and graphical elements, such as buttons and icons. Products in this software category include Adobe Persuasion, Astound, Asymetrix Compel, Corel Click & Create, HyperCard, Lotus Freelance, and Microsoft PowerPoint.

Multimedia Authoring Software

To move beyond creating simple business presentations, you can consider using a full-featured multimedia authoring tool like Macromedia Director. Tools in this category provide much greater control over media elements, synchronization, and interactivity. Although these features may not be critical for creating slide-based presentations to the board of directors or for organizing your lecture notes, they are extremely important for developing interactive titles that must capture and retain your audience's attention. Some products that can help in this category include Allen Communication's Quest, Macromedia Director, mFactory mTropolis, and QuarkImmedia.

The typical authoring environment for Macromedia Director 5.0

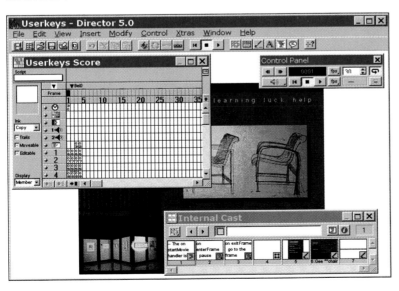

Director

Macromedia Director is the most popular multimedia authoring software available, with more than 350,000 users worldwide. Because you can develop and play back titles on both the Windows and Macintosh platforms, the Director authoring environment is popular among creative designers, graphic artists, businesspeople, educators, and students. Director is distributed and sold as the primary component in a comprehensive suite of multimedia software, including a 3-D modeling and animation program

(Extreme 3D), sound editing software for either the Macintosh (SoundEdit 16) or Windows (Sound Forge XP) platforms, and bit-mapped manipulation software (xRes).

Director is a timeline and scripting-based authoring program used for creating business presentations, product demonstrations, advertising and marketing material, Web-based multimedia content, and CD-ROM titles. You use Director to place and synchronize multimedia content, including text, graphics, animation, sound, and movies, along a timeline. Once your media elements are in place, you can easily animate objects and add interactivity using pull-down menus and other options. For even more functionality, Director provides extensible programming through the Lingo scripting language, Xtras, C++, and Java. In addition to supporting Progressive Network's RealAudio audio Web streaming technology, Director also enables you to create hybrid CD-ROM and Internet applications, stream Shockwave audio and graphical content across the Internet, and play Java applets. Director titles are distributed via self-running executable files, called Projectors, or over the Web using Macromedia Shockwave.

Quest

Since its introduction in 1984 as the first DOS-based multimedia development tool, *Quest* has developed a small but loyal following of users. In its current release, called Quest Net+, Allen Communications is directly targeting developers of Web-based multimedia presentations, educational programs, and entertainment sites. With its peer-to-peer TCP/IP connectivity and client-server capabilities, Quest can provide real-time interaction and Internet delivery of training simulations and remote presentations. Two additional software products from Allen Communications, called Designer's Edge and Manager's Edge, enable developers to manage the design, administration, and maintenance of multimedia presentations and educational courseware.

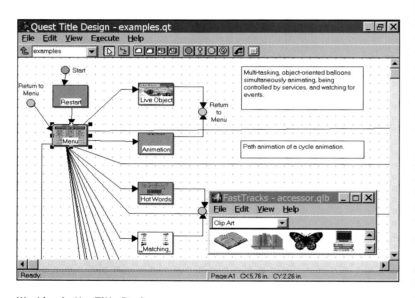

Working in the Title Design mode of Allen Communications' Quest Net+ multimedia authoring software

Quest provides an intuitive software environment that capitalizes on the best features of the flowchart and book authoring metaphors. In the Title Design mode, for example, you gain a macro perspective of your project using an icon-based layout, which allows you to easily manipulate and rearrange icons representing the actual screens in your project. Using the toolbar and the Quick Frame libraries, you can quickly structure the logic and flow of your program by simply clicking and dragging with the mouse. Switching to the WYSIWYG ("what you see is what you get") Frame Edit mode, you create and edit the screen content, insert media objects, and build interactivity into your program using the Quest C script box. Since ANSI C is embedded in Quest, you can extend your programs with the power of C by directly linking to other executable programs and external dynamic link libraries. As with most programs in this category, Quest supports object animation, screen transitions, and the typical text, graphic, sound, and video file formats.

Multimedia CBT Authoring Software

Approximately 80% of the authoring tools purchased today are used in the development of computer-based training. Aside from the development process, the features required for administering and managing computer-based instruction far exceed the capabilities of today's presentation software. Authoring software for computer-based training (CBT) must support high levels of interactivity and complex evaluation methods, along with exceptional media and device handling. Therefore, computer-based authoring software is typically much more advanced, complex, and costly than presentation-oriented authoring software. Products in this software category include AimTech IconAuthor, Asymetrix Toolbook, and Macromedia Authorware.

Authorware

Setting button properties for a multimedia application in Macromedia Authoring 3.0 (the user clicks on buttons to move through the application)

Arguably the most popular development software for multimedia computer-based training programs, *Macromedia Authorware's* icon-based flowchart model has set the ease-of-use standard that other developers strive to meet. You use Authorware to create highly interactive and visual programs for informational kiosks, advertising and promotion, reference materials, product demonstrations, and, most commonly, education. Because it is cross-platform and uses a relatively simple authoring model, Authorware is used extensively by corporations, educational institutions, and government agencies.

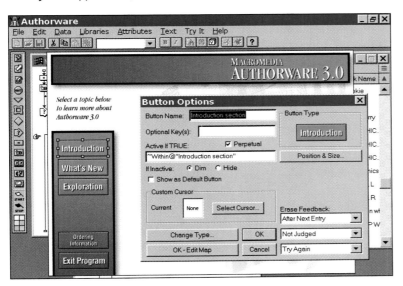

To build a multimedia production using Authorware, you simply drag icons onto a flow line. The arrangement and sequence of icons determines the progression, logic, and structure of the program. For more complex applications, you add more layers for grouping and nesting icons. Once the icons are placed on the flow line, you add content to the presentation by opening up and editing the individual icons.

Toolbook

Asymetrix produces multimedia presentation and authoring software. In addition to its flagship authoring software called *Multimedia Toolbook,* Asymetrix produces a Java (✔ p. 10.28) development environment called SuperCede, a three-dimensional animation software called 3D F/X, a desktop video editing software called Digital Video Producer, and presentation software called Compel. The Toolbook product line includes an entry-level, wizard-driven program for content developers called Assistant, a full-featured CBT development environment called Instructor, and a Java-based course management system for Web servers called Librarian. In addition to providing plug-ins and ActiveX controls for viewing applications using browser software, Toolbook applications can also be exported to HTML files and Java applets for nonproprietary Internet delivery.

Unlike most of the authoring products mentioned previously, Toolbook does not use the flowchart metaphor for its development environment. Instead, Toolbook relies on the trusted book and page metaphor first made popular by Hyper-Card. To create a multimedia program, you add content and media objects to pages within a book. You must then tell Toolbook how to react to user events, such as mouse clicks and keystrokes, by selecting object properties and by writing code called *scripts*. The scripting language, called OpenScript, is an interpreted Visual Basic derivative that enables you to easily customize and enhance your program's behavior. Along with hundreds of design templates, Toolbook provides pre-scripted CBT and Internet "widget" objects for quickly prototyping multimedia programs for both CD-ROM and Web-based delivery.

In designing and evaluating computer-based training solutions, teaching professionals, instructional designers, content experts, and technology advisors must strive to use media types appropriate to meeting the learning objectives, build in interactivity and interaction, and ensure effective and efficient communication. In other words, a successful solution capitalizes on the strengths of the medium without assuming that any multimedia product can meet each and every learning style. The target audience must remain at the forefront in both the educators' and designers' minds when developing and implementing educational multimedia.

Career Opportunities in Multimedia

Developing a multimedia production requires many skilled and talented people. Although you may be able to assemble content yourself using one of the previously mentioned authoring tools, few people have the expertise required to create all the necessary media elements. To be successful working alone requires that you identify the people or companies to whom you can *outsource* work. Some roles and responsibilities that you may require in completing a multimedia production include:

■ *Producer/director:* The producer or director acts as the manager of a multimedia production. This role requires competence in planning and budgeting, cost control and analysis, resource scheduling, and personnel management. This person is also responsible for directing the content, focusing and motivating the team, and dealing with the client. Project management software (✔ p. 6.26) may come in handy here.

■ *Scriptwriter/content expert:* The scriptwriter or content expert researches the topic and prepares a written treatment for the multimedia production. This role requires excellent research, writing, and communication skills. In addition to being directly involved in storyboarding, this person works closely with the producer and media content developers throughout the production process.

■ *Editor/proofreader:* The editor and proofreader refines the script and ensures consistency among the storyboards and written treatment. In other words, this person is responsible for finalizing and polishing all the written material on-screen for interest, clarity, and accuracy. In many cases, the editor or proofreader also acts as a tester as the production nears completion.

■ *Interface designer:* The interface designer provides the "look and feel" of a production. This person prepares the initial storyboards from the written treatment, designs the flow and navigation controls, and establishes the program's physical and logical structure, also called a *map*. Working closely with the art director and producer, the interface designer selects the fonts, colors, illustrations, and images, and then determines the placement of all media elements.

■ *Artist/illustrator:* The graphic artist or illustrator helps develop the storyboards with the interface designer and prepares the final graphics for the production. This person is responsible for producing vector illustrations and other graphics, scanning images and photographs, and acquiring stock content from libraries and catalogs.

- *Animator:* The animator is responsible for preparing the final animation clips used in a production. With smaller production teams, this person also acts as the artist or illustrator. The animator is responsible for specifying path animation used for text and graphic objects, producing two- and three-dimensional animated sequences for digital video playback, and creating models and rendered objects for backgrounds, buttons, and icons.

- *Audio technician:* The audio technician is responsible for preparing, producing, and digitizing the background music, sound effects, and voice-over narration. This person must also research existing stock content from libraries and catalogs.

- *Video Technician:* The video technician is responsible for staging, filming, and digitizing the required video clips. The role also includes researching existing stock content from libraries and catalogs.

- *Programmer:* The programmer writes the code that integrates all the media elements and builds interactivity into the production. This role typically requires several people with specific skills in a variety of authoring software and programming languages. For example, one programmer may combine the media and implement the navigational controls using an authoring tool, such as Macromedia Director. Another programmer may use the C (✔ p. 10.19) language to create special programs for improving the performance of the title and for adding functions not found in the authoring software. And yet another programmer may be responsible for producing an optimized Internet version of the multimedia production based on the Java language.

- *Evaluator/tester:* The testing process for a multimedia production is often separated into an alpha and a beta stage. In the *alpha* stage, only internal testers review and provide feedback on the production. In the *beta* stage, the production is released to outside testers for their feedback.

The Internet allows multimedia producers to access talented content developers from around the world. Take, for example, Paul D. Hibbitts of Software Usability Design Associates (SUDA), a one-person multimedia development company used by some of Canada's largest universities and colleges. Working from his home-based studio in Vancouver, British Columbia, Paul works with talented artists, writers, and programmers from across Canada to create educational multimedia courseware. Paul credits his success to "being a people-person" and having a strong sense for interface design. "With my understanding and past experience in human-computer interface design, I am able to visualize and communicate how a product will be used by someone during the planning stage."[5] Truly an entrepreneur, Paul is not alone as an independent multimedia producer who prefers contracting out to hiring a production team. He is successful because he keeps the audience at the forefront in his mind, and he understands the value of skilled content developers.

Do you think you would enjoy working in the multimedia industry? If so, what aspects would you specialize in?

Artificial Intelligence (AI)

The field of artificial intelligence (AI) attempts to develop machines that emulate human activities and functions. AI includes the areas of robotics, perception systems, natural language processing, expert systems, neural networks, genetic algorithms, virtual reality, and fuzzy logic, as well as building computers that can pass the Turing Test.

You're having trouble with your new software program. You call the "help desk" at the software maker. Do you get a busy signal or get put on hold to listen to music for several minutes? Technical support lines are often swamped, and waiting is commonplace. Or, to deal with your software difficulty, do you find yourself dealing with . . . other software?

This event is not unlikely. Programs that can walk you through a problem and help solve it are called *expert systems* (✔ p. 11.17). Expert systems are one of the most useful applications of an area known as *artificial intelligence.*

Artificial intelligence (AI) is a group of related technologies used in an attempt to develop machines to emulate human-like qualities, such as learning, reasoning, communicating, seeing, and hearing. AI evolved from early attempts to write programs that would allow computers to compete with humans in games such as chess and to prove mathematical theorems.

What Is AI Supposed to Do?

The aim of AI is to produce a generation of systems that will be able to communicate with us by speech and hearing, use "vision" (scanning) that approximates the way people see, and be capable of intelligent problem solving. In other words, AI refers to computer-based systems that can mimic or simulate human thought processes and actions. Some of the primary areas of research within AI that are of particular interest to business users are robotics, natural language processing, fuzzy logic, expert systems, neural networks, and virtual reality.

Robotics

Robotics is a field that attempts to develop machines that can perform work normally done by people. The machines themselves, of course, are called robots. According to *Webster's Tenth New Collegiate Dictionary,* a **robot** is an automatic device that performs functions ordinarily ascribed to human beings or that operates with what appears to be almost human intelligence. It derives from the Polish word *robotnik,* which means "slave."

All robots are preprogrammed. That is, they can only respond to situations for which they have been specifically programmed. *(See Figure 13.1.)* The most extensive uses of robots so far have been in automobile manufacturing or in dangerous environments. Dante II, for instance, is an eight-legged, 10-foot-high, satellite-linked robot used by scientists to explore the inside of Mount Spurr, an active volcano in Alaska.

Perception Systems

Robots that emulate the human capabilities of sight, hearing, touch, and smell and then respond based on the new information are called *intelligent robots,* or

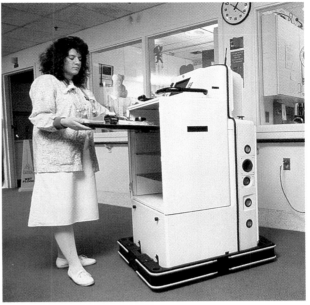

Figure 13.1 Robots

(*Top left*) Dante II explores Alaska's active Mount Spurr volcano; for much of the time, it was without human guidance. (*Top right*) HelpMate robot serves meals at a Connecticut hospital. (*Bottom left*) Robots weld cars on a Hyundai production line in Ulsan, South Korea. (*Bottom right*) The robotic arm of a police robot reaches down to scoop up a live bomb during a test of the bomb squad device. The robot is operated via remote control from the police van behind the robot.

perception systems. One future application of intelligent robotics is a machine that is small enough to be swallowed. It will be able to scan intestinal walls with a miniature camera, searching for possible tumors, and send the images to a doctor watching a monitor. Then, under instructions from the doctor, it will take a tissue sample. Obviously, this robot is very sensitive to touch.

Robot vision has already been successfully implemented in many manufacturing systems. To "see," a computer measures varying intensities of light reflected off a shape; each intensity has a numbered value that is compared to a template of intensity patterns stored in memory. One of the main reasons for the importance of vision is that production-line robots must be able to discriminate among parts. General Electric, for example, has Bin Vision Systems, which allows a robot to identify and pick up specific parts in an assembly-line format.

Another area of interest is the "personal" robot, familiar to us from science fiction. Existing personal robots exhibit relatively limited abilities, and whether a sophisticated home robot can be made cost-effective is debatable. B.O.B. (Brains On Board) is a device sold by Visual Machines that can speak (using prerecorded

GO TEAM, GO!

Just as some jobs are best handled by teams of people working together, other tasks might be tackled by groups of cooperative robots. That's the premise behind work at Brandeis University and MIT. Brandeis computer scientist Maja Matarie and colleagues have assembled 24 robots that can move around, pick up objects, and transmit and receive radio signals. Matarie has trained the robots to decide when to aggregate or disperse, travel in a flock, and search for "food," sharing information to maximize group yield.

So far the robots, known as the Nerd Herd, have mastered the art of foraging for pucks scattered throughout Matarie's lab and can collect them efficiently without trampling one another in the process. She's recently added four larger and smarter robots to the group. "I can envision a system of natural leaders and followers eventually evolving," says Matarie. Before long, she predicts, robots could take over dangerous jobs like disabling mines, putting out fires, and cleaning up toxic spills.

James McLurkin, a research scientist at MIT's Artificial Intelligence Lab, is pursuing a slightly different tack. He's studying ant colonies to learn engineering principles that might be applied to his matchbook-sized "ant" robots. "Nature doesn't worry about getting things right all the time," McLurkin says. "It's OK to lose a few ants [robotic or real], for the success of the community."

He now has a dozen robots that communicate via infrared signals. One "ant," for instance, might announce: "I found food." Others relay the message: "I found an ant that found food." A similar scheme could work at landfills, with robots gathering salvageable materials.

—Steve Nadis with Jerry Shine, "Go Team, Go," *Popular Science*

phrases), follow people around using infrared sensors, and avoid obstacles by using ultrasonic sound. Software will allow the robot to bring its owner something to drink from the refrigerator. Another type of personal robot is the Spimaster, built by Cybermotion. This security robot patrols up to 15 miles per shift, collecting video images and recording data. If it senses a problem, it heads for the trouble zone and sounds alarms on-site and at security headquarters.

What kind of robot would you build that would be most useful to society?

The performance limitations of personal robots reflect the difficulties in designing and programming intelligent robots. In fact, we have just begun to appreciate how complicated such mundane tasks as recognizing a can of Pepsi in the refrigerator can be. Another concern is that if a robot does in fact become intelligent, what would stop it from deciding that work is something to avoid?

Natural Language Processing

Natural languages are ordinary human languages, such as English. (A second definition is that they are programming languages, called fifth-generation languages, that give people a more natural connection with computers; ✔ p. 10.17.) **Natural language processing** is the study of ways for computers to recognize and understand human language, whether in spoken or written form. The primary difficulty in implementing this kind of communication is the sheer complexity of everyday conversation. For example, we readily understand the sentence "The spirit is willing, but the flesh is weak." One natural language processing system, however, understood this sentence to mean "The wine is agreeable, but the meat has spoiled." It also understood the phrase "out of sight, out of mind" to mean "blind idiot." It turns out that the system must have access to a much larger body of knowledge than just a dictionary of terms. People use their world knowledge to help them understand what another person is saying. For example, we know the question "Coffee?" means "Do you want a cup of coffee?" But a computer would have difficulty understanding this one-word question.

Most existing natural language systems run on large computers; however, scaled-down versions are now available for microcomputers. Intellect, for example, is the name of a commercial product that uses a limited English vocabulary to help users orally query databases on both mainframes and microcomputers. One of the most successful natural language systems is LUNAR, developed to help users analyze the rocks brought back from the moon. It has access to extensive detailed knowledge about geology in its knowledge database and answers users' questions. The U.S. Postal Service is currently using a language-processing system that was developed by Verbex to speed up the sorting and delivery of mail that doesn't include a zip code. After the human mail sorter reads the address into a microphone, the computer responds in an electronic voice with the correct zip code.

Fuzzy Logic

One relatively recent concept being used in the development of natural languages is fuzzy logic. Classical logic has been based on either/or propositions. For example, to evaluate the phrase "The cat is fat," classical logic requires a single cutoff point to determine when the cat is fat, such as a specific weight for a certain length. It is either in the set of fat cats or it is not. However, "fat" is a vague, or "gray," notion; it's more likely that the cat is "a little fat." **Fuzzy logic** is a method of dealing with imprecise data and vagueness, with problems that have many answers rather than one. Unlike traditional "crisp" digital logic, fuzzy logic is more like human reasoning: it deals with probability and credibility. That is, instead of being simply true or false, a proposition is *mostly* true or *mostly* false, or *more* true or *more* false.

REAL LESSONS FROM A PSEUDOTUTOR

If Herman and his kind can live up to the initial raves of students at Martin Middle School in Raleigh, North Carolina, teachers will soon be getting help from pseudospace. A bug-like alien dreamed up by researchers at North Carolina State University is just a computer simulation, but a savvy one.

He's a tour guide for the Design-a-Plant program. To teach botany to children aged 9 to 14, Herman takes them to four planets and explains the different ecologies. Then Herman challenges each student to devise a plant suited for that planet. By analyzing the responses to periodic questions. Herman's artificial-intelligence component sizes up its human students and adjusts the interactive presentation accordingly. For families that can't afford a personal tutor, Herman the pseudotutor could be the next best thing.

—Otis Port, "Developments to Watch," *Business Week*

A frequently given example of an application of fuzzy logic is in running elevators. How long will most people wait for an elevator before getting antsy? About a minute and a half, say researchers at the Otis Elevator Company. The Otis artificial intelligence division has done considerable research into how elevators may be programmed to reduce waiting time. Ordinarily when someone on a floor in the middle of a building pushes the call button, the system will send whichever elevator is closest. However, that car might be filled with passengers, who will be delayed by the new stop (perhaps making them antsy). Another car, however, might be empty. In a fuzzy logic system, the computer assesses not only which car is nearest but also how full the cars are before deciding which one to send.

Fuzzy logic circuitry is also used in autofocus cameras to enable the camera to focus properly.

Expert Systems: Human Expertise in a Computer

We described expert systems in Chapter 11, Information Management, in relation to its uses by management and nonmanagement personnel to solve specific problems, such as how to reduce production costs or improve workers' productivity. In this section we describe expert systems in more detail. As you may recall from Chapter 11, an *expert system* is a set of computer programs that performs a task at the level of a human expert. To expand on that definition, an **expert system** is an interactive computer program that can apply rules and data to input questions or problems in such a way as to generate conclusions. The program helps users solve problems that would otherwise require the assistance of a human expert. *It is important to emphasize that expert systems are designed to be users' assistants, not replacements. Also, their success depends on the quality of the data and rules obtained from the human experts.*

An expert system solves problems that require substantial expertise to understand. The system's performance depends on the body of facts (knowledge) and the heuristics (rules of thumb) that are fed into the computer. Knowledge engineers gather, largely through interviews, the expert knowledge and the heuristics from human experts in the field for which the computer-based system is being designed to support decisions—fields such as medicine, engineering, or geology. (For example, in the field of medicine, one question that might be asked of an expert system is whether one treatment is better for a patient than another one.) The responses recorded during the interviews are codified and entered into a knowledge base that can be used by a computer. An expert system has the capacity to store the collection of knowledge and manipulate it in response to user inquiries; in some cases, it can even explain its responses to the user.

An expert system has three major program components *(see Figure 13.2)*:

1. *Knowledge base:* A **knowledge base** is an expert system's database of knowledge about a particular subject. This includes relevant facts, information, beliefs, assumptions, and procedures for solving problems. One basic unit of knowledge is expressed as an IF-THEN-ELSE rule ("IF this happens, THEN do this, ELSE do that"). Programs can have as many as 10,000 rules (heuristics), which express the reasoning procedures of experts on the subject. A system called ExperTAX, for example, which helps accountants figure out a client's tax options, consists of more than 2000 rules.

2. *Inference engine:* The **inference engine** is the software that controls the search of the expert system's knowledge base and produces conclusions. It takes the problem posed by the user of the system and fits it into the rules in the knowledge base. It then derives a conclusion from the facts and rules contained in the knowledge base. *Reasoning* refers to the way the

Figure 13.2 Components of an expert system The three components are the user interface, the inference engine, and the knowledge base.

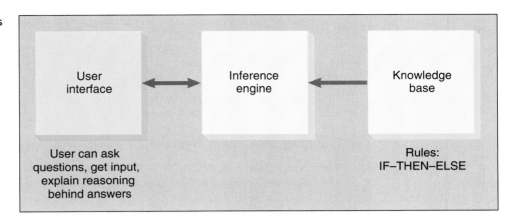

User interface

Inference engine

Knowledge base

User can ask questions, get input, explain reasoning behind answers

Rules: IF–THEN–ELSE

inference engine attacks problems. There are several types of reasoning processes too technical to go into here. In any case, the system must be able to explain its reasoning process to the user, if requested.

3. *User interface:* The user interface is what appears on the display screen for the user to interact with. It gives the user the ability to ask questions and get answers.

Expert systems include stand-alone microcomputers, as well as workstations and terminals connected to servers and larger computer systems in local area networks and/or wide area networks (✔ p. 7.28).

Expert Systems at Work

One of the most famous expert systems—an older system since replaced by updated ones—is MYCIN, a system that diagnoses infectious diseases and recommends appropriate drugs. For example, bacteremia (bacteria in the blood) can be fatal if it is not treated quickly. Unfortunately, traditional tests for it require 24 to 48 hours to verify a diagnosis. However, MYCIN provides physicians with a diagnosis and recommended therapy within minutes. To use MYCIN, the physician enters data on a patient; as the data is being entered, MYCIN asks questions (for example, "Is patient a burn patient?"). As the questions are answered, MYCIN's inference engine "reasons" out a diagnosis: "IF the infection is primary bacteria, AND the site of the culture is a gastrointestinal tract, THEN there is evidence (0.7) that the identity of the organism causing the disease is Bacteroides." The "0.7" means that MYCIN "thinks" there is a 7 out of 10 chance that this diagnosis is correct. This pattern closely follows that of human thought; much of our knowledge is inexact and incomplete, and we often reason using odds (such as "There's a 40% chance it's going to rain") when we don't have access to complete and accurate information.

Gensym Corporation's G2 Real-Time Expert system is used in Mrs. Baird's Bakery (a large independent bakery in Fort Worth) for scheduling and monitoring the production of baked goods. The system takes care of scheduling such tasks as ingredient mixing and oven operations—don't plan on finding a burned cookie at Mrs. Baird's!

The Residential Burglary Expert System (REBES) is an expert system that uses certain rules of thumb to help a detective investigate a crime scene. REBES, which acts like a partner to the detective, might ask "Did the intruder search the entire house? If so, an accomplice might be involved" or "Was valuable jewelry taken but cheaper jewelry left behind? If so, thieves may be professionals/repeaters."

Examples of other expert systems are XCON, a system that puts together the best arrangement of Digital Equipment Corporation (DEC) computer system components for a given company; DENDRAL, a system that identifies chemical compounds; PROSPECTOR, a system that evaluates potential geological sites of oil, natural gas, and so on; and DRILLING ADVISOR, a system that assists in diagnosing and resolving oil-rig problems. CLUES (Countrywide Loan Underwriting Expert System) evaluates home-mortgage-loan applications. CRUSH takes a body of expert advice and combines it with worksheets reflecting a user's business situation to come up with a customized strategy to "crush" competitors.

Building an Expert System

Capturing human expertise for the computer is a time-consuming and difficult task. **Knowledge engineers** are trained to elicit knowledge (for example, by interview) from experts and build the expert system. The knowledge engineer may program the system in an artificial intelligence programming language, such as LISP or PROLOG, or may use system-building tools that provide a structure. Tools allow faster design but are less flexible than languages. An example of such a tool is EMYCIN, which is MYCIN without any of MYCIN's knowledge. A knowledge engineer can theoretically enter any knowledge (as long as it is describable in rules) into this empty shell and create a new system. The completed new system will solve problems as MYCIN does, but the subject matter in the knowledge base may be completely different (for example, car repair).

Expert systems are usually run on large computers—often dedicated artificial intelligence computers—because of these systems' gigantic appetites for memory; however, some scaled-down expert systems (such as the OS/2 [✔ p. 5.20] version of KBMS, Knowledge Base Management System) run on microcomputers. Negotiator Pro from Beacon Expert Systems for IBM and Apple Macintosh computers helps executives plan effective negotiations with other people by examining their personality types and recommending negotiating strategies. Scaled-down systems generally do not have all the capabilities of large expert systems, and most have limited reasoning abilities. LISP and PROLOG compilers (✔ pp. 10.21–10.22) are available for microcomputers, as are some system-building tools such as EXPERT-EASE, NEXPERT, and VP-Expert, which allow relatively unsophisticated users to build their own expert system. Such software tools for building expert systems are called *shells*.

Implications for Business

Expert systems are becoming increasingly important to business and manufacturing firms. However, it is difficult to define what constitutes "expertise" in business. Unlike some other areas—notably math, medicine, and chemistry—business is not made up of a specific set of inflexible facts and rules. Some business activities, however, do lend themselves to expert system development. DEC has developed several in-house expert systems, including ILPRS (which assists in long-range planning) and IPPMS (which assists in project management).

Another issue that inhibits the use of expert systems in business is that businesses want systems that can be integrated into their existing computer systems. Many existing expert systems are designed to run in a stand-alone mode. Furthermore, who will use the expert system? Who will be responsible for its maintenance? Who will have authority to add and/or delete knowledge in the expert system? What are the legal ramifications of decisions made by an expert system? These and other questions will have to be answered before expert systems are fully accepted in the business environment.

Cost is also a factor. Associated costs include purchasing hardware and software, hiring personnel, publishing and distribution costs (if the expert system is used at more than one location), and maintenance costs, which are usually more than the total of any costs already incurred. The costs can easily run into the many thousands of dollars. However, over the last few years, the number of

> Do you have any expertise that would be useful to someone building an expert system? If so, what kind of system would it be? If you were the person building the system, what kinds of questions would you ask yourself to elicit the appropriate information?

implementations of expert systems has exploded from the hundreds to the thousands as businesses realize the benefits of better performance, reduced errors, and increased efficiency. In addition, less expensive micro-based tools are becoming increasingly powerful and available to businesses.

Neural Networks

Artificial intelligence and fuzzy logic principles are also being applied to the development of neural networks. **Neural networks** use physical electronic devices or software to mimic the neurological structure of the human brain. *(See Figure 13.3.)* Because they are structured to mimic the rudimentary circuitry of the cells in the human brain, they learn from example and don't require detailed instructions.

To understand how neural networks operate, let us compare them to the operation of the human brain.

■ *The human neural network:* The word *neural* comes from *neurons,* or nerve cells. The neurons are connected by a three-dimensional lattice called *axons.* Electrical connections between neurons are activated by synapses.

Figure 13.3 Neural networks are based on the brain's cell circuitry (*right*).

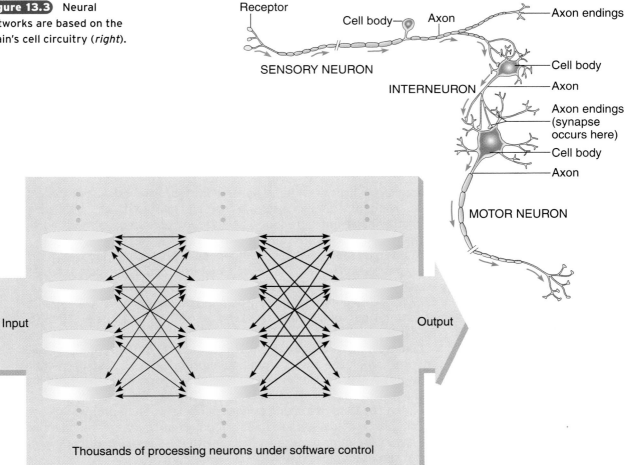

The human brain is made up of about 100 billion neurons. However, these cells do not act as "computer memory" sites. You could eliminate any cell—or even a few million—in your brain and not alter your "mind." Where do memory and learning lie? In the electrical connections between cells, the synapses. Using electrical pulses, the neurons send "on/off" messages along the synapses.

■ *The computer neural network:* In a hardware neural network, the nerve cell is replaced by a transistor, which acts as a switch. Wires connect the cells (transistors) with one another. Synapses are replaced by electronic components called *resistors,* which determine whether cells should activate the electricity to other cells. A software neural network emulates a hardware neural network, although it doesn't work as fast.

Computer-based neural networks use special AI software and complicated fuzzy-logic processor chips to take inputs and convert them to outputs with a kind of logic similar to human logic.

Ordinary computers mechanically obey instructions according to set rules. However, neural-network computers, like children, learn by example, problem solving, and memory by association. The network "learns" by fine-tuning its connections in response to each situation it encounters. (In the brain, learning takes place through changes in the synapses.) If you're teaching a neural network to speak, for example, you train it by giving it sample words and sentences as well as the pronunciations. The connections between the electronic "neurons" gradually change, allowing more or less current to pass.

Using software from a neural-network producer, Intel has developed a neural-network chip that contains many more transistors than the Pentium. Other chip makers are also working on neural-network chips. Over the next few years, these chips will begin to bring the power of these silicon "brains" not only to your PC but also to such tasks as automatically balancing laundry loads in washing machines.

Neural networks are already being used in a variety of situations. One such program learned to pronounce a 20,000-word vocabulary overnight.[6] Another

FROM DOWN UNDER, NEURAL-NET PCS

Anthony J. Richter grew up in poverty in Western Australia in the early 1950s, living for a time in a tent in the sand hills south of Perth. Now he's a millionaire entrepreneur who's vowing to change computing with hardware and software that mimic the human brain.

Richter, an industrial psychologist, calls his technology Neuronetics. It's used for security and voice-mail systems sold by his company, Perth-based Formulab Neuronetics Corp. But Richter has bigger ambitions . . . a $99 Windows-compatible programming language, a $300 plug-in circuit card for personal computers, and a $6000 stand-alone computer, all based on Neuronetics.

Like a brain, Neuronetics hardware consists of neuron-like circuits that "fire" when the inputs from neighboring neurons reach a certain threshold. Unlike ordinary neural nets, whose inner workings are hard to decipher, Neuronetics systems can be easily checked and adjusted. Programming consists of making connections between neurons and setting the firing thresholds. It's especially good for such jobs as recognizing patterns in sound or pictures, dealing with missing data, or coping with several simultaneous events.

—Peter Coy, "Developments to Watch," *Business Week*

helped a mutual-fund manager to outperform the stock market by 2.3–5.6 percentage points over three years.[7] At a San Diego hospital emergency room in which patients complained of chest pains, a neural-network program was given the same information given doctors. It correctly diagnosed patients with heart attacks 97% of the time, compared to 78% for the human physicians.[8] In Chicago, a neural-net system has also been used to evaluate patient X rays to look for signs of breast cancer. It outperformed most doctors in distinguishing malignant tumors from benign ones.[9] Banks use neural-network software to spot irregularities in purchasing patterns associated with individual accounts, thus often noticing when a credit card is stolen before its owner does.[10]

Genetic Algorithms

A **genetic algorithm** is a program that uses Darwinian principles of random mutation to improve itself. The algorithms are lines of computer code that act like living organisms. Different sections of code haphazardly come together, producing programs. Like Darwin's rules of evolution, many chunks of code compete with one another to see which can best perform the desired solution—the aim of the program. Some chunks will even become extinct. Those that survive will combine with other survivors and will produce offspring programs.

Expert systems can capture and preserve the knowledge of expert specialists, but they may be slow to adapt to change. Neural networks can sift through mountains of data and discover obscure causal relationships, but if there is too much or too little data they may be ineffective—garbage in, garbage out. Genetic algorithms, by contrast, use endless trial and error to learn from experience—to discard unworkable approaches and grind away at promising approaches with the kind of tireless energy of which humans are incapable.[11]

The awesome power of genetic algorithms has already found applications. Organizers of the 1992 Paralympic Games used it to schedule events. LBS Capital Management Fund of Clearwater, Florida, uses it to help pick stocks for a pension fund it manages. In something called the FacePrints project, witnesses have used a genetic algorithm to describe and identify criminal suspects. Texas Instruments is drawing on the skills that salmon use to find spawning grounds to produce a genetic algorithm that shipping companies can use to let packages "seek" their own best routes to their destinations. A hybrid expert system–genetic algorithm called Engenous was used to boost performance in the Boeing 777 jet engine, a feat that involved billions of mind-boggling calculations.

Computer scientists still don't know what kinds of problems genetic algorithms work best on. Still, as one article pointed out, "genetic algorithms have going for them something that no other computer technique does: they have been field-tested, by nature, for 3.5 billion years."[12]

Artificial Life, the Turing Test, and AI Ethics

Genetic algorithms would seem to lead us away from mechanistic ideas of artificial intelligence and into more fundamental questions: "What is life, and how can we replicate it out of silicon chips, networks, and software?" We are dealing now not with artificial intelligence but with artificial life. *Artificial life,* or *A-life,* is a field of study concerned with "creatures"—computer instructions or pure information—that are created, replicate, evolve, and die as if they were living organisms.[13]

Of course, "silicon life" does not have two principal attributes associated with true living things—it is not water- and carbon-based. Yet in other respects such "creatures" mimic life: if they cannot learn or adapt, they perish.

How can we know when we have reached the point where computers have achieved human intelligence? How will you always know, say, when you're on the phone, whether you're talking to a human being or to a computer? Clearly, with the strides made in the fields of artificial intelligence and artificial life, this question is no longer just academic.

Interestingly, this matter was addressed back in 1950 by Alan Turing, an English mathematician and computer pioneer. Turing predicted that by the end of the century computers would be able to mimic human thinking and converse so naturally that their communications would be indistinguishable from a person's. Out of these observations came the Turing test. The **Turing test** is a test or game for determining whether a computer is considered to possess "intelligence" or "self-awareness."

In the Turing test, a human judge converses by means of a computer terminal with two entities hidden in another location. One entity is a person typing on a keyboard. The other is a software program. As the judge types in and receives messages on the terminal, he or she must decide whether the entity is human. In this test, intelligence and the ability to think is demonstrated by the computer's success in fooling the judge. *(See Figure 13.4.)*

Judith Anne Gunther participated as one of eight judges in the third annual Loebner Prize Competition, which is based on Turing's ideas. (Hugh Loebner, a New York businessman, with support from the National Science Foundation and the Alfred P. Sloane Foundation, has offered a $100,000 prize for the first computer system that can pass the Turing test by fooling the subject into thinking he or she is communicating with a person.) The "conversations" are restricted to predetermined topics, such as baseball. This is because today's best programs have neither the databases nor the syntactical ability to handle an unlimited number of subjects. Conversations with each entity are limited to 15 minutes. At the end of the contest, the program that fools the judges most is the one that wins.

Gunther found that she wasn't fooled by any of the computer programs. The winning program, for example, relied as much on deflection and wit as it did on responding logically and conversationally. (For example, to a judge trying to discuss a federally funded program, the computer said: "You want logic? I'll give you

Figure 13.4 Turing test. In this test, a human judge converses via computer terminal with two entities in another location. One is a human being, the other a computer program. The task of the judge is to figure out whether the "intelligence" he or she is conversing with is human or not. Often the computer just gives itself away by being illogical, as in this "conversation."

"**Computer:** As a psychoanalyst, I am familiar with discussing such marital troubles with you as the patient on the couch. If you don't have a bad marriage just pretend that you do. Please start with 'My wife . . .' or 'My husband . . .'.
Judge: Ok, I'll pretend I have a bad marriage. Let's say the reason is because he never picks up his dirty underwear. Is this marriage irreparable?
Computer: Well, if you think I'm hopeless, you can always just swear at me."

—Judith Anne Gunther, "An Encounter with A.I.," *Popular Science*

logic: shut up, shut up, shut up, shut up, shut up, now go away! How's that for logic?") However, Gunther *was* fooled by one of the five humans, a real person discussing abortion. "He was so uncommunicative," wrote Gunther, "that I pegged him for a computer."[14]

With the century's end in sight, no machine has consistently passed the Turing test. And on those few occasions when interrogators have been fooled by computers, the transcripts reveal a less-than-penetrating interrogation. (Hence one problem with the Turing test: is it measuring the thinking power of the machines or of the humans?)[15]

Behind everything that has to do with artificial intelligence and artificial life—just as it underlies everything we do—is the whole matter of ethics. In his book *Ethics in Modeling,* William A. Wallace, professor of decision sciences at Rensselaer Polytechnic Institute, points out that many users are not aware that computer software, such as expert systems, is often subtly shaped by the ethical judgments and assumptions of the people who create it.[16] In one instance, he points out, a bank had to modify its loan-evaluation software after it discovered that it tended to reject some applications because it unduly emphasized old age as a negative factor. Another expert system, used by health maintenance organizations (HMOs), instructs doctors on when they should opt for expensive medical procedures, such as magnetic resonance imaging tests (MRIs). HMOs like the systems because they help control expenses, but critics are concerned that doctors will have to base decisions not on the best medicine but simply on "satisfactory" medicine combined with cost cutting.[17] Clearly, there is no such thing as completely "value-free" technology. Human beings build it, use it, and have to live with the results.

Also, some people think that AI is dangerous because it does not address the ethics of using machines to make decisions nor does it require machines to use ethics as part of the decision-making process. And . . .

> It isn't just that as these machines get more powerful they do more jobs once done only by people, from financial analysis to secretarial work to world-class chess playing. It's that, in the process, they seem to underscore the generally dispiriting drift of scientific inquiry. First Copernicus said we're not the center of the universe. Then Darwin said we're just protozoans with a long list of add-ons—mere "survival machines," as modern Darwinians put it. And machines don't have souls, right? Certainly Deep Blue [the chess-playing IBM computer that defeated Gary Kasparov in 1997] hasn't mentioned having one. The better these seemingly soulless machines get at doing things people do, the more plausible it seems that we could be soulless machines, too.[18]

"The mystery grows more acute," says philosopher David Chalmers, whose book *The Conscious Mind* deals with the enigma of human consciousness. "The more we think about computers, the more we realize how strange consciousness is."[19]

Do you really want computers to achieve the level of human intelligence? Why or why not?

When Kasparov lost Game 1, he was gloomy. Could Deep Blue ever feel deeply blue? Does a face-recognition program have the experience of recognizing a face? Can computers—even computers whose data flow precisely mimics human data flow—actually have subjective experience? This is the question of consciousness, or mind. The lights are on, but is anyone home?[20]

Figure 13.5 Virtual reality. (*Top*) Man wearing interactive sensory headset and glove. When the man moves his head, the 3-D stereoscopic views change. (*Middle left*) What the man is looking at—a simulation of an office. When the man moves his glove, sensors collect data about his hand movements. The view then changes so that the man feels he is "moving" over to the bookshelf and "grasping" a book. (*Middle right*) Virtual reality glove. (*Bottom left*) During a virtual reality experiment in Chapel Hill, North Carolina, a man uses a treadmill to walk through a virtual reality environment. (*Bottom right*) Two medical students study the leg bones of a "virtual cadaver."

Virtual Reality (VR)

Want to take a trip to the moon? Be a race car driver? See the world through the eyes of an ocean-bottom creature or your cat? Without leaving your chair, you can experience almost anything you want through the form of AI called virtual reality (VR). **Virtual reality** is a kind of computer-generated artificial reality that projects a person into a sensation of three-dimensional space. *(See Figure 13.5.)* In virtual reality, the user is inside a world instead of just observing an image on

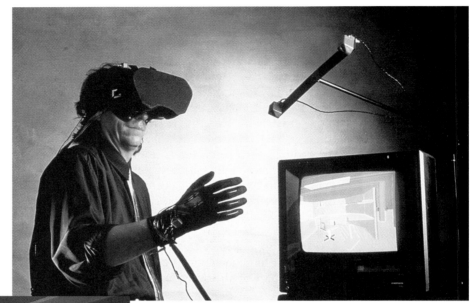

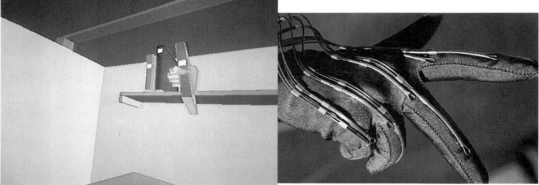

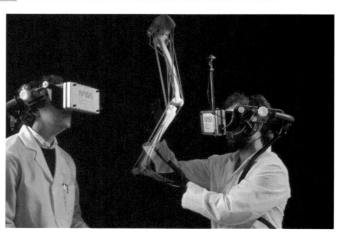

the screen. To put yourself into virtual reality, you need the following interactive sensory equipment:

■ *Headgear:* The headgear—which is called *head-mounted display (HMD)*—has two small video display screens, one for each eye, that create the sense of three-dimensionality. Headphones pipe in stereophonic sound or even "3-D" sound. Three-dimensional sound makes you think you are hearing sounds not only near each ear but also all around you.

■ *Glove:* The glove has sensors that collect data about your hand movements.

■ *Software:* Software gives the wearer of this special headgear and glove the interactive sensory experience that feels like an alternative to real-world experiences.

You may have seen virtual reality used in arcade-type games, such as Atlantis, a computer simulation of The Lost Continent. You may even have tried playing golf on a virtual golf range or driven a virtual racing car. There are also a few virtual-reality home video games. However, there are far more important uses, one of them being in simulators for training.

Simulators are devices that represent the behavior of physical or abstract systems. Virtual-reality simulation technologies are applied a great deal in training. For instance, they have been used to create lifelike bus control panels and various scenarios such as icy road conditions to instruct bus drivers. They are used to train pilots on various aircraft and to prepare air-traffic controllers for equipment failures. They also help children who prefer hands-on learning to explore subjects such as chemistry.

Of particular value are the uses of virtual reality in health and medicine. For instance, surgeons-in-training can rehearse their craft through simulation on "digital patients." Virtual-reality therapy has been used for autistic children and in the treatment of phobias, such as extreme fear of public speaking or of being in public places or high places. It has also been used to rally the spirits of quadriplegics and paraplegics by engaging them in plays and song-and-dance routines. As one patient said, "When you spend a lot of time in bed, you can go crazy."[21]

Perhaps the largest problem facing virtual-reality developers is how to keep users from getting sick. Although improvements in head tracking, force feedback, and tactile feedback have made virtual reality a better experience, users still get headaches, experience nausea, and are disoriented at times during total immersions.[22] Because many virtual-reality systems have not achieved a high level of visual depth and a sophisticated method of anticipating head motion, the systems cause delays that confuse the brain. Any delays between the computer images and the user's movement increase the opportunity for simulator sickness.[23]

Another problem can be caused by HMDs. They place low levels of radiation, in the form of X rays, close to the eyes and brain. It's possible that an electromagnetic field of intense magnitude can cause brain cell damage as well as damage to the genetic makeup of the brain and eyes. Also, prolonged exposure to X rays can have a detrimental effect on visual acuity.[24]

Overall, the ability to interact with computers in a virtual world may soon take on the paradigm suggested by artist Char Davies, director of Visual Research at SoftImage, Inc., in Montreal, Canada. In her artificial world, Osmose, participants are immersed in a sea of images based on the physical elements contained in nature. Navigation comes by breathing in and out, and participants float through the space. As they encounter objects, they have the opportunity to become one with each element, including the very code that makes up the program.

This dream world offers an example of how virtual reality will soon open up new insights into how we behave, interact, and move through cyberspace—and ultimately into the tools we create for navigating artificial worlds.[25]

Cloning Buildings: In Dresden, in the former East Germany, there lie the ruins of a centuries-old cathedral called *die Frauenkirche.* Bombed out during the Allied air raids in World War II, this legendary European landmark has literally been a pile of rubble in the middle of the city for nearly 50 years. But now, thanks to German reunification and some IBM computers and software, Dresden is rebuilding the church with astonishing accuracy in a $177 million project. This project, which won't be completed until 2003, marks a turning point for virtual reality.

The Dresden project is arguably the most creative and useful application of virtual reality ever attempted. Using the original architectural plans and old photos, engineers have been able to recreate (simulate), on their computers, in impeccable detail the interior and exterior of the church exactly as it stood before its destruction.

Using 3-D models, the engineers can literally walk through the virtual church and examine its facades, ceilings, and metalwork up closely. In the process, they've managed to identify nearly a third of the original stones in the church and "place" them where they belong. Specialists in Eastern European Baroque interiors are using the same technology to recreate the church's vast, complex inner environments. Meanwhile, the real construction has begun, and there's a multimedia kiosk at the construction site where you can preview the reconstructed church.

Until now, landmarks destroyed by natural or human disaster stayed that way or were rebuilt as modern imitations. Now, with today's computer graphics and improving VR techniques, aging and ruined wonders can reappear before us and future generations. Can Rome rise again?

Digitized Battlefield: Bradley Fighting Vehicles turned their guns on the soldier as he ran to a tree line for cover. Comanche attack helicopters buzzed through the night air, accompanied by the sporadic pounding of bombs.

The soldier peered through his night-vision goggles to locate the source of the fire. He began moving toward higher ground, but 155-mm. Howitzer shells turned him back. Debris from the shells fell all around, and the soldier re-

treated down the hill to the tree line, firing a Beretta pistol at the approaching enemy.

When it was over, no one had suffered so much as a scratch. In fact, no one had truly been in danger—or anywhere near a battlefield. The encounter had taken place in a new type of computerized combat simulator at Fort Belvoir, Virginia. The idea is to expose foot soldiers to the confusion, noise, and shock of battle without the cost and danger of live-fire exercises.

The trainee starts by putting on a virtual-reality helmet, in which tiny screens display images of a battlefield; the scene changes as the head is moved. The soldier walks on a stair-stepping exercise device, which offers more resistance when hills are climbed and less during a descent, to "move" around the simulated scene. An electronic pistol is the soldier's weapon.

Simulated Tours: In matters of tourism, art not only imitates life, it sometimes is better than life. Thus a new generation of attractions has sprung up on the coattails of established tourist destinations, appealing to those who want the travel experience without necessarily putting in much time or effort. Destination Cinema, Inc., runs IMAX theaters at the Grand Canyon, Honolulu, Seattle, Yellowstone Park, and Niagara Falls. Other types of synthetic destinations are also popping up at resort hotels, in malls, in major cities, and on cruise ships.

Driving these new attractions is technology such as virtual reality, big-screen projection, motion simulators, and computerized rides.

Grand Canyon IMAX attracts about 1 million visitors a year and offers viewers stunning views of the canyon that they otherwise would have to hike, fly, and raft to see. Some 650,00 visitors were attracted in 1995 to New York Skyride on the second floor of New York City's Empire State Building. The ride takes tourists on a simulated flight around the city. Ride Niagara offers a journey "over" the falls in a computerized motion simulator.

—"Virtual War Can Be Mindgoggling," *San Francisco Chronicle;* Jeff Glasser, *Washington Post;* Susan Carey, "Unnatural Wonders: Simulated Tours Beat the Real Thing," *Wall Street Journal.*

Intelligent Agents, Information Filtering, and Avatars

Intelligent agents are computer programs that help users deal with information overload by acting as electronic secretaries, e-mail and information filters, and electronic news clipping services. Avatars graphically represent users on a display screen.

What the online world really needs is a terrific librarian. "What bothers me most," says Christine Borgman, chair of the UCLA Department of Library and Information Science, "is that computer people seem to think that if you have access to the Web, you don't need libraries. But what's on the Web now is just a fraction of what's in the average-sized library."[26] And what's in a library is standardized and well organized, and what's on the Web is unstandardized and chaotic.

As a solution, scientists have been developing so-called *intelligent agents* to send out to computer networks to find and filter information. And to make them more friendly they have invented graphical on-screen personifications called *avatars*.

Intelligent Agents

An **intelligent agent** is a computer program that performs work tasks on your behalf, including roaming networks and compiling data. It acts as an electronic assistant that will perform, in the user's place, such tasks as filtering messages, scanning news services, and performing similar secretarial chores. It will also travel over communications lines to nearly any kind of computer database, collecting files to add to a database. In this context, **filtering** refers to using a program to construct a type of custom-made electronic barrier through which only selected or desired data is passed.

Examples of agents are the following.[27]

- *Electronic secretaries:* Wildfire is a voice recognition system (✔ p. 3.15), an electronic secretary that will answer the phone, take messages, track you down on your cell phone and announce the caller, place calls for you, handle e-mail and faxes, and remind you of appointments.

- *E-mail filters:* The ease of e-mail has resulted in a flood of unimportant messages; and people often express opinions they might otherwise have kept to themselves. Programs like BeyondMail will filter your e-mail, alerting you to urgent messages, telling you which require follow-up, and sorting everything according to priorities. For people whose e-mail threatens to overwhelm them with "cyberglut," such an agent is a great help.

- *Electronic clipping services:* Several companies offer customized electronic news services (Heads Up, I-News, Journalist, Personal Journal, News Hound, the Personal Internet Newspaper) that will scan online news sources and publications looking for information that you have previously specified using keywords. Some will rank a selected article according to how closely it fits your request. Others will pull together articles in the form of a condensed electronic newspaper.

■ *Internet agents—spiders, crawlers, and robots: Search engines,* as mentioned in Chapter 8 (✔ p. 8.25), are Web pages containing forms into which you type text on the topic you want to search for. The search engine then looks through its database and presents a list of Web sites matching your search criteria. Examples of search engines are AltaVista and Meta Crawler. Of particular interest here, however, are the intelligent agents used to assemble the database that a search engine searches. Most such databases are created by spiders. *Spiders,* also known as *crawlers* or *robots,* are software programs that roam the Web, looking for new Web sites by following links from page to page. When a spider finds a new page, it adds information about it—its title, address, and perhaps a summary of the contents—to the search engine's database. (However, with the millions of pages on the Web and the constant changes being made to many of them, there's no way anyone can keep on top of it all, even with information filters and Internet agents.)

Newer agents can be instructed in plain English to scour the Web for relevant information. For example, they can understand phrases such as "comparative prices and features of sport utility vehicles" and "best places to visit in Southeast Asia."[28] The program from Autonomy, Inc. (*www.agentware.com*), for example, uses little animated dogs to search out and retrieve information. The agents get smarter with use, and they can be set up to go information hunting while you're not at the computer.

Avatars

Want to see yourself—or a stand-in for yourself—on your computer screen? Then try using a kind of cyberpersona called an *avatar.* An **avatar** is either (1) a graphical image of you or someone else on a computer screen or (2) a graphical personification of a computer or a process that's running on a computer.[29]

Figure 13.6 Avatars. This screen shows some avatars from a chat site that one can choose to interact with.

■ *Avatar as yourself or others:* The on-screen version of yourself could be "anything from a human form to a pair of cowboys boots with lips," wrote technology columnist Denise Caruso. "Users move them around while talking (via keyboard) with other avatars on the same screen."[30] On the Internet, users participating in online chat rooms furnished like cartoon sets can get together with other users each of whom can construct an avatar from a variety of heads, clothing, shoes, and even animal identities. *(See Figure 13.6.)*

To view an avatar, click once to get a cursor; then click on a poster.

■ *Avatars representing a process:* "The driving force behind avatars is the ongoing search for an interface that's easier and more comfortable to use," says one writer, "especially for the millions of people who are still computerphobic."[31] One difficulty with designing computer-controlled avatars—also called *agents, characters,* and *bots*—is making sure people don't react negatively to them. Thus, instead of faces or personifications, it may be better to use pictures of notepads, checkbooks, and similar objects.

There still remains much room for improvement in the areas of intelligent agents, information filtering, and avatars before they can really help us deal efficiently with information overload. Says Jon Dvorak, a seasoned writer on the topic of computers and information technology:

> Until the filtering mechanisms on the Web and for e-mail are substantially improved, all of us parked in front of our PCs are going to continue wasting far too much time. . . . The simple fact is that the Web and the Net revolution have removed the natural barriers between us and the carload of information we would normally never see. The loss of these natural filters is problematic, and the only solution is to create filters artificially that reestablish a wall between ourselves and the information floodwaters.[32]

A FLASH OF REASONING POWER?

Computers are whizzes when it comes to the grunt work of mathematics. But for creative and elegant solutions to hard mathematical problems, nothing has been able to beat the human mind. That is, perhaps, until now.

A computer program written by researchers at Argonne National Laboratory in Illinois has come up with a major mathematical proof that would have been called creative if a human had thought of it. In doing so, the computer has, for the first time, got a toehold into pure mathematics, a field described by its practitioners as more of an art form than a science. And the implications, some say, are profound, showing just how powerful computers can be at reasoning itself, at mimicking the flashes of logical insight or even genius that have characterized the best human minds.

Computers have found proofs of mathematical conjectures before, of course, but those conjectures were easy to prove. The difference this time is that the computer has solved a conjecture that stumped some of the best mathematicians for 60 years. And it did so with a program that was designed to reason, not to solve a specific problem. In that sense, the program is very different from chess playing computer programs, for example, which are intended to solve just one problem: the moves of a chess game. . . .

[T]he result also may challenge the very notion of creative thinking, raising the possibility that computers could take a parallel path to reach the same conclusions as great human thinkers. Or it may be that since no one has any idea how humans think, the magnificent bursts of creativity that spring apparently full blown from the minds of geniuses are actually a result of hidden, computer-like drudge work in the unconscious recesses of the brain.

—Gina Kolata, "With Major Math Proof, Brute Computers Show Flash of Reasoning Power," *New York Times*

WHAT IT IS
WHAT IT DOES

WHY IT IS IMPORTANT

artificial intelligence (AI) (LO 2, p. 13.14) Group of related technologies used in an attempt to develop machines to emulate human-like qualities, such as learning, reasoning, communicating, seeing, and hearing.

AI is important for enabling machines to do things formerly possible only with human effort.

avatar (LO 9, p. 13.30) Graphical image of you or someone else on a computer screen; (2) graphical personification of a computer or process that's running on a computer.

It is hoped that avatars will make information technologies easier to use.

expert system (LO 5, p. 13.18) Interactive computer program that can apply rules to input in such a way as to generate conclusions. The program helps users solve problems that would otherwise require the assistance of a human expert.

Expert systems allow users to solve problems without the assistance of a human expert; they incorporate both surface knowledge ("textbook knowledge") and deep knowledge ("tricks of the trade").

filtering (LO 9, p. 13.29) Using a program to construct a type of custom-made electronic barrier through which only selected or desired data is passed.

Filtering helps limit and monitor the data and/or information the user receives.

fuzzy logic (LO 4, p. 13.17) Method of dealing with imprecise data and vagueness, with problems that have many answers rather than one.

Unlike traditional "crisp" digital logic, fuzzy logic is more like human reasoning: it deals with probability and credibility.

genetic algorithm (LO 6, p. 13.23) Program that uses Darwinian principles of random mutation to improve itself.

Genetic algorithms use trial and error to learn from experience, thus constantly improving themselves.

inference engine (LO 5, p. 13.18) Software that controls the search of the expert system's knowledge base and produces conclusions.

An inference engine fits the user's problem into the knowledge base and derives a conclusion from the rules and facts it contains.

intelligent agent (LO 9, p. 13.29) Computer program that performs work tasks on your behalf, including roaming networks and compiling data.

Agents scan databases and electronic mail; clerical agents answer telephones and send faxes, user-interface agents learn individual work habits.

kiosk (LO 1, p. 13.3) Small, self-contained structure such as a newsstand or a ticket booth. Unattended multimedia kiosks dispense information via computer screens. Keyboards and touch screens are used for input.

Kiosks are designed to offer information to a large number of people. With more advanced multimedia authoring software, corporations are creating in-house advertising and promotional programs for display using kiosks at trade shows and during product demonstrations.

knowledge base (LO 5, p. 13.18)   Expert system's database of knowledge about a particular subject.

A knowledge base includes relevant facts, information, beliefs, assumptions, and procedures for solving problems.

knowledge engineers (LO 5, p. 13.20)   Persons who are trained to elicit knowledge (for example, by interview) from experts and build an expert system.

Capturing human expertise for the computer is a time-consuming and difficult task. The expert system is only as good as the quality of the data and rules obtained from the human experts.

MPC classifications (LO 1, p. 13.4)   The set of minimum hardware standards for personal computer multimedia use that are published by the Multimedia PC Marketing Council.

The Multimedia PC Marketing Council publishes the MPC classifications to help consumers identify a minimum system configuration for playing back multimedia on Intel-based and similar computers.

natural languages (LO 4, p. 13.16)   Programming languages, called fifth-generation languages, that give people a more natural connection with computers.

Natural languages make it easier for users to work with computers.

natural language processing (LO 4, p. 13.16)   Study of ways for computers to recognize and understand human language, whether in spoken or written form.

Natural language processing could further reduce the barriers to human/computer communications.

neural networks (LO 6, p. 13.21)   Field of artificial intelligence; networks that use physical electronic devices or software to mimic the neurological structure of the human brain, with, for instance, transistors for nerve cells and resistors for synapses.

Neural networks are able to mimic human learning behavior and pattern recognition.

perception system (LO 3, p. 13.15)   Robot that emulates the human capabilities of sight, hearing, touch, and smell and then responds to the new information; also called *intelligent robot.*

Intelligent robots are used in factories for inspecting quality of products and in security patrols, among other things.

robot (LO 3, p. 13.14)   Automatic device that performs functions ordinarily ascribed to human beings or that operates with what appears to be almost human intelligence.

Robots are performing more and more functions in business and the professions, including situations that would be too dangerous for humans to work in.

robotics (LO 3, p. 13.14)   Field that attempts to develop machines that can perform work normally done by people.

See *robot.*

simulators (LO 8, p. 13.27)   Devices that represent the behavior of physical or abstract systems.

Virtual-reality simulators are used to train pilots on various aircraft and to prepare air-traffic controllers for equipment failures. They are used for many other virtual-reality simulations as well.

Turing test (LO 7, p. 13.24)   A test or game for determining whether a computer is considered to possess "intelligence" or "self-awareness." In the Turing test, a human judge converses by means of a computer terminal with two entities hidden in another location.

Some experts believe that once a computer has passed the Turing test, it will be judged to have achieved a level of human intelligence.

virtual reality (VR) (LO 8, p. 13.26)   Computer-generated artificial reality that projects a person into a sensation of three-dimensional space.

With virtual reality you can experience almost anything you want without ever leaving your chair. Virtual reality has become instrumental as simulators in training programs of many types.

SELF-TEST EXERCISES

1. A(n) _____ is an automatic device that performs functions that are ordinarily performed by a human being.

2. A concept being used in the development of natural language processing is _____ _____, which doesn't base decisions on either/or propositions.

3. The goal of _____ _____ _____ is to enable the computer to communicate with the user in the user's native language.

4. A robot that can hear, see, smell, and touch is referred to as a(n) _____ _____.

5. A(n) _____ _____ is a computer-based system that attempts to mimic the activities of the human brain.

SHORT-ANSWER QUESTIONS

1. What does the term *avatar* refer to?

2. What is meant by the term *artificial intelligence*?

3. What is an expert system?

4. What do you need in order to experience virtual reality?

5. Describe the relationship between the Turing test and research into artificial intelligence and natural language processing.

MULTIPLE-CHOICE QUESTIONS

1. To which of the following are the terms *knowledge base, inference engine,* and *user interface* most closely related?
   a. artificial intelligence
   b. fuzzy logic
   c. expert system
   d. knowledge engineers
   e. all the above

2. Which of the following could you use to roam a computer network to find information?
   a. intelligent agent
   b. avatar
   c. simulator
   d. head-mounted display (HMD)
   e. all the above

3. Which of the following is necessary in order to experience virtual reality?
   a. intelligent agent
   b. avatar
   c. simulator
   d. head-mounted display (HMD)
   e. all the above

TRUE/FALSE QUESTIONS

1. To run multimedia software, your hardware requirements are the same as those of someone who creates multimedia titles. (true/false)

2. Text is the primary media element for communicating information in a multimedia production. (true/false)

3. Software programs that roam the Web are commonly referred to as *spiders.* (true/false)

4. Vector graphics are superior in quality to bit-mapped graphics. (true/false)

5. The main limitation of expert systems is that they aren't interactive. (true/false)

ETHICS, PRIVACY, SECURITY, AND SOCIAL QUESTIONS

Computing for Right Living

PREVIEW

When you have finished this chapter, you will be able to:

1. Discuss how the use of computers raises new kinds of ethical problems

2. Discuss how privacy can be invaded

3. Describe intellectual-property matters that relate to copyright, software and network piracy, plagiarism, and the ownership of media

4. Describe how in art and journalism computers can be used to alter sounds, photos, videos, and facts

5. Discuss major free-speech issues

6. Describe the major threats to computers and communications system

7. Describe some methods for making computers and communications systems more secure

8. Discuss social issues related to computing

WHY IS THIS CHAPTER IMPORTANT?

One morning a magazine writer who had recently published an article about Microsoft chairman Bill Gates checked into his computer e-mail to find the following reaction to his story from an anonymous reader: "Listen, you toadying [*deleted*] scumbag . . . remove your head [*three words deleted*] long enough to look around and notice that real reporters don't fawn over their subjects, pretend that their subjects are making some sort of special contact with them, or, worse, curry favor by TELLING their subjects how great the [*deleted*] profile is going to turn out and then brag in print about doing it. . . ."

On reading the message, the writer rocked back in his chair. "Whoa," he said aloud to himself. "I got flamed."[1] A form of speech unique to online communication, *flaming* is writing an online message that uses derogatory, obscene, or inappropriate language. Flaming, often done anonymously, is a new wrinkle in human communications, evidence once again that information technology gives us more possibilities of nearly every sort. Not only does the use of computers provide us with different ways of working, thinking, and playing; it also presents us with some different moral choices—determining right actions in the digital and online universe.

In this chapter we discuss several matters pertaining to right actions:

- Computer ethics
- Computers and privacy
- Intellectual property rights
- Truth in art and journalism
- Free speech, civility, pornography, and censorship
- The threats to computers and communications systems
- Security issues relating to computers and communications systems
- Social questions related to computers

Computer Ethics

Ethics is concerned with principles governing conduct. Because of their speed and scale, unpredictability, and complexity, computers raise new kinds of ethical problems.

Every reader of this book at some point will have to wrestle with ethical issues related to computer technology. **Ethics** is defined as a set of moral values or principles that govern the conduct of an individual or group.

Here, for instance, are three aspects of computers that affect ethics in human affairs, as pointed out by Tim Forester and Perry Morrison in their book *Computer Ethics:*[2]

- *Speed and scale:* Great amounts of information can be stored, retrieved, and transmitted at a speed and on a scale not possible before. Despite the benefits, this has serious implications "for data security and personal privacy (as well as employment)," they say, because the security of information technology can never be considered certain.

- *Unpredictability:* Computers and communications are pervasive, touching nearly every aspect of our lives. However, unlike other pervasive technologies—such as electricity, television, and automobiles—information technology is a lot less predictable and reliable.

- *Complexity:* The on/off principle underlying computer systems may be simple, but the systems themselves are often incredibly complex. Indeed, some are so complex that they are not always understood even by their creators. "This," say Forester and Morrison, "often makes them completely unmanageable," producing massive foul-ups or spectacularly out-of-control budgets.

The speed and scale, unpredictability, and complexity of computers affect several important areas of our lives, ranging from privacy to environmental questions. Let us consider them.

Computers and Privacy

The important right of privacy is affected by information technology, particularly through misuse of databases and electronic networks. Some rules and laws in the United States protect citizens against certain abuses by computers. Nevertheless, some argue, privacy may have to be limited for the greater good.

Privacy is the right of people not to reveal information about themselves—the right to keep personal information, such as medical histories, personal e-mail messages, student records, and financial information from getting into the wrong hands. Information technology, however, puts constant pressure on this right.

Think your medical records are inviolable? Actually, private medical information is bought and sold freely by various companies since there is no federal law prohibiting it. (And they simply ignore the patchwork of varying state laws.)[3]

A worker monitors rail activities from a computer workstation at a control center in Hokaido, Japan.

Think the boss can't snoop on your e-mail at work? The law allows employers to "intercept" employee communications if one of the parties involved agrees to the "interception." The party "involved" is the employer. Indeed, employer snooping seems to be widespread. Thus a good rule of thumb, suggests one writer, is to "think of an e-mail message not as a sealed letter but as a postcard—and, moreover, a postcard that might well be read and copied in every post office it passes through, then kept on file for years afterward." (Using the little trash-can "delete" symbol on your display screen doesn't mean your e-mail is really deleted; most networks routinely store backups of all messages that pass through them.)

Think your student records are protected? Actually, attorneys, auditors, therapists, and some others can view them now anyway. But in addition, colleges are beginning to implement systems of transferring transcripts, disciplinary reports, and other student records by electronic means, such as through the SPEEDE/ EXPRESS electronic system. "Brick by innocent brick, the edifice of lifelong electronic student dossiers is being constructed without any recognition by the general public of what is being done," warns privacy advocate Gordon Cook.

Think there are adequate controls on financial information collected about you? Then pray you're never the victim of identity theft, one of the fastest-growing forms of fraud. A relatively new crime, *identity theft* is the stealing of identifying information about you—from loan documents, credit card offers, bank statements, utility bills, and the like—then using it to establish new credit accounts. San Francisco couple Leonard and Olga Dudin, for instance, found themselves in a one-year nightmare, their credit ruined, after a co-worker obtained Leonard's Social Security number and used it to open several charge accounts, racking up more than $200,000 in bills. The Dudins didn't learn about it for a while because the fake Dudin put his own address on the new accounts.

A great many people are concerned about the loss of their right to privacy. Indeed, a recent survey found that 80% of the people contacted worried that they had lost "all control" of the personal information being collected about them and tracked by computers.[4] One study found that 94% of 9300 online respondents were so concerned that marketers would misuse their personal information that they said they would not give retail, medical, or financial information to firms online that they'd had no previous dealings with.

Most computer-related privacy issues involve the use of large databases and electronic networks, particularly the Internet. Let us consider these.

Databases

Large organizations around the world are constantly compiling information about most of us. Worldwide the number of online databases—70% of which are in the United States—has skyrocketed from about 400 in 1980 to 4465 in 1990 to 10s of thousands in 1996.

As explained earlier, the means by which related records are pulled together in databases is the use of a *key field* (↘ p. 12.6) to do the linking. In the United States, the Social Security number is the most frequently used key field. This number was intended principally to be used to help collect taxes for the federally administered retirement system and for disbursing its payments to individuals. It was not designed as a kind of "universal identifier" for Americans, but that is what it has become, used by banks, insurance companies, loan companies, employers, and so on. Unfortunately, one's Social Security number can be obtained from a variety of sources. Indeed, for a while, the Social Security Administration even offered a Web site that allowed anyone with enough information to access personal Social Security records.

Of course, there are other kinds of identifying numbers (key fields), and it's surprising how easy some of them are to find. For instance, computer columnist Gina Smith discovered that having an unlisted telephone number only meant that people couldn't find it in the phone book. "I was surprised to find out your fingers can still do the walking to my phone number if they happen to be holding a mouse." Apparently, the online phone directories on the Web are good places to find unlisted phone numbers because these databases are assembled from mailing lists and warranty cards, not phone companies.

This illustrates just how sophisticated the building of databases has become. Professional data gatherers, or "information resellers," collect personal data and sell it to fund-raisers, direct marketers, and others. In the United States, even some motor-vehicle departments sell the car-registration data they store. From this database, companies have been able to collect names, addresses, and other information about the majority of American households. Some privacy experts estimate that the average person is on 100 mailing lists and in 50 databases at one time. *(See Figure 14.1.)*

One last point: Even when people volunteer information about themselves for seemingly the most innocuous of reasons, it can end up being used in astonishing ways. For instance, when Texas resident Beverly Dennis filled out a written questionnaire about her buying habits in return for free product samples, she didn't realize that prison inmates were processing data from such questionnaires—until she got a disturbing letter from an imprisoned rapist.

Electronic Networks

"When most people surf the Net," writes one technology reporter, "they assume nobody knows where they go or what they do. They're wrong." Says Janlori Goldman of the Center for Democracy and Technology, "The danger of the Internet now is the illusion of anonymity that's completely false. People think they're invisible."

Say you visit a cigarette company's Web site and give it your name or e-mail address in order to get discount coupons for cigarettes. The Web site deposits—on *your* computer—a so-called **cookie,** a special file that keeps track of your activities and visits. The cookie can connect your name or e-mail address to any future visit to that Web site. There's no requirement that you be notified that this information is being gathered. Moreover, there are practically no restrictions on how the information may be disseminated or otherwise used. Thus, for example, your

Figure 14.1 Junk mail: How your name gets on mailing lists. Lists are compiled from two principal sources about you: List brokers use public information sources. List brokers use commercial transactions in which you have been involved. Compilers and brokers then sell your name to each other and to various direct mailers.

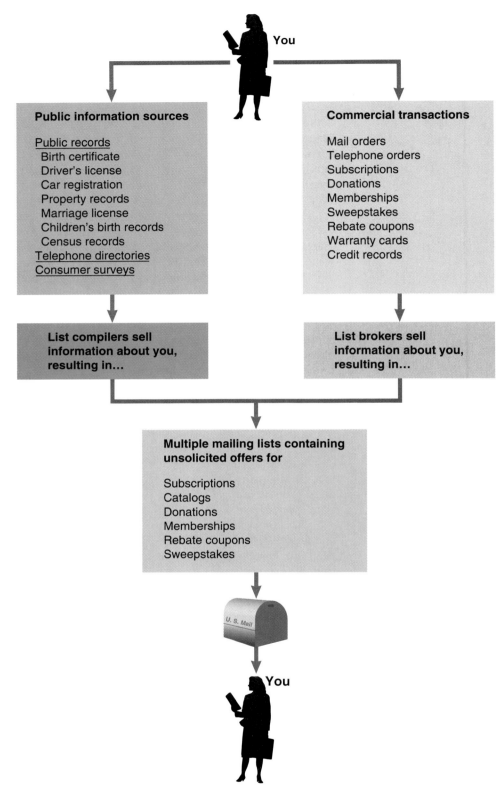

health or life insurance company could eventually get hold of the information and decide to raise the premiums of people it believes are smokers. (You can set up your Web browser to notify you when a cookie is being sent, and you can delete cookies from your hard disk; look for a folder called "cookies.")

What about online services, such as AOL, CompuServe, MSN, and Prodigy? All of them can and do sell information about you to marketers, to be used for direct marketing purposes. Most (but not all) of the services allow you to specify that you don't want information about you disclosed in this way, but you have to take the initiative.

Most people using electronic networks rely on privacy by obscurity. In the case of the Internet, says writer Matthew Hawn, they hope "that the sheer volume of data that flows over the Net each day will keep browsing anonymous." Actually, tracing your travels on the Net is probably easier than you might think. Deja News (*http://www.dejanews.com*), as Hawn points out, is a site that has catalogued and indexed more than 15,000 Usenet news groups (✔ p. 8.20), the Internet's bulletin board, since 1995. One feature of Deja News is a usage profile of each person who posts messages on Usenet. Hawn ran a search for Tim May, a privacy advocate, and found that May had posted 527 messages to Usenet in 18 months' time, including postings to 32 different news groups like the Cypherpunk mailing list, a beer news group, and a fan group for Debbie Reynolds. "No one ever said that Usenet was a private way to exchange information," writes Hawn, "but it can still be shocking to see one's own postings indexed and sorted by frequency and topic."

Rules and Laws on Privacy

In the 1970s the U.S. Department of Health, Education, and Welfare developed a set of five Fair Information Practices. These rules have since been adopted by a number of public and private organizations. The practices also led to the enactment of a number of laws to protect individuals from invasion of privacy.

Perhaps the most important law is the Federal Privacy Act, or Privacy Act of 1974. The *Privacy Act of 1974* prohibits secret personnel files from being kept on individuals by government agencies or their contractors. It gives individuals the right to see their records, see how the data is used, and correct errors. Another significant piece of legislation was the U.S. Freedom of Information Act, passed in 1970. The *Freedom of Information Act* allows ordinary citizens to have access to data gathered about them by federal agencies.

Most privacy laws regulate only the behavior of government agencies or government contractors. For example, the *Computer Matching and Privacy Protection Act of 1988* prevents the government from comparing certain records to try to find a match. This law does not affect most private companies.

Banking and credit are two private industries for which there are federal privacy laws on the books. The *Fair Credit Reporting Act of 1970* allows you to have access to and gives you the right to challenge your credit records. If you have been denied credit, this access must be given to you free of charge. The *Right to Financial Privacy Act of 1978* sets restrictions on federal agencies that want to search customer records in banks.

The Case for Limiting Privacy: Should We Really Fear "Data Rape"?

Employers read our e-mail and medical records. Strangers listen to our cellular-phone conversations. Is our privacy rapidly being stripped away? Should we seek even more laws to protect us from "data rape"?

Not so fast, says sociologist Amitai Etzioni. Restoring old-fashioned privacy is about as likely as vanquishing nuclear weapons, he says. "The genie is out of the bottle. We must either return to the Stone Age (pay cash, use carrier pigeons, and forget insurance) or learn to live with shrunken privacy."

Are you concerned about protecting your privacy? What online actions would you avoid to protect your privacy?

Actually, Etzioni argues, "giving up some measure of privacy is exactly what the common good requires." After all, do we really want banks to be able to hide large amounts of money from drug transactions, prohibit schools from screening out security personnel who have been child abusers, enable incompetent physicians who have caused patient deaths to cross state lines to continue practicing? All these are prevented through computer cross-checks.

While we should tolerate new limitations on privacy *only* when there is a compelling need, says Etzioni, it must be accepted that privacy is not an absolute value.

PROTECTING YOUR PRIVACY ONLINE

You may not know it, but that line running from the back of your computer to the Internet could be opening a door on your privacy. In fact, there may already be personal information about you online. Here are some tips for maintaining your privacy in the digital era:

■ **Personal Information** Whether you're registering for a Web site, personalizing a service, or creating your own home page, think twice about giving out personal information. Some Web sites don't allow you to register unless you've filled in all the entries. If they ask for information you don't want to disclose, don't register—or use fake data.

■ **Privacy Policy** Many Web sites and online services now publish a privacy notice when they request personal information. Look for this guarantee that your name and data won't be shared with anyone without your permission. You also can check for a privacy policy before subscribing to an electronic mailing list.

■ **Unwanted Mailings** During the sign-up process, many content providers ask whether you'd like to receive mailings, either from the company or from a third party. Usually, the "yes" box is selected, meaning you have to change it to "no" if you don't want to be included in a mailing list.

■ **Search Databases** If you don't want your home address, phone number, or e-mail address listed on any search site on the Web, you can request that this information be deleted. The problem is, you

have to write to each service that lists the data. The Four11 White Page Directory FAQ, the Bigfoot FAQ, and the Internet Address Finder FAQ all explain how you can remove your e-mail address from their archives. Switchboard and Yahoo's People Search tell you how to suppress your phone number and address from their database.

■ **Search Archives** You can exclude your Usenet posts from some search archives (such as Deja News and AltaVista) by typing the phrase *x-no-archive:yes* at the beginning of each post.

■ **Use Different Screen Name** If you use a service like America Online, you can set up different screen names under one account. Use a separate screen name (and e-mail address) when you register for Web sites, post to Usenet, and so on, so you can track how your name is shared and confine your junk e-mail to a separate address.

■ **Talk Back** If you start receiving unwanted e-mail that you can track to a particular company, let that company know you'd like to be taken off its list. To express your opinion on a wider scale, you can sign up for the Federal Trade Commission's privacy mailing list, which is soliciting input toward the development of privacy principles. There are also several privacy advocacy organizations on the Net.

—Adapted from C/Net, "Some Tips to Protect Privacy," *San Francisco Chronicle*

Intellectual Property Rights

Intellectual property rights involve areas of copyright, software and network piracy, plagiarism, and ownership of media.

Information technology has presented legislators and lawyers—and you—with some new ethical issues regarding rights to intellectual property. **Intellectual property** consists of the products of the human mind, tangible or intangible. There are three methods of protecting intellectual property. They are *patents* (as for an invention), *trade secrets* (as for a formula or method of doing business), or *copyrights*.

Copyright

Of principal interest to us is copyright protection. A **copyright** is a body of law that prohibits copying of intellectual property without the permission of the copyright holder. The law protects books, articles, pamphlets, music, art, drawings, movies, and other expressions of ideas. It also protects computer software.

A copyright protects the *expression* of an idea but not the idea itself. Thus, others may copy your idea for, say, a new shoot-'em-up video game but not your particular variant of it. Copyright protection is automatic and lasts a minimum of 50 years; you do not have to register your idea with the government (as you do with a patent) in order to receive protection.

These matters are important because the use of computers has made the act of copying far easier and more convenient than in the past. Copying a book on a photocopying machine might take hours and cost 20 dollars, so people felt they might as well buy the book. Copying a software program (✔ p. 6.35) might take just seconds and cost little or nothing. Digitization threatens to compound the problem. For example, current copyright law doesn't specifically protect copyright material online. Says one article:

> Copyright experts say laws haven't kept pace with technology, especially digitization, the process of converting any data—sound, video, text— into a series of ones and zeros that are then transmitted over computer networks. Using this technology, it's possible to create an infinite number of copies of a book, a record, or a movie and distribute them to millions of people around the world at very little cost. Unlike photocopies of books or pirated audiotapes, the digital copies are virtually identical to the original.[5]

Three copyright-related matters deserve our attention: software and network piracy, plagiarism, and ownership of images, sounds, and other media.

Software and Network Piracy

It may be hard to think of yourself as a pirate (no sword or eye patch) when all you've done is make a copy of some commercial software for a friend. However, from an ethical standpoint, an act of piracy is like shoplifting the product off a store shelf—even if it's for a friend.

Piracy is theft or unauthorized distribution or use. A type of piracy is to appropriate a computer design or program. This is the piracy that Apple Computer claimed in a suit (since rejected) against Microsoft and Hewlett-Packard, saying that items in its interface, such as icons and windows, had been copied. **Software piracy** is the unauthorized copying of copyrighted software. One way is to copy a program from one diskette to another or to make a duplicate CD-ROM. Another is to download a program from a network and make a copy of it. **Network piracy** is using electronic networks to distribute unauthorized copyrighted materials in digitized form. Record companies, for example, have protested the practice of computer users' sending unauthorized copies of digital recordings over the Internet.[6]

The easy rationalization is to say that "I'm just a poor student, and making this one copy isn't going to cause any harm." But it is the single act of software piracy multiplied millions of times that is causing the software publishers a billion-dollar problem. They point out that the loss of revenue cuts into their budget for offering customer support, upgrading products, and compensating their creative people. Piracy also means that software prices are less likely to come down; if anything, they are more likely to go up.

Quite apart from ethics, there are plenty of reasons of self-interest for staying legal:

- *Staying up-to-date:* When you buy a software program and register your purchase with the manufacturer, you're generally entitled to discounts on new versions, so you can keep software up-to-date economically.

- *Ability to get help:* If you crash your computer or network with a pirated version of a software program, there's no one you can call for help.

- *Risk of getting a virus:* Every time you obtain illegal software, whether via diskette or off the Internet, you risk getting a software virus. As we explain in a few pages, a virus can corrupt or destroy your data or software.

- *Risk of getting caught:* If you, your company, or your college is caught using pirated software, the results can be unpleasant, to say the least. You or your organization could face civil fines of up to $100,000. The illegal software will be destroyed and you'll have to replace it with legal products at current retail prices. Finally, you may have to endure humiliating publicity and end up with a criminal record.

Software piracy is rampant, representing 26% of all software in use in the United States, according to the Business Software Alliance, a trade group charged with enforcing policies against piracy. In time, anticopying technology may be developed that, when coupled with laws making the disabling of such technology a crime, will reduce the piracy problem. Regardless, publishers, broadcasters, movie studios, and authors must be persuaded to take chances on developing online and multimedia versions of their intellectual products. Such information providers need to be able to cover their costs and make a reasonable return. If not, suggests one writer, the information superhighway will remain "empty of traffic because no one wants to put anything on the road."[7]

Plagiarism

Plagiarism is the expropriation of another writer's text, findings, or interpretations and presentation of it as one's own. Information technology puts a new face on plagiarism in two ways. On the one hand, it offers plagiarists new opportunities to go far afield for unauthorized copying. On the other hand, the technology offers new ways to catch people who steal other people's material.

Electronic online journals are not limited by the number of pages, and so they can publish papers that attract a small number of readers. In recent years, there has been an explosion in the number of such journals and of their academic and scientific papers. This proliferation may make it harder to detect when a work has been plagiarized, since few readers will know if a similar paper has been published elsewhere.[8]

Yet information technology can also be used to identify plagiarism. Scientists have used computers to search different documents for identical passages of text. In 1990, two "fraud busters" at the National Institutes of Health alleged after a computer-based analysis that a prominent historian and biographer had committed plagiarism in his books. The ensuing uproar shook the academic community for four years. The historian, who said the technique turned up only the repetition of stock phrases, was later exonerated in a scholarly investigation.[9]

Ownership of Media

Scanners, digital cameras (still and video), and the like make it possible to alter movies, images, and sounds to be almost anything you want. What does this mean for the original copyright holders? An unauthorized sound snippet of James Brown's famous howl can be electronically transformed by digital sampling into the background music for dozens of rap recordings.[10] Images can be appropriated by scanning them into a computer system, then altered or placed in a new context. Universities have found themselves threatened with copyright-infringement lawsuits because their students have used the comic-strip characters of "Calvin and Hobbes" and "Dilbert" and the "Playmates" of *Playboy* magazine in creating Web home pages without much thought as to who might own the copyrights.

The line between artistic license and infringement of copyright is not always clear-cut. In 1993, a Federal appeals court in New York upheld a ruling against artist Jeff Koons for producing ceramic art of some puppies. It turned out that the puppies were identical to those that had appeared in a postcard photograph copyrighted by a California photographer.[11] But what would have been the judgment if Koons had scanned in the postcard, changed the colors, and rearranged the order of the puppies?

In any event, to avoid lawsuits for violating copyright, a growing number of artists who have recycled material have taken steps to protect themselves. This usually involves paying flat fees or a percentage of their royalties to the original copyright holders.

Truth in Art and Journalism

In art and journalism, sounds, photos, videos, and even facts can be manipulated without it being clear that this has been done.

The ability to manipulate digitized images and sounds has brought a new tool to art but a big new problem to journalism. How can we now know that what we're seeing or hearing is the truth? Consider the following issues.

Manipulation of Sound

Frank Sinatra's 1994 album *Duets* pairs him through technological tricks with singers like Barbra Streisand, Liza Minnelli, and Bono of U2. Sinatra recorded solos in a recording studio. His singing partners, while listening to his taped performances on earphones, dubbed in their own voices. This was done not only at different times but often, through distortion-free phone lines, from different places. The illusion in the final recording is that the two singers are standing shoulder to shoulder.

Newspaper columnist William Safire loves the way "digitally remastered" recordings recapture great singing he enjoyed in the past. However, he called *Duets* "a series of artistic frauds." Said Safire, "The question raised is this: When a performer's voice and image can not only be edited, echoed, refined, spliced, corrected, and enhanced—but can be transported and combined with others not physically present—what is a performance? . . . Enough of additives, plasticity, virtual venality; give me organic entertainment."[12] Another critic said that to call the disk *Duets* seemed a misnomer. "Sonic collage would be a more truthful description."[13]

Some listeners feel that new technology changes the character of a performance for the better—that the sour notes and clinkers can be edited out. Others, however, think the practice of assembling bits and pieces in a studio drains the music of its essential flow and unity.

Whatever the problems of misrepresentation in art, however, they pale beside those in journalism. Could not a radio station edit a stream of digitized sound to achieve an entirely different effect from what actually happened?

Manipulation of Photos

When O. J. Simpson was arrested on suspicion of murder, the two principal newsmagazines both ran pictures of him on their covers.[14,15] *Newsweek* ran the mug shot unmodified, as taken by the Los Angeles Police Department. *Time,* however, had the shot redone with special effects as a "photo-illustration" by an artist working with a computer. Simpson's image was darkened so that it still looked like a photo but, some critics said, with a more sinister cast to it.

Should a magazine that reports the news be taking such artistic license? Should *National Geographic* in 1982 have moved two Egyptian pyramids closer together so that they would fit on a vertical cover? Was it even right for *TV Guide* in 1989 to run a cover showing Oprah Winfrey's head placed on Ann-Margret's body?

The potential for abuse is clear. "For 150 years, the photographic image has been viewed as more persuasive than written accounts as a form of 'evidence,'" says one writer. "Now this authenticity is breaking down under the assault of technology."[16] Asks a former photo editor of the *New York Times Magazine,* "What would happen if the photograph appeared to be a straightforward recording of physical reality, but could no longer be relied upon to depict actual people and events?"[17]

Do you believe that photo manipulation is acceptable? Under what circumstances?

Many editors try to distinguish between photos used for commercialism (advertising) versus journalism, or for feature stories versus news stories. However, this distinction implies that the integrity of photos applies only to some narrow definition of news. In the end, it can be argued, tampered photographs pollute the credibility of all of journalism. For this reason new types of digital film are becoming available that allow examiners to determine if any pixels have been manipulated.

Manipulation of Video

The technique of morphing, used in still photos, takes a quantum jump when used in movies, videos, and television commercials. In **morphing,** a film or video image is displayed on a computer screen and altered pixel by pixel, or dot by dot. *(See Figure 14.2.)* The result is that the image metamorphoses into something else—a pair of lips into the front of a Toyota, for example.

Figure 14.2 Morphing

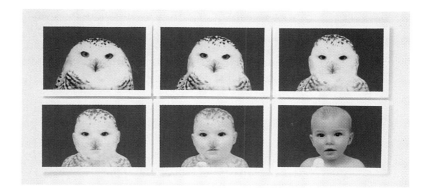

Morphing and other techniques of digital image manipulation have had a tremendous impact on filmmaking. Director and digital pioneer Robert Zemeckis (*Death Becomes Her*) compares the new technology to the advent of sound in Hollywood. It can be used to erase jet contrails from the sky in a western and to make digital planes do impossible stunts. It can even be used to add and erase actors. In *Forrest Gump,* many scenes involved old film and TV footage that had been altered so that the Tom Hanks character was interacting with historical figures.

Films and videotapes are widely thought to be somewhat accurate versions of reality (as evidenced by the reaction to the amateur videotape of the Rodney King beating by police in Los Angeles). Thus, the possibility of digital alterations raises some real problems. One is the possibility of doctoring videotapes supposed to represent actual events. Another concern is for film archives: Because videotapes suffer no loss in resolution, there are no "generations." Thus, it will be impossible for historians and archivists to tell whether the videotape they're viewing is the real thing or not.

Information technology increasingly is blurring humans' ability to distinguish between natural and artificial experience, say Stanford University communication professors Byron Reeves and Clifford Nass.[18] For instance, they have found that showing a political candidate on a large screen (30 or 60 inches) makes a great difference in people's reactions. In fact, you will actually like him or her more than if you watch on a 13-inch screen. "We've found in the laboratory that big pictures automatically take more of a viewer's attention," said Reeves. "You will like someone more on the large screen and pay more attention to what he or she says but remember less." Our visual perception system, they find, is unable to discount information—to say that "this is artificial"—just because it is symbolic rather than real.

If our minds have this inclination anyway, how can we be expected to exercise our critical faculties when the "reality" is not merely artificial but actively doctored?

Manipulation of Facts

"Rumors have probably been around as long as humans have been able to speak," points out technology observer Tom Abate, "and social scientists say during crises, conflicts, or catastrophes people tend to spread stories that sound plausible but aren't true. . . . Now the Internet allows us to send messages around the world at the speed of light, exponentially increasing the power of rumormongers. . . ."

There's one problem: Internet rumors shouldn't be accepted as being *news* in the true sense of the word. Says veteran computer journalist Walter Mossberg:

News isn't gossip or rumor or speculation. It isn't claims or conspiracy theories passed around by people who've done no research or reporting. And it isn't merely news releases issued by companies, government agencies, interest groups, and others. But these categories make up a lot of what's considered news on-line."[19]

Real news is the reporting of events by trained journalists who aren't involved directly in events or trends but have witnessed them or interviewed people involved.

What can you do to guard against being misled by online reports parading as "news"? The same thing you should do with stories reported elsewhere, as on TV or in newspapers: You should take advantage of a range of choices of news sources, and you should exercise critical judgment in evaluating the report, such as ascertaining the legitimacy of the source.

Free Speech, Civility, Pornography, and Censorship

Free-speech issues in cyberspace must be concerned with issues of civility and "netiquette," pornography, and censorship.

In Saudi Arabia, officials try to police taboo subjects (sex, religion, politics) on the Internet.[20] In China, Net users must register with the government, which has also blocked access to as many as 100 Web sites.[21] In Germany, prosecutors indicted the manager of CompuServe Deutschland on charges of trafficking in pornography—material its customers obtain from sites on the Internet—thus holding the online service responsible for carrying material it had no part in producing.[22] In the United States, however, free speech is protected by the First Amendment to the Constitution.

But how free should free speech be in a cyberspace universe where children can access pornography and swindlers can fool the unsophisticated? Some people think federal regulators should curb "indecency" on the Internet and crack down on supposed consumer fraud. Others fear any regulation could slow growth and innovation of the Net and online services. "No form of electronic media in history has grown as fast as the Internet, and the Internet has grown precisely because it isn't regulated," says the head of the National Technology and Information Administration.

Let us consider some of these matters.

Civility: Online Behavior and "Netiquette"

Civility is important, even online. The anonymity of the Internet allows for a wide range of behavior, some of it pretty obnoxious. However, the flaming attack described at the beginning of this chapter is probably unusual, since most flaming happens when someone violates online manners or "netiquette." Many online bulletin boards or chat forums have a set of "FAQs"—frequently asked questions—that newcomers, or "newbies," are expected to become familiar with before joining in any chat forums. Most FAQs offer **netiquette,** or "net etiquette," guides to appropriate behavior while online.

Examples of netiquette blunders are typing with the CAPS LOCK key on—the Net equivalent of yelling—discussing subjects not appropriate to the forum, repetition of points made earlier, sending "I agree" and "Me, too" messages, and improper use of the software. **Spamming,** or sending unsolicited mail, is especially irksome; a spam includes chain letters, advertising, or similar junk mail.

One of the great things about the Internet is that it has got Americans to start writing again. However, writing shouldn't be sloppy. "Most people who see poor spelling and poor grammar think the writer is a dummy," says Virginia Shea, author of a book called *Netiquette,* who is said to be the Emily Post or Miss Manners of cyberspace. "You'd think some people never opened a dictionary in their lives from the spelling in their e-mail. They just dash off a note and figure that it doesn't matter how it reads. That is a big mistake."[23]

For more information on netiquette, visit the Web site *http://www.yahoo.com/ Computers_and_Internet/Information_and_Documentation/Beginners_Guides/ Netiquette/.*

Pornography and Censorship

If a U.S. court decides *after* you have spoken that you have defamed or maliciously damaged someone, you may be sued for slander (spoken speech) or libel (written speech) or charged with harassment, but you cannot be stopped beforehand. However, "obscene" material is not constitutionally protected free speech. Obscenity is defined as sexually explicit material that is offensive as measured by "contemporary community standards"—a definition with considerable leeway, depending on localities.

In 1996, Congress passed legislation, as part of its broad telecommunications law overhaul called the Communications Decency Act, that imposed heavy fines and prison sentences on people making available "patently offensive," sexually explicit material over the Internet in a manner available to children. This part of the law was blocked by a federal judge as being constitutionally vague. In 1997, the U.S. Supreme Court ruled that this part of the law was indeed unconstitutional.

Since computers are simply another way of communicating, there should be no surprise that a lot of people use them to communicate about sex. Yahoo, the Internet directory company, says that the word "sex" is the most popular search word on the Net.[24] All kinds of online X-rated bulletin boards, chat rooms, and Usenet newsgroups exist. A special problem is with children having access to sexual conversations, downloading hard-core pictures, or encountering odious adults tempting them into a meeting. "Parents should never use an online service as an electronic baby sitter," says computer columnist Lawrence Magid. People online are not always what they seem to be, he points out, and a message seemingly from a 12-year-old girl could really be from a 30-year-old man. "Children should be warned never to give out personal information," says Magid, "and to tell their parents if they encounter mail or messages that make them uncomfortable."[25]

Not only are parents concerned about pornography in electronic form, so are employers. Many companies are concerned about the loss of productivity—and the risk of being sued for sexual harassment—as workers spend time online looking at sexually explicit material. What can be done about all this? Some possibilities:

■ *Blocking software:* Some software developers have discovered a golden opportunity in making programs like SurfWatch, Net Nanny, and CYBERsitter. These "blocking" programs screen out objectionable matter typically by identifying certain nonapproved keywords in a user's request or comparing the user's request for information against a list of prohibited sites.[26] (The screening is sometimes imperfect: The White House Web site was once accidentally put off-limits by SurfWatch because it used the supposedly indecent term "couples" in conjunction with the vice president and his wife.)

■ *Browsers with ratings:* Another proposal in the works is browser software that contains built-in ratings for Internet, Usenet, and World Wide Web files. Parents could, for example, choose a browser that has been endorsed by the local school board or the online service provider.

■ *The V-chip:* The 1996 Telecommunications Law officially launched the era of the V-chip, a device that may be required equipment in most new television sets. The V-chip allows parents to automatically block out programs that have been labeled as high in violence, sex, or other objectionable material. Who will do the ratings (of 600,000 hours of programming currently broadcast per year) and whether the system is really workable remains to be seen. However, as conventional television and the Internet converge, the V-chip could become a concern to Net users as well as TV watchers.

The difficulty with any attempts at restricting the flow of information, perhaps, is the basic Cold War design of the Internet itself, with its strategy of offering different roads to the same place. "If access to information on a computer is blocked by one route," writes the *New York Times*'s Peter Lewis, "a moderately skilled computer user can simply tap into another computer by an alternative route." Lewis points out an Internet axiom attributed to an engineer named John Gilmore: "The Internet interprets censorship as damage and routes around it."[27]

Security: Threats to Computer and Communications Systems

Computers can be disabled by a number of occurrences. They may be harmed by people, procedural, and software errors; by electromechanical problems; and by "dirty data." They may be threatened by natural hazards and by civil strife and terrorism. Criminal acts perpetrated against computers include theft of hardware, software, time and services, and information; and crimes of malice and destruction. Computers may be harmed by software worms and viruses. Computers can also be used as instruments of crime. Criminals may be employees, outside users, hackers, crackers, and professional criminals.

There will probably always be a need for paper towels or the equivalent. That is because there will always be household accidents and mistakes—spills, messes, leaky pipes. Similarly, accidents and other disasters will probably disable computer and communications systems from time to time, as they have in the past. What steps should we take to minimize them, and how should we deal with them when they do happen?

Here we discuss the following threats to computers and communications systems:

■ Errors and accidents

■ Natural and other hazards

■ Crimes against information technology

■ Crimes using information technology

■ Worms and viruses

Errors and Accidents

ROBOT SENT TO DISARM BOMB GOES WILD IN SAN FRANCISCO, read the headline.[28] Evidently, a hazardous-duty police robot started spinning out of control when officers tried to get it to grasp a pipe bomb. Fortunately, it was shut off before any damage could be done. Most computer glitches are not so spectacular, although they can be almost as important.

In general, errors and accidents in computer systems may be classified as people errors, procedural errors, software errors, electromechanical problems, and "dirty data" problems.

People Errors

Recall that one part of a computer system is the people who manage it or run it. For instance, Brian McConnell of Roanoke, Virginia, found that he couldn't get past a bank's automated telephone system to talk to a real person. This was not the fault of the system so much as of the people at the bank. McConnell, president of a software firm, thereupon wrote a program that automatically phoned eight different numbers at the bank. People picking up the phone heard the recording, "This is an automated customer complaint. To hear a live complaint, press. . . ."[29] Quite often, what may seem to be "the computer's fault" is human indifference or bad management.

Procedural Errors

Some spectacular computer failures have occurred because someone didn't follow procedures. Consider the 2½-hour shutdown of NASDAQ, the nation's second largest stock market. NASDAQ is so automated that it likes to call itself "the stock market for the next 100 years." In July 1994, NASDAQ was shut down by an effort, ironically, to make the computer system more user-friendly. Technicians

This dispatcher is monitoring the computers at a 911 emergency control center.

were phasing in new software, adding technical improvements a day at a time. A few days into this process, the technicians tried to add more features to the software, flooding the data-storage capability of the computer system. The result was a delay in opening the stock market that shortened the trading day.

Software Errors

We are forever hearing about "software glitches" or "software bugs." A *software bug* is an error in a program that causes it not to work properly (✔ p. 10.11). *(See Figure 14.3.)* An example of a somewhat small error is the one a school employee in Newark, New Jersey, made in coding the school system's master scheduling program. When 1000 students and 90 teachers showed up for the start of school at Central High School, half the students had incomplete or no schedules for classes. Some classrooms had no teachers while others had four instead of one.[30]

Especially with complex software, there are always bugs, even after the system has been thoroughly tested and "debugged." However, there comes a point in the software development process where debugging must end. That is, the probability of the bugs disrupting the system is considered to be so low that it is not worth searching further for them.

Electromechanical Problems

Mechanical systems, such as printers, and electrical systems, such as circuit boards, don't always work. They may be faultily constructed, get dirty or overheated, wear out, or become damaged in some other way. Power failures (brownouts and blackouts) can shut a system down. Power surges can burn out equipment.

Figure 14.3 A software error caused automatic teller machines to deduct more than they should from customers' accounts.

Whether electromechanical failure or another problem causes it, computer downtime is expensive. A survey of about 450 information system executives picked from Fortune 1000 companies found that companies on average suffer nine 4-hour computer-system failures a year. Each failure costs the company an average of $330,000. Because of them, companies are unable to deliver a service, complete production, earn fees, or retrieve data. Moreover, employees lose productivity because of idle time.

"In one of the biggest computer errors in banking history, Chemical Bank mistakenly deducted about $15 million from more than 100,000 customers' accounts on Tuesday night, causing consternation among its customers around the New York area.

The problem stemmed from a single line in an updated computer program installed by Chemical on Tuesday in its Somerset, N.J. computer center that caused the bank to process every withdrawal and transfer at its automated teller machines twice. Thus a person who took $100 from a cash machine had $200 deducted, although the receipt only indicated a withdrawal of $100....

[T]he obvious suspect was a small section of new software that had been installed as part of a year-long effort by Chemical to improve the software it uses to operate its A.T.M.'s.

The problem line of the computer program was meant to be 'dormant,' until further changes in the system were made. ...What it did, however, was to send an electronic carbon copy of every A.T.M. withdrawal and transfer that was made to a second computer system used for processing paper checks. That meant money was deducted from customers' accounts once by the A.T.M. system and then a second time by the check system."

—Saul Hansell, "Cash Machines Getting Greedy at a Big Bank," *The New York Times*

"Dirty Data" Problems

When keyboarding a research paper, you undoubtedly make a few typing errors (which, hopefully, you clean up). Typos are also a fact of life for all the data-entry people around the world who feed a continual stream of raw data into computer systems. A lot of problems are caused by this kind of "dirty data." **Dirty data** is data that is incomplete, outdated, or otherwise inaccurate.

A good reason for having a look at your records—credit, medical, school—is so you can make any corrections to them before they cause you complications.

Natural and Other Hazards

Some disasters do not merely lead to temporary system downtime, they can wreck the entire system. Examples are natural hazards, and civil strife and terrorism.

Natural Hazards

Whatever is harmful to property (and people) is harmful to computers and communications systems. This certainly includes natural disasters: fires, floods, earthquakes, tornadoes, hurricanes, blizzards, and the like. If they inflict damage over a wide area, as did the 1997 floods in the West and the Great Plains, natural hazards can disable all the electronic systems we take for granted. Without power and communications connections, the automated teller machines, credit-card verifiers, and bank computers are useless.

Civil Strife and Terrorism

We may take comfort in the fact that wars and insurrections seem to take place in other parts of the world. Yet we are not immune to civil unrest, such as the so-called Rodney King riots that wracked Los Angeles in 1992. Nor are we immune, apparently, to acts of terrorism, such as the 1995 truck-bombing of Oklahoma City's Federal Building. Following the 1993 bombing of New York's World Trade Center, companies found themselves frantically moving equipment to new offices and reestablishing their computer networks.

Crimes Against Computers and Communications

An **information technology crime** can be of two types. It can be an illegal act perpetrated *against* computers or telecommunications. Or it can be the *use* of computers or telecommunications to accomplish an illegal act. Here we discuss the first type.

Crimes against information technology include theft—of hardware, of software, of computer time, of cable or telephone services, of information. Other illegal acts are crimes of malice and destruction. Some examples are as follows.

Theft of Hardware

Stealing of hardware can range from shoplifting an accessory in a computer store to removing a laptop or cellular phone from someone's car. Professional criminals may steal shipments of microprocessor chips off a loading dock or even pry cash machines out of shopping-center walls.

A particularly interesting case was the theft in December 1990 of a laptop computer from the car of a British officer right before the Gulf War. It happened to contain U.S. General Norman Schwarzkopf's preliminary military plans for the invasion of Iraq. Fortunately, the war plans were not compromised by the event.

SCARY THOUGHTS ABOUT STOLEN CHIPS

"Computer chips are the dope of the 90s," Sgt. Jim McMahon is saying. "They're easier to steal than dope. Worth more money than dope. And for the people who steal them, here's the best part: Once stolen, they're almost untraceable."

It's a Monday morning in May, and McMahon, head of the High-Tech Crime Unit of the San Jose Police Department, is standing outside an evidence room at headquarters....

McMahon ... lifts a computer chip that sits nearby. The tiny silicon unit has been implanted in a PGA, the prong-and-grid array that plugs into a computer. Ready for action, the chip and its PGA are smaller and thinner than a Saltine cracker.

McMahon flips the assembly between his fingers. "On the street," he says, "the most valuable chips are worth between $400 and $600. And do you see any marks on this? Any serial numbers? I don't. Neither do the robbers. The guys who make them keep it that way."

Thanks to an $80 billion annual boom in silicon-chip-equipped technology, automobiles, computers, medical equipment, children's toys, magazine ads, and even greeting cards use them—demand has never been greater....

A wave of "takeover style" robberies began in 1991, and it has washed over every corner of the computer industry. From Osaka, Japan, to Portland, Oregon, bands of heavily armed men have forced their way into factories, stealing chips and beating one or two of the witnesses to secure a fearful silence....

"The chips change hands 8 to 15 times within 72 hours after they've been stolen," McMahon says. "They may go overseas or out of town by FedEx or UPS. They're incredibly hard to track." At each step in the chain, the price of the chips rises until their value nears that of the marketplace. Then, with everyone having made money and the chips carrying a price that seems legitimate, new receipts are drawn up, and the chips are sold into the lawful marketplace....

"Despite the attributes black-market dealers of computer chips claim their wares have," McMahon says, "the quality of these batches of chips is often less than perfect."

Many times, he says, computer chips haven't been tested when they're stolen, or, even worse, during the helter-skelter of the robbery, batches of faulty chips may be mixed with fully functional ones....

"This is where things get scary," says McMahon, "since many chips these days are purchased for uses other than personal computers.

"Do you want a faulty, black-market chip running the navigation system on your commercial aircraft?" he asks. "How about the blood-temperature machine in a surgical lab when you're going under the knife?"

—Donovan Webster, "Chips Are a Thief's Best Friend,"
The New York Times Magazine

Theft of computers has become a major problem on many campuses. Often the thieves, who may be professionals, don't take the peripheral devices, only the system unit. If the computers are bolted down, thieves often open the systems units and steal the RAM chips, drives, and processors.

Theft of Software

Stealing of software can take the form of physically making off with someone's diskettes, but it is more likely to be copying of programs. Software makers secretly prowl electronic bulletin boards in search of purloined products, then try to get a court order to shut down the bulletin boards.[31] They also look for companies that "softlift"—buying one copy of a program and making copies for as many computers as they have. Many pirates are reported by co-workers or fellow students to the "software police," the Software Publishers Association. The SPA has a toll-free number (800/388-7478) on which anyone can report illegal copying, to initiate antipiracy actions. In mid-1994, two New England college students were indicted for allegedly using the Internet to encourage the exchange of copyrighted software.[32]

Another type of software theft is copying or counterfeiting well-known software programs (DOS, Windows, Seventh Guest). These pirates often operate in Taiwan, Mexico, Russia, and various parts of Asia and Latin America. In some countries, more than 90% of U.S. microcomputer software in use is thought to be illegally copied.[33]

Theft of Time and Services

The theft of computer time is more common than you might think. One way is people using their employer's computer time to play games. Some also run sideline businesses. The biggest abuse, however, is probably wasting time with electronic mail and the Internet. One analysis of e-mail logs of three companies (IBM, Apple, AT&T) found that employees visited Penthouse magazine's Web site 12,823 times in a single month. (Based on an average visit of 13 minutes, that works out to 347 eight-hour days, a considerable loss of work time.)

Theft of telephone services has increased significantly. For instance, high-tech thieves use sophisticated radio scanners to pluck out of the air the phone numbers and electronic serial numbers broadcast by cellular phones. These numbers are then programmed into the microchips of other phones—a fraud called "cloning"—that enables illegal users to make calls that are charged to innocent users. As a result, U.S. cellular phone companies lose an estimated $2 million every day.

Theft of Information

In 1992, "information thieves" were caught infiltrating the files of the Social Security Administration, stealing confidential personal records, and selling the information. Thieves have also broken into computers of the major credit bureaus and stolen credit information. They have then used the information to charge purchases or have resold it to other people. On college campuses, thieves have snooped on or stolen private information such as grades.

Crimes of Malice and Destruction

Sometimes criminals are more interested in abusing or vandalizing computers and telecommunications systems than in profiting from them. For example, a student at a Wisconsin campus deliberately and repeatedly shut down a university computer system, destroying final projects for dozens of students. A judge sentenced him to a year's probation, and he left the campus.[34]

There are many devices, principally involving programming tricks, for entering into computer systems and wreaking havoc. Some of these are listed in the accompanying box. *(See Table 14.1.)*

Table 14.1

SOME TYPES OF COMPUTER CRIME

■ *Carding:* Obtaining, using, or selling other people's credit card numbers.

■ *Data diddling:* Changing the data before or as it enters into the computer system.

■ *Data leakage:* Removing copies of confidential data from within a system without any trace.

■ *Phreaking:* Any manipulation of phone systems, such as simulating tones to get free calls.

■ *Piggybacking:* Using access permission belonging to someone else to gain entry to a computer system.

■ *Salami shaving:* Diverting small dollar amounts from larger ones to unauthorized sources without being noticed.

■ *Scavenging:* Searching trash cans for printouts, memos, carbons, and so on that contain confidential information not intended for public distribution.

■ *Superzapping:* Bypassing all security systems by means of specialized software packages.

■ *Trapdoor:* Using systems escapes to gain illegitimate access to a computer system.

■ *Trojan horse:* Placing covert instructions that would allow unauthorized access to a computer system from within a legitimate program.

■ *Warez trading:* Exchanging or selling pirated software.

Crimes Using Computers and Communications

Just as a car can be used to assist in a crime, so can a computer or communications system. For example, four college students on New York's Long Island who met via the Internet used a specialized computer program to steal credit-card numbers, then, according to police, went on a one-year, $100,000 shopping spree. When arrested, they were charged with grand larceny, forgery, and scheming to defraud.[35]

In addition, investment fraud has come to cyberspace. Many people now use online services to manage their stock portfolios through brokerages hooked into the services. Scam artists have followed, offering nonexistent investment deals, phony solicitations, and manipulating stock prices.

Information technology has also been used simply to perpetrate mischief. For example, three students at a Wisconsin campus faced disciplinary measures after distributing bogus e-mail messages, one of which pretended to be a message of resignation sent by the university's chancellor.[36]

Worms and Viruses

Worms and viruses are forms of high-tech maliciousness. A **worm** is a program that copies itself repeatedly into memory or onto a disk drive until no more space is left. An example is the worm program unleashed by a student at Cornell University that traveled through an e-mail network and shut down thousands of computers around the country.

A **virus** is a "deviant" piece of computer code or program that overwrites or attaches itself to programs or documents and destroys or corrupts data (✔ p. 5.7). Some viruses just cause inane messages, such as "Happy birthday, Joshi," to appear on your display screen. Some cause minor glitches such as making it seem as if a couple of keys on your keyboard are stuck. The worst, however, may erase all the contents of your hard drive, to the point where your computer won't even start again. Or a virus may evade your detection and spread its havoc elsewhere.

Viruses, then, are passed in two ways:

- *By diskette:* The first way is via an infected diskette, such as one you might get from a friend or a repair person. It's also possible to get a virus from a sales demo disk or even (in 3% of cases) from a shrink-wrapped commercial disk.

- *By network:* The second way is via a network, as from e-mail, an electronic bulletin board, or the Internet. This is why, despite all the freebie games and other software available online, you should use virus-scanning software to check downloaded files.

  "A pure-text file can't contain a virus," points out computing writer Phillip Robinson. "Most viruses infect programs that you run on your computer. But newer ones, called *macro viruses,* are especially scary because they use programming languages built into some of the latest applications such as word processors or spreadsheets. If you get an infected document via e-mail and merely open it, the virus goes to work."[37] An example of this type of virus is the Microsoft Word "Concept" virus.

Some 10,000 viruses have been collected by IBM's Thomas J. Watson Research Center, and the Symantec Anti-Virus Research Center estimates that six to nine new ones are found daily. Some of them have become quite well known. (Examples: Brain, Vienna, Jerusalem, Stoned, Form, Michelangelo, Concept.) However, only about 130 or so of them have been found "in the wild," or in general circulation and actually infecting people's computers, and of these you're likely to encounter only a handful. Even so, the cost of all computer viruses to users in terms of lost time, cleanup, and repair is estimated at more than $2 billion a year, according to the National Computer Security Association.

Viruses may take several forms. The three main traditional ones are *boot-sector viruses, file viruses,* and *multipartite viruses. (See Table 14.2.)* A recent one, as mentioned, is the *macro virus,* which attaches to documents rather than programs. The Concept macro virus, for example, hitches rides on e-mail and attaches itself to documents created by Microsoft's popular word processing program, Microsoft Word 6.0 or higher. Another macro virus, Laroux, infects Microsoft Excel spreadsheets the same way.

The rise in use of the Internet raises the risk of contagion even further, especially with the appearance of new Internet programming languages such as Sun Microsystems' Java (✔ p. 10.28). These languages work by invisibly downloading and running files on your computer, presenting an opportunity for [virus] infection every time you surf the Web. Such programming languages will only make the virus problem worse because they have security loopholes that virus creators will be able to take advantage of.

Table 14.2

TYPES OF VIRUSES

■ *Boot-sector virus:* The boot sector is that part of the system software containing most of the instructions for booting, or powering up, the system. The boot sector virus replaces these boot instructions with some of its own. Once the system is turned on, the virus is loaded into main memory before the operating system. From there it is in a position to infect other files. Any diskette that is used in the drive of the computer then becomes infected. When that diskette is moved to another computer, the contagion continues. Examples of boot-sector viruses: AntCMOS, AntiEXE, Form.A, NYB (New York Boot), Ripper, Stoned.Empire.Monkey.

■ *File virus:* File viruses attach themselves to executable files—those that actually begin a program. (In DOS these files have the extensions .com and .exe.) When the program is run, the virus starts working, trying to get into main memory and infecting other files.

■ *Multipartite virus:* A hybrid of the file and boot-sector types, the multipartite virus infects both files and boot sectors, which makes it better at spreading and more difficult to detect. Examples of multipartite viruses are Junkie and Parity Boot.

  A type of multipartite virus is the *polymorphic virus,* which can mutate and change form just as human viruses can. Such viruses are especially troublesome because they can change their profile, making existing antiviral technology ineffective.

  A particularly sneaky multipartite virus is the *stealth virus,* which can temporarily remove itself from memory to elude capture. An example of a multipartite, polymorphic stealth virus is One Half.

■ *Macro virus:* Macro viruses take advantage of a procedure in which miniature programs, known as macros, are embedded inside common data files, such as those created by e-mail or spreadsheets, which are sent over computer networks. Until recently, such documents have typically been ignored by antivirus software. Examples of macro viruses are Concept, which attaches to Word documents and e-mail attachments, and Laroux, which attaches to Excel spreadsheet files. Fortunately, the latest versions of Word and Excel come with built-in macro virus protection.

■ *Logic bomb:* Logic bombs, or simply *bombs,* differ from other viruses in that they are set to go off at a certain date and time. A disgruntled programmer for a defense contractor created a bomb in a program that was supposed to go off two months after he left. Designed to erase an inventory tracking system, the bomb was discovered only by chance.

■ *Trojan horse:* The Trojan horse covertly places illegal, destructive instructions in the middle of a legitimate program, such as a computer game. Once you run the program, the Trojan horse goes to work, doing its damage while you are blissfully unaware. An example of a Trojan horse is FormatC.

A variety of virus-fighting programs are on the market, often available in the utility section in software stores. **Antivirus software** scans a computer's hard disk, diskettes, and main memory to detect viruses and, sometimes, to destroy them. Such virus watchdogs operate in two ways. First, they scan disk drives for "signatures," characteristic strings of 1s and 0s left by known viruses. Second, they look for suspicious virus-like behavior, such as attempts to erase or change areas on your disks. You can employ antivirus programs as constant sentries. Like metal detectors scanning people entering an airport, antivirus monitors can detect any viruses trying to enter your computer.

Among the antiviral programs available are Dr Solomon's Anti-Virus Toolkit, F-PROT Professional, IBM AntiVirus, McAfee VirusScan, Norton AntiVirus, ThunderByte Anti-Virus Utilities, TouchStone PC-Cillin, and (for Macs) Disinfectant. IBM and Symantec are working on technologies that will automatically destroy viruses that haven't been analyzed by researchers. (A detailed list of antivirus software can be found on the World Wide Web at *http://www.ncsa.com.*)

What are the basic steps to take to avoid viruses?

Computer Criminals

What kind of people are perpetrating most of the information-technology crime? More than 80% may be employees, and the rest are outside users, hackers and crackers, and professional criminals.

Employees

"Employees are the ones with the skill, the knowledge, and the access to do bad things," says Donn Parker, an expert on computer security at SRI International in Menlo Park, California. "They're the ones, for example, who can most easily plant a 'logic bomb'. . . ." Dishonest or disgruntled employees, he says, pose "a far greater problem than most people realize."[38] Says Michigan State University criminal justice professor David Carter, who surveyed companies about computer crime, "Seventy-five to eighty percent of everything happens from inside."[39]

Most common frauds, Carter found, involved credit cards, telecommunications, employees' personal use of computers, unauthorized access to confidential files, and unlawful copying of copyrighted or licensed software. In addition, the increasing use of laptops off the premises, away from the eyes of supervisors, concerns some security experts. They worry that dishonest employees or outsiders can more easily intercept communications or steal company trade secrets.

Workers may use information technology for personal profit or steal hardware or information to sell. They may also use it to seek revenge for real or imagined wrongs, such as being passed over for promotion. Sometimes they may use the technology simply to demonstrate to themselves that they have power over people. This may have been the case with a Georgia printing-company employee convicted of sabotaging the firm's computer system. As files mysteriously disappeared and the system randomly crashed, other workers became so frustrated and enraged that they quit.

TEN SECURITY TIPS FOR PC USERS

■ *Password security:* Choose strong passwords. Never use your name or the name of a loved one, or even a word in the dictionary. Use a mix of alphanumeric characters, but make it easy to remember.

■ *Social engineering:* The hacker's most effective tool isn't technological at all—it's the manipulation of humans. Be suspicious of unfamiliar requests, whether over the phone or via mail [or e-mail]. Never disclose your password or details of your computer system to strangers whose motives, need to know, or identity you cannot verify.

■ *Credit card security:* Don't send your credit card number "in the clear" (that is, without encryption) over the Internet.

■ *Terminate connections:* Don't leave modem lines or Internet connections open when you're not using them. Turn off your computer when you leave it.

■ *Anti-virus defense:* Install anti-virus scanning software and use it unceasingly.

■ *Access control and encryption:* Consider using a PC security package that demands passwords for computer access and encrypts data resident on the hard disk.

■ *Physical security:* Consider installing key-locked diskette drive security devices to prevent unauthorized access via diskette.

■ *Backup:* Make frequent backups of vital data and store it in a different physical locale from the computer.

■ *Buy smart:* When buying operating systems or applications software, inquire about available security features. At the very least, does the package offer password protection? Does it offer an encryption option? If it is a product to be used by more than one person, does it offer access control so you can decide who sees what?

■ *Ask about security:* In the workplace, ask your manager or network administrator about the company's information security policies and procedures for users.

—Computer Security Institute, San Francisco.
Printed in the *San Francisco Examiner*

Outside Users

Suppliers and clients may also gain access to a company's information technology and use it to commit crimes. With both, this becomes a greater possibility as electronic connections such as Electronic Data Interchange systems (✔ p. 8.32) have become more commonplace.

Hackers and Crackers

Hackers are people who gain unauthorized access to computer or telecommunications systems for the challenge or even the principle of it. For example, in 1996, Swedish hackers broke into the Web site of the CIA, the American Central Intelligence Agency, and posted a message declaring it the "Central Stupidity Agency." (CIA officials said their home page is not linked to mainframe computers containing secrets.)

Eric Corley, publisher of a magazine called *2600: The Hackers' Quarterly,* believes that hackers are merely engaging in "healthy exploration." In fact, by breaking into corporate computer systems and revealing their flaws, he says, they are performing a favor and a public service. Such unauthorized entries show the corporations involved the leaks in their security systems.[40] Indeed, at one point, Netscape launched a so-called Bugs Bounty program, offering a cash reward to the first hacker to identify a "significant" security flaw in its latest Web browser software.[41]

Crackers also gain unauthorized access to information technology but do so for malicious purposes. (Some observers think the term *hacker* covers malicious intent, also.) Crackers attempt to break into computers and deliberately obtain information for financial gain, shut down hardware, pirate software, or destroy data.

The tolerance for "benign explorers"—hackers—has waned. Most communications systems administrators view any kind of unauthorized access as a threat, and they pursue the offenders vigorously. Educators try to point out to students that universities can't provide an education for everybody if hacking continues.[42] The most flagrant cases of hacking/cracking are met with federal prosecution. Two young Berkeley, California, men ages 20 and 21 who broke into a Tower Records security network and downloaded a file containing 1700 credit-card numbers had no plans to exploit their find, only to show off their accomplishment at a hackers' convention. Contrary to the hacker myth that says if you don't actually use the numbers you cannot be prosecuted, the pair were sentenced to many months in federal prison.[43]

Professional Criminals

Members of organized crime rings don't just steal information technology. They also use it the way that legal businesses do—as a business tool, but for illegal purposes. For instance, databases can be used to keep track of illegal gambling debts and stolen goods. Not surprisingly, the old-fashioned illegal booking operation has gone high-tech, with bookies using computers and fax machines in place of betting slips and paper tally sheets.

Drug dealers have used pagers as a link to customers. Microcomputers, scanners, and printers can be used to forge checks, immigration papers, passports, and driver's licenses. Telecommunications can be used to transfer funds illegally. For instance, in 1995, Russian computer hackers broke into a Citibank electronic money transfer system and stole more than $10 million before they were caught.

As information-technology crime has become more sophisticated, so have the people charged with preventing it and disciplining its outlaws. Campus administrators are no longer being quite as easy on offenders and are turning them over to police. Industry organizations such as the Software Publishers Association are going after software pirates large and small. (Commercial software piracy is now a felony, punishable by up to five years in prison and fines of up to $250,000 for anyone convicted of stealing at least ten copies of a program, or more than $2500 worth of software.) Police departments as far apart as Medford, Massachusetts, and San Jose, California, now have police patrolling a "cyber beat." That is, they cruise online bulletin boards looking for pirated software, stolen trade secrets, child molesters, and child pornography.

In 1988, after the last widespread Internet break-in, the U.S. Defense Department created the Computer Emergency Response Team (CERT). Although it has no power to arrest or prosecute, CERT provides round-the-clock international information and security-related support services to users of the Internet.

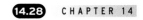

Whenever it gets a report of an electronic snooper, whether on the Internet or on a corporate e-mail system, CERT stands ready to lend assistance. It counsels the party under attack, helps them thwart the intruder, and evaluates the system afterward to protect against future break-ins.

Security: Safeguarding Computers and Communications

Information technology requires vigilance in security. Four areas of concern are identification and access, encryption, protection of software and data, and disaster-recovery planning.

Does your Social Security number say anything about you? Indeed it does. The first three numbers, called area numbers, generally tell in which state you were born or, if you recently emigrated, where you lived when you received your working papers. The next six digits can tell government officials whether a Social Security Number is fraudulent.

It's usually nobody's business but your own where you came from, but you'd like to keep it that way. However, the ongoing dilemma of the Digital Age is balancing convenience against security. **Security** is a system of safeguards for protecting information technology against disasters, systems failure, and unauthorized access that can result in damage or loss. We consider four components of security:

- Identification and access
- Encryption
- Protection of software and data
- Disaster-recovery planning

Identification and Access

Are you who you say you are? The computer wants to know.

There are three ways a computer system can verify that you have legitimate right of access. Some security systems use a mix of these techniques. The systems try to authenticate your identity by determining (1) what you have, (2) what you know, or (3) who you are.

What You Have—Cards, Keys, Signatures, Badges

Credit cards, debit cards, and cash-machine cards all have magnetic strips or built-in computer chips that identify you to the machine. Many require you to display your signature, which someone may compare as you write your signature. Computer rooms are always kept locked, requiring a key. Many people also keep a lock on their personal computers. A computer room may also be guarded by security officers, who may need to see an authorized signature or a badge with your photograph before letting you in.

Of course, credit cards, keys, and badges can be lost or stolen. Signatures can be forged. Badges can be counterfeited.

What You Know—PINs, Passwords, and Digital Signatures

To gain access to your bank account through an automated teller machine (ATM), you key in your PIN. A *PIN,* or *personal identification number,* is the security number known only to you that is required to access the system. Telephone credit cards also use a PIN. If you carry either an ATM or a phone card, *never* carry the PIN written down elsewhere in your wallet (even disguised).

A *password* is a special word, code, or symbol that is required to access a computer system. Passwords are one of the weakest security links, says AT&T security expert Steven Bellovin. *(See Figure 14.4.)* Passwords can be guessed, forgotten, or stolen. Too many passwords, like your mother's maiden name, are easily guessed by outsiders. Some intruders are aided by password-guessing software. The most common password is the users' name; the second-place choice is the word "secret." To reduce a stranger's guessing, Bellovin recommends never choosing a real word or variations of your name, birthdate, or those of your friends or family. Instead you should mix letters, numbers, and punctuation marks in an oddball sequence of no fewer than eight characters.[44]

The advice is sound, but the problem today is that many people have to remember several passwords. "Now password overload has become a plague, with every computer online service, voice-mail box, burglar-alarm disarmer, and office computer network demanding a unique string of code," says technology writer William Bulkeley.[45] Still, in line with Bellovin's suggestions, he offers these possibilities as good passwords: *2blorNOT2b%. Alfred!E!Newman7.* He also reports the strategy of Glenn Maxwell, a computer instructor from Farmington, Michigan, who uses an obvious and memorable password, but shifts the position of his hands on the keyboard, creating a meaningless string of characters.

Skilled hackers may break into national computer networks and detect passwords as they are being used. Or they pose on the telephone as computer technicians to cajole passwords out of employees. They may even find access codes in discarded technical manuals in trash bins.[46]

Some computer security systems have a "call-back" provision. In a *call-back system,* the user calls the computer system, punches in the password and hangs up. The computer then calls back a certain preauthorized number. This measure will block anyone who has somehow got hold of a password but is calling from an unauthorized telephone.

A relatively new technology is the digital signature, which security experts hope will lead to a world of paperless commerce. A *digital signature* is a string of characters and numbers that a user signs to an electronic document being sent by his or her computer. The receiving computer performs mathematical operations on the alphanumeric string to verify its validity. The system works by using a *public-private key system.* That is, the system involves a pair of numbers called a private key and a public key. One person creates the signature with a secret private key, and the recipient reads it with a second, public key. "This process in effect notarizes the document and ensures its integrity," says one writer.[47]

Figure 14.4 Most commonly used passwords

1. Your first, last, or kid's name	6. "Bonkers"
2. "Secret"	7. The current season ("Winter,"
3. Stress-related words ("Deadline," "Work")	8. "Spring") Your ethnic group
4. Sports teams or terms ("Bulls," "Gikfer")	9. Repeated characters ("AAAAA," "BBBBB")
5. "Payday"	10. Obscenities, sexual terms

For example, when you write your boss an electronic note, you sign it with your secret private key. (This could be some bizarre string beginning 479XY283 and continuing on for 25 characters.) When your boss receives the note, he or she looks up your public key. Your public key is available from a source such as an electronic bulletin board, the Postal Service, or a corporate computer department. If the document is altered in any way, it will no longer produce the same signature sequence.

Who You Are—Your Physical Traits

Some forms of identification can't be easily faked—such as your physical traits. Biometrics tries to use these in security devices. *Biometrics* is the science of measuring individual body characteristics.

For example, before a number of University of Georgia students can use the all-you-can-eat plan at the campus cafeteria, they must have their hands read. As one writer describes the system, "a camera automatically compares the shape of a student's hand with an image of the same hand pulled from the magnetic strip of an ID card. If the patterns match, the cafeteria turnstile automatically clicks open. If not, the would-be moocher eats elsewhere."[48]

Besides handprints, other biological characteristics read by biometric devices are fingerprints (computerized "finger imaging"), voices, the blood vessels in the back of the eyeball, the lips, and even one's entire face.

Encryption

PGP is a computer program written for encrypting computer messages—putting them into secret code. **Encryption,** or enciphering, is the altering of data so that it is not usable unless the changes are undone. PGP (for *Pretty Good Privacy*) is so good that it is practically unbreakable; even government experts can't crack it. (This is because it uses a two-keys method similar to that described above under digital signatures.)

Encryption is clearly useful for some organizations, especially those concerned with trade secrets, military matters, and other sensitive data. However, from the standpoint of our society, encryption is a two-edged sword. For instance, police in Sacramento, California, found that PGP blocked them from reading the computer diary of a convicted child molester and finding links to a suspected child pornography ring. *Should* the government be allowed to read the coded e-mail of its citizens? What about its being blocked from surveillance of overseas terrorists, drug dealers, and other enemies?

Protection of Software and Data

Organizations go to tremendous lengths to protect their programs and data. As might be expected, this includes educating employees about making backup disks, protecting against viruses, and so on.

Other security procedures include the following:

■ *Control of access:* Access to online files is restricted only to those who have a legitimate right to access—because they need them to do their jobs. Many organizations keep a transaction log that notes all accesses or attempted accesses to data. (Most LAN management software includes this function.)

■ *Firewalls:* For security, organizations with their own internal networks often install guarded gateways known as firewalls. A **firewall** is software or hardware that prevents hackers and others from infiltrating a computer or internal network from an outside network, usually the rough-and-tumble Internet.

A firewall admits only those outside communications you decide to admit. If you want to close off your network to everyone except Sue at International, communicating by e-mail at certain hours of the day, you can do that. Everyone else will be kept away—even if Sue picks the wrong time or communications method. Besides allowing those with need-to-access to access an Internet network, a firewall should log suspicious events and alert system administrators when attempts are made to breach security.

- *Audit controls:* Many networks have *audit controls* to track which programs and servers were used, which files opened, and so on. This creates an *audit trail,* a record of how a transaction was handled from input through processing and output.

- *People controls:* Because people are the greatest threat to a computer system, security precautions begin with the screening of job applicants. That is, resumes are checked to see if people did what they said they did. Another control is to separate employee functions, so that people are not allowed to wander freely into areas not essential to their jobs. Manual and automated controls—input controls, processing controls, and output controls—are used to check that data is handled accurately and completely during the processing cycle. Printouts, printer ribbons, and other waste that may yield passwords and trade secrets to outsiders are disposed of through shredders or locked trash barrels.

Disaster-Recovery Plans

A **disaster-recovery plan** is a method of restoring information-processing operations that have been halted by destruction or accident. "Among the countless lessons that computer users have absorbed in the hours, days, and weeks after the [New York] World Trade Center bombing," wrote one reporter, "the most enduring may be the need to have a disaster-recovery plan. The second most enduring lesson may be this: Even a well-practiced plan will quickly reveal its flaws."[49]

Mainframe computer systems are operated in separate departments by professionals, who tend to have disaster plans. Mainframes are regularly and frequently backed up. However, many personal computers, and even entire local area networks, are not backed up. The consequences of this lapse can be great. It has been reported that, on average, a company loses as much as 3% of its gross sales within eight days of a sustained computer outage. In addition, the average company struck by a computer outage lasting more than 10 days never fully recovers.[50]

A disaster-recovery plan is more than a big fire-drill. It has the following characteristics:

- *Priorities of business functions:* It includes a list of all business functions, ranked in priority according to which functions must be back in operation first. Thus, most companies would consider it more important for programs computing customer billing and accounts receivable to be up and running before the programs computing employee pension plans. A college would want its payroll programs in operation before its alumni contribution lists.

- *Support resources needed:* The disaster-recovery plan includes a list of everything and everybody needed to support these business functions: the hardware, software, data, facilities, and people needed.

■ *Backup sites:* The disaster-recovery plan includes the ongoing process of backing up and storing programs and data in another location, either a hot site or a cold site. A *hot site* is a fully equipped computer center, with everything needed to resume business functions. A *cold site* is a building or other suitable environment in which a company can install its own computer system.

■ *Procedures for implementing plan:* The recovery plan describes ways of getting access to the support resources, procedures for alerting necessary personnel, and the steps to take to implement the plan. The action plan should describe how input and output data is to be handled at a different site.

■ *Training and practice:* The plan describes how the people involved should be trained and practice for disasters.

Sometimes organizations join with other organizations in a consortium or mutual-aid arrangement, so that even competitors, for example, will share resources until the emergency is over.

How fancy should the alternate arrangements be? The best way to judge is to figure out how long it would take to duplicate the present arrangements. At the World Trade Center before the bombing, said an executive with a company offering recovery services, "traders had two or three terminals on each desk. That is a lot of communications to duplicate."[51]

Social Questions: Will Information Technology Make Our Lives Better?

Information technology can create problems for the environment, including energy consumption and environmental pollution; people's mental health (isolation, gambling, Net addiction, and stress); and the workplace (misuse of technology and information overload). Many people worry that jobs are being reduced due to the effects of information technology. They also worry that it is widening the gap between the haves and have-nots. However, information technology also promises great benefits in the areas of education and information, health, commerce and electronic money, entertainment, and government and electronic democracy.

Much of our society is built on an abiding faith that technology is good, that innovation drives progress. Clearly, however, it is not that simple. Here let us examine information technology in relation to several key areas:

■ Environmental problems

■ Mental-health problems

■ Workplace problems

■ Economic issues and employment

High school students in a computer training session at the Instituto Technologico in Mexico

- Education and information
- Commerce and electronic money
- Entertainment
- Government and electronic democracy

Environmental Problems

As the upgrade merry-go-round continues, as it has since the birth of the computer industry, more and more people are getting in on the Digital Revolution. Everyone hopes, of course, that the principal effects of this growth will be beneficial. But you need not be anti-technology to wonder just what negative impact computerization will have. How, for instance, will it affect the environment—energy consumption and environmental pollution, for example?

Energy Consumption and "Green PCs"

All the computers and communications devices discussed in this book run on electricity. Much of this is simply wasted. Computers themselves have in the past been built in ways that used power unnecessarily. An office full of computers also generates a lot of heat, so that additional power is required to run air-conditioning systems to keep people comfortable. Finally, people leave their computer systems on even when they're not sitting in front of them—not just during the day but overnight and weekends as well.

In recent years, the Environmental Protection Agency launched Energy Star, a voluntary program to encourage the use of computers that consume a minimal amount of power. The goal of Energy Star is to reduce the amount of electricity microcomputers and monitors use from the typical 150 watts of power to 60 watts or less. This goal is about the power requirements for a moderately bright light bulb. (Half the wattage would be for the system unit, the other half for the monitor.) As a result, manufacturers are now coming forth with Energy Star–compliant "green PCs."

"If you use your PC for 8 hours a day but always leave it on," says one writer, "a green PC could save about $70 a year. If everyone used only green PCs, $2 billion could be saved annually."[52]

Environmental Pollution

Communities like to see computer manufacturers move to their areas because they are viewed as being nonpolluting. Is this true? Actually, in the past, chemicals used during the manufacturing process of semiconductors polluted air, soil, and groundwater. Today, however, computer makers are literally cleaning up their act.

The rush to obsolescence has produced numbers of computers, printers, monitors, fax machines, and so on, that have wound up as junk in landfills, although some are stripped by recyclers for valuable metals. More problematic is the disposal of batteries, as from portable computers. Nickel-cadmium batteries contain the toxic element cadmium, which can leach from a landfill garbage dump into groundwater supplies. Disposal of such batteries should be through local toxic-waste disposal programs. Newer battery technology, such as nickel-hydride and lithium cells, may eventually replace nickel-cadmium.

If you have an old-fashioned computer system, consider donating it to an organization that can make use of it. Don't abandon it in a closet. Don't dump it in the trash. "Even if you have no further use for a machine that seems horribly antiquated," writes *San Jose Mercury News* computing editor Dan Gillmor, "someone else will be grateful for all it will do."[53]

Several nonprofit groups exist that accept or pass along used computer equipment to deserving organizations. However, there are some practical steps you should take to ensure that the system ends up doing some good. *(See Figure 14.5.)*

Software packaging also poses a problem. Some estimates state that about 40 million software boxes and other packaging materials are thrown away and that less than 30% of all packaged software is recycled, according to the Software Manufacturer's Association. Add to these facts that more than 1 billion diskettes are thrown away each year. It takes a diskette more than 450 years to decompose in a landfill. In light of this information, one can clearly see the advantages of downloading software from suppliers over the Internet.

Mental-Health Problems: Isolation, Gambling, Net Addiction, Stress

From a mental-health standpoint, will being wired together really set us free? Consider:

Isolation

Automation allows us to go days without actually speaking with or touching another person, from buying gas to playing games. Even the friendships we make online in cyberspace, some believe, "are likely to be trivial, short lived, and disposable—junk friends." Says one writer, "We may be overwhelmed by a continuous static of information and casual acquaintance, so that finding true soul mates will be even harder than it is today."[54]

Gambling

Gambling is already widespread in North America, but information technology could make it almost unavoidable. Although gambling by wire is illegal in the U.S., all kinds of moves are afoot to get around it. For example, host computers for Internet casinos and sports books are being set up in Caribbean tax havens, and satellites, decoders, and remote-control devices are being used so TV viewers can do racetrack wagering from home.[55-57]

Some mental-health professionals are concerned with the long-range effects. "About 5% [of the users or viewers] will be compulsive gamblers and another 10%

"If you're going to donate a used machine, don't just leave it on the doorstep somewhere. A little planning will ensure that your well-meaning gift actually goes to a good cause.

And before you give it away, make sure you've moved your personal data—letters, financial information, etc.—onto your new computer, using machine-to-machine software such as LapLink or copying the data to floppies and then to the new computer.

If you plan to keep the software you were using before, you should delete it from the machine you give away. Otherwise you're committing piracy; even in a good cause that's not a good idea.

When you're ready to give the computer away, call the school, church or organization first. Some will be unable to use the model you're offering even if it works well.

Some groups, however, welcome computers of any age and in almost any condition (though you should still call them before you donate)."

–Dan Gillmore, "Old Computer Will Mean a Lot to Those in Need," *San Jose Mercury News*

California
Plugged In
1923 University Ave.
East Palo Alto, CA 94303
800-225-PLUG

Detwiler Foundation Computer for Schools Program
470 Nautilus St., Suite 300
La Jolla, CA 92037
800-939-6000

The Computer Recycling Center
1245 Terra Bella Ave.
Mountain View, CA 94043
415-428-3700

CompuMentor
89 Stillman St.
San Francisco, CA 94107
415-512-7784

The Shareware Project
410 Townsend St. Suite 408
San Francisco, CA 94107
415-543-0500

Connecticut
The National Christina Foundation
591 West Putnam Ave.
Greenwich, CT 06830
800-274-7846

Illinois
Information Technology Resource Center
59 East Van Buren, Suite 2020
Chicago, IL 60605-1219
312-939-8050

Massachusetts
CONNECT
Technical Development Corporation
30 Federal St., 5th floor
Boston, MA 02111
617-728-9151

East-West Education Development Foundation
55 Temple Place
Boston, MA 02111
617-542-1234

New York
Nonprofit Computer Exchange
Fund for the City of New York
121 Sixth Ave., 6th floor
New York, NY 10013
212-925-5101

Connecticut
Gifts in Kind America
700 North Fairfax St., Suite 300
Alexandria, VA 22314
703-836-2121

Figure 14.5 Groups accepting used computers

to 15% will be problem gamblers," says Kevin O'Neill of New Jersey's Council on Compulsive Gambling. "Compulsive gamblers want action, which is what interactive television [or computers] can give you."[58]

Net Addiction

Don't let this happen to you: "A student e-mails friends, browses the World Wide Web, blows off homework, botches exams, flunks out of school."[59] This is the downward spiral of the "Net addict," often a college student—because schools give students no-cost/low-cost linkage to the Internet—though it can be anyone. Some become addicted (although some professionals feel "addiction" is too strong a word) to chat groups, some to online pornography, some simply to the escape from real life.[60,61] Indeed, sometimes the computer replaces one's spouse or boyfriend/girlfriend in the user's affections. In one instance, a man sued his wife for divorce for having an "online affair" with a partner who called himself The Weasel.[62–65]

Stress

In a survey of 2802 American PC users, three-quarters of the respondents (whose ages ranged from children to retirees) said personal computers had increased their job satisfaction and were a key to success and learning. However, many found PCs stressful: 59% admitted getting angry at them within the previous year. And 41% said they thought computers have reduced job opportunities rather than increased them.[66]

Psychologist and sociologist Sherry Turkle of MIT believes that, when it comes to mental health, information technology is neither a blessing nor a curse. In fact, she holds, "The Internet is not a drug." Rather, people who seem addicted may be "working through important personal issues in the safety of life on the screen."[67]

Workplace Problems

First the mainframe computer, then the desktop stand-alone PC, and now the networked computer were all brought into the workplace for one reason only: to improve productivity. How is it working out? Let's consider two aspects: the misuse of technology and information overload.

Misuse of Technology

"For all their power," says an economics writer, "computers may be costing U.S. companies tens of billions of dollars a year in downtime, maintenance and training costs, useless game playing, and information overload."[68]

Consider games. Employees may look busy, staring into their computer screens with brows crinkled. But often they're just hard at work playing Quake or surfing the Net. Workers with Internet access average 10 hours a week online.[69] However, fully 23% of computer game players use their office PCs for their fun, according to one survey.[70] A study of employee online use at one major company concluded that the average worker wastes $1\frac{1}{2}$ hours each day.[71]

Another reason for so much wasted time is all the fussing that employees do with hardware and software. Says one editor, "Back in the old days, when I toiled on a typewriter, I never spent a whole morning installing a new ribbon. . . . I did not scan the stores for the proper cables to affix to my typewriter or purchase books that instructed me on how to get more use from my liquid white-out."[72] One study estimated that microcomputer users waste 5 billion hours a year waiting for programs to run, checking computer output for accuracy, helping co-workers use their applications, organizing cluttered disk storage, and calling for technical support.[73]

Many companies don't even know what kind of microcomputers they have, who's running them, or where they are. The corporate customer of one computer consultant, for instance, swore it had 700 PCs and 15 users per printer. An audit showed it had 1200 PCs with one printer each.[74]

A particularly interesting misuse is the continual upgrade. Ask yourself, Do I really need that slick new product? "I use an old version of WordPerfect on my PC," says Ron Erickson, former chairman of the Egghead Software stores and now a technology consultant. "The one thing I don't need is a new version of WordPerfect—or of any of the other software on my machine for that matter."[75] Erickson's advice to consumers: "Don't get the new version if the old one is working O.K." As for many businesses, he says, the rule should be: "Stop buying new software, and train employees on what you have."

Information Overload

"My boss basically said, 'Carry this pager seven days a week, 24 hours a day, or find another job,'" says the chief architect for a New Jersey school system. (He complied, but pointedly notes that the pager's "batteries run out all the time.")[76] "It used to be considered a status symbol to carry a laptop computer on a plane," says futurist Paul Saffo. "Now anyone who has one is clearly a working dweeb who can't get the time to relax. Carrying one means you're on someone's electronic leash."[77]

The new technology is definitely a two-edged sword. Cellular phones, pagers, fax machines, and modems may free employees from the office, but they tend to work longer hours under more severe deadline pressure than do their counterparts who stay at the office, according to one study.[78] Moreover the gadgets that once promised to do away with irksome business travel by ushering in a new era of communications have done the opposite—created the office-in-a-bag that allows business travelers to continue to work from airplane seats and hotel desks.[79]

What does being overwhelmed with information do to you, besides inducing stress and burnout? One result is that because we have so many choices to entice and confuse us we become more adverse to making decisions. Home buyers now take twice as long as a decade earlier to sign a contract on a new house, organizations take months longer to hire top executives, and managers tend to consider worst-case scenarios rather than benefits when considering investing in a new venture.[80]

"The volume of information available is so great that I think people generally are suffering from a lack of meaning in their lives," says Neil Postman, chair of the department of culture and communication at New York University. "People are just adrift in the sea of information, and they don't know what the information is about or why they need it."[81]

Economic Issues: Employment and the Haves/Have-Nots

People who don't like technology in general, and today's information technology in particular, have been called *neo-Luddites.* The original Luddites were a group of weavers in northern England who, while proclaiming their allegiance to a legendary King Ludd, in 1812–1814 went about smashing modern looms that moved cloth production out of the hands of peasant weavers and into inhumane factories. Some of today's neo-Luddites make the alarming case that technological progress is actually no progress at all—indeed, it is a curse. The two biggest charges (which are related) are, first, that information technology is killing jobs and, second, that it is widening the gap between the rich and the poor.

Technology, the Job Killer?

Technological advances play a variety of roles, good and bad, in social progress. But is it true, as Jeremy Rifkin says in *The End of Work,* that intelligent machines are replacing humans in countless tasks, "forcing millions of blue-collar and white-collar workers into temporary, contingent, and part-time employment and, worse, unemployment"?[82]

This is too large a question to be fully considered in this book. Many factors are responsible for the decline in economic growth, the downsizing of companies, and the rise of unemployment among many sectors of society. The U.S. economy is undergoing powerful structural changes brought on not only by the widespread diffusion of technology but also by the growth of trade's role, the shift from manufacturing to service employment, the weakening of labor unions, more rapid immigration, and other factors.[83,84]

Many economists seem to agree that the boom times of economic growth that the United States enjoyed in the 1950s and 1960s won't return until there is more public investment and more personal saving instead of spending—savings that could be used for machinery and other tools of a thriving economy. Investment in recent years has been concentrated in computers. Surprisingly, however, as one economics writer points out, "so far computers have not yielded the rapid growth in production that came from investments in railroads, autos, highways, electric power, and aircraft—all huge outlays, involving government as well as the private sector, that changed the way Americans lived and worked."[85]

Gap Between Rich and Poor

"In the long run," says Stanford University economist Paul Krugman, "improvements in technology are good for almost everyone. . . . Unfortunately, what is true in the long run need not be true over shorter periods."[86] We are now, he believes, living through one of those difficult periods in which technology doesn't produce widely shared economic gains but instead widens the gap between those who have the right skills and those who don't.

A U.S. Department of Commerce survey of "information have-nots" reveals that about 20% of the poorest households in the U.S. do not have telephones. Moreover, only a fraction of those poor homes that do have phones will be able to afford the information technology that most economists agree is the key to a comfortable future.[87] The richer the family, the more likely it is to have and use a computer.

Schooling—especially college—makes a great difference. Every year of formal schooling after high school adds 5–15% to annual earnings later in life.[88] Being well educated is only part of it, however; one should also be technologically literate. Employees who are skilled at technology "earn roughly 10–15% higher pay," according to the chief economist for the U.S. Labor Department.[89]

Advocates of information access for all find hope in the promises of NII (National Information Infrastructure) proponents for "universal service" and the wiring of every school to the Net. But this won't happen automatically. Ultimately we must become concerned with the effects of growing economic disparities on our social and political health. "Computer technology is the most powerful and the most flexible technology ever developed," says Terry Bynum, chair of the American Philosophical Association's Committee on Philosophy and Computing. "Even though it's called a technical revolution, at heart it's a social and ethical revolution because it changes everything we value."[90]

A supercomputer's simulation of the earth (blue) with continents (green), displaying clusters of black dots that represent oil field disasters

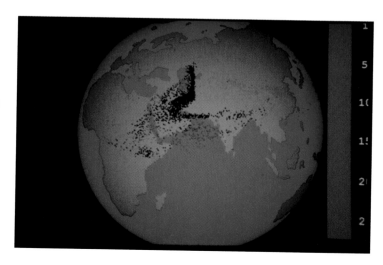

Education and Information

The government is interested in reforming education, and technology can assist that effort. Presently the United States has more computers in its classrooms than other countries, but the machines are older and teachers aren't as computer-literate. A recent study shows that 61.2% of urban schools have phone lines they could use for Internet access, while 42% own modems. The poorer the school district, the less likely it is to have modems.[91] President Clinton proposed a "high-tech barn-raising," a government-industry collaboration to put computers in every school in the nation by the year 2000.[92]

Computers can be used to create "virtual" classrooms not limited by scheduled class time. Some institutions (Stanford, MIT) are replacing the lecture hall with forms of learning featuring multimedia programs, workstations, and television courses at remote sites. The Information Superhighway could be used to enable students to take video field trips to distant places and to pull information from remote museums and libraries.[93–95]

As we have seen, making information available—and having it make sense—is one of our greatest challenges. Can everything in the Library of Congress be made available online to citizens and companies? What about government records, patents, contracts, and other legal documents? Or satellite-generated geographical maps? Indeed, satellite imaging based on technology from Cold War spy satellites will soon be so good that companies, cities, and other buyers could use it to get views of land use, traffic patterns—and even of your back yard. (The technology also has some people worried about privacy invasion and a free-for-all expansion of espionage.)

Of particular interest is distance learning, or the "virtual university." *Distance learning* is the use of computer and/or video networks to teach courses to students outside the conventional classroom. At present, distance learning is largely outside the mainstream of campus life. That is, it concentrates principally on part-time students, those who cannot easily travel to campus, those interested in non-credit classes, or those seeking special courses in business or engineering. However, part-timers presently make up about 45% of all college enrollments. This, says one writer, is "a group for whom 'anytime, anywhere' education holds special appeal."[96]

Health

Another goal of the Information Superhighway is to improve health care. The government is calling for an expansion of "telemedicine." *Telemedicine* is the use of telecommunications to link health-care providers and researchers, enabling them to share medical images, patient records, and research. Of particular interest would be the use of networks for "teleradiology" (the exchange of X rays, CAT scans, and the like) so that specialists could easily confer. Telemedicine would also allow long-distance patient examinations, using video cameras and, perhaps, virtual-reality gloves that would transmit and receive tactile sensations.[97, 98]

Another application is technology for translating human anatomy into billions of bytes of computer memory. Such models would help medical students with their training, surgeons with preoperative planning, and furniture designers with building better chairs. Another important health goal is to bring interactive, multimedia materials to the public to promote health and outline healthcare options.

Still another health goal is to eliminate *repetitive stress injury* (*RSI*), which can be caused by repetitive tasks, such as typing on a computer keyboard and using a mouse or touch pad. RSI symptoms are tightness, stiffness, tingling, numbness, pain in the hands, wrists, fingers, forearms, neck, or back. Keyboard manufacturers are developing new styles of keyboards to help alleviate this problem. Users can also help themselves by using good posture, taking breaks, and stretching. (For advice about choosing a keyboard and avoiding RSI, try these Web sites: *http://engr-www.unl.edu/ee/eeshop/rsi/html; http://ergo.human. cornell.edu; http://www.cs.princeton.edu/~dwallach/tifaq/keyboards.html; http://web. mit.edu:1962/tiserve.mit.edu/9000/32823.html; http://www.agilecorp.com/ergonomics/ AboutThisSite.html.*)

Commerce and Electronic Money

Businesses clearly see information technology as a way to enhance productivity and competitiveness. However, the changes will probably go well beyond this.

The thrust of the original Industrial Revolution was separation—to break work up into its component parts to permit mass production. The effect of computer networks in the Digital Revolution, however, is unification—to erase boundaries between company departments, suppliers, and customers.

Indeed, the parts of a company can now as easily be global as down the hall from one another. Thus, designs for a new product can be tested and exchanged with factories in remote locations. With information flowing faster, goods can be sent to market faster and inventories kept down. Says an officer of the Internet Society, "Increasingly you have people in a wide variety of professions collaborating in diverse ways in other places. The whole notion of 'the organization' becomes a blurry boundary around a set of people and information systems and enterprises."[99]

The electronic mall, in which people make purchases online, is already here. Record companies, for instance, are putting sound and videos of new albums on Web sites, where you can sample the album and then order it sent as a cassette or CD. Banks in cyberspace are allowing users to adopt avatars or personas of themselves and then meet in three-dimensional virtual space on the World Wide Web where they can query bank tellers and officers and make transactions. Wal-Mart Stores and Microsoft have developed a joint online shopping venture which allow shoppers to browse online and buy merchandise.

Cybercash, or E-cash, will change the future of money. Whether it takes the form of smart cards or of electronic blips online, cybercash will probably begin to displace (though not completely supplant) checks and paper currency. This would change the nature of how money is regulated as well as the way we buy and sell.

Entertainment

Among the future entertainment offerings could be movies on-demand, video games, and gaming ("telegambling"). *Video on-demand* would allow viewers to browse through a menu of hundreds of movies, select one, and start it when they wanted. This definition is for true video on-demand, which is like having a complete video library in your house. (An alternative, simpler form could consist of running the same movie on multiple channels, with staggered starting times.) True video on-demand will require a server, a storage system with the power of a supercomputer that would deliver movies and other data to thousands of customers at once.

Government and Electronic Democracy

Will information technology help the democratic process? There seem to be two parts to this. The first is its use as a campaign tool, which may, in fact, skew the democratic process in some ways. The second is its use in governing and in delivering government services.

Santa Monica, California, established a computer system, called Public Electronic Network (PEN), which residents may hook into free of charge. PEN gives Santa Monica residents access to city council agendas, staff reports, public safety tips, and the public library's online catalog. Citizens may also enter into electronic conferences on topics both political and nonpolitical; this has been by far the most popular attraction.

What, in your opinion, are the most significant disadvantages of using computers? What do you think can be done about these problems?

PEN could be the basis for wider forms of electronic democracy. For example, electronic voting might raise the percentage of people who vote. Interactive local-government meetings could enable constituents and town council members to discuss proposals.

Information technology could also deliver federal services and benefits. In 1994, the government unveiled a program in which Social Security pensioners and other recipients of federal aid without bank accounts could use a plastic automated-teller-machine card to walk up to any ATM and withdraw the funds due them.

Onward Toward the Future

The four principal information technologies—computer networks, imaging technology, massive data storage, and artificial intelligence—will affect probably 90% of the workforce by 2010.[179] Clearly, information technology is driving the new world of jobs, leisure, and services, and nothing is going to stop it.

Where will you be in all this? People pursuing careers find the rules are changing very rapidly. Up-to-date skills are becoming ever more crucial. Job descriptions of all kinds are metamorphosing, and even familiar jobs are becoming more demanding. Today, experts advise, you need to prepare to continually upgrade your skills, prepare for specialization, and prepare to market yourself. In a world of breakneck change, you can still thrive. The most critical knowledge, however, may turn out to be self-knowledge.

AITP

Vision Statement

AITP is dedicated to providing industry leadership and professional development to members of the Information Technology profession.

Mission Statement

It is the mission of AITP to provide superior leadership and education in Information Technology. AITP is dedicated to using the synergy of Information Technology partnerships to provide education and benefits to our members and to working with the industry to assist in the overall promotion and direction of Information Technology.

AITP Code Of Ethics

I acknowledge:

That I have an obligation to management, therefore, I shall promote the understanding of information processing methods and procedures to management using every resource at my command.

That I have an obligation to my fellow members, therefore, I shall uphold the high ideals of AITP as outlined in its Association Bylaws. Further, I shall cooperate with my fellow members and shall treat them with honesty and respect at all times.

That I have an obligation to society and will participate to the best of my ability in the dissemination of knowledge pertaining to the general development and understanding of information processing. Further, I shall not use knowledge of a confidential nature to further my personal interest, nor shall I violate the privacy and confidentiality of information entrusted to me or to which I may gain access.

That I have an obligation to my College or University, therefore, I shall uphold its ethical and moral principles. That I have an obligation to my employer whose trust I hold, therefore, I shall endeavor to discharge this obligation to the best of my ability, to guard my employer's interests, and to advise him or her wisely and honestly.

That I have an obligation to my country, therefore, in my personal business and social contacts, I shall uphold my nation and shall honor the chosen way of life of my fellow citizens.

I accept these obligations as a personal responsibility and as a member of this Association.

I shall actively discharge these obligations and I dedicate myself to that end.

If you have any questions, call our Membership Department at
800.224.9371, FAX 847.825.1693 or CompuServe 70430,35

Association of INFORMATION TECHNOLOGY PROFESSIONALS
505 Busse Highway
Park Ridge, IL 60068-3191

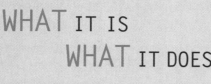

WHAT IT IS
WHAT IT DOES   WHY IT IS IMPORTANT

antivirus software (LO 7, p. 14.25) Program that scans a computer's hard disk, diskettes, CD-ROMs, and main memory to detect viruses and, sometimes, to destroy them.

Computer users must find out what kind of antivirus software to install in their systems to protect them against damage or shutdown.

cookie (LO 2, p. 14.5)   A special file that keeps track of your activities and visits on the Web. It's automatically created on your hard disk when you visit certain Web sites.

Without notifying you, cookies can connect your name or e-mail address to any Web site that you visit. Moreover, there are practically no restrictions on how the information may be disseminated or otherwise used.

copyright (LO 3, p. 14.9)   A body of law that prohibits copying of intellectual property without the permission of the copyright holder.

Copyright matters are important because computers and networks have made the act of copying far easier and more convenient than in the past.

crackers (LO 6, p. 14.27)   People who gain unauthorized access to information technology for malicious purposes.

Crackers attempt to break into computers to deliberately obtain information for financial gain, shut down hardware, pirate software, or destroy data.

dirty data (LO 6, p. 14.19)   Data that is incomplete, outdated, or otherwise inaccurate.

Dirty data can cause information to be inaccurate.

disaster-recovery plan (LO 7, p. 14.31) Method of restoring information-processing operations that have been halted by destruction or accident.

A disaster-recovery plan is important if a company desires to resume its computer and business operations in short order.

encryption (LO 7, p. 14.30)   Also called *enciphering;* the altering of data so that it is not usable unless the changes are undone.

Encryption is useful for users transmitting trade or military secrets or other sensitive data.

ethics (LO 1, p. 14.3)   A set of moral values or principles that govern the conduct of an individual or group.

Every reader of this book at some point will have to wrestle with ethical issues related to computer technology.

firewall (LO 7, p. 14.30)   Software or hardware that prevents hackers and others from infiltrating a computer or internal network from an outside network.

Firewalls protect an organization's data and systems.

hackers (LO 6, p. 14.26)   People who gain unauthorized access to computer or telecommunications systems for the challenge or even the principle of it.

The acts of hackers create problems not only for the institutions that are victims of break-ins but also for ordinary users of the systems.

information technology crime (LO 6, p. 14.19) (1) An illegal act perpetrated *against* computers or telecommunications. (2) The *use* of computers or telecommunications to accomplish an illegal act.

Crimes against information technology include theft—of hardware, of software, of computer time, of cable or telephone services, of information. Other illegal acts are crimes of malice and destruction.

intellectual property (LO 3, p. 14.9)   Consists of products of the human mind, tangible or intangible.

Information technology has presented legislators and lawyers—and you—with some new ethical matters regarding rights to intellectual property.

morphing (LO 4, p 14.12)   Altering a film or video image displayed on a computer screen pixel by pixel, or dot by dot.

Morphing and other techniques of digital image manipulation can produce images that misrepresent reality.

netiquette (LO 5, p. 14.14)   "Net etiquette"; guides to appropriate behavior while online.

Netiquette rules help users to avoid offending other users.

network piracy (LO 3, p. 14.10)   Using electronic networks to distribute unauthorized copyrighted materials in digitized form.

An example of network piracy is computer users' sending unauthorized copies of digital recordings over the Internet. Network piracy is illegal.

plagiarism (LO 3, p. 14.10)   The expropriation of another writer's text, findings, or interpretations and presentation of it as one's own.

Information technology puts a new face on plagiarism in two ways. On one hand, it offers plagiarists new opportunities to go far afield for unauthorized copying. On the other hand, the technology offers new ways to catch people who steal other people's material.

privacy (LO 2, p. 14.3)   The right of people not to reveal information about themselves—the right to keep personal information, such as medical histories, personal e-mail messages, student records, and financial information from getting into the wrong hands.

Information technology puts constant pressure on privacy.

security (LO 7, p. 14.28)   System of safeguards for protecting information technology against disasters, systems failure, and unauthorized access that can result in damage or loss.

With proper security, organizations and individuals can minimize linformation technology losses from disasters, system failures, and unauthorized access.

software piracy (LO 3, p. 14.10)   The unauthorized copying of copyrighted software.

One act of software piracy is to copy a program from one diskette to another. Another is to download a program from a network and make a copy of it. Software piracy is illegal.

spamming (LO 5, p. 14.15)   Sending unsolicited mail.

A spam includes chain letters, advertising, or similar junk mail, which take up server space and annoy e-mail recipients.

virus (LO 6, p. 14.23)   Deviant program that overwrites or attaches itself to programs and/or documents and destroys or corrupts data.

Viruses can cause users to lose data or files or can even shut down entire computer systems.

worm (LO 6, p. 14.23)   A program that copies itself repeatedly into memory or onto a disk drive until no more space is left.

Worms can shut down computers.

SELF-TEST EXERCISES

1. _____ is a set of moral values or principles that govern the conduct of an individual or group.

2. Computer _____ are "deviant" programs that can cause destruction to computers that contract them.

3. _____ is the expropriation of another writer's text, findings, or interpretations and presentation of it as one's own.

4. _____ _____ is using electronic networks to distribute unauthorized copyrighted materials in digitized form.

5. _____, or enciphering, is the altering of data so that it is not usable unless the changes are undone.

SHORT-ANSWER QUESTIONS

1. What is meant by the term *intellectual property*?
2. What is software piracy?
3. What does the Privacy Act of 1974 do?
4. Provide a few examples of information technology crimes.
5. What danger might exist in electronically manipulating photos and other illustrations?

MULTIPLE-CHOICE QUESTIONS

1. Which of the following threatens computers and communications systems?
   a. crackers
   b. errors and accidents
   c. worms
   d. viruses
   e. all the above

2. One form of security, called _____, is the science of measuring individual body characteristics.
   a. encryption
   b. flaming
   c. spamming
   d. biometrics
   e. all the above

3. To keep track of your activities, certain Web sites may deposit a

   _____ on your computer.
   a. morphed image
   b. spammed document
   c. cookie
   d. CERT
   e. all the above

4. Which of the following provides round-the-clock international information and security-related support services to users of the Internet?
   a. CERT
   b. hacker
   c. call-back system
   d. firewall
   e. all the above

5. Which of the following should you use to protect your own internal network from unauthorized access?
   a. CERT
   b. hacker
   c. call-back system
   d. firewall
   e. all the above

TRUE/FALSE QUESTIONS

1. The Freedom of Information Act of 1970 gives citizens the right to look at data concerning themselves that is stored by the U.S. government. (true/false)

2. Crackers gain unauthorized access to information technology for malicious reasons. (true/false)

3. The V-chip is used primarily with the Internet to block out Web pages that have been labeled as high in violence. (true/false)

4. Junk mail on the Internet is commonly referred to as a *spam*. (true/false)

5. Most computer-related privacy issues involve the use of large databases and electronic networks. (true/false)

KNOWLEDGE IN ACTION

1. What's your opinion about the issue of free speech on an electronic network? Research some recent legal decisions in various countries, as well as some articles on the topic, and then give a short report about what you think. Should the contents of messages be censored? If so, under what conditions?

2. Contact the Software Publishers Association, 1730 M Street, NW, #700, Washington, DC 20036 (202/452-1600, *www.spa.org*). Ask for guidelines and literature on keeping software legal. Give a short report based on the information you receive.

3. Contact the Electronic Privacy Information Center (EPIC), 666 Pennsylvania Avenue, SE, Suite 301, Washington, DC 20003 (202-544-9240, *www.epic.org/*). Request a copy of a document that addresses "the A to Zs of privacy." Prepare a short report describing the major privacy issues identified in the document.

4. In your opinion, have people become less ethical with the invention and widespread use of computers and related technology, or is some unethical behavior just more obvious now because news can travel so much faster and farther? Explain your answer.

EPISODE 5

WELCOME TO EARTH'S BIGGEST BOOKSTORE . . . . . .

Amazon.com

Now that your site is up and running, your job is over, right? Wrong. Aside from managing the day-to-day operations of your business, including taking and filling orders, you must take steps to ensure that customers will keep visiting your site. In this Episode, we explore some of these considerations in more detail.

On May 15, 1997, Amazon.com Inc. made headlines (see below) when it went public and became valued at $438 million. Jeff Bezos, the company's founder, is now one of the richest Internet entrepreneurs given that he and his family control 52% of the company's common stock.

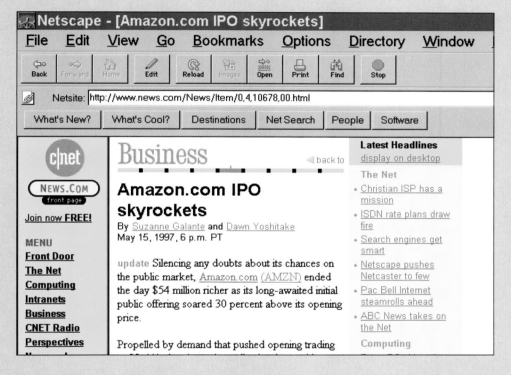

Is this the last chapter in the Amazon.com story? Hardly. In fact, after you consider some of the plans Bezos has for his company, the Amazon.com story may just be beginning.

PLANNING FOR THE FUTURE AT AMAZON.COM

By the year 2000, Bezos would like Amazon.com to be one of the world's leading bookstores. How will this be accomplished? Bezos's strategies include investing heavily in technology, customer service, and marketing and advertising.

Amazon.com plans to continue making improvements to its Web site and transaction processing systems. For example, "One thing that interactive retailing holds for the future is that you can redecorate the store for every customer. Right now we're not doing anything with that type of thing. But it would certainly make sense to me that if we know that every time you come to the store you buy science fiction, we should redecorate the store and show you the latest science fiction,"[1] says Bezos.

High-quality customer service factors greatly into the current and future success of Amazon.com because it encourages customers to make repeat visits and purchases. Amazon.com uses a team of customer support representatives to respond to customer inquiries about their orders. Many Amazon.com support services are currently automated, including the process used to send customers an e-mail notice acknowledging the receipt of an order. In the future, Amazon.com plans to automate additional customer support services.

Amazon.com also intends to invest heavily in marketing and promotion in the years ahead, and may incorporate advertising into its site. "Maybe one of the things that we can do is when you come in and you search for books on kayaks, we'll show you the list of 225 books we have on kayaks, but we'll also show you an advertisement for a company that sells kayaks. And you can click on that and go to their Web site and buy a kayak. So I do think there are a lot of ways we could start to help put people together with the products they want,"[2] says Bezos.

MANAGING YOUR WEB SITE

One customer commented that the Amazon.com site almost seems alive. For example, the books featured on the Amazon.com home page one day may be different the next day, and new author interviews and book reviews from professional sources are frequently added to the site.

For your Web business to have any future at all, make sure you develop a plan for managing your site and then stick to the plan. Nothing will turn customers off more than outdated information. Perform the following management tasks on a daily or weekly basis:

1. Keep the content fresh by adding new information.

2. Update existing information.

3. Verify that your site correctly references the file locations of your graphics files.

4. Verify that your site's navigation buttons work correctly and that other internal links are correct.

5. Verify that any links to external sites work correctly.

WHAT DO YOU THINK?

1. Describe your online business in a two- to three-page report and then (optionally) present the report to your class. Include the following elements:

   ■ The name of your business

   ■ Your product

   ■ The features of your home page

   ■ Your online catalog

   ■ Your plan for taking orders and collecting payment

   ■ Steps you plan to take in order to establish a Web presence

   ■ How you plan to gather, and then use, information about your customers

   ■ What will be your competitive advantage? How will you survive competitive pressures from other Web-based businesses?

   ■ Your hopes for the future expansion of your business

2. What tasks do you anticipate performing to manage your site on an ongoing basis?

Purchasing a Microcomputer System

Many different microcomputers—with different features and processing capabilities—exist on the market today. If you, or your company, are in the market to purchase a microcomputer you should consider carefully your processing needs. Not only should you define your software and hardware requirements clearly before you purchase a microcomputer system, but you should also investigate the company from which you are buying the computer to make sure it will offer support in the long run. In addition, you should plan for future expansion (upgrading).

In this appendix we provide you with the basic information that will help you purchase a microcomputer system and maintain it over time.

Purchasing a System: What to Consider

"You need at least a 1-GB hard disk." "You must purchase a PostScript laser printer." "By all means, purchase this word processing package." Purchasing a microcomputer system involves doing some research, listening to a lot of advice, and ultimately making a number of different purchasing decisions. Many people will buy hardware and software on just the recommendation of a friend. Although recommendations are helpful, if you don't do additional research, you may find yourself spending a lot of money for a system that offers features you will never use.

In this section we provide advice on choosing software and hardware to support your processing needs and explain what to consider before you purchase a particular brand of microcomputer or a microcomputer clone—that is, a microcomputer that is virtually identical to and compatible with the brand of computer it is copying. In addition, we describe some factors that should affect where you purchase a microcomputer system.

What Software and Hardware Will You Need?

If you are a firsttime buyer of a microcomputer, you should choose your applications software first, after you identify your processing needs. For example, do you want to generate documents? Budgets? Graphics? In color? Will others use the computer? If so, what are their processing needs? Will you need to send messages and files to others or access the Internet/Web? Depending on your needs, you will need to purchase one or more applications software packages.

Once your applications software needs have been determined, choose the compatible hardware models and system software that will allow you to use your applications software efficiently. (The system software is usually included with the computer.)

The documentation (user's manual) that accompanies the applications software you purchase will list the minimum hardware requirements necessary to run the software. For example, your microcomputer must have a *minimum* of 8 MB RAM to run most of the software applications on the market today—many programs require 16–32 MB RAM. And if your objective is to output graphics, you must make sure that your software is compatible with the printer you want to use; that is, make sure the software contains the *printer driver* (software instructions) that tells the software how to communicate with your printer. Unless you plan on purchasing an obscure printer, such as one sold by a small computer company with few sales, the software you use will most likely support the printer you want to use.

By choosing your applications software first, you will ensure that all your processing requirements will be satisfied: you won't be forced to buy a software package that is your second choice simply because your first software choice wasn't compatible with the hardware or systems software already purchased.

When you go to work in an office, chances are that the computer hardware and system software will already be in operation, so if you have to choose anything, it will most likely be applications software to help you do your job. If you do find yourself in a position to choose applications software, make sure not only that it will satisfy the processing requirements of your job, but also that it is compatible with your company's hardware and existing software.

PC Clones: A Good Bet?

Yes, usually. If you ask some important questions before making a purchase, you will end up with a compatible system for a good price. These systems use Intel or Intel-compatible processors.

■ Is the microcomputer accompanied by proper and adequate documentation? This is extremely important. If your microcomputer needs to be repaired or upgraded, the computer technician will want to look at the technical documentation that accompanies your system. No matter what the price, if the system comes without documentation, you should not buy it.

■ Are the characteristics of the motherboard—the main circuit board—similar to those of the PC's motherboard? If they are, then PC adapter boards (such as expanded memory or video adapter boards) will work in the clone.

■ Is the system covered by a warranty? The system should be covered by at least a 12-month warranty. If something fails during that time, the manufacturer should repair it at no cost. Does the manufacturer have a technical support line?

■ If the system fails after the warranty period, will parts be available? The manufacturer should service your computer after the warranty period expires. In other words, watch out for fly-by-night manufacturers.

Companies have conducted studies that prove their computers are 100% compatible with the microcomputer they are cloning. This type of information is useful to the microcomputer clone buyer; ask your dealer about such studies.

Because IBM microcomputers used to be very popular in the business environment, computer makers still manufacture Intel-based IBM clones and sell them with their own manufacturing label. Don't think that a microcomputer with an IBM label is better than a clone—clones are sometimes more powerful and typically are less expensive than the machines they copy.

Macintoshes

As we mentioned in Chapter 5, System Software, many more applications programs have been written for the IBM-type, Intel-based PC than for the Motorola-based Mac. However, although desktop publishing programs—such as Quark XPress and PageMaker—are now available for the PC, the high-end Quadra and the Power Mac are still preferred by many people in desktop publishing and related areas.

Basically, the Mac can do anything the IBM can do, and many people still insist it's easier to use than IBM microcomputers—even those with Windows. It's getting easier to swap files between the two systems—with extra, inexpensive software all Macs can accept diskettes formatted on an IBM PC. (Macs with System 7 and later operating system software include this special software.) Some Power Macs have two kinds of chips to enable the computer to support both Mac- and

PC-based programs; and, as with all Macs, networking capability is built in. However, this system is still relatively expensive.

Where to Go

The following three factors should greatly influence where you purchase a microcomputer:

1. The company's reputation
2. The warranty agreement and technical support availability
3. The price

Since each of these factors influences the others, they can't be described independently. If a local computer store has been in business for a few years, you can be reasonably confident that it has tested the waters and won't go out of business. When deciding where to purchase a computer, consider the following:

■ Manufacturers generally support warranties on computers sold through dealers. Should anything happen to the computer in 6–12 months, parts and labor are covered by the manufacturer's *warranty,* or agreement between the manufacturer (and sometimes the seller) and purchaser. If a computer has a problem, you will likely experience it in the first 6–12 months anyway, so this warranty is a fair deal. If a computer is sold through someone other than an authorized dealer—computers sold in this way are referred to as *gray-market computers*—many manufacturers ignore the manufacturer's warranty.

■ When purchasing a computer from a local store, you have a convenient place to take the computer if it needs to be serviced. However, even if you purchase a computer from a mail-order company, you can often pack up the computer in its original box and send it back to the company for service.

■ When you purchase from a local computer company, you have the advantage of establishing personal contacts at the computer store should you have questions about your system.

You can also purchase a microcomputer and peripheral equipment from a mail-order company for a substantial discount. Make sure the hardware you purchase is supported by a warranty. Computer magazines all contain advertisements for mail-order companies. Although many mail-order companies have solid reputations, some don't. Do the following homework before buying from a mail-order company:

■ Check back issues of the magazine to see if the advertisement has been running regularly. If it has, the company has been paying its bills.

■ Check the ad for a street address. If no street address exists—only a P.O. box—it is possible that the company may be a temporary operation.

■ Compare the prices offered by different mail-order companies. If the price you are eyeing is more than 25% lower than the competition, you might be looking at something that is too good to be true.

■ Make sure the system's price includes all the features and peripherals that you want. For example, make sure the price includes a monitor and a keyboard.

■ As mentioned previously, make sure the system you purchase is covered by a manufacturer's warranty. Some major computer manufacturers don't honor warranties on computers sold through mail-order companies.

■ Pay by credit card. If you have an unresolved complaint about the product, U.S. federal law says that the credit card company can't bill you if you report your complaint to them promptly.

■ In addition, you may want to check with the Better Business Bureau or local consumer protection department in the company's area to find out more details about the company.

Other Practical Considerations

Following are a few more guidelines that will help you in choosing a microcomputer system:

1. Determine the maximum amount of money you can spend. *Don't spend money on fancy hardware and software functions you don't need or may never use!*

2. After you decide what you want the system to do for you and have chosen your software, determine what the minimum hardware requirements are to run the software. These requirements are listed in the documentation that accompanies each software program. Pay special attention to RAM requirements, as well as processor speed and multimedia capabilities. In general, it makes sense to use most of your purchase money to invest in a good motherboard and processor, because it's harder to upgrade these components later. It's relatively easy to upgrade RAM and secondary storage later.

3. Determine if any of your hardware needs to be portable.

4. To ensure the possibility of upgrading the computer in the future, choose one with sufficient slots for RAM expansion modules and other types of expansion cards and sufficient interfaces (ports) for hooking up the peripheral devices you need.

5. Determine if your system must be compatible with another system—either in your office or in another context—or with software you or your colleagues are already using. If so, be sure to choose compatible hardware, and make sure that any systems software that comes with the computer is compatible also.

6. If possible, buy everything (computer, keyboard, monitor, printer, and so on) at one place, so you have to make only one phone call to ask questions and solve problems.

7. If you purchase from a local computer store, practice on the computer for a while before you decide to purchase it. Take special care to make sure you're comfortable with the keyboard and monitor.

8. Determine how much secondary storage you will need and buy accordingly. If you're going to be dealing with a lot of graphics, sound, and video, you should probably get a 2-GB hard-disk drive and a hard-disk cartridge drive such as Syquest, Zip, or Jaz for portability of files and backup. If you'll be dealing only with text, a lesser-capacity hard drive and a tape backup unit may be sufficient (and will be less expensive).

9. Determine if you need to print in color. For highest-quality and high-quantity output, use a color laser printer (expensive!). For low-quantity color output of a lesser quality, buy an inkjet printer. (The higher the

resolution, the more expensive.) Black-and-white laser printers and inkjet printers are recommended if you're planning to print mostly text documents with few graphics. If speed is an issue, determine the printer's ppm (pages per minute rate).

10. Determine your communications needs: Are fax-modem capabilities sufficient, or will you also need to access a network? Do you plan to get an ISDN hook-up?

11. Determine what, if any, scanning capabilities you need. Scanners increase in price according to resolution and color capability. High-end desktop publishing may require a 600 dpi color scanner, whereas low-end document storage and retrieval could use a 300 dpi black-and-white scanner.

12. Determine sound and video input/output needs, and purchase compatible support boards and software.

Following is a checklist you can take with you when purchasing a microcomputer system. One final note: magazines such as *Consumer Reports* offer up-to-date guidelines for this, as well as rating computer stores. Also, talk to other users and read hardware/software reviews in computer magazines. If you have access to the Internet, you can also do searches on the hardware/software names you want information on.

Portable Checklist for Buying a Microcomputer System

Copy this list and take it along when you're shopping for a microcomputer system.

Desired Price Range (including peripherals and software)

_____	up to $1000	_____	up to $2000	_____	up to $3000
_____	up to $4000	_____	up to $5000	_____	more than $5000

Uses (software needed)

(Note: All applications software chosen must run with compatible systems software. Note the applications software's operating system—OS—requirements.)

Cost:

_____ Writing letters and reports; preparing professional papers (word processing software).

_____ Personal finance; budgeting and planning; taxes (spreadsheet software).

_____ Business applications; finance management; accounting; planning; scheduling; inventory; sales management (spreadsheet, DBMS, project management, and presentation software).

_____ Entertainment (game software).

_____ Education (tutorial, reference, and other instructional software).

_____ Mailing lists (word processing and DBMS software).

_____ Publishing newsletters and brochures (word processing, graphics, scanning, and photo manipulation software; also desktop publishing software for complicated projects).

_____ Creating art and other graphics for use in published materials (drawing, painting, scanning, photo manipulation, and desktop publishing software).

_____ Multimedia presentations (word processing and presentation software; possibly scanning and photo manipulation).

_____ Personal record keeping (personal information management software).

_____ Communications software for general hookups and Internet use.

_____ Browser software for using the World Wide Web.

_____ Web page creation software.

_____ Networking software (_____ needs to be compatible with other networks? What kind: _____; otherwise)

_____ CAD/CAM software.

_____ Antivirus software.

_____ Conversion software for cross-platform use (for example, IBM/Macintosh).

_____ Data compression software.

_____ Other utilities : ——————————————————.

TOTAL projected cost for software $ _____

Hardware

(Check your chosen software's documentation for minimum hardware requirements and compatibility restrictions; when no requirements are given in the documentation, check your own preferences. Be sure to save all packaging that hardware comes in, in case you have problems and have to send something back to the manufacturer.)

Note cost in blank where appropriate.

1. _____ System must be compatible with other systems? (Y/N) If yes, what kind: _____

2. _____ Uses what kind of system software? Will your chosen applications software run with it?

3. _____ How much memory do I need? _____ 8 MB _____ 16 MB _____ 24 MB _____ 32 MB _____ other

4. _____ 16-bit processor; _____ 32-bit processor (number of bits the processor handles at once). Check the bus architectures: _____ ISA; _____ EISA; _____ MCA; _____ PCMCIA; _____ SCSI; _____ PCI; _____ USB

5. _____ Processor speed: _____ less than 166 MHz; _____ 166 MHz; _____ 200 MHz; _____ 233 MHz; _____ more than 233 MHz; _____ supports multimedia

6. _____ Microcomputer must be portable? (Y/N)

7. _____ Color screen (_____ RAM requirements; low emission _____; active matrix _____)

8. _____ Super VGA; _____ XGA (note screen resolution, or clarity of image: _____; make sure you get the appropriate software driver to support number of colors you want)

9. _____ Screen can tilt and swivel? (Y/N)

10. _____ Size of screen (appropriate to needs and screen resolution?)

11. _____ System cabinet can be put on floor to save desk space? (Y/N)

12. _____ QWERTY keyboard; _____ other keyboard (ergonomically correct?)

13. _____ Number of required functions keys present? (check your applications software requirements)

14. _____ Voice input?

15. _____ Single diskette drive; _____ dual diskette drives (note diskette capacity: _____)

16. _____ Hard disk drive: _____ 1 GB; _____ 2 GB; _____ other

17. _____ Tape backup

18. _____ Portable hard-disk cartridge drive (for portability and backup) _____ Zip; _____ Jaz; _____ Syquest

19. _____ Surge suppressor; _____ uninterrupted power supply

20. _____ Mouse; _____ trackball; _____ touch pad

21. _____ Dot-matrix printer (for simple, black-and-white, mostly text jobs and multiple-part forms); _____ laser printer; _____ inkjet printer; (_____ color capability; _____ speed; _____ top resolution; _____ PostScript driver needed? _____ cost of ink and paper supplies) (also check how to purchase additional fonts for your printer)

22. _____ Modem (_____ internal; _____ external): _____ 14,400 bps; _____ 28,800 bps; _____ 33,600 bps; _____ 56,000 bps (or planning to get ISDN hookup? _____)

23. _____ Fax (dedicated fax machine or internal fax/modem; _____)

24. _____ Scanner (_____ color? _____ just gray-scale? _____ slides? _____ photos?) Note the resolution: _____

25. _____ Sound/video input?

26. _____ Sound/video output?

27. _____ Is system easily upgradable? (Y/N)

28. _____ Any special needs (such as voice output/braille input for a blind person, special keyboard for a disabled person)
29. _____ CD-ROM drive? Note speed: _____
30. _____ Any other multimedia hardware needs? _____

(Note: If you need video and sound capability make sure the cards are compatible with the software you plan to use. Sound and video cards use different standards.)

TOTAL projected cost for hardware: $ _____

Support

Investigate the following:

- Manufacturer's reputation and length of time in business

- Dealer's reputation and length of time in business

- Warranties

- Quality of documentation (both printed and online)—easy to follow? detailed?

- Hotline/online technical support for solving problems. Is it free?

- Location and availability of repair services

- Availability of training

- Will dealer put the system together for you, install the software, and get your communications setup working?

As a simple guide, we recommend the following minimum requirements for a microcomputer system:

- At least 8 MB RAM for Windows 3.1, 16 MB RAM for Windows 95, and 32 MB for Windows NT; more if you plan to work with multimedia

- 15-inch, 17-inch, 19-inch, or 21-inch SVGA monitor, 28 mm dot pitch

- Pentium 166 MHz processor or better with MMX

- At least a 1-GB hard disk drive (multimedia programs may require up to 4 GB or more)

- Mouse or other pointing device

- One or two 3 1/2-inch diskette drives

- Fax/modem or modem and fax machine; 33.6 Kbps or 56 Kpbs (check compatibility with your system)

- Keyboard

- Surge protector

- Extra expansion slots for upgrading later

- Upgradable RAM

- CD-ROM drive, 8-speed (8X) or higher

- 32-bit sound card, speakers, and driver software, if multimedia software will be used

- A backup method; diskettes, tape, hard disk cartridges, depending on the amount of data you have to back up regularly

- Graphics card capable of displaying 65 K colors at 1024 x 768 resolution

- Printer

Your need for video capability, scanner, and other peripherals depends on what you plan to use your system for.

APPENDIX B

Answers to Selected Exercises

CHAPTER 1
Self-Test Questions
1. teleshopping 3. Peripheral 5. computer

Short-Answer Questions
1. (a) *Hardware* is the physical equipment of the computer.
(b) *Software* describes the instructions that direct the hardware.
(c) *Data* is processed into (d) *information* using computer processing. (e) *Procedures* in the form of documentation manuals and reference manuals contain guidelines for using hardware and software. (e) *Communications* is a sixth element when one or more computers are connected together. 3. Whereas systems software runs the basic operations of the computer system, applications software runs the operations you ask it to—in other words, it performs useful tasks that increase your productivity.
5. [answers will vary]

Multiple-Choice Questions
1. e 3. d 5. a

True/False Questions
1. f 3. f 5. f

CHAPTER 2
Self-Test Questions
1. kilobyte, megabyte, gigabyte 3. machine language 5. word size

Short-Answer Questions
1. A parity scheme is used to ensure that bytes are transmitted correctly. Error detection is accomplished using a ninth bit, called the *parity bit*. In an even-parity scheme, the ninth bit is set to 0 or 1 so that the number of 1 bits adds up to an even number. In an odd-parity scheme, the ninth bit is set to 0 or 1 so that the number of 1 bits adds up to an odd number. When the number of 1 bits doesn't match the chosen parity scheme an error message will appear on the screen. 3. Registers hold data that is needed immediately by the processor. Data is transferred from RAM into the registers before processing. 5. The ALU (arithmetic/logic unit) is the component of the processor that performs arithmetic and logical operations and controls the speed of those operations.

Multiple-Choice Questions
1. b 3. d 5. c

True/False Questions
1. f 3. t 5. f

CHAPTER 3
Self-Test Questions
1. input controls 3. keyboard 5. ergonomics

Short-Answer Questions
1. An imaging system uses an image or graphics scanner to convert text and images into a digital form that can then be stored and further edited on the computer. 3. resolution, dot pitch, refresh rate 5. A terminal is an input/output device that uses a keyboard for input and a monitor for output.

Multiple-Choice Questions
1. e 3. d 5. c

True/False Questions
1. t 3. t 5. t

CHAPTER 4
Self-Test Questions
1. terabyte 3. magnetic tape 5. backup

Short-Answer Questions
1. Hard disks can store more than diskettes and allow faster access to data. 3. Systems software stores data on a diskette or hard disk at the intersection of a track (concentric rings) and a sector (wedge-shaped sections). 5. data storage, encyclopedias, catalogs, games, edutainment, magazines and books, movies

Multiple-Choice Questions
1. d 3. d 5. b

True/False Questions
1. t 3. f 5. t

CHAPTER 5
Self-Test Questions
1. applications software 3. communications 5. compression utilities, lossy compression utilities

Short-Answer Questions
1. Without systems software, your computer wouldn't even be able to start. It is the principal coordinator of all hardware components and applications software programs. 3. Whereas *multitasking* refers to the execution of more than one program concurrently for a single user, *timesharing* refers to the processing of several programs for several users. 5. The term *platform* refers to the type of computer architecture that a computer uses. The platform is determined by the type of processor chip inside the computer and the choice of operating system.

Multiple-Choice Questions
1. c 3. b 5. d

True/False Questions
1. t 3. t 5. t

CHAPTER 6
Self-Test Questions
1. word processing 3. installed 5. groupware

Short-Answer Questions
1. communications 3. Integrated software combines the features of several applications into one application. A software suite is several applications that have been bundled together and sold for a discounted price. 5. Multimedia authoring software enables users to combine text, graphics, animation, video, music, voice, and sound into a software product.

Multiple-Choice Questions
1. c 3. a 5. c

True/False Questions
1. f 3. f 5. f

CHAPTER 7
Self-Test Questions
1. modem 3. full-duplex 5. fiber-optic

Short-Answer Questions
1. The faster the modem, the less time you have to spend on the telephone collecting charges from your telephone company. 3. You upload data from your computer to another computer. You download data from another computer to your computer. When data is uploaded and downloaded, it is

usually copied. 5. A portion, or bandwidth, of the electromagnetic spectrum has been allocated by the FCC for communications purposes. The wider the bandwidth, the faster the transmission speed.

Multiple-Choice Questions
1. e 3. a 5. e

True/False Questions
1. t 3. t 5. t

CHAPTER 8
Self-Test Questions
1. Internet 3. workgroup computing 5. telecommuting

Short-Answer Questions
1. You can connect to the Internet through your school or work, through an online information service, or through an Internet service provider (ISP). 3. e-mail, discussion groups, file transfer, remote access, information searches

Multiple-Choice Questions
1. c 3. d 5. c

True/False Questions
1. f 3. t 5. t

CHAPTER 9
Self-Test Questions
1. system 3. data flow diagram 5. prototyping

Short-Answer Questions
1. CASE (computer-aided software engineering) tools are software programs that automate various activities of the SDLC in several phases. 3. JAD is used to jointly define and design systems using highly organized workshops that bring together system owners, users, analysts, and designers. 5. In a structured interview, preset questions are asked. Unstructured interviews are more free-flowing.

Multiple-Choice Questions
1. d 3. c 5. a

True/False Questions
1. f 3. t 5. t

CHAPTER 10
Self-Test Questions
1. first 3. Structured 5. programming

Short-Answer Questions
1. Natural languages, or fifth-generation languages, allow questions or commands to be framed in a more conversational way than languages of previous generations. 3. Visual programming is a method of creating programs by using icons that represent common programming routines. 5. Program documentation helps train newcomers and provides the basis for maintaining the existing system.

Multiple-Choice Questions
1. a 3. a 5. b

True/False Questions
1. t 3. t 5. t

CHAPTER 11
Self-Test Questions
1. tactical 3. downsizing 5. exception

Short-Answer Questions
1. An expert system is a set of computer programs that helps users solve problems that would otherwise require the assistance of a human expert. 3. An executive information system is an easy-to-use DSS made especially for top managers and specifically supports strategic decision making. 5. Research and development, production, marketing, accounting and finance, human resources

Multiple-Choice Questions
1. e 2. b 3. c 4. e 5. d

True/False Questions
1. t 2. t 3. t 4. f 5. t

CHAPTER 12
Self-Test Questions
1. character, field, record, file, and database 3. data dictionary 5. database administrator

Short-Answer Questions
1. In batch processing, data is collected over a period of time and then processed all at once in what is referred to as a *batch*. In online processing, the updating of master files occurs in real-time as the transaction takes place. 3. A query language refers to an easy-to-use language for retrieving information from database. 5. Privacy Act of 1974

Multiple-Choice Questions
1. a 3. e 5. b

True/False Questions
1. f 3. t 5. f

CHAPTER 13
Self-Test Questions
1. robot 3. natural language processing 5. neural network

Short-Answer Questions
1. An avatar is an onscreen representation of an individual or a process. Avatars are used to simplify computerized user interfaces. 3. An expert system is a set of computer programs that can solve problems that would otherwise require the assistance of a human expert. 5. The Turing test is used to measure whether a computer possesses intelligence. The success of the test is a direct result of the artificial intelligence technologies implemented in the computer.

Multiple-Choice Questions
1. c 3. d 5. b

True/False Questions
1. f 3. t 5. f

CHAPTER 14
Self-Test Questions
1. ethics 3. plagiarism 5. encryption

Short-Answer Questions
Intellectual property consists of products of the human mind, tangible or intangible. 3. The Privacy Act of 1974 prohibits secret personnel files from being kept on individuals by government agencies or their contractors. 5. It becomes impossible to know for sure whether a photo depicts reality.

Multiple-Choice Questions
1. e 3. c 5. d

True/False Questions
1. t 3. f 5. t

APPENDIX C

Notes

CHAPTER 1

1. Richard Bolles, cited in T.Minton, "Job-Hunting Requires Eyes and Ears of Friends," *San Francisco Chronicle*, January 25, 1991, p. D5.
2. Field Institute survey, reported in Jonathan Marshall, "High-Tech Often Equals Higher Pay," *San Francisco Chronicle*, September 3, 1996, p. A5
3. Alan Krueger, Princeton University, cited in Marshall, 1996.
4. Richard Atcheson, "A Woman for *Lear's*," *Lear's*, November 1993, p. 87.
5. Merritt Jones, quoted in "FYI," *Popular Science*, November 1995, pp. 88–89.
6. William J. Cook, "Ahead of the Weather," *U.S. News & World Report*, April 29, 1996, pp. 55–57.
7. Glen Martin and Kevin Fagan, "High-Tech Help for Firefighters," *San Francisco Chronicle*, August 22, 1996, pp. A1, A11.
8. Kerry Pechter, "Office Memos: Some Predictions About the Workplace of the Future," *Wall Street Journal*, June 4, 1990, p. R5.
9. Sandra D. Atchison, "The Care and Feeding of 'Lone Eagles,'" *Business Week*, November 15, 1993, p. 58.
10. Link Resources, cited in Carol Kleiman, "At-Home Employees Multiplying," *San Jose Mercury News*, November 12, 1995, pp. 1PC–2PC.
11. *Internet World*, December, 1996, p. 47.
12. Susan N. Futterman, "Quick-Hit Research of a Potential Employer," *CompuServe Magazine*, September 1993, p. 36.
13. J. Peder Zane, "Now, the Magazines of 'Me,'" *New York Times*, May 14, 1995, sec. 4, p. 5.
14. R. U. Serius, "Virtual Banality," *San Francisco Examiner*, June 30, 1996, pp. C-5, C-6.
15. Elizabeth Wasserman, "Software Giant Goes On-Line with Magazine," *San Jose Mercury News*, pp. 1A, 12A.
16. *Ibid.*
17. *Catherine Arnst, Paul M. Eng, Richard Brandt, and Peter Burrows*, "The Information Appliance," *Business Week*, November 22, 1993, pp. 98–110.

EPISODE 1

1. Karen Southwick, Interview with Jeff Bezos of Amazon.com, October 1996, *http://www.upside.com.*
2. Vince Emery, *How to Grow Your Business on the Internet* (Scottsdale, AZ: Coriolis Group Books, 1996), p. 73.

CHAPTER 2

1. Randy Pausch, quoted in John W. Verity and Paul C. Judge, "Making Computers Disappear," *Business Week*, June 24, 1996, pp. 118–119.
2. Dan Gillmor, "Tiny Chips Have Transformed the World," *San Jose Mercury News*, October 20, 1996, pp. 1A, 22A.
3. Michael S. Malone, "The Tiniest Transformer," *San Jose Mercury News*, September 10, 1995, pp. 1D–2D; excerpted from *The Microprocessor: A Biography* (New York: Telos/Springer Verlag, 1995).
4. *Ibid.*
5. *Internet World*, December, 1996.
6. Rick Satava, quoted in Gary Taubes, "Surgery in Cyberspace," *Discover*, December 1994, pp. 85–94.
7. Laurence Block, quoted in Jeffrey Young, "Lab on a Chip," *Forbes*, September 23, 1996, pp. 210–211.
8. Joshua Cooper Ramo, "Doc in a Box," *Time*, Special Issue, Fall, 1996, pp. 55–57.
9. *Ibid.*

10. Dennis J. Streveler, "Telemedicine: A Primer," *California Medicine*, May 1996, pp. 17–18.
11. Los Angeles Times technology poll, reported in Greg Miller, "Southlanders Gaga Over Computers, Poll Says," *San Francisco Examiner*, October 6, 1996, p. C-7; reprinted from *Los Angeles Times*.
12. Kathleen Travers, quoted in Miller, 1996.
13. Alan Freedman, *The Computer Desktop Encyclopedia* (, New York: AMACOM, 1996), P. 547.
14. Alan Greenspan, quoted in James Worsham, "The Flip Side of Downsizing," *Nation's Business*, October 1996, pp. 18–25.
15. U.S. Bureau of Labor Statistics, reported in Worsham, 1996.
16. Lloyd McPherson, quoted in Thomas E. Weber, "Add Internet to List of Useful Farm Tools," *Wall Street Journal*, May 28, 1996, pp. A21. A26.
17. Greg Nolan, quoted in Weber, 1996.
18. Barbara Carton, "Farmers Begin Harvesting Satellite Data to Boost Yields, " *Wall Street Journal*, July 11, 1996, p. B4.

CHAPTER 3

1. Payment Research Systems, Inc., cited in Nikhil Deogun, "Newest ATMs Dispense More Than Cash," *Wall Street Journal*, June 5, 1996, pp. B1, B10.
2. Arthur M. Louis, "Verifone Unveils Your Very Own ATM," *San Francisco Chronicle*, September 30, 1996, pp. E1, E2.
3. *PC Novice*, March 1997, p. 27.
4. Vincent J. Alabiso, quoted in Otis Port, "Digital Finds Its Photo Op," *Business Week*, April 15, 1996, pp. 71–72.
5. *Ibid.*
6. Stephen Manes, "Digital Photos as Fuzzy Snapshots," *New York Times*, March 19, 1996, p. B9.
7. John Holusha, "Kodak Shows Digital Model of Camera Set Under $350," *New York Times*, June 4, 1996, p. C4.
8. Bruce Schwartz, "Turning PCs into Photo Labs," *USA Today*, September 5, 1996, p. 1D.
9. Nichols Van den Berghe, quoted in Jon Swartz, "Battle Begins Over Web Photo Software," *San Francisco Chronicle*, September 12, 1996, pp. B1, B9.
10. *PC Magazine*, March 25, 1997, p. 176.
11. *Ibid.*
12. *Ibid.*
13. Larry Slonaker, "Entrepreneur Trades Software for Soft Blankets, " *San Jose Mercury News*, October 27, 1996, pp. 1E, 3E.
14. *U.S. News*/Bozell poll, reported in Amy Saltzman, "You, Inc.," *U.S. News & World Report*, October 28, 1996, pp. 66–79.
15. IDC/Link, cited in Leta Herman, "An Office at Home," *San Francisco Chronicle*, October 2, 1996, Section (Z-5), pp. 1, 3.
16. Stuart Weiss, "Will Working at Home Work for You?" *Business Week*, August 19, 1996, p. 84E8.
17. Michael J. Prince, quoted in Roger Ricklefs, "Working at Home Proves Too Cozy for Entrepreneur," *Wall Street Journal*, September 12, 1996, p. B2.
18. Diana Berti, quoted in Timothy L. O'Brien, "Aided by Computers, Many of the Disabled Form Own Businesses," *Wall Street Journal*, October 8, 1993, pp. A1, A5.

CHAPTER 4

1. Audrey Choi, "Storage Devices Take Spotlight in Computer Industry," *Wall Street Journal*, April 22, 1996, p. B4.
2. Thomas Lahive, quoted in Choi, 1996.
3. Alan Freedman, *The Computer Desktop Encyclopedia* (New York: AMACOM), p. 374.
4. "MR Heads: The Next Step in Capacity and Performance," Seagate Technology, Inc., April 24, 1997, *http://www.seagate.com/new/sep96/mr_techp.shtml.*
5. William M. Bulkeley, "Publishers Deliver Reams of Data on CDs," *Wall Street Journal*, February, 1993, p. B6.
6. Peter H. Lewis, "Besides Storing 1000 Words, Why Not Store a Picture, Too?" *New York Times*, November 11, 1992, sec 3, p. 8.
7. Dennis Normile, "Get Set for the Super Disc," *Popular Science*, February 1996, pp. 55–58.
8. *Ibid.*
9. Janet L. Fix, "Deal Secures First Data's Credit Lead," *USA Today*, September 18, 1995, pp. 1B, 2B.

10. Brian Bremner, Joan Warner, and Jonathan Ford, "Hold It Right There, Citibank," *Business Week,* March 25, 1996, p. 176.

11. Adam Zagorin, "Cashless, Not Bankless," *Time* September 23, 1996, p. 52.

12. Saul Hansell, "With I.B.M., Big Banks Will Go Electronic, *New York Times,* September, 10, 1996, p. C2.

13. Paul Saffo, quoted in Jared Sandberg, "CyberCash Lowers Barriers to Small Transactions at Internet Storefronts," *Wall Street Journal,* September 30, 1996, p. B6.

14. Julianne Malveaux, "Web Banking: Its Promise, Its Problems," *San Francisco Examiner,* June 2, 1996, p. D-2.

CHAPTER 5

1. Alan Robbins, "Why There's Egg on Your Interface," *New York Times,* December 1, 1996, sec 3, p. 12.

2. Mark Maremont, "No Waiting at This DMV," *Business Week,* August, 19, 1996, p.6.

3. Sana Siwoloop, "Imagine Finding Your Picture on a Virtual Post Office Wall," *New York Times,* November 10, 1996, sec. 3, p. 3.

4. Michelle Locke, "Wells Uses the Web to Catch Criminals," *San Francisco Chronicle,* November 30, 1996, pp. D1, D7.

5. Raoul V. Mowatt, "Cable TV Show Helps Uncover Fugitives," *San Jose Mercury News,* September 8, 1996, pp. 1B, 5B.

6. Carolyn Zinko and Michael McCabe, "High-Tech Hunt Sped Rescue of Missing San Jose Bay," *San Francisco Chronicle,* December 7, 1996, pp. A1, A11.

7. Gordon Witkin, "Making Mean Streets Nice, Computer Maps That Take the 'Random' Out of Violence," *U.S. News & World Report,* December 30, 1996/January 6, 1997, p. 63.

8. Associated Press, "Exhibit A May Be on Hard Drive B," *San Francisco Examiner,* November 29, 1996, p. A14.

9. Julie Chao, "High-Tech Tools Foil Car Thieves," *San Francisco Examiner,* November 17, 1996, pp. C-1, C-4.

10. Berry Eberling, "Future Cops Learn How to Sleuth in Cyber-space," *San Francisco Examiner,* December 15, 1996, p. C-6, reprinted from *Fairfield Daily Republic.*

11. Joe McGarvey, "Next UP for Unix," *Interactive Week,* January 13, 1997.

12. David Kirkpatrick, "Mac vs. Windows," *Fortune,* October 4, 1993, pp. 107–114.

13. Robert Frankenberg, quoted in Richard Buck, "Novell Is Trying to Connect All of Us," *Sun Jose Mercury News,* May 21, 1995, pp. 1E, 6E; reprinted from *Seattle Times.*

14. Lawrence M. Fisher, "Novell Readies a Response to Windows," *New York Times,* September 18, 1995, pp. C1, C10.

15. *Ibid.*

16. "A New Model for Personal Computing," *San Jose Mercury News,* August 13, 1995, p. 27A.

17. Some of this material adapted from: Lee Gomes, "Hollow Dreams," *San Jose Mercury News,* November, 12, 1995, pp. 1D, 3D; Joseph Jennings, "The End of Wintel?" *San Francisco Examiner,* December 17, 1995, pp. B-5, B-7; Mark Fleming and Mike McGowan, "Present at the Creation of the Net," *Business Week,* December 25, 1995, p. 12.

18. Brent Schlender, "Whose Internet Is It Anyway/" *Fortune,* December 11, 1995, pp. 120–142.

19. *Ibid.*

20. *Ibid.*

21. Amy Cortese, Kathy Rebello, Robert D. Hof, and Catherine Yang, "Win 95, Lose 96?" *Business Week,* December 18, 1995, pp. 34–35.

22. Alan Freedman, *The Computer Desktop Encyclopedia* (New York: AMACOM), p. 609.

CHAPTER 6

1. "Get with the Programs," *Business Week,* November 4, 1996, p. 144.

2. Jakob Nielsen, quoted in Amy Cortese, "Software's Holy Grail," *Business Week,* June 24, 1996, pp. 83–92.

3. Alan Deutschman, "Mac vs. Windows,: Who Cares?" *Fortune,* October 4, 1993, p. 114.

4. Peter H. Lewis, "In a Battle of the Spreadsheet, Borland Acts 'the Barbarian,'" *New York Times,* August 29, 1993, sec. 3, p. 8.

5. "A New Model for Personal Computing," *San Jose Mercury News,* August 13, 1995, p. 27A.

6. David Kirkpatrick, "Groupware Goes Boom," *Fortune,* December 27, 1993, p. 100.

7. Gary McWilliams, "Lotus 'Notes' Get a Lot of Notice," *Business Week,* March 29, pp. 84–85.

8. Kirkpatrick, 1993, pp. 11–101

9. Steve Lohr, "Microsoft Seeks to Pad Wide Lead in PC Suites," *New York Times,* October 15, 1993, p. C3.

10. Edward Rothstein, "Between the Dream and the Reality Lies the Shadow. Or Is It the Interface?" *New York Times,* December 11, 1995, p. C3.

11. Bob Frost, "Technomad," *West Magazine, San Jose Mercury News,* December 29, 1996, p. 4.

12. Laurie M. Grossman, "Truck Cabs Turn Into Mobile Offices as Drivers Take on White-Collar Tasks," *Wall Street Journal,* August 3, 1993, pp. B1, B5.

13. Jon Swartz, "Computers Fuel Race Car Teams' Success," *San Francisco Chronicle,* September 7, 1996, pp. D1, D7.

14. Carl Nolte, "Traffic Help as Near as the Phone," *San Francisco Chronicle,* October 21, 1996, pp. A1, A11.

15. Faith Bremner, "Sensors Make Snowy Roads Safer," *Reno Gazette-Journal,* pp. 1A, 10a.

16. Michelle Krebs," Cars That Tell You Where to Go," *New York Times,* December 15, 1996, sec. 11, p. 35A.

17. Frank Vizard, "Cars That Talk You There," *Popular Science,* September 1996, p. 39.

18. Reuters, "Smart Cars Are Wave of Future," *San Francisco Chronicle,* October 25, 1996, p. A12.

19. Michael Krantz, "Robots of the Road," *Time,* November 4, 1996, pp. 76–78.

20. Thaai Walker, "Gadget May End Lengthy Bus Waits," *San Francisco Chronicle,* November 25, 1996, A13, A20.

21. Stacey Richardson, Quoted in Peter H. Lewis, "Pairing People Management with Project Management," *New York Times,* April 11, 1993, sec. 3, p. 12.

22. Glenn Rifkin, "Designing Tools for the Designers," *New York Times,* June 18, 1992, p. C6.

23. Bernie Ward, "Computer Chic," *Sky,* April 1993, pp. 84–90.

24. Alan Freedman, *The Computer Glossary,* 6th ed., (New York: AMACOM, 1993), pp. 196–197.

25. *Ibid.*

26. *PC Novice,* March, 1997.

27. Some of this material is adapted from Ron Wodaski, *Multimedia Madness* (Englewood Cliffs: NJ, 1994.)

28. Barbara Kantrowitz, Andrew Cohen, and Melinda Lieu, "My Info Is NOT Your Info," *Newsweek,* July 18, 1994, p. 54.

29. David Edelson, "What Price Superhighway Information?" (letter) *New York Times,* January 16, 1994, p. 16.

30. David L. Wheeler, "Computer Networks Are Said to Offer New Opportunities fro Plagiarists," *Chronicle of Higher Education,* June 30, 1993, pp. A17, A19.

31. Denise K. Magner, "Verdict in a Plagiarism Case," *Chronicle of Higher Education,* January 5, 1994, pp. A17, A20.

32. Robert Tomsho, "As Sampling Revolutionizes Recording, Debate Grows Over Aesthetics, Copyrights," *Wall Street Journal,* November 5, 1990, p. B1.

33. William Grimes, "A Questions of Ownership of Images," *New York Times,* August 20, 1993, p. B7.

34. Jennifer Larson, "Try Before You Buy," *PC Novice,* March 1993, p. 41.

35. Andy Ihnatko, "Right-Protected Software," *MacUser,* March 1993, pp. 29–30.

EPISODE 3

1. David Cook and Deborah Sellers *Launching a Business on the Web* (Indianapolis: Que Corp., 1996), p. 307.

2. Karen Southwick, Interview with Jeff Bezos of Amazon.Com, October 1996.

CHAPTER 7

1. Thomas A. Stewart, "The Information Age in Charts," *Fortune,* April 4, 1994, pp. 75–79.

2. Tom Mandel, in "talking About Portables," *Wall Street Journal,* January 23, 1997, pp. B1, B6.

3. Gautem Naik, "In Digital Dorm, Click on Return for Soda," *Wall Street Journal,* January 23, 1997, pp. B1, B6.

4. Marshall Toplansky, quoted in Jennifer Larson, "Telecommunications and Your Computer," *PC Novice,* March 1993, pp. 14–19.

5. Leslie Cauley, "Babt Bells Rediscover Fast ISDN Service," *Wall Street Journal,* January 22, 1996, p. B5.

6. Peter Coy, "The Big Daddy of Data Haulers?" *Business Week,* January 29, 1996, pp. 74–76.

7. Lucien Rhodes, "The Race for More Bandwidth," *Wired,* January 1996, pp. 140–145.

8. Chuck Guilford, quoted in Kelly McCollum, "Web Site Treats Writer's Block," *The Chronicle of Higher Education,* September 20, 1996, p. A33.

9. Kenneth C. Green, *1996 Campus Computing Survey,* Claremont Graduate School, Claremont, CA, reported in Thomas J. Deloughry, "Campus Computer Use Is Increasing, But Not as Fast as in Previous Year," *The Chronicle of Higher Education,* November 22, 1996, pp. A21–A22.

10. "At Stanford, a Class-Lab Friendly to Computers," *New York Times,* April 3, 1996, p. B10.

11. Vikas, Bajaj, "U. of Southern California Plans Cinema Class on the Internet," *The Chronicle of Higher Education,* September 13, 1996, p. A31.

12. Thomas J. Deloughry, "New School for Social Research Bolsters Flagging Enrollment with 90 On-Line Courses," *The Chronicle of Higher Education,* September 20, 1996, pp. A27–A28.

13. Joann S. Lublin, "Schools Boot Up to Offer On-Line M.B.A.'s," *Wall Street Journal,* September 24, 1996, pp. B1, B7.

14. Mary Beth Marklein, "Computers Allow a Virtual Shift in Higher Learning," *USA Today,* December 19, 1996. p. 7D.

15. Anthony Ramirez, "Cheap Beeps: Across Nation, Electronic Pagers Proliferate," *New York Times,* July 19, 1993, pp. A1, C2.

16. Mark Lewyn, "Beep If Your Pager Sends Voice Mail," *Business Week,* September 25, 1995, p. 147.

17. Kevin Maney, "Pager Offers Sports Fans Scores, News," *USA Today,* November 2, 1995, p. 1B.

18. Adapted from Betsy Wagner, *U.S. News & World Report,* January 27, 1997.

19. Edmund L. Andrews, "Washington Is a Guinea Pig in Test of Wireless System," *New York Times,* November 15, 1995, p. C7.

20. Walter S. Mossberg, "New PCS Phones Beat Cellular System in Quality and Cost," *Wall Street Journal,* February 29, 1996, p. B1.

21. David J. Lynch, "Telecom Giants Enter Crowded, High-Cost Race," *USA Today,* November 21, 1995, pp. 1B, 2B.

22. *Ibid.*

23. Jeff Cole, "In New Space Race, Companies Are Seeking Dollars from Heaven," *Wall Street Journal,* October 10, 1995, pp. A1, A10.

24. David J. Lynch, "AT&T Links Up with DirectTV," *USA Today,* January 23, 1996, p. 1B.

25. C. Michael Armstrong, quoted in Cole, 1995.

CHAPTER 8

1. Kurt Andersen, "The Age of Unreason," *The New Yorker,* February 3, 1997, pp. 40–43.

2. Elizabeth Fernandez, "Homeless But Wired," *San Francisco Examiner,* January 28, 1996, pp. A-1, A-14.

3. Peter H. Lewis, "The Good, the Bad, and the Truly Ugly Faces of Electronic Mail," *New York Times,* September 6, 1994, p. B7.

4. Walter S. Mossberg, "With E-Mail, You'll Get the Message Without the Hang-Ups," *Wall Street Journal,* April 20, 1995, p. B1.

5. *Ibid.*

6. Lewis, 1994.

7. Michelle Quinn, "E-Mail Is Popular—But Far from Perfect," *San Francisco Chronicle,* April 21, 1995, pp. B1, B8.

8. David Cay Johnston, "Not So Fast: E-Mail Sometimes Slows to a Crawl," *New York Times,* January 7, 1996 sec. 4, p. 5.

9. "Postmarks on E-Mail," *Business Week,* April 24, 1995, p. 47.

10. Steven Levy, "Dead Men Walking," *Newsweek,* January 22, 1996, pp. 71–72.

11. David J. Lynch, "On-Line Services Shake-Out Ahead," *US Today,* January 5, 1996, p. B11.

12. Elizabeth P. Crowe, "The News on Usenet," *Bay Area Computer Currents,* August 8–21, 1995, pp. 94–95.

13. Susan Chandler, "The Grocery Cart in Your PC," *Business Week,* September 11, 1995, pp. 63–64.

14. Steven Levy, "Dead Men Walking," *Newsweek,* January 22, p. 66.

15. Thomas E. Weber, "AT&T to Move On-Line Service onto the Web," *Wall Street Journal,* January 5, 1996, p. B11.

16. David J. Lynch, "On-line Service Shake-Out Head," *USA Today,* January 5, 1996, p. 1B.

17. Julie Schmit, "On-Line Services Experience Static," *USA Today,* February 22, 1996, p. 3B.

18. "A Great Lost Cause: France vs. the Internet," *U.S News & World Report,* April 21, 1997, p. 57.

19. Forrester Research Inc., cited in Paul M. Eng, "War of the Web," *Business Week,* March 4, 1996, pp. 71–72.

20. Elizabeth P. Crowe, "The News on Usenet," *Bay Area Computer Currents,* August 8–21, 1995, pp. 94–95.

21. Mary Ann Pike, *Using the Internet,* 2nd ed., (Indianapolis: Que Corp., 1995), p. 638.

22. Mike Branigan, "The Cost of Using an Online Service," *PC Novice,* January 1992, pp. 65–71.

23. Michael H. Martin, "Digging Data Out of Cyberspace," *Fortune,* April 1, 1996, p. 147.

24. Richard Scoville, "Find It on the Net," *PC World,* January 1996, pp. 125–130.

25. "On-Line Stores," *Internet World,* October 1997.

26. *Ibid.*

27. *Ibid.*

28. "Planning for Push," *Internet World,* May 1997, p. 49.

29. Adapted from *The new Republic,* February 17, 1997, pp. 15–18.

30. "Where the Information Highway Is Taking Us," *San Francisco Chronicle,* March 14, 1996, p. A23.

31. Bart Ziegler, "IBM's Gerstner Vows Funds for Lotus in Microsoft Duel and Internet Battle," *Wall Street Journal,* January 23, 1996, p. B7.

32. Mark Shapiro, "Bulletin Board Systems Cover Just About Every Topic Imaginable," *San Jose Mercury News,* July 23, 1995, pp. 1F, 4F.

33. Bud Konheim, quoted in Jared Sandberg, "The Internet Pulsates with All the Pros and Cons of AT&T's Free-Access Offer," *Wall Street Journal,* February 29, 1996, pp. B1, B3.

34. Alvin Toffler, quoted in Marianne Roberts, "Computers Replace Commuters," *PC Novice,* September 1992, p. 27.

35. Bob Spoer, quoted in Marilyn Lewis, "Tethered to Work," *San Jose Mercury News,* October 1, 1995, pp. 1A, 18A.

36. Peter Hart, quoted in Lewis, 1995.

CHAPTER 9

1. Jeffrey L. Whitten and Lonnie Bentley, *Systems Analysis and Design Methods,* 4th ed. (Burr Ridge, IL; Irwin/McGraw-Hill, 1997), pp. 99, 100.

2. *Ibid.*

3. James O'Brien, *Introduction to Information Systems,* 8th ed. (Burr Ridge, IL: Irwin/McGraw-Hill, 1997) p. 385.

4. *Ibid.*

5. Penny A. Kendall, *Introduction to Systems Analysis and Design: A Structured Approach,* 3rd ed. (Burr Ridge, IL: Irwin/McGraw-Hill), p. 53.

6. Whitten/Bentley, 1997, p. 126.

7. Whitten/Bentley, 1997, p. 104.
8. *Ibid.*
9. *Ibid.*
10. O'Brien, 1997.
11. O'Brien, 1997, p. 410.
12. Hal Lancaster, "Technology Raises Bar for Sales Jobs; Know Your Dress Code," *Wall Street Journal*, January 21, 1997, p. B1.
13. Ingrid Wickelgren, "Treasure Maps for the Masses," *Business Week/Enterprise*, 1996, pp. ENT22–24.
14. Tim McCollum, "New Horizons in Communications," *Nation's Business*, August 1996, pp. 38–39.
15. Laura Casteneda and Jon Swartz, "Kicking Virtual Tires," *San Francisco Chronicel*, October 15, 1996. P. C4
16. Kathy Balog, "On-Line Cyber Shoppers Post record Buying," *USA Today*, December 24, 1996, p. 1B.

CHAPTER 10

1. James Randi, "Help Stamp Out Absurd Beliefs," *Time*, April 13, 1992.
2. Hy Ruchlis and Sandra Oddo, *Clear Thinking: A Practical Introduction* (Buffalo, NY: Prometheus, 1990), p. 109.
3. Ruchlis and Oddo, 1990.
4. R. Wild, "Maximize Your Brain Power," *Men's Health* April, 1992, pp. 44–49.)
5. Gene Wang, *The Programmer's Job Handbook* (New York: McGraw-Hill, 1996), p. 129.
6. *Ibid.*, p. 144.
7. Alan Freedman, *The Computer Glossary*, 6th ed. (New York: AMACOM, 1993, p. 370.
8. *Internet World*, February, 1997, p. 67.
9. *Ibid.*, p. 73.
10. Peter D. Varhol, "Visual Programming's Many Faces," *Byte*, July, 1994, pp. 187–188.
11. Edward Baig, "A World Wide Web of Sports," *Business Week*, October 14, 1996, pp. 134E4–134E6.
12. Steve Lohr, "Electronics Replacing Coaches' Clipboards," *New Your Times*, May 5, 1993, pp. C1, C5.
13. Ron Kroichick, "Candid Camera," *San Francisco Chronicle*, December 11, 1996, pp. B1, B8.

CHAPTER 11

1. Gil Gordon, cited in Sue Shellenberger, "Overwork, Low Morale Vex the Mobile Office," *Wall Street Journal*, August 17, 1994, pp. B1, B4.
2. Shellenberger, 1994.
3. John Diebold, "The Next Revolution in Computers," *The Futurist*, May–June, 1994, pp. 34–37.
4. Jonathan Marshall, "Contracting Out Catching On," *San Francisco Chronicle*, August 22, 1994, pp. D1, D3.
5. David Greising, "Quality: How to Make It Pay," *Business Week*, August 8, 1994, pp. 54–59.
6. William Cats-Baril and Ronald Thompson, *Information Technology and Management* (Burr Ridge, IL: Irwin/McGraw-Hill, 1997, p. 159.
7. James O'Brien, *Management Information Systems* (Burr Ridge, IL: Irwin/McGraw-Hill, 1996, pp. 376–377.
8. *Ibid.*, p. 375.
9. Cats-Baril/Thompson, 1997, p. 163.
10. Robert Benfer, Jr., Louanna Furbee, and Edward Brent, Jr., quoted in Steve Weinber, "Steve's Brain," *Columbia Journalism Review*, February, 1991, pp. 50–52.
11. Jane Bowar Zastrow, "Database Can Plug You Into Homes Similar to Your Own," *San Francisco Examiner*, October 13, 1996, pp. E-1, E-5.
12. *Ibid.*
13. *Ibid.*
14. Jane Bowar Zastrow, "Designing in 3-D," *San Francisco Examiner*, September 8, 1996, pp. E-1, E-5.

CHAPTER 12

1. Doug Rowan, quoted in Ronald B. Lieber, "Picture This: Bill Gates Dominating the Wide Word of Digital Content," *Fortune*, December 11, 1995, p. 38.

2. *Ibid.*
3. Wendy Bounds, "Bill Gates Owns Otto Bettmann's Lifework," *Wall Street Journal*, January 17, 1996, pp. B1, B2.
4. Paul Saffo, quoted in Steve Lohr, "Huge Photo Archive Bought by Software Billionaire Gates," *New York Times*, October 11, 1995, pp. A1, C5.
5. David M. Kroenke, *Database Processing*, 5th ed. (Upper Saddle River, NJ: Prentice Hall, 1995), p. 453.
6. *Ibid.* p. 454.
7. Mike Snider and Kevin Maney, "Patience I a Plus as System Keeps Evolving," *USA Today*, February 16, 1996, pp. 1D, 2D.
8. Richard T. Watson, *Data Management* (New York: Wiley, 1996), p. 366.
9. Kroenke, 1995, p. 22.
10. James A. Larson, *Database Directories* (Upper Saddle River, NJ: Prentice Hall PTR, 1995).
11. Alan Freedman, *The Computer Desktop Dictionary* (New York: AMACOM, 1996), p. 199.
12. Kroenke, 1995, p. 271.
13. Larson, 1995.
14. Kroenke, 1995, p. 467.
15. Jonathan Berry , John Verity, Kathleen Kerwin, and Gail DeGeorge, "Database Marketing," *Business Week*, September 5, 1994, pp. 56–62.
16. Sara Reese Hedberg, "The Data Gold Rush," *Byte*, October 1995, pp. 83–88.
17. Cheryl D. Krivda, "Data-Mining Dynamite," *Byte*, October 1994, pp. 97–103.
18. Edmund X. DeJesus, "Data Mining," *Byte*, October 1995, p. 81.
19. Karen Watterson, "A Data Miner's Tools," *Byte*, October 1995, pp. 91–96.
20. *Ibid.*
21. *Ibid.*
22. *Ibid.*
23. Richard Lamm, quoted in Christopher J. Feola, "The Nexis Nightmare," *American Journalism Review*, July/August, 1994, pp. 39–42.
24. *Ibid.*
25. Penny Williams, "Database Dangers," *Quill*, July/August, 1994, pp. 37–38.
26. Lynn Davis, quoted in Williams, 1994.
27. Associated Press, "Many Companies Are Willing to Give a Cat a Little Credit," *San Francisco Chronicle*, January 8, 1994, p. C1.
28. Jeffrey Rothfelder, "What Happened to Privacy?" *New York Times*, April 13, 1993, p. A15.
29. Ken Hoover, "Prisoner's Long-Distance Victims," *San Francisco Chronicle*, June 1, 1993, pp. A1, A6.
30. David Linowes, cited in Joseph Anthony, "Who's Reading Your Medical Records?" *American Health*, November 1993, pp. 54–58.
31. *Ibid.*
32. Erik Larson, quoted in Martin J. Smith, "Marketers Want to Know Your Secrets," *San Francisco Examiner*, November 21, 1993, pp. E-3, E-8.
33. Deborah L. Jacobs, "They've Got Your Name. You've Got Their Junk," *New York Times*, March 13, 1994, sec. 3, p. 5.
34. Erik Larson, quoted in Martin J. Smith, "Tactics for Evading Nosy Marketers," *San Francisco Examiner*, November 21, 1993, p. E-3.
35. Jacobs, 1994.
36. John R. Emshwiller, "Firms Find Profits Searching Databases," *Wall Street Journal*, January 25, 1993, pp. B1, B2.
37. Adapted from "Flour Power: A Small Town Keeps Its Doughty Christmas Tradition," *Wall Street Journal*, December 4, 1996, p. B1.

CHAPTER 13

1. *Business Week*, December 9, 1996, p.148.
2. *Ibid.95.*
3. *Ibid.*
4. John Villamil-Casanova and Louis Molina, *An Interactive Guide to Multimedia* (Indianapolis: Que Education and Training, Macmillan, 1996), p. 8.

5. Personal.

6. Gene Bylinsky, "Computers That Learn by Doing," *Fortune*, March 13, 1995.

7. Robert McGrough, "Fidelity's Bradford Lewis Takes Aim at Indexes with His 'Neural Network' Computer Program," *Wall Street Journal*, October 27, 1992, pp. C1, C21.

8. Michael Waldholz, "Computer 'Brain' Outperforms Doctors Diagnosing Heart Attack Patients," *Wall Street Journal*, December 2, 1991, p. B78.

9. Otis Port, "A Neural Net to Snag Cancer," *Business Week*, March 13, 1995, p. 95.

10. Otis Port, "Computers That Think Are Almost Here," *Business Week*, July 17, 1995, pp. 68–72.

11. Port, 1995.

12. Sharon Begley and Gregory Beals, "Software au Naturel," *Newsweek*, May 8, 1995, pp. 70–71.

13. Peter H. Lewis, "'Creatures' Get a Life, Although It Is an Artificial One," *New York Times*, October 13, 1993, p. B7.

14. Judith Anne Gunther, "An Encounter With AI," *Popular Science*, June 1994, pp. 90–93.

15. "Can Machines Think?," *Time*, March 25, 1996, p. 52.

16. William A. Wallace, *Ethics in Modeling* (New York: Elsevier Science, Inc., 1994).

17. Laura Johannes, "Meet the Doctor: A Computer That Knows a Few Things," *Wall Street Journal*, December 18, 1995, p. B1.

18. *Time*, 1996.

19. *Time*, 1996.

20. "The Conscious Mind Is Still Baffling to Experts of All Stripes," *New York Times*, April 16, 1996. P. B9.

21. Osvaldo Arias, Quoted in N.R. Kleinfield, "Stepping into Computer, Disabled Savor Freedom," *New York Times*, March 12, 1995, sec. 1. P. 17.

22. Michael Sommermeyer, "What Virtual Reality Needs to Get Real," *High Technology Careers Magazine*, October–November 1996, p. 52.

23. *Ibid*.

24. *Ibid*.

25. *Ibid*

26. Christine Borgman, quoted in Gary Chapman, "What the On-Line World Really Needs Is an Old-Fashioned Librarian," *San Jose Mercury News*, August 21, 1995, p. 3D; reprinted from the *Los Angeles Times*.

27. John W. Verity and Richard Brandt, "Robo-Software Reports for Duty," *Business Week*, February 14, 1994, pp. 110–113; Katie Hafner, "Have Your Agent Call My Agent," *Newsweek*, February 22, 1995, pp. 76–77; Laurie Flynn, "Electronic Clipping Services Cull Cyberspace and Fetch Data for You, But They Can't Think for You," *New York Times*, May 8, 1995, p. C6; Peter Wayner and Alan Joch, "Agents of Change," *Byte*, March, 1995, pp. 97–104; Kury Indermaur, "Baby Steps," *Byte*, March 1995, pp. 97–104; Peter Wayner, "Free Agents," *Byte* March 1995, pp. 105–114.

28. Richard Scoville, "Find It on the Net," *PC World*, January 1996, pp. 125–130.

29. Tom R. Halfhill, "Agents and Avatars," *Byte*, February 1996, pp. 125–130.

30. Denise Caruso, "Virtual-World Users Put Themselves in a Sort of Electronic Puppet Show," *New York* Times, July 10, 1995, p. C5.

31. *Ibid*.

32. John C. Dvorak, "Avoiding Information Overload," *PC Magazine*, December 17, 1996, p. 87.

CHAPTER 14

1. John Seabrook, "My First Flame," *The New Yorker*, June 6, 1994, pp. 70–79.

2. Tom Forester and Perry Morrison, *Computer Ethics: Cautionary Tales and Ethical Dilemmas in Computing* (Cambridge, MA: the MIT Press, 1990), pp. 1–2.

3. Gina Kolata, "When Patients' Records Are Commodities for Sale," *New York Times* November 15, 1995, pp. A1, B7.

4. Survey by Equifax and Louis Harris and Associates, cited in Bruce Horovitz, "80% Fear Loss of Privacy to Computers, *USA Today*, October 31, 1995, pp. A1, B7.

5. Barbara Kanotrowitz, Andrew Cohen, and Melinda Lieu, "My Info Is NOT Your Info," *Newsweek*, July 18, 1994, p. 54.

6. Teresa Riordan, "Writing Copyright Law for an Information Age," *New York Times*, Juky 7, 1994, pp. C1, C5.

7. David Edelson, "What Price Superhighway Information?" (letter), *New York Times* January 16, 1994, p. 16.

8. David L. Wheeler, "Computer Networks Are Said to Offer New Opportunities for Plagiarists," *Chronicle of Higher Education*, June 30, 1993, pp. A17, A19.

9. Denise K. Magner, "Verdict in a Plagiarism Case," *Chronicle of Higher Education*, January 4 5, 1994, pp. A17, A20.

10. Robert Tomsho, "As Sampling Revolutionizes Recording, Debate Grows Over Aesthetics, Copyrights," *Wall Street Journal*, November 5, 1990, p. B1.

11. William Grimes, "A Question of Ownership of Images," *New York Times*, August 20, 1993, p. B7.

12. William Safire, "Art vs. Artifice," *New York Times*, January 3, 1994, p. A11.

13. Hans Fantel, "Sinatra's 'Dutes'; Music Recording or Wizardry?" *New York Times*, January 1, 1994, p. 13.

14. Cover. *Newsweek*, June 27, 1994.

15. Cover, *Time*, June 27, 1994.

16. Jonathan Alter, "When Photographs Lie," *Newsweek*, July 30, 1990, pp. 44–45.

17. Fred Ritchlin, quoted in Alter, 1990.

18. Kathleen O'Toole, "High Tech TVs, Computer Blur Line Between Artificial, Real," *Stanford Observer*, November-December 1992, p. 8.

19. Faiza S. Ambah, "An Intruder in the Kingdom," *Business Week*, August 21, 1995, p. 40.

20. Associated Press, "China Tells Internet Users to Register with the Police," *San Francisco Chronicle*, February 166, 1996, p. A15.

21. John Markoff, "On-Line Service Blocks Access to Topics Called Pornographic," *New York Times*, December 29, 1995, pp. A1, C4.

22. Edmund L. Andrews, "Telecommunications Bill Signed, And New Round of Battles Starts, *New York Times*, February 14, 1996, pp. A1, C2.

23. Virginia Shea, quoted in Ramon G. McLeod, "Nettiquette—Cyberspace's Cryptic Social Code," *San Francisco Chronicle*, March 6, 1996, pp. A1, A10.

24. Yahoo!, cited in Del Jones, "Cyber-Porn Poses Workplace Threat," *USA Today*, November 27, 1995, p. 1B.

25. Lawrence J. Magid, "Be Wary, Stay Safe in the On-Line World," *San Jose Mercury News*, May 15, 1994, p. 1F.

26. David Einstein, "SurfWatch Strikes Gold as Internet Guardian," *San Francisco Chronicle*, March 7, 1996, pp. D1, D2.

27. Peter H. Lewis, Limiting A Medium Without Boundaries," *New York Times*, January 15, 1996, pp. C1, C4.

28. Associated Press, "Robot Sent to Disarm Bomb Goes Wild in San Francisco," *New York Times*, August 28, 1993, p. 7.

29. "Frustrated Bank Customer Lets His Computers Make Complaint," *Los Angeles Times*, October 20, 1993, p. A28.

30. Joseph F. Sullivan, "A Computer Glitch Causes Bumpy Starts in a Newark School," *New York Times*, September 18, 1991, p. A25.

31. G. Pascal Zachary, "Software Firms Keep Eye on Bulletin Boards," *Wall Street Journal*, November 11, 1991, p. B1.

32. Thomas J. De Loughry, "2 Students Are Arrested for Software Piracy," *Chronicle of Higher Education*, April 20, 1994, p. A23.

33. Suzanne P. Weisband and Seymour E. Goodman, "Subduing Sofwtare Pirates," *Technology Review*, October 1993, pp. 31–33.

34. David L. Wilson, "Gate Crashers," *Chronicle of Higher Education*, October 20, 1993, pp. A22–A23.

35. John T. McQuiston, "4 College Students Charged with Theft Via Computer," *New York Times*, March 18, 1995, p. 38.

36. Jeremy L. Milk, "3 U. of Wisconsin Students Face Punishment for Bogus E-Mail Messages," *Chronicle of Higher Education*, October 20, 1993, p. A25.

37. James Kim, "Understanding Concept Virus Is Key to Prevention," *USA Today*, March 11, 1996, p. 5B.

38. Donald Parker, quoted in William M Carley, "Rigging Computers for Fraud or Malice Is Often an Inside Job," *Wall Street Journal*, August 27, 1992, pp. A1, A4.

39. David Carter, quoted in Associated Press, "Computer Crime Usually Inside Job," *USA Today,* October 25, 1995, p. 1B.

40. Eric Corley, cited in Kenneth R. Clark, "Hacker Says It's Harmless, Bellcore Calls It Data Rape," *San Francisco Examiner,* September 13, 1992, p. B-9; reprinted from Chicago Tribune.

41. Philip Elmer-Dewitt, "Bugs Bounty," *Time*, October 23, 1995, p. 86.

42. Wilson, 1993.

43. Joshua Quittner, "Hacker Homecoming," *Time*, January 23, 1995, p. 61.

44. Steven Bellovin, cited in Jane Bird, "More Than a Nuisance," *The Times* (London), April 22, 1994, p. 31

45. William M Bulkeley, "To Read This, Give Us the Password, . . . OOOps! Try It Again," *Wall Street Journal*, April 19, 1995, pp. A1, A8.

46. Anthony Ramirez, "How Hackers Find the Password," *New York Times*, July 23, 1992, p. A12.

47. Robert Lee Hotz, "Sign on the Electronic Dotted Line," *Los Angeles Times*, October 19, 1993, pp. A1, A16.

48. Eugene Carlson, "Some Forms of Identification Can't Be Handily Faked," *Wall Street Journal*, September 14, 1993, p. B2.

49. John Houlsha, "The Painful Lessons of Disruption," *New York Times*, March 17, 1995, pp. C1, C5.

50. The Enterprise Technology Center, cited in "Disaster Avoidance and Recovery Is Growing Business Priority," special advertising supplement in *LAN Magazine*, November 1992, p. SS3.

51. John Painter, quoted in Holusha, 1995.

52. Brian Nadel, "Power to the PC," *PC Magazine*, April 26, 1994, pp. 114–183.

53. Dan Gilmor, "Old Computers Will Mean a Lot to Those in Need," *San Jose Mercury News*, December 23, 1995, p. 1F.

54. Andrew Kupfer, "Alone Together," *Fortune*, March 20, 1995, pp. 94–104.

55. William M. Bulkeley, "Electronics Is Bringing Gambling into Homes, Restaurants, and Planes," *Wall Street Journal*, August 16, 1995, pp. A1, A5.

56. Linda Kanamine, "Despite Legal Issues, Virtual Dice Are Rolling," *USA Today*, November 17, 1995, pp. 1A, 2A.

57. James Sterngold, "Imagine the Internet as Electronic Casino," *New York Times*, October 22, 1995, sec. 4, p. 3.

58. Kevin O'Neill, quoted in David Lieberman, "Racetracks Are Betting on Interactive TV," *USA Today*, October 25, 1995, p. 1B.

59. Marco R. della Cava, "Are Heavy Users Hooked or Just On-Line Fanatics?" *USA Today,* January 16, 1996, p. B2.

60. Laura Evenson, "Losing a Mate to the Internet," *San Francisco Chronicle,* August 9, 1995, pp. A1, A13.

61. Unabomber letter to David Gelernter, quoted in Bob Ickes, "Die, Computer, Die," *New York Times*, July 24, 1995, pp. 22–26.

62. Steven Levy, "The Luddites Are Back," *Newsweek*, June 12, 1995, p. 55.

63. Jeremy Rifkin, "Technology's Curse: Fewer Jobs, Fewer Buyers," *San Francisco Examiner*, December 3, 1995, p. C-19.

64. Michael J. Mandel, "Economic Anxiety," *Business Week*, March 11, 1996, pp. 50–56.

65. Bob Herbert, "A Job Myth Downsized," *New York Times*, March 8, 1996, p. A19.

66. Survey by Microsoft Corp., reported in Don Clark and Kyle Pope, "Poll Finds Americans Like Using PCs but May Find Them to Be Stressful," *Wall Street Journal*, April 10, 1995, p. B3.

67. Sherry Turkle, quoted in Susan Wloszczyna, "MIT Prof Taps into Culture of Computers," *USA Today*, November 27, 1995, pp. 1D, 2D.

68. Jonathan Marshall, "Some Say High-Tech Boom Is Actually a Bust," *San Francisco Chronicle,* July 10, 1995, pp. A1, A4.

69. Yahoo!/Jupiter Communication survey, reported in Del Jones, "On-Line Surfing Costs Firms Time and Money," *USA Today*, December 8 1995, pp. 1A, 2A.

70. Coleman &Associates survey, reported in Julie Tilsner, "Meet the New Office Party Pooper," *Business Week*, January 29, 1996, p. 6.

71. Webster Network Strategies survey, reported in Jones, 1995.

72. Steven Levy, quoted in Marshall, 1995.

73. STB Accounting Systems 1992 survey, reported in Jones, 1995.

74. Ira Sager and Gary McWilliams, "Do You Know Where Your PCs Are?" *Business Week*, March 6, 1995, pp. 73–74.

75. Ron Erickson, "More Software. Gee," *New York Times*, August 4, 1995, p. A19.

76. Alex Markels, "Words of Advice for Vacation-Bound Workers: Get Lost," *Wall Street Journal*, July 3, 1995, pp. B1, B5.

77. Paul Saffo, quoted in Laura Evenson, "Pulling the Plug," *San Francisco Chronicle,* December 18, 1994, "Sunday" section, p. 53.

78. Daniel Yankelovich Group report, cited in Barbara Presley Noble, "Electronic Liberation or Entrapment," *New York Times*, June 15, 1995, p. C4.

79. Leslie Wayne, "If It's a Tuesday, This Must Be My Family," *New York Times*, May 14, 1995, sec 3, pp. 1, 12.

80. Anette Kornblum, "Maybe, Maybe Not," *San Jose Mercury News*, March 10, 1996, pp. 1C, 5C; reprinted from the *Washington Post.*

81. Neil Postman, quoted in Evenson 1994.

82. Rifkin, 1995.

83. Mandel, 1996.

84. Herbert, 1996.

85. Louis Uchitelle, "It's a Slow-Growth Economy, Stupid," *New York Times*, March 17, 1996, sec 4, pp. 1, 5.

86. Paul Krugman, "Long-Term Riches, Short-Term Pain," *New York Times*, September 25, 1994, sec 3, p. 9.

87. Department of Commerce survey, cited in "The Information 'Have Nots'" (editorial), *New York Times*, September 5, 1995, p. A12.

88. Beth Belton, "Degree-Based Earnings Gap Grows Quickly," *USA Today*, February 16, 1996, p. 1B.

89. Alan Kreuger, quoted in LynNell Hancock, Pat Wingert, Patricia King, Debra Rosenberg, and Allison Samules, "The Haves and the Have Nots," *Newsweek*, February 27, 1995, pp. 50–52.

90. Terry Bynum, quoted in Lawrence Hardy, "Tapping into New Ethical Quandries," *USA Today*, August 1, 1995, p. 6D.

91. Tamara Henry, "Many Shcools Can't Access Net Offer," *USA Today,* November 3, 1995, p. 7D

92. Susan Yoachum and Edward Epstein, "Clinton Goal—Internet in Every School," *San Francisco Chronicle,* September 22, 1995, p. A1, A19.

93. Bill Workman, "Media Revolution in Stanford Future," *San Francisco Chronicle,* February 16, 1994, p. A12.

94. Edward Barrett, "Collaboration in the Electronic Classroom," *Technology Review*, February/March 1993, pp. 51–55.

95. Louis Freedberg,, "A Plan to Make Books Obsolete," *San Francisco Chronicle*, July 15, 1993, pp. A1, A12.

96. Robert L. Johnson, "Extending the Reach of 'Virtual' Classrooms," *Chronicle of Higher Education*, July 6, 1994, pp. A19–A23.

97. Ronald Smothers, "New Video Technology Lets Doctors Examine Patients Many Miles Away," *New York Times*, September 16, 1992, p. B6.

98. John Eckhouse and Ken Siegmann, "A Medical Version of the Superhighway," *San Francisco Chronicle*, January 19, 1994, p. B4.

99. Tony Rutkowski, quoted in Schnaidt, 1993.

EPISODE 5

1. Karen Southwick, Interview with Jeff Bezos of Amazon.com, October, 1996, *http://www.upside.com.*

2. Southwick 1996.

Photo Credits

Page **1.3** (top) Stock South, © 1992; (bottom) Rainbow, © Dan McCoy, 1994; **1.4** (left and right) Rainbow, ©Dan McCoy, 1994; **1.6** © Rainbow, 1995; **1.7** IBM; **1.8** © 1996 PhotoDisc, Inc.; **1.9** (top) Peter Fox, Apple Computer, Inc.; (bottom) Intel Corp.; **1.10** (top) Intel Corp.; (bottom) Centron Electronics; **1.11** (top) Hewlett-Packard; (second from top) Sony; (bottom two) © 1996 PhotoDisc, Inc.; **1.13** Cray Research; **1.14** (top three) IBM; (bottom) Intel Corp.; **1.15** (top left) Silicon Valley, Inc.; (middle left) Sony; (middle bottom) Toshiba; (top right) U.S. Robotics; (middle right) Sharp Electronics Corp.; (bottom right) IBM; **1.17** (a-c) IBM Archives; (d-e) Smithsonian Institution; (f) IBM Archives; **1.18** Unisys Archives; **1.28** Sharp Color Zaurus; **2.3** Stock, Boston, © 1990 Matthew Borkoski; **2.8** Phototake, © 1994 Richard Nowitz; **2.10** IBM; **2.11** Intel Corp.; **2.13** (top) Centron Electronics; (bottom) Stock, Boston, © 1991 Peter Menzel; **2.18** Stock South, © 1994 Tommy Thompson; **2.20** Word & Pictures, © 1995 Ann Purcell, Carl Purcell; **2.27** Hayes; **3.6** (left) John Greenleigh, Apple Computer, Inc.; (right) Microsoft Corp.; **3.7** (a, b, c) Logitech, (d, e) Input Center; **3.8** IBM; **3.9** (left and right) FTG; **3.10** (top) Hewlett-Packard; (middle) Calcomp Ultraslate; (bottom left and bottom right) Stylistic 1000; **3.11** (left, middle) IBM; (right) NCR; **3.12** (top) © 1991 James Lukosi; (bottom) CheckMate Electronics; **3.13** (middle) Lanier Worldwide, Inc.; (bottom) Hayes; **3.14** (top) Black Star, © 1989 Arnold Zann; (middle left) Pagescan; (middle right) Logitech; (bottom right) Microscribe Immersion Corp.; **3.17** US Pro; **3.18** (middle) Digital Technology Association; **3.20** Tom Burdete, U.S. Geological Society; **3.24** Hewlett-Packard; **3.26** (top, bottom) Calcomp; **3.27** Okidata; **3.29** (left, right) Planar; **3.34** Contact Press Images, © 1992 Dilip Mehta; **3.35** (top) The Image Works; **3.36** (top) Mondex; (bottom) AT&T Global Info/Solution; **4.9** IBM; **4.10** (both) © 1996 PhotoDisc., Inc.; **4.14** IBM; **4.15** (bottom) AP/Wide World Photos/IBM; **4.17** (left) Iomega; (right) Syquest; **4.18** IBM; **4.21** (left) Toshiba; (right) IBM; **4.22** © Frank Bevans; **4.23** SureStore CD Writer; **4.24** © Greenlar, The Image Works; **4.26** (top) Toshiba; **4.28** Sun Disk; **5.4** Stock, Boston, © 1988 Charles Gupton; **5.16** © 1992 Peter Menzel; **6.15** Microsoft Corp.; **6.16** (bottom) Intersolv Multilink; **6.28** (left) Autodesk; (right) IBM; **7.5** (top) Hayes; (bottom) Multitech Systems; **7.12** (bottom left) U.S. Sprint; (others) AT&T; **7.14** Newfoundland Telephone Co.; **7.15** Rainbow, © Hank Morgan; **7.17** (top) Nokia; **7.18** Nokia; **8.8** (top) Tony Stone Images; **9.11** © 1996 PhotoDisc, Inc.; **9.14** © 1996 PhotoDisc, Inc.; **9.21** (top) © 1996 PhotoDisc, Inc.; (bottom) Iconix; **9.24** © 1996 PhotoDisc, Inc.; **9.25** © 1996 PhotoDisc, Inc.; **9.28** © 1996 PhotoDisc, Inc.; **10.11** Naval Surface Warfare Center, Dahlgren, Virginia; **11.3** © 1993 Matthew Borkoski; **11.15** © Mapinfo; **12.4** AP/Wide World Photos; **13.3** © 1987 Laurence Migdale; **13.15** (top left) NASA; (top right) Transitions Research Corp.; (bottom left) © 1987 Spencer Grant; (bottom right) © Dennis Budd Gray; **13.24** © 1996 PhotoDisc, Inc.; **13.26** (top and middle left) Autodesk; (middle right) UPL Research, Inc.; (bottom left) © 1991 Charles Gupton; (bottom right) © 1990 Peter Menzel; **14.4** Black Star, © 1988 Paul van Riel; **14.13** Elastic Reality, Inc.; **14.17** Phototake, © 1994 Tom Carroll; **14.33** Stock, Boston, © Bob Daemmrich; **14.35** © Everett Collection, New York; **14.38** Phototake, © 1994 Ray Nelson.

Text and Art Credits

Page **1.25** Osborne Series, McGraw-Hill; **2.24** adapted from Alan Freedman, *The Computer Desktop Encyclopedia* (New York: AMACOM, 1996), pp. 670–671; **3.9** (top) adapted from *MacWorld*, May 1996, p. 101; © 1996, *USA Today*, reprinted with permission; **3.37** adapted from *Wall Street Journal*, September 17, 1996, p. B1, reprinted by permission of *Wall Street Journal*, © 1996, Dow Jones & Co., Inc., all rights reserved worldwide; **4.26** (middle) © April 21, 1997, *U.S. News & World Report*; (bottom) adapted from *PC Novice,* May, 1997, p. 38; **4.29** adapted from *LAN Times*, June 5, 1995, p. 51; **6.10** adapted from *PC Novice*, May, 1996, p. 26; **7.8** adapted from *Time*, September 23, 1996, p. 55; **7.16** adapted from Jared Schneidman, "How It Works," *Wall Street Journal*, February 11, 1994, p. R5, and *Popular Science;* © March 3, 1997, *U.S. News & World Report*; **7.21** adapted from *Byte*, September 9, 1996, p. 69; **7.27** adapted from Alan Freedman, *The Computer Desktop Encyclopedia* (New York: AMACOM, 1996), p. 617; **8.7** adapted from *Newsweek*, April 21, 1997, p. 89; **8.18** adapted from "How Internet Mail Finds Its Way," *PC Magazine*, October 11, 1994, p. 121; **8.27** *Newsweek*, January 1, 1997, p. 84; **9.6** information rom *San Francisco Chronicle*, December 18, 1996, pp. A10–A11, *New York Times* April 16, 1996, p. A13, and May 11, 1996, p. 17; **9.7** adapted from Penny A. Kendall, *Introduction to Systems Analysis & Design: A Structured Approach*, 3rd ed. (Burr Ridge, IL: Irwin/McGraw-Hill, 1996), p. 8; **9.8** adapted from Penny A. Kendall, *Introduction to Systems Analysis & Design: A Structured Approach*, 3rd ed. (Burr Ridge, IL: Irwin/McGraw-Hill, 1996), p. 21; **9.10** (top) Penny A. Kendall, *Introduction to Systems Analysis & Design: A Structured Approach*, 3rd ed. (Burr Ridge, IL: Irwin/McGraw-Hill, 1996), p. 30, reprinted with permission of the McGraw-Hill Companies; (bottom) Whitten/Bentley, *Systems Analysis and Design Methods* (Burr Ridge: IL, Irwin/McGraw-Hill, 1997), p. 21, reprinted with permission of the McGraw-Hill Companies; **9.20** Penny A. Kendall, *Introduction to Systems Analysis & Design: A Structured Approach*, 3rd ed. (Burr Ridge, IL: Irwin/McGraw-Hill, 1996), p. 171, reprinted with permission of the McGraw-Hill Companies; **9.27** James O'Brien, *Introduction to Information Systems* (Burr Ridge: IL, Irwin/McGraw-Hill, 1997), p. 410, reprinted with permission of the McGraw-Hill Companies; **10.7** adapted from Elizabeth A. Dickson, *Computer Program Design* (Burr Ridge, IL: Irwin/McGraw-Hill, 1996), pp. 30–31; **10.8** Julia Case Bradley *Quick BASIC and QBASIC Using Modular Structure* (Burr Ridge, IL: Irwin/McGraw-Hill, 1996), p. 15; **10.16** adapted from Alan Freedman, *The Computer Desktop Encyclopedia* (New York: AMACOM, 1996), p. 159; **10.27** adapted from Brenden P. Kehoe, *Zen and the Art of the Internet* (Englewood Cliffs, NJ: Prentice Hall PTR, 1996), pp. 203–208; **10.29** information from *San Francisco Chronicle*, March 6, 1997, p. A4 and November 15, 1996, p. E2, *Popular Science*, February 1997, p. 26, *San Jose Mercury News*, May 12, 1996, p. E1; **11.6** both from *Management Information Systems* (Burr Ridge, IL: Irwin/McGraw-Hill, 1996), pp. 314, 319, reprinted with permission of the McGraw-Hill Companies; **11.17** reprinted from *Columbia Journalism Review*, January/February 1991, © 1991 by Columbia Journalism Review; **11.18** James O'Brien, *Introduction to Information Systems* (Burr Ridge: IL, Irwin/McGraw-Hill, 1996), p. 281, reprinted with permission of the McGraw-Hill Companies; **11.19** William Cats-Baril, *Information Technology and Management* (Burr Ridge, IL: Irwin/McGraw-Hill, 1997), p. 109, reprinted with permission of the McGraw-Hill Companies; **11.20** adapted from Del Jones, "Information Gridlock," *USA Today*; **12.3** adapted from David M Kroenke, *Databse Processing* (Englewood Cliffs, NJ: Prentice Hall, 1995) p. 9; **12.22** adapted from "Data Mining Process," illustrated by Victor Gad, © 1995, p. 84, in Sara Reese Hedberg, "The Data Gold Rush," *Byte*, October 1995, pp. 83–88; **13.16** "Go Team Go," Steve Nadis with Jerry Shine, *Popular Science,* May 1996; **13.17** Otis Port, "Developments to Watch," *Business Week*, March 25, 1996, p. 87; **13.22** Peter Coy, "Developments to Watch," *Business Week,* December 9, 1996; **13.31** Copyright © 1996 by the New York Times Co., reprinted by permission; **14.8** *San Francisco Chronicle*, June 11, 1996; **14.20** copyright © 1994 by the New York Times Co., reprinted by permission; **14.42** Association of Information Technology Professionals, reprinted with permission.

INDEX

Abacus, 1.17
Abate, Tom, 14.13
Access security, 12.19, 14.28–14.30
Access time, **4.16**
Accounting and finance department, 11.6
Accuracy of databases, 12.24
Active-matrix display, **3.28**
ActiveX controls, 8.23
Ada programming language, **10.21**
Add-ons
    boards, 2.25
    programs, 8.23
Addresses
    Internet, 8.16–8.19
    main memory, 2.14
ADSL (asymmetric digital subscriber line), 7.8
After-image records, 12.20
Agricultural computers, 2.17
AI. *See* Artificial intelligence
Algorithms, **10.3**
    genetic, **13.23**
    hashing, 12.10
Alias, 8.6
Allen, George, 1.16
Alpha testing, 10.11
Amazon.com Web site
    catalog shopping on, E3.1–E3.4
    design of, E2.1–E2.2
    future of, E5.1–E5.2
    marketing success of, E4.1–E4.3
    origins of, E1.1–E1.2
America Online, 8.10
American Analytical Information
    Management System
    (AAIMS), 11.14–11.15
American National Standards
    Institute (ANSI), 10.19
Amplitude, **7.3**
Analog cellular phones, 7.16
Analog signals, **1.7**, 3.16, **7.3**
Analytical graphics, **6.12**–6.13
Analyzing systems. *See* Systems
    analysis
Andersen, Kurt, 8.2
Andreeson, Marc, 5.27
Animation, 13.7
Anonymous FTP sites, 8.20
ANSI (American National Standards Institute), 10.19
Antivirus software, **5.7**–5.8, **14.25**

APL (A Programming Language),
    10.22
Apple Macintosh. *See* Macintosh
    computers
Applets, 5.27–5.28
Application generator, 10.17
Applications development cycle.
    See Systems development life
    cycle
Applications software, **1.12**,
    5.3–5.4, 6.2–6.38
    basic categories of, 6.2–6.4
    common features of, 6.4–6.7
    communications, **6.18**–6.19
    compatibility issues, 6.6–6.7
    computer aided design/computer-aided manufacturing
    (CAD/CAM), **6.29**
    computer-aided design (CAD),
    6.27–6.29
    database, **6.15**–6.17,
    12.12–12.20
    desktop accessories, **6.20**
    desktop publishing (DTP),
    6.25–6.28
    drawing and painting programs,
    6.29–6.30
    groupware, **6.19**
    installing, 6.33
    integrated software packages,
    6.21
    multimedia authoring,
    6.30–6.33, 13.9–13.10
    personal finance, **6.13**–6.14
    personal information manager
    (PIM), **6.20**
    presentation graphics, **6.15**
    productivity tools, 6.3, 6.7–6.22
    project management, **6.26**–6.27
    software suites, **6.21**
    specialty tools, 6.3–6.4,
    6.24–6.33
    spreadsheet, **6.11**–6.13
    updating, 6.33–6.34
    Web browsers, **6.22**
    word processing, 6.7, **6.8**–6.11
    See also System software
Archie utility, **8.20**
Arithmetic operations, 2.10
Arithmetic/logic unit (ALU), **2.10**
Arithnometer, 1.17
Armstrong, C. Michael, 7.19

Arrow keys, 3.6
Artificial intelligence (AI),
    13.14–13.28
    aim of, 13.14
    artificial life and, **13.23**–13.24
    educational use of, 13.17
    ethical issues, 13.25
    expert systems, **13.18**–13.21
    fuzzy logic, **13.17**–13.18
    genetic algorithms, **13.23**
    natural language processing,
    13.16–13.17
    neural networks, **13.21**–13.23
    perception systems, **13.14**–13.16
    robotics, **13.14**, 13.15
    third-generation languages for,
    10.21–10.22
    Turing test of, **13.24**–13.25
    virtual reality, **13.26**–13.28
Artificial life, **13.23**–13.24
ASCII (American Standard Code
    for Information Interchange)
    coding scheme,
    2.4 files, **4.4**
Assemblers, 10.15
Assembly language, 10.15
Association of Information Technology Professionals (AITP),
    14.44
Asymetrix Multimedia Toolbook,
    13.11–13.12
Asynchronous transfer mode
    (ATM), 7.25
Asynchronous transmission, **7.23**,
    7.24
ATMs (automated teller
    machines), 3.2, 3.34
Attributes, 12.16
Audio board, 3.16
Audio CDs, 4.19
Audio files, **4.4**
Audio input devices, **3.16**
Audio output hardware, 3.30,
    3.32–3.33
    sound output devices, **3.32**–3.33
    voice output devices, **3.32**
Audio teleconferencing, 8.8
Audit controls, 14.31
Auditing systems, 9.28
Authoring process, 13.8–13.9
Authoring software, **6.30**–6.33,
    13.9–13.12

for computer-based training programs, 13.11–13.12
Automatic backups, 4.28
Automation, 11.3
Avatars, **13.30**–13.31
Axons, 13.21

Background tasks, 5.12
Backup utility, **5.7**
Backups, 4.27–4.28
Backward compatibility
for chips, 2.21
for software, 5.15, 6.34
Backward recovery, 12.20
Balkema, Grant, 7.7–7.8
Band printers, 3.22
Bands, **7.9**
Bandwidths, **7.9**, 7.20
Banking, electronic, 4.30
Banner advertising, E4.3
Baptiste, Valerie, 4.30
Bar charts, 6.12
Bar codes, **3.11**
Bar-code readers, **3.11**–3.12
BASIC (Beginner's All-purpose Symbolic Instruction Code), **10.21**
Batch processing, **12.8**
Baud rates, 2.29, 7.6
Bellovin, Steven, 14.29
Berners-Lee, Tim, 5.27, 8.22
Berry, Neal, 8.3
Beta testing, 10.12
Bezos, Jeffrey P., E1.1, E1.2, E3.4, E5.1
Binary coding schemes, 2.4–2.5
Binary digits (bits), **1.6**
Binary system, **1.6**, **2.4**
Biometric systems, 3.20, 14.30
BIOS (basic input/output system), **5.6**
Biotechnology, 2.28
Bisbee, Mark, 1.16
Bit, **1.6**, **2.8**, 12.6
Bit depth, 3.29
Bit-mapped display screens, 3.30
Bit-mapped graphics, 6.38, 13.6
Bits per second (bps), 2.29, **7.6**
Bloatware, 5.26
Block, Lawrence, 2.6
Blocking software, 14.15–14.16
Body suits, 3.20
Bolles, Richard, 1.2
Book authoring format, 13.8
Bookmarks, E4.2
Books, CD-ROM, 4.22
Boot routine, 5.5

Booting the computer, 5.5
Boot-sector viruses, 14.24
Borgman, Christine, 13.29
Brain-wave devices, 3.20
Bricklin, Daniel, 6.11
Bridges, **7.33**
Browsers. *See* Web browsers
Bubble-jet printers, 3.24
Buchanan, Charlotte, 8.28
Bugs, software, 14.18
Bulkeley, William, 14.29
Bulletin board systems (BBSs), 6.18, **8.11**
Bundled programs, 6.21
Bus line, **2.25**
Bus network, **7.35**
Buses, 2.10, **2.25**–2.27
Business
effects of information technology on, 14.40
expert systems in, 13.20–13.21
multimedia in, 13.2–13.3
online, 8.27–8.28
specialty software for, 6.3
See also Web businesses
Business graphics, 6.12–6.13
Business process redesign (BPR), 9.12
Buttons, **6.5**
Bynum, Terry, 14.38
Byte, **1.6**, **2.8**, 12.6

C programming language, **10.19**, 10.21
C++ programming language, 10.25
Cable modems, 7.7–**7.8**
Cache memory, **2.22**–2.23
CAD (computer-aided design) software, **6.27**–6.29
CAD/CAM (computer-aided design/computer-aided manufacturing) software, **6.29**, 11.5
Calculating tools, 1.17
Calendaring programs, 6.20
California Department of Forestry, 1.16
Call-back system, 14.29
Campbell, John, 12.27
Campbell, Matt, 7.2
Capacity, 2.29
diskette, 4.12
main memory, 2.15
secondary storage device, 4.3
Carey, Susan, 13.28
Car-navigation systems, 6.24

Carrier wave, 7.3
Carter, David, 14.25
Cartridge tape units, 4.9
Caruso, Denise, 13.30
CASE (computer-aided software engineering) tools, 9.16, **9.21**–9.22
Case control structure, 10.10
Catalogs
CD-ROM, 4.22
online, E3.1–E3.4
Cathode-ray tubes (CRTs), **3.27**, 3.28
CBT programs. *See* Computer-based training (CBT) programs
CDEs (erasable optical disks), **4.25**
CD-R disks, **4.23**–4.24
CD-ROM disks, **4.20**–4.24
multimedia and, 4.22–4.23
uses for, 4.21–4.22
CD-RWs (rewritable optical disks), **4.25**
Cell address, **6.12**
Cell pointer, 6.12
Cells, **6.12**
Cellular Digital Packet Data (CDPD), 7.17
Cellular phones
analog, 7.16
digital, 7.17
Censorship, 14.15–14.16
Central processing unit (CPU), **1.9**, **2.9**–2.11
Chain printers, 3.22
Chalmers, David, 13.25
Character-recognition devices, 3.12–3.13
Characters, **12.6**
Chat rooms, 8.11
Chat sessions, 8.8
Check bit, 2.5
Child records, 12.13–12.14
Chips, **2.10**
coprocessor, 2.12
creating, 2.11
downward-compatible, 2.21
DRAM, 2.13
EEPROM, 2.22
EPROM, 2.22
PROM, 2.22
RAM, 2.13, 2.21, 2.25
RISC, 2.12
ROM, 2.22
specialized, 2.12
SRAM, 2.13
theft of, 14.20

Chips, *(continued)*
  upward-compatible, 6.33–6.34
  VRAM, 2.23
Circuit switching, 7.25
CISC processors, 2.12
Civil hazards, 14.19
Clark, James, 5.27
Clicking, 3.8
Client application, 5.20
Clients, 3.34, 7.31–7.32
  thin, 5.26–5.27
Client-server LANs, **7.31**–7.32
Clipboard, **6.6**
Clock speed, 2.29
Clusters, 4.4
CMOS technology, 2.13
Coaxial cable, 7.13, **7.14**
COBOL (Common Business Ori-
  ented Language), **10.18**–10.19
Codecs, 5.9
Coding, 10.3, **10.10**–10.11
Coding schemes, 2.4–2.5
Collaborative computing, 8.32
Colmerauer, Alan, 10.22
Color depth, 3.29
Color display screens, 3.29–3.30
Column headings, 6.11
COM ports, 2.23–2.24
Command-driven interface, 5.13
Commerce. *See* Business
Communications, **1.5**, **7.2**
Communications channels, **7.9**–7.19
  analog cellular, 7.16
  Cellular Digital Packet Data
    (CDPD), 7.17
  coaxial cable, 7.13, **7.14**
  communications satellites, **7.14**,
    7.18–7.19
  digital cellular, 7.17
  electromagnetic spectrum and,
    7.9–7.10, 7.12
  fiber-optic cable, 7.13, **7.14**
  Global Positioning System
    (GPS), **7.14–7.15**
  microwave systems, **7.13**–7.14
  packet-radio, 7.16–7.17
  pagers, 7.15–7.16
  personal communications ser-
    vices (PCS), 7.17–7.18
  satellite-based systems, **7.14**,
    7.18–7.19
  specialized mobile radio (SMR),
    7.18
  twisted-pair wire, **7.12**
Communications controller, 7.26
Communications Decency Act
  (1996), 14.15

Communications hardware, **1.11**
Communications networks. *See*
  Networks
Communications protocols, **5.6**
Communications satellites, **7.14**,
  7.18–7.19
Communications services, 8.2–8.36
  electronic data interchange
    (EDI), **8.32**
  e-mail, **8.6**–8.7
  extranets, **8.33**
  fax messages, **8.4**–8.5
  the Internet, **1.24**, **8.13**–8.21,
    8.30–8.31
  intranets, **8.33**
  online information services,
    1.23–1.24, **8.9**–8.13
  picture phones, **8.9**
  telecommuting, **8.34**
  videoconferencing, **8.8**–8.9
  virtual offices, **8.34**–8.35
  voice mail, **8.5**–8.6
  workgroup computing, **5.19**,
    8.32
  World Wide Web, **1.24**,
    8.22–8.31
Communications software,
  6.18–6.19, 7.6–7.7
Communications technology,
  7.2–7.36
  ADSL technology, 7.8
  cable modems, 7.7–**7.8**
  channels used in, 7.9–7.19
  communications software,
    7.6–7.7
  data transmission factors,
    7.20–7.27
  ISDN phone lines, **7.7**
  measurement terms for, 2.29
  modems, **7.4**–7.6
  networks, 7.27–7.29
  practical uses of, 8.2–8.4
  satellite dishes, 7.8–7.9
  types of signals in, 7.3–7.4
Compatibility issues
  applications software, 6.6–6.7
  downward compatibility, 2.21,
    5.15, 6.34
  upward compatibility, 6.33–6.34
Compilers, **10.16**
CompuServe, 8.10
Computer competency, **1.3**
Computer conferencing, 8.8
Computer Emergency Response
  Team (CERT), 14.27–14.28
Computer Ethics (Forester and
  Morrison), 14.3

Computer literacy, **1.3**
Computer Matching and Privacy
  Protection Act (1988), 12.25,
  14.7
Computer operators, 1.3
Computer professionals, **1.2**–1.3
Computer programmers, 1.2, 10.29
Computer-aided design (CAD)
  software, **6.27**–6.29
Computer-aided design/computer-
  aided manufacturing
  (CAD/CAM) software, **6.29**,
  11.5
Computer-aided software engineering (CASE) tools, 9.16,
  9.21–9.22
Computer-based information systems, **1.4**–1.5, 11.6,
  11.10–11.18
Computer-based training (CBT)
  programs, 13.8
  authoring software for,
    13.11–13.12
Computers, **1.4**
  development of, 1.17–1.20
  digital basis of, 1.6
  ethics of using, 14.3
  generations of, 1.18–1.20
  hardware for, 1.8–1.11
  language of, 2.3–2.9
  measurement terms used for, 2.29
  privacy rights and, 14.3–14.8
  software for, 1.11–1.12
  types of, 1.13–1.15, 2.15–2.16,
    2.18
  See also Microcomputers
Concentrators, **7.26**
Concurrent-use license, **6.37**
Conference calls, 8.8
Connectivity, 1.5, **1.22**–1.23
  practical uses of, 8.2–8.3
  tools of, 8.3–8.4
  See also Communications ser-
    vices
Connectivity diagrams, **9.16**, 9.19
Conscious Mind, The (Chalmers),
  13.25
Consumer information, 12.26
Control structures, 10.5, **10.7**,
  10.9, 10.10
Control unit, **2.9**, 2.10
Controller cards, 2.25
Controllers, 3.16
Convergence, 1.28
Conversion
  date, 10.29
  system, 9.26, 9.27

Cook, David, E3.3
Cook, Gordon, 14.4
Cookies, 8.28, **14.5–14.6**
Copen, John L., 4.9
Coprocessing, 5.13
Coprocessors, **2.12**, 5.13
Copyrights, **6.34**–6.35, **14.9**
Core process redesign, 11.4
Corley, Eric, 14.27
Corporations. *See* Organizations
Courseware, **13.3**
Coy, Peter, 13.22
CPU (central processing unit), **1.9**, **2.9**–2.11
Crackers, **14.27**
Crawlers, 13.30
Creative thinking, 13.31
Credit records, 12.25, 14.42
Crime, computer, **14.19**–14.22
  perpetrators of, 14.25–14.28
  See also Security issues
Criminal records, 14.42
Cross-life cycle activities, 9.8
CRTs (cathode-ray tubes), **3.27**, 3.28
Cursor, **1.8**, **3.5**, **6.4**
Cursor-movement keys, 3.5–**3.6**
Custom software, 5.4
Cut, copy, and paste commands, 6.8
Cyber gloves, 3.20
Cybercash, 14.40
Cyberspace, 8.3
Cylinder method, 4.14

Daisy chain, 2.24
Data, **1.5**
  analyzing, 9.15–9.19
  cleansing or scrubbing, 12.21
  computer representation of, 2.3–2.9
  converting, 9.26
  gathering, 9.14–9.15
  security procedures, 14.30–14.31
  storage methods, 4.5–4.8
Data communications software, **6.18**–6.19
Data compression
  communications software and, 7.7
  techniques of, 5.9–5.10
  utility programs for, **5.8**–5.9
Data dictionary, **9.16**, **12.17**
Data files, 2.7, **4.3**–4.4, **12.8**
Data flow diagram (DFD), **9.16**, 9.17
Data integrity, 12.11

Data management, **5.6**
Data mining (DM), 12.20–12.23
Data processing, 1.17, 12.8–12.9
Data recovery utility, **5.7**
Data redundancy, 12.11
Data storage hierarchy, **12.6**–12.7
Data transmission, 7.20–7.27
  asynchronous, **7.23**, 7.24
  full-duplex, **7.23**
  half-duplex, **7.22**–7.23
  line configurations, 7.21
  multiplexing, **7.25**–7.26
  packet switching, **7.24**–7.25
  parallel, **7.22**
  protocols, **7.26**–7.27
  rate of, 7.20
  serial, **7.21**
  simplex, **7.22**
  synchronous, **7.24**
Data warehouse, 12.20, 12.21–12.22
Database administrators (DBAs), **12.5**–12.6
Database management systems (DBMS), 6.15, **12.12**–12.20
  access security, 12.19
  advantages and disadvantages of, 12.12–12.13
  data dictionaries, **12.17**
  for multimedia productions, 13.5–13.6
  object-oriented, **12.16**–12.17
  organizational arrangements, 12.13–12.17
  query languages, **12.18**
  report generators, **12.19**
  system recovery features, 12.19–12.20
  utilities, **12.17**–12.18
Database saves, 12.19
Database server, 7.32
Database software, **6.15**–6.17
Databases, **1.23**, 6.15, 12.2–12.28
  accuracy and completeness issues, 12.24
  data mining, 12.20–12.23
  data storage hierarchy, **12.6**–12.7
  defined, **12.7**
  distributed, **12.5**
  ethics of using, 12.23–12.26
  hierarchical, **12.13**–12.14
  key field, **12.7**
  managing, 12.5–12.6
  network, **12.14**
  privacy issues, 12.24–12.26, 14.5
  relational, **12.14**, 12.15, 12.16

shared, **12.5**
software for managing, 12.12–12.13
Date conversion, 10.29
Davies, Char, 13.27
DBMS. *See* Database management systems
Debugging, **10.11**
Decision support system (DSS), **11.13**–11.16
  components of, 11.14
  examples of, 11.14–11.16
Decision tables, **9.16**, 9.20
Default values, **6.5**
Defraggers, **5.11**
Defragmentation, 5.11
Deleting text, 6.8
Democracy, electronic, 14.40–14.41
Demodulation, 7.4
Dennis, Beverly, 14.5
Denver International Airport (DIA), 9.6
Departments, organizational, 11.5–11.7
Designing systems. *See* Systems design
Desk-checking, **10.11**
Desktop, 5.17
Desktop publishing (DTP), 3.13
  software for, **6.25**–6.28
Desktop-accessory programs, **6.20**
Diagnostic program, **5.7**
Diagnostic routines, 5.5–5.6
Diagnostics, 10.11
Dialog box, **6.5**
Dial-up Internet connections, 8.14–8.15
Diebold, John, 11.3
Digital audio tape (DAT), 4.9
Digital cameras, 3.17–**3.18**, 3.19
Digital cellular phones, 7.17
Digital convergence, **1.28**
Digital signals, **1.6**, 7.3–7.4
Digital signatures, 14.29
Digitizing, 2.6
Digitizing tablet, **3.9**–3.10
Direct access storage, **4.5**, 4.8, 12.9
Direct file organization, **12.10**
Direct implementation, **9.26**, 9.27
Directories, Internet, **8.25**–8.26
  adding your Web site to, E4.1
Dirty data, **14.19**
Disaster-recovery plans, **14.31**–14.32
Disk drives, **4.10**–4.11

Diskettes, **4.9**–4.13
  caring for, 4.13
  characteristics of, 4.11–4.12
Disks
  floppy (diskette), **4.9**–4.13
  hard, **4.13**–4.19
  optical, **4.19**–4.27
Display adapter cards, 2.25
Distance learning, 14.39
Distributed databases, **12.5**
Distributed object technology,
  10.25–10.26
Document files, **4.4**
Documentation, **6.6**
  for programs, 10.12
  in systems development, 9.26,
  9.27
Documentation manuals, **1.5**
Documents
  creating, 6.8
  editing, 6.8
  formatting, **6.8**–6.10
  printing, 6.10–6.11
Domain Name System (DNS),
  8.16–8.19
Donahoe, Tom, 10.30
DOS (Disk Operating System),
  5.15
Dot pitch, 2.29, **3.29**
Dot-matrix printers, 3.22
Double-clicking, 3.8
Downlinking, 7.14
Downloading files, 6.18, **7.29**, 8.12
Downsizing, 7.36, 11.3
Downward compatibility
  for chips, 2.21
  for software, 5.15, 6.34
Dpi (dots per inch), 2.29
Draft-quality output, 3.22
Dragging and dropping, 3.8
DRAM chips, 2.13
Drawing programs, **6.29**–6.30
Drive door, 4.10
Drivers, **3.26**, **5.7**
Drum plotters, 3.25
DSS. *See* Decision support system
DTP. *See* Desktop publishing
Dudin, Leonard and Olga, 14.4
Dumb terminals, 3.33
DVD-ROM disks, **4.25**–4.27
Dvorak, Jon, 13.31
Dynamic linking, 6.12

EBCDIC (Extended Binary Coded
  Decimal Interchange Code),
  2.4
E-cash, 14.40

Eck, John, 5.16
Economic issues, 14.37–14.38
Editing documents, 6.8
Education/reference software, 6.3
Educational technology, 7.11,
  14.39
  multimedia as, 13.3
Edutainment, 4.22
EEPROM chips, 2.22
EISA (Enhanced Industry Stan-
  dard Architecture), 2.26
Electroluminescent (EL) display,
  3.28
Electromagnetic spectrum,
  7.9–7.10, 7.12, 7.36
Electromechanical problems, 14.18
Electronic computers, 1.4
Electronic data interchange (EDI),
  8.32
Electronic democracy, 14.40–14.41
Electronic imaging, 3.15
Electronic money, 4.30
Electronic Numerical Integrator
  and Computer (ENIAC), 1.18
Electronic performance support
  systems (EPSS), 9.28, 13.3
Electronic ticketing machines, 3.2
Ellis, Peter, 9.29
Ellison, Larry, 1.27
E-mail (electronic mail), 1.22,
  8.6–8.7
  filtering agents, 13.29
  privacy issues, 14.4
  software for, **6.18**–6.19, 8.20
Embouchure, 3.33
Emery, Vince, E1.2
Emoticons, 8.29
Employee crimes, 14.25
Employment
  job-related databases, 8.36,
  12.28
  privacy issues, 12.26
Empowerment, 11.4
Encapsulation, 10.24
Encryption, **14.30**
Encyclopedias, CD-ROM,
  4.21–4.22
End of Work, The (Rifkin), 14.37
End-users, 1.3
Energy consumption issues, 14.33
Energy Star program, 14.33
Enhanced Integrated Drive Elec-
  tronics (EIDE), **4.16**
Enter key, **3.5**
Entertainment
  future of, 14.40
  multimedia, 13.3–13.4

  online, 8.12
  software, 6.3
Environmental issues, 14.33–14.34
EPROM chips, 2.22
Erasable optical disks (CDEs), **4.25**
Ergonomics, **3.6**
Erickson, Ron, 14.36
Error correction, 7.6
Errors
  people, 14.17
  procedural, 14.17–14.18
  software, 14.18
Ethernet, 7.35
Ethics, **14.3**
  artificial intelligence and, 13.25
  database use and, 12.23–12.26
Ethics in Modeling (Wallace),
  13.25
Etzioni, Amitai, 14.7–14.8
Evaluating systems, 9.28
Even parity, 2.5
Executable files, **4.3**
Execution cycle (E-cycle), **2.14**
Execution programs, 2.7–2.8
Executive information system
  (EIS), **11.16**
Executive support system (ESS),
  11.16
Expansion buses, 2.25–2.26
Expansion cards (boards), 2.20,
  2.25
Expansion slots, 2.20, **2.25**
Expert systems, 2.6, **11.17**–11.18,
  13.14, **13.18**–13.21
  building, 13.20
  business use of, 13.20–13.21
  examples of, 13.19–13.20
  major components of,
  13.18–13.19
Extended-density (ED) diskettes,
  4.12
External hard disk drives, 4.17
External modems, 7.5
Extranets, **8.33**
E-zines, 1.25

Fact-finding, 9.8
Facts, manipulating, 14.13–14.14
Fair Credit Reporting Act (1970),
  12.25
FAQs (Frequently Asked Questions), **8.20**, 8.29
Fault-tolerant systems, 5.13
Fax (facsimile transmission)
  machines, **3.13**
  messages, **8.4**–8.5
  servers, 7.32

FDDI (Fiber Distributed Data Interface) network, **7.35**–7.36
Feasibility study, 9.11–9.13
FED (field emission display), 3.30
Federal Communications Commission (FCC), 7.12, 7.36, 8.17
Feola, Christopher, 12.24
Fiber-optic cable, 7.13, **7.14**
Fields, **6.17**, **12.6**
Fifth-generation programming languages, 10.17–10.18
File allocation tables (FATs), 4.4
File management systems, **12.10**–12.11
File manager, 6.16, 12.10
File server, **7.32**
File viruses, 14.24
Files, **6.17**, **12.6**
  converting, 9.26
  managing, 4.5, 12.8–12.11
  organizing, 12.9–12.10
  storage methods, 4.5–4.8
  transferring, 6.18
  types of, 4.3–4.4, 12.8
Filtering data, **13.29**
Finances
  online management of, 8.12
  privacy issues, 12.25, 14.4
Firewalls, **8.33**, **14.30**–14.31
Firmware, 2.22
First-generation programming language, 10.15
Fixed disk drives, 4.18
Flaming, 14.2
Flash memory (RAM) cards, **2.23**, 4.28–**4.29**
Flatbed plotters, 3.25
Flatbed scanners, 3.14
Flat-file management systems, 6.16
Flat-panel displays, **3.27**–3.28
Flipbook, 13.7
Floating-point operations per second, **2.16**
Floppy disks. See Diskettes
Flops, **2.16**
Flowchart authoring format, 13.8
Flowcharts
  program, **10.6**–10.7, 10.8
  systems, **9.16**, 9.18
FM synthesis, 3.32
Focus group, 9.11
Fonts, 4.4, **6.9**, 6.10
Foreground tasks, 5.12
Forester, Tim, 14.3
Formatting
  disks, **4.12**
  documents, **6.8**–6.10

Formulas, **6.12**
FORTH programming language, 10.22
Forward recovery, 12.20
Fourth-generation programming languages (4GLs), 10.17
Fowler, Donald, 10.29
Fractions of a second, 2.29
Fragmentation, 5.11
Frame-grabber video card, 3.17
Frankenberg, Robert, 5.24
Frazier, Tom, 7.2
Freedman, Alan, 10.24
Freedom of Information Act (1970), 12.25, 14.7
Free-speech issues, 14.14–14.16
Freeware, **6.36**–6.37
Frequency, **7.3**, 7.9, 7.20
Friday, Elbert, 1.16
Front-end processors, **7.26**
FTP (File Transfer Protocol), **8.20**
Full backup, 4.28
Full-duplex transmission, **7.23**
Full-motion video card, 3.17
Function keys, 1.8, **3.6**
Functions (spreadsheet), 6.12
Furbee, Louanna, 11.17
Fusing system, 3.23
Fuzzy logic, **13.17**–13.18

Gallium arsenide, 2.27
Gambling, 14.34–14.35
Game ports, 2.24
Games
  CD-ROM, 4.22, 4.23
  multimedia, 13.3–13.4
  online, 8.12
Gantt chart, 6.26, 9.22
Gates, Bill, 2.3, 7.18, 12.2
Gateways, **7.34**
Gaunt, Wheeling, 12.27
Genetic algorithms, **13.23**
Geographic information system (GIS), 1.16, 11.15–11.16
Geostationary orbits, 7.14
Gesture recognition, 3.10
Gibson, William, 8.3
Gigabyte (GB), **2.9**, 4.3
Gillmor, Dan, 2.2, 14.34
Gilmore, John, 14.16
Gingrich, Newt, 7.18
GIS. See Geographic information system
Glasser, Jeff, 13.28
Global Positioning System (GPS), 2.17, **7.14**–7.15
Goldman, Janlori, 14.5

Gopher, **8.21**
Gosling, James, 5.27
Government and electronic democracy, 14.40–14.41
GPS. See Global Positioning System
Grammar checker, 6.8
Graphical user interface (GUI), **5.14**
Graphics
  analytical, **6.12**–6.13
  multimedia, 13.6
  presentation, **6.15**
Graphics adapter cards, 2.25
Graphics coprocessor chip, 2.12
Graphics scanner, 3.20
Gray-scale, 3.29
Greenspan, Alan, 2.17
Grid charts, **9.16**, 9.19
Group decision support systems, 11.16
Groupware, **6.19**, 8.32
Guilford, Chuck, 7.11
Gunther, Judith Anne, 13.24–13.25

Haas, Carl, 6.23
Hackers, **14.26**–14.27
Half-duplex transmission, **7.22**–7.23
Half-height drives, 4.17
Hamilton, Katie and Gene, 8.11
Hammond, Lou Ann, 9.29
Handheld scanners, 3.14
Handshaking, 7.26
Handwriting recognition, 3.10
Hard disk cartridges, **4.17**
Hard disks, **4.13**–4.19
  external, 4.17
  future technology for, 4.19
  internal, 4.14–4.16
  for large computer systems, 4.18–4.19
  power and portability of, 4.17
  removable, 4.17
  virtual memory and, **4.18**
Hardcopy output, 1.11, 3.21
Hardware, **1.4**, 1.8–1.11
  acquiring for systems development, 9.24
  communications, **1.11**
  converting, 9.26
  input, **1.8**–1.9, **3.3**, 3.4–3.21
  output, **1.11**, 3.21–3.33
  processing, **1.9**–1.10, 2.9–2.14
  storage, **1.11**
  theft of, 14.19–14.20

Hart, Peter, 8.35
Hashing algorithm, 12.10
Hawn, Matthew, 14.7
Hazards, computer, 14.19
HDTV (high-definition television), 3.30
Head crash, 4.16
Head-mounted display (HMD), 13.27
Headphones, 3.33
Health issues, 14.39–14.40
Help menu, **6.5**
Hertz (Hz), **7.9**
Hesselbein, Frances, 11.19
Hibbitts, Paul D., 13.13
Hierarchical databases, **12.13**–12.14
Hierarchies, organizational, 11.18–11.19
Hierarchy chart, 10.5, 10.6
High-density (HD) diskettes, **4.12**
High-resolution display, 3.30
Hoff, Ted, 1.20
Home pages, **8.23**, 8.24–8.25
Home/personal software, 6.3
Home-based careers, 3.31
Host adapter, 4.16
Host computer, **7.28**
Hoteling, 8.34
HTML (Hypertext Markup Language), 5.27, 6.30, **8.22**, **10.26**–10.28
HTTP (Hypertext Transfer Protocol), 6.30, **8.22**
Human resources department, 11.6
Human-biology input devices, 3.20
Hybrid network, **7.35**
Hydra printers, 3.26
Hygrant, Carl, 8.5
HyperCard, 6.30, 6.31, 10.25
Hypertalk programming language, 10.25
Hypertext, **6.30**, 6.31, **8.22**

IBM calculating machine, 1.17
IBM-compatible computers (clones), 2.3, 2.20
Icons, 4.4, **5.14**, **6.5**
Identity
  authentication of, 14.28–14.30
  theft of, 14.4
IF-THEN-ELSE structure, 10.7
Image files, **4.4**
Imaging systems, **3.13**–3.15
Impact printers, 3.22
Implementing new systems, 9.25–9.28

Incremental backup, 4.28
Indexed-sequential access method (ISAM), 4.8
Indexed-sequential file organization, **12.10**
Inference engine, **13.18**–13.19
Information, **1.5**
  properties of, 11.10
  theft of, 14.21
Information appliances, 1.24, 1.26–1.27
Information brokering, 12.27
Information explosion, 1.20
Information overload, 14.37
Information technology crime, **14.19**–14.22
Information technology trends, 1.21–1.28
  connectivity, 1.21–1.23
  digital convergence, **1.28**
  interactivity, **1.24**, 1.26–1.28
  online information access, 1.23–1.24
  social issues and, 14.32–14.41
Information utilities, 12.4
Infrared ports, 2.25
Inheritance, 10.24
Initializing disks, **4.12**
Inkjet printers, **3.24**
Input controls, **3.21**
Input hardware, **1.8**–1.9, **3.3**, 3.4–3.21
  audio input devices, **3.16**
  controls, **3.21**
  digital cameras, 3.17–**3.18**
  human-biology input devices, 3.20
  keyboard, **1.8**, **3.4**–3.6
  mouse, **1.8**
  multimedia, 3.20
  pointing devices, **3.4**, 3.7–3.10
  scanning devices, **3.11**–3.15
  sensors, **3.18**, 3.20
  source-data entry devices, **3.4**, 3.11–3.20
  video cards, 3.17
  voice-recognition systems, **3.15**–3.16
Input/output (I/O) devices, 3.2–3.3
  optical cards, 3.36
  retinal display systems, 3.36–3.37
  smart cards, **3.35**–3.36
  terminals, **3.33**–3.35
  touch screens, **3.36**
  See also Input hardware; Output hardware
Inserting text, 6.8

Insertion point, 1.8, 3.5, 6.4
Installing
  applications software, 6.33
  printers and plotters, 3.26
Instruction cycle (I-cycle), **2.14**
Integrated circuits, **1.19**
Integrated software packages, **6.21**
Intel chips, 2.20–2.21
Intellectual property, **6.34**–6.38, **14.9**–14.11, 14.43
Intelligent agents, 12.23, **13.29**–13.30
Intelligent terminals, 3.34
Interactive presentations, 13.8
Interactivity, **1.24**, 1.26–1.28, 4.22–4.23
Interfaces, 5.2
  system software, 5.13–5.14
Internal hard disk drives, 4.14–4.16
Internal memory, 2.12
Internal modems, 7.5
Internal Revenue Service (IRS), 9.6
International Data Corporation (IDC), E1.1
Internet, **1.24**, **8.13**–8.21
  address system on, 8.16–8.19
  connecting to, 8.14–8.16
  downside issues related to, 8.30–8.31
  features of, 8.19–8.21
  forthcoming improvements to, 8.17
  origins of, 8.13–8.14
  privacy issues, 14.5–14.7
  See also World Wide Web
Internet II, 8.17
Internet Explorer (Microsoft), 5.28
Internet PC, 5.26
Internet service providers (ISPs), **8.14**–8.15
  tips for choosing, 8.16
  See also Online information services
Interpreters, **10.16**
Interviews, systems analysis, 9.14–9.15
Intranets, **8.33**
Investment software packages, 6.14
IS technicians, 9.9
ISA (Industry Standard Architecture), 2.26
ISDN (Integrated Services Digital Network) lines, **7.7**
Isolation, 12.19, 14.34
ISPs. *See* Internet service providers

Iteration control structure, 10.9, **10.10**
Iverson, Kenneth, 10.22

Jacquard loom, 1.17
Java programming language, 5.27–5.28, **10.28**
Jewell, Jan, 3.31
Job hunting, 8.36, 12.28
Joint applications development (JAD), 9.4
Joystick, **3.8**
JPEG compression, 5.9
Junk mail, 14.6, 14.42–14.43

Kaplan, Jerry, 1.12
Kasparov, Gary, 13.25
Kay, Alan, 10.25
Kemeny, John, 10.21
Kettering, Charles, 1.28
Key field, **12.7**, 14.5
Keyboards, **1.8**, **3.4**–3.6
Kilobits per second (Kbps), **7.6**
Kilobyte (KB), **2.8**–2.9, 4.3
King, Rodney, 14.13, 14.19
Kiosk, **13.3**
Kirkpatrick, David, 5.22
Knowledge base, **13.18**
Knowledge discovery, 12.20–12.23
Knowledge engineers, 11.17, **13.20**
Knowledge management, 11.20
Knowledge system, 11.17–11.18
Kobrin, Rob, 1.12
Kolata, Gina, 13.31
Koons, Jeff, 6.36, 14.11
Krugman, Paul, 14.38
Kurtz, Thomas, 10.21

Lamm, Richard, 12.23
Landmarks, virtual, 13.28
Lanford, Jim and Audri, 8.28
Language translators, 2.8, **5.11**, **10.15**
LANs. *See* Local area networks
Laparoscope, 2.6
Large-scale integrated (LSI) circuits, 1.19
Larson, Erik, 12.26
Laser printers, **3.22**–3.24
Latency, **4.16**
Law enforcement technology, 5.16–5.17
Lawton, Cheryl, 5.17
Leibniz Wheel, 1.17
Levy, Steven, 8.12
Lewin, Darin, 9.29
Lewis, Peter, 8.6, 14.16
Light pen, **3.9**

Line discipline, 7.26
Line graphs, 6.12
Line printers, 3.22
Linear slide-based presentations, 13.8
Line-of-sight systems, 3.20, 7.13, 7.14
Liquid-crystal display (LCD), **3.28**
LISP programming language, 10.21–10.22
List brokers, 14.6
Listservs, 8.20
LMDS (local multipoint distribution service), 8.17
Local area networks (LANs), **1.14**, 5.19, **7.30**–7.36
  components of, 7.32–7.34
  impact of, 7.36
  topology of, 7.34–7.36
  types of, 7.31–7.32
Local buses, 2.25, 2.26–2.27
Local networks, **7.28**, 7.30–7.36
Loebner, Hugh, 13.24
Logic bombs, 14.24
Logic errors, **10.11**
Logic structures. *See* Control structures
Logical operations, 2.10
Logo programming language, 10.22
Loop control structure, **10.10**
Lossless compression utilities, 5.10
Lossy compression utilities, 5.9
Lower-level management
  computer-based information systems for, 11.12
  responsibilities of, 11.8–11.9

Mac OS, **5.22**
Machine cycle, **2.14**
Machine language, 2.7, **10.15**
Macintosh computers, 2.3, 2.21
  operating system for, **5.22**–5.23
Macro viruses, 14.23, 14.24
Macromedia Authorware, 13.11
Macromedia Director, **13.9**–13.10
Macros, **6.5**
Maez, Robert, 5.16
Magazines, CD-ROM, 4.22
Magid, Lawrence, 14.15
Magnetic tape, **4.8**–4.9
Magnetic-ink character recognition (MICR), **3.12**
Magneto-optical disk, 4.25
Magnetoresistive read head (MRH) technology, 4.19
Mail servers, 7.32

Mailing lists
  e-mail, 8.20
  junk mail, 14.6
Main memory (RAM), 1.10, 2.9, **2.12**–2.13, 2.15, 2.21
Mainframe computers, **1.14**
  processing speed, 2.16
Maintenance
  program, 10.12
  system, 9.28
Malone, Michael, 2.2
Malveaux, Julianne, 4.30
Management
  database, 12.5–12.6
  file, 4.5, 12.8–12.10
Management information system (MIS), **11.12**–11.13
Managers
  computer-based information systems for, 11.10–11.18
  levels and responsibilities of, 11.7–11.9
  participation in systems development by, 9.9
  tasks of, 11.7
  types of information for, 11.9–11.10
Manes, Stephen, 3.19
Maremont, Mark, 5.16
Marketing
  data mining and, 12.20–12.21
  information technology for, 9.29
  online, 8.27–8.28, 9.29, E4.1–E4.3
Marketing department, 11.6
Mark-recognition devices, 3.12
Martin, John and Alice, 7.18
Mass media, 8.3
Massively parallel processing (MPP) computers, 12.22
Master file, **12.8**
Matarie, Maja, 13.16
Math coprocessor chip, 2.12
Mathematical reasoning programs, 13.31
Maxwell, Glenn, 14.29
May, Tim, 14.7
MCA (Micro Channel Architecture), 2.26
McCarthy, John, 10.22
McCaw, Craig, 7.18
McConnell, Brian, 14.17
McLurkin, James, 13.16
McMahon, Jim, 14.20
McPherson, Lloyd and Disa, 2.17
Measurement terms for computers, 2.29

Media rights, 14.11
Medical records, 12.25–12.26, 14.3, 14.42
Medical technology, 2.6–2.7, 14.39
Meeting software, 6.19
Megabyte (MB), **2.9**, 4.3
Megahertz (MHz), **2.16**
Memory, **1.10**, **2.12**–2.13
  cache, **2.22**–2.23
  expansion cards, 2.25
  flash, **2.23**, 4.28-**4.29**
  random access (main), 1.10, 2.9, 2.12–2.13, 2.15, 2.21
  read-only, **2.22**
  video, **2.23**
  virtual, **4.18**
Memory-management utilities, 5.10–5.11
Mental-health problems, 14.34–14.36
Menu bar, **6.5**
Menu-driven interface, 5.13–5.14
Messaging protocols, **5.6**
Metropolitan area networks (MANs), **7.28**
Microchips. *See* Chips
Microcomputers, **1.14**
  components of, 2.18–2.27
  development of, 2.2–2.3
  processing speed, 2.16
Microcontrollers, **1.14**
Microphone, 3.20
Microprocessor: A Biography, The (Malone), 2.2
Microprocessors, 1.9, 2.2–2.3, **2.9**, 2.20–2.21, 13.2
Microsoft Network, 8.10
Microwave systems, **7.13**–7.14
Middle management
  computer-based information systems for, 11.12–11.13
  responsibilities of, 11.8
MIDI (Musical Instrument Digital Interface), 3.16, 13.7
Midsize computers, 2.16
Milestones, 6.26
Millennium Bug, 10.29
Millimeter waves, 7.36
Miniaturization, 1.20
  of hard disk drives, 4.17
MIPS (millions of instructions per second), **2.16**, 2.29
Mirroring, 12.19
MIS (management information system), **11.12**–11.13
Mobile office, 11.2

Mobile telephone switching office (MTSO), 7.16
Modems, 1.7, **7.4**–7.6
  cable, 7.7–**7.8**
  external vs. internal, 7.5
  transmission speed, 7.6
Modularization, 10.5
Modulation, 7.4
Money, electronic, 4.30
Monitors, 1.11, 3.26–3.30
  bit-mapped display, 3.30
  cathode-ray tube (CRT), **3.27**, 3.28
  color standards for, 3.29–3.30
  flat-panel display, **3.27**–3.28
  future display technology for, 3.30
  screen clarity of, 3.28–3.29
Monochrome display screens, 3.29
Moore, Charles, 10.22
Morphing, **14.12**–14.13
Morrison, Perry, 14.3
Morse, Samuel, 7.3
Morse code, 7.3–7.4
Mossberg, Walter, 7.18, 14.13
Motherboard, 1.9, **2.20**
Motorola chips, 2.21
Mouse, **1.8**, **3.7**–3.8
Mouse pointer, **3.7**
MPC standards, 4.23, **13.4**
MPEG compression, 5.9
MPP (massively parallel processing), 2.12
Multidimensional analysis (MDA) tools, 12.23
Multifunction devices, **3.26**, 3.27
Multimedia, **1.24**, 13.2–13.13
  authoring process, 13.8–13.9
  authoring software, **6.30**–6.33, 13.9–13.12
  business uses for, 13.2–13.3
  career opportunities in, 13.12–13.13
  CBT authoring software, 13.11–13.12
  CD-ROMs and, 4.22–4.23
  creating, 13.4–13.7
  educational uses for, 13.3
  entertainment and games, 13.3–13.4
  input devices, 3.20
  operating system support for, 5.24
  output devices, 3.33
  presentation software, 13.9
  system requirements for, 13.4
  utility programs, 5.10

Multipartite viruses, 14.24
Multiple-user license, **6.37**
Multiplexers, **7.25**–7.26
Multiplexing, **7.25**–7.26
Multipoint line, 7.21
Multiprocessing, **5.12**–5.13
Multiprogramming, **5.12**
Multitasking, **5.11**–5.12

Nadis, Steve, 13.16
Nanotechnology, 2.28
Nass, Clifford, 14.13
National Information Infrastructure (NII), 14.38
National Weather Service, 1.16
Natural hazards, 14.19
Natural language processing, **13.16**–13.17
Natural languages, **10.17**–10.18, 12.18, **13.16**
NC Reference Profile, 5.26
Near-letter-quality (NLQ) output, 3.22
Near-typeset-quality (NTQ) output, 3.22
Nelson, Bob, 8.27–8.28
Nelson, Ted, 6.30
Net addiction, 14.35
Netiquette, 8.29, **14.14**–14.15
Netscape Navigator, 5.27
NetWare, 5.23–5.24
Network adapter, 7.26
Network computers (NCs), 1.26–1.27, 5.26–5.27
Network databases, **12.14**, 12.15
Network interface card, **7.32**
Network operating system (NOS), **5.6**, **5.23**, 7.28
Network piracy, **6.35**, **14.10**
Network service providers (NSPs), 8.14–8.15
Network Solutions, Inc., 8.18–8.19
Networks, 1.11, 7.27, **7.28**–7.29
  advantages of, 7.29
  features of, 7.28–7.29
  local, **7.28**, 7.30–7.36
  local area (LANs), **1.14**, 5.19, **7.30**–7.36
  metropolitan area (MANs), **7.28**
  topology of, 7.34–7.36
  wide area (WANs), **7.28**
Neural networks, **13.21**–13.23
Neuromancer (Gibson), 8.3
Neurons, 13.21–13.22
Newbies, 8.29
Newman, Paul, 6.23

News
    manipulation of, 14.13–14.14
    online, 8.11
Newsgroups, **8.20**
Nielsen, Jakob, 6.2
Node, **7.29**
Nolan, Greg, 2.17
Nonimpact printers, 3.22–3.25
Nonprocedural languages, 10.17
Nonvolatile memory, 2.23, 4.29
Nordin, Sarah, 5.17
Novell, 5.23–5.24
NuBus architecture, 2.26
Num Lock key, 3.6
Numeric keypad, **3.6**

Object, **10.23**, **12.16**
Object code, 10.16
Object linking and embedding
    (OLE), **5.20**, **6.5**–6.6
Object-oriented analysis (OOA),
    9.16
Object-oriented database manage-
    ment system (OODBMS),
    12.16–12.17
Object-oriented programming
    (OOP), **10.23**–10.26
Obscenity, 14.15
O'Connor, Mike, E1.2
Odd parity, 2.5
Office automation systems (OASs),
    11.18
Offline storage, **12.9**
Off-the-shelf software, 5.4
OLE (object linking and embed-
    ding), **5.20**, **6.5**–6.6
O'Neill, Kevin, 14.35
One-to-many relationship,
    12.14
One-way communications,
    7.14–7.16
Online businesses. *See* Web busi-
    nesses
Online information services,
    1.23–1.24, **8.9**–8.13
    accessing, 8.10–8.11
    as information utilities, 12.4
    the Internet and, 8.12–8.13,
        8.14
    offerings of, 8.11–8.12
    privacy issues, 14.7
Online processing, **12.9**
Online storage, **12.9**
Open architecture, 2.25
Operating system (OS), **5.5**–5.6,
    5.14–5.24
Operator documentation, 10.2

Optical cards, 3.36
Optical character recognition
    (OCR), **3.12**–3.13, 13.6
Optical disks, **4.19**–4.27
    CD-R, **4.23**–4.24
    CD-ROM, **4.20**–4.24
    DVD-ROM, **4.25**–4.27
    erasable or rewritable, **4.25**
Optical mark recognition (OMR),
    3.12
Opto-electronic processing, 2.28
Organizational chart, 11.8
Organizations, 11.5–11.10
    departments in, 11.5–11.7
    hierarchical structure in,
        11.18–11.19
    management levels in, 11.7–11.9
    tasks of management in, 11.7
    types of information in,
        11.9–11.10
Ort, Harold, 7.18
OS/2 (Operating System/2),
    5.20–5.21
OSI (Open Systems Interconnec-
    tion), **7.26**
Output hardware, **1.11**, **3.3**,
    3.21–3.33
    audio, 3.30, 3.32–3.33
    drivers, **3.26**
    monitors, 3.26–3.30
    multifunction devices, **3.26**, 3.27
    multimedia, 3.33
    plotters, **3.25**
    printers, **3.21**–3.25
Outsourcing, 11.3

Packaged software, 5.4
Packet switching, **7.24**–7.25
Packet-radio transmission,
    7.16–7.17
Packets, **7.24**
Page description language (PDL),
    3.24
Pagers, 7.15–7.16
Painting programs, **6.29**–6.30
Papert, Seymour, 10.22
Paradigm Online Writing Assis-
    tant, 7.11
Parallel data transmission, **7.22**
Parallel implementation, **9.26**, 9.27
Parallel ports, **2.23**
Parallel processing, 2.12, 5.13
Parent records, 12.13–12.14
Parity bit, **2.5**
Parker, Donn, 14.25
Pascaline calculator, 1.17
Passive-matrix display, 3.28

Passwords, 8.6, 14.29
Patches, 8.12
Patents, 6.34, 14.9
Pausch, Randy, 2.2
PBXs (private branch exchanges),
    7.28, **7.30**
PC cards, 2.27
PC/TVs, 1.28
PCI (Peripheral Component Inter-
    connect), 2.26
PCMCIA (Personal Computer
    Memory Card International
    Association), **2.27**
Peer-to-peer LANs, **7.32**
Pen-based computer systems, **3.10**
Pentium chips, 2.21
People, **1.5**
    errors caused by, 14.17
    security controls and, 14.31
Perception systems, **13.14**–13.16
Peripheral devices, **1.8**
Personal communications services
    (PCS), 7.17–7.18
Personal computers (PCs), 1.14
Personal digital assistants (PDAs),
    1.28
Personal finance software,
    6.13–6.14
Personal information manager
    (PIM), **6.20**
PERT chart, 6.26, 9.22
PGP (Pretty Good Privacy), 14.30
Phased implementation, **9.26**, 9.27
Philanthropy, 12.27
Phonemes, 3.32
Photo CDs, 4.23–4.24
Photography
    digital, 3.17–3.18, 3.19
    technological manipulation of,
        14.12
Photolithography, 2.11
Picture phones, **8.9**
Pie charts, 6.12
Pilot implementation, **9.26**, 9.27
PIN (personal identification num-
    ber), 14.29
Pipeline-burst cache, 2.23
Piracy, 6.35, 14.9–14.10, 14.21,
    14.43
Pixelation, 4.27
Pixels, **3.27**
Plagiarism, **6.35**–6.36, **14.10**–14.11
Platforms, 2.7, **5.15**, 5.24–5.25
Plotters, **3.25**
    installing, 3.26
Plug-and-play products, 5.18–5.19
Plug-ins, 8.23

"Plunge" implementation, **9.26**
Point-and-shoot, 3.8
Pointing devices, **3.4**, 3.7–3.10
Point-of-sale (POS) terminals, **3.34**, 3.35
Point-to-point line, 7.21
Point-to-point protocol (PPP), 8.16
Pollution problems, 14.34
Polymedia, 3.33
Polymorphism, 10.24–10.25
Pop-up menus, **6.5**
Pornography, 14.15–14.16
Port, Otis, 13.17
Portable computers, 1.15
Portable Document Format (PDF), 6.25
Portable operating system, 5.21
Portable terminals, 3.34
Ports, **2.23**–2.25
Postman, Neil, 14.37
Power supply, **2.20**
Power-on self test (POST), 2.22
Practology, 5.2
Precision farming, 2.17
Preliminary investigation, **9.11**–9.13
Presentation software
    graphics, **6.15**
    multimedia, 13.9
Primary storage, 1.10, 2.12
Prince, Michael, 3.31
Print server, 7.32
Printers, **3.21**–3.25
    impact, 3.22
    installing, 3.26
    nonimpact, 3.22–3.25
Printing documents, 6.10–6.11
Privacy, **14.3**–14.8
    the case for limiting, 14.7–14.8
    databases and, 12.24–12.26, 14.5
    electronic networks and, 14.5–14.7
    junk-mail issues and, 14.42–14.43
    obtaining your own information files, 14.42
    rules and laws on, 14.7
    tips for protecting, 14.8
Privacy Act (1974), 12.25, 14.7
Private branch exchanges (PBXs), 7.28, **7.30**
Procedural errors, 14.17–14.18
Procedural languages, 10.16
Procedures, **1.5**
Process innovation, 11.4
Process model, 9.16
Processing hardware, **1.9**–1.10, 2.9–2.14

central processing unit (CPU), **1.9**, **2.9**
    coprocessors, **2.12**
    main processor, 2.9–2.12
    memory, **1.10**, **2.12**–2.13
    microprocessor, 1.9, 2.2–2.3, **2.9**
    registers, 2.13–2.14
Processing speeds, 2.16, 2.18
Processor, **2.9**
Processor bus, 2.25
Prodigy, 8.10
Production department, 11.5–11.6
Productivity software, 6.3, 6.7–6.22
    communications, **6.18**–6.19
    database, **6.15**–6.17
    desktop accessories, **6.20**
    groupware, **6.19**
    integrated software packages, **6.21**
    personal finance, **6.13**–6.14
    personal information manager (PIM), **6.20**
    presentation graphics, **6.15**
    software suites, **6.21**
    spreadsheet, **6.11**–6.13
    Web browsers, **6.22**
    word processing, 6.7, **6.8**–6.11
Program files, **12.8**
Program flowcharts, **10.6**–10.7, 10.8
Program independence, 12.11
Programmers, 1.2
    preparing documentation for, 10.12
    year 2000 problem for, 10.29
Programming, **10.3**
    future of, 10.29
    object-oriented, **10.23**–10.26
    steps in, 10.3–10.13
    structured, **10.5**–10.10
    visual, **10.26**
Programming languages, 1.12, **10.11**, 10.13–10.22
    assembly language, 10.15
    generations of, 10.13–10.18
    high-level, 10.16, 10.18–10.22
    machine language, **10.15**
    natural, **10.17**–10.18
    query languages, 10.17
    traditional, 10.18–10.22
    very-high-level, **10.17**
    for Web pages, 10.26–10.28
    See also names of specific languages
Programs, 1.12
    execution, 2.7–2.8
    maintaining, 10.12

utility, **5.7**–5.11
    See also Applications software
Project management software, **6.26**–6.27, 9.22
Projects, 6.26
PROLOG programming language, 10.22
PROM chips, 2.22
Proprietary software, **6.37**–6.38
Protocols, **7.26**–7.27
Prototypes, **9.22**
Prototyping, **9.22**
Prusak, Larry, 11.20
Pseudocode, **10.6**, 10.7
Public domain software, **6.36**
Public Electronic Network (PEN), 14.41
Public-private key system, 14.29
Pull-down menus, **6.5**
Punched cards, 1.17, 1.20
Push technology, 8.28–8.29

Quarter-Inch Cartridge (QIC) standard, 4.9
Queries, database, 6.17, 12.18
Query by example (QBE), 12.18
Query languages, 10.17, **12.18**
Query-and-reporting tools, 12.23
Quest Net+, 13.10
Questionnaires, systems analysis, 9.15
Quicken, 6.14
QWERTY keyboard layout, 3.4

Radio scanners, 7.18
RAID storage systems, **4.18**–4.19, 12.21–12.22
RAM (random access memory), 1.10, 2.12–2.13
    capacity, 2.15
RAM chips, 2.13, 2.21, 2.25
Randi, James, 10.2
Random file organization, 12.10
Rapid application development (RAD) tools, 10.17
Raster graphics, 6.38, 13.6
Reading data, **4.10**
    on optical disks, 4.20
Real estate technology, 11.21
Real-time processing, 12.9
Recalculation feature, 6.11, 6.12
Records, **6.17**, **12.6**
Reengineering, 11.4–11.5
Reeves, Byron, 14.13
Refresh rate, **3.29**
Registers, 2.9, 2.10, 2.13–2.14
Relational databases, **12.14**, 12.15, 12.16

Releases, software, 5.15, 6.33
Remote-control software, 7.7
Removable hard disks, 4.17
Removable packs, 4.18
Repetitive stress injury (RSI),
    14.39–14.40
Report generators, 10.17, **12.19**
Reports
    database, 6.17
    systems analysis, 9.19
Reprocessing, 12.19–12.20
Research, online, 8.11
Research and development (R&D)
    department, 11.5
Resistors, 13.22
Resolution, **3.28**–3.29
Retinal display systems,
    3.36–3.37
Rewritable optical disks (CD-RW),
    4.25
RGB monitors, 3.29
Richter, Anthony J., 13.22
Rifkin, Jeremy, 14.37
Right to Financial Privacy Act
    (1978), 12.25, 14.7
Ring network, **7.34**–7.35
RISC processors, 2.12
Robbins, Alan, 5.2
Roberts, Steve, 6.23
Robinson, Phillip, 14.23
Robotics, **13.14**, 13.15
Robots, **13.14**, 13.15, 13.30
Rollback, 12.20
Rollforward, 12.20
ROM (read-only memory), **2.22**
ROM BIOS (basic input/output
    system), **2.22**
ROM bootstrap, 2.22
ROM chips, 2.22
Root record, 12.13–12.14
Rothfeder, Jeffrey, 12.25
Routers, **7.34**
Row headings, 6.11–6.12
Rowan, Doug, 12.2
RS-232 port, 2.23
Ruestman, Arlen, 2.17
Ryder, Nick, 6.13–6.14

Saffo, Paul, 4.30, 12.2, 14.37
Safire, William, 14.12
Sales technology, 9.29
Sampling, 3.16, 13.6–13.7
Satava, Rick, 2.6
Satellite dishes, 7.8–7.9
Satellite-based communications
    systems, **7.14**, 7.18–7.19
Scanning devices, **1.8**–1.9,
    3.11–3.15

bar-code readers, **3.11**–3.12
character-recognition devices,
    3.12–3.13
fax machines, **3.13**
imaging systems, **3.13**–3.15
mark-recognition devices, 3.12
Scanning tunneling microscope
    (STM), 4.29
Scheduling software, 6.19, 6.20
Schoenbrun, Cynthia, 12.27
Screens. *See* Monitors
Scripts, 13.12
Scrolling, 6.4
SCSI (Small Computer System
    Interface)
    bus, 2.27
    hard disk architecture, **4.16**
    ports, **2.24**
Search and replace feature, 6.8
Search engines, **8.25**–8.26, 13.30
    adding your Web site to, E4.1
Searching the Web
    tips for, 8.26–8.27
    tools for, 8.25–8.26
Secondary storage, 1.10, **4.2**–4.3
    advanced technology for, 4.29
    capacity of devices for, 4.3
    data access methods, 4.5–4.8
    on diskettes, **4.9**–4.13
    file management for, 4.5
    file types and, 4.3–4.4
    on flash-memory cards, **2.23**,
      4.28–**4.29**
    on hard disks, **4.13**–4.19
    on magnetic tape, **4.8**–4.9
    on optical disks, **4.19**–4.27
    organizing files for, 12.9–12.10
Second-generation programming
    languages, 10.15
Sectors, **4.11**–4.12
Security issues, 14.16–14.32
    computer criminals,
      14.25–14.28
    database access, 12.19
    disaster-recovery plans,
      14.31–14.32
    encryption, **14.30**
    errors and accidents,
      14.17–14.19
    identification and access proce-
      dures, 14.28–14.30
    information technology crime,
      14.19–14.22
    natural hazards, 14.19
    security tips for PC users, 14.26
    societal hazards, 14.19
    software and data protection,
      14.30–14.31

for Web businesses, E3.3–E3.4,
    E4.3
worms and viruses, 14.23–14.25
Seek time, **4.15**–4.16
Selection control structure, **10.7**,
    10.9, 10.10
Self-employed people, 3.31
Sellers, Deborah, E3.3
Semiconductor, 2.10–2.11
Semistructured information, 11.10
Sensors, **3.18**, 3.20
Sequence control structure, **10.7**,
    10.9, 10.10
Sequential file organization,
    12.9–12.10
Sequential storage, **4.5**, 12.9
Serial data transmission, **7.21**
Serial ports, **2.23**–2.24
Serial processing, 2.12
Servers, **1.14**, **7.29**, 7.31–7.32
Service bureaus, 6.29
Set-top boxes, 1.24, 1.26
SGML (Standard Generalized
    Markup Language), 8.22,
    10.26
Shared databases, **12.5**
Shared resources, 8.31–8.33
Shareware, **6.37**
Shea, Virginia, 14.15
Sheetfed scanners, 3.14
Shells, 13.20
Shine, Jerry, 13.16
Shopping, online, 8.12, 14.40
    See also Web businesses
Shrink-wrap licenses, **6.37**
Shuler, Gregg, 11.21
"Siftware" tools, 12.23
Silicon, 2.10–2.11
SIMMs, 2.13, 2.25
Simplex transmission, **7.22**
Simpson, O. J., 14.12
Simulators, **13.27**
Sinatra, Frank, 14.11
Single-user license, **6.37**
Site license, **6.38**
Smalltalk programming language,
    10.25
Smart boxes, 1.24, 1.26
Smart cards, **3.35**–3.36, 4.30
Smith, Gina, 14.5
Social issues in information tech-
    nology, 14.32–14.41
    business and commerce, 14.40
    economic issues, 14.37–14.38
    education and information, 14.39
    entertainment, 14.41
    environmental problems,
      14.33–14.34

Social issues in information technology *(continued)*
government services, 14.40–14.41
health care, 14.39–14.40
mental-health problems, 14.34–14.36
workplace problems, 14.36–14.37
Social security information, 14.42
Softcopy output, 1.11
Software, **1.4**, 1.11–1.12
acquiring for systems development, 9.24
bugs in, 14.18
converting, 9.26
custom, 5.4
downloading, 8.12
intellectual property rights and, **6.34**–6.38, 14.9–14.11
off-the-shelf (packaged), 5.4
security procedures, 14.30–14.31
theft of, 14.21
types of, 1.12, 5.3–5.4
See also Applications software; System software
Software engineering. *See* Programming
Software license, **6.37**
Software package, 1.12
Software piracy, **6.35**, 14.9–**14.10**, 14.21, 14.43
Software Publishers Association (SPA), 6.7, 6.38, 14.21, 14.27
Software suites, **6.21**
Software Usability Design Associates (SUDA), 13.13
Sorting database records, 6.17
Sound
multimedia, 13.6–13.7
technological manipulation of, 14.11–14.12
Sound cards, 3.16, 3.20, 3.33
Sound output devices, **3.32**–3.33
Source code, 10.16
Source program files, **4.3**
Source-data entry devices, **3.4**, 3.11–3.20
audio input devices, **3.16**
digital cameras, 3.17–**3.18**
human-biology input devices, 3.20
scanning devices, **3.11**–3.15
sensors, **3.18**, 3.20
video cards, 3.17
voice-recognition systems, **3.15**–3.16

Spaghetti code, 10.7
Spamming, 8.29, **14.15**, E4.1
Speakers, 3.33
Specialized mobile radio (SMR), 7.18
Specialized processor chips, 2.12
Specialty software, 6.3–6.4
computer aided design/computer-aided manufacturing (CAD/CAM), **6.29**
computer-aided design (CAD), **6.27**–6.29
desktop publishing (DTP), **6.25**–6.28
drawing and painting programs, **6.29**–6.30
multimedia authoring, **6.30**–6.33
project management, **6.26**–6.27
Speech coding, 3.32
Speech synthesis, 3.32
Spelling checker, 6.8
Spiders, 8.25, 13.30
Spoer, Bob, 8.35
Sports technology, 10.30
Spreadsheet cursor, 6.12
Spreadsheet software, **6.11**–6.13
SRAM chips, 2.13
Star network, **7.34**
Stoll, Clifford, 8.31
Storage
direct access, **4.5**, 4.6–4.7, 4.8, 12.9
indexed-sequential, 4.6–4.7, 4.8
offline, **12.9**
online, **12.9**
primary, 1.10, 2.12
secondary, 1.10, **4.2**–4.3
sequential, **4.5**, 4.6–4.7, 12.9
volatile, 2.13
See also Main memory; Secondary storage
Storage hardware, **1.11**, 4.8–4.27
diskettes, **4.9**–4.13
flash-memory cards, 4.28–**4.29**
hard disks, **4.13**–4.19
magnetic tape, **4.8**–4.9
optical disks, **4.19**–4.27
Stress, 14.36
Streveler, Dennis, 2.7
Stroustrup, Bjarne, 10.25
Structured development life cycle. *See* Systems development life cycle
Structured information, 11.10
Structured programming, **10.5**–10.10

Structured Query Language (SQL), 12.18
Structured walkthrough, **10.10**
Style sheet, 6.25
Subprograms, 10.5
Sullivan, Virginia, 12.26
Supercomputers, **1.13**
processing speed, 2.16, 2.18
Superconductors, 2.27–2.28
Supervisor, 5.5
Supervisory management. *See* Lower-level management
Surge protectors, 2.20
SVGA (super video graphics array), **3.30**
Swapping, 5.11
Synapses, 13.22
Synchronous transmission, **7.24**
Syntax, **10.11**
Syntax errors, **10.11**
System, **9.2**
System board, 1.9, 2.10, 2.20
System clock, **2.16**
System diagnostics, 5.7
System recovery features, 12.19–12.20
System software, **1.12**, **5.3**–5.28
capabilities, 5.11–5.13
components, 5.4–5.14
interfaces, 5.13–5.14
online computing model and, 5.24–5.25
operating systems, **5.5**–5.6, 5.14–5.24
utility programs, **5.7**–5.11
See also Applications software
System testing, **9.24**–9.25
System unit, **1.9**, 1.10, **2.18**–2.19
Systems analysis, **9.13**–9.20
analyzing data, 9.15–9.19
gathering data, 9.14–9.15
report based on, 9.19
Systems analysts, 1.2–1.3, **9.9**, 9.10
Systems design, **9.20**–9.23
detailed, 9.22–9.23
preliminary, 9.20–9.22
report based on, 9.23
Systems development, **9.23**–9.25
acquiring software and hardware, 9.24
examples of problems with, 9.6
reasons for failure of, 9.4–9.5
testing the system, 9.24–9.25
user participation in, 9.3–9.5
Systems development life cycle (SDLC), **9.2**, 9.7–9.28
analyzing the system, 9.13–9.20

designing the system, 9.20–9.23
developing the system, 9.23–9.25
implementing the system, 9.25–9.28
maintaining the system, 9.28
participants in, 9.9–9.11
phases in, 9.7–9.9
preliminary investigation phase, 9.11–9.13
Systems flowcharts, **9.16**, 9.18
Systems implementation, **9.25**–9.28
compiling final documentation, 9.26, 9.27
converting to the new system, 9.26, 9.27
training users, 9.28
Systems integration, 9.4
Systems maintenance, **9.28**

Tabulating machine, 1.17
Tape storage, 4.8–4.9
Tape streamers, 4.9
Tax software programs, 6.14
Taylor, Lee, 1.21
TCP/IP (Transmission Control Protocol/Internet Protocol), **8.13**
Telecommunications, 1.21–1.23, **7.2**–7.3
See also Communications technology
Telecommunications Act (1996), 8.9, 14.16
Telecommuting, 1.22, **8.34**
Teleconferencing, 8.8
Telemedicine, 2.7, 14.39
Telephone services theft, 14.21
Telephone-related communications, 8.4–8.7
e-mail, **8.6**–8.7
fax messages, **8.4**–8.5
voice mail, **8.5**–8.6
Telephony, 8.23
Teleprocessing (TP) monitor, **5.6**
Teleshopping, 1.22
Telework, 8.34
Telnet, **8.21**
Terabyte (TB), **2.9**, 4.3
Terminal emulation mode, 6.18
Terminal emulation software, 7.7
Terminals, **3.33**–3.35
Terrorism, 14.19
Testing, system, 9.24–9.25
Text
multimedia, 13.6
word processing, 6.8

Theft, information technology, 14.19–14.21
Thermal printers, 3.24, 3.25
Thin clients, 5.26–5.27
Third-generation programming languages, 10.16, 10.18–10.22
code comparison for, 10.20
Time slicing, 5.12
Timeline authoring format, 13.8
Time-sharing, **5.12**
Toffler, Alvin, 8.33
Toner, 3.23
Toolbar, **6.5**
Top management
computer-based information systems for, 11.13–11.16
responsibilities of, 11.7–11.8
Top-down program design, **10.5**, 10.6
Topology, LAN, 7.34–7.36
Total quality management (TQM), 11.3–11.4
Touch screens, **3.36**
Touchpad, **3.8**–3.9
Tours, virtual, 13.28
Tower units, 1.14
TP monitor, **5.6**
Trackball, **3.8**
Tracks, **4.11**
Tracks per inch (TPI), 4.11
Trade secrets, 6.34, 14.9
Traditional programming languages, 10.18–10.22
Training users, 9.28
Transaction file, **12.8**
Transaction processing system (TPS), **11.12**
Transactions, **11.12**
Transmission. See Data transmission
Transportation technology, 6.23–6.24
Travel services, online, 8.12
Traven technology, 4.9
Travers, Kathleen, 2.15
Trojan horse, 14.24
TRON OS, 5.28
True color, 3.30
Tuples, 12.16
Turing, Alan, 13.24
Turing test, **13.24**–13.25
Turkle, Sherry, 14.36
Tutorials, **6.6**
Twain, Mark, 6.7
Twisted-pair wire, **7.12**
Two-way communications, 7.16–7.17

Typeface, 6.9
Typing keys, 3.4–3.5
Typos, 14.19

Unicode, **2.5**
Unit testing, **9.24**
UNIVAC I, 1.19
Universal Product Code, 3.11
Universal Serial Bus (USB), 2.27
Unix, **5.21**–5.22
Unstructured information, 11.10
Updating software, 6.33–6.34
Uplinking, 7.14
Uploading files, 6.18, **7.29**
UPS (uninterruptible power supply) units, 2.20
Upward compatibility, 6.33–6.34
URLs (Universal Resource Locators), **8.23**–8.24
Urpens, Ted, 9.29
Usenet newsgroups, **8.20**
User interface, 5.2, **5.13**, 13.19
Users, **1.3**
participation in systems development, 9.3–9.5, 9.9
preparing program documentation for, 10.12
training, 9.28
Utility programs, **5.7**–5.11
for database management systems, **12.17**–12.18

Values, 6.12
vBNS (very high speed backbone network service), 8.17
V-chip, 14.16
Vector graphics, 6.38, 13.6
Verdon, Lina, 12.27
Veronica utility, 8.21
Versions, software, 5.15, 6.33
Very-high-level languages, **10.17**
Very-large-scale integrated (VLSI) circuits, 1.19–1.20
VESA (Video Electronics Standard Association), 2.26
VGA (video graphics array), **3.29**–3.30
Video
multimedia, 13.7
technological manipulation of, 14.12–14.13
Video adapter ports, **2.24**
Video cards, 3.17, 3.20, 3.33
Video disks, 4.25, 4.27
Video files, **4.4**
Video memory, **2.23**, 3.27
Video on-demand service, 14.40

Video Privacy Protection Act (1988), 12.26
Videoconferencing, **8.8**–8.9
Virtual acoustics, 3.32–3.33
Virtual memory, **4.18**, 5.10–5.11
Virtual office, **8.34**–8.35, 11.2, 11.4
Virtual reality (VR), **13.26**–13.28
Viruses, **14.23**–14.25
  protection against, 5.7–5.8, 14.25
  types of, 14.24
  See also Security issues
Visual programming, **10.26**
V-mail (video mail), 8.9
Vo, Thao, 7.36
Voice mail, 1.22–1.23, **8.5**–8.6
Voice output devices, **3.32**
Voice-recognition systems, **3.15**–3.16, 13.29
Volatile memory, 1.10, 2.13
VRAM (video RAM), 2.23, 3.27
VRML (Virtual Reality Markup Language), **10.28**

Wafers, 2.11
WAIS (Wide Area Information Server), **8.21**
Wallace, William A., 13.25
Wand reader, 3.12
Warp (OS/2), 5.21
Wars, virtual, 13.28
Watson, Thomas J., 2.15
Wavelength, 7.9
Weather forecasting, 1.16
Web browsers, 1.24, 5.27, **6.22**, **8.23**
  site rating systems, 14.16
Web businesses, 8.27–8.28
  creating online catalogs, E3.1–E3.2
  future of, E5.1–E5.2
  gathering customer information, E4.3

  hardware recommendations, E2.3
  host location for, E2.1
  inventory tracking for, E3.4
  managing, E5.2
  marketing, 9.29, E4.1–E4.3
  naming, E1.2
  security considerations, E3.3–E3.4, E4.3
  site design for, E2.1–E2.2
  software recommendations, E3.4
  starting, E1.1–E1.3
  taking orders, E3.2–E3.3
  See also World Wide Web
Web pages, 1.24
Web publishing, 1.25
Web Review, The, 1.25
Web sites, **8.23**
Webster, Donovan, 14.20
Webzines, 1.25
Weinberg, Steve, 11.17
"What if" function, 6.12
Wide area networks (WANs), **7.28**
Williams, Penny, 12.24
Windows (desktop feature), **5.14**, 5.17, **6.4**
Windows operating environments/systems (Microsoft)
  Windows 3.x, **5.17**
  Windows 95, **5.17**–5.19
  Windows CE, 5.19
  Windows NT, **5.19**–5.20
WinZip program, 6.37
Wired communications, 7.12–7.13
Wireless communications, 7.13–7.19, 7.36
Wizards, **6.5**
Word processing software, 6.7, **6.8**–6.11
Word size, **2.15**–2.16, 2.29
Word wrap, 6.8
Workflow software, 6.19

Workgroup computing, **5.19**, **8.32**, 11.16
Workplace
  changes in, 11.2–11.5
  problems caused by technology in, 14.36–14.37
Workplace Shell (WPS), 5.20
"Works" programs, 6.21
Workstations, **1.14**
  processing speed, 2.16
World Wide Web, **1.24**, **8.22**–8.29
  browsers for, **6.22**, **8.23**
  downside issues related to, 8.30–8.31
  finding information on, 8.25–8.27
  intelligent agents on, 13.30
  job hunting via, 8.36, 12.28
  law enforcement on, 5.16–5.17
  marketing and business on, 8.27–8.28, 9.29
  online computing model, 5.24–5.25
  privacy issues, 14.5–14.7
  publications on, 1.25
  push technology on, 8.28–8.29
  real estate information on, 11.21
  speed of data transfer on, 8.27
  sports information on, 10.30
  See also Internet; Web businesses
Worms, **14.23**
Write-protect features, 4.12
Writing data, **4.10**
  on optical disks, 4.20

XGA (extended graphics array), **3.30**

Year 2000 problem, 10.29
Yield management system, 11.15

Zemeckis, Robert, 14.13
Zines, 1.25, 8.25